Hedging Commodities

HARRIMAN HOUSE LTD
3A Penns Road
Petersfield
Hampshire
GU32 2EW
GREAT BRITAIN

Tel: +44 (0)1730 233870
Fax: +44 (0)1730 233880
Email: enquiries@harriman-house.com
Website: www.harriman-house.com

First published in Great Britain in 2014.

ISBN: 9780857193193

British Library Cataloguing in Publication Data
A CIP catalogue record for this book can be obtained from the British Library.

Hedging Commodities

A practical guide to hedging strategies with futures and options

Slobodan Jovanović

Hh

PREFACE

Markets are eccentric formations moving in erratic and unpredictable fashion. Global commodity markets are no exception: their movement is not governed by consistent and rigid rules typical for natural sciences (in the sense of rigorous and predictable cause-effect patterns – that similar causes prove similar effects and that similar effects prove similar causes). Hence, the market's future direction is difficult to anticipate.

Only a few years ago, five American investment banks – the pride of the nation's financial system – collapsed within a matter of weeks, propelling the crisis into a global panic. Metals markets were also hit hard; copper in particular. The financial crises in the second half of 2008 resulted in the first ever breakdown in copper prices – from $8000 to $2000. What seems to be the lasting truth in regard to markets is that outcomes often diverge from expectations.

Successful investors use different routines and strategies to achieve positive returns. However, it would be misleading to regard success as a consequence of good fortune. Favourable prospects are just wishful thinking; therefore, an investor must reject any affinity towards predicting price movements. Luck may come once or twice, but generally success does not occur because investors are lucky. Success is neither luck nor a divine gift, but something that should be contemplated merely as an encounter of opportunity and the readiness to react.

Rather than guessing where the economy is headed, successful commodity traders are consistently focused on monitoring and managing price risk activity in an attempt to exploit a momentous opportunity. To become consistently successful, all traders, investors, and company risk managers must first acquire a clear understanding of derivatives' basic features and – before entering a trade – become familiar with hedging strategies that have been designed to achieve that cardinal rule of investing – eliminate the market risk exposure.

Futures hedging – often quoted as a zero-sum game – should provide predictable results: secure that "nothing's gained and nothing's lost." Yet, in some instances, the vagaries of market conditions leave potential for a fortuitous profit. These exceptional cases require an instantaneous reaction from the hedgers – to unwind the hedge strategy already instituted and alter the outcome to their advantage.

Option hedging is different, as is the nature of strategy profile and the risks it implies. Every option's hedge is an exceptional, singular phenomenon. For this reason, *Hedging Commodities* pays critical attention to options versatility and accentuates a wide picture of alternative scenarios. This approach is supposed to provide eligible investors with the criteria to refine risk parameters and implement the best fit strategy against all market uncertainties.

Great consideration has been devoted to visual design as it becomes increasingly common in business literature and textbooks. To enhance the learners-memorizing capacity, the author's analysis reveals the strategy concept – whenever possible – in a way clearly perceptible to the senses, so that the human eye can grasp quickly, and brain extract and correlate the essential meaning from it.

Plentiful illustrations and visually compelling figures, with practical solutions and case studies, have been developed to monitor strategy execution and learn from performance. For those with no relevant prior knowledge of hedging concepts and strategies, *Hedging Commodities* is a resourceful guide to distinctive exchange-based terms and concepts that explicates price risk protection fundamentals and derivative-based hedging solutions – and eventually – enunciates its ultimate goal: to allow the market risk hedges become visible.

Slobodan JOVANOVIĆ

CORE OBJECTIVES

HEDGING COMMODITIES ADDRESSES THE THREE MOST pronounced and intricate strands in the world of finance: derivatives, risk, and hedging.

Derivatives

In the dynamic world of finance, the derivatives industry is an intriguing spectrum growing at a rapid pace especially within the last two decades. Its global popularity comes as a consequence of decidedly dissimilar aspects of their application: to afford protection and speculation.

Hedgers are using derivatives mainly as a key mechanism for removing the risk associated with physical assets, while speculators are assuming the risk motivated by desire of acquiring out-sized profits.

In the broadest sense, derivatives are defined as contracts whose value is derived from the value of an underlying financial asset: currency, interest rate, equity, and commodity. Although there are many types of derivatives (with new types constantly emerging), *Hedging Commodities* builds upon the two fundamental exchange-traded contract types – futures and options. Forwards and swaps – the major OTC contract types – are also extensively reviewed and illustrated. Throughout this work, the emphasis is placed on commodity markets and the role derivatives play in managing the risk associated with physical assets.

Risk

The theory of finance distinguishes various types of risk: financial and non-financial risk; systematic and non-systematic risk; counter-party risk; market risk; credit risk; operational risk, and the alike. The *Hedging Commodities* focus is on the market risk – the intimidating phenomenon entwined in all business activities enclosing the exchange-trading arena. The book introduces an impressive number of case-scenarios and examples showing a key set of criteria for measuring the risk and drawdowns against the expected gains. Guided by pragmatic solutions, readers may find what many investors are looking for – a useful trajectory on how to preserve asset value and overcome the 'paralyzing inertia' in implementing risk-related decisions.

Hedging

To hedge a risky position is to minimize, mitigate, or even eliminate the omnipresent menacing threat of an adverse price move. Hence, the increased need of businesses and company leaders to reconsider and invigorate their approach to risk management. This book abounds with examples of managing risk using derivative instruments and in particular the risk exposure within metals industry complex. An emphasis has been placed on real-world risk scenarios.

Diverse hedge strategies, showing the payoff profiles and performance metrics, have been designed in an effort to achieve the ultimate goal – to convey the essential information to students, traders, and risk managing teams to develop and improve their practical abilities in managing and handling the increased uncertainty implicit in commodities trading.

PARTS AND CHAPTERS REVIEW

The two commodity features, in view of exchange trading in particular – standardization and price volatility – recommend them as convenient items for analyzing the framework of risk management challenges: protecting against events that dramatically influence the correlation between supply and demand; wars, climate changes (floods, hurricanes, droughts), and hedging against market risk relating to future price variations.

Hedging examples are elaborated within the context of commodity exchanges, mainly LME and CME, and on real tangible assets – copper and gold – the most commonly exchange-traded commodities also known as "inflation assets" or "safe-haven" assets.

The *Hedging Commodities* main body is segmented into five general heads,discussing in detail the role of commodity derivatives and hedging, disclosing the main features, concepts, strategies, and terms.

Part 1: Forwards, Futures and Swaps

Part 1 focuses on three types of derivatives given in chronological order: forwards, futures, and swaps. Along with the basic characteristics and features of each derivative type, Part 1 reviews the fundamentals of futures pricing theory and offers an in-depth analysis of futures hedge strategies with many worked-out examples – hedge patterns.

Chapters 1 to 4 discuss the basic characteristics of forwards and futures contracts and the fundamental concepts of futures pricing and hedging. Great effort has been invested in order to develop a new approach and usage of graphic visualization – a concept that will attempt to facilitate an understanding of futures hedge basic features, application, and performance.

In Chapter 5 an emphasis has been given on practical, real-world examples in different market environments with visual patterns, and performance analysis.

The concept of futures hedge patterns is designed to enable the reader with two things:

- to actually see the hedge developing, and
- to provide clear and straightforward graph pattern recognition for every hedge strategy.

Chapter 6 offers an innovative graphic approach to futures spread trading. The ways of generating increased profits with minimum risk are illustrated with the breakthrough graphics displaying the nature of the strategy profile and riskiness it implies.

Chapter 7 introduces the concept of basis analyzed in two different market environments; London Metal Exchange (LME), and Chicago Mercantile Exchange (CME).

SWAPS, the most frequent derivative in OTC markets are described and analyzed in Chapter 8.

Part 2: Options Basic Features and Strategies

Part 2 provides an integrated approach to option's hedging and its benefits in comparison to the uncertainties of holding an open market position.

Chapters 9 and 10 cover: options fundamental features and characteristics, payoff profiles, and four basic directional trading strategies.

Chapter 11 contains "Options One Page Lesson" the most concise presentation of key options features synthesized in a "Diamond Graph." This chapter, using real-context risk scenarios, offers a meticulous review of options risk hedges that should enable the reader:

- to learn how to identify the risk exposure
- to learn how to configure four essential strategies to protect commodities from an adverse price movement
- to scrutinize the ultimate payoff diagrams
- to tabulate the data and examine the performance metrics
- to determine and calculate the break-even points.
- to develop the "Three-Strategies Comparison" model and review the effects of manipulating strike prices.

Chapter 12 is devoted to a typical equity hedging strategies and their characteristics.

Part 3: Options Pricing Models

Part 3 is meant to serve as an introductory survey of the principles of option pricing models.

Chapter 13 introduces main determinants of an option's value. Every single factor is analyzed in detail with graphical and tabular illustrations to assist in understanding the logic of how the change in variables influence option's price.

Chapter 14 examines options pricing bounds in a concise and pragmatic manner.

Chapters 15 and 16 provide captivating insight into two fundamental option pricing models – Black Scholes and Binomial Options Pricing Model (BOPM). The famous Black-Scholes formula – one of the most complex topics related to options valuation – is expounded using a simplified intuitive approach.

Elaboration of the Binomial Options Pricing Model begins with a geometrical exposition aimed to deploy flashlight on this no less complicated topic. The model unfolds gradually from the two-period towards the multi-period binomial tree, depicting the essential features and methods of calculating the call option's premium value. The chapter ends with Dynamic Hedge Primer that synthesizes the concept through a practically worked-out example.

Chapter 17 introduces the concept of the so-called "Put Call Parity." It begins with one integrated diagram – a concise-graphic elucidation on how options, futures, and underlying assets interrelate to each other. The concept of arbitrage, as a phenomenon of a mispriced instrument configuring the put-call parity, is scrutinized in every aspect – theoretical, graphical, and practical – underpinned with the payoff diagram illustrations and straightforward numeric examples.

Memorizing these models is an important facility in quantifying the potential risk and choosing the proper follow-up actions needed to improve risk management conceptions.

Part 4: Advanced Hedging Strategies

Part 4 deals with various advanced-hedging strategies that are merely more complex extensions of previous strategies elaborated in Part 2.

Chapters 18 through 22 cover topics that are rarely encountered and explained, such as: hedging the long underlying with a bear call spread; hedging the short underlying with a bull call spread; collars and fences; and conversions and reversals.

Chapter 23 describes multiple ways of implementing protective strategies on a position that has already accumulated profit.

Part 5: Options Spreads and Combinations

The final Part 5 examines numerous option spread strategies with imaginative graphics and clear-cut explanations.

Chapter 24 presents the family of "Spread Strategies" characterized by a specific range-bound risk profile highlighting the factors that explain the differences in payoff profiles.

Chapters 25 and 26 describe call and put ratio spreads with a proper attention to their inversely correlated performance metrics.

Chapter 27 introduces strategies configured between put and call options designated "Options Combinations." Variations of straddles and strangles are punctiliously exact leaving no space for ambiguity.

Chapter 28 discusses "Synthetic Instruments." The study is segmented into three subdivisions: combinations between options and underlying instrument; between only options; and combinations excluding options. Aiming to facilitate their meaning and application, the author has devised clarifying illustrations to depict specific steps of enacting each single instance of "synthetic" instrument transformation.

KEY FEATURES OF THE BOOK

Hedging Commodities tackles major issues related to financial risk management. Challenging the conventional narrative discourse, it emphasizes visualization, believing that graphical presentation, handled expertly, can communicate with greater efficiency and richer meaning than text alone. In that respect, the author developed a unique set of graphic payoff illustrations and tabular strategy performance metrics to help explain complex and often obscure hedging transactions leaving aside the multifarious quantitative aspect that underlies the subject. One of the main goals of this book is to elucidate hedging strategies, and by virtue of graphic depiction, make them more transparent.

Accordingly, every strategy, every concept is elaborated in multiple ways – by means of four different methods: graphical, algebraic, symbolic, and numerical.

An emphasis has been placed on practical, real-world context of the probable risk scenarios, hence, the case studies and examples are obvious and conclusive. By strictly adhering to simple and effective criteria of weighing the risk against reward – based on strategy selection, related performance metrics, and graphic exposition of the risk profiles – it provides a valuable insight on how the physical risk exposure can be identified, quantified, and contained by applying proper hedging strategies.

More than 200 practical and innovative tables and figures were designed to contribute to that ultimate goal – to convey the knowledge of containing the risk to a wider audience – students, traders, risk managers and professionals.

Rather than providing isolated aspects of risk management, the author has managed to capture an integrated corpus of interrelated conceptions, allowing investors to compare numerous avenues of handling risk exposure and better adapt to unpredictable market occurrences.

Who should benefit:

In the first place, organizations related to the metal industry complex can learn how to recognize the typical risk profiles, deal with them, and develop necessary skills to mitigate or even eradicate the element of uncertainty in future cash flows due to volatile price movements. On the second level – since hedging principles can be universally applied to any price risk-sensitive position – a better understanding of hedging strategies with futures and options may benefit not only industries and participants related to commodity markets, but also to all financial institutions dealing with exchange-traded securities.

The *Hedging Commodities* strives to convey an integrated coverage of the field of finance: price protection, and exchange-based trading, upon which finance and non-finance students, college and university student, risk executives and businesses in general can build an effective conceptual framework for risk measurement and management.

With these comprehensive examples of risk challenges and major hedging strategies that can be applied on exchange traded commodities, we hope, *Hedging Commodities* succeeded in developing a trusted guidance that will serve well all market participants and executives in price-sensitive industries to plan ahead and better manage, control and contain the risk exposure encountered in exchange-traded commodities across all market adversities.

SHORT CONTENTS

CONTENTS

PART 1

FORWARDS, FUTURES AND SWAPS

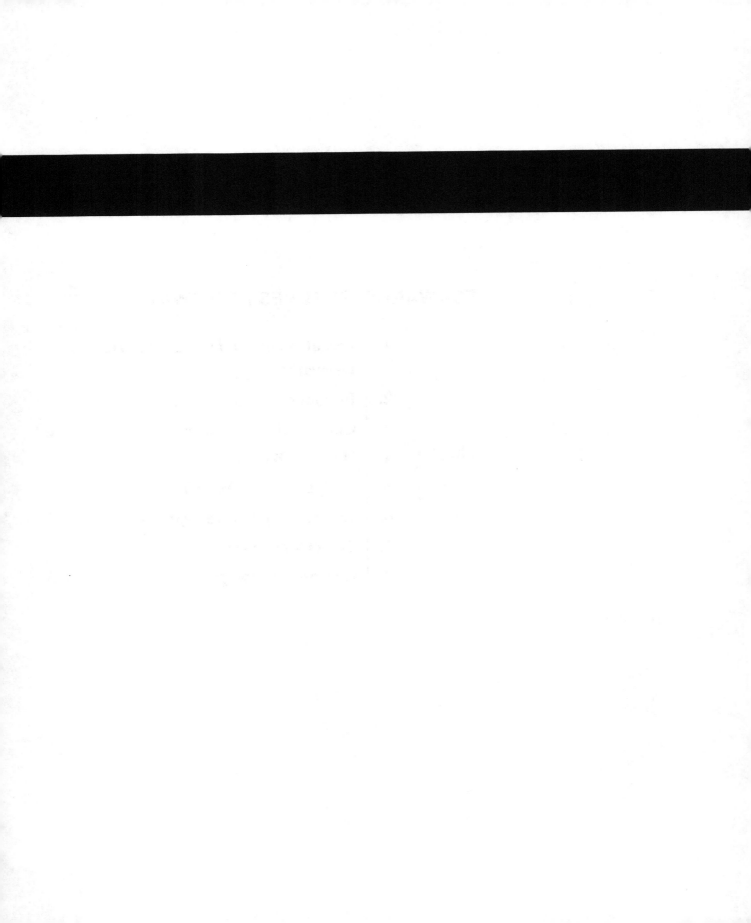

CHAPTER 1

EVOLUTION OF TRADE: FROM PHYSICAL TO DERIVATIVE

CHAPTER OBJECTIVES

- To understand the evolution of forwards
- To define and explain forward contracts
- To describe forwards' main features
- To explain forwards' pricing principles
- To highlight forwards' main advantages and disadvantages

EVOLUTION OF TRADE: FROM PHYSICAL TO DERIVATIVE

A MAJOR TRANSFORMATION, FROM PHYSICAL CASH TRADING TO DERIVATIVES, TOOK place in nineteenth century Chicago, which has become widely acclaimed as the trading centre in agricultural products. Commodity exchanges have evolved from the times when closing a trade compelled farmers to haul bushels of wheat and corn to the local market.

In the 1800s, as the agricultural products trade was rapidly underway, market participants became aware that the great supply and demand volatility as well as the price disparity between the cash market and prices in the off-season, were usually the cause of huge losses. The prevailing market environment and existing price mechanisms were incapable of managing price risk.

The evolution of forwards began with trade instruments called "to arrive contracts" clearly indicating the concept of forward delivery – agreements to establish a price now and allow for the payment and delivery to take place at some point in the future.

Forward agreements allowed exactly that – they enabled the trader to deliver or receive commodities on a particular future date based on predetermined terms and conditions (unlike cash transactions that called for immediate execution). In this way forwards facilitated elevation to a higher stage; long-term planning, and risk management.

These instruments were designed to prevent market instability and institute mechanisms for reducing price risk at different stages of crop cycles, from harvesting to marketing and food processing.

This was a critical innovation that led to the development of commodity futures exchanges.

Versatility of products and trading terms, normally associated with exchange markets, has proved to be time consuming and unproductive. The demand for standardized contracts that would enable efficient flow of commodities from producers to consumers matured over time and led to the development of today's modern futures contracts – contracts set forth by exchange authorities with harmonized terms in respect of quantity, quality and delivery terms.

Although you will encounter many types of derivatives traded on exchanges globally, fundamentally it could be argued that there are only two types of derivatives: forwards and options (futures being treated as an exchange traded forward contract). From the viewpoint of their imminent cash flow obligations or payoffs this division is justifiable; forwards display linear and symmetric payoff obligations; options display nonlinear and asymmetric payoff obligations.

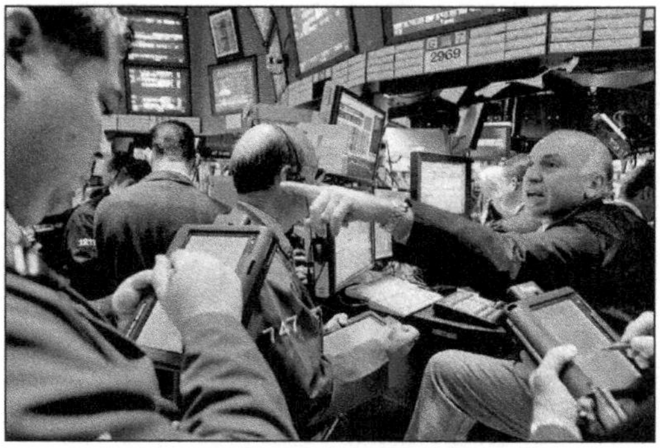

Exchange Floor

In view of the type of underlying asset, exchange-traded derivatives may be categorized broadly as follows; FX derivatives, interest rate derivatives, commodity derivatives, and equity-linked derivatives.

Another equally judicious classification emphasizes the difference between derivative instruments based on the type of the market at which the trade is executed. In this respect all derivatives fall into two classes:

Exchange Traded	Over the Counter (OTC)
Futures	Exotic options
Options	Forwards
Futures options	Swaps

As the two classic exchange traded derivatives, futures and options will be discussed profoundly throughout this book. At this point it will suffice to say that **derivatives** are "financial market instruments representing an obligation or right to execute an exchange at some forward date." Why are they called derivatives? The term itself, in view of semantics, leaves no space for dilemma – they are called derivatives simply because they "derive" their value from the price of an underlying asset.

Key Terms

derivatives
financial market instruments representing an obligation or right to execute an exchange at some predetermined forward date. They are called derivatives simply because they "derive" their value from the price of an underlying asset

Derivatives trading is an ever increasing activity. According to Triennial Central Bank Survey (BIS), as of April 2010, average daily turnover of derivatives in advanced economies only reached an astonishing figure of $13.8 trillion:

- Exchange-traded derivatives (comprised of futures and options) $8.2 trillion
- OTC derivatives (comprised of FX derivatives and interest rate derivatives) $5.6 trillion

If we add the rapidly increasing daily turnover in Emerging Market Economies of $1.2 trillion for the same period, we arrive at a total derivatives daily average turnover of $15 trillion!

There are at least three features responsible for derivatives' burgeoning popularity:

1. The fact that you don't buy and sell the physical assets themselves, but enter a legally binding contract to buy or sell the assets at a predetermined price for delivery on a predetermined date.
2. The fact that these contracts allow their users to transfer an unwanted risk held in one asset class to another party and assume a different kind of risk that will be executed in the future rather than today.
3. Ease of entering and exiting the trade.

I FORWARDS OVERVIEW

Key Terms

forward contract
a derivative contract agreed between two parties, the buyer and the seller to exchange a specified commodity at a specified date in the future at a predetermined price

long forward
the contract obliging the party to buy an asset

short forward
the contract obliging the party to sell an asset

delivery date
the date specified in the contract on which the delivery of the commodity must be executed

delivery price
the price fixed at the outset and paid at maturity of the contract

A **forward contract** is a derivative contract agreed between two parties, the buyer and the seller for delivery of a specified commodity at a specified date in the future with a price agreed upon today. When you initiate a forward contract there are only two positions you can take – **long and short.** By entering a long forward contract you are committing to buy the asset and by entering a short forward contract you are committing to sell the asset.

The terms of a forward contract are not standardized but rather fitted for a particular purpose and according to preferences of parties involved. The contract price is called the **delivery price**.

Forward contracts have been around ever since the Roman times. They are very common in everyday life. Every purchase that calls for delivery of the goods at some future point in time and at a price concluded today is in fact a forward contract. If you've ever subscribed to a newspaper or magazine, you have entered into a type of forward contract. Every time you rent an apartment you are making a forward agreement in which price and the term of the contract are fixed at the outset. You would be probably obliged to pay the first rent up front (a collateral) and then you will be paying the fixed amount every last date of the current month, for the next, let's say three years. The contract will stipulate that you cannot cancel the rent or if you do you must announce cancellation 6 months in advance. Another kind of common forward contract involves the purchase of a new car. The dealer may not have the exact car with all of the options you require, so he may have to order the car from the factory where these specific requests can be added.

Imagine for a moment that you are visiting the "Geneva International Motor Show." You are fascinated with the new "Porsche" design and since you just inherited a fortune, you can not resist to have that very model. You enquire with the dealer but to your great disappointment, the dealer informs you that this model has to be returned to the factory and therefore is not for sale. The best he can do is to put you on a list and make delivery in three months from now. You decide it is worth waiting and now you can ask the dealer to adapt the model to your particular preferences – you want leather seats in the same colour as the car, and the colour to be "blue violet with a big pink star on the bonnet," than the dashboard to be made of reddish mahogany and the steering wheel to be in the style of one in a Formula 1 car, and you also want to have an additional horn that sounds like a South African "vuvuzele"! The price now, of course, will be a bit different than for the regular model. The dealer makes a few phone calls and comes up with a modified price. You have no reason to doubt the credibility of Porsche and the dealer has checked your creditworthiness so the deal is done. You sign a contract and now you can brag as the fresh owner of a new Porsche. Congratulations, you have just completed a forward contract. It cost you nothing to enter the deal (although the provision of some kind of collateral is usually requested), and you are now confident that in three months time, on the date specified in the contract you will have a new Porsche parked in front of your home. Accordingly, the **delivery date** of the forward contract is the date when delivery of the commodity must be executed. Now all you will have to do is to close out your part of the obligation – to pay the delivery price; the price fixed at the outset and paid at maturity in exchange for the asset. Once fixed the delivery price cannot be changed.

From the aforementioned fictional narrative, it is obvious that forwards trading is accompanied with certain advantages as well as disadvantages.

Advantages:

- First, forward contracts convey an explicit obligation to either buy or sell, and consequently they eliminate uncertainty; the actual exchange will take place at the contract maturity with all the specific features of the contract determined up front.
- Forwards are privately negotiated deals, tailored to specific needs, offering great flexibility in view of the amount, quality and terms of delivery.
- Forwards are settled at maturity principally through delivery and require no daily settlements in the interim.

Disadvantages:

- Forwards are unique and non-standardized contracts; accordingly it may be difficult to find a counterparty; hence they are less liquid.
- Tying up capital – forwards typically require some form of guarantee or collateral.
- Subject to default risk. Forwards are merely a pledge to execute a certain contractual obligation at a future date, and indeed the contract execution is actually backed only by the reputation of the firm(s).

PRINCIPLES FOR CALCULATING A FORWARD PRICE

Calculation of forward prices rests upon the following factors:

- no arbitrage principle, and
- risk free interest rate

One of the ways to demonstrate how these factors relate to each other is through a simplified hypothetical example. Suppose that a copper tubes manufacturer need to sell 1000 tons of copper tubes for a delivery six months forward. The manufacturer is concerned that the price in the future might fall and looks for the way to fix the price six months in advance. How can he do it? One way to avoid this uncertainty is to enter into a forward contract. Let us suppose that the LME copper settlement price today is $8975/ton. The prevailing annual interest rate is R = 4.5 percent. So, the question is: what would be the right price for the 100 tons of copper cathodes agreed today for delivery in six months' forward time?

Today (t = 0)

- Copper converter borrows funds to buy 100 tons of copper today
- Buy 100 tons of copper today at $8975/ton based on the current cash price on the LME
- Enter a forward contract for delivery six months from now at delivery price K.
- Value of the forward contract V0, today (t = 0) is zero.
  V0 = 8975 – 8975 + 0 = 0

At Maturity, T= ½ (six months forward)

- Copper converter repays the loan $8975 x $(1+.045)^{0.5}$ = $9174.71
- Delivers 100 tons of copper pipes
- Receives the delivery price K

- Value of the forward contract at time T, VT, is zero to satisfy no-arbitrage principle.
- If $V_T > 0$ there is an arbitrage opportunity
- If $V_T < 0$ there is an arbitrage opportunity
- Under assumptions of no-arbitrage $V_T = 0$, and consequently
  $V_T = -\$9174.71 + K + 0 = K - \$9174.71 = 0$
  $K = \$9174.71$
- Final selling price would normally include the following provisional costs: $1150 manufacturing cost, $100 billet premium and a profit of $100 but these costs do not affect the principals for calculating the forward price.

SUMMARY

A forward contract is a private negotiation made in the present that establishes the price of a commodity to be delivered at some definitive point of time in the future.

These are "customized contracts," in the sense that all the principal features of the contract:

- quantity
- quality
- delivery date, and
- delivery point
- are dependant upon the will of the contracting parties.

The forward price, one of the principal factors of every contract, is also subject to a bilateral agreement that is negotiated directly between the contractual parties.

These privately negotiated contracts, designed specifically to respond to particular preferences of the parties involved, are representative examples of OTC (over-the-counter)contracts and all trading activities are restricted to OTC markets.

- Forward contracts cannot be marked-to-market.
- Collateral deposited as guarantee, if any, is set once, on the day of the initial transaction.
- The commodity does not change hands until the predetermined delivery date.
- The investor has to wait for the delivery date to realize the profit or loss on the position.
- The risk of default—each party involved in the trade is faced with the default of the other.
- Most common parties to a forward contract involve corporations, banks, financial institutions and governments.

KEY TERMS

derivatives
forward contract
long forward
short forward
delivery date
delivery price
OTC contract

CHAPTER 2

INTRODUCTION TO FUTURES

CHAPTER OBJECTIVES

- To define and explain a futures contract
- To accentuate the distinction between hedgers and speculators
- To explain the mechanics of a futures trade
- To illustrate the difference between cash and physical settlement
- To identify futures' basic building blocks

I FUTURES OVERVIEW

Key Terms

futures contract
a commitment to either purchase or sell a specific underlying commodity or financial instrument at some future date for a specified price that is determined today

commodity
a basic good standardised in terms of quality, with a specific utility used primarily as inputs in the production of other goods and services or to satisfy some particular consumer needs

THE USUAL WAY OF DEFINING A FUTURES CONTRACT GOES LIKE THIS: "THE **FUTURES contract** is a commitment to either purchase or sell a specific underlying **commodity** and/or financial instrument at some future date for a specified price which is determined today."

At LME (the London Metal Exchange) the world's premier nonferrous metals market, for example, this underlying asset is either a steel billet or one of eight nonferrous metals; aluminum, aluminum alloy, copper, lead, nickel, tin, zinc or NASAAC (a North American Special Aluminium Alloy Contract) and of standardized shape and quality. In February 2010 two minor metals were introduced—cobalt and molybdenum.

But on other exchanges, as far as commodities are concerned, the underlying asset may represent anything from pork bellies, coffee, orange juice, wheat, corn, sugar, precious metals—such as gold, platinum and silver, crude oil, electricity, gas, and many other products. Commodities futures are most commonly divided into two subcategories: Agricultural and Metals & Energy. Other major groups of underlying asset are: interest rates, foreign currency futures, equity indices.

Let us take a look at an arbitrary selection of futures contracts traded at New York's Comex/Nymex:

Table 2.1 Futures Contract Quotes: Comex/Nymex

Contract	Quoted Units	Trading Unit	Minimum Fluctuation	Initial Margin	Maintenance Margin
Corn	US $ per bushel	5000 bu.	¼ C ($12.50)	$1350	$1000
Coffee	US $ per pound	37,500 lbs.	0.0005 ($18.25)	$4900	$3500
S&P 500	index points	$250 x S&P	0.10 pt ($25)	$22,500	$18,000
Goldman Sachs	GSCI index points	$250 x GSCI	0.05 pt ($12.5)	$12,000	$8000
Oil	US $ per barrel	1000 net barrels	1 US cent per barrel	$7288	$5830
Gold	US $ per troy ounce	100 tr. oz	10 pts=$10	$4300	$3250
Copper HG	US $ per pound	25,000 pounds	5 pts=$12.50	$7763	$5750

Value of one contract = price x contract amount

Remember This! Futures Early Origins

The first futures exchange market was registered in Japan around 1730 and it was linked to Yodoya Komeichi (rice market) in Osaka, a rice trade centre with an amazing 91 warehouses. During the Tokugava shogunate government, this market was reorganized as the "Dojima Rice Exchange," the world's only futures exchange until 1860. The Dojima futures exchange developed all the main features of a modern exchange market: precise definitions of quality, delivery date and place, and a clearing house. Almost two centuries after Yodoya Komeichi, in 1848 the largest derivative exchange in the world the Chicago Board of Trade (CBOT)—was established in Chicago. It is generally accepted that futures contracts, in their contemporary meaning, have been in use since 1860. Guided by some bizarre coincidence, these two examples set in distant areas—and equally distant cultures, clearly evidence that emergence of modern-day futures exchanges was closely related to the sequence of fortunes and calamities in grain harvests—their abundance and oversupply in one period and scarcity in another—which force farmers and traders to seek predictability in forward grain prices, while at the same time trying to mitigate the severe damage which can arise from drastic seasonal price fluctuations.

Since then, futures contracts have not changed much and have remained more or less in the same form, to the present day.

What seems odd at first glance and causes difficulties in understanding a futures contract, is that peculiarity, that unique feature which allows an owner to sell something he does not have. Common sence would suggest that things you do not have you can buy—but to sell things you do not have sounds rather odd. Yet the futures contract permits exactly that—both the right to buy first and sell later and the right to sell first and then buy back at some later date.

Maybe comprehension of this odd situation would be much easier if you consider a futures contract as a be: a bet against your personal projection of market development—or, more specifically, the direction you expect prices to take. All market participants do have their own estimate of futures' market performance based on current trends. In this respect, the market is recognizing a simple division of its participants: the ones that are anticipating a price increase are labelled with a distinctive term—**bulls;** and those who are anticipating a price decline are labelled as—**bears.** Bulls earn money in rising markets, buying first then selling later at a higher price (buy low, sell high), whereas bears earn money in declining markets—by selling first and buying later at a lower price (sell high, buy low). Figure 2.1 is a graphic illustration of this relationship.

Key Terms

bulls
market participants expecting price increase

bears
market participants expecting price decrease

Figure 2.1 Long & Short Futures: Profit & Loss Diagrams

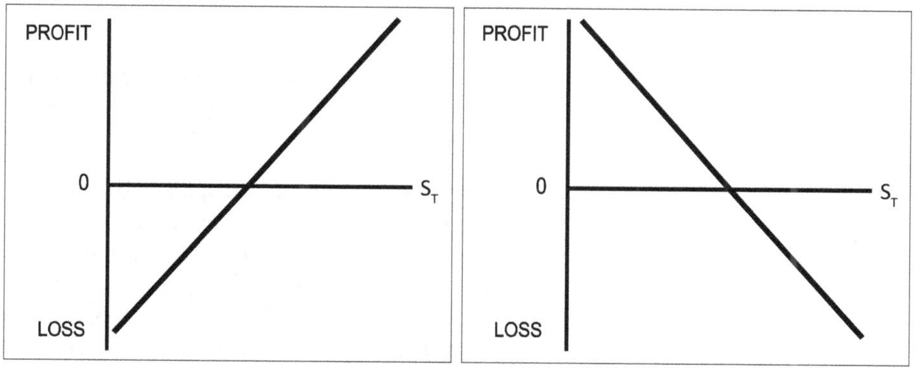

NB: The futures payoff pattern is symmetric and linear meaning that the change in the value of the futures is in the same direction and proportion with the value of the underlying asset.

A futures contract has a finite life. Before the expiry date a futures holder must decide what to do—to close out the contract with a reversal, to offset a sale or purchase, or to make or take delivery. If delivery takes place, then the futures contract becomes physical and is converted (in the case of LME contracts) into a steel billet or one of those eight nonferrous metals.

Looking at data for LME transactions, it can be ascertained that the historic ratio between cash settlement and physical delivery is around 99 to 1 per cent. So futures markets are purely financial markets—financial instruments are bought and sold either for speculative purposes or for hedging risks against an adverse price change. Physical delivery, although possible, is rarely contemplated and is considered only as a harbour of last resort.

The majority of futures contracts are closed out prior to expiry. The buyer of a futures contract (the party taking a long position), closes out the position by executing an offsetting sale (selling back the same contract). The seller of a futures contract, (the party taking a short position) closes out the position by executing an offsetting purchase (buying back the same contract). The futures contract is a convenient tool designed to give protection against an adverse change in underlying asset prices. In that capacity it is massively used in configuring hedging strategies.

COMMODITY MARKET PARTICIPANTS

The modern futures market evolved from a need to transfer risk. The futures market makes it possible for those who want to manage price risk—**hedgers,** to transfer that risk to those who are willing to accept it in the hope of a profit—**speculators.**

Futures exchanges represent a unique forum where hedgers, representing one side of the market, effectively manage the risk of fluctuating prices related to the sale and purchase of their physical supplies. Exchanges worldwide, organised either on a non-profit basis (where members have voting rights and hold exchange memberships which allow them to trade on the exchange) or as for-profit organizations (where members receive shares of stocks) offer standardized futures contracts on different underlying assets; agriculture products, metals and energy; equity indices; currencies, and interest rates. Gradually, the futures contract has come to be an indispensable instrument in the hedging programmes of all companies seeking to gain protection from an adverse price move or to evade the risks immanent in commodities trading.

Key Terms

hedger
market participant seeking to eliminate risk of an adverse price change related to the sale and purchase of their physical commodities

speculator
independent market participant who enters the market with no implicit risk exposure aiming to make profit from anticipated price change

Hedgers are risk averse and tend to hedge away price risk.

Speculators take on risk for hedgers and willingly subject themselves to the consequences of their own opinion on where the commodity price is heading.

The driving force behind hedgers is the need to eliminate the price risk exposure embedded in their physical assets, while speculators—the inescapable counterparty—enter the market with no implicit risk, aiming to make a profit from price changes.

Hedgers and speculators fit together as two parts of a whole, with their motives reciprocally interrelated. The coexistence of both categories is necessary for carrying out the normal function of any futures exchange, as the gains credited to one party are attributed at the expense of the other.

Remember This! Hedgers vs. Speculators

Generally speaking, market participants are classified into three major groups: *hedgers, speculators* and *arbitrageurs.*

Hedgers use the market to offset the price risk existing between the cash commodity market and different maturities of the underlying futures market. Their essential purpose for entering the market is to avoid the risk associated with holding a physical commodity.

Speculators are the second major group of market participants attracted by luring prospects of high returns. These participants approach the market with no initial exposure—unlike smelters, refiners, fabricators or merchants they have no natural long nor short position that they might seek to offset.

Their raison d'être is to make a profit by assuming risk. Speculators enter the market with the idea of unbalancing neutral position. They intend to gain exposure by entering a futures position.While hedgers' main preoccupation is to reduce—or eliminate completely—losses even at a cost of losing windfall profits, speculators are risking a loss with the hope of gaining precarious profits. The idea behind speculation is simple but bears incommensurate risk—speculators are in the market to make a profit by buying and selling futures contracts: "buying low/selling high" in the case of going long, "selling high/buying low" in the case of going short. Their actions are based solely on their anticipation of the market's future direction with no firm clues or guarantees—the outcome is more presumed than predicted. Nevertheless, the role of speculators is very important to futures markets. By assuming the risks which hedgers avoid they are adding essential liquidity to the market, making it more cost-efficient and reducing the risk of default for the market as a whole. In effect, investing in futures—especially from the viewpoint of a speculator—can be, and often is "a high risk/high return game."

Arbitrageurs are looking for opportunities to lock-in a riskless profit by simultaneously buying and selling the same or closely related financial instrument in different market. Consistent with their predominant trading style s and activities, speculators are divided into three categories, commonly referred to as:

- Scalpers
- Day traders, and
- Position traders

Having outlined the subject we can now define futures the contract a bit more explicitly and say that:

> "*A futures contract is a legally binding commitment to execute a trade (to deliver or take delivery) of an exchange standardized asset (commodity, equity or financial instrument) at a predetermined forward date (t_1) for a price contracted now (t_0).*"

But there is much more to it! In order to explore the full meaning of the term we shall soon arrive at one of the most extensive futures contract definition, that will aid us in understanding the complexity of the subject matter and its essential features.

Key Terms

prompt date
the delivery date of a futures contract, entered at London Metal Exchange, and the last date an open futures position can be closed is two business-days before prompt

FUTURES TRADE ILLUSTRATION

Commodity futures may be closed out in two different ways:

- Cash settlement – futures contracts are closed by an offsetting trade, in most cases this transaction is executed prematurely (i.e. prior to the settlement date). At LME the last date for cash settlement is two days before the **prompt date**.
- Physical delivery - if held through to the delivery date, the futures contract is settled by physical delivery of the underlying metal.

In the following graphics we shall try to visualize the distinction with the help of the arrow symbols. The white arrows will represent a futures contract—in our example a sale or purchase on the LME market—and the shaded arrow will represent sale or purchase of physical metal.

Notations:
(t_0) – initial time, today
(T) – maturity, no specific date, (days/months/years)
(T–t) – if the contract is closed at any time before maturity – at time t, the time to maturity is T–t (days/months/years)
$F_{(0,T)}$ – initial futures price at time t_0
$F_{(T\text{-}t)}$ – final futures price at time T–t
S_T – final spot price at time T
(at expiration $F_T = S_T$, so that $F_0 - F_T = F_0 - S_T$)

Most commonly, futures contracts are not carried to maturity or the settlement date. On the LME the settlement date is referred to as the prompt date; and the vast majority of futures contracts (almost 99 per cent) are closed out prematurely by assuming an equal and opposite position to an original futures with the same prompt date!

For those who enter a short futures position, the closing or offsetting transaction will be to go long that futures with the same maturity date.

For those who enter a long futures position, the closing or offsetting transaction will be to go short that futures with the same prompt date.

The distinction also has to be made with regard to the stage of the settlement. In this respect we may differentiate between:

- a futures contract closed out prematurely—before the maturity date, and
- a futures contract closed out at the maturity date—i.e., keeping with the LME provisions, two days before the prompt date.

Figure 2.2 Futures Trade Illustration—Closing Out Prematurely

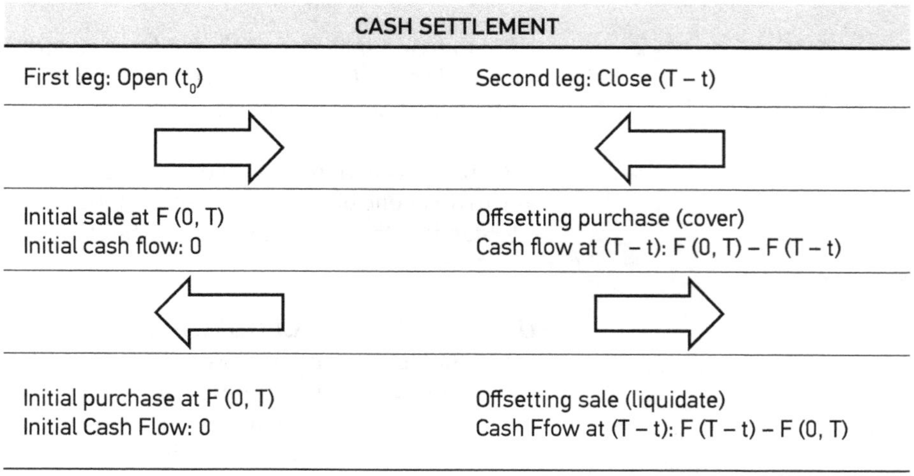
CASH SETTLEMENT
First leg: Open (t_0)
Second leg: Close (T – t)
Initial sale at F (0, T)
Initial cash flow: 0
Offsetting purchase (cover)
Cash flow at (T – t): F (0, T) – F (T – t)
Initial purchase at F (0, T)
Initial Cash Flow: 0
Offsetting sale (liquidate)
Cash Ffow at (T – t): F (T – t) – F (0, T)

If a commodity futures is not closed out before maturity it may be settled either in cash or by actual delivery of the underlying commodity.

Figure 2.3 illustrates the essentials of cash settlement versus physical settlement transactions.

Figure 2.3 Futures Trade Illustration—Closing Out on the Prompt Date

CASH SETTLEMENT		PHYSICAL SETTLEMENT	
First leg: Open **(t_0)**	Second leg: Close **(T)**	First leg: Open **(t_0)**	Second leg: Close **(T)**

Initial sale at **F (0, T)** Initial cash flow: 0	Offsetting purchase Cash flow at **(T)**: F (0, T) – S_T	Initial sale at **F (0, T)**	Delivery at **F (0, T)**

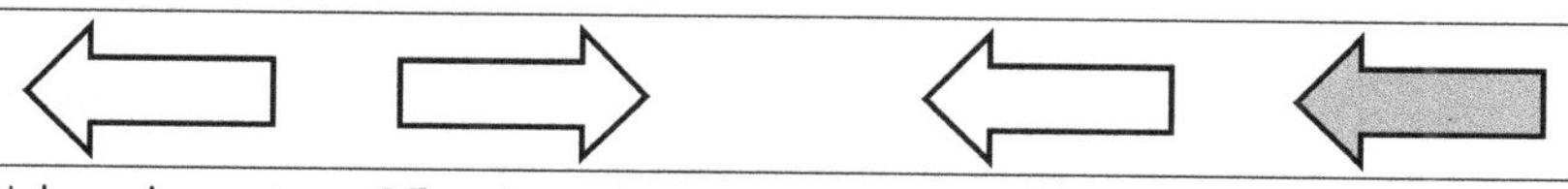

Initial purchase at **F (0, T)** Initial cash flow: 0	Offsetting sale Cash flow at **(T)**: S_T – F (0, T)	Initial purchase at ***F (0, T)***	Accept delivery at **F (0, T)**

The arrow symbols are really an introduction to Chapter 5, in which they will be intensely used to illustrate different hedging strategies. We will look into the main characteristic of each particular strategy, how it may develop and how changing market circumstances may be applied to a trading system to improve and enhance its overall performance.

Example: Physical Delivery Settlement

Long copper futures contract fixed at $9250/t
Exchange: LMEContract size: 25 metric tons

If the long futures contract is not closed out by an offsetting trade—prior to the prompt date—you are committed to accept delivery:

- you will end up paying the original futures price F (0, T) at time (t_0) is $9250/t x 25 tons (the size of the contract).

Net cost: $231,250 (excluding commissions).

But since futures are subject to daily settlement (marking-to-market) this net cost consists of two components: the spot price you pay at maturity (that is two days before the prompt date), and the closing margin balance, resulting from daily adjustments—gains and losses on your margin account—recorded during the life of the contract.

We assume that the closing spot price (S_T) at time (T) is $9600.

The balance equals the sum of cumulative daily gains and losses! Accordingly, your margin account will show a credit of $350.

At the end, you are effectively paying the original futures price F(0, T):
$9600 – $350 = $9250.

DEFINITION & FUTURES BUILDING BLOCKS

"A futures contract is a contract concluded on standardized terms on a centralized market. Under this contract, a financial asset representing a given quantity of some underlying asset, which is either a standardized physical commodity available at a given future date and given location, or some financial asset available at some given future date, is either bought or sold between a given date and the date of availability of the underlying asset (called the maturity of the contract). This implies that any quantity of the financial asset available on the futures market, once it has initially been either bought or sold, may be, respectively, sold back or bought back at any subsequent time before maturity of the contract, thus ending any commitment with respect to the quantity of asset. At maturity, the contract may be fulfilled by the seller through the actual delivery of the asset under some standardized conditions and by the buyer through paying the initial futures price. To avoid any default or liability, an initial deposit which is a significant fraction of the value of the contract has to be paid in cash or marketable securities at the beginning of any contract, with daily settlements of any liability or claim resulting from any daily difference in the value of the contract due to daily market variations. If necessary, other liability settlements (margin calls) are required to maintain a minimum deposit."

(Ephraim Clark, Jean-Baptist Lesourd & Rene Thieblemont).

From this lengthy definition, which looks like a huge multi-storey building, we shall try to extract the key building blocks for the sake of further clarification.

BUILDING BLOCK NO. 1 STANDARDIZATION

Futures contracts are highly standardized in the sense that all specific terms of the contract—such as, quality, quantity, delivery date, settlement location, and price—are determined by the exchange. On the LME, for example, for each underlying commodity the exchange supplies a list of approved brands and warehouse locations.

BUILDING BLOCK NO. 2 CENTRALIZED MARKET; EXCHANGE

Futures contracts are traded on centralized markets i.e., on organized and strictly regulated exchanges. Exchanges are places which can be physically located—they have their addresses, offices and trading floors—or trading rings—where the real trading takes place. The price discovery process is held in a transparent manner usually in the form of "open outcry" and is based on the influence of market forces.

BUILDING BLOCK NO. 3 LONGS AND SHORTS

Each futures trade has two legs. First leg—opening or initial trade (buy or sell). Second leg—closing or offsetting repurchase or resale. So, those who open trade with a purchase are said to be long futures. Longs agree to take delivery of the underlying commodity at the futures contract price on a pre-agreed forward date—the **maturity date**. Shorts agree to deliver the underlying commodity at the futures contract price on pre-agreed forward date—maturity date.

Repurchase (buy back), closes the short futures.
Resale (sell back), closes the long futures.

Key Terms

maturity date
the date when the futures contract must be settled either by delivery of the physical goods or in cash. Also delivery date

This second leg, or reversal trade, can be executed on any exchange trading date during the life of the contract or before the expiry date.

BUILDING BLOCK NO. 4 MATURITY

Maturity of a futures contract can be defined as the date when a futures contract that has not been closed or cancelled by an opposite transaction (sale—in the case of initial purchase, and purchase—in the case of initial sale) must be settled by delivery of a physical commodity or other underlying instrument: such as stocks, bonds currency and the like. The fulfilment of contract obligations that end up with a delivery unfolds as follows: the "longs" are obliged to accept delivery of the underlying metal and the "shorts" are obliged to deliver the same underlying metal.

BUILDING BLOCK NO. 5 INITIAL DEPOSIT

The initial deposit—in cash or other acceptable collateral—that a client must pay before opening a futures position (to buy or sell) is commonly called the "margin." Since these funds must to be deposited at the outset of a futures transaction, futures exchange lingo addresses these funds more precisely as the **initial margin.**

The amount of the initial margin is a meticulously balanced calculation designed to reconcile the need for safety and protection of the clearing house against any default of the exchange and its innumerable clients on one side, and, on the other, to procure liquidity and a flow of market transactions by establishing a level which is high enough to avoid the inconvenience of frequent minor adjustments, since the futures prices are marked-to-market on a daily basis. From the viewpoint of an exchange it is also considered to be a "good faith deposit" which is required from both sides (sellers as well as buyers).

This deposit is paid out at the opening of the contract and is a certain percentage of the full value of the asset underlying the contract—the usual range for LME contracts is between five and15 per cent and depends predominantly upon the volatility of the particular commodity.

Another closely related term frequently encountered is the **maintenance margin.** Maintenance margin refers to the minimum level of money that must be kept in the margin account in order to maintain a futures position. It can also be interpreted as the lower level of the initial margin after which the clearing house issues a margin call. Minimum levels for initial and maintenance margins are at the discretion of the exchange - not a broker.

Key Terms

initial margin
initial deposit as a collateral against possible losses arising from holding a position in futures market

maintenance margin
the predetermined minimum level of margin that must be maintained throughout the validity of the contract

marked to market
expiry date is the date at which the final settlement of a futures contract (a reversal trade) has to be executed or the delivery will be enforced

Remember This! Types of Brokers

Should you consider trading commodities with your own money, the very first thing you should do is choose a commodity broker. Basically there are two types of commodity brokers: the *full service commodity broker* and the *online commodity broker*. Both choices bearing specific benefits and dangers. All novice traders should make the first choice: a full service commodity broker can help them learn the mechanics and order flow of the particular exchange market. Experienced traders—who devote almost all their time to market research, can offer valuable advice and prevent you from making some of the erratic and foolish mistakes which are characteristic of new traders. On the other hand, if you are familiar with exchange procedures and have a trading plan, then you may opt for an online broker. Almost all online brokers will provide an excellent trading platform with real time quotes, charts, futures news and technical analysis programmes enabling easy trading. The commissions are also considerably lower, making access to numerous trading strategies more feasible.

Key Terms

margin call
request from the clearinghouse to a customer to add funds necessary to bring the margin back to the initial level

mark-to-market
the daily revaluation of futures position with regard to current market prices, to calculate the daily profits and losses

variation margin
the cash transfer of payables and receivables as a consequence of daily settlement procedure of market prices flowing from the party who has lost money to the party who has gained money

To clear things up, let us illustrate this with an example:

Example: Maintenance Margin

Sell May S&P500@856.56 Initial $22,500 Maintenance $18,000

	Price	Change	Action	Margin Call	Balance
Day 1	861.46	4.9	1225		21,275
Day 2	868.86	7.4	1850		19,425
Day 3	885.26	16.4	4100	7175 call	22,500
Day 4	887.56	2.3	575		21,925
Day 5	875.56	12.0	3000		24,925
Day 6	866.56	9.0	2250		27,175
Day 7 Close	851.56	15.0	3750		30,925

Your final gain, less commissions, should be $5.0 x 250 = $1250
You sold an S&P futures contract at $22,500. Your total outlay is $22,500.

The level of maintenance margin should be set at around 80% of the initial -$18,000. This implies that until the drop in your balance does not reach that level you will not receive a margin call.

From the illustrated example you can follow the provisional seven day scenario. The price drop in the first two days will not alarm the clearing house since your margin is still above the maintenance level. On the third day the index price drops below the maintenance level, so the margin call is triggered and you have to bring the margin back to its initial level.

The final outcome shows a positive return of $1250 – the difference between the initial price of the index $856.56 and the price at the close $851.56. You will arrive to the same result if you subtract the losses—($7750) from the gains ($9000) accrued during the seven-day period.

But beware! Having entered in the position you have also undertaken responsibility for the total value of moves in the market—whatever direction they may take. Theoretically, the price of a futures contract can rise infinitely or it can go all the way down to zero just like stocks—or stock index!

BUILDING BLOCK NO. 6 DAILY SETTLEMENTS

A margin call comes as a consequence of the daily evaluation of an open position in a procedure commonly referred to as **marking-to-market.** Marking-to-market is a daily —or even intra daily—procedure of evaluating an open position, with regard to the current market price of the underlying instrument, to calculate daily profits and losses. Accordingly, if a client's losses drop below the predetermined lower level—called the maintenance margin—they will receive a margin call to add additional funds, in order to top up the margin account to the initial margin level and thus keep the position alive. **A Variation margin** is a modification of a daily settlement procedure at some exchanges (LME for example) which refers to the cash transfer of payables and receivables posted each day as a consequence of the mark-to-market convention. The money transfer of actual credits and debits goes from the margin account of the party who has lost money to the margin account of the party who has gained money on each particular day with no reference to the maintenance margin. Daily valuation of market prices prevents default by either party as payables/receivables are immediately settled as they arise. This way the clearing house effectively prevents the risk of default by the losing party and guarantees the viability of each futures contract.

Example: Variation Margin

Imagine a client sells a May copper contract at LME for $6850 on day one, paying an initial margin of $7763. If the price of the contract goes up on day two to $6876, client will be called on to pay an unrealized loss of twenty six dollars or a total of $26 x 25 = $650. Similarly, if the price on day three falls from $6876 to $6835, his account will be credited for a total of $1025 (gain of $41 x 25). As we see future contracts are marked-to-market and must be settled daily as the price changes. Such payments calculated against daily gains and losses are known as variation margins. On day four your position gains another $23 or a total of $575. On day five you decide to offset the contract by buying at $6840. Overall, client's position recorded a profit of $250: $6850 – $6840 = $10 x 25 = $250.

			Initial	Variation	Variation Margin Balance
Day 1	Sell1 May LME copper	$6850	($7763)		
Day 2	Settlement price	$6876		($650)	($650)
Day 3	Settlement price	$6835		$1025	$375
Day 4	Settlement price	$6812		$575	$950
Day 5	Buy 1 May LME copper	$6840	$7763	($700)	$250

It should be noted that the initial margin of $7763 virtually serves as a "good faith deposit" and remains intact during the life of the contract. It is returned to the client only as the contract has been terminated

BUILDING BLOCK NO. 7 LEVERAGE

As you will have noticed above, the size of the initial margin an investor has to deposit prior to acquiring a futures position is much smaller than the cost of acquiring the underlying asset. This brings us to the notion of **leverage**. Futures contracts are rightly denoted highly leveraged instruments, implying that you can control a huge amount of commodities or other underlying assets, with only a proportion of their value—the margin investment. The term "leverage," in this context, simply means an allowance not to pay the full price for an underlying asset at the outset. Unlike stocks, for example, you do not need to pay the full price upfront to buy a package of, say 100 ABC stocks—worth $3500. Instead, you only need to pay a fraction of its value—$350. In this way, with a modest amount of capital ($350) you can open a position of much greater value ($3500) in just the way that a person using a lever can lift a heavier weight than his physical strength would otherwise allow him to do.

Key Terms

leverage
utilizing typically borrowed money in financing a derivative venture with an effect of gaining or losing far in excess of your initial cash outlay

The leverage ratio can be expressed mathematically as the reciprocal of the initial margin—in our example, 1/0,1 = 10 (350 : 3500 = 0.1).

So leverage makes it possible to invest small amount of money and reap considerable profits quickly—but at a risk. In our example a one dollar price change on a leveraged position will either credit or debit $1000 from client's account. If the price

Example: Leverage

Unleveraged Equity Position		
ABC Shares	Case A	Case B
Purchase price per share	35	35
No. of shares purchased	100	100
Total investment	3500	3500
Stock price after 3 m	28	42
Total value after 3 m	2800	4200
Return	–20%	20%

Leveraged Futures Position		
ABC Futures	Case A	Case B
Purchase price per share	35	35
No. of shares purchased	1000	1000
Initial margin	3500	3500
Stock price after 3 months	28	42
Total value after 3 months	(7000)	7000
Return	–200%	200%

of ABC shares goes up by $7 (which is the normal and highly probable scenario), then the stock position will earn $700—or a yield of 20 per cent. Conversely, it could well happen that the price of ABC shares drops by $7; in which case, the client's position will score a $700 loss—negative yield of 20 per cent. At the same time profits and losses on client's leveraged position will be magnified ten times.

Accordingly, we may offer the following definition of leverage:

> *Leverage refers to utilizing money (typically borrowed) to finance a derivative venture which will have the effect of gaining or losing far in excess of the initial cash outlay.*

It is worth emphasizing that flat futures transactions can be highly risky and should not be undertaken by novices and individual investors. But anyone who is prepared to try his luck in this hazardous game should bear in mind the ultimate nature of leverage—its essence: you can be on the hook for amounts far greater than you have invested.

Margin requirements may differ from market to market, but generally they reflect market volatility and the overall exposure of the broker members—the net balance of the overall long and short positions opened. On LME, for example, they have developed a bespoke computer program—the SPAN algorithm (Standard Portfolio ANalysis of risk)—which is applied to each clearing member on a daily basis.

The other specific features which apply to trading procedures—such as delivery dates, daily price limits, minimum price change and position closing—tend to be standardized, but may also vary significantly. Knowing the procedure at one specific exchange does not imply that a client will qualify as an experienced trader on another. Thus, before contracting a trade on any exchange it has become an imperative that each client study the exchange's rules, its governance and regulations.

BUILDING BLOCK NO. 8 THE CLEARING HOUSE

One thing which is in common to all futures exchanges is the existence of a clearing house. Since its first appearance in the USA, back in the 1920's, the clearing house's operations have been constantly modernized in effort to meet the ever increasing needs of member clients, and smooth out and facilitate futures trading. The role of the clearing house can be summarized in the following way:

Each party entering a futures position is obliged to make that "good faith deposit" called the margin with their broker. Should the market development be favourable on any particular day and the position earns money, unrealized gains will be credited to the margin account. It also implies that, on the other side of the transaction, there is an invisible counterpart whose account will record a loss to exactly the same extent and will be debited accordingly for the same amount. Hence, every transaction has two parties—for every buyer there is a seller. The clearing house makes it possible because every deal, before being passed for "clearing," has to be "matched." The matching is done through the exchange computing system, where computers compare the inputs from all parties to the contract until it picks up the two that coincide in all particulars—then the transaction has been matched.

Now the role of the clearing house comes into play. The margin received by the broker is required to be deposited into the clearing house account. At this point the clearing house will register the existence of the contract. When a deal is registered it means that responsibility for daily settlements is assumed by the clearing house. This process is called "Novation." From that moment on, the parties on each side of the transaction enter into a direct contractual relationship with the clearing house as their counterparty. As a result, both parties have passed their risk exposure to the clearing house, which is considered to be risk neutral since both clients have deposited the margin set out by the exchange at a level which is high enough to secure protection against daily fluctuations in contract value. In addition to margin requirements, the system itself is effectively protected by marking-to-market, a routine which constantly monitors changes in each contract's value. At the end of each trading day accounts that lose value are required to transfer funds immediately up to the margin level. This represents the satisfactory protection for the clearing house.

In essence, the clearing house serves as a trustworthy go-between in charge of crediting the accounts of winners on behalf of losers on a daily basis.

Finally, the clearing house takes responsibility for managing delivery on maturity of the contract.

Example: Clearing House Offsetting Cash Flows

Price rise $100

LONG +$100 credits ← CLEARING HOUSE ← debits −$100 **SHORT**

Price fall $235

LONG −$235 debits → CLEARING HOUSE → credits +$235 **SHORT**

Under the normal state of affairs, delivery is an undesirable outcome. In order to avoid it, brokers issue warnings to their clients that the delivery date is approaching, so that they can close out active positions in time. In practice, however, the clients—those who fail to close out their positions before the final trading day—do find themselves having to deal with delivery. So, what happens in that case? The longs—those who have opened the position by buying a futures—will have to take delivery (accept the corresponding tonnage of the underlying commodity), and the shorts—those who have opened the position by selling a futures—will have to make a delivery (submit or hand over the underlying commodity to the exchange). The whole procedure is facilitated by the clearing house, which is responsible for providing a smooth procedure regarding the quality of the merchandise, where and when it is to be delivered, storage costs and other details. Here again it should be emphasized that delivery does not suggest that clients are obliged to hand over or receive the commodity itself. Instead they exchange the delivery instruments—the documents of possession authorizing the bearer to take delivery at some particular approved warehouse facility.

In the case of LME the delivery instrument covering the underlying commodity is in the form of a warrant. The warrant is a bearer document specifying the brand of the commodity, its quality, shape and weight, the size of the lot and the specific LME-approved warehouse location. Exchange of warrants from the seller to the buyer takes place on the prompt date. By this transaction the seller authorizes the holder of the warrant with the right to take possession of the specific metal at the specific LME warehouse. The quality and brand of metal from the warrant must conform to the relevant contract specification.

SUMMARY

Exchange-traded futures contracts are a flexible and convenient tool for managing the price risk inherent in the cash market or tangible commodity positions. Like other open markets, where large numbers of potential buyers and sellers compete for the best prices, futures markets provide an indispensable environment for risk management and hedging programmes designed to meet the versatile requirements of individual companies. In addition, these markets provide the opportunity for leveraged investments, which in turn attract large pools of risk capital.

As a result, futures markets are among the most liquid of all global financial markets, providing simplicity, low transaction costs, easy-to-enter-and exit procedures, and capital efficiency. Because of their ever-rowing popularity we shall repeat some of the key characteristics deemed liable for their universal acceptance:

- Futures contracts are standardized in terms of quality, quantity, price and location of delivery;
- Futures contracts are traded on organized and highly regulated markets;
- The last day on which the futures contract must be closed with an offsetting transaction is called the maturity date;
- Futures contracts are marked-to-market each day at their end-of-day settlement prices, in order to establish a day-to-day account of profits and losses;
- When the sum of these profits exceeds the original margin amount deposited, the trader is entitled to withdraw his excess profits without waiting for the existing position to be terminated; the trader of an unprofitable account whose losses fall behind the maintenance margin must deposit additional funds to ensure his ability to meet the contract's obligations;
- Futures contracts can be closed prematurely. The majority of futures contracts are closed out by reversal transaction (i.e., an equal and opposite transaction to the one that initiated the position) at any time prior to the contract's expiration;
- Physical delivery is considered to be an exceptional way of terminating a futures contract as they are primarily designed to be instruments of price protection;
- In case of eventual physical delivery, the "longs" (those who initially bought a futures contract) are obliged to receive the underlying asset and pay the contracted futures price; and the "shorts" (those who initially sold a futures contract) are obliged to handover or deliver the asset underlying the contract at the contracted futures price;
- The clearing house acts as the ultimate buyer to all sellers and seller to all buyers, thus eliminating the possibility of default by the other parties.

KEY TERMS

futures contract	speculator	margin call
commodity	prompt date	mark-to-market
bulls	maturity date	variation margin
bears	initial margin	leverage
hedger	maintenance margin	

CHAPTER 3

COMMODITY FUTURES PRICING

CHAPTER OBJECTIVES

- To introduce the cost of carry concept
- To define and explain the concept of arbitrage
- To describe and demonstrate the case of cash and carry arbitrage
- To describe and demonstrate the case of reverse cash and carry arbitrage
- To exhibit and define the meaning of convenience yield
- To exhibit and define the meaning of forward curves – contango and backwardation
- To highlight the major differences between forward and futures contracts

COST OF CARRY CONCEPT

Most futures contracts can be priced on the basis of no-arbitrage, implying that the futures contract, if priced right, should cost the same as a strategy of buying and storing the underlying commodity.

For an asset (stock) that provides no-income/interest, the generally accepted formula which connects spot prices (S_0), and futures prices (F_0), should endorse the following equality:

$$\text{Discrete: } F0 = S0\ (1 + r)\ T$$

$$\text{Continuously Compounded: } F0 = S0e^{rT}$$

For storable goods the equation is modified to reflect the cost of carry:

$$\text{Discrete: } F0 = S0\ (1 + C\ 0, T)\ T$$

$$\text{Continuously Compounded: } F0 = S0\ e^{cT}$$

Example: Continuously Compounded Interest Rate

Time Periods	n	r/n	$[1+(r/n)]^n$	PV	$FV=PV[1+(r/n)]^n$
Annually	1	.045	1.0450	100	104.50
Semiannually	2	.0225	1.0455	100	104.55
Quarterly	4	.01125	1.0458	100	104.58
Monthly	12	.00375	1.0459	100	104.59
Weekly	52	.00086538	1.0460	100	104.60
Daily	365	.00012328	1.046025	100	104.6025

$e^{(0.45)} = 1.046028$

Continuous compounding is the term which denotes that interest payments are fragmented to an infinite number of periods, so that interest is earned on previously earned interest incessantly.

Notations:
S (0) = Spot price
F (0, T) = Forward price for time – T, as of time – 0
C (0, T) = Cost of carry

Futures pricing theory for storable goods rests upon the "cost of carry" concept and no-arbitrage principle.

The concept of cost of carry is used to calculate the "fair value" of the futures contract.

The no arbitrage principle assumes that the value of an asset acquired through a futures contract, and the value of acquiring that same asset spot and storing it until the forward date, should be the same.

The **cost of carry** refers to the costs associated with holding a commodity until the futures contract's expiry. This model is the most pragmatic concept that connects the current futures price (F0), with the spot price (S0) of the underlying asset.

Key Terms

cost of carry
the costs related to financing the commodity up to some date in the future (interest + storage costs + insurance)

The cost of carry includes interest, insurance and storage.
The relationship is soundly logical as nothing could be more natural than to regard the price of the futures contract as the correspondent to its underlying spot price plus the cost associated with carrying the position from the current date to time T—the expiration date (maturity of the contract). So, in a normal state of affairs, the futures price is higher for the riskless rate of interest per period (traditionally attached to the Treasury Bill, which is considered riskless), the storage and insurance costs. These costs are also treated as a "negative yield," since they increase the cost of carry.

If this equation does not hold then prospective investors can avail themselves of arbitrage opportunities.

An example of discrete storage cost calculation:

$$F(0, T) = S0\,[1 + (C\,0, T)\,T]$$

In the following examples, for simplicity reasons we shall assume that storage costs for physical commodities—as in precious metals markets—are negligible and will be excluded from the calculation.

S (0) = \$1090
C (0, T) = r, interest riskfree rate 4.5%
Then, for example, the futures contract would be priced as follows:
T = 0.5
F (0, T) = S0 [1+(C 0, T) T]
F (0, T) = \$1090 x $(1 + .045)^{0.5}$
F (0, T) = \$1090 x 1.0225
F (0, T) = \$1114.255

The price obtained is the equilibrium price or "arbitrage free forward price." If this equation is unbalanced an "arbitrage opportunity" would be possible—an opportunity to make an up-front riskless profit, either as "cash and carry," or "reverse cash and carry" arbitrage (as illustrated below).

CASH AND CARRY ARBITRAGE

$$\text{Overpriced Futures } F(0, T) > S0\,[1+(C\,0,T)T]$$

S (0) = \$1090
S0 [1 + (C 0, T) T] = \$1114.255 = arbitrage free forward price
C(0, T) = r, risk-free interest rate 4.5%
T = 0.5
F (0, T) = \$1130 = actual futures price
\$1130 > \$1114.255

The cash and carry is a spot-forward arbitrage strategy exploiting the situation in which the futures quoted price—F0,T exceeds the "arbitrage free forward price."

The term "cash and carry arbitrage, "correlates directly to the set of transactions needed to constitute the strategy: the investor uses borrowed money (cash) to buy the asset spot; the investor then stores it—i.e., carries that asset until the maturity of the short futures contract. At maturity the investor delivers the spot asset to cover the short futures sale.

This strategy is also known as "self-financing arbitrage."

Alternative I:
Immediate gain at the outset, no risk of loss in the future.

F (0,T) 1130	Time (0)	Time (T)
Borrow PV (F0, T) **"Cash"**	$1105.13	
Buy Asset Spot and **"Carry"** Forward	–$1090.00	
Short a Futures	0.00	
Repay Loan + Interest		–$1130.00
Deliver Asset Against Short Futures		$1130.00
Portfolio	$15.13	0.00

Alternative II :
Zero cost investment at the outset, positive cash inflow at the close.

F (0,T) 1130	Time (0)	Time (T)
Borrow S0 **"Cash"**	$1090.00	
Buy Asset S0 and **"Carry"** Forward	–$1090.00	
Short a Futures	0.00	
Repay Loan S0 [1 + (C 0, T) T		–$1114.25
Deliver Asset S0 Against Short Futures		$1130.00
Portfolio: [F0 – S0 [1 + (C 0, T) T]	0.00	$15.75

REVERSE CASH AND CARRY ARBITRAGE

Underpriced futures F (0, T) < S0 [1+(C 0,T)T]

S (0) = $1090
S0 [1+(C 0,T)T] = $1114.255 = arbitrage free forward price
C(0, T) = r, risk-free interest rate 4.5%
T = 0.5
F (0, T) = $1100 = actual futures price
$1100 < $1114.255

The reverse cash and carry is a variant of spot-forward arbitrage strategy exploiting the situation in which the futures quoted price (F0,T), is lower than the "arbitrage free forward price."

This stream of transactions is inverted compared to cash and carry arbitrage: the investor sells the asset short—performing the "reverse cash" part of the strategy—and invests the proceeds from the short sale for time T—thereby carrying the proceeds until maturity. This is the "carry" part of the strategy. At maturity, the investor takes delivery against the long futures and covers the short asset sale.

This sequence of transactions brings the following outcome:

Alternative I:
Immediate gain at the outset, no risk of loss in the future.

F (0,T) 1100	Time (0)	Time (T)
Sell Asset Short **"Cash"**	$1090.00	
Lend PV (F0, T) and **"Carry"** Forward	–$1075.80	
Buy a Futures	0.00	
Collect Loan + Interest		$1100.00
Take Delivery and Cover Short Asset		–$1100.00
Portfolio	$14.20	0.00

Alternative II:
Zero cost investment at the outset, positive cash inflow at the close.

F (0,T) 1100	Time (0)	Time (T)
Sell Asset Short S0 **"Cash"**	$1090.00	
Lend S0 and **"Carry"** Forward	–$1090.00	
Buy a Futures	0.00	
Collect Loan S0 [1 + (C 0, T) T		$1114.25
Take Delivery F0 and Cover Short Asset		–$1100.00
Portfolio: [S0 [1+ (C 0, T) T – F 0]	0.00	$14.25

Key Terms

contango
market term structure in which current futures prices stand at a premium relative to spot or cash prices;

backwardation
market term structure in which current futures prices stand at a discont relative to spot or cash prices; also inverted market

The cost of carry is a valuation method which explains the relationship between spot and future prices as well as why the level of **contango** must equal the carrying costs. But the real price-term structure of storable commodities is not one dimensional.

In times of market disruptions, with low inventories and when a scarcity today is more pronounced than the one anticipated in the future, then a large convenience yield will overpower the cost of carry, causing the term structure of futures prices to flip from contango to **backwardation**.

One of the major shortcomings of the futures pricing formula is that it cannot explain how low prices may go, and how or why the basis could be negative. In an attempt to overcome this apparent deficiency, the authors of" Managing Metals Price Risks with the LME," incorporated the factor X in the formula—the influence of nearby supply and demand. This slightly modified equation looks like this:

$$F = N + I + S - X$$

Notations:
F – futures price
N – nearby prices
I – riskless rate
S – storage costs
X – supply and demand influence

The formula could be paraphrased as follows:

- As long as X is zero—and assuming that supply and demand are in balance—forward prices will equal nearby prices plus the sum of I + S.
- At the same time, the maximum possible contango is determined by the sum of I + S. If it rises above this level—as we saw in the previous equation—you will be better off borrowing to buy metal and making a profit from the interest rate.
- Contango will prevail as long as $X < (I + S)$.
- Backwardation will prevail as long as $X > (I + S)$.

CONVENIENCE YIELD

Another observation of the influence of nearby supply and demand on futures prices relates to the concept of **convenience yield.** This was introduced by H. Working and S. Hoss and may be defined as the benefit accruing to the owner of a physical inventory compared to that of a distant futures contract. It rests on the following premises:

- Storage costs are not constant—they vary with the passage of time. When a commodity is in plentiful supply storage costs tend to be higher as capacity is limited; convenience yield is nonexistent and the level of a forward price is determined by the sum of storage costs and interest rate.
- As the level of stocks diminishes, storage costs tend to fall accordingly. When inventories are dried out the storage costs decline and the convenience yield rises, thus making the basis negative. Figure 3.1 illustrates this relationship.

Key Terms

convenience yield
the benefit or the premium accrued to owners holding physical goods rather than a distant derivative contract

Figure 3.1 Storage Costs, Convenience Yield and Level of Stocks

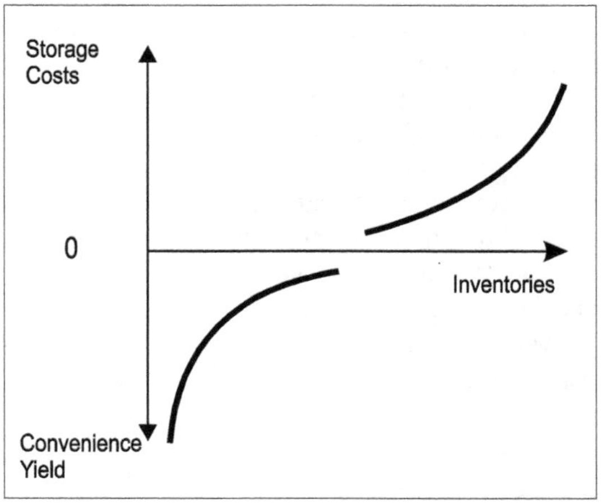

Rearranging the previous formula we arrive at the following equation:

$$F = SP + I + \text{STORAGE COSTS} - \text{CONVENIENCE YIELD}$$

Or expressed in terms of continuous compounding:

$$F_0 = S_0\, e^{(r+u-y)T}$$

Where (r) is a riskless rate, (u) storage costs, and (y) convenience yield.

Lower inventories make physical commodities more valuable and raise the convenience yield. The logic is straightforward. With low inventory levels—relative to current consumption requirements—the probability of stock-outs and associated costs increase as well. When the equilibrium of supply and demand is distorted—in the sense that demand exceeds supply—than the pendulum of price appreciation shifts from owners of futures delivery contracts to owners of physical commodities. In that respect, convenience yield may be defined also as a commodity shortage which appreciates on the market through price increase.

We find clear manifestations of this situation during a **squeeze** such as one we had in 1990, during the Iraq-Kuwait oil crises, when spot prices rallied to $40 per barrel overwhelming the futures price level of $24 per barrel and driving the market into steep backwardation.

Key Terms

squeeze
pressure on a particular delivery date which makes the price of that date higher in relation to other dates

A recent example, presented in the following graph, illustrates the correlation between zinc metal prices and the relative inventories held at the LME. It also exhibits the anomaly of a zinc price collapse, which was fuelled by a report that Red Kite Management Ltd.—a $1 billion metals' trading hedge fund—has suffered losses at the beginning of 2007.

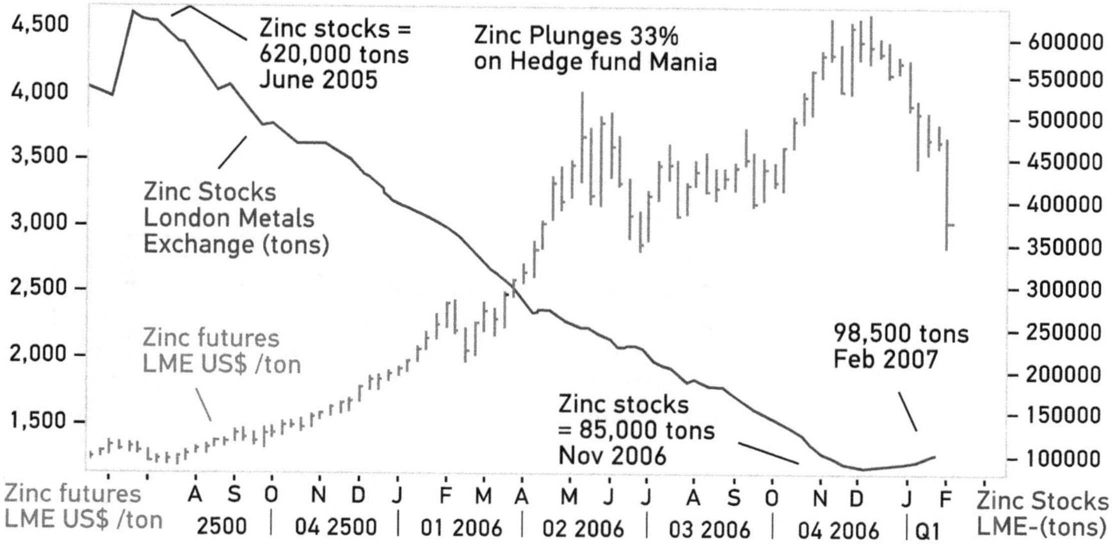

In mathematical terms the convenience yield is defined as:

$$\text{Forward Price} \times (1 + CY) = \text{Spot Price} \times (1 + \text{Interest Rate})$$

Key Terms

forward curve
the relationship between cash and futures prices across different maturities

Discrete compounding

Spot price = 100
Forward price = 104
Interest rate = 6%
Forward price x (1+ CY) = Spot price x (1+interest rate)
1 + CY = Spot price x (1+interest rate)/ forward price)
1 + CY = $106/$104 = 1.01923
CY as a % of forward price = 0.01923 = 2
$104 x 1.01923 = $100 x 1.06 = $106
Forward price = Spot price + interest rate – convenience yield = $100 + 6 – 2 = $104

Continuous compounding

$F_0 = S_0 e^{(r-y)T}$
$r = 6\%; y = 2\%$
$F_0 = \$100 \times 2.71828^{(0.06-0.02)1} = \$104.08$
$Y = S(t) - F(t,T) \exp[-(r+c)(T-t)] = \$100 - (\$104.08 \times 2.71828^{-.06x1}) = \$100 - \$98.0188 = \$1.9811$
$F(t,T) = (S(t) - Y) \exp[(r+c)(T-t)] = (\$100 - \$1.9811)e^{.06x1} = \$104.08$

Figure 3.2 illustrates the relationship between cash and futures prices across different maturities. These, so-called "**forwards curves**" or "futures price curves" typically manifest themselves either as contango or backwardation.

Figure 3.2 Forward Curves—Futures Price Curves

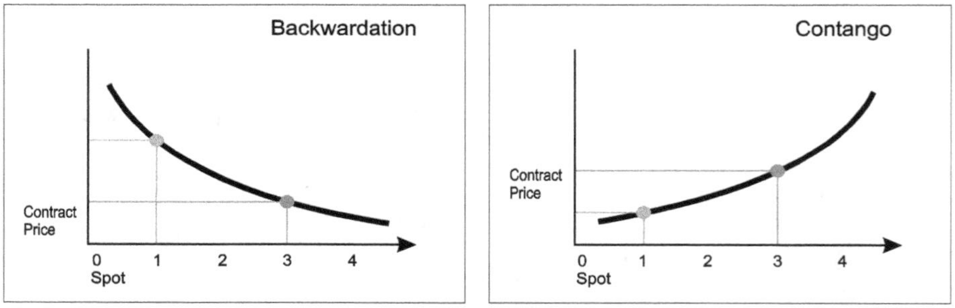

Contango A market structure in which current futures prices in successive delivery months command a premium relative to near term or spot prices. The size of contango is fairly predictable subject to limits given by the sum of the cost of carry (interest + storage costs); the futures prices in the successive delivery months are linearly higher than the spot or cash price, therefore:

Contango is Depicted as an Upward-Sloping Forward Curve.

Backwardation A market structure in which current futures prices in succeeding delivery months stand at a discount relative to near term or spot prices. There is no predictable limit to the size of backwardation, prices in forward (distant) delivery months could be progressively lower compared to spot prices. Spot prices can rise to exceptional levels. Hence,

Backwardation is Depicted as a Downward-Sloping Forward Curve.

The steepness of the curve might assume a more dramatic shape. It is important to emphasize that the main cause influencing the steepness of the backwardation curve is the rise of cash commodity prices, rather than the fall of forward prices, which sustain their existing level.

Another essential observation relates to the term structure of the forward curves. Forward, or "yield curves"— depicted in the form of contango and backwardation— are not of uniform structure across different maturities but develop in rather volatile fashion. Due to the uneven shape of the yield curve, on any particular date, different contracts and their relative expirations offer a variety of different yields. Look carefully at the LME real-time data in the following table.

Table 3.1 Forward Prices Term Structure

LME OFFICIAL PRICES (US$/tone) for 26 Sept 2011			
TERM STRUCTURE	**COPPER**	**ALUMINIUM**	**TIN**
Cash Buyer	7225.00	2195.00	20,795.00
Cash Seller & Settl.	7226.00	2195.50	20,800.00
3 Months Buyer	7240.00 c	2220.50 c	20,550.00 b
3 Months Seller	7240.50 c	2221.00 c	20,555.00 b
15 Months Buyer	7275.00 c	2305.00 c	20,690.00 b
15 Months Seller	7285.00 c	2310.00 c	20,740.00 b
27 Months Buyer	7270.00 c	2385.00 c	N/A
27 Months Seller	7280.00 c	2390.00 c	N/A

This property of the yield curve—to change randomly across different maturities—retains a potential which in futures trading may be turned into an unforeseen source of profit.

Remember This! Forward Curve Common Misapprehension

A forward curve is not to be understood as a projection, or a market expectancy of future spot prices! The forward curve (aka "Forward Yield" or "Yield Curve") is a real time exposition of the forward prices available for trading at a particular moment in time! The actual price differential between spot and forward prices will determine the shape of the forward curve.
Accordingly, we have distinguished that the market is in contango if spot or near month prices are lower than the next near month's prices, or in backwardation if the market structure is reversed and spot or near month prices are higher than next near month's price. The forward curves and its associated contango and backwardation rates, develop in a rather unpredictable fashion across time.

The reasons that drive the market in backwardation are numerous and subject to a variety of influences. Broadly speaking they can be grouped into two categories: those pertaining to fundamental changes in economic data—such as production, consumption and all sorts of differing causes of disruptions on the supply side (strikes, natural disasters, wars etc.,); and those related to noneconomic data, either technical or psychological (including financial speculations), that might have an impact on market behaviour. The two groups of influences are, of course, not mutually exclusive and the market response is usually a hybrid of the two.

Whatever the cause, the reality is that the supply and demand are rarely in equilibrium; consequently the contangos and backwardations overwhelm each other in a random sequence. An increase in demand—or a sudden fall in supply—normally drives prices up. In such instances the magnitude of the change will affect near-term prices to a much greater extent than those in the long-term.

In the case of natural catastrophes, political tensions, or open military conflict, spot prices can reach extreme levels—often beyond rational expectations. Commodities particularly sensitive to this kind of anomalies are gold, oil and at an earlier time in history, copper and zinc, as they have been extensively used in ammunition production.

Forecasting market behaviour very often proves to be erroneous and unrewarding, irrespective of expertness and diligent observance of related price analysis.

> *The market is manic-depressive, subject to wild swings in emotions and valuations.*
>
> Charles Munger, Berkshire Hathaway

Therefore, no analysis has adequate capacity to predict the unscientific nature of markets or to obviate the uncertainty principle so deeply embedded in futures trading.

Remember This! Commodities Main Characteristics

Contemporary definition designates commodities as goods with a specific utility, used primarily as inputs in the production of other goods and services, or to satisfy some particular consumers needs, usually produced in large quantities by many independent producers. They are also standardized in terms of quality, quantity and delivery terms and fungible (the property denoting that commodities of the same class are easily replaceable with one another). Commodity prices are determined, most often, by supply and demand interactions in the global marketplace. The process of the price discovery and trade transparency is governed and supervised by exchange authorities.

There are several ways of dividing commodities into classes. One practical method separates the diversity of commodity shapes and designations into "hard" and "soft" categories.

Hard commodities are also qualified as nonperishable assets and further divided as:

- Energy Products – Crude Oil, Natural Gas, Gasoline
- Precious Metals – Gold, Platinum, Palladium, Silver
- Industrial Metals – Aluminum, Copper, Nickel, Zinc, Lead, Tin
- Timber – Lumber, paper products

Soft commodities are perishable and consumable assets such as:

- Agricultural products – Corn, Wheat, Soybeans, Sugar, Cotton, Cocoa and Coffee
- Livestock – Cattle, Pork

The most popular investable Commodity Indices are: Goldman Sachs Commodity Index (GSCI), 24 commodities; Dow Jones-AIG Commodity Index, 19 commodities; S&P Commodity Index, 17 commodities; Deutsche Bank Liquid Commodity Index; Reuters Jefferies CRB, 19 commodities.

I FORWARDS VS. FUTURES

One of the last observations concerns similarities and dissimilarities between futures and forward contracts. Because they are so similar in nature and their differences so delicate they are often mistaken for each other.

Certain features which are seemingly inherent to the concept of forward commitments and future execution—such as the promise that the exchange of money and asset will take place at a future date—are mutual contracts, but the differences are many and should be duly distinguished.

As we emphasized earlier, forward contract are "customized contracts," in the sense that they are tailored specifically to meet the particular preferences of the parties involved. Therefore, forward trading activities are restricted to OTC markets. The advantage is that contract details can be freely negotiated between parties to meet their own particular needs. A forward contract does not require margin deposit and is not subject to daily settlement.

All the principal parameters of the contract:

- quantity,
- quality,
- delivery date,
- delivery point, and
- the price

are dependent upon the will of the contracting parties.

A futures contract is different. It also represents a legally binding commitment to buy or sell a commodity at some predetermined future date. But, contrary to forwards, futures contracts are transacted on major futures exchanges and can only be traded on the exchange that created them, under the rules and regulations set by that exchange and its regulator.

All the key features of futures contracts are predetermined, except the price:

- quantity,
- quality,
- delivery date (set of forward delivery dates determined by the relevant exchange), and
- delivery point.

These features are responsible for making futures contracts a handy vehicle for the transference of risk through hedging strategies, whereas

- futures price

is the only variable which is discovered through an order-routing system on the trading floor of an organized futures exchange.

Price negotiation is made public by futures exchanges through a process termed "**price discovery**." This is an ongoing daily referendum in which competition between market participants, buyers and sellers, is translated into the language of market prices. Hence, futures prices are changing constantly to reflect current market conditions—the current interrelationship of supply and demand factors.

Key Terms

price discovery
ongoing daily referendum in which the competition between market participants, purchasers and sellers, is translated into the language of market prices

Futures vs. Forwards final settlement procedure:

Forward contract	Futures contract
Settled at maturity	Daily settled due to marking-to-market

The differences in settlement procedures are reflected also in futures and forwards payoffs.

FORWARDS PAYOFF

The value of a forward contract at the outset is 0 (zero). It costs nothing (excluding commissions and a collateral that is typically required) to enter into a forward contract, and no margin deposit is required.

Initial cash flow = 0

The value of a forward position at maturity depends on the relationship between the delivery price (K) and the underlying price (PT) at that time. Hence, the payoff from the forward contract would also be the P&L from the contract.

Notations:
K is the original forward price (aka delivery price)
PT is the price of the underlying asset

	Initial Cash Flow	Final Cash Flow
For a long position, the payoff is:	0	PT – K
For a short position, the payoff is:	0	K – PT

FUTURES PAYOFF

Notations:
F (0,T) is the original futures price (aka delivery price)
F (T–t) is the futures contract price when it is closed out
$\mathbf{S_T}$ is the spot price of the underlying at maturity ($S_T = F_T$)

The value of the futures contract at the outset differs as it requires an initial margin deposit. The value of a futures position at maturity depends on the difference between the original (initial) price of the futures contract, and the market price when it is closed out.

In that respect we may conclude that there is no large drift between the performance of a forward contract and the corresponding futures contract.

If and when the futures contract is closed out—settled at maturity date—the futures price will converge to the actual spot price ($F_T = S_T$), and the payoff would be as follows:

Profit and loss for futures position held to maturity

Profit for long futures position:	$S_T - F_0$ (spot – original futures price)
Profit for short futures position:	$F_0 - S_T$ (original futures price – spot)

Key Terms

pit
the physical trading place of the exchange

ring
refers specifically to the trading floor at the LME

position limit
the maximum number of contracts that may be held by any single market participant

price limit
the maximum price rangedefined by an exchange that a commodity can trade in a single day. Also daily trading limits

The key difference between forwards and futures is that a futures contract allows early termination; in association with the movement of prices, profits and losses are calculated on a daily basis in a process designated "marking-to-market."

Consequently, if a futures contract is closed out prior to maturity date, its payoff would be as follows:

Profit and loss for futures position not held to maturity	
Profit for long futures position:	$F(T - t) - F_0$
Profit for short futures position:	$F_0 - F(T - t)$

From this particular aspect we may deduce that a futures contract is an exchange -traded modification of a forward-like contract—subject to daily settlement—which pays incremently (losses are deducted and gains credited to margin accounts) due to marking-to-market.

The whole procedure related to price discovery takes place right in front of the eyes of the public—usually on the central trading floor: the **pit,** or the **ring** of the exchange—and may be screened on the electronic trading system panels.

In futures trading, the negotiating counterparty is not a particular individual and contract performance is guaranteed by a clearing house.

If you want to fix a price you can do so through an authorized exchange dealer by locking-in an instant price for future delivery as they appear on the screen.

Locking-in the price is like a snapshot of the electronic screen taken at one particular point in time.

Regulation and governance of the exchange markets and brokerage houses involved in trade procedures are entrusted to and supervized by the independent government bodies such as:

In the US:

- The Commodity Futures Trading Commission (CFTC), and
- The National Futures Association (NFA)

In the UK:

- The Financial Conduct Authority (FCA), and
- The Prudential Regulation Authority (PRA).

The principal role of these bodies is to provide and guarantee a legislative framework, to reduce financial crime and provide confidence in the integrity of the market.

Futures exchanges also contribute to an orderly market by deciding upon both **position limits**—the maximum number of contracts that may be held by any single market participant—and **price limits**— the maximum price range defined by an exchange that a commodity can trade in a single day.

SUMMARY

The futures pricing theory is based upon two premises:

- Cost of carry explains the relationship between spot and futures prices.
- The no-arbitrage principle assumes that the value of an underlying commodity acquired through a futures contract, maturing at some forward date, and the value of acquiring that same commodity outright and financing it until the same forward date, should be the same. If this principle does not hold then an investor is able to conduct "cash and carry arbitrage" or "reverse cash and carry arbitrage"—that will earn riskless profits.

Further observations, relating to the futures pricing principles, explain the concept of forward curves and contango and backwardation rates. This brings into focus the concept of convenience yield that explicates how and why the basis can become negative. Finally, because futures and forwards are prone to misunderstanding and confusion let us outline the similarities and dissimilarities between these two contracts:

Forwards & Futures

Similarities:

- Forwards and futures are concluded in advance of delivery.
- Both contracts convey an explicit commitment either to buy or sell specific goods at a set price on a future delivery date.
- There is no initial exchange of payment, but a collateral and a margin payment respectively are normally required.
- Both forwards and futures have linear and symmetrical payoffs.

Having outlined the similarities, let us also single out the major differences:

Dissimilarities

Futures:	**Forwards**:
Standardized contract terms, dealers market	Bilateral agreement, non standardized terms
Traded on Exchange floor	Traded on OTC
Settled daily; initial margin + variation	No daily settlements; no margin
Initial margin obligation	Collaterals negotiable
Final settlement predominantly cash	Forwards are normally closed out with physical delivery
Generally closed out prior to maturity	Fixed delivery date, cannot be closed prematurely
Less risk of default; execution guaranteed by the clearing house	Lightly-regulated; risk of delivery/payment default

KEY TERMS

cost of carry	contango	ring
convenience yield	backwardation	position limit
squeeze	price discovery	price limit
forward curve	pit	

CHAPTER 4

HEDGING BASICS

CHAPTER OBJECTIVES

- To define and explain the basic concept of hedging
- To explain and illustrate hedging mechanics
- To outline different types of hedging:
  - Concept of the long hedge
  - Concept of the short hedge
- To define and explicate different types of hedgers:
  - Price fix hedgers
  - Price offset hedgers

I DEFINING HEDGE

Hedge is a fence or barrier formed by bushes set close together. To hedge, accordingly, means to surround, guard or hem in with or as with obstructions or barriers.

(*Definition taken from "Funk & Wagnall's Standard Dictionary)."

THE CONTEMPORARY USE OF THE WORD HEDGE—IN VIEW OF ITS LEXICAL association with modern financial markets jargon—derives its meaning from its original roots: it implies some kind of protection. In the context of financial markets the term has very specific meaning. Among the myriad of hedge definitions, to begin with, the first one is very conspicuous as it defines "hedge" in a way probably the old Laconians would have; it simply says: "Hedge = Reduce risk." It is short, no doubt about it, and it is correct; it tells you the essence of what a financial hedge is. But the problem with definition is that it does not tell you what it is not.

So, we can say that every hedge is reducing risk but conversely we cannot say that every reduced risk is a hedge. For example, there are back-to-back arrangements that cannot only reduce your risk but eliminate it completely. Although you are perfectly protected and insured, this instance of price protection cannot be considered a hedge. Others may seek to reduce risk—and they often do—by limiting or diminishing the scope of investment, by diversifying their portfolio, by predicting the market following sophisticated charts and market analysis, or listening to smart market wizards—but still they are not hedging their position.

What we should have in mind when hedge transactions are concerned is that every hedge must comply to certain rules—characteristics that differentiate the hedge from other risk-reducing activities. Here are those that are inextricably implied in all hedge transactions.

Hedge distinctive features imply:

- that assets are registered and tradable on exchange markets: securities, stocks, stock indexes, currencies or some tangible assets—i.e., commodities such as metals, oils, grains, livestock, softs etc.,
- that the asset at risk is counterbalanced by a hedge instrument—either futures or options—at the exchange,
- that the opening and closing of the futures position must be made at the same time that the physical contract is priced in order to eliminate further exposure to unfavourable price moves, and
- that all trade transactions are subject to the exchange's governance and regulations.

Key Terms

hedging
transaction initiated to offset the risk of an adverse price change emanating from a position held in the physical market by establishing an equal and opposite position in the futures market

If you are missing any of the above features you do not have a hedge.

In financial lingo "hedging" is the act, exercised by exchange-market participants, of taking an offsetting position in a related commodity (or a security) in order to reduce or eliminate the risk of adverse price changes.

Taking into consideration the aforementioned presumptions, let us focus on the following definition of hedging more broadly by stating that:

"***Hedging** is a transaction initiated to offset the risk of an adverse price change emanating from a position held in the physical market by establishing an equal and opposite position in the futures market.*"

HEDGING MECHANICS

Every hedge is a risk-reduction or risk-eliminating strategy. Therefore, it necessarily includes two different transactions:

- One performed in the physical market—the sale or purchase of a physical commodity based on a relevant current exchange (LME) price, and
- the other, an offsetting transaction entered in the financial-exchange market. This is done through the mechanism of a futures trade—i.e., by buying or selling an equal and opposite futures position which matches the delivery date anticipated for the physical transaction.

And at least two phases:

1. The initial phase—at which the hedger instructs his or her broker to open a corresponding futures position, equal and opposite to that held in the physical market, and
2. The closing phase—at maturity or delivery date the hedger instructs his or her broker, prevalently, to financially settle the initial position by buying or selling back the original futures contract based on the current market price.

In between these two phases the original hedge strategy may evolve into a set of different intermediary transactions; these will be the subject of detailed analysis in subsequent chapters.

Holding two different assets—"tangible goods" on the one side, and "paper-based" assets on the other, inversely correlated—puts a hedger in a rather fortuitous position, as losses in one asset will be compensated by gains in the other. In that respect we may designate the general concept of hedging as a "zero-sum game" in which:

> *Nothing's gained and nothing's lost.*
>
> With apologies to The Rolling Stones.

As we are going to illustrate our hedge examples mainly through LME metals transactions, let it be noted that the instruments available there are: futures, options, TAPO's or the LME Index. The subject matter of this book will be confined to futures and options as the most prevalent instruments of price protection. Moreover, as we shall mainly use the London Metal Exchange as the arena for exhibiting hedging transactions, we shall acquaint you with one of the most comprehensive hedging definitions, as follows:

HEDGING DEFINITION

"Hedging is a technique used in futures markets whereby a financial position is taken to offset price risk inherent in a firm's physical operations. It is important to note that the financial position is taken on exchange as an activity in a firm's risk management department that runs parallel to the physical purchase and sale of the underlying products which continue as normal in the firm's commercial department.

In terms of LME, hedging describes the process undertaken by users of the market to lock-in the prices they will pay (or receive) for future deliveries. This is done because the hedger wants to lock-in the known price on a particular operation, or because the prices currently available on the forward market are attractive and the hedger wishes to fix these prices against anticipated business. The hedger will start with price risk exposure from its physical operations, and will buy or sell a futures contract to offset this price exposure in the futures market."

(London Metal Exchange)

DIFFERENT TYPES OF HEDGING

LONG HEDGE

Every hedge begins either as a purchase or a sale of a specific quantity of futures depending on a position held in a physical market.

Long hedgers in general seek to protect a short position in the underlying commodity against a possible price rise.

For instance a metal fabricator makes a firm commitment on May 1 to sell copper wire rods to his regular customer, at a price fixed now, for delivery on June 30. The forward price on that particular date happens to be $7170. He needs 30 days to convert the raw material (copper cathodes) into a finished product (copper wire). He has not yet purchased the necessary quantity of copper cathodes but he hopes to do so in the next 30 days. The fabricator is therefore said to be holding a **short physical position.** In the meantime, he is exposed to price fluctuations, and will generate a loss if the copper price rises. That risk—being short of physical metal—is offset by opening a long futures position: i.e., by buying the equivalent quantity of futures as a hedge. The date of physical purchase, May 30, has to be matched with the futures position closing date. The loss incurred on the physical commodity (due to an increase from $7170 to $7350 between the dates May 1 and May 30), is offset with an equal gain in the futures position.

Key Terms

long hedge
a position initiated by buying a futures, benefits if the underlying market price increase

short physical position
not owning a commodity for which you have a forward commitment

Hedge Buying (Long Hedge) is designed to protect against possible price rise.
It appreciates in value with the price rise: "buy low, sell dear."

We shall illustrate this situation using arrows:

Figure 4.1 Buying (Long) Hedge

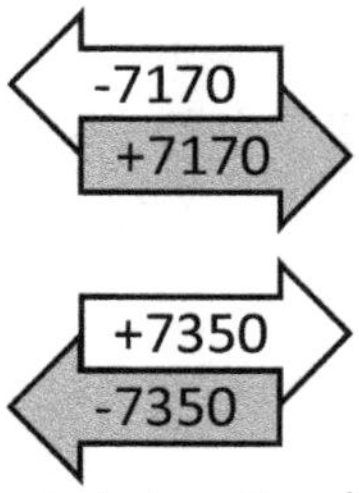

Price on the opening of the hedge in US$ – **May 1st.**

Price on the closing of the hedge in US$ – **May 30th.**

NB: in the context mentioned the term "short position" pertains to being short specifically in physical metal and therefore related to physical market operations. The difference between long of physical/long of futures, and short of physical/short of futures is a very important distinction and must be dully emphasized. Otherwise, as in many other instances, the same terms will appear confusedly mingled or logically inconsistent. A long physical position is offset with opening a short futures position; and vice versa, a short physical position is offset with opening a long futures position.

Figure 4.2, shows a short physical position diagram represented by a long diagonal descending from left to right. Obviously, the short position benefits from the price fall as its profit potential is on the down-side; in rising markets, however, short positions generate a loss.

Profits as well as losses are commensurate with the change of the relative market price.

Figure 4.2 Short Physical Position—Generates a Loss in Case of Price Increase

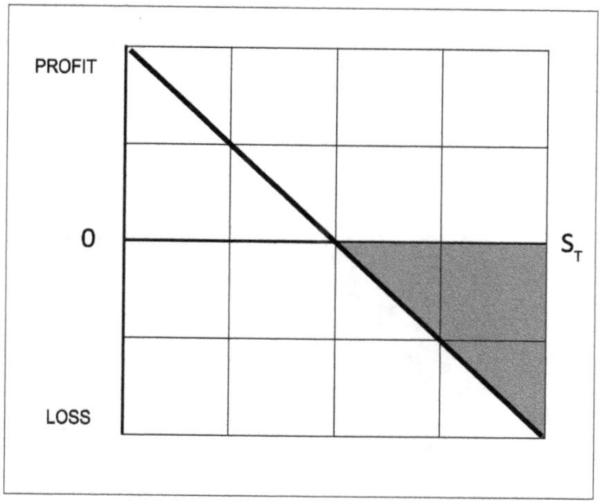

To offset the potential losses arising from being short in a physical commodity the holder takes an equal and opposite offsetting position in the futures market!

Figure 4.3 Inception of Long Hedge

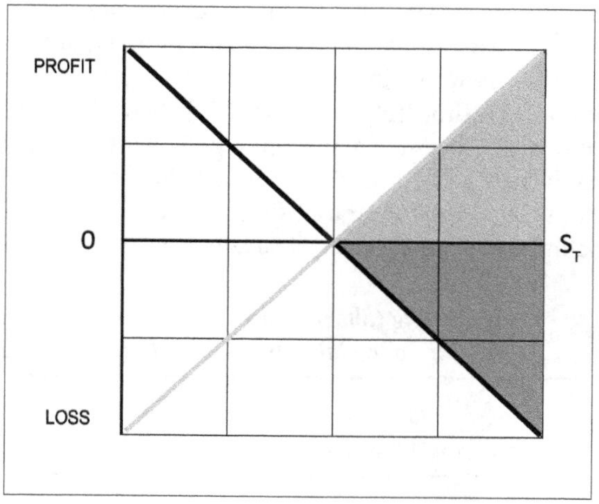

The profit on a futures position, which is closed now by selling back at a higher price, will counterbalance or offset the loss on the physical side—the difference between a price fixed on May 1 and the increase in the price of the cash metal that a fabricator will have to cover. As the prices increased, the physical position generated a loss and the futures position a profit. Because their payoff is symmetrical, gains and losses are equal and opposite. Profits and losses are in balance so the hedge has served its purpose perfectly.

In the case of a price fall the result would be reversed, as shown in the following graph. With a price fall your physical position generates a profit but your futures position generates an equivalent loss, so the final outcome is the same—zero.

Figure 4.4 Long Hedge—Price Fall Illustration

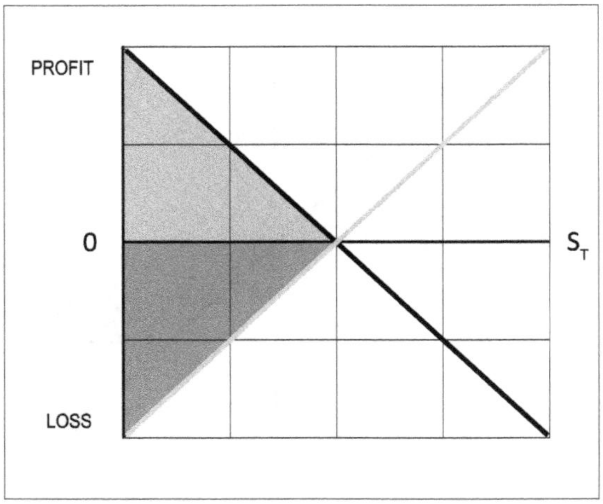

Key Terms

short hedge
initiated by selling a futures, benefits if the underlying market price decrease

long physical position
owning a commodity for which you do not have a forward commitment

SHORT HEDGE

On the other side of the coin we have those who are seeking protection against a possible price fall. Short hedgers sell futures to protect a long position in the underlying commodity against a possible price fall.

The metal on stock, which has been bought but remains unsold, will generate a loss if metal prices fall. Normally, the most sensitive participants in metal business to price decline are miners, and metal producers—smelters or refineries; namely, all those who are, by the nature of their business, holding a **long physical position.**

The risk which investors incur by being long in physical metal is therefore offset by initiating a short futures position (on May 1), i.e., by selling the equivalent quantity of futures as a hedge. Their pricing policy has to be insured in every possible way as the fixed costs of their operation do not allow for sudden and unpredictable price fluctuations. To secure this, the closing date of the futures position has to be matched with the actual sale date of the physical commodity (June 30).

Hedge Selling (Short Hedge) is designed to protect against a possible price fall. It appreciates in value with the price fall: "sell high, buy low."

Figure 4.5 Selling (Short) Hedge

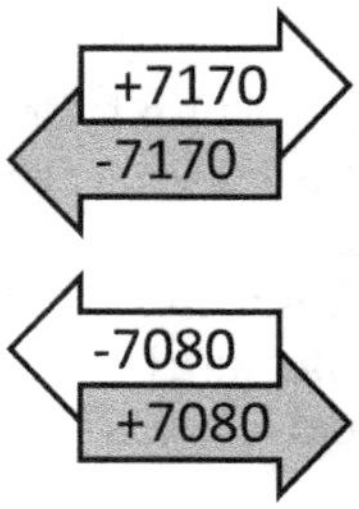

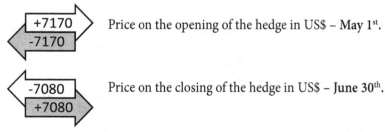

Price on the opening of the hedge in US$ – **May 1st.**

Price on the closing of the hedge in US$ – **June 30th.**

The loss incurred on the cash or physical metals price due to a price fall is offset against the profit arising from a futures transaction which closed (was bought back) at a price lower than on opening.

Figure 4.6 Long Physical Position—Generates a Loss if Price Falls

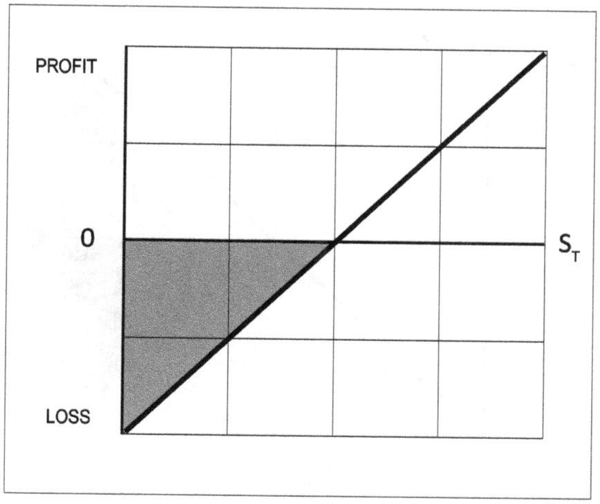

To offset the potential losses arising from being long in a physical commodity the holder takes an equal and opposite position in the futures market.

Figure 4.7 Inception of Short Hedge

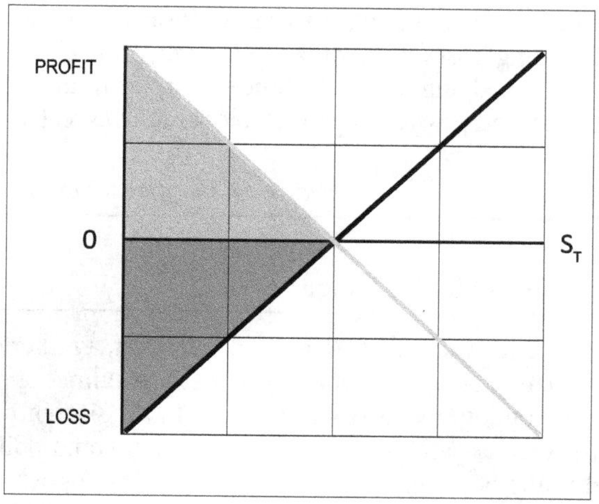

In falling markets, an unhedged long physical position will generate a loss commensurate with the market price decline.

Short futures effectively offset the risk of a price fall, fulfilling the basic hedging principle—elimination of an adverse price change.

Figure 4.8 gives a basic resume of a short hedge performance in the case of price increase.

A price rise will produce results that are directly opposite to that of the price fall; in rising markets, your long physical position now generates a profit (buy low, sell high). But the position in futures generates an equivalent loss (sell low, buy high) so the final outcome is the same = 0.

Figure 4.8 Short Hedge—Price Rise Illustration

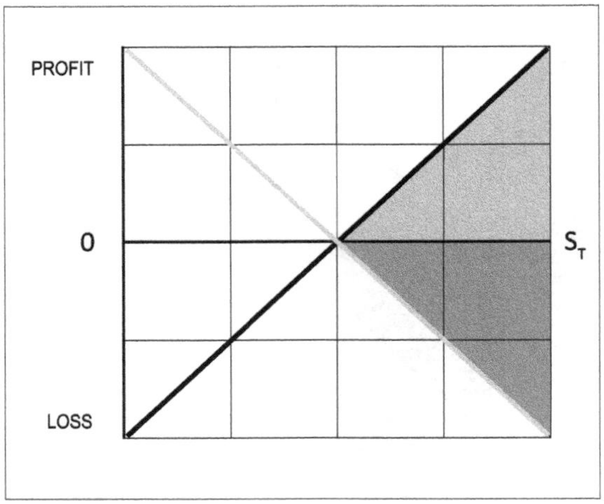

Leaving a position unhedged, in commodity markets, where there is so much uncertainty, often proves to be a hazardous venture ending with a huge loss. Protection of an existing commodity position from such losses—commensurate with the risks being taken—is the focus of many prudent investors, and the crucial safeguarding principle that underlies all investment and trading strategies.

The core idea behind hedging is in managing performance issues; evaluating future outcomes by weighing risk against reward, with the emphasise on containing risk and "avoiding losses" rather than "acquiring profits."

The hedging eliminates uncertainty of future price moves across all market scenarios, and provides a predictable result irrespective of price direction.

Hedging = Indifference to Price Direction

Remember This! London Metal Exchange

The London Metal Exchange is presently located at 56, Leadenhall Street, a rather quiet street in the heart of the Square Mile, the most eminent square mile in the world (2.6 km^2) that outlines one of the world's major business and financial centres—the City of London. Its history traces back in the sixteenth century—the reign of Queen Elizabeth—during which the first regular gatherings of metal and other commodity traders were recorded. The LME modern history is related to the beginnings of exchange-based trading which goes back to the late nineteenth century when the London Metals and Mining Company was founded in 1877.

Today the London Metal Exchange, which is a UK Recognized Investment Exchange, is the world's premier nonferrous metals market, responsible for more than 90 percent of global on-exchange trading in base metals derivatives. The "official cash settlement price" published daily—is used as a reference price by over 95 per cent of the world's physical metals trading. Its annual turnover in 2011, exceeded 146 million lots, the equivalent of 3.5 billion tonnes and $15.4 trillion in notional value. To obtain such a huge trading volumes, LME uses three trading platforms: ring trading (the open outcry market); Inter-office telephone market, and the LME Select market.

Ring Sessions During Ring Sessions, members, sitting around an open-outcry trading floor, the world-famous "Ring", with its scarlet leather seats, trade each LME contract in specific 5-minute periods. At present, there are 12 "ring dealers." Each metal is traded during two sessions—morning and afternoon, four times a day as well as during the "kerb" sessions when all metals are traded simultaneously.

I DIFFERENT TYPES OF HEDGERS

In the world of exchange markets, prices normally fluctuate on a daily basis. Their movements are highly dynamic. Here is an example of copper price fluctuations on a yearly basis (2007–2010):

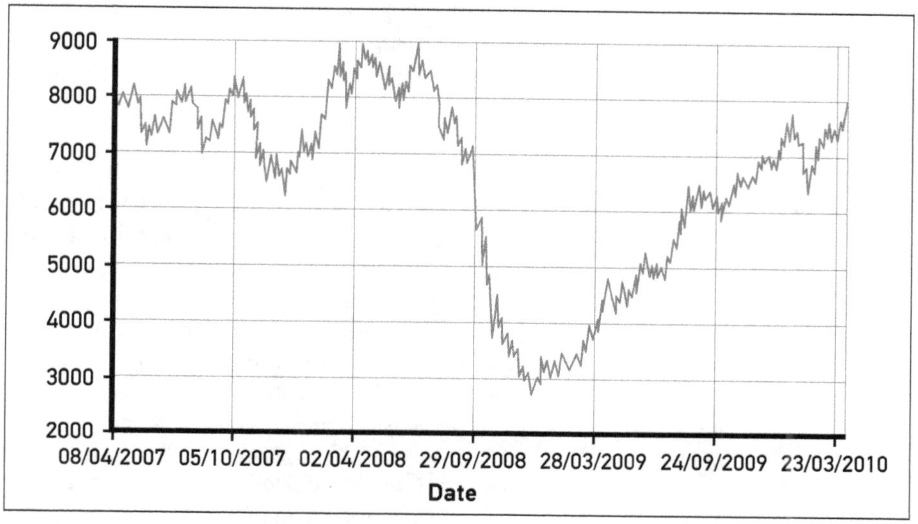

The price diagram more or less repeats itself—you have ups and you downs, depending mostly on over- or under-supply factors, but many other causes are involved too. Therefore, it is fairly difficult to predict where the prices will end at some point in the future. Markets are never wrong—but predictions usually are.

That makes the job of risk managers or management teams very complex and difficult. Their task is to employ hedging strategies to minimize—at least, and eventually completely offset—the exposure to their price-sensitive position. The nature and types of hedging strategy that are supposed to eliminate the risk of an adverse price movement suggest that hedgers may be differentiated into two distinct categories.

Key Terms

price fix hedgers
those who aim to eliminate the uncertainty of forward price movements by locking-in the target price, where a futures contract serves as a price fixing instrument

price offset hedgers
those who aim to create an equal and opposite position in futures market to protect the value of a specific physical position

PRICE FIX HEDGERS

The objective of price fix hedgers is to eliminate price uncertainty and lock-in the target price no matter whether they are buyers or sellers. Price fix hedgers remove the speculative element from their forward price commitments by securing the convenient metal price level, which is known at the outset.

PRICE OFFSET HEDGERS

The basic objective of offset hedgers is to create an equal and opposite futures position in order to eliminate exposure originated from holding a physical position. Offset hedge is performed by those who both buy and sell on a metals price-sensitive basis. The pricing of the metal on the one side—whether a sale or a purchase—must be outweighed by the opposite transaction on the LME. Matching the exact tonnage, and the choice of transaction dates are of paramount importance. The opening transaction (either a sale or a purchase at the LME) must be fully synchronized with the time the physical contract is priced.

The closing transaction—**resale** against the hedge purchase, or **repurchase** against the hedge sale—must also match the date the physical price is fixed.

The following chapters will introduce and review the basic futures hedging strategies and their applications. Chapter 5 lays emphasis on hedging graphical interpretation—hedge patterns, covering a wide range of alternative hedge scenarios.

Key Terms

resale
selling back the long futures (a position initiated with a futures purchase)

repurchase
buying back the short futures (a position initiated with a futures sale)

SUMMARY

In this chapter we have examined the basics of different types and forms of hedging strategies. The purpose of all risk management—regardless of the nature of business—is to plan ahead and manage price risk exposure. A short hedger sells futures to hedge a long position in the underlying commodity, while a long hedger buys futures to hedge a short position in the underlying commodity.

Price fix hedgers seek to eliminate uncertainty and lock-in the target price of a forward commitments; they establish long and short futures positions as a temporary substitute for the physical sale or purchase that is going to be realized at some forward point in time.

A price offset hedger's objective is to institute an equal and opposite futures position to match the price risk originating from holding a physical position.

Hedging strategies create the security that losses in the value of actuals are compensated by gains in the value of futures, and vice versa. This clearly demonstrates that hedging is not designed to be a means of making profits. The aftermath of a properly employed hedging solution should adhere to a conclusive paradigm (fundamental hedging principle)—"nothing's gained and nothing's lost."

KEY TERMS

hedging	short hedge	repurchase
long hedge	long physical position	price fix hedgers
short physical position	resale	price offset hedgers

CHAPTER 5

HEDGE PATTERNS WITH FUTURES

CHAPTER OBJECTIVES

- To introduce and visualization basic hedge patterns with futures
- To explain the difference between a price fixing hedge and a price offsetting hedge
- To show how the hedge reduces risks encountered in commodities trading
- To illustrate the concept of rolling a futures hedge
- To explain and illustrate the mechanics of average price hedging
- To explain the procedure and the main types of futures order placement

I HEDGE PATTERNS WITH FUTURES

AT THIS POINT WE SHALL EMPLOY THE CONCEPT OF HEDGE PATTERNS TO EXPLAIN the price fix hedge strategy aimed to protect firstly metal sellers, and then metal buyers.

Notations:
t_0 – denotes initial time. It can be any date in any month available on related exchange calendar.
Cash column—refers to the spot price at which the futures contract, held to maturity, is closed out by an opposite trade.
Columns 1 month, 2 months and 3 months refer to forward spread:
t_0+ 30/60/90 days respectively.
In the following patterns we assume that t_0 is one day in January not specifying which one in particular as this would only complicate the concept. Hedge patterns exhibited below also bear two more restrictions: they do not reflect the bid/ask spread, and for simplicity reasons, they do not reflect the LME specific – the two days cash to prompt execution. I believe, however, that these reservations will have no detrimental effect on conceptual consistency. Transaction costs also have been ignored.

Before we actually begin to elaborate different hedging strategies let us focus once again on the fundamental nature of a futures contract, in a somewhat simplified form. In view of the LME as an exchange arena, a futures contract can be defined simply as an obligation to buy or sell a commodity. The time at which the futures contract is initiated and the price of the underlying commodity fixed, is referred to as t_0, whereas the imposition entailed—to deliver or take delivery at some specified forward date—is referred to as t_1, also called the prompt date.

On the LME, for example, all trading dates between now and three months forward are available as prompt dates. From that point in time, the prompt dates are reduced to every Wednesday for the next three months, and then every third Wednesday of the month, from 7 to 123 months forward, depending on the particular underlying commodity.

It seems worth emphasizing that a firm commitment to execute the ultimate contractual obligation—to deliver the commodity in the case of a futures sale, or take delivery in the case of a futures purchase—can be cancelled out, or closed, by the reversal purchase or sale prior to the prompt date—the maturity of the futures contract. The last date you are allowed to do that—to offset the futures contract—is two days prior to the prompt date.

Before we delve into the different hedging strategies, depicted in this chapter and the following one, there is one important notice you should be acquainted with: the relationship between spot and futures prices is driven by continually changing forces of supply and demand.

As a consequence of this dynamic phenomenon, the market structure in which futures contracts are transacted is defined either as a "contango" or "backwardation."

Contango: Occurrence in which Futures Prices > Spot Prices.

Backwardation: Occurrence in which Futures Prices < Spot Prices.

Referring to the relationship between spot and forward prices, it is very important to put emphasis on the following commonly encountered occurrence: looking down the "forward curve" of a particular commodity at a particular market you may observe that the term structure in effect spreads unevenly over the different contract month maturities.

So, it is theoreticall—possible, and quite often empirically verified (especially in the case of LME, with expiration going many months forward)— to see that the settlement prices for various contract months do not necessarily move in tandem. Thus, at any given date, different contract maturities offer different yields—you may have the near month contract closing up in contango for the day and the further month contract closing down in backwardation for the day, or vice versa.

This repeated occurence comes as a consequence of the fact that the settlement price of each contract month is determined independently—founded on expectations and dynamic market factors such as supply and demand—which put explicit weight on the forward contract months. Hence, different contract maturities will vary in a price significantly.

In the examples presented below, for the sake of clarity we have assumed that the forward curve (term structure) is either in contango or in backwardation respectively, not implying that this particular case is the norm in the LME market.

When it comes to hedge strategies specifically, a great effort has been employed in creating new instruments and concepts that will prove to be superior to classic scholastic interpretations.

Narrative explications, so predominantly encountered, would only manage in typical fashion, to stir and obfuscate what is really going on. Elaborate strategies often sound ambiguous and confusing. Consequently, I have tried to uncover a different concept with a powerful design application of the strategy execution. The idea was to select and adapt an exciting new approach to disseminate and share information—how the futures hedging works, the logic why it works that way, and how it may develope subject to unexpected swings in prices.

Finally, we have succeeded to tabulate the concept in this respect, and interpret each hedging case with the aid of a visual recognition—in other words, we have managed to assign a "pattern" to each case study.

So now, as we are going to demonstrate in the coming pages, each particular strategy receives its visual identity and comes forward with radical clarity.

The case studies in this chapter, in particular, will provide you with:

- an innovative and illuminating approach to choosing a best-fit hedging strategy,
- an accurate and comprehensive view of the repercussions of each strategy,
- instant visual recognition of the different alternatives associated with futures hedging strategies and evaluation of its performance metrics as they develop, and finally,
- a tool that makes it possible to simulate performance and analyze restructuring opportunities as they unfold.

PRICE FIXING HEDGE—SELLING FORWARD

The following tables reveal the logic of price fixing transactions. Note that the number of arrows in the price fix hedges is odd: two of them represent futures transactions while one represent a physical transaction. And now, let us proceed with our first example.

Table 5.1 Price Fixing Hedge; Selling Forward

FORWARD / CURRENT	CASH	1 MONTH	2 MONTHS	3 MONTHS
JANUARY (to)	7520	7530	7540	+7550
FEBRUARY	7480	7490	7500	7510
MARCH	7440	7450	7460	7470
APRIL	+7400 −7400	7410	7420	7430

Price fall, contango market
Cash metal price $7400 + Profit on futures $150
Net selling price = $7550

Selling a futures contract on the LME, as a temporary substitution for an anticipated forward sale, provides protection from a price fall, whether the market is in contango (as in our example) or in backwardation. The hedge transaction locks-in the net selling target price of $7550, offsetting the actual physical metal price decline.

This is a selling hedge. It begins by selling a futures at a date corresponding to the projected physical sale of the metal. In other words, for this emblametic transaction the exchange's lingo would use the proverbial expression "selling short," or **short a futures**.

Key Terms

short futures
opening position on LME (or any other exchange) with a sale of futures

Price Fixing Hedge; Selling Forward—Price Falling

The repercussions in the case of prices falling would unfold as follows:

- If you hedged your position the eventual losses on the physical side would be compensated for with the profit earned on the futures.
- If you did not hedge then your position would generate a loss

This is one scenario. But, of course, the outcome could have been different. Instead of falling, the prices could have risen, lets say to $7720. In which case, we would obtain the same final result—the net selling price of $7550 remains the same except now the futures transaction generates a loss of $170. If we apply the same logic to a price increase then the situation is as follows:

Price Fixing Hedge; Selling Forward—Price Rising

The repercussions in the case of a rising price are as follows:

- If you hedged your position the gain on the physical side would offset the loss on the futures.
- If you did not hedge then your position would generate a profit.

In the event of rising prices, instead of falling, it is obvious that our metal seller would have been much better off had he not hedged his position—he would have achieve a price of $7720. A hedge, in this case, means that the potential gain arising from the price increase has been lost. But you will remember that hedging is designed to remove the speculative element from your forward commitment, and not as a source of generating profits. Once the hedge is instituted it leaves no room for a windfall profit. Potential profits arising from the favourable price move are forfeited.

PRICE FIXING HEDGE—BUYING FORWARD

Buying a futures contract on the LME, as a temporary substitute for an anticipated forward purchase, provides protection from a price rise, no matter if the market is in contango (as in our example) or in backwardation.

Table 5.2 Price Fixing Hedge; Buying Forward

FORWARD / CURRENT	CASH	1 MONTH	2 MONTHS	3 MONTHS
JANUARY (to)	7520	7530	7540	← −7550
FEBRUARY	7560	7570	7580	7590
MARCH	7600	7610	7620	7630
APRIL	+7640 → / ← −7640	7650	7660	7670

Price rise, contango market
Cash buying price −$7640 + Profit on futures $90
Net purchase price = $7550

The hedge transaction locks-in the target price of $7550, thus compensating for the actual physical metal price rise. This is a buying hedge. It begins with buying a futures at a date corresponding to our projected physical purchase of metal, which in the exchange terminology would be referred to as “buying long” or **long a futures.**

As in our previous example, here again the outcome could have been different—instead of rising the price could have declined, with the opposite repercussions to those stated in our selling example.

Key Terms

long futures
opening position at LME (or any other exchange) with a futures purchase

Price Fixing Hedge; Buying Forward—Price Rising

A price rising involve the following:

- If you hedged your position, the losses on the physical side would be compensated by the gains on the futures.
- If you did not hedge then you would generate a loss.

Price Fixing Hedge; Buying Forward—Price Falling

A price falling involve the following:

- If you hedged your position, the gains on the physical side would offset against the losses on the futures.
- If you did not hedge, then your position would generate a profit.

OFFSET HEDGE BASIC PATTERNS

As our intention is not to write a hedging Bible illustrating innumerable variations of hedging transactions we shall confine our endeavour to the four basic strategieslisted

listed below. We use the term "basic patterns," believing that once they have been depicted they can easily be visualized and stored in your memory. Therefore, we shall divide them into two distinctive groups: buying forward and selling forward.

OFFSET HEDGE BASIC PATTERNS—BUYING FORWARD

1.1	Perfect Hedge	Figure 5.3
1.2	Imperfect Hedge	Figure 5.4/5.5
1.3	Carry by Borrowing	Figure 5.6/5.7
1.4	Carry by Lending	Figure 5.8/5.9

NB: The tables presented in this chapter contain graphic elaborations of numerous hedging case studies and their final results. Our examples are meant to illustrate key concepts and hedging opportunities for market participants whether they be miners, fabricators or merchants. We assume they all have only one thing in common—the use of considerable amounts of copper as an input.

These examples represent an integration of theoretical issues and necessarily abstract two important factors—the bid-offer ratio and LME specific—i.e., two day cash to prompt execution (on LME the last date that a futures can be closed is two days before prompt) valid for transactions on the London Metal Exchange. However, we consider that this is not an essential simplification as the strategy outcomes principally would not differ from the real trade outcome.

You will remember from the beginning that a buying hedge begins as a hedge purchase and is designed to give protection from a price rise. Therefore in the opening example we assume rising markets and contango prevailing conditions as they represent a rather typical state of affairs.

1.1. Perfect Hedge; Closing a Buy Hedge on the Prompt Date

In Table 5.3, we assume that on 1 January the producer has agreed to sell the physical metal (copper rods) based on a three months forward price at 1 April of $7550. The producer has sold the finished product although he has not yet purchased the raw material (copper cathodes) but he plans to do so before the delivery date.

Table 5.3 Perfect Hedge; Closing a Buy Hedge on the Prompt Date, Contango Market

CURRENT \ FORWARD	CASH	1 MONTH	2 MONTHS	3 MONTHS
JANUARY (t0)	7520	7530	7540	+7550 / −7550
FEBRUARY	7560	7570	7580	7590
MARCH	7600	7610	7620	7630
APRIL	+7640 / −7640	7650	7660	7670

Price rise, contango market
Loss on cash metal price –$90 + Profit on futures $90
Net result = 0

NB: The total number of arrows in price offset hedges is always even.

At that moment he cannot possibly know where the copper prices will end up three months ahead. In the interim, he is exposed to the risk of rising prices. In that case he will incur a loss. In order to protect his metal position, on 1 January, the producer buys an equivalent amount of futures as a hedge. As our example illustrates a perfect hedge, we also assume that the purchase of the physical metal (copper cathodes) coincides with the prompt date—the date at which the short hedge has to be closed by reversal purchase. As these dates are matched our producer is perfectly hedged and the risk of price rising entirely eliminated.

The loss on the physical side is compensated in full by the gain on the futures.

The net result would not change even if the market was falling. The direction of price change therefore has no significance for the perfect hedge outcome—only that the profits and losses would change sides.

The net results remain unaffected too, even if the market was in backwardation.

1.2. Imperfect Hedge; Closing a Buy Hedge Before the Prompt Date

We are still with the same producer and his initial position remains the same.

Table 5.4 Imperfect Hedge; Closing a Buy Hedge Before Prompt Date, Contango Market

FORWARD / CURRENT	CASH	1 MONTH	2 MONTHS	3 MONTHS
JANUARY (to)	7520	7530	7540	+7550 / −7550
FEBRUARY	−7560	7570	+7580	7590
MARCH	7600	7610	7620	7630
APRIL	7640	7650	7660	7670

Price rise, contango market
Loss on cash metal price –$10 + Profit on futures $30
Net result = +$20 equal to 2 months contango

But, for a change, let us assume that our producer decides to take advantage of the prevailing contango and closes his hedge before the prompt date—in our case, in February or in other words, two months early. Now the significance of contango and backwardation comes into play. In all situations in which there is a time lag between the spot purchase (or sale) and the futures position closing transaction, you are no longer perfectly hedged, and your position is open to an unfavourable outcome—which could end up in considerable losses. From our pattern it is obvious that the hedger is in no danger of closing early as long as the market stays in contango. On the contrary, he will be better off by exactly the sum of the prevailing contango.

Table 5.4, clearly illustrates the case of an imperfect hedge, closing a buy hedge before the prompt date to the benefit of the hedger, a future gain of $30, which outpaces the physical position losses ($10), producing a positive net return of $20. Position gains are commensurate with the amount of the two-months prevailing contango—the higher the better.

In a backwardation market the final result would be reversed; the producer would suffer a loss equal to the sum of prevailing backwardation.

Table 5.5 Imperfect Hedge; Closing a Buy Hedge Before the Prompt Date, Back Market

CURRENT \ FORWARD	CASH	1 MONTH	2 MONTHS	3 MONTHS
JANUARY (to)	7520	7510	7500	+7490 → / ← −7490
FEBRUARY	← −7560	7550	+7540 →	7530
MARCH	7600	7590	7580	7560
APRIL	7640	7630	7620	7610

Price rise, backwardation market
Loss on cash metal price –$70 + Profit on futures $50
Net result = –$20 equal to 2 months backwardation

Table 5.5 illustrates the repercussions of an imperfect hedge in a backwardation market structure.

Key Terms

carry trade
simultaneous trade consisting of two legs – purchase and sale of futures contracts, not necessarily in that order

1.3. Carry by Borrowing; To Bring Nearer the Prompt Date

At this point we introduce the concept of **carry trade.**

You can move the prompt date and yet remain perfectly hedged—and even make a profit. The example below illustrates how. What is a carry? A carry is the simultaneous purchase and sale of the same futures contracts with different maturities. The general term is used to denote both borrowing and lending, two inverse transactions:

Table 5.6 Carry by Borrowing; To Bring Nearer the Prompt Date, Contango Market

CURRENT \ FORWARD	CASH	1 MONTH	2 MONTHS	3 MONTHS
JANUARY (to)	7520	7530	7540	+7550 → / ← −7550
FEBRUARY	7560	← −7570	+7580 →	7590
MARCH	+7600 → / ← −7600	7610	7620	7630
APRIL	7640	7650	7660	7670

Price rise, contango market
Loss on cash metal price $50 + Profit on futures $50
Borrowing in contango earns $10
Net result = +$10 equal to 1 month contango

Key Terms

borrowing
buying the near date futures and simultaneous sale of a more distant one

lending
selling the near date futures and simultaneous purchase of a more distant one

Borrowing as in the above example, is a transaction of buying a near date and the simultaneous sale of further forward date; whereas **lending** is a reciprocal transaction —selling the near date and buying the more distant date in the future. What are the consequences? As you can see in the table above, borrowing in contango is beneficial for the hedger as it earns money equal to one month's contango. In the above case a carry made it possible for our producer to acquire a $10 better price.

In the case of backwardation, as you can imagine, the result will be reversed. The producer will end up with a loss equal to the prevailing backwardation—in our case it is a one month backwardation = $10. The table below illustrates this situation.

Table 5.7 Carry by Borrowing; To Bring Nearer the Prompt Date, Back Market

CURRENT \ FORWARD	CASH	1 MONTH	2 MONTHS	3 MONTHS
JANUARY (to)	7520	7510	7500	+7490 / −7490
FEBRUARY	7560	−7550	+7540	7530
MARCH	+7600 / −7600	7590	7580	7570
APRIL	7640	7630	7620	7610

Price rise, backwardation market
Loss on cash metal price $110 + Profit on futures $110
Borrowing in backwardation loses $10
Net result = −$10 equal to 1 month backwardation

1.4. Carry by Lending; Extending the Prompt Date

Finally, we shall examine the concept of carry by lending. A lending transaction involves selling a near date and the simultaneous purchase of a further forward date.

Carry by lending, applied to a buying hedge, is designed to extend the maturity date. There may be various reasons for that, but on this particular occasion let us suppose that the producer, or merchant is unable to buy his physical metal on the due date for which the hedge was instituted—in our case, the three months forward date, i.e., 1 April. Therefore, he is forced to delay the purchase or extend the due date until some point in the future (namely 1 May). To do this the producer sells the due date (1 April) and buys the more distant one (1 May). Consequently, on 1 May he buys the physical metal and closes out his hedge purchase with an offsetting hedge sale.

The sequence of actions in both contango and backwardation markets is illustrated in Tables 5.8 & 5.9:

Remember This! Coins & Alloys

Mixing copper with other metals produces alloys of different colors. Contemporary technology is capable of producing as many as 400 different copper and copper-alloy compositions loosely grouped into categories including: Copper, Brasses, Bronzes, Nickel Silver, Nickel-Brass or Cupro-Nickel and others. Two of these specific copper alloys were initially used for the first production of the eight new Euro coins back in 2002. 184,000 tones of copper were used for this purpose, by 16 European mints, to produce around 52 billion coins, with a total value of €15.75 billion. (European Central Bank):

- €2 and €1 coins made of an alloy called Nickel-Brass, €1 ring / €2 centre; Cupro-Nickel, €2 ring / €1 centre.
- 10, 20 and 50 cent coins made of an alloy called Nordic Gold, and
- 1, 2 and 5 cents are copper-coated steel.

Table 5.8 Carry by Lending; Extending the Prompt Date, Contango Market

FORWARD / CURRENT	CASH	1 MONTH	2 MONTHS	3 MONTHS
JANUARY (to)	7520	7530	7540	+7550 −7550
FEBRUARY	7560	7570	7580	7590
MARCH	7600	7610	7620	7630
APRIL	+7640	−7650	7660	7670
MAY	+7680 −7680	7690	7700	7710

Price rise, contango market
Loss on cash metal price $130 + Profit on futures $130
Lending in contango Loses $10
Net result = –$10 equal to 1 month contango

As you may well notice from the pattern exhibited, in a contango market, carry by lending will produce a loss equal to the amount of contango prevailing in the period for which the carry transaction has been instituted. That period is one month and the contango is $10—therefore the net result is –$10. If the carry needs to be extended for a longer period, say three months, then the end result would be different, in our example -$30, but the net result would always remain negative.

Table 5.9 Carry by Lending; Extending the Prompt Date, Backwardation Market

FORWARD / CURRENT	CASH	1 MONTH	2 MONTHS	3 MONTHS
JANUARY (to)	7520	7510	7500	+7490 −7490
FEBRUARY	7560	7550	7540	7530
MARCH	7600	7590	7580	7570
APRIL	+7640	−7630	7620	7610
MAY	−7680 +7680	7670	7660	7650

Price rise, backwardation market
Loss on cash metal price $190 + Profit on futures $190
Lending in backwardation earns $10
Net result = +$10 equal to 1 month backwardation

In a backwardation market the net result, due to carry by lending, would always be opposite to that in a contango market—i.e., the net result would always be positive since the near date (selling) price, in backwardation, is always higher than the more distant date (purchase) price.

OFFSET HEDGE BASIC PATTERNS—SELLING FORWARD

2.1	Perfect Hedge	Figure 5.10
2.2	Imperfect Hedge	Figure 5.11/5.12
2.3	Carry by Lending	Figure 5.13/5.14
2.4	Carry by Borrowing	Figure 5.15/5.16

In selling hedge illustrations we assume a falling market as this type of hedge is designed to provide protection from price falls. Therefore, illustrations of contangos and backwardations alternate to emphasize their different outcomes.

2.1. Perfect Hedge; Closing a Sell Hedge on the Prompt Date

In the example below—closing the sell hedge on a prompt day (Table 5.10)—we have an inverse situation.

As a selling hedge is designed to give protection from a price fall it is initiated by selling forward on the LME—i.e., protecting the physical metal position at risk by selling the equivalent amount of futures as a hedge. The assumptions are the same as in a buying hedge except that we have assumed, as a necessary consequence, a falling market—a selling hedge's primary objective is to provide protection in declining markets.

Table 5.10 Perfect Hedge; Closing a Sell Hedge on the Prompt Date, Contango Market

FORWARD / CURRENT	CASH	1 MONTH	2 MONTHS	3 MONTHS
JANUARY (to)	7520	7530	7540	−7550 +7550
FEBRUARY	7480	7490	7500	7510
MARCH	7440	7450	7460	7470
APRIL	+7400 −7400	7410	7420	7430

Price fall, contango market
Loss on cash metal price $150 + Profit on futures $150
Net result = 0

The pattern above can be interpreted as follows: on 1 January a merchant buys an LME metal for delivery three months forward and agrees to pay based on the LME three months price (for 1 April). The purchase price is known but he has to sell the metal and cannot yet find a customer. In the meanwhile the merchant runs the risk of loss if the price declines. On the other hand, if the prices increases, he will end up with a profit. To protect his position from eventual loss, our merchant decides to exclude the speculative element and opts in favour of a hedge: so he sells the futures contract which is equivalent to his physical position, three months forward on the LME. Furthermore, we assume that the trader manages to find a customer and conclude his sale on 1 April. The selling price is established by the cash settlement price on that date (1 April). Accordingly, the net result is zero—the loss on the physical side which originated from a price decline—is exactly counterbalanced by the profit on the LME transaction.

So, the positional exposure has been successfully eliminated regardless of the actual contango or backwardation prevailing.

2.2. Imperfect Hedge; Closing a Sell Hedge Before the Prompt Date

In the following examples (Figure 5.11) and (Figure 5.12), the net results are exactly the opposite—closing the sell hedge early in contango market will produce a loss equal to the contango prevailing for the relevant period, whereas in a backwardation market it will earn a profit equal to backwardation prevailing in the same period.

Table 5.11 Imperfect Hedge; Closing a Sell Hedge Before the Prompt Date, Contango Market

FORWARD / CURRENT	CASH	1 MONTH	2 MONTHS	3 MONTHS
JANUARY (to)	7520	7530	7540	−7550 / +7550
FEBRUARY	+7480	7490	−7500	7510
MARCH	7440	7450	7460	7470
APRIL	7400	7410	7420	7430

Price fall, contango market
Loss on cash metal price –$70 + Profit on futures $50
Net result = –$20 equal to 2 months contango

Table 5.12 Imperfect Hedge; Closing a Sell Hedge Before the Prompt Date, Back Market

FORWARD / CURRENT	CASH	1 MONTH	2 MONTHS	3 MONTHS
JANUARY (to)	7520	7510	7500	−7490 / +7490
FEBRUARY	+7480	7470	−7460	7450
MARCH	7440	7430	7420	7410
APRIL	7400	7390	7380	7370

Price fall, backwardation market
Loss on cash metal price –$10 + Profit on futures $30
Net result = +$20 equal to 2 months backwardation

2.3. Carry by Lending; To Bring Nearer the Prompt Date

There is an inverse relationship between a buying hedge and a selling hedge. In the figures shown below we illustrate a lending operation "to bring nearer the selling hedge prompt date." You will note that in the corresponding buying example—"to bring nearer the buying hedge prompt date"—we have used carry by borrowing. In carry by lending the initial hedge transaction on 1 January, is opened by selling the three month futures on the LME—on 1 April. In order to bring the prompt date nearer, you have to sell the nearer date (1 March) and repurchase the more distant one (1 April).

Table 5.13 Carry by Lending; To Bring Nearer the Prompt Date, Contango Market

FORWARD / CURRENT	CASH	1 MONTH	2 MONTHS	3 MONTHS
JANUARY (to)	7520	7530	7540	−7550 / +7550
FEBRUARY	7480	+7490	−7500	7510
MARCH	+7440 / −7440	7450	7460	7470
APRIL	7400	7410	7420	7430

Price fall, contango market
Loss on cash metal price $110 + Profit on futures $110
Lending in contango Loses $10
Net result = –$10 equal to 1 months contango

Tables 5.13 and 5.14 exhibit precisely the sequence of transactions both in contango and in backwardation markets, with the corresponding results.

Table 5.14 Carry by Lending; To Bring Nearer the Prompt Date, Backwardation Market

FORWARD / CURRENT	CASH	1 MONTH	2 MONTHS	3 MONTHS
JANUARY (to)	7520	7510	7500	+7490 / −7490
FEBRUARY	7480	+7470	−7460	7450
MARCH	+7440 / −7440	7430	7420	7410
APRIL	7400	7390	7380	7370

Price Fall, Backwardation Market
Loss on Cash Metal Price $50 + Profit on Futures $50
Lending in backwardation earns $10
Net result = +$10 equal to 1 month backwardation

2.4. Carry by Borrowing; Extending the Prompt Date

The last pair of examples illustrates a borrowing transaction—with the idea of extending the hedge selling prompt date. For this purpose a carry by borrowing has been instituted on premises exactly opposite to the transactions in the buying hedge example where the lending operation was used. Tables 5.15 and 5.16 illustrate a succession of transactions in contango and in backwardation markets respectfully.

Needless to say, the net results originating from extending the selling hedge prompt date are exactly reciprocal to those illustrated in buying hedge examples (Figures 5.8 & 5.9).

Table 5.15 Carry by Borrowing; Extending the Prompt Date, Contango Market

FORWARD / CURRENT	CASH	1 MONTH	2 MONTHS	3 MONTHS
JANUARY (to)	7520	7530	7540	−7550 / +7550
FEBRUARY	7480	7490	7500	7510
MARCH	7440	7450	7460	7470
APRIL	−7400	+7410	7420	7430
MAY	+7360 / −7360	7370	7380	7390

Price fall, contango market
Loss on cash metal price $190 + Profit on futures $190
Borrowing in contango Earns $10
Net result = +$10 equal to 1 month contango

Table 5.16 Carry by Borrowing; Extending the Prompt Date, Backwardation Market

FORWARD / CURRENT	CASH	1 MONTH	2 MONTHS	3 MONTHS
JANUARY (to)	7520	7510	7500	−7490 / +7490
FEBRUARY	7480	7470	7460	7450
MARCH	7440	7430	7420	7410
APRIL	−7400	+7390	7380	7370
MAY	+7360 / −7360	7350	7340	7330

Price fall, backwardation market
Loss on cash metal price $130 + Profit on futures $130
Borrowing in backwardation loses $10
Net result = −$10 equal to 1 month backwardation

These examples lead to unequivocal conclusions:

Extending the prompt date on a position initially entered as a hedge selling generates a profit equal to contango which prevails for the time period of the borrow (Figure 5.15). Alternatively, it generates a loss equal to the backwardation prevailing for the time period of the borrow (Figure 5.16).

And finally, to put things into context—and to avoid possible confusion and misapprehension—we shall exhibit the two alternative methods which can be used to gradually unfold the transactions in any of the previously exhibited patterns.

Table 5.17 Hedge Transactions Unfolding

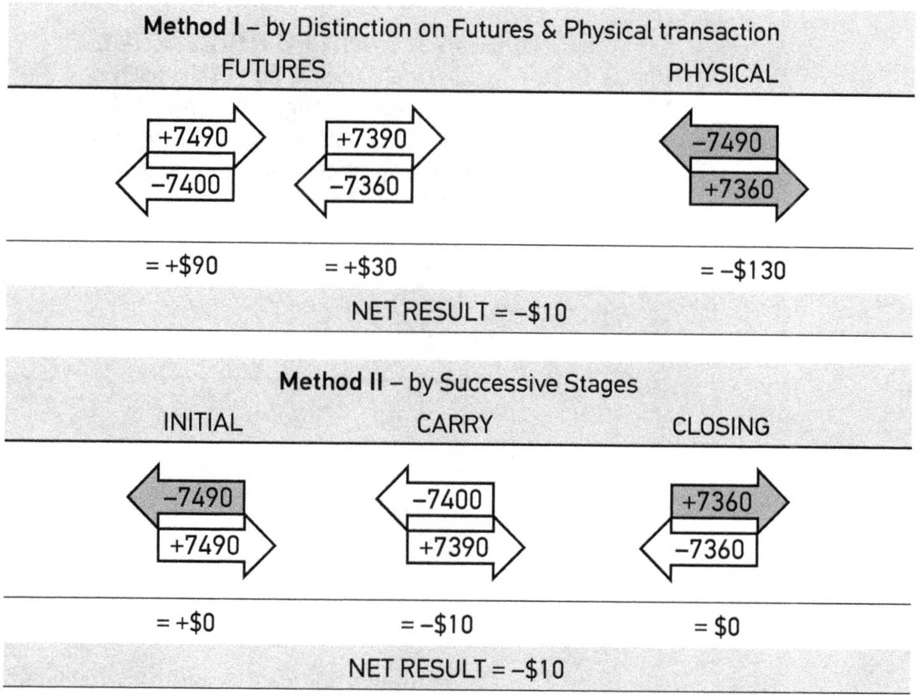

DISAMBIGUATION

There's a fair degree of diversity in the terms denoting the same notion/idea/conception. This is particularly valid for the so-called "closing out" outstanding futures. The related terms you may encounter are as follows:

negate/cancel out/reverse/offset/exit/unwind/cover/liquidate

all pointing to the same procedure: terminating the original contractual commitment to buy or sell with an opposite transaction.

ROLLING A FUTURES HEDGE

The main reason for rolling a futures hedge from one nearby contract to the next, is most commonly driven by pressure of market circumstances, in which a hedger is required to extend the hedged position (long or short) over a period of time and to avoid physical delivery.

Consequently, **"roll yield"** would be the return from extending a futures contract while assuming the spot market will remain unchanged. It reflects the difference between the price at which the original futures contract is sold (or bought), and the next (more distant) futures contract is purchased (or sold).

Roll yield can take either a positive or a negative value depending on the shape of the yield curve at the time the rolling transaction is instituted.

Key Terms

roll yield
the return from extending a futures contract assuming the spot market remains unchanged

ROLLING A LONG FUTURES HEDGE

Roll Yield, from the viewpoint of the party with the long position in the futures.

If you are initially long, rolling forward a futures contract assumes "carry by lending"—selling back a nearby contract to buy further into the forward curve.
Hence, assuming prices and the shape of the curve remain constant—rolling a long futures contract in backwardation will yield a positive return.

Figure 5.1 Lend in Backwardation: Positive Roll Yield

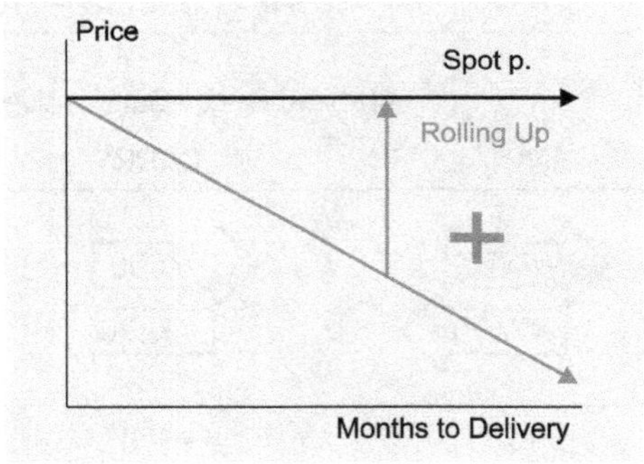

The nearby futures contract is sold back *high* and the next futures contract is purchased low. And conversely, rolling a long futures contract in contango will yield a negative return.

Figure 5.2 Lend in Contango: Negative Roll Yield

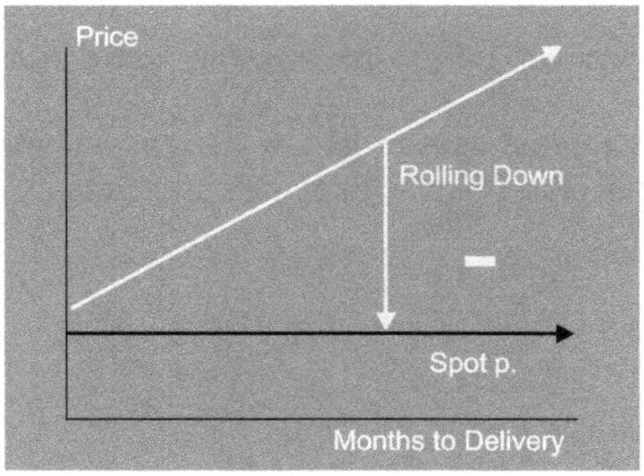

The nearby futures contract is sold back *low* and the next futures contract is purchased *high*!

ROLLING A SHORT FUTURES HEDGE

Roll Yield, from the viewpoint of the party with a short position in the futures.

If you are initially short, rolling a futures contract assumes "carry by borrowing" (buying back the nearby futures to sell further into the forward curve).

Hence, under the same assumptions, rolling a short futures contract in contango will yield a positive return!

Figure 5.3 Borrow in Contango: Positive Roll Yield

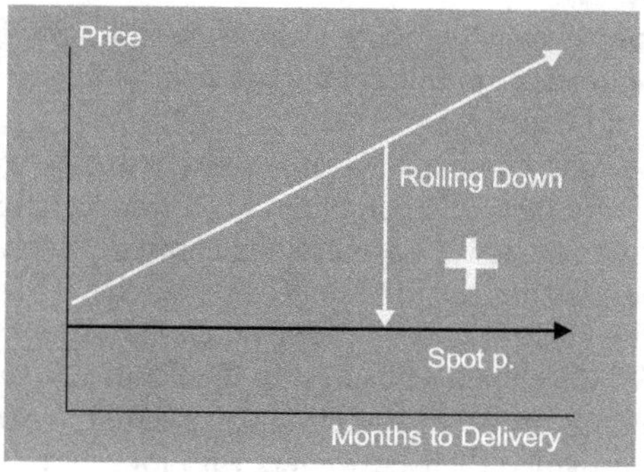

The nearby futures contract is bought back *low* and the next futures contract is sold *high*.

And conversely, if the commodity yield curve is in backwardation, rolling a short futures contract will yield a negative return.

Figure 5.4 Borrow in Backwardation: Negative Roll Yield

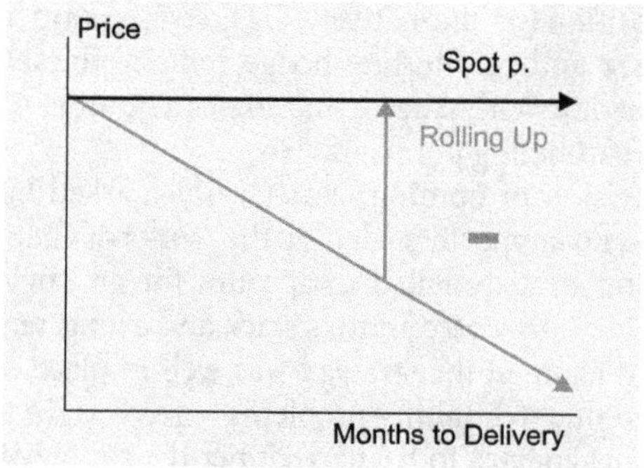

The nearby futures contract is bought back *high* and the next futures contract is sold *low*!

A CASE OF A NOTORIOUS HEDGING DEBACLE

Metallgesellschaft AG; When a Hedge Is Not a Hedge!

At the beginning of 1994, MGR&M's losses from trading in oil futures accumulated to nearly $1.4 billion and brought Metallgesellschaft AG, the parent company, to the brink of bankruptcy. MG's Supervisory Board responded by liquidating MGR&M's derivative positions and forward supply contracts and by replacing MG's top management. The rescue plan required a $1.9 billion emergency bailout from 150 German and international creditors to prevent bankruptcy.

The use of stack-and-roll futures hedges remains the subject of widespread debate to this day.

The controversial hedging strategy used by MGR&M, and its aftermath, aroused not only enormous public debate but also a vehement debate within the financial media. How did it all begin?

The German company **Metallgesellschaft A.G.** was founded in 1881, with its head office in Frankfurt. The company was a traditional metal producer and trader. Over a century of successful business, the company evolved into a huge conglomerate involved, besides metals, in finance, energy, chemicals, engineering and contracting as well. At the beginning of the 1990s their subsidiary MG Refining and Marketing Inc. (MGR&M) developed a business in the US in charge of refining and marketing petroleum products. In 1992 MGR&M in an attempt to eliminate the price risk of oil-related products provided their customers with long-term supply contracts, stretching up to ten years. These contracts guaranteed, at prices fixed in 1992, the purchase of a certain amount of petroleum products every month. By September 1993 the MGR&M total commitment to sell amounted to 154 million barrels. In other words MGR&M intentionally created a short physical position of 154 million barrels of petroleum products. From Chapter 4 we learned that a "long hedger" buys futures to hedge a short position in the underlying commodity. Accordingly, MGR&M developed a hedge strategy to protect their long term price exposure by entering into unleaded and heating oil long futures position (or alternatively, OTC swap contracts). The strategy employed, a "one-to-one stack-and-roll" futures hedge, remains the subject of widespread controversy to the present day. Within academic circles a number of related articles have been written involving conflicting points of view.

The division of opinions was clearly marked between critics—led by Mello and Parsons—and supporters—led by the works of Culp and Miller. The first claimed that the hedging strategy failed to account for an obvious maturity structure mismatch between the short-dated futures stack and a long-term fixed-price commitment, while the second claimed the strategy was well in place and—had it not been prematurely terminated due to liquidity problems—was certain to yield a positive return.

But let us go back to try to decipher the strategy itself, a one-to-one-stack-and-roll futures hedge. The "one-to-one" part of the hedge refers to the parity ratio between the contracted delivery volume and the underlying volume—for every 1000 barrels of petroleum in the MGR&M short physical position the company bought futures contracts for the equivalent of 1000 barrels.

The second part, "stack-and-roll" describes a position in which the whole volume of underlying futures was "stacked" (one on top of the other) in the nearby month rather than spread over different month maturities. This means that only the portion of nearby futures which fell due were unwound and the outstanding "stack" was rolled forward to the next-to-nearest contract. Each time the stack of futures neared maturity, the contracts were sold and new next-month contracts were purchased. Thus, as time passed the futures position was commensurately reduced.

Example:

Contracted delivery commitment; 154 million barrels spread out to 10 years forward = 120 months

Size of Futures Stack = 154 million barrels
Monthly Supply Contracts 154/120 = 1.28
Size of Futures Stack after first maturity: 154 – 1.28 = 152.72
Size of Futures Stack after second maturity 152.72 – 1.28 = 151.44
Size of Futures Stack after third maturity 151.44 – 1.28 = 150.2
- - - - - - - - - -
Size of Futures Stack after last maturity = 0

The reason for establishing a short-term stack hedge was due to illiquidity problems—at that time futures contracts on petroleum products, purchased at NYMEX were only actively traded a few months forward.

As a result, MGR&M's fixed-price delivery commitments spread ten years, whereas their NYMEX petroleum futures contracts were stacked on to the next-to-nearest month. MGR&M effectively and deliberately created an over-hedged position equal to the long speculative position in the outstanding futures. Why? The conception was supported on the grounds that the oil market yield curve had traditionally been downward-sloping—in backwardation. When markets are in backwardation it is possible to offset a long futures position at a profit. Believing that the market would remain in backwardation, MGR&M was aiming to capture the rolling yield arising from offsetting the outstanding stack at a higher spot price. The one-to-one stack hedge was put forth as an absolute and dependable tenet. It emphatically endorsed the idea of a continuous market trend and perpetual backwardation based on historic spot-futures price relationships.

But backwardation and contango states of affairs alternate in random and unpredictable fashion. While rolling forward in backwardation yields a profit, in contango roll incurs losses.

So, when in September 1993, the NYMEX futures market for crude oil flipped into contango, MGR&M's naked futures position was faced with margin calls. The "rolling yield" aspect turned from a source of trading profit to one of trading losses. The losses generated from rolling the outstanding futures stack (the entire stack of short-dated futures contracts), had to be settled by the end of the month. On the other side, the eventual compensating gains produced by partial deliveries are realized only gradually over the course of the remaining ten-year delivery term.

The disaster began to unfold! As the market continued to fall, mark-to-market losses on MGR&M's long futures position increased until they reached the point of a full-scale insolvency crisis that led to termination of the hedge position and most of the long-term supply contracts.

Figure 5.5 is designed to reveal the effect of rolling the long futures hedge in falling markets and in a contango market structure—the long futures position Ft (the short-dated stack of futures contracts) is closed out spot at a lower market price FT producing a loss (sell high, buy low)—and the position is then rolled forward to the next short dated futures at a higher than spot price, triggering the margin calls.

Figure 5.5 Rolling Naked Futures: One-to-One-Stack-and-Roll Hedge

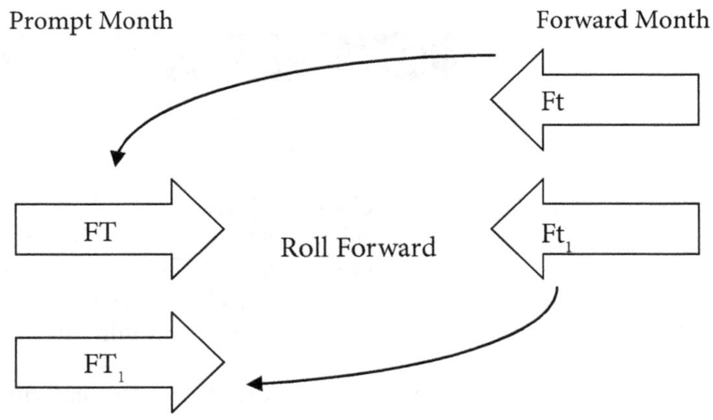

Long hedge, market falling FT < Ft; $FT_1 < FT_1$ = Negative return
Long hedge, market rising FT > Ft; $FT_1 > Ft_1$ = Positive return

Rolling an over-hedged stack forward creates virtually a new position—an independent, separate directional trade, that might end either positive or negative; the final return is irrelevant to the prevailing yield curve and has nothing to do with the basis risk. If you do not close the hedge when the futures stack falls due, you do not have exposure to the basis risk: your exposure is a margin risk.

If we can manage to focus clearly on the change of market structure and its repercussions on the relevant hedging position (this particular stack-and-roll hedge) then we shall come to the inevitable conclusion that the *emergence of contango alone does not necessarily imply a negative result.* If we assume that prices will continue to rise, instead of fall, and the existing yield curve for the same period will persist to be in contango, the position would yield a positive return irrespective of the actual contango forward curve! We can illustrate that kind of scenario in the following graph:

Figure 5.6 Rolling Naked Futures in Contango, Rising Market

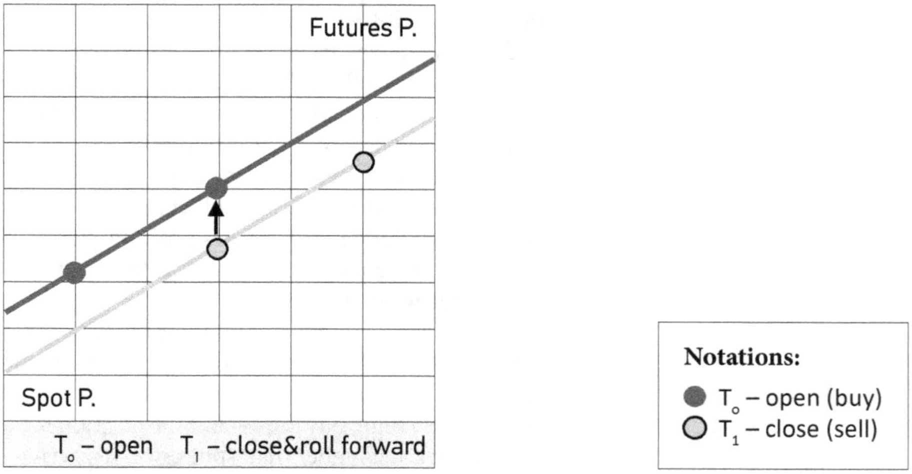

Positive Yield (buy low t_0, sell high t_1)

In addition to the contango forward curve, a steady decline in spot prices was necessary for the position to generate losses. In the case of MGR&M, the losses accumulated on long outstanding stack were not produced because the actual yield curve flipped from backwardation to contango, but were exclusively created as a result of falling prices.

Figure 5.7 Rolling Naked Futures in Contango, Falling Market

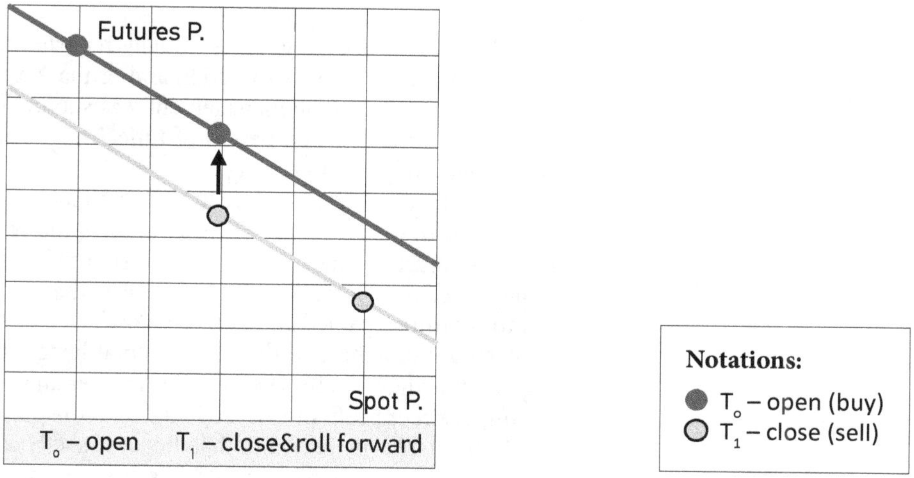

Negative yield (buy high t_0, sell low t_1)

Likewise, it would be also possible to perceive a model in which the same stack-and-roll position would yield a negative return in backwardation (and falling market).

An entire spectrum of market circumstances would fall into four categories:

1. Contango rising market.
2. Contango falling market.
3. Backwardation rising market.
4. Backwardation falling market.

Effects on cash flow as a consequence of a long "stack-and-roll" hedge in each scenario:

1. Contango rising market—positive roll yield.
2. Contango falling market—negative roll yield.
3. Backwardation rising market—positive roll yield.
4. Backwardation falling market—negative roll yield.

In falling markets, negative yield irrespective of forward yield curve i.e., contango or backwardation.

In rising markets, positive yield irrespective of forward yield curve i.e., contango or backwardation

With 20–20 hindsight we may conclude that the real problem of MGR&M came from two principle flaws: the first was definitely the maturity mismatch; and secondly the position was disproportionately over-hedged (effectively MGR&M was holding a huge naked futures position stacked in the near month).

The stack-and-roll hedge was a conflicting strategy. The model was predicated on two autonomous variables in the locked-in ratio—continuous backwardation and rising markets.

It failed to postulate the probability of changes in market trend and forces and to incorporate the impact of potential risk profiles under all market conditions—falling market and rising market, backwardation as well as contango.

> *"You must never delude yourself into thinking that you are investing while you are speculating."* Benjamin Graham

If MGR&M were hedging, as initially reported in the press, they would be indifferent to a change in price direction and or market structure. On the other hand, the strategy presented to the management was supposed to generate profits under given conditions for a specified period of time. The presumption of profit contradicts the very essence of perfect hedging.

Recall that a perfect hedge, in the first place, implies that maturity of futures is matched with the contracted delivery of the underlying asset. Second, the futures contract size must be the same as the position held in the underlying asset. As a consequence of these core hedging principles, the perfect hedge result substantiate the motto "nothing's gained and nothing's lost."

A failure to adhere to this fundamental hedging goal would produce a variety of imperfect hedges. An imperfect hedge implies an uncertain and unstable situation resulting in either profit or loss attributable to the prevailing market structure.

While there is no guidance that dictates exactly what is the most appropriate strategy for a particular set of circumstances, there are some pitfalls you should by all means try to avoid.

This is a good time to point out the ultimate hedging guidelines:

1. Hedging's principal aim is to provide safety against losses in all reasonably foreseeable conditions and deviations.
2. If any set of parameters initially applied to a hedge strategy guarantees permanent profitability, a red light should be flashing, as it contradicts the very nature of hedging.
3. The probability of a strategy performing without failure for a specified period of time and the ensuing price protection and future returns, cannot rest upon a subjective predilection that antecedent states of affairs (be it a backwardation market and rising prices or some other configuration) would continue to be the norm in the future.

I. AVERAGE PRICE HEDGING

In real life, the pricing of physical contracts related to the LME are predominantly based upon average month prices rather than a single day. When it comes to pricing, you will find that the formula most commonly used would indicate the QP (Quotation Period) as the pricing period. One of the typical pricing clauses may be paraphrased as follows:

Example:

PRICE: LME Grade A, Copper Cash Settlement Quotation averaged over the QP (quotation period) plus a premium of USD 62 (Sixty two) per metric ton FCA (nominated place of destination).

QUOTATIONAL PERIOD: For the tonnage under this contract the Q/P shall be the average of the calendar month of the month of delivery. (with variations such as... prior to the month of delivery (referred as M – 1) or... following the month of delivery (referred as M + 1).

The implications of this observed propensity of metal-based contracts may imply, at first sight, that things might get a bit more complicated if you are supposed to hedge the average price of distant forward months—i.e., when the maturity of the risk to be hedged falls more than three months forward.

We shall use a provisional example to illustrate the sequence of relative transactions that should serve to obtain the hedge protection when the pricing month is more than three months away.

Assumptions: Hedge selling on the LME against a possible price fall. Time span—more than three months forward, where only third Wednesdays are available as prompts. Current forward prices quoted on the LME would provide a satisfactory selling price, but the profit margin could be significantly endangered in a sharp price decline.

Hedge strategy unfolds in four stages:

- Initial (t_0)
- Spreading (t_1)
- Closing out (unwinding/lifting the hedge) (t_2)
- Physical sale (t_3)

Initial—Feb. 15th (t_0)

Sell futures for the third Wednesday of September (Sept the 16th) **40 lots @7020**

Spreading—2 July (t_1)

This is the first date on which the full range of relevant prompts become available. You need not execute the spread on that day. The actual transaction can be performed on any subsequent LME day.

You have to instruct your broker to spread the dates from the third Wednesday across the whole of September (1 Sept—30 Sept). Spreading in this respect would imply a carry transaction that would effectively disseminate the 40 lots from the third Wednesday (16 September) across the whole of September: 22 LME days (40/22 = 18*

2 and 4* 1 lots).

But before you instruct your broker to make the necessary arrangements, you have to be very careful about the selection of respective prompt dates. Remember, your goal is to achieve the September *Average Cash Settlement Price.* In order to obtain that you have to select LME prompt dates properly. That will explain why 2 July was the first date we could start the spreading procedure! So, let us have a look at the September 2009 calendar:

SEPTEMBER						
S	M	T	W	T	F	S
		1	2	3	4	5
6	7	8	9	10	11	12
13	14	15	16	17	18	19
20	21	22	23	24	25	26
27	28	29	30	1	2	

There are 22 LME tradable dates within that month but, due to the LME's ruling procedure of "2 day cash to prompt," you have to flip the prompt dates two days ahead of the dates completing the September average. It means simply that the 3 September prompt will have a cash settlement price set for 1 September. And the last cash settlement date in September will close on the corresponding prompt of 2 October. Consequently, the set of actual prompts will have to include the period from 3 September until 2 October.

All being set, you may begin "spreading" the hedge with "carry by lending"—to bring nearer the third Wednesday prompt date from 16 September to the beginning of September (buy back two lots daily from third Wednesday quota and spread from 3 September until 16 September).

From 17 September until the end of September, keep on "spreading" the hedge from third Wednesday, now with a reverse transaction, "carry by borrowing"—to extend the prompt date from third Wednesday forward (from 16 September to 2 October). In this period there are 12 prompt days available. Accordingly, you will have to spread 8* 2 lots and 4* 1 lot.

Now, to be unreservedly explicit, we shall bring in some provisional prices in order to disclose the underlying principle.

So, let's suppose that on 2 July when you initiate spreading, the forward copper price for 16 September (which is the third Wednesday) is quoted at $6910. The market is in contango. In a contango market structure, prices for nearer dates—1 September—are lower than prices for distant dates—16 September. In order to bring the third Wednesday nearer—to 3 September—you should initiate a "carry by lending;" that is, sell the near date (3 September), and buy back the more distant date (16 September). You repeat the same procedure for each prompt date available until 16 September. From this date on, you need to reverse the transaction to a "carry by borrowing" for all available prompt dates until 2 October.

For the sake of illustration, we shall consider the hypothetical case that a one month contango during the relevant period was $21, spread evenly over 22 prompt days.

The model is designed to allow an insight into the set of transactions taking place in a reference time frame and tries to capture and visualize the whole process as it develops.

In the following table we have adopted a sequence of transactions: "lending" and "borrowing" with actual prompt dates and hypothetical prices to clarify the process.

Figure 5.8 The Average Month Spreading Transaction

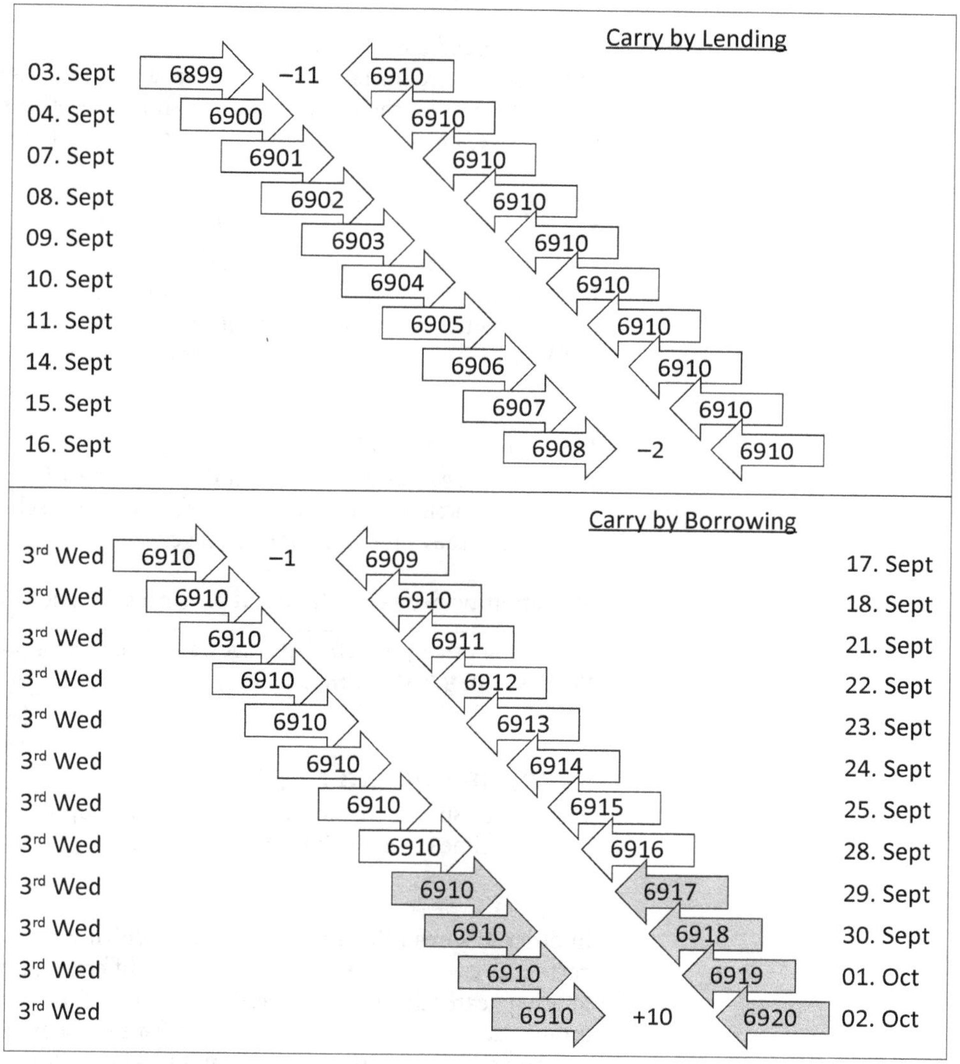

NB: You can manipulate/adjust the hedge (choice of dates and number of lots) to your benefit depending on the prevailing term structure!

You have extinguished the third Wednesday contract. It is now spread across the whole of September leaving two lots each day from 3-28 September (18 LME days) and one lot on each of four LME days: 29/30 September and 1/2 October.

The initial third Wednesday (40 lots futures contract), has been disseminated into 18 x two and 4 x one lot contracts—22 separate contracts.

Spreading transactions results in an average spread cost, either profit or loss, depending upon the prevailing market structure. In our hypothetical example, using the figures shown in Table 5.18, the actual calculation would bring the following results:

Average spread cost = –$3300 + $1900 = –$1400/1000 t = –$1.4/t
(Average spread calculus = spread difference per each prompt date x no. of lots);
3 Sept – $11 x 50t (2 lots) = $550; 4 Sept – $10 x 50t (2 lots) = $500
and so on until 02 Oct + $10 x 25t (1 lot)
Subtract the total minus values from the total plus values/1000 tons

Average spread cost = $1.4/t
In this set of circumstances it would be appropriate to place 4*1 lot contracts at the very beginning of the spread to diminish the negative spread cost. If you have done that the overall spread cost will be a positive +$0.4/t or +$400 on the position.

Closing out—1 September (t_2)
Two days prior to the first September prompt date—on Tuesday, 1 September, you close the first prompt date, which is Thursday 3 September. You continue lifting the hedge by buying back "each LME day" from 1 September throughout September. You have 22 September cash dates to offset 22 prompt dates spread out from 3 September until 2 October, thus locking in the September average, say $683:

40 lots @$6835

Physical sale—1 October (t_3)
After the hedge has been "unwound," successfully locking-in the September Official Cash Settlement Average Price, on 1 October you sell the physical position to your customer at the same September average: **40 lots @$6835**

The offsetting hedge purchase and physical sale cancel each other so you are left with:

Net selling price = $7020 – Average spread cost ($1.4) = $7018.60
Final result: $7018.60/ton.

AVERAGE SPREAD COSTS

The average spread cost would depend entirely upon the price term structure prevailing at the time the spreading was instituted.

Contango Prevailing

In order to spread the third Wednesday (which is de facto 16 September 2009 in this particular case) you have to perform two different carry transactions. First you have to bring nearer the third Wednesday from 16 September to the range of available LME prompt dates within 3 to 16 September. This set of available LME dates happens to be ten. You can do with the carry by lending—i.e., selling the near dates and buying back the third Wednesday, as we have described above. Throughout this period your broker will be selling two lots each day and buying back 2 lots from the "big" third Wednesday contract, thus splitting the big contract into numerous small ones.

> *Carry by Lending loses money (–) in a contango market as you will be selling low and buying high.*

From 17 September onwards (until the end of September, plus 2 LME dates in October) there are 12 prompt days. You continue the spreading now with the carry by borrowing, i.e., buying back the near date and selling the more distant date. To be exact, as per our factual data, between 17 September and 2 October you will be selling 8*2 lots and 4*1 lots to match exactly the original hedged tonnage from the inception of the hedge.

Carry by Borrowing earns money (+) in a contango market as you will be buying low and selling high.

The hedge is now reinstituted, leaving you with 18*2 lots of contracts plus 4*1 lots contracts—altogether 40 lots spread over 22 prompt days across the month of September plus 1 and 2 October.

In a contango market the forward prices within any one month fall within a very narrow price range. Costs suffered from "carry by lending" should even out with gains accrued from "carry by borrowing." Therefore, the overall cost of spreading the position from the third Wednesday across the whole month should result in only a tiny differential—either plus or minus.

Backwardation Prevailing

Carry by Lending earns money (+) as you sell high and buy low.

Carry by Borrowing loses money (–) as you buy high sell low.

Again, gains and losses should offset each other, but the final result might get out of proportion.

The concise pattern created by a set of transactions as described above is presented in the following table:

Table 5.18 Average Month Spread Resume

	Cash	1 Month	2 Months	3 Months	4 Months	5 Months	6 Months 3rd Wed.
t_0 March 16							7020 →
t_1 July 02				Lend dates 03–16. Sept (10 Prompt dates) → ← 3rd W Borrow dates 17–30. Sept. (12 Prompt dates) ← 3rd W → Average Spread Cost +/–			
t_2 Sep 01	← 6835 22 dates						
t_3 Oct 01	6835 →						$7020 +/– Average Spread Cost

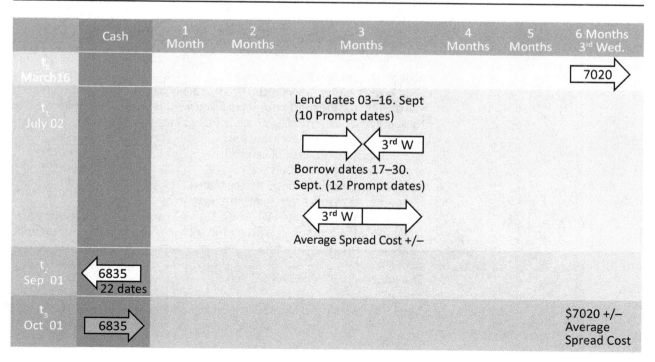

FUTURES ORDER PLACEMENT

This section aims to provide the basic order types menu that should be carefully considered prior to entering into futures trading. Different choices will enable you to fine tune your risk appetite before you initiate the position. And before you do, make sure that you inquire thoroughly with your broker as to the specifics of each order and how they really work. Different exchanges might have different regulations and different execution rules even in relation to the same order types. Read the Clients Account Contract very carefully, especially the Disclaimer Statement in order to apprise yourself of the risks involved. Although these statements vary considerably they all come to the same point which is conventionally most often formulated as follows:

- Trading in futures and options involves a high degree of risk and may not be suitable for everyone.
- Past performance is no guarantee of future results.
- Losses from using managed futures/option investments can be substantial.

Provisional Futures Order Ticket: NYMEX Light Sweet Crude Oil; December, 2008 Futures Price $93.00

This table illustrates the data required for futures order placement:

Table 5.19 Futures Order Placement

1.	2.	3.	4.	5.	6.	7.	8.
Peter Jones acc. no. 123	Buy or Sell	5	Dec 2010	NYMEX Crude Oil	$93	Market	Day order
Name & Acc. no.	**Market Action**	**Qty.**	**Delivery Month**	**Exchange Contract**	**State the Price**	**Order Type**	**Order Action**

1. State your name and account number.
2. State market action: whether this order is a buy or sell. A word of caution! If you are holding the short position and you want to cover, your order is—buy back, not sell! Conversely, if you are holding a long position you want to liquidate your order is—sell back, not buy.
3. State the quantity, number of contracts.
4. State the delivery month and year.
5. State the exchange and contract to be traded.
6. State the price at which you want your order to be activated.
7. Order type: Market. If you state "Market" you do not need to specify the price! It is implied that your order will be executed at the best possible current price available at the time the order is entered. Different order types will be discussed below.
8. State order action. All orders fall into two categories:

1. **Day Order** is valid only for the trading session during which you placed it. If your order is not filled you have to re-enter your order for the next session, if you wish so.

2. **Good Till Cancelled Order ("GTC" or Open order).** This order type remains valid until: it is filled; it is cancelled by you; or until it expires.

NB: All orders, except Market Orders, can be cancelled and replaced with a different order unless filled prior to cancellation.

3 BASIC ORDER TYPES ON FUTURES CONTRACT

1. Market Order

This is the most common order type. You use this order when you want to get filled immediately—irrespective of price. The priority is laid on speed of execution.

Example: Buy Dec. Crude **Oil AT THE MARKET** (no price specified)

1.1. Market on Close ("MOC")

A MOC order is an instruction to fill the order, at market, but only in the closing range (the range is determined by the individual exchanges).

1.2. Market on Open

An order that is to be filled in the official exchange opening range. If any part of the order cannot be filled during this period, it will automatically be cancelled.

2. Limit Order

A limit order may be executed only at the specified price or better! By entering this type of order you are securing either a maximum buying price or a minimum selling price.

Sell Limit – is always placed above the market price. The order will be filled only if the market trades at a specified price or better—**higher.** Sell 10 Crude Oil at $52.00 LIMIT (when the market is trading at $50.00)

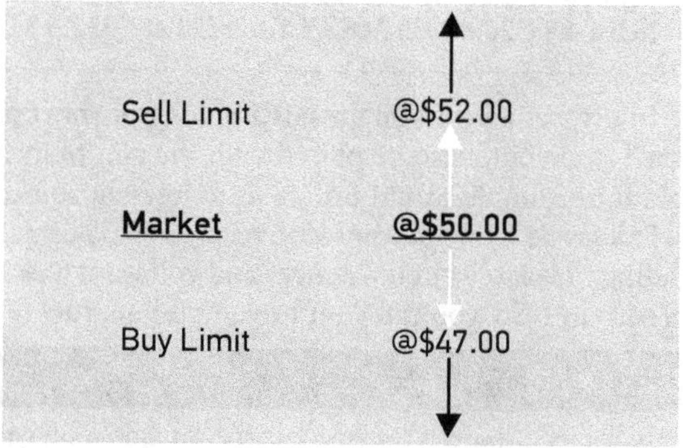

Buy Limit – is always placed below the market price. The order will be filled only if the market trades at a specified price or better—**lower.** Buy 10 Crude Oil at $47.00 LIMIT (when the market is trading at $50.00)

3. Stop Order

Stop Order is not executed until the market reaches a given price, at which time it becomes the Market Order.

Buy Stop – is always placed above the "Ask" market price. Your order will be triggered only when and if the "Ask" market price is at or above the Stop price.

Sell Stop – is always placed below the "Bid" market price. Your order will be triggered only when and if the "Bid" market price is offered at or below the Stop price.

Stop orders are commonly used to achieve one of the following targets:

A. To initiate a new long or short position

You can use this order to open long and short positions in the wake of the trend confirmation you are waiting for. Therefore, if you want to enter the market going long and the current crude oil trades at $93.60 you decide to make a trade only if the market signals that a new uptrend is confirmed and the price goes above $93.75. So, your instruction to the broker will be as follows:

Example:

Buy 1 Dec 2008, NYMEX Crude Oil at $93.75 STOP.GTC
Conversely, if your idea is to go short and you wait for the down trend to be signalled, you will instruct the broker to:
Sell 1 Dec 2008, NYMEX Crude Oil at $93.45 STOP. GTC

B. To protect a profit on an existing long or short position

A sell stop could also be placed with the aim of locking in the profit. Using the same data this example would unfold as follows: at some point the crude oil price goes up to, let's say $94.15. Your position records $0.55 cents per unit but you feel the market is trading in volatile circumstances and you want to secure your position from a possible turnaround. So, you call your broker and instruct him to:

Example:

Sell 1 Dec 2008, NYMEX Crude Oil at $93.95 STOP. GTC
In this way the sell stop will protect your position from a price decline and secure your position with a profit of $0.35 cents per unit.
Otherwise if you enter the market with a short position on crude oil at $93.60 and the current price is trading in line with your expectations at $93.15 you might want to lock in the profit by setting the level at which you want to exit the market. Your instruction to the broker would be as follows:
Buy 1 Dec 2008, NYMEX Crude Oil at $93.30 STOP. GTC
With the price level set at $93.30 stop you are instructing your broker to close the position as soon as the market hits the buy stop price, thus securing a profit on your position of $0.30 cents per unit traded.

C. To minimize a loss on a long or short position

A sell stop order could be also used to prevent further losses on a long position. It is also labelled as a "stop loss" order and its mechanics work as follows: you enter a market going long on a December crude oil contract at $93.60 and the price starts falling. Your major concern is to prevent the position from heavy losses so you instruct your broker as follows:

Example:

Sell 1 Dec 2008, NYMEX Crude Oil at $93.45 STOP. GTC
Conversely, if you enter the market at $93.60 by shorting the crude oil and the price is trading at $93.70 you may want to prevent further losses if the market continues to rise, so you call the broker and place the following order:

Buy1 Dec 2008, NYMEX Crude Oil at $93.75 STOP. GTC
With this order you are instructing the broker to close your position as soon as the market hits the buy stop thus preventing further losses.

NB: Securities are bought at ASK price and sold at BID price.

SUMMARY

In this chapter we have analysed in detail the basic hedging strategies. Different strategies in different markets have been introduced with simple examples—hedge patterns. We have shown that price protection initiated by the original hedging strategy is valid under given conditions and a specified time frame and that a perfect hedge is not always possible. Numerous cases, with practical hedging strategies, were reviewed with the discovery that quite often hedging strategies are closed prematurely: if, for whatever reason, the hedger is forced to move the prompt date the hedging aftermath will be dictated by the prevailing market circumstances—contangos and backwardations. In all cases of imperfect hedging—those positions suffering from a maturity mismatch between a futures and a physical position—the future returns and the risk originating from the change in market structure cannot be unfailingly predicted. Next, we covered the role of carry transactions—borrowing and lending—with explicit illustrations and their implications. We have seen that a change in timing —to bring nearer and/or extend the prompt date—can produce either beneficial or adverse effects.We have tabulated all the major cases and their repercussions. Here is a summary of the basic futures hedge advantages and disadvantages:

Advantages:
Confines price risk.
No credit risk.
Attractive margin requirements.
Possibility of closing out prior to maturity.
Possibility of extending the delivery date.
Highly standardized contracts in terms of quality, quantity and delivery location.
High liquidity.

Disadvantages:
Daily settlement – margin calls.
Limited profit potential.
Uncertainty of future returns in case of moving the prompt date.

Average price hedging is rarely explained in detail and is frequently a source of misunderstanding. We have offered a meticulous graphic presentation in four stages. We believe that graphic illustrations promote clear understanding and leave no room for ambiguity. The logic of the tabular exposition leads to an obvious conclusion: the aftermath of an average price hedge equals the initial futures price plus or minus the average spread cost.

KEY TERMS

short futures
long futures
carry trade
borrowing
lending
roll yield

CHAPTER 6

COMMODITY FUTURES SPREADS

CHAPTER OBJECTIVES

- To introduce the concept of commodity futures spreads
- To explain and illustrate the mechanics of calendar spread trading
- To outline the distinction between buying a spread and selling a spread
- To investigate how developments of market structure affects the final outcome of spread trading

COMMODITY FUTURES SPREADS

Key Terms

spread
one trade consisting of two legs-one short and one long, initiated simultaneously, and aiming to exploit opportunities dependent upon the change in correlation between the two legs of the spread

inter-market spread
transaction involving a purchase of a futures on one asset and a sale of a futures with the same maturity in another usually closely related asset

calendar spread
a position initiated by entering simultaneously a long and short futures position (not necessarily in that order) on the same underlying asset but with different maturity dates

buying a spread
go long the higher priced contract

CALENDAR (TIME) SPREAD

In this chapter we explore the rules of commodity spread trading. A spread may be defined as one trade consisting of two legs—one short and one long—initiated simultaneously and aiming to exploit opportunities arising from the change in relationship between the two legs of the spreads. Here is a brief overview of spread trading related terms:

Intermarket Spread Refers to futures markets and describes a transaction involving a purchase of a futures on one asset and a sale of a futures with the same maturity in another usually closely related asset: for example, purchase of Brent crude oil and sale of gas oil. Also referred to as intercommodity spread.

Calendar Spread Establishing a position in the futures market by simultaneously entering a long and short position (not necessarily in that order) on the same underlying asset but with different maturity dates (for example, purchase of a March contract and sale of a September contract), aiming to profit from the relative price change. Also referred to as intramarket and interdelivery spreads.

You can establish a calendar spread with any of the carry transactions—so four different openings are available to you:

- borrow the contango,
- borrow the backwardation,
- lend the contango, and
- lend the backwardation

Offsetting of the calendar spread must be performed by two simultaneous but opposite transactions:

If you open a position with a borrow you have to close it with a lend and vice versa.

It is important to recognize that in the spread trading transactions, the nominal price of the futures contract itself becomes irrelevant and does not represent the source of profit.

What actually matters is to monitor the size of the spread and how it has evolved from the time it was instituted—time t_0; and the time when the spread is closed by an offsetting transaction—time t_1.

The only relevant and most critical factor in spread trading, is the evolution of the spread—the structural change in the forward curve configuration which is noticeable as contango and backwardation.

Buying a Spread: BiB & LiC

If you initiate a so-called **buy spread** (go long the higher-priced contract), in terms of market structure these positions are recognized as:

- **L**ending **in C**ontango (LiC)
- **B**orrowing **in B**ackwardation (BiB)

In both cases you are actually betting that the relative price difference between the two contracts will "widen"—implying that the spread between the two contracts at the close will be wider than the spread at the outset.

If your prediction was right you would close a winning trade.

Let us illustrate these two examples:

Example: Buying a Spread

I. Lending in Contango (LiC): Arrows Converging
Initial transaction (April, 11)
Sell the near month (June 15) | Go "long" the higher priced contract (Aug. 30)

Initial outlay: Negative −$22
Closing transaction:

Contango Widening
Closing transaction: Borrow in Contango
Buy back June, 15 | Sell back Aug. 30

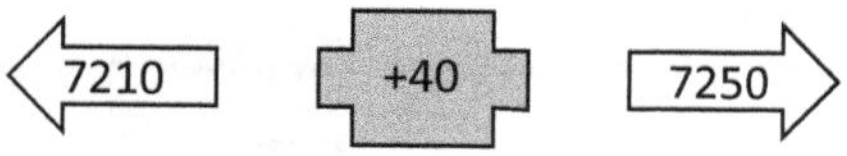

Closing outlay: Positive +$40
Final outcome +$18

II. Borrowing in Backwardation (BiB): Arrows Diverging
Initial transaction (Jan. 17)
Go "long" the higher priced contract (March 22) | Sell the further month (May, 25)

Initial outlay: Negative −$30
Closing transaction:

Backwardation Widening
Closing transaction: Lend in Backwardation
Sell back Feb, 12 | Buy back May, 2

Closing outlay: Positive +$95
Final outcome +$65

In conclusion: there is one, and one only, positive market scenario. All others – back narrowing and back turning in contango, contango narrowing & contango turning in backwardation – are losing positions!

Key Terms

selling a spread
go short the higher priced contract

Selling a Spread: BiC & LiB

If you initiate a so-called **sell spread** (go short the higher priced contract), in terms of market structure these positions are recognized as borrowing in contango or lending in backwardation (BiC & LiB respectively).

In both cases you are actually betting that the relative price difference between the two contracts will "narrow"— the spread between the two contracts at the close will be narrower than the spread at the outset.

In selling a spread trade there is more than one winning scenario.

Or to express it more precisely; in selling a spread, there is one and one only losing scenario—contango widening, in case of borrowing in contango (Figure 6.1) and backwardation widening, in case of lending in backwardation (Figure 6.2).

On the basis of evidence from historical or empirical data related to non-ferrous metals markets, and especially considering the probability aspect of the two scenarios, we may deduce that the first scenario—contango widening—is far less probable than the second—backwardation widening. The size of contango has its limits and is a predictable variable that could be factored in with a high degree of certainty. On the other hand, backwardation is a highly unpredictable, random event which may go off at any time at a magnitude just as unpredictable as it is surprising.

In Figure 6.1 we have devised the sequence of transactions that outline "Borrowing in Contango" (BiC); in that respect the entire market scenario has been segmented into three sections: Section I, Contango Widening; Section II, Contango Narrowing; and Section III, Contango Turns into Backwardation. The initial position is represented with the two black grid circles; the blank circle represents a buy side, the shaded circle represents a sell side. The position is initiated in contango, thus producing a

Figure 6.1 Borrowing in Contango (BiC)

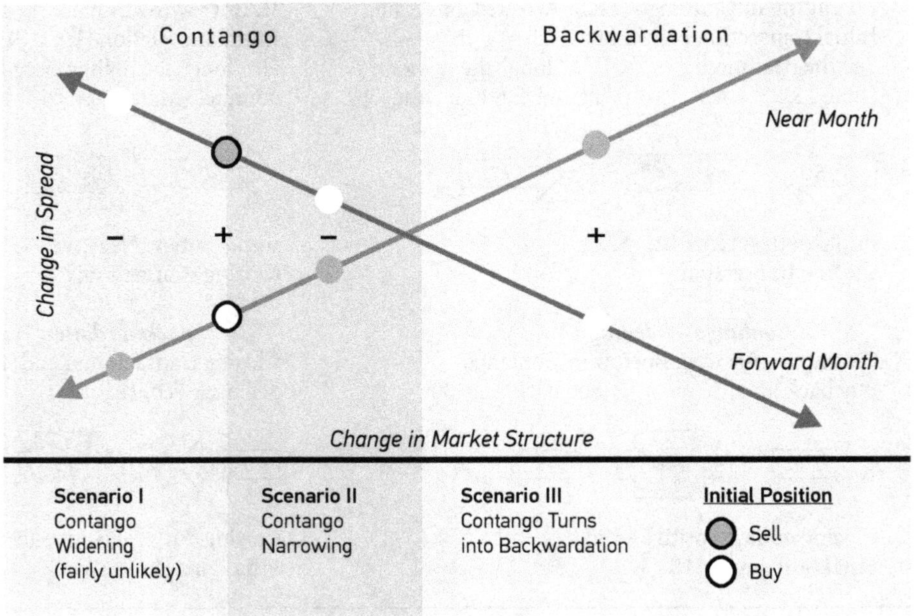

positive net outlay, since the lower priced contract is purchased and the higher priced contract is sold. From that point onward, we follow how the spread might unfold in three respective market scenarios subject to change in the market structure.

• **Initial position** – Borrowing in Contango [BiC]:	
Buy near month, sell forward month: Buy low, sell high	Initial outlay (+)
• **Scenario I Contango widening**	
Closing position: Lend in contango	Closing outlay (–)
Sell back low; Buy back high	– > + = –
Portfolio return: Loss	(–)
• **Scenario II Contango narrowing**	
Closing position: Lend in contango	Closing outlay (–)
Sell back low; Buy back high	– < + = +
Portfolio return: Gain	(+)
• **Scenario III Entering Backwardation**	
Closing position: Lend in backwardation	Closing outlay (+)
Sell back high; Buy back low	+, + = +
Portfolio return: Gain	(+)

Figure 6.2 Lending in Backwardation (LiB)

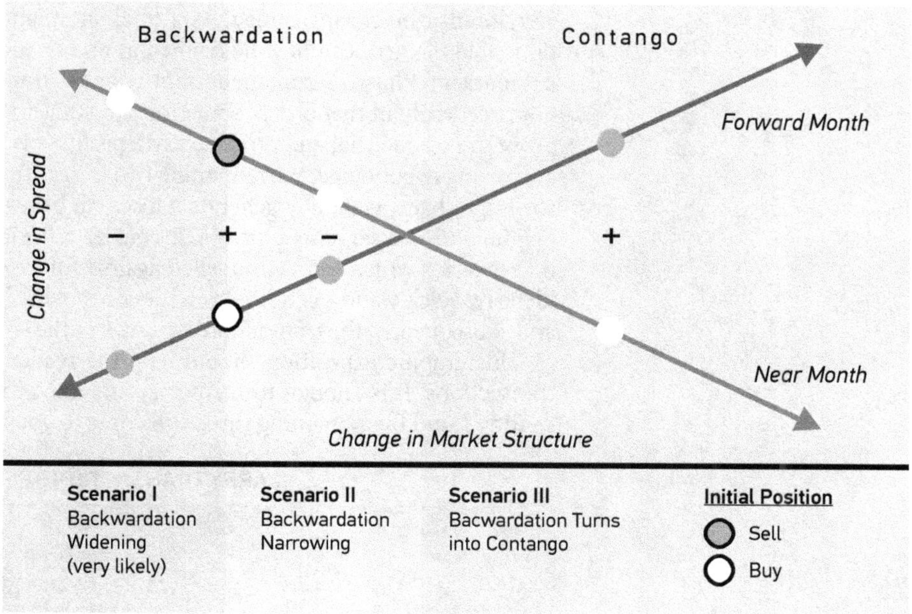

As was the case with Borrowing in Contango, the same logic applies to lending in backwardation. Note, however, that a selling spread position, now initiated in a backwardation market structure, also generates a net positive outlay, since the lower priced contract is bought and the higher priced contract is sold.

- **Initial position** – Lending in Backwardation [LiB]:
  Sell near month, buy forward month: Sell high, buy low — Initial outlay (+)
- **Scenario I Backwardation widening**
  Closing position: Borrow in backwardation — Closing outlay (–)
  Buy back high; Sell back low — – > + = –
  Portfolio return: Loss — (–)
- **Scenario II Backwardation narrowing**
  Closing position: Borrow in backwardation — Closing outlay (–)
  Buy back high; Sell back low — – < + = +
  Portfolio return: Gain — (+)
- **Scenario III Entering Contango**
  Closing position: Borrow in contango — Closing outlay +
  Buy back low; Sell back high — +, + = +
  Portfolio return: Gain — (+)

SUMMARY

The profitability of the spread strategy hinges upon the relative difference between the long and short sides of the spread at the time the spread is initiated—the initial outlay— and the relative difference between the inverse contract positions at the time they are closed—the closing outlay. As a final summation we introduce a carry transaction table. A carry can now be defined as an instance of fixing differentials on terminal market with two simultaneous but opposite transactions - buying and selling, but not necessarily in that order! Sometimes locking-in these differentials in a spread will prove to be beneficial and produce extra profits—as is the case of lending in back, and borrowing in contango; the remaining two transactions—lending in contango and borrowing in back, generally generate a loss. We believe that the table presented is truly helpful and will serve its purpose. It enables a flexible comparison of different "what if" scenarios which can be modelled against future expectations. It also allows you to identify, quickly and easily, the consequences of the likely changes in market structure, and subsequently, the transaction exposure of the spread strategy employed.

This graphic exposition should help the reader remember the integrity of carry transactions. It is enough to memorize any one of these patterns—the one most appealing—and the remaining three will come to you by the logic of opposites.

CARRY TRANSACTIONS RESUME

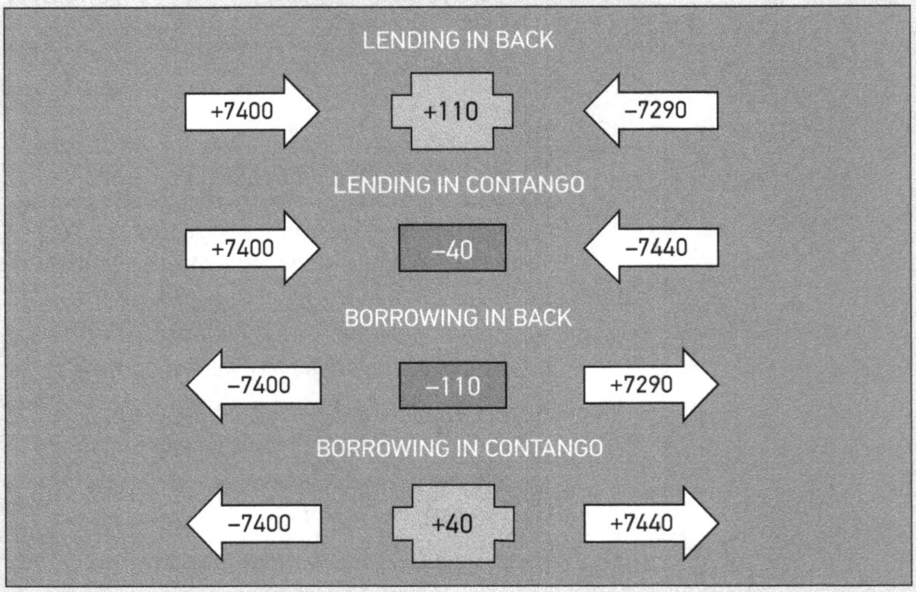

NB: The figures given in the "Carry Transactions" table are only arbitrary, used to illustrate the differentials and are not relevant for concept apprehension!

For example:

Suppose you start with lending in backwardation?

Then the logic of opposites unfolds as follows:

- If lending in backwardation is (+), then lending in contango is (–);
- If lending in backwardation is (+), then borrowing in backwardation is (–);
- If borrowing in backwardation is (–), then borrowing in contango is (+).

KEY TERMS

intermarket spread	buying a spread
calendar spread	selling a spread

CHAPTER 7

BASIS CONTROVERSY

CHAPTER OBJECTIVES

- To highlight and explain the different concepts of basis
- To examine and define the notion of price convergence
- To introduce basis diagrams and emphasize the differences between "basis weakening" and "basis strengthening"
- To explain the relationship between a basis risk and a maturity mismatch
- To analyze and depict different hedging outcomes deriving from a change in basis
- To discuss practical applications in different market environments with respect to forward prices fluctuations
- To illustrate the specifics of basis movement in the CBOT environment
- To illustrate the specifics of basis movement in the LME environment

DIFFERENT CONCEPTS OF BASIS

When we were explaining the imperfect hedge and its implications, the idea was to point out the importance of contango and backwardation relative to the final outcome of the hedge strategy. As we have seen, when futures' prompt dates do not match perfectly with the maturity of the risk to be hedged, the hedge might not eliminate all risk. Thus, the prevailing market conditions and the choice of maturity dates will affect in one way or another the effectiveness of the hedge strategy.

Since commodities and other assets are traded in the spot and futures markets simultaneously, sometimes matching the dates involved in the hedge is not possible—or, at least, it would be overly optimistic to expect that the maturity of the futures contract would always correspond perfectly with the maturity of the cash position at risk.

When the maturity date is far in the future, the relationship between spot and futures prices will fluctuate in an unpredictable fashion—very often beyond rational proportions.

Consequently, these price variations will cause responsive succession in contangos and/or backwardations prevailing in the period observed.

At maturity time t, however, the futures price inches towards or becomes equal to the spot price. The essential reason that drives the futures price to converge to that of the spot price is the credibility of the delivery arrangement (the obligations entailed in physically settled futures contracts to make or take delivery). Once confidence in delivery is ensured, price convergence is ensured as well, since efficient markets, in principle, must provide conditions in which risk-free arbitrage is precluded. Otherwise, traders would be able to speculate excessively.

If this were not so, the price divergence between cash and the futures price at expiration would allow traders to the endless possibility of "buying low and selling high," —or vice versa—thereby achieving a permanent and riskless profit.

Figure 7.1 Price Convergence

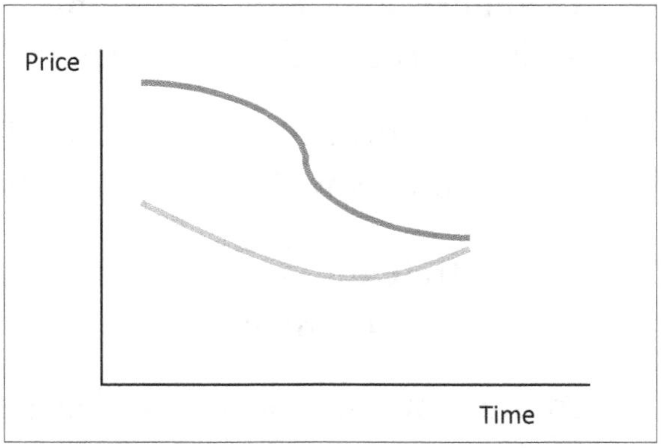

Key Terms

price convergence
property of commodity markets driven by dependability and integrity of delivery mechanism, ensuring that the futures prices converge upon spot prices during the delivery month

Accordingly, we may deduce that **price convergence** reflects the property of commodity markets which are driven by dependability and integrity of delivery mechanism, ensuring that the futures prices "converge" upon spot prices during the delivery month.

Figure 7.1 illustrates the universally observed rule of price convergence, which implies that the futures price of a commodity (the LME settlement price) approaches its spot/physical price when it approaches maturity time t.

Key Terms

basis
the difference in between current futures price and current spot price

Some authors identify a sequence of market conditions, defined as contango and backwardation, with the concept of "basis risk."

The **basis** itself is a market phenomenon that describes the relationship between the cash/spot price and its related futures price.

It is logical to assume that the following definition is the most coherent and hence most persuasive:

Basis is the difference between the current futures price and the current spot price. When it is positive it is called contango, when it is negative it is called backwardation.

Basis = Futures price – Cash price

- Fp > Sp = Positive basis: Contango
- Fp < Sp = Negative basis: Backwardation

But here comes the terminology confusion. Some authors define the basis from a different perspective and hence with an opposite sign the basis is viewed as the difference between the local cash price and the current futures price:

Basis is the difference between the local cash price of a commodity and the current futures price on the same commodity at any given point in time.

Basis = Local Cash price – Futures price

Consequently,

- Sp < Fp = Negative basis: Contango
- Sp > Fp = Positive basis: Backwardation

As we have seen, in many instances jargon does more to confuse than clarify: the same terms do not have only one referent. Moreover, their meaning is sometimes expressed in an ambiguous manner, denoting two or even more different things within a given context. This is particularly true in the jargon of basis. Therefore, it is very important to pay utmost attention to verbal distinctions of the terms applied and their precise connotations.

BASIS AND MATURITY OF FUTURES CONTRACT

Enumerating the distinctive features of hedging from the beginning of the chapter we pointed out:

"....that the opening and closing of the futures position must be made at the same time as the physical contract is priced so as to avoid further exposure to unfavourable change in price moves."

But on many occasions this will not prove possible and the hedger will be exposed to **basis risk.** Basis risk is the risk associated with an unexpected widening or narrowing of basis within the time interval between initiation and reversal of the futures position. Basis movement can also be exploited as an opportunity to improve a position already initiated by closely monitoring the development of the basis over time and choosing the proper moment to close the hedge before maturity.

Key Terms

basis risk
the risk associated with an unexpected widening or narrowing of basis

Likewise, basis movement can also motivate a speculator to attempt to lock-in a profit originating from the expected basis rise or fall. The critical point to decide upon would obviously be the right timing to reverse the trade.

In the basis diagrams that follow we shall exhibit the eight possible basis movement scenarios.

Table 7.1 Basis Movement and Effects on Hedging

MARKET STRUCTURE			LONG HEDGE	SHORT HEDGE
BASIS RISE	Contango widening	FP rise faster	+	–
		FP falls slower	+	–
	Back narrowing	FP rise faster	+	–
		FP falls slower	+	–
BASIS FALL	Contango narrowing	FP falls faster	–	+
		FP rise slower	–	+
	Back widening	FP falls faster	–	+
		FP rise slower	–	+

Table 7.1 above is a display of market conditions arranged in accordance with eight different scenarios relative to the repercussions on instituted hedging positions. From a first glance we may extract a few apparent conclusions:

- The basis is not constant as the ratio between futures and spot prices is changing continuously, hence the basis can rise or it can fall.
- The long hedgers benefit from a rise in the basis.
- The short hedgers benefit from a fall in the basis.
- The basis can find itself in two different environments: contango and backwardation.

Key Terms

basis rise
the futures prices rise faster or fall slower than the spot prices

basis fall
the futures prices fall faster or rise slower than the spot prices

Table 7.1 also offers some useful logical shortcuts worth emphasizing: Since the long hedge is designed to give protection from a price rise, it is obvious that it benefits from a **basis rise** and vice versa; since a short hedge is instituted to protect from a price fall, it obviously benefits from a **basis fall.**

So, the basis can rise and it can fall! What do these terms really mean?

By definition:

"A basis rise implies that futures prices rise faster or fall slower than spot prices"
And,
"A basis fall implies that futures prices fall faster or rise slower than spot prices."

If you think it is not confusing enough, we can turn it the other way around and say that:

"A basis rise implies that spot prices rise slower or fall faster than the futures price"
And,
"A basis fall implies that spot prices fall slower or rise faster than the futures price."

Admittedly, this sounds rather confusing! Figures 7.2 and 7.3 aim to untangle the intricacy of basis movements by means of graphic depiction. In this analytical exposition, variations in basis movement over time are split into two different market environments—contango and backwardation. Figure 7.2 illustrates the evolution of a basis spread in a contango market, and in Figure 7.3 we pursue the evolution of basis spread in a backwardation market.

Figure 7.2 Basis Movement Diagrams – Contango Market

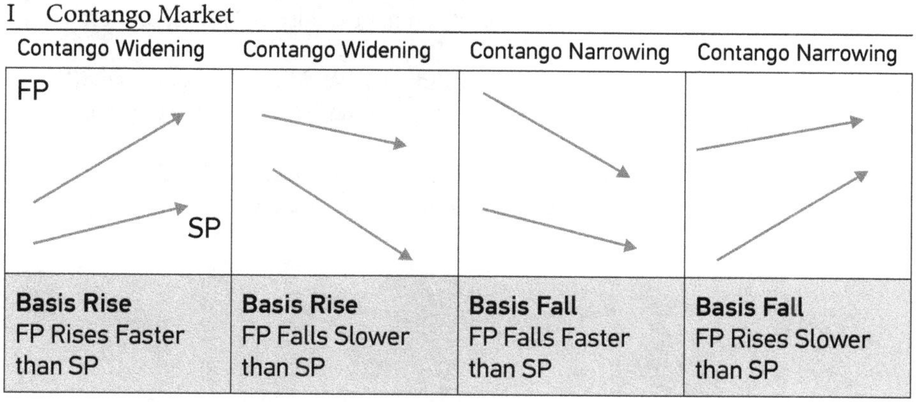

I Contango Market
Contango Widening
Contango Widening
Contango Narrowing
Contango Narrowing
FP
SP
Basis Rise
FP Rises Faster than SP
Basis Rise
FP Falls Slower than SP
Basis Fall
FP Falls Faster than SP
Basis Fall
FP Rises Slower than SP

The basis, as we have already pointed out, can be found in two different circumstances.

I. In a contango market basis can rise just as it can fall.

If it rises it can also be in two different market conditions:

- Rising market—FP rises faster than SP
- Falling market— FP falls slower than SP

But in a contango market the basis can also fall. The fall of the basis can also be manifested in two different market conditions:

- Falling market—FP falls faster than SP
- Rising market—FP rises slower than SP

The same relevance is valid in case of backwardation market.

Figure 7.3 Basis Movement Diagram, Backwardation Market

II Backwardation Market

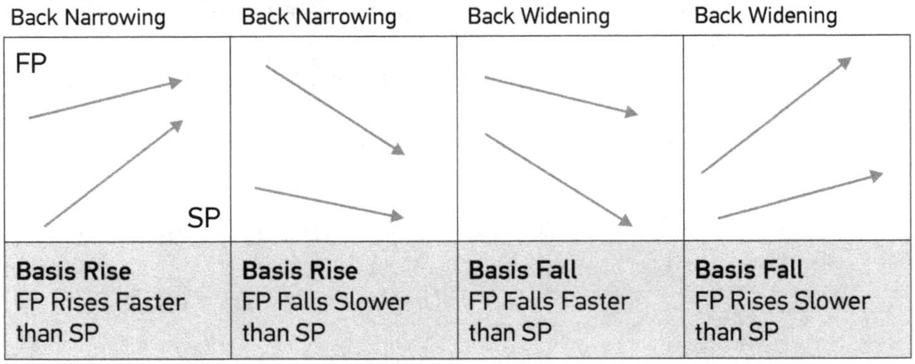
Back Narrowing
Back Narrowing
Back Widening
Back Widening
FP
SP
Basis Rise
FP Rises Faster than SP
Basis Rise
FP Falls Slower than SP
Basis Fall
FP Falls Faster than SP
Basis Fall
FP Rises Slower than SP

II. In a backwardation market accordingly, the basis can rise just as it can fall. If it rises it can happen in two different market conditions:

- Rising market—FP rises faster than SP
- Falling market—FP falls slower than SP

If it falls it can happen also in two different market conditions:

- Falling market—FP falls faster than SP
- Rising market—FP rises slower than SP

Now we can skip to the headline "Hedging and Basis Risk", where we will acquaint you with different market situations and their repercussions on profit/loss proceeds.

I HEDGING AND BASIS RISK

A PRIMER FROM CBOT

Key Terms

maturity mismatch
lifting a futures hedge on a date that is not matched with the date the cash trade is executed

If we take the CBOT (Chicago Board Of Trade) as a referent market for agricultural products—wheat and corn, for example—we see that "**maturity mismatch**" is almost the norm. This is due to the fact that futures are traded at monthly expiration dates and it is seldom possible to match exactly the date of the physical trade with the offsetting position in the corresponding futures.

CBOT wheat futures Contract Months: July, Sep, Dec, Mar, May

Basis = Local Cash Price – Futures Price

An instance of "negative basis:" Contango	
Mar '11 Local cash price	860 (cent/bushel)
Dec '11 Futures price	–900 c/bushel
Basis	–0.40 c/bushel

An instance of "positive basis:" Backwardation	
Mar '11 Local cash price	860 (cent/bushel)
Sep '12 Futures price	825 c/bushel
Basis	0.35 c/bushel

Because a basis reflects local market conditions, aside from the regular costs of carry (such as transportation costs, interest/storage costs, etc.), the basis will also be directly influenced by grains specific factors including:

- local supply and demand conditions, such as grain quality, availability, need, local weather, handling costs and profit margins.

For this reason, price convergence is not always perfect—even for the same maturity date, so it may happen that at maturity the spot and futures prices do not fully converge to zero.

Although every hedge is designed to remove most of the risk associated with adverse price changes, it will not eliminate basis risk and its repercussions must be taken into account upfront.

As the basis risk is constantly changing in a more or less predictable fashion, every risk management or prudent investor should reconsider carefully the following aspects before setting definitive hedging strategy:

- Would you be better off to enter into a forward deal?
- Is the market structure in favour of the particular occurrence (purchase or sale)?
- What is the most appropriate forward month in which to place a hedge?
- When is the best time to lift the hedge?
- What are the risks associated with the offsetting trade?

In Figure 7.4 we have illustrated the case of change in basis as it may develop within the Chicago Board of Trade, pointing to the basic terms associated with the relative change in market structure.

Figure 7.4 Basis Movement Illustration – CBOT Case

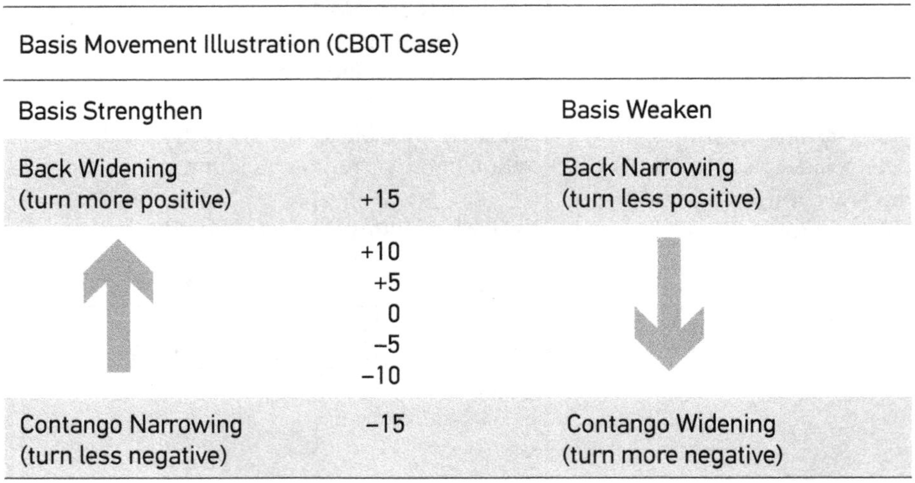
Basis Movement Illustration (CBOT Case)
Basis Strengthen
Basis Weaken
Back Widening
(turn more positive)
+15
Back Narrowing
(turn less positive)
+10
+5
0
–5
–10
Contango Narrowing
(turn less negative)
–15
Contango Widening
(turn more negative)

Namely, the difference between futures and spot prices will either expand—go wide, or diminish—go narrow. In CBOT terminology these variations are referred to as, in the first case,—**basis strengthening** (contango narrowing and/or backwardation widening), or—**basis weakening** (contango widening and/or backwardation narrowing) in the second.

Key Terms

basis strengthens
contango narrowing and/or backwardation widening

basis weakens
contango widening and/or backwardation narrowing

The terms "strengthening basis", and "weakening basis" both refer to a change in the price relationship between the cash and futures prices and are utterly indifferent to a change in price direction.

From the moment the hedge is instituted, the ultimate market price loses its significance and ceases to matter. The only important factor to watch is a change in basis.

SHORT HEDGE

So, more often than not, hedgers will have to execute the physical trade at one date and simultaneously lift the hedge on the futures (close the futures position) at another date (due to the divergence in maturity dates).

In other words, a hedger is repeatedly faced with a maturity mismatch or a "maturity gap," which is the point where the basis risk comes into play, shaping the final result of the instituted hedge.

In the short hedge examples that soon follow, we shall observe a farmer producing wheat at a cost of 800 c/bushel. He needs to protect his production against a possible downturn in wheat prices. Therefore he enters into a short hedge by selling a May wheat future at 840 c/bushel.

Assumptions Our farmer is aware that there is a real potential for the basis to strengthen (expecting contango narrowing) so he decides to initiate a hedge by selling a May futures contract accordingly.

His decision is supported by a historical evidence that the local basis in early April averages 30 under (–30 c/bushel) the May futures contract. If his expectations are correct and the basis narrows, he will be able to achieve a higher selling price for his wheat.

The net selling price would be calculated according to the formula:

Futures Price t_0 + (–Expected Basis) = Expected Selling Price

BASIS MOVEMENT—THREE POSSIBLE SCENARIOS

The farmer initiates a short hedge by selling a futures contract as a temporary substitute for a physical sale that is going to take place at some forward date. Since we elaborate performance of the short hedge, which is primarily designed to protect the forward selling price and offset the risk of falling prices, we assume a falling market.

We emphasize once again that local prices may vary substantially from the relative futures price subject to prevailing local market conditions.

Initial position: Contango market	
Cash price at t_0	800 c/bushel
May futures price t_0	840 c/bushel
Basis	–40 c/bushel

During the time left to the futures contract expiry, the change in basis may develop into one of three possible states: "basis strengthening," "basis weakening," and "basis unchanged."

The following examples are to examine in detail all three possible scenarios, and demonstrate how the change in basis affects hedging outcomes. We begin our analysis with the case of basis strengthening.

Case no. 1: Basis Strengthening

In the first case we assume that contango narrows conveniently from (–\$0.40) to (–\$0.30): becomes less negative, causing the basis to strengthen.

As we lift the hedge at some point in early April the result should unfold as follows:

May futures price t_1	820 c/bushel
Basis early April delivery	–30 c/bushel
April cash price t_1	790 c/bushel

I. Original Futures Price t_0 + (–Actual Basis) = Final Selling Price

840 + (–30) = 810 c/bushel

Paraphrasing the above formula we may verify that, if the above set of circumstances materialized, the hedger would obtain a 10 c/bushel better selling price compared to the producer price: 810 compared to 800.

Subject to individual preference, one may choose from two more algebraic alternatives which arrive at the same result:

II. Difference in Basis +/– Original Cash price t_0 = Final Selling Price

+\$10 + \$800 = \$810 c/bushel

Initial basis	–\$40 c/bushel
Closing basis	–\$30 c/bushel
Difference	+\$10 c/bushel

III. Cash Price at t_1 +/− Profit/Loss on Futures Position = Final Selling Price

790 + 20 = 810 c/bushel

Cash price t_1	790 c/bushel
Futures gain (sells 840/c – buys 820/c)	20 c/bushel
Net selling price	810 c/bushel

In the circumstances described above, the hedge succeeded in providing protection from falling wheat prices, and due to favourable basis development it managed to secure a price that fully corresponded to our expectations.

From the time t_0, the point the hedge was instituted, the final sale price would remain indifferent to a change in price direction.

The only relevant factor that affects the final sale price is the relative change between the cash and the futures prices—the change in basis.

Indeed, if futures prices were to rise instead of fall, the final outcome would not be altered. For example, if futures price rallied to 860, maintaining the same basis proportion of −0.30, then the actual cash price at time t_1 would be 830. The final selling price would remain the same—810.

FINAL RESULT: GAIN 10 c/bushel

Case no. 2: Basis Unchanged

Basis strengthening as shown in Case no. 1, is to be considered only as an advantageous disposition and not a custom set of circumstances: there can be no guarantees in regard to forward price movement. The next example is the case of unchanged basis:

May futures price t_1	820 c/bushel
Basis early April delivery	– 40 c/bushel)
April cash price t_1	780 c/bushel

I. Original Futures Price t_0 + (−Actual Basis) = Final Selling Price

840 + (−40) = 800 c/bushel

II. Difference in Basis +/−Original Cash Price t_0 = Final Selling Price

0 + 800 = 800 c/bushel

Initial basis:	−40 c/bushel
Closing basis	−40 c/bushel
Difference	+0 c/bushel

III. Cash Price at t_1 +/− Profit (Loss) on Futures Position = Final Selling Price

780 + 20 (840 – 820) = 800 c/bushel

Cash price t_1	780 c/bushel
Futures gain (sells 840/c – buys 820/c)	20 c/bushel
Net selling price	800 c/bushel

If the basis remains unchanged in the course of the period observed, the final price will be no worse than the initial forward price = 800 c/bushel.

FINAL RESULT: UNCHANGED

Case no. 3: Basis Weakening

If you initiate a futures position with an idea to take advantage of anticipated term structure of the yield curve, then you are speculating a bit and you have to take into account the risk of an adverse price movement. In the next example we will check out how the weakening basis worsens the projected hedge result.

May futures price t_1	830 c/bushel
Basis early April delivery	–55 c/bushel)
April cash price t_1	775 c/bushel

I. Original Futures Price t_0 + (–Actual Basis) = Final Selling Price

840 +(–55 basis) =785 c/bushel

II. Difference in Basis +/– Original Cash Price t_0 = Final Selling Price

–15 + 800 = 785 c/bushel

Initial basis:	–40 c/bushel
Closing basis	–55 c/bushel
Difference	–15 c/bushel

III. Cash Price at t_1 +/– Profit (Loss) on Futures Position = Final Selling Price

775 + 10 (840 – 830) = 785 c/bushel

Cash price t_1	775 c/bushel
Futures gain (sells 840/c – buys 830/c)	10 c/bushel
Net selling price	785 c/bushel

If at time t_1 the basis was weaker than initially (–55 t_1 comparing to –40 t_0) because, contrary to our expectations, contango moved in the opposite direction—became more negative (widened instead of narrowed), you would receive less than 800 for the wheat. This is the only scenario in which the hedge instituted would bring a negative result—a lower wheat selling price.

FINAL RESULT: LOSS 15 c/bushel

Short hedgers benefit from basis strengthening and suffer from basis weakening.

LONG HEDGE

It is the beginning of September 2010. The company XYZ will need to purchase soybean oil in January 2011. The soybean oil user needs to decide whether to protect its forward purchase price by initiating a hedge, or to fix the forward deal with a local supplier based on current market prices.

Initial position: Backwardation market	
Current January forward delivery	\$0.28/lb
January futures contract	\$0.25/lb
Current basis	+\$0.03/lb

Assumptions Looking at historical records, the producer notices that the basis average by January, in general, moves around half a cent, (+\$0.005/lb). Company's XYZ anticipation is that towards January the backwardation will narrow, driving the basis to its historic average. In other words, expectations are that the basis will weaken. The soybean oil price of \$0.28 for January delivery, is currently the best available on the market. Accordingly, company XYZ decides to reject the forward purchase offer, since the current futures (\$0.25/lb) is lower than the cash forward (\$0.28/lb), and enters into a long futures hedge.

A long hedge is initiated by buying a futures contract as a temporary substitute for a physical purchase that is going to take place at some forward date.

Under the premises the expected buying price is obtained by the formula:

Original Futures Price + Expected Basis = Expected Purchase Price

\$0.25/lb + (+\$0.005) = \$0.255/lb

BASIS MOVEMENT—THREE POSSIBLE SCENARIOS

Again we shall investigate the three hypothetical cases of basis movement in backwardation market.

Case no.1: Basis Weakening

Time goes by and we are in late December. The futures price has supposedly increased to \$0.27. Also, the correlation between cash and futures price has moved in line with our expectations, so that backwardation has in fact narrowed—become less positive. The basis has weakened from \$0.03 to \$0.005.

The farmer unwinds the hedge by purchasing January soybean oil requirements for cash (-\$0.275), and simultaneously closes the futures position by selling back the January futures contract for \$0.27 earning a positive return of \$0.20/lb.

The final results calculated using three different algebraic methods, are:

I. Cash Price at t_1 + Profit on Futures = Final Purchase Price

–\$0.275/lb + \$0.020/lb = –\$0.255/lb

Cash soybean oil t_1	–\$0.275/lb
Futures gain (sells \$0.27 – buys \$0.25)	\$0.020/lb
Net purchase price	–\$0.255/lb

II. Original Futures Price t_0 + Actual Basis = Final Purchase Price

–(\$0.25 + \$0.005) = –\$0.255/lb

Jan. futures price t_1	\$0.25 /lb
Actual Basis	+\$0.005 /lb
December Cash price t_1	\$0.255 /lb

III. Difference in Basis – Original Forward Price = Final Purchase Price

+$.025/lb – $0.28/lb = –$0.255/lb

Initial basis	$0.03/lb
Closing basis	$0.005/lb
Difference	+$0.025/lb

The long hedger's major concern is to provide protection against rising prices. In the above example, the futures price has moved higher but backwardation has narrowed—become less positive—driving the basis weaker, which is in accordance with his expectations. A weakening basis results in a better soybean oil purchase price.

FINAL RESULT: GAIN $.025/lb

Case no. 2: Basis Unchanged

Cash soybean oil at t_1	$0.29/lb
January futures contract at t_1	$0.26/lb
Current basis	+$0.03/lb

Cash Price at t_1 + Profit (Loss) on Futures = Final Purchase Price

Cash soybean oil	–$0.29/lb
Futures gain (sells $0.26 – buys $0.25)	$0.010/lb
Net purchase price	–$0.28/lb

Had the basis remained unchanged, the final soybean oil purchase price would be equivalent to the forward cash price that was available from the outset. The ultimate soybean oil purchase price of $0.28/lb is the same as if no hedge had been instituted. It is worth noticing that the final soybean oil purchase price remains unaffected, regardless of the change in price direction.

FINAL RESULT: UNCHANGED

Case no. 3: Basis Strengthening

Cash soybean oil at t_1	$0.30/lb
January futures contract at t_1	$0.25/lb
Current basis	+$0.05/lb

Cash Price at t_1 + Profit (Loss) on Futures = Final Purchase Price

Cash soybean oil at t_1	–$0.30/lb
Futures gain (sells $0.25 – buys $0.25)	$0/lb
Net purchase price	–$0.30/lb

Lastly, had the basis gone in another direction as a consequence of backwardation widening, the hedge would have produced a negative outcome—a higher soybean oil purchase price.

FINAL RESULT: LOSS $.020 /lb

In conclusion, we may affirm that the final soybean oil purchase price, in all exhibited examples, would remain the same regardless of the change in price direction.

Long hedgers benefit from basis weakening and suffer from basis strengthening.

Figure 7.5 Basis Movement and Imperfect Hedging Aftermath Resume (CBOT)

Basis Position	Long Hedgers	Short Hedgers
Basis Strengthening	–	+
Contango Narrows/Back Widens		
Basis Weakening	+	–
Contango Widens/Back Narrows		

NB: Useful mnemonics, CWBW – Contango widening, Basis Weakening.

In CBOT terminology variations in basis are referred to as:

- basis strengthening (contango narrowing and/or backwardation widening) or
- basis weakening (contango widening and/or backwardation narrowing).

The terms; "strengthening basis" and "weakening basis," both refer to a change in the price relationship between the cash and futures prices—and are utterly indifferent to a change in price direction.

I hope that these elaborations help investors attain a wide picture of basis alternative movements and their ramifications.

Figure 7.5 goes into the correlation between two variables—basis risk and hedging— and looks at how a change in basis affects the strategy performance.

A PRIMER FROM LME

At the very beginning of this chapter we ventured to clarify the differences or conflicting implications associated with the term "basis".

From the facts offered we may derive a conclusion that definitions of basis are a matter of convention and both definitions offered are convincingly justified.

However, we deem it prudent to underline the dissimilarities once again:

American Exchanges predominantly are referring to:

> Basis = Spot price – Futures price

- Spot price < Futures price = Negative basis = Contango
- Spot price > Futures price = Positive basis = Backwardation

The LME is exclusively referring to:

> Basis = Futures price – Spot price

- Futures price > Spot price = Positive basis = Contango
- Futures price < Spot price = Negative basis = Backwardation

In the same context, we shall remind ourselves of the two more related definitions: the term "basis rise" refers to the situation in which futures prices rise faster or fall slower than spot prices, and "basis fall" refers to the situation in which futures prices fall faster or rise slower than spot prices.

Within the LME, investors are available to trade every LME date up to three months forward: matching the dates proves to be one of the greatest conveniences for all investors trading on the London Metal Exchange.

In "*Managing Metals Price Risks*" (the LME Edition), the authors, analyzing the basics of hedging on the LME related to the basis phenomenon, proposed the following conclusion:

> *As the LME's settlement prices are the global "pricing standard" for the metals covered, its use for hedging elegantly avoids any problem of "basis risk."*

Once the physical transaction has been concluded, the hedger initiates an equal and opposite futures position for the same delivery date as their physical transaction.

In this way, the hedger will have locked in the future price, regardless of any subsequent price change, thus executing the "perfect hedge."

Accessibility of matching the maturity dates up to three months forward on the LME and using "LME Settlement Price" to price both sides of the trade—physical and futures—effectively eliminates the basis risk.

This is possible because cash and futures prices tend to converge as each delivery contract month approaches maturity.

However, basis risk may come into play whenever there is a divergence along the forward curve between the futures price and the cash price of the underlying commodity which is being hedged.

Inside the LME environment, divergence takes place predominantly in cases where the hedger is forced (for whatever reason) to close the physical side of the trade at a time that is not exactly the same as the delivery (prompt) date of the futures.

This imperfect correlation between cash and futures prices will then unlock the predicted result, adding incalculable risk to the strategy already instituted. The difference between cash and futures prices may go wide or narrow relative to the initial position, causing the forward yield curve to shift from contango to backwardation, and vice versa.

At LME, the basis risk is manifested either as contango (positive basis) or backwardation (negative basis). Once encountered in a hedging strategy, basis risk will create the potential for excess gains or losses. The final result, in general, will be determined by the size of contango and/or backwardation prevailing at time T (the time the hedge is lifted).

Predicting forward buying and selling prices based on basis movement and not depending on price fluctuations, is a very frequent way of profiling hedge strategies.

The basis examples that follow aim to disclose how the evolution of the basis (contango and backwardation) are influencing hedge positions that have already been instituted. In a variety of possible situations, emanating from the term structure of the forward curve, some will prove to be beneficial and some detrimental. From the moment the position has been initiated, either as a forward purchase or a sale, an experienced hedger has every interest to watch closely and re-estimate how the contango and/or backwardation have evolved since the initial hedge, and be ready to turn the favourable price movement into an advantage.

Understanding the mechanics of closing the hedge before maturity, and how to calculate the net selling or buying price resulting from a change in price structure, may prove to be indispensable information in analyzing the perspective of any cash market excess gains and losses.

Figure 7.6 Basis Movement Illustration (LME Case)

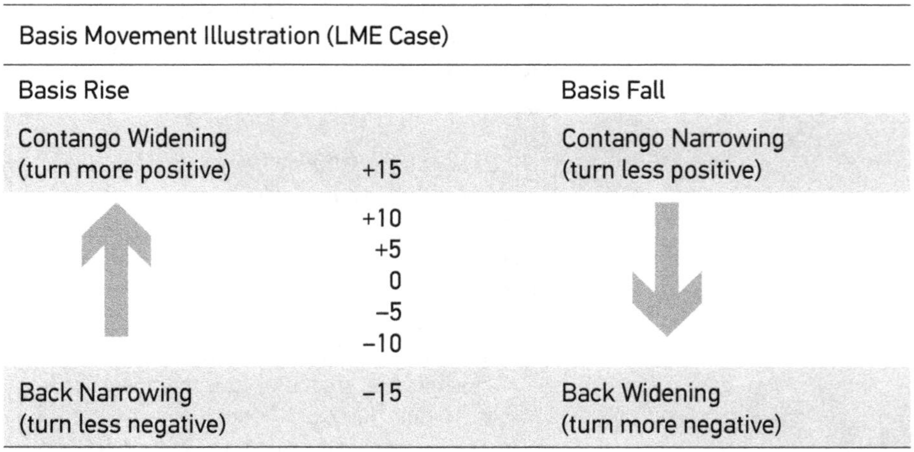
Basis Movement Illustration (LME Case)
Basis Rise
Basis Fall
Contango Widening
(turn more positive)
+15
Contango Narrowing
(turn less positive)
+10
+5
0
–5
–10
Back Narrowing
(turn less negative)
–15
Back Widening
(turn more negative)

Before we begin to analyze various scenarios there are some observations that need to be underlined. With reference to LME term structure and related manifestations of contango and backwardation yield curves, there are two noteworthy remarks:

Contango never goes beyond carrying costs, which are directly observable, and therefore the scale of contango is fairly predictable. Consequently, it would be unrealistic, or highly improbable, to expect that contango will go wide as each contract month nears expiration.

Backwardation, characterized by a conspicuous gap between spot and futures prices, is rightfully deemed an "inverted market" and is usually treated as a transitory disturbance of the normal state between supply and demand, predisposed to be short-lived. The emergence and size of backwardation is hard to predict.

In what follows we shall analyze two probable market scenarios encountered with a basis risk and the repercussions thereof:

- Price Fixing Hedge—Buying Forward
- Price Fixing Hedge—Selling Forward

LONG HEDGE—BUYING FORWARD

Hedging a short position in a commodity naturally begins with a long futures position as a temporary substitute for the anticipated metal purchase, which is to be negotiated at some predetermined date in the future.

Price Fixing Hedge; Buying Forward, Backwardation Market

At the beginning of January, a copper producer is facing a short position of 100 tons of copper cathodes that will be needed in three months time. The copper price is currently quoted at $7520. This price level is satisfactory, but buying the material now will tie up capital unnecessarily and incur storage costs. A short position in commodities will generate a loss if there is a price increase. As a three months period is a long time our producer wants to take some kind of protection against unexpected swings in copper price.

The market is in backwardation, so the three month futures is available at a lower price of $7490. A long price fixing hedge will secure a purchase price of $7490, leaving the hedger indifferent to a price change.

So, let us assume the hedger initiates in January a long price fixing hedge by purchasing four April futures contracts to match his physical forward purchase.

At the beginning of March the backwardation narrows, futures prices rise faster than spot prices and the cash price goes from $7520 to $7600—a rise of $80, while the futures price goes from $7490 to $7590—a rise of $100.

This scenario would be denoted a "basis rise."

Considering the circumstances, the hedger may be induced to lift the hedge prematurely.

Depending on the timing he chooses, and the correlation between the futures and spot prices, the hedge payout efficiency will be affected for better or worse. The predictions of how the price of the futures contract will evolve relative to the spot price, and the choice of maturity date, therefore becomes crucial for the hedge's effectiveness.

The scenario of lifting the buying hedge prematurely is illustrated in Table 7.2.

Table 7.2 Imperfect Hedge; Buying Forward, Backwardation Narrowing, Market Rising

FORWARD / CURRENT	CASH	1 MONTH	2 MONTHS	3 MONTHS
JANUARY (to)	7520	7510	7500	−7490
FEBRUARY	7560	7550	7540	7530
MARCH	−7600	+7590	7580	7570
APRIL	7640	7630	7620	7610

1. Comparing to Initial Spot Price ($7520)
Backwardation Narrowed: FP Rise Faster than SP
Spot Price went from $7520 to −7600 = −$80
Futures Price went from −$7490 to $7590 = +$100
Net Purchase Price: −$7520 + $20 (Basis Gain)
Net Purchase Price: −$7500
Net effect: +$20 (Basis Gain)

The end result—the final purchase price (−$7500)—differs from what would be the expected outcome delivered by a price fixing hedge, had it been closed out at maturity ($7490).

However, this result may be interpreted from the viewpoint of three different aspects: the first aspect compares the final outcome to the initial spot price ($7520); the second compares the final outcome to the fixed forward price ($7490), and the third compares the results to the actual spot price ($7600).

Table 7.2 reflects the hedging outcome of an imperfect hedge. When a perfect hedge is not possible, basis risk must be incorporated into the hedging outcome.

In our example, due to a change in the basis, the final purchase price is $20 better than the initial target price: −$7500, compared to −$7520.

But because of accessibility to match maturity dates up to three months forward on LME and advantage of using "LME Settlement Price" to price both sides of the trade—physical and futures—the basis risk could be viewed from a different perspective. Obviously, the hedger would be better off if the closing transaction is left to be lifted at maturity. If left intact, the price fixing hedge would secure a purchase price of $7490 irrespective of where the closing spot price may finish.

Due to basis rise, the final purchase price is $10 worse than what would have been secured with a perfect price fixing hedge: (−$7500) compared to (−$7490).

2. Comparing to Fixed Forward Price (−$7490)
Backwardation Narrowed: FP Rise Faster than SP
Closing Backwardation= −$10
Net Purchase Price: −$7490 −$10 (Actual Basis; Backwardation)
Net Purchase Price: −$7500
Net effect: −$10 (Actual Basis)

3. Comparing to Closing Spot Price (–$7600)
Backwardation Narrowed: FP Rise Faster than SP
Net Purchase Price: –$7600 + $100 (Futures Gain)
Net Purchase Price: –$7500
Net effect: +$100 (Futures Gain)

Relative to an unhedged position, the imperfect hedge outcome is $100/t better.

However, on the day the hedge is lifted, the basis might be quite different. The basis is genuinely a "random variable" as the two prices—cash and forward—move independently over time. When the basis changes, hedging outcomes change too. Imperfect hedges, in all instances, must incorporate the shape of the futures curve into the hedging outcome.

Changes in market structure are quite common in the metals market and, in some cases, may be exploited to your advantage. In the example exhibited in Table 7.2 the benefit could be even more pronounced if, during the validity of futures contract, the forward yield curve shifted from backwardation to contango.

Price Fixing Hedge; Buying Forward, Backwardation Flips to Contango

Therefore, in our next example, we shall assume that in March the copper market evolves from backwardation to contango, so that the one month forward price hits $7610. The basis has moved favourably, so the hedger may now unwind the hedge purposefully to his advantage. If he lifts the hedge in this market scenario, the final purchase price would be $7480. The price achieved is $10 better than the price he would acquire if the hedge is lifted at expiration ($7490), and $40 better than the initial spot price ($7520).

In the LME market lingo we would say that "backwardation flipped to contango."

This scenario is illustrated in the following Table 7.3.

Table 7.3 Imperfect Hedge; Buying Forward, Backwardation Flips to Contango

CURRENT \ FORWARD	CASH	1 MONTH	2 MONTHS	3 MONTHS
JANUARY (to)	7520	7510	7500	–7490
FEBRUARY	7560	7550	7540	7530
MARCH	–7600	+7610	7620	7630
APRIL	7640	7650	7660	7670

1. Comparing to Initial Spot Price ($7520)
Backwardation Turns to Contango
Spot Price went from $7520 to –7600 = –$80
Futures Price went from –$7490 to $7610 = +$120
Net Purchase Price: –$7520 + $40 (Basis Gain)
Net Purchase Price: –$7480
Net effect: +$40 (Basis Gain)

2. Comparing to Fixed Forward Price (–$7490)
Backwardation Turns to Contango
Closing Contango: +$10
Net Purchase Price: –$7490 + $10 (Actual Basis; Contango)
Net Purchase Price: –$7480
Net Effect: +$10 (Actual Basis)

3. Comparing to Closing Spot Price (–$7600)
Backwardation Turns to Contango
Net Purchase Price: –$7600 + $120 (Futures Gain)
Net Purchase Price: –$7480
Net effect: +$120 (Futures Gain)

NB: The correlation between algebraic variables remains intact and indifferent to the shape of the futures price curve.

Price Fixing Hedge; Buying Forward, Contango Market

Let us suppose now that, instead of backwardation, the market is in contango, so that the three month futures is available at higher price—$7550. Narrowing contango may produce positive effects on hedging outcomes, so the hedgers avail themselves of an opportunity to close the hedge early and capture windfall profits.

The scenario of lifting the buying hedge prematurely, in a contango market, is illustrated in Table 7.4:

Table 7.4 Imperfect Hedge; Buying Forward, Contango Narrowing

FORWARD / CURRENT	CASH	1 MONTH	2 MONTHS	3 MONTHS
JANUARY (to)	7520	7530	7540	–7550
FEBRUARY	7560	7570	7580	7590
MARCH	–7600	+7605	7620	7630
APRIL	7640	7650	7660	7670

1. Comparing to Initial Spot Price ($7520)
Contango Narrowed: FP Rise Slower then SP
Spot Price went from $7520 to –7600 = –$80
Futures Price went from –$7550 to $7605 = +$55
Net Purchase Price: –$7520 – $25 (Basis Loss)
Net Purchase Price: –$7545
Net effect: –$25 (Basis Loss)

In our example, compared to the initial spot price ($7520), the change in basis has moved adversely (–$25 basis loss), causing the increase in the final purchase price: from -$7520 to –$7545. The remaining two comparisons follow:

2. Comparing to Fixed Forward Price (–$7550)
Contango Narrowed: FP Rise Slower then SP
Closing Contango = +$10
Net Purchase Price: –$7550 + $10 (Actual Basis; Contango)
Net Purchase Price: –$7545
Net effect: +$5 (Actual Basis)

3. Comparing to Closing Spot Price (–$7600)
Contango Narrowed: FP Rise Slower then SP
Net Purchase Price: –$7600 + $55 (Futures Gain)
Net Purchase Price: –$7545
Net effect: +$55 (Futures Gain)

Long hedgers benefit from basis rise and suffer from basis fall.

SHORT HEDGE—SELLING FORWARD

On the other side, the market participants who are initially long are seeking protection against a price fall. Hedging a long position in commodities naturally begins with initiating a short futures position as a temporary substitute for anticipated metal sale which is to be negotiated at some predetermined forward date.

Price Fixing Hedge; Selling Forward, Contango Market

The current market price is $7520. This price level is considered to be acceptable for the copper producer and would bring in a positive return. On top of that, the market happens to be in contango and the three months forward price is quoted at $7550.

If left intact, the price fixing hedge would guarantee a selling price at $7550 irrespective of eventual price fall. The hedge would also be indifferent to basis risk, as price convergence at expiration would secure that the cash and futures prices become one. The only possible scenario that could unbalance the projected hedging outcome is lifting the hedge prior to expiration date.

At the beginning of March the contango narrows, the cash price goes from $7520 to $7480 (a fall of $40), while the futures price goes from $7550 to $7490 (a fall of $60). Futures prices fell faster than spot prices!

In terms of basis this scenario is designated as a "basis fall."

Considering the circumstances, the hedger may be induced to lift the hedge prematurely. His target price was $7520, so if he unwinds the hedge early he would lock-in the selling price of $7540—that is $20/ton better than his target price.

The scenario of lifting the selling hedge prematurely is illustrated in the following Table 7.5:

Table 7.5 Imperfect Hedge; Selling Forward, Contango Narrowing, Market Falling

FORWARD / CURRENT	CASH	1 MONTH	2 MONTHS	3 MONTHS
JANUARY (to)	7520	7530	7540	+7550 →
FEBRUARY	7500	7510	7520	7530
MARCH	+7480 →	← −7485	7500	7510
APRIL	7460	7470	7480	7490

1. Comparing to Initial Spot Price (–$7520)
Contango Narrowed: FP Fell Faster than SP
Spot Price went from –$7520 to + $7480 = –$40
Futures Price went from +$7550 to –$7485 = +$65
Net Selling Price: $7520 + $25 (Basis Gain)
Net Selling Price: +$7545
Net Effect: +$25 (Basis Gain)

2. Comparing to Fixed Forward Price ($7550)
Contango Narrowed: FP Fell Faster than SP
Closing Contango = –$5
Net Selling Price: $7550 –$5 (Actual Basis; Contango)
Net Selling Price: +$7545
Net Effect: –$5 (Actual Basis)

3. Comparing to Closing Spot Price ($7480)
Contango Narrowed: FP Fell Faster than SP
Net Selling Price: $7480 + $65 (Futures Gain)
Net Selling Price: +$7545
Net Effect:+$65 (Futures Gain)

In the case of a "basis rise"—contango widening—the hedging outcome would be negative, but this scenario would contradict the basic postulation of futures pricing theory, and as such should be considered exceptional, if not utterly impossible.

Price Fixing Hedge; Selling Forward, Contango Flips to Backwardation

The change in basis could prove to be even more beneficial if, during the validity of a futures contract, the shape of the futures yield curve flips from contango to backwardation.

This scenario is frequently encountered in the metals markets. The repercussions are illustrated in Table 7.6:

Table 7.6 Imperfect Hedge; Selling Forward, Contango Flips to Backwardation

FORWARD / CURRENT	CASH	1 MONTH	2 MONTHS	3 MONTHS
JANUARY (to)	7520	7530	7540	+7550 ⇨
FEBRUARY	7500	7510	7520	7530
MARCH	+7580 ⇨	⇦ −7520	7520	7550
APRIL	7550	7510	7500	7520

1. Comparing to Initial Spot Price (–$7520)
Contango Flips to Backwardation
Spot Price went from –$7520 to +$7580 = +$60
Futures Price went from +$7550 to –$7520 = +$30
Net Selling Price: $7520 + $90 (Basis Gain)
Net Selling Price: +$7610
Net Effect: +$90 (Basis Gain)

2. Comparing to Fixed Forward Price ($7550)
Contango Flips to Backwardation
Closing Backwardation = +$60
Net Selling Price: $7550 + $60 (Actual Basis; Backwardation)
Net Selling Price: +$7610
Net Effect: +$60 (Actual Basis)

3. Comparing to Closing Spot Price ($7580)
Contango Flips to Backwardation
Net Selling Price: $7580 + $30 (Futures Gain)
Net Selling Price: +$7610
Net Effect: +$30 (Futures Gain)

In some instances, as we can see in the examples elaborated in this chapter, it may be advantageous to interrupt an existing hedging strategy if the shift in the futures yield curve turns out to be rewarding. By doing that, not only does the hedger maintain the protection of his initial position, but he also generates increased returns.

Price Fixing Hedge; Selling Forward, Backwardation Market

Now let us assume that the market is in backwardation, so that the three month futures is available at lower than the spot price—$7490.

After a two-month period, the futures price has fallen slower than the spot price, causing the backwardation to narrow.

This scenario and the repercussions of lifting the selling hedge prematurely in backwardation is illustrated in Table 7.7.

Table 7.7 Imperfect Hedge; Selling Forward, Backwardation Narrowing

CURRENT \ FORWARD	CASH	1 MONTH	2 MONTHS	3 MONTHS
JANUARY (to)	7520	7510	7500	+7490
FEBRUARY	7500	7490	7480	7470
MARCH	+7480	−7470	7460	7450
APRIL	7460	7450	7440	7430

1. Comparing to Initial Spot Price (−$7520)
Backwardation Narrowed: FP Fell Slower than SP
Spot Price went from −$7520 to $7480 = −$40
Futures Price went from +$7490 to −$7470 = +$20
Net Selling Price: +$7520 − $20 (Basis Loss)
Net Selling Price: +$7500
Net effect: −$20 (Basis Loss)

2. Comparing to Fixed Forward Price ($7490)
Backwardation Narrowed: FP Fell Slower than SP
Closing Backwardation = +$10
Net Selling Price: +$7490 + $10 (Actual Basis; Backwardation)
Net Selling Price: +$7500
Net effect: +$10 (Actual Basis)

3. Comparing to Closing Spot Price ($7480)
Backwardation Narrowed: FP Fell Slower than SP
Net Selling Price: +$7480 + $20 (Futures Gain)
Net Selling Price: +$7500
Net effect: +$20 (Futures Gain)

Short hedgers benefit from basis fall and suffer from basis rise.

Markets in general are full of opportunities. The examples exhibited herewith aim to explore a broad range of market opportunities and occasions, which could be exploited to hedgers' advantage, and improve the returns relative to those initially envisaged. Aside from predetermined "perfect hedge" returns, there are evident arguments for investigating alternative outcomes associated with the imperfect hedge repercussions.

The recognition of the versatility of hedging outcomes, subject to a change in the term structure of the forward yield curve, may only add a discretionary supplement to metals price risk managements, and assist in profiling a strategy capable of utilizing favourable market opportunities.

In response to a variety of market conditions, hedgers may compare hypothetical hedging outcomes in different market scenarios and term structures of commodities, and develop the most suitable strategy, based on the trade-off between the risks being taken and expected future results. Profiling the hedge effectiveness is therefore largely dependent upon the analysis of alternative outcomes and methods which allow hedgers to monitor performance and act in real-time. Referring to the "initial spot price" we can confirm that the entire spectrum of relations between the cause (basis risk), and the effect (hedging outcome), may be synthesized in the following causality resume::

Figure 7.7 Basis Movement and Imperfect Hedging Causality Resume (LME)

Basis Position	Long Hedgers	Short Hedgers
Basis Rise	**+**	**–**
Contango Widens	+	–
Back Narrows	+	–
Back Flips to Contango	+ +	– –
Basis Fall	**–**	**+**
Back Widens	–	+
Contango Narrows	–	+
Contango Flips to Back	– –	+ +

SUMMARY

As a final summation we should emphasize what, we hope, is readily apparent from the exhibited examples:

In all instances of the so called "imperfect hedge" (where the closing futures price does not match with the price of the physical contract being hedged), the hedger is exposed to basis risk.

The hedging position—instituted originally to minimize or offset completely the risk of an adverse price movement—will turn out to be exposed and vulnerable to changes in the term structure of the yield curve.

Conditioned upon the development of the basis, an imperfect hedge will result either in windfall profits or excess losses.

In different Exchange Market environments—CBOT and LME—the basis concept is treated differently:

American Exchanges define basis as:
Spot price – Futures price = Positive basis, backwardation (+); Negative basis; contango (–);

LME defines basis as:
Futures price – Spot price = Positive basis, contango (+); Negative basis, backwardation (–)
Consequently, the divergence in prices between a futures contract and a spot price of a commodity being hedged is also subject to different terminology:

CBOT:
Basis weakening
Contango widening (turn more negative); Backwardation Narrowing (turn less positive).
Basis Strengthening
Backwardation widening (turn more positive); Contango Narrowing (turn less negative).

LME:
Basis rise
Contango widening (turn more positive); backwardation narrowing (turn less negative).
Basis fall;
Contango narrowing (turn less positive); backwardation widening (turn more negative).

Hence the change in basis within specific time periods and for certain contract maturities would generate different outcomes.

CBOT
Short hedgers benefit from basis strengthening and suffer from basis weakening;
Long hedgers benefit from basis weakening and suffer from basis strengthening.

LME
Long hedgers benefit from basis rise and suffer from basis fall;
Short hedgers benefit from basis fall and suffer from basis rise.

In all instances, however, the prudent hedger needs to apprehend the idiosyncratic basis risk and assume the overall perspective that shapes the term structure of the yield curve to be able to turn the risk into an advantage.

KEY TERMS

price convergence
basis
basis risk
basis rise
basis fall
maturity mismatch
basis strengthens
basis weakens

CHAPTER 8

COMMODITY SWAPS

CHAPTER OBJECTIVES

- To define and explain the swap arrangement
- To identify basic characteristics and features of swaps
- To introduce the principles of swap pricing
- To explain and illustrate swap arrangement mechanics
- To discuss the principal relationship between swap buyer and swap seller
- To distinguish between fixed price payers and floating price payers

SWAPS OVERVIEW

COMMODITY PRICES ARE LIKELY TO FLUCTUATE ERRATICALLY. MARKETS WITH volatile commodity prices sustain increasing uncertainty about future costs, so that managing the risks in commodity-related companies becomes more demanding.

A swap arrangement is yet another instrument designed to provide means to hedge a stream of risky payments.

The swap market is very large and, to a certain extent, has managed to evade strict governmental supervision. Swap markets have none of the regulatory provisions that the futures and options markets do and are not governed with the austerity of authorized exchange bodies. On the other hand, swaps have a measure of privacy and can be negotiated for unique quantities, qualities, and other specific contract terms.

Remember This! Swaps History Timeline

Swap arrangements entered the financial world in the late 1970s and soon gained a credibility that paved the way for a fast expansion.

- The first swap was a currency swap (cross-currency interest rate swap) involving the World Bank and IBM as counterparties. The swap was engineered by the Salomon Brothers banker Jon Rotenstreich in London 1981. It allowed the World Bank to obtain Swiss francs and Deutschmarks to finance its operations in Switzerland and West Germany without having to borrow from the Swiss and West German capital markets directly.
- The first interest rate swap entered the scene soon after in 1982 in the U.S. when Student Loan Marketing Association (Sallie Mae) contracted a "fixed-for-floating" interest rate swap.
- Commodity swaps were first engineered in 1986 when the Chase Manhattan Bank executed the first ever oil commodity swap
- Equity Swaps were introduced in 1989, by one of the largest commercial banks in the United States, Bankers Trust Co.

Due to apparent cost-reducing benefits, and a variety of risk-management applications, swaps have become unquestionably the leading force in today's international financial network. According to the Switzerland-based "Bank for International Settlements," notional amounts outstanding in June 2012 were as follows:

- Total contracts $638.289 billion
- Commodity contracts $12 billion
- Gold $523 billion
- Forwards and swaos $1,659 billion

Another independent source, Kevin McPartland of the TABB Group, publicized that the combined notional turnover for the single year (OTC and exchange traded) was around $3.7 quadrillion.

Swaps, in general, offer more flexibility as they are tailored to meet the unique requirements of producers and consumers and are not traded on large competitive markets or exchanges. They are offered off-exchange and hence considered OTC products.

SWAP DEFINITION

Essentially a **swap,** as implied by its name, is a bilateral agreement entered into by counterparties to swap (exchange) cash flows at specified maturities (once or periodically).

Key Terms

swap
a bilateral agreement entered into by counterparties to swap (exchange) cash flows at specified maturities (once or periodically)

A commodity swap is a financial product that is exercised by participants in the physical commodity markets involving a mutual exchange of commitments.

Market participants, such as producers and consumers, aim to eliminate, mitigate, or hedge the exposure to adverse price movements over an elected period of time. The principal goal of any swap arrangement is to lock-in the known price, in advance of the expected physical commodity forward purchase or sale, t.

For example, a cable wire producer who needs to purchase a fixed quantity of copper cathodes every month needs to hedge his forward purchase against rising copper prices ahead of copper wire production.

On the other side, a copper smelter (a producer of copper cathodes) that sells a regular monthly quota to its customers may wish to hedge the exposure to falling copper prices ahead of delivery—sale.

If, for whatever reason (nonstandard quality, quantity, a specific pricing period, etc.), the market participants are unable to hedge their exposure through standardized derivative instruments such as futures and option contracts, or they find these instruments unsuitable for their particular objectives, they may enter into a swap agreement with a financial institution commonly referred to as a "swap bank."

Swaps share the features of a fixed forward pricing in the commodity markets and permit the counterparties to the transaction to negotiate specific, nonstandard terms, such as: quality, quantity, the tenor, and the number of calculation periods, in a private bilateral agreement.

A single-payment swap is the same thing as a cash-settled forward contract.

A multi-payment swap may be regarded as a convenient way of packaging a strip of forward contracts; each with a different maturity date, but with the same forward price.

SWAP FEATURES

The contracting parties are called counterparties. A swap dealer, or a commodity broker, negotiates the agreement between the counterparties.

Commodity swaps are purely financial arrangements: swap settlement between the parties is effected by exchanging payments—**cash settlement amounts**—calculated with reference to the fixed price and the floating price.

Key Terms

cash settlement amount
the difference between the fixed price and the floating price in a swap transaction

There is no exchange of physical commodities.

Upon settlement, the two counterparties buy and sell the actual cash commodity through the usual market channels.

The floating price or the "commodity reference price" in a particular swap deal is based on the settlement price of an agreed futures contract for the underlying commodity on a referent futures exchange, or on the settlement price quoted in an agreed trade journal for the physical underlying.

However, in oil and metal swaps particularly it is a fairly common procedure to have the variable payment spread over a longer period in order to obtain the average price of the commodity, rather than the price of the commodity quoted on a single settlement date.

In this way firms wish to remove the risks of extreme single day settlement highs and lows associated with uncommonly high volatility.

Key Terms

swap bank
a financial institution whose main goal is to regulate and facilitate the exchange between counterparties

notional amount
the amount of the underlying commodity that is used to establish the actual cash flows

The fixed price is determined by the **swap bank.**

The "Swap Bank" is a generic term that relates to a financial institution whose main goal is to facilitate the exchange between the counterparties. Hence, the swap bank can serve either as a broker or a dealer. As a broker, the swap bank matches counterparties but does not assume any of the risks of the swap. Acting as a dealer, the swap bank assumes the risk by taking either side of a swap, and then offsets the risk, or matches it with a counterparty.

Although the commodities subject to the swap arrangement are not actually exchanged, one of the first things to be determined is the **notional amount** of the swap: for example: 7500 oz. of gold; 12,000 barrels of oil; 7750 mt. of copper cathodes, etc. The notional value (notional amount x price) is then used to calculate the cash settlement payment that will be exchanged between the two parties.

Swap transactions are executed on only one, single-calculation date, or can be split into multi-calculation dates.

Other common features are:

- Effective date; the starting date of the swap.
- Termination date; ending date.
- Fixed Maturity or Tenor; the time span between the effective date and the termination date.

Example: Commodity Swap Terms Sheet

Trade date: 1 June 2007
Transaction type: Commodity Swap
Commodity: Gold
Quantity: 250kg
Buyer (Fixed Price Payer): ABC, Hamburg, Germany
Seller (Floating Price Payer): UBS Bank
Reference Price:
NYMEX gold average July 2010 futures contract settlement price, on the Commodity Pricing Date, converted by the Calculation Agent in good faith from:
(i) tr.oz to metric tonnes at the Conversion Rate on the Commodity Pricing Date; and
(ii) USD to Euro at the Currency Reference Rate on the Currency Pricing Date
Fixed Price: $1350.00/tr.oz
Commodity Pricing Date: 1 Aug 2010
Conversion Rate:
Currency Reference Rate: Euro/USD 9.45am Hedge Settlement Rate as published by Reuters
Currency Pricing Date: 1 Aug 2008
Calculation Agent: UBS Bank
Settlement Date: 3 Aug 2010

SWAP PRICING

The calculation of a fixed swap price takes place at the origination of the swap arrangement. The provisional assumptions are as follows:

Trade date: 15 Feb 2011
Transaction type: Commodity swap
Commodity: Gold/Quantity: 1250 kg (40,188.40 tr.oz)
Commodity reference price: COMEX gold futures contract settlement price, on the Commodity Pricing Date
Commodity Pricing Date: will be every year, beginning four months from today.
Tenor of the swap will be 52 months (4 years +1/3)
The floating price will be the spot price of gold on each commodity pricing date.

COMEX Feb 15 gold futures prices are:

Months to Next Pricing Date	Gold Futures Price
t_1 (4 months) Jun 11	1486.80
t_2 (16 months) Jun 12	1495.20
t_3 (28 months) Jun 13	1522.00
t_4 (40 months) Jun 14	1570.10
t_5 (52 months) Jun 15	1632.60

Corresponding interest rates (usually the zero-coupon bond yields) with time expressed in years are:
$r_1 = 0.028$ (0.33); $r_2 = 0.030$ (1.33); $r_3 = 0.032$ (2.33); $r_4 = 0.035$ (3.33); $r_5 = 0.038$ (4.33)

Calculation unfolds as follows:

- the PV of these expected floating payments is:

PV = \$1486.80 / (1.028) 0.33 + \$1495.20 / (1.03) 1.33 + \$1522.00 / (1.032) 2.33 + \$1570.10 / (1.035) 3.33 + \$1632.60 / (1.038) 4.33
PV = \$1473.31 + \$1437.56 + \$1414.30 + \$1400.06 + \$1389.14 = \$7114.37

The present value of the agreement to sell gold at the fixed price (P fixed) is:

P fixed {1 / (1.028) 0.33 + 1 / (1.03) 1.33 + 1 / (1.032) 2.33 + 1/(1.035) 3.33 + 1 / (1.038) 4.33} = \$7114.37
P fixed {0.99093 + 0.96145 + 0.92924 + 0.89176 + 0.85087} = \$7114.37
P fixed {4.62425} = \$7114.37
P fixed = \$1538.49/oz

SWAP MECHANICS

The market convention has it that the party paying the fixed price is called the buyer and takes the "long" side of the swap. The party paying the floating price is called the seller and takes the "short" side of the swap. This division is consistent with the nature of derivatives—forwards and futures to be precise.

The seller of a commodity (holding a long physical position) naturally seeks protection against a possible price fall.

The seller of the commodity would also be the seller of a swap which is an equivalent position to a short futures hedge.

Seller of the Commodity = Seller of the Swap = Floating Price Payer

Key Terms

floating price payer
the party paying the floating price takes the short side of the swap; also swap seller

Key Terms

fixed price payer
the party paying the fixed price takes the long side of the swap; also swap buyer

The buyer of a commodity (holding a short physical position) is seeking protection against the eventual price rise.

The buyer of the commodity would also be the buyer of the swap which is an equivalent position to a long futures hedge.

Buyer of the Commodity = Buyer of the Swap = Fixed Price Payer

At inception, a swap value is set to be zero—both parties have zero value, meaning that it costs nothing to enter into the contracts.

However, changes in commodity prices over the life of the swap contract will drive its value to be either positive or negative.

In financial swaps, a noteworthy feature is that the counterparties to a swap execute cash settlement payments that are separated in time and mutually exclusive. In a commodity swap, at any one subsequent swap calculation date (aka "the commodity pricing date"), only one party pays the cash settlement amount; one party pays fixed (the Fixed Price Payer), whilst the other pays a floating price (the Floating Price Payer) subject to the relationship between fixed price and the commodity reference price—the floating price.

Exchange from the Perspective of a Swap Buyer

If on the swap settlement date the fixed price exceeds the floating price—fixed price > floating price—then the swap buyer is obliged to pay the cash settlement amount—the difference between the fixed price and the floating price.

For the sake of illustration let us put in some provisional figures.

Swap Buyer = Fixed Price Payer if Fixed price > Spot/Floating price

The swap buyer agrees to buy the gold at $1320/tr.oz. At the first calculation date the gold spot declines to $1300 so that fixed price > floating price. Just as in offsetting the futures position the swap buyer pays –$20/tr.oz to the swap counterparty (buys at $1320 sells at $1300 = –$20), and buys the gold spot at $1300. The overall net position for the gold buyer is –$20 – $1300 = –$1320. The counterparty earns $20/tr.oz. If the deal was to be set by physical delivery, the counterparty would buy the gold spot for $1300 and sell it to the swap buyer at $1320, incurring a $20/tr.oz profit. For the gold buyer the financial position would be unchanged –$1320.

If on the swap settlement date the price relationship is inverted and the fixed price is below the floating price—fixed price < floating price—then the swap counterparty must pay the cash settlement amount to the Swap buyer.

We follow up on the eventual price increase.

At the subsequent calculation date, the gold spot price increases to $1330, so that now fixed price < floating price. If the deal was to be settled by physical delivery the counterparty would have to purchase the gold at increased spot price = $1330 and sell it at $1320. Instead the counterparty would offset the deal at a loss and pay $10/tr.oz to the swap buyer. The financial position for the gold buyer would be again the same –$1320 (receive $10, buy spot –$1330 = –$1320).

Figure 8.1 is a graphic sketch of a swap transaction from the standpoint of a (buyer) consumer indicating the cash flows between the counterparties.

Counterparty A	Counterparty B
CONSUMER Fixed Payer (Floating Price Receiver)	SWAP COUNTERPARTY Floating Payer (Fixed Price Receiver)

Figure 8.1 Consumer—Seeking Protection Against Price Rise

SWAP COUNTERPARTY	Floating P. > Fixed P. →→ Receives	CONSUMER
		FIXED PAYER
SWAP COUNTERPARTY	Floating P. < Fixed P. ←← Pays	CONSUMER

Assumptions:

- The gold consumer needs to buy ten contracts of gold each month in the next 5 months.
- The swap fixed price agreed upon a trade date is $1320 tr.oz.
- The swap reference floating price of the underlying commodity will be the NYMEX gold spot settlement price on predetermined calculation dates—commodity pricing dates.

Table 8.1 Exchange from the Perspective of the Consumer (Buyer)

Time	Floating P. (Spot)	Gold Consumer	
		Receives (+)	Pays (–)
t_1	$1300		–$20,000
t_2	$1330	+$10,000	
t_3	$1260		–$60,000
t_4	$1360	+$40,000	
t_5	$1422	+$102,000	

Unhedged position: Σ floating prices x 100 tr.oz x 10 contracts =	–$ 6,672,000,00
Sum received: $152,000	+$ 152,000,00
Sum paid: Σ $80,000	–$ 80,000,00
Final purchase price: Σ –$6,600,000.00/5 = $1320	–$ 6,600,000.00

- By locking-in the fixed price of $1320, the gold producer has protected himself against the fall in gold prices. The eventual adverse price change is compensated from the swap counterparty.
- If the price of gold rises, the gold producer is unable to participate in a favourable price increase. A beneficial price change has been forfeited.

I. Time t_1: Swap (fixed price) > Spot floating price; $1320 > $1300
User "Swap Buyer" (pays the cash settlement amount –$20,000)
(Floating price – swap price) – floating price = –Swap price
$1300 – $1320 – $1300 = –$1320
Swap payment: –$20,000

Swap Buyer = Fixed Price Payer if Fixed price > Spot/Floating price

II. Time t_2: Swap (fixed price) < Spot floating price; $1320 < $1330
User "Swap Buyer" (receives the cash settlement amount +$10,000)
(Floating price – swap price) – floating price = –Swap price
$1330 – $1320 – $1330 = –$1320 (always!)
Swap payment: +$10.000

Swap Buyer = Floating Price Receiver if Spot/Floating price > Fixed price

Exchange from the Perspective of a Swap Seller

If on the swap settlement date the actual spot price exceeds the fixed price—floating price > fixed price—then the swap seller (producer), just as in any long trade, has effectively contracted a winning scenario (the selling price is higher than the purchase price). But since the parties to a swap have no possibility of profiting from a favourable price move, the swap seller is obliged to compensate the swap counterparty with a cash settlement in excess of the fixed price. The summarised cash flow streams are demonstrated in the following equation:

Swap Seller = Floating Price Payer if Floating price > Fixed price

In the case that on the swap settlement date the price relationship is inverted and the floating price is below the fixed price—floating price < fixed price—then the swap counterparty must pay the cash settlement amount to the swap seller.

Swap Seller = Floating Price Receiver if Floating price < Fixed price

In Figure 8.2 we have outlined a swap transaction between a producer, the floating price payer, and the swap counterparty, the fixed price payer, indicating the direction of the streams of cash flows between the two swap participants: counterparty A and counterparty B.

Counterparty A	Counterparty B
PRODUCER	SWAP COUNTERPARTY
Floating Payer	Fix Payer
(Fixed Price Receiver)	(Floating Price Receiver)

Figure 8.2 Producer—Seeking Protection Against Price Fall

PRODUCER	Floating P. > Fixed P. Pays →→	SWAP COUNTERPARTY
FLOATING PAYER		
PRODUCER	Floating P. < Fixed P. Receives ←←	SWAP COUNTERPARTY

Assumptions:

- A gold producer needs to sell ten contracts of gold each month in the next 5 months.
- The swap fixed price agreed upon a trade date is $1320 tr. oz
- The swap reference price—the floating price of the underlying commodity—will be the NYMEX gold spot settlement price on predetermined calculation dates (commodity pricing dates).

Table 8.2 Exchange from the Perspective of the Producer (Seller)

Time	Floating P. (Spot)	Gold Producer	
		Receives (+)	Pays (–)
t_1	$1300	+$20,000	
t_2	$1330		–$10,000
t_3	$1260	+$60,000	
t_4	$1360		–$40,000
t_5	$1422		–$102,000

Unhedged position: Σ floating prices x 100 tr.oz x 10 contracts =	+$6,672,000.00
Sum paid: Σ $152,000	–$ 152,000.00
Sum received: Σ $80,000	+$ 80,000.00
Final selling price: Σ 6,600,000/5 = $1320:	+$6,600,000.00

- Locking in a fixed price of $1320, the gold producer has protected itself against the fall in gold prices. Adverse price changes have been compensated for by the swap counterparty.
- If the gold price rises, the gold producer is unable to participate in a favourable price increase; beneficial price change is forfeited.

I. Time t_1: Spot (floating price) < Swap fixed price; 1300 < 1320
Producer "Swap Seller" (receives the cash settlement amount +20,000)
(Swap price – floating price) + floating price = + Swap price
(\$1320 – \$1300) + \$1300 = +\$1320
Swap payment: +\$20,000

II. Time t_2: Spot (floating price) > Swap fixed price; \$1330 > \$1320
Producer "Swap Seller" (pays the cash settlement amount –\$10,000)
(Swap price – floating price) + floating price = + Swap price
(\$1320 – \$1330) + \$1330 = +\$1320 (always)
Swap payment: –\$10,000

Figure 8.3 Commodity Swaps Resume

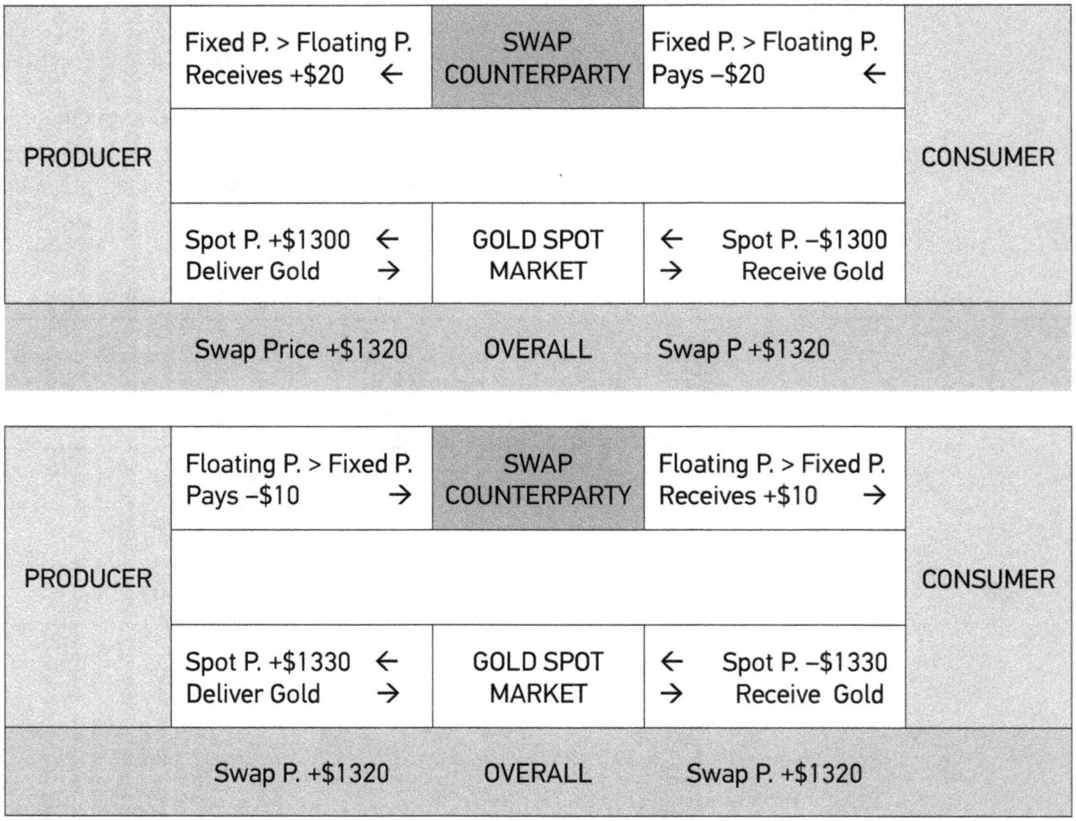
PRODUCER
Fixed P. > Floating P.
Receives +$20 ←
SWAP COUNTERPARTY
Fixed P. > Floating P.
Pays –$20 ←
CONSUMER
Spot P. +$1300 ←
Deliver Gold →
GOLD SPOT MARKET
← Spot P. –$1300
→ Receive Gold
Swap Price +$1320
OVERALL
Swap P +$1320
PRODUCER
Floating P. > Fixed P.
Pays –$10 →
SWAP COUNTERPARTY
Floating P. > Fixed P.
Receives +$10 →
CONSUMER
Spot P. +$1330 ←
Deliver Gold →
GOLD SPOT MARKET
← Spot P. –$1330
→ Receive Gold
Swap P. +$1320
OVERALL
Swap P. +$1320

We conclude the swaps elaboration where we began; Figures 8.4 and 8.5 identify the two risky position profiles, which are in fact the geometric transposition of the "Commodity Swaps Resume" depicted in Figure 8.3. P & L diagrams in Figure 8.4 represent the swap seller (gold seller) holding the long position and Figure 8.5 represents the swap buyer (gold buyer) holding the short position. Initial positions are set to zero. The final outcome is either positive or negative, based upon the correlated events—the position of the floating price (dashed line diagram) relative to the fixed price (solid line diagram).

Figure 8.4 Illustration of Swap Mechanics—Gold Buyer

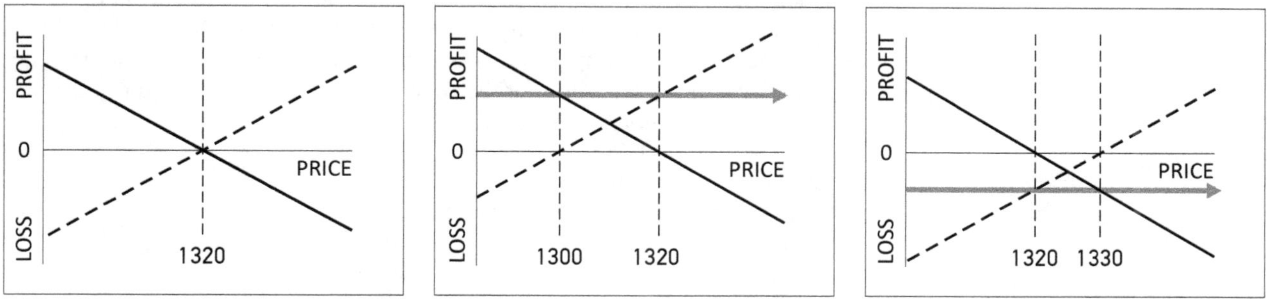

time t_0
Swap value = 0

time t_1
Swap value = +$20

time t_2
Swap value = –$10

Notations:
--- Hedge instrument = Long futures
— Unhedged position/Gold Seller's Risk profile
→ Net Inflow/Outflow

Figure 8.5 Illustration of Swap Mechanics—Gold Seller

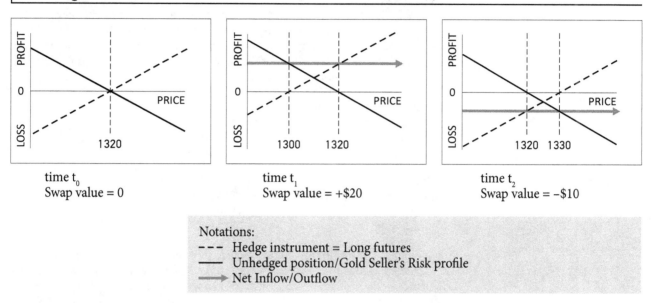

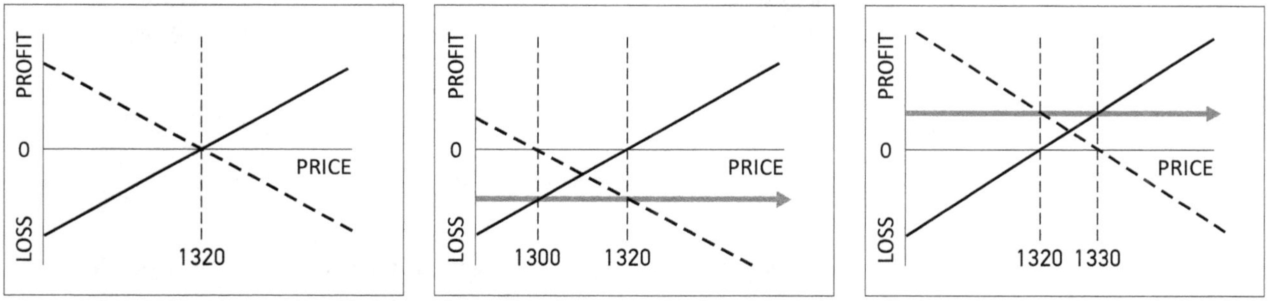

time t_0
Swap value = 0

time t_1
Swap value = –$20

time t_2
Swap value = +$10

Notations:
--- Hedge instrument = Short futures
— Unhedged position/Gold Seller's Risk profile
→ Net Inflow/Outflow

The point, in sum, is that in the swap agreement, the losers get compensated by the winners—the parties to a swap effectively "swap" their loss for another party's profit, and vice versa.

Thus, the swap has proved itself to be an effective vehicle that offers a favorable balance of risk versus profit potential for those who attempt to evade the unexpected swings in value of their price sensitive commodities.

SUMMARY

In this chapter we have introduced the basic features and characteristics of a commodity swap arrangement.

From the illustrated exchange between swap parties, we may conclude that the swap arrangement managed to secure desired prices for both parties. It seems like a zero sum game. But is it really? If you take a look at cash settlement amounts being paid and received during the course of the swap from the perspective of the gold seller (the producer) you will notice the following:

Gold buyer:

paid in total the sum of	–$80,000
Received in total	+$152,000
Net cash inflow	+$72,000

Gold seller:

paid in total the sum of	–$152,000
received in total	+$80,000
Net cash outflow	–$72,000

With the benefit of hindsight we may deduce that the swap arrangement proves to be more advantageous to one of the parties at the expense of the other party. In this particular case, the gold seller apparently would have achieved a much better price had he not entered into a swap: $1334.40 (the sum of the periodical gold prices; 6672/5) compared to effective swap price of $1320/tr.oz. The eventual gain of $14.40 has been forfeited. At the same time, from the perspective of the gold buyer, the swap turned out to be commensurately beneficial.

. In this respect one of the peculiarities of a swap transaction, as you may notice from the above, is that a party to a swap is exposed to credit risk only if the financial position is positive:

- In case of a commodity buyer, the cash outflow occurs when spot prices are falling!
- In a case of a commodity seller, the cash outflow occurs when spot prices are rising!

The risk management is a trade-off between the reliability or revelance of safe returns on the one side and prospective revenues on the other.

As should be self-evident, efforts seeking merely to eliminate the risk are paid for by sacrificing future gains. The gains credited to one party are financed by the losses debited from the other party.

"There's no such thing as a free lunch."

This concept of sacrificing the upside potential in exchange for downside protection could prove particularly useful and attractive to many investors that shy away from predicting market direction.

Advantages:

- Flexible, tailored terms and easy to use.
- No initial costs when entering into a commodity swap.
- The facility to lock-in a known price for a commodity at a future date
- Lower costs compared to futures and options.

- No initial or maintenance margins.
- Settlement at maturity.

Disadvantages:

- Credit or counterparty risk
- Costs associated with getting out before maturity (early termination)
- Forfeited profit potential originating from a favourable price movement during the term of the commodity swap: "opportunity loss" for the seller if the commodity reference price is greater than the fixed price—the seller of the swap will have to pay the cash settlement difference to the buyer; "opportunity loss" for the buyer if the commodity reference price is less than the fixed price—the buyer of the swap will have to pay the cash settlement difference to the seller
- Collateral in the form of some solid asset as land or property, may be required.

KEY TERMS

swap
opportunity loss
fixed price payer
swap seller
swap bank
cash settlement amount
swap counterparty
notional amount
floating price payer
swap buyer

PART 2

BASIC FEATURES AND STRATEGIES OF OPTIONS

CHAPTER 9

INTRODUCTION TO OPTIONS

CHAPTER OBJECTIVES

- To define and explain option contracts
- To introduce and explain key option components
- To highlight the three different ways, and the implications, of closing out an option contract

I OPTIONS BASICS

Key Terms

premium
the price established at the outset at which options are bought or sold. The price of the option contract paid by the buyer and received by the seller

bullish
market sentiment based on expectation that prices will rise

bearish
market sentiment based on expectation that prices will fall

exercise date
the last date on which the option contract can be either liquidated or exercised

WHEN WRITING ABOUT OPTIONS, MANY AUTHORS LIKE TO EMPHASIZE THE resemblance between options and insurance: buying options is like buying insurance, and selling options is similar to selling insurance. For a small portion of money called a **premium**, you are protecting your asset—a car or a house—from dire consequences; a car crash, a flood, an earthquake or a fire. It is your choice whether to claim your rights arising from the insurance policy and cover the damage. On the other hand, the insuring company is obliged to indemnify you in full, thus running the risk of much greater losses than the premium received.

The similarity stands. Option buyers pay an upfront price called a premium for the privilege of having the choice to claim their rights, at the same time limiting the downside risk to the amount of the premium paid. On the other side, option writers collect that premium in return for taking on larger losses should the option holders claim their right to exercise the option.

In this respect options could be viewed and treated like betting tickets. They have the potential to win unlimited profits for a limited risk which is known from the outset—at the cost of a premium which you think you can afford to lose. So, what are you betting against?

In general, you are betting against the market. It is the matter of your choice at which exchange and which asset class you are going to trade (stocks, stock indices, commodities, currencies, interest rates, etc.).

Once you are in the market you enter into this endless and exciting game of result forecasting. Exchange markets are very sophisticated and highly regulated places where market participants place their trades. The most basic trade is that the asset price of your choice will either rise—if you are **bullish** in your expectation—or fall—if you feel **bearish**.

In futures markets you can do this by buying futures in anticipation of a price increase, or by selling futures in anticipation of a price decline.

You can do the same with options—bet that prices will rise or fall. But when it comes to options it gets a bit more interesting. Why? Because options markets, aside from the two mentioned choices, offer two more "options"—you can also bet that the prices will not rise, and you can bet that prices will not fall. Figure 9.1 illustrates a comparison between futures' and options' available alternatives and the relevant payoff diagrams.

The illustration is designed primarily to underly the most essential distinction between futures and options—the payoff geometry at expiration, where linear and symmetric futures payoffs—signifying the unlimited profit and loss potential in both directions—are confronted with the alternative choices of linear and asymmetric risk-reward payoff diagrams of option contracts.

The four possibilities, or choices, offered by options contracts should be clearly recognized. They are as follows:

- You can bet that the market **price will rise.**
- You can bet that the market **price will fall.**
- You can bet that the market **price will not rise.**
- You can bet that the market **price will not fall.**

Options are highly standardized and legally binding contracts traded on exchange markets, allowing participants to challenge the price direction of a specific asset at some point of time in the future—**the exercise date.**

Figure 9.1 Futures and Futures Options Comparison

VARIETY OF CHOICES
Futures vs. Futures Options

I LONG	FUTURES	II SHORT
Price will go up	**CHOICE**	Price will go down
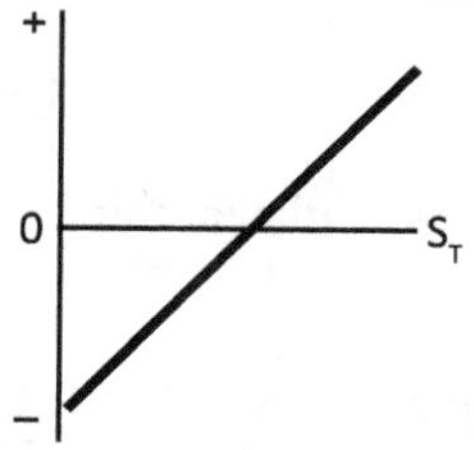	Linear and Symmetric Payoffs	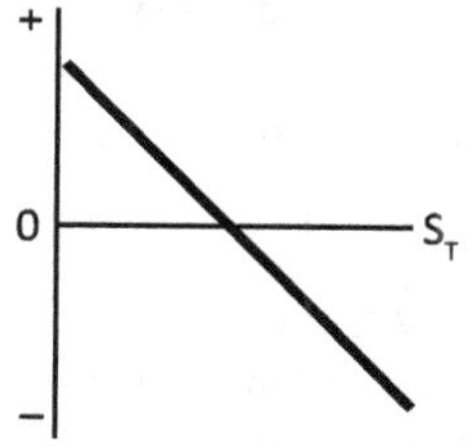

III SHORT CALL	I LONG CALL	OPTIONS ON FUTURES	II LONG PUT	IV SHORT PUT
Price will *not* go up	Price will go up	**CHOICE**	Price will go down	Price will *not* go down
OBLIGATION	RIGHT		RIGHT	OBLIGATION
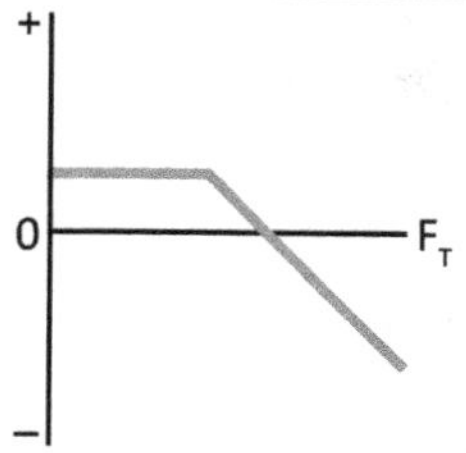	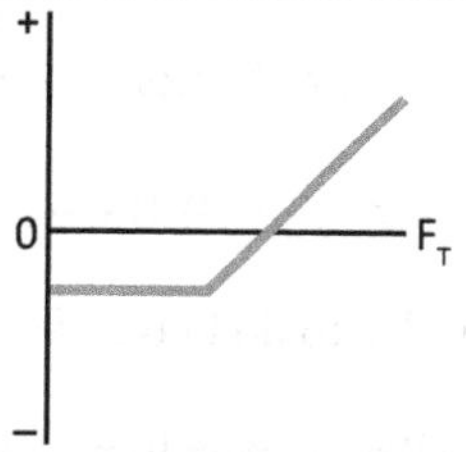	Linear and Asymmetric Payoffs	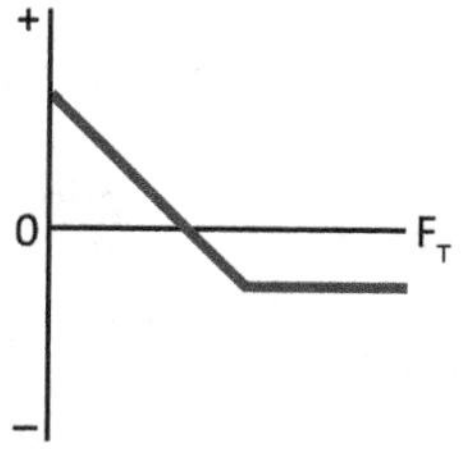	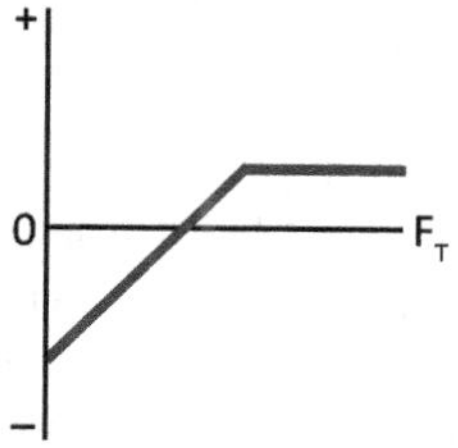
Collect Premium	Pay Premium	Initial Cash Flow	Pay Premium	Collect Premium
To sell futures at the strike price	To buy futures at the strike price	**IF EXERCISED**	To sell futures at the strike price	To buy futures at the strike price

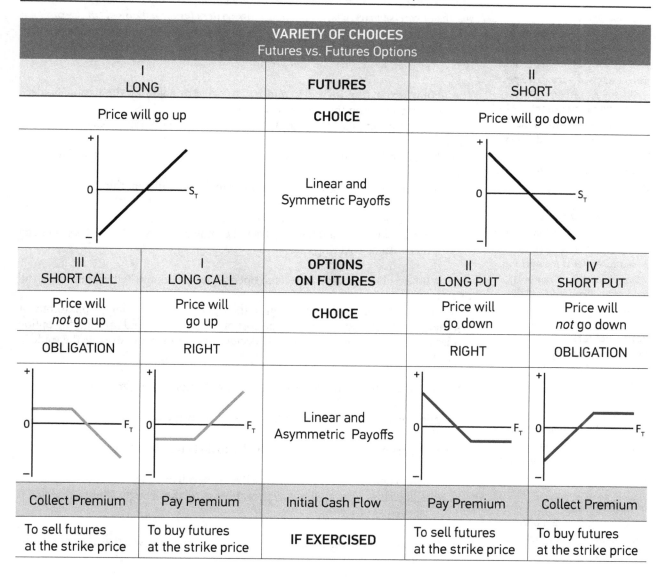

The challenge can be initiated in one of four ways:

- If you choose the first alternative, buy a call option.
- If you choose the second alternative, buy a put option.
- For the third alternative, sell a call option.
- For the fourth alternative, sell a put option.

Four alternatives, four different option contracts. They are also tradable instruments. You can buy them, and you can sell them—sell back the one you have bought in the first place, or buy back the one you have initially sold.

In light of these factors, let's define options more specifically:

Key Terms

exercise price
the price specified in the option contract at which the underlying security will be bought or sold when exercised—see strike price

underlying instrument
a specific asset on which the derivative price is based. It may be anything from commodities, securities, currencies, stocks and stock indices

option writers/grantors
those who sell an option contract (call or put) to open a short position. Writer is the norm in US markets while Grantor is used more commonly in UK markets

option holders
those who buy an option contract (call or put) to open a long position

covering
buy back the same option you have sold in the first place to close a position. Sell first and then buy back to close

offsetting
sell to close a position opened with a purchase. Buy first and then sell to close

An option is a contract which conveys the rights to its ***holders,*** *to buy (in the case of a call), or sell (in the case of a put), the* ***instrument underlying*** *the option contract at a specified* ***exercise price,*** *and obligations to its* ***writers*** *(grantors), to sell (in the case of a call) or to buy (in the case of a put), that same underlying instrument. For the privilege to execute rights without obligations option holders pay a* ***premium*** *and, for submission to oblige, option writers receive that premium.*

The option writer (the invisible counterparty) has to abide by the option holder's choice, whatever action the holder decides to take.

If the put option holder chooses to sell, the put option writer is obligated to purchase.

If the call option holder chooses to buy, the call option writer is obligated to sell.

Option buyers may purchase option contracts to do two different things:

1. Buy to open a long position; to buy either a call or a put.
2. Buy to close a position; to buy back the same option they sold (in option slang this is called **covering**).

Option holders buy option contracts to open a long position whether they buy a call or a put.

Consequently, option holders acquire the right, but not the obligation, to buy or sell the underlying instrument. For the cost of the premium paid upfront, the option holder is granted a choice to ultimately decide whether or not to execute the trade in the future.

For every option buyer (holder) there must be an option writer (grantor).

The option premium paid by the holder is received by the writer.

Option writers may sell option contracts also to do two different things:

1. Sell to open a short position; to sell either a call or a put.
2. Sell to close a position; to sell the same option they bought (this transaction is labelled as **offsetting**).

Option writers sell option contracts to open a short position whether they are selling calls or puts.

Consequently, option writers acquire obligations inherent in the terms of the contract—to deliver (when selling a call option), or to take delivery of the underlying instrument (when selling a put option).

THREE WAYS TO LIQUIDATE AN OPTION CONTRACT

Key Terms

exercise
the option holder's declaration to purchase (call) or sell (put) the asset underlying the option contract at the strike (exercise) price or to convert the option into long futures (call) or short futures (put)

American-style option
an option that can be exercised at any time prior to the expiration date

European-style option
an option that can be exercised only at the expiration date

1. Exercising
2. Covering or Offsetting
3. Abandoning

EXERCISING

Exercising is the privilege of options holders. By exercising a call option, the option holder acquires the right to purchase the underlying instrument at the exercise price. By exercising a put option, the option holder acquires the right to sell the underlying instrument at the exercise price. In this respect it is necessary to point out the distinction between two different options types:

- American-style options.
- European-style options.

Holders of **American-style** options may claim their right to exercise any time prior to the expiration date.

Exercise date # Expiration date

Holders of **European-style** options may claim their right to exercise only at a strictly predetermined date—the expiration date.

Exercise date = Expiration date

The origin and lexicology of the terms "call" and "put" seem to be derived from these two fundamental options features:

Call option—by exercising their right, a call option holder is entitled to "call" the underlying asset (stock, currency or corresponding futures contract) from the option writer. Put option—by exercising their right, a put option holder is entitled to "put" the underlying asset to the option writer.

When an option holder declares the right to exercise, the option writer receives a Notice of Assignment.

Remember This! Options assignment

Is a procedure governed by a clearing house of the relevant exchange and may take place randomly any time prior to/at the expiration date, providing that the option is in-the-money. When assigned, an option writer–the assignee—is obligated to sell the underlying asset at the exercise price—in the case of a call writing, or to buy the underlying asset—in the case of put writing. Since each option, on both sides of the process (long option interest and short option interest) has equal probability of being drawn, the procedure of matching the long option holders—who have declared their intent to exercise—and short option holders—to whom exercise will be assigned—is termed "Random Assignment" or "Random Pairing" of exercisers and assignees.

OFFSETTING

An offsetting transaction is the reversal of the original opening transaction. Both parties (option holders as well as option writers) are entitled to offset their positions at any time prior to or at expiration, and this represents the most frequent method of liquidating an options contract. But the motives are divergent.

Option holders offset their options to exit a long trade at a profit. If the opening position is a long call, then the offsetting or closing transaction would be "sell to close" that very same call (same exercise price and maturity). In the case that you initially bought a long put, then you have to "sell to close" exactly the same put (with the same exercise price and maturity). The net return will be the difference between the premium originally paid to buy the option, and the higher option premium received when you exit the trade.

Option writers buy back their short options primarily to minimize loss, or to avoid assignment. If you are "short a call" then your offsetting transaction is "buy to close" exactly the same call (same exercise price and expiration date). In the case you are "short a put" then the offsetting transaction would imply ordering your broker to "buy to close" the very same put (same exercise price and expiration date). The net return will be the difference between the premium originally received for writing the option and the premium paid to offset the option.

ABANDONING

If at expiration the option you hold has no intrinsic value it will expire worthless. The option is said to have been abandoned and the option holder loses the entire premium invested.

Conversely, the writer of that option will earn the premium invested by the option the holder.

Key Terms

abandonment
letting the option contract expire unexercised

Remember This! Early Beginnings of Options

If we disregard the historical traces of option trading described in the Code of Hammurabi and Aristotle's "Politics" and skip to modern times, we might rightfully ascertain that Chicago is entitled to claim itself as the home of yet another derivative instrument. On April 26, 1973, the Chicago Board Options Exchange (CBOE) was the first Exchange to begin trading equity call options contracts. The first 16 stocks originally listed belonged to the following companies:

AT&T, Atlantic Richfield; Brunswick, Eastman Kodak; Ford; Gulf & Western; Loews; McDonald; Merck; Northwest Airlines; Pennzoil; Polaroid; Sperry Rand; Texas Instruments; Upjohn and Xerox.

The volume on the first opening day was 911 call option contracts.

Put trading was introduced in 1977 and in October 1982 the Chicago Board of Trade introduced the first options on futures contracts—options on US Treasury Bond futures.

Standardization of the option contract, in tandem with security of performance and trade execution, as well as the practical ability to open and close the options trade at any time during the exchange open hours, contributed enormously to the success of options markets not only in US but abroad as well.

This achievement was largely to the the credit of one of the exchange's managers—Joseph W. Sullivan who proposed and implemented options standardization with respect to the exercise price, expiration date, size, and other relevant contract terms. He also recommended the creation of an intermediary—the Option Clearing Corporation—as a guarantor responsible for all options trades.

Other exchanges were soon to follow: the American Stock Exchange (AMEX) and the Philadelphia Stock Exchange (PHLX) began trading listed options in 1975. The Toronto Stock Exchange (TSE) listed stock options in 1976, followed, in 1978, by the London Traded Option Market (LTOM) and the London International Financial Futures Exchange (LIFFE) in 1982. The latter two merged together in 1992 to create the London International Financial Futures and Options Exchange (LIFFO) the biggest futures and options exchange in Europe.

Today, option contracts are traded on all major exchanges around the globe, enormously helping market participants to manage and transfer price risk. To get an idea of how immensely the market has evolved since let's look at the numbers: daily traded contract on CBOE alone, were in 2009, around 1,900.000; the dollar volume reached $610 billion.

DISAMBIGUATION

The diversity in terminology used in the Options Industry calls for an additional note of clarification:

Option buyer	is synonymous with: **Holder; Owner; Taker** (all indicating long option positions)
Option seller	is synonymous with: **Writer; Giver; Grantor** (all indicating short option positions)
Exercise price	(E or X) is synonymous with Strike price (K)

SUMMARY

This Chapter has focused on the basic characteristics of an option. We have defined options as contracts that convey rights to their holders and obligations to their writers. We have outlined the basic option types: the long call, the long put, the short call and the short put—as well as the differences in the corresponding risk profiles. A long call option conveys the right to buy an asset at a specified strike price. A long put option conveys the right to sell an asset at a specified strike price. A short call option writer has the obligation to sell an asset at a strike price, and a short put option writer has the obligation to buy an asset at a strike price.

We highlighted the distinction between American options (allow exercise at any date during the life of the option) and European options (allow exercise only on the expiration date).

Following from this, we emphasized the differences in option payoffs and those of futures contracts. We showed that option payoffs are nonlinear and asymmetric while futures payoffs are linear and symmetric. We have seen that options are far more flexible and offer more alternatives than futures contracts. Finally, the three basic ways of liquidating an options contract were discussed; Exercising, Offsetting or Covering and Abandoning, outlining the specifics of each alternative.

KEY TERMS

premium
bullish
bearish
exercise date
exercise price
underlying instrument
option writers/grantors
option holders
covering
offsetting
exercise
American style options
European style options
abandonment

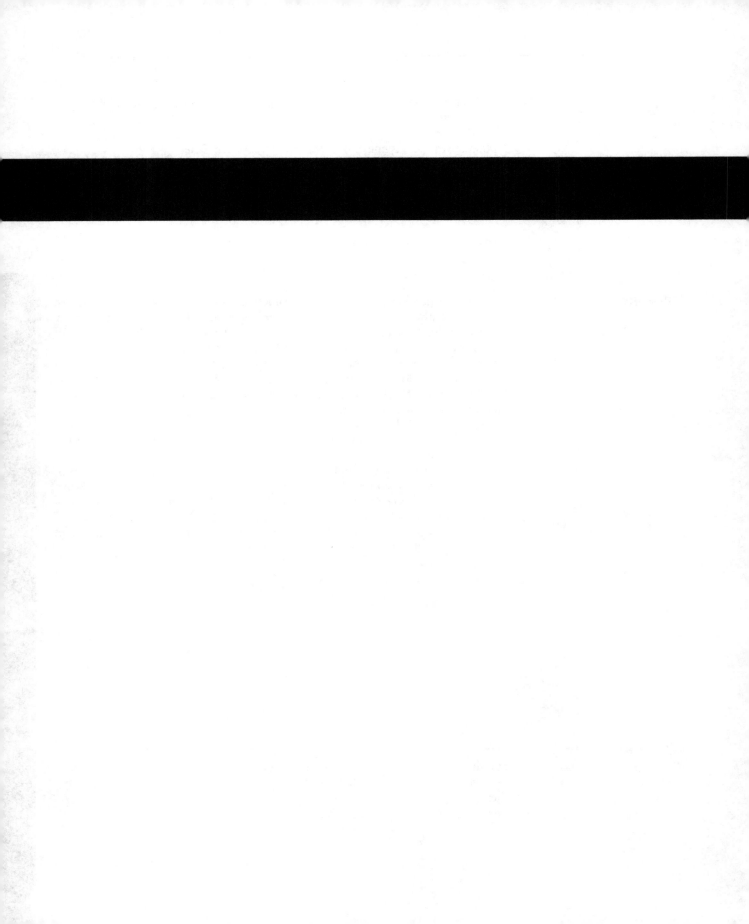

CHAPTER 10

BASIC DIRECTIONAL STRATEGIES USING OPTIONS

CHAPTER OBJECTIVES

- To identify and describe basic option types
- To highlight the specifics of option payoff diagrams
- To emphasize the potential benefits and drawbacks of alternative options strategies
- To synthesize the complexity of options features in a one-page lesson, "Diamond Graph."

I INTRODUCTION

THE BASICS OF OPTIONS DIRECTIONAL TRADING, FOR SIMPLICITY REASONS, WILL BE illustrated through stock options examples. Specifically, we shall use the data for 3M Co. NYSE (MMM), November 2011 Options Chain as of 4 October 2011.

Equity options always expire on the third Saturday of the relevant month, though the last trading day will be the Friday preceding the third Saturday. Prior to options expiration, option holders are entitled to exercise their rights to buy or sell the underlying stock at the exercise price. Options sellers take the opposite side, inheriting only obligations to execute the contractual commitment to sell 100 shares of the underlying stock in the case of a call, or to buy 100 shares of the underlying stock in the case of a put.

3M Co.(MMM)   November 2011 Options Chain as of 4 October 2011.

CALLS — Expire at close Friday* November 18, 2011

Strike	Symbol	Last	Chg	Bid	Ask	Vol	Int
60.00	MMM111119C00060000	n.a.	n.a.	11.35	12.70	n.a.	n.a.
65.00	MMM111119C00065000	8.12	-2.08	7.05	7.20	5	146
67.50	MMM111119C00067500	6.30	+0.60	5.15	5.30	42	116
70.00	MMM111119C00070000	3.91	-0.14	3.55	3.65	47	497
71.01	**Stock Price Last as of 10.04/2011 04:02:02 PM**						
72.50	MMM111119C00072500	2.40	-0.36	2.25	2.30	325	790
75.00	MMM111119C00075000	1.43	-0.15	1.30	1.34	503	1,291
77.50	MMM111119C00077500	0.78	-0.07	0.68	0.71	327	1,588
80.00	MMM111119C00080000	0.40	-0.01	0.32	0.35	116	2,492
82.50	MMM111119C00082500	0.19	-0.01	0.14	0.17	82	3,032
85.00	MMM111119C00085000	0.07	-0.01	0.06	0.10	72	4,845
87.50	MMM111119C00087500	0.06	+0.02	0.01	0.06	13	1,807
90.00	MMM111119C00090000	0.04	-0.01	0.01	0.04	10	2,968
95.00	MMM111119C00095000	n.a.	n.a.	11.35	12.70	n.a.	n.a.

PUTS — Expire at close Friday* November 18, 2011

Strike	Symbol	Last	Chg	Bid	Ask	Vol	Int
60.00	MMM111119P00060000	0.44	+0.19	0.44	0.48	73	586
65.00	MMM111119P00065000	1.12	+0.17	1.12	1.16	195	3,477
67.50	MMM111119P00067500	1.61	-0.03	1.73	1.77	87	397
70.00	MMM111119P00070000	2.23	+0.06	2.59	2.65	441	2,547
71.01	**Stock Price Last as of 10.04/2011 04:02:02 PM**						
72.50	MMM111119P00072500	3.45	+0.10	3.75	3.85	158	2,222
75.00	MMM111119P00075000	5.11	+0.71	5.30	5.45	30	4,437
77.50	MMM111119P00077500	6.71	+0.16	7.20	7.30	14	2,233
80.00	MMM111119P00080000	8.90	+1.71	8.80	9.45	106	4,399
82.50	MMM111119P00082500	10.70	+1.20	11.60	11.75	20	1,287
85.00	MMM111119P00085000	12.35	+0.50	14.05	14.20	2	3,033
87.50	MMM111119P00087500	15.85	+1.50	16.50	16.65	9	1,091
90.00	MMM111119P00090000	17.00	-0.30	18.95	19.15	15	2,673
92.50	MMM111119P00092500	17.65	-0.50	19.80	21.65	1	1,509
95.00	MMM111119P00095000	20.79	-0.78	22.30	24.15	145	783

*Stock Options expire always on the third Saturday (which is November 19 in our case) but the last day options can be traded is the Friday before the third Saturday of the relative month.

Before we begin to elaborate each individual case let us pay attention to the options terminology used in the above table:

Strike Stands, of course, for the option strike price (also exercise price) which is the price at which the owner of an option can purchase (in the case of a call) or sell (in the case of a put) the underlying stock of shares, security or commodity

Symbol A new format option symbol has replaced the previous configuration of the OPRA codes and fractional strike price values. Changes in options symbology, introduced by the OCC (Options Clearing Corporation), took place between January and May 2010.

Symbology key for 3M Co. Option strike $77.50

MMM111119C00077500

Root symbol **MMM** (may be extended to max. 6 bytes) + Expiration Year **11** (2 bytes) + Expiration Month **11** (2 bytes) + Expiration Day **19**
(2 bytes) + Call/Put Indicator (C or P) + Strike price Dollar **00077** (5 bytes) Strike price fraction **500** (3 bytes)

Altogether 18 characters (bytes), maximum 21!

Last Refers to the "last trade"—the most recent price at which a specific security was traded.

Change Refers to the dollar change and percentage change of the last buy or sell.

Bid Refers to the current dollar amount a buyer is willing to pay for a share of stock.

Ask Refers to the current dollar amount a seller is willing to accept for a share of stock.

Volume Indicates the total number of contracts that have been traded on a given exchange market on a single trading day.

Open Interest Represents the total number of outstanding contracts that are held by market participants at the end of each day or the total number of transactions that have been opened on a given day. Open interest goes up or down based on the number of new traders entering and old traders leaving the market. To explain this let us look at the open interest figure from our example — 2.492 for $80 Call Strike. If the next day this figure rises to 2.540, for example, it would mean that 48 new contracts have been created, i.e., 48 new buyers and 48 new sellers have entered the market. For each seller of an option contract there must be a buyer of that contract so that total number of longs equals the total number of shorts. Thus a seller and a buyer come together to create only one contract. Open interest and volume charts are good indicators of the flow of money into the futures market and are among the favourites used by technicians to determine market trend.

BUYING CALL—LONG CALL

Key Terms

long call
an option contract that gives its holder the right but not the obligation to buy a specific asset at a set price called the strike price on or before the fixed date in the future – the expiration date

in-the-money
for a call option a position when the current spot price of the underlying is above the call exercise price. The converse applies for a put option – the strike price needs to be higher than the spot price

As we said earlier, if you are opting for the first choice—betting that the market price will rise significantly—then you will be buying a call option. Buying a call option gives you the right but not the obligation to buy a specific amount of shares or stock at the price which is set at the opening of the transaction, and which is called, as we have already learned—the exercise price. The privilege to have that choice will cost you money, which is in the options world called a premium. A call option buyer pays a premium to acquire the right to purchase the stock at the exercise price.

So every option deal has two transactions; it begins with the opening transaction, in this case a purchase of the call option, and it ends in any of the following three ways: offsetting, exercise or abandonment.

For the long call option example we shall take the following data:

Long call exercise price: $67.50
Premium: $6.30

This particular 3M Co. call option, as you may observe from the 3M Options Chain, is initially in-the-money, as its exercise price ($67.50) is below the current 3M stock price ($70.01).

The most compelling reason for purchasing a call option would be to capture anticipated upward price movement while containing the risk if the market drifts in the opposite direction. With long options trading, calls as well as puts, you can adjust the amount of risk you feel comfortable with by choosing the strike price and corresponding premium levels. This is clearly visible from the 3M Options Chain table.

Now, in light of this essential introduction, we shall proceed with different market scenarios and discuss the profit and loss potential of each. In the first place, let's suppose that your market predictions were correct and the price before expiration did rise: the 3M stock market price went above the option's strike.

SCENARIO I: PRICE RISE; IN-THE-MONEY

Offsetting Once the underlying stock price rises above the strike price, a call option gets **in-the-money.** The long call option now yields a payoff that rises one-for-one with the price of underlying stock.

Since the call option has gained in value, the option holder can now make an exit with an offsetting transaction—sell the option back to the market. You can execute an offsetting trade any time prior to the expiration date. As the offsetting sale is executed at a higher option price the option holder is left with extra money on his account—the net profit will equal the difference between the premium initially paid and the appreciated value of the premium received when the option is liquidated.

Example: Offsetting Long Call Option

A trade is initiated with a long call $67.50 MMM111119C00067500 at $6.30. We suppose also that 3M price increased to $75 and the current option premium increased to $9.10. By offsetting the long call option (selling it back to the market) your net return on the position will equal the difference between the premium paid (–$6.30) and the premium received (+$9.10), which is $2.80 x 100 shares = $280.
This provisional calculation does not include transaction costs and commission charges.

Key Terms

out-of-the-money
for a call option when the current spot price of the underlying is below the strike price, for a put option if the spot price of the underlying is higher than the strike price

Exercising If a call option gets in-the-money—the current market price rises above the option's strike price—then an option holder has a second choice, to declare his right to exercise.

Holding a call stock option gives you the right to purchase 100 shares of stock at the strike price ($67.50) and resell it immediately at a higher market price (suppose $75.00). Your profits will equal the price difference ($75.00 – $67.50) less the premium paid ($6.30), which is $1.20 x 100 = $120. The gain is commensurate with the increase of the underlying stock market price. Theoretically, these gains are unlimited in the sense that there is no upper limit to the price rise.

Net Profit if Exercised: (Current UI Price – Exercise Price) – Premium Paid

SCENARIO II: PRICE FALL; OUT-OF-THE-MONEY

Abandonment But if the "market made a mistake" and the stock prices did fall instead of rise, well it's no big deal: you would abandon the option and lose that fixed portion of money called the premium. Your option would expire worthless as it ended **out-of-the-money.** For a call option this is a situation in which the market price of the underlying is below the exercise price. In any case, the loss is limited to the premium paid ($630).

Figure 10.1 illustrates long call profit/loss performance.

Notations:
Call options: _______
Put options: _ _ _ _ _
Exercise (Strike) price point ○
Break-even point ●
Shaded area: In-the-money zone (ITM)
Blank area: Out-of-the-money zone (OTM)

Figure 10.1 Long Call Profit & Loss Diagram

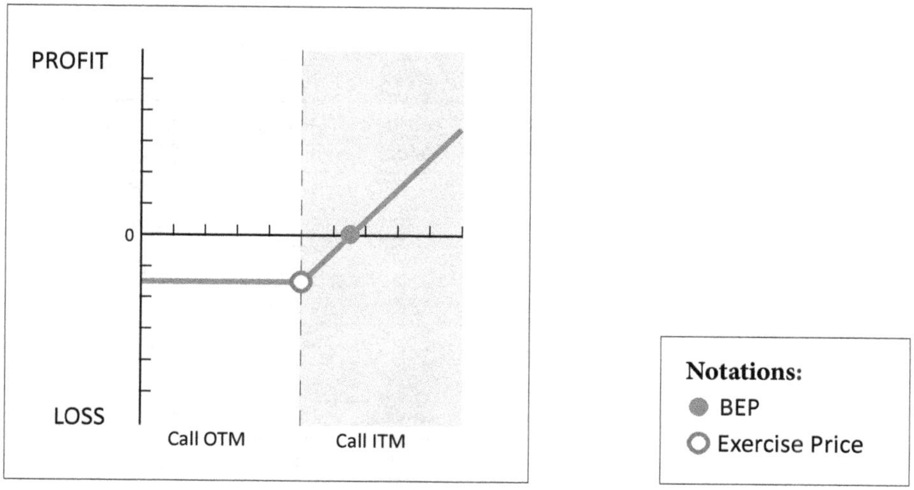

Key Terms

break-even point
a point at which an option neither loses nor gains money

BEP and the profit potential are on the upside.

Maximum Loss: Limited to Premium Paid

Referring to Figure 10.1, you will notice that the long call option payout profile is asymmetric and always twists at the exercise price point. The difference between the x-axis and the flat part of the option's strategy diagram outlines the premium value. From the strike price point—or the twist point—the part of the diagram slanting upwards at a 45 degree angle reflects the one-to-one gain relationship between the option value and the price of the underlying instrument at maturity. That twist, being at-the-money, also marks the point at which strategy shifts from the out-of-the-money zone to the in-the-money zone.

If you take a good look you will see it all clearly: the in-the-money zone, the out-of-the-money zone, and of course, the at-the-money point which we have when the strike price is at the same level as the underlying stock price. The maximum risk is limited to the premium paid and the potential profits are theoretically unlimited. You can also determine very easily the **break-even point** (BEP). This is the point at which an option neither loses nor gains money. In the case of a long call, the BEP is on the upside, and can be simply calculated like this:

BEP = Exercise Price + Premium Paid

To yield a profit, the price of the underlying stock would have to go a bit above the BEP of the long call before expiration. Although, as may easily be observed from the graph, any price increase above the strike price will be beneficial to the option holder as the cost of the premium paid will start to recover until it reaches the BEP—the point at which the strategy net payout is equal to zero. From that point onwards, theoretically, there is no limit to potential profits.

Maximum Profit: Unlimited

Table 10.1 Long Call Profit & Loss Metrics

Long Call Strike Price $67.50 BEP = $67.50 + $6.30 = $73.80			
Stock Price $	Intrinsic Value	Premium Paid	Net P&L
60.00	0	−6.30	**−6.30**
65.00	0	−6.30	**−6.30**
67.50	0	−6.30	**−6.30**
70.00	2.50	−6.30	**−3.80**
73.80	6.30	−6.30	**0**
75.00	7.5	−6.30	**1.20**
77.50	10	−6.30	**3.70**
80.00	12.50	−6.30	**6.20**

Long Call Strike Price (X) $67.50 Resume	
Break-Even Point	Strike Price + Premium Paid
Potential Profit	Variable = UI – BEP when Price of UI is Above BEP
Potential Loss	Limited = Premium Paid if UI is Below X
Time Decay Impact	Negative

BUYING PUT—LONG PUT

Key Terms

long put
an option contract giving its holder the right but not the obligation to sell a specific asset at a set price called the strike price on or before a fixed date in the future – the expiration date

If you opt for the second alternative—price decline—you will buy a put option—a **long put.** The put option gives you the right to sell the underlying instrument at a price which is also set at the opening of the transaction—the exercise or strike price. Therefore, the most basic incentive for purchasing a put option would be to capture anticipated price decline while containing the risk if the price of 3M stock goes in the opposite direction. We shall pay close attention to the two alternative scenarios.

For the long put option example we shall take the following data:

Long put exercise price: $72.50
Premium: $3.45

The 3M Co. Long Put option, as you may observe from the 3M Options Chain, is also initially in-the-money, as its exercise price ($72.50) is above the current 3M stock price ($70.01).

SCENARIO I: PRICE FALL; IN-THE-MONEY

Offsetting Suppose that the expectations of a put option holder come to fruition and the stock price falls. The stock price decline will drive the put option into the in-the-money zone. For a put option that is in-the-money, this implies that the current market price of the UI is below the exercise price. A long put option now yields a payoff that rises one-for-one with the price fall of the underlying stock.

Now your offsetting transaction (sell to close) will be executed at a price higher than the initial price at which the option was purchased, earning a profit. An offsetting transaction can be executed any time prior to expiration. Net profit would equal the difference between the premium initially paid and the appreciated value of the premium received when the option was liquidated.

Example: Offsetting Long Put Option

You initiated a trade with November long put $72.50 MMM111119P00072500 at $3.45. We suppose that before expiration the 3M price declines to $67.50 and that the actual option premium supposedly increases to $5.10.
By offsetting the long put option (sell back to close) your net return on the position will equal the difference between the premium you paid (–$3.45) and the premium you received (+$5.10), which is $1.65 x 100 shares = $165.
This provisional calculation excludes transaction costs and commission charges.

Exercising With an in-the-money put, the option holder may choose another alternative—to declare his right to exercise. Upon exercise the put option holder acquires the right to sell the stock at the strike price. So, he buys the stock at the current market price and sells it at the strike price, which is now higher than the stock market price, thus earning a profit. The option writer is left with the obligation to purchase the stock from the option holder at the exercise price. In the case of cash settled options the holder would receive the cash settlement amount and the option writer would have to pay for it.

Net Profit if Exercised: (Exercise Price – Current UI Price) – Premium Paid

For a long put option the price of the underlying asset would have to drop down, below the BEP, in order to earn money. However, the put holder will benefit from any price decrease below the exercise price as the cost of the premium paid will start to recover until it reaches the BEP—the point at which the strategy net payoff is equal to zero. If the stock price falls past that point, the strategy will begin to earn money. Ultimate profits are limited only by the fact that, in the real world, the price of an asset cannot decline below zero.

Example: Exercising Long Put Option

We assume that you initiated a trade with a November $72.50 put; MMM111119P00072500 at $3.45. We suppose also that 3M price decreased to $67.50.
By exercising the put option your net return on the position is equal to the difference between the strike price ($72.50) and the current market price for the 3M stock ($67.50), less the premium paid ($3.45), which is :
($72.50 –$67.50) – $3.45 = $1.55 x 100 = $155 on the position.
This provisional calculation excludes transaction costs and commission charges.

SCENARIO II: PRICE RISE; OUT-OF-THE-MONEY

Abandonment Should your expectations fail and the stock price during the life of the option does not fall but goes up, your option goes out-of-the-money—the current stock market price is higher than the strike price—and your option expires worthless. You will lose the entire sum paid for the premium. But again, the premium paid is the maximum you can lose.

Maximum Loss = Limited to Premium Paid

Each option has its expiration date. That means the life of an option is not indefinite; its value diminishes as the expiration date nears. For this reason, options are coined with the term "wasting assets," denoting that options have limited life and lose value over time. When you are long an option, time value works against you. With the passage of each day, a portion of the option's time value is lost. At the expiration date, an out-of-the-money option will lose all 100% of its time value and end up with no value at all. Time value is a clear disadvantage to option holders. Therefore, it is worth pointing out that, in order to make a profit, you do not have to be right only in the direction of the price but, also, you need to be right about when the anticipated change will occur. The anticipated change in price direction must take place before an option's expiration date. Otherwise you will lose all of your initial investment.

The fact is that, holding an option, you can never lose more than your initial investment—the value of the premium paid. The risk of loss in long option trading is limited and predictable; nevertheless, you may easily finish by losing the entire 100% of whatever your initial investment was. No loss should ever be justified just on the grounds that it was limited.

Figure 10.2 Long Put Profit & Loss Diagram

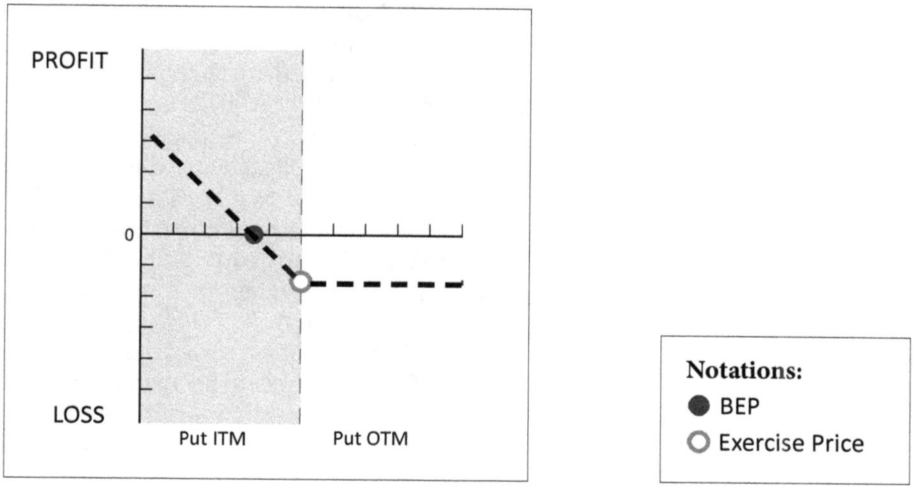

BEP and the profit potential are on the down-side.

Maximum Profit = Unlimited

The break-even point for a put option is:

BEP = Exercise Price – Premium Paid

Here again, our seemingly logical conclusion shall be supported with figures, as in the previous example:

Table 10.2 Long Put Profit & Loss Metrics

Long Put Strike Price $72.50 BEP = $72.50 – $3.45 = $69.05			
Stock Price $	Intrinsic Value	Premium Paid	Net P&L
60.00	12.50	–3.45	**9.05**
65.00	7.50	–3.45	**4.05**
67.50	5	–3.45	**1.55**
69.05	3.45	–3.45	**0**
72.50	0	–3.45	**–3.45**
77.50	0	–3.45	**–3.45**
80.00	0	–3.45	**–3.45**
82.50	0	–3.45	**–3.45**

Long Put Strike Price (X) $72.50 Resume	
Break-Even Point	Strike Price – Premium Paid
Potential Profit	Variable = BEP – UI when Price of UI is Below BEP
Potential Loss	Limited = Premium Paid if UI is Above X
Time Decay Impact	Negative

SELLING CALLS—NAKED CALL WRITING

Key Terms

short call
an option contract that conveys obligation to its writer to sell the specific asset at a set price called the exercise price on or before the fixed date in the future – the expiration date

naked call
an instance when a call option writer does not possess the underlying instrument on which the call is written. Also 'uncovered call'

An option holder enters the trade in anticipation of a favourable price move which will drive his option in-the-money. Quite to the contrary, an option writer enters the trade anticipating that such a price change will not occur.

By selling a call, a **short call,** the option writer grants the right to the option buyer to purchase the underlying instrument at the strike price. The writer receives the premium and acquires an obligation to sell/deliver the underlying instrument if assigned.

Selling calls is neutral to a bearish strategy. Call writers expect that the price at expiration will remain flat or decline below the strike price and they will retain the premium received. Compared to futures trading, this is one of options' remarkable advantages. In options trading you can make money even if the price of the underlying asset does not move at all. If stock prices remain unchanged during the life of the option, the call writer will realize a profit equal to the premium received.

On the other hand, in case the market prices drift in the opposite direction, the potential losses are unlimited. In writing uncovered calls especially, it is of crucial importance to remember that your strategic view of the market is based on the premise that the price will not rise.

Call writers may expect to receive the notice of assignment any time during the life of the option, i.e., till the very last trading day. If the call writer is assigned an exercise he will have to sell or deliver the underlying shares of stock to the option buyer. In the case of **naked call** writing—the situation when the call writer does not possess the underlying instrument on which the call is written—the sequence of transactions could unfold as follows:

For the short call option example we shall take the following data:

Short call exercise price: $67.50
Premium: $6.30

SCENARIO I: PRICE RISE; IN-THE-MONEY

Assignment With the stock price increase the call option enters the in-the-money zone—the stock price exceeds the strike price and the call option holder is entitled to exercise the option at a profit. Accordingly, the call option writer is obliged to deliver the underlying shares of stock at the strike price.

Example: Short Call Assignment

The option writer receives a premium of $630 for writing a call option of $67.50. The price of 3M Co. shares jumps to $90, the call option gets in-the-money. As the writer has written a naked call it means his portfolio consists only of the short call option. To satisfy his obligation on the call he will have to purchase 100 shares of stock at current market price of $90 and simultaneously deliver shares of stock at the strike price of $67.50.

His net position is –$16.20 per share resulting from –($90 – $67.50) + $6.30 = –$22.50 + $6.30 = –$16.20 x 100 = –$1620.

All of the premium is wiped out and on top of that you "earn" a negative return of 157.14 percent (630 – 1620/630 = 1.5714). Now you can see why writing uncovered calls is considered to be a very risky investment and a very hazardous attempt to make a profit.

Net Loss if Assigned: –(Current UI Price – Exercise Price) + Premium Received

Single stock options imply physical delivery at the time of exercise whereas most index options are cash settled, meaning that in-the-money holders receive the excess cash settlement amount upon exercise.

Remember This! Options Margin

Referring to equity options trading it is worth emphasizing that whenever you are writing short options, whether calls or puts, you will be obliged to make a margin deposit in an options broker account as collateral to ensure the ability to execute obligations imposed by options contracts sold. As a general rule, the margin level for writing naked calls is 20 percent of the stock price less the call option premium.
Margin requirements are reviewed on a daily basis, very much as in futures trading, implying that a naked call writer may expect to receive a margin call for an additional deposit in order to maintain the position.
By writing a call option you undertake an obligation to sell the underlying stock to the holder of the long side. If assigned an exercise you are obligated to buy the underlying stock from the market at a higher price so the margin deposit serves as an assurance that you will be able to fulfil your obligation.
In case you write a put option, you undertake an obligation to buy the underlying stock from the put option holder so the margin deposit serves the same cause.
In both instances the entire risk of loss may be even higher than the margin deposit.

SCENARIO II: PRICE FALL; OUT-OF-THE-MONEY

Abandonment For a short call writer, the price of the underlying shares of stock would have to stay out-of-the-money (at or below the strike price) in order for the strategy to prove beneficial. If that is the case, the option will expire worthless and the option writer will be entitled to retain the premium.

Maximum Profit: Limited to Premium Received

Figure 10.3 Short Call Profit & Loss Diagram

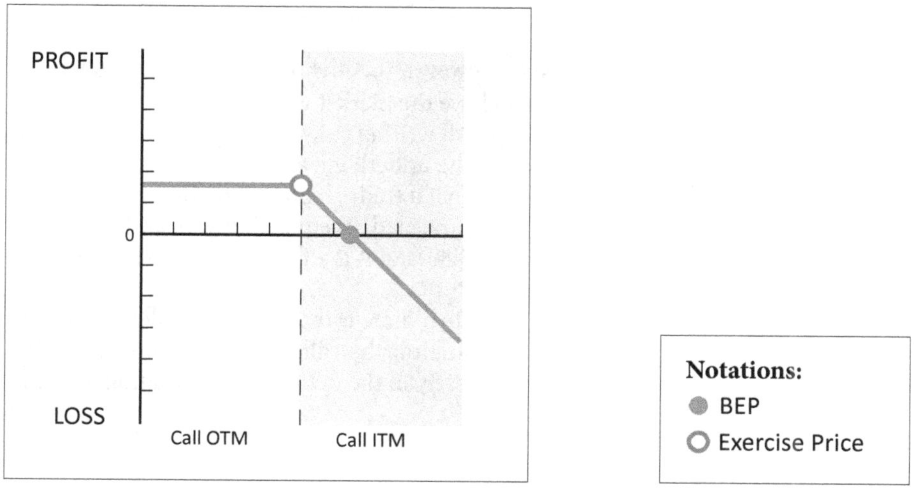

BEP and the loss potential are on the upside.

Maximum Loss = Unlimited

The break-even point for the short call option is:

BEP = Exercise Price + Premium Received

And again, as in the case of a long call, the BEP of the short call is on the upside denoting that any price increase above the strike price would have a negative effect on the option premium. From the strike price onwards, the value of the premium starts to erode until it reaches the BEP—the point at which the strategy net payoff will be equal to zero. If the price continues to rise so will your losses too.

Table 10.3 illustrates short call strategy performance.

Table 10.3 Short Call Profit & Loss Metrics

Short Call Exercise Price $67.50 BEP = $67.50 + $6.30 = $73.80			
Stock Price $	Intrinsic Value	Premium Received	Net P&L
60.00	0	6.30	**6.30**
65.00	0	6.30	**6.30**
67.50	0	6.30	**6.30**
70.00	−2.50	6.30	**3.80**
73.80	−6.30	6.30	**0**
75.00	−7.5	6.30	**−1.20**
77.50	−10	6.30	**−3.70**
80.00	−12.50	6.30	**−6.20**

Short Call Exercise Price (X) $67.50 Resume	
Break-Even Point	Exercise Price + Premium Received
Potential Profit	Limited = Premium If Price of UI is Below BEP
Maximum Loss	Unlimited = UI − BEP, if UI is Above BEP
Time Decay	Positive

Note, however, that the main idea in option writing is based upon the price direction you believe the market will not take.

The call writing risk-reward profile may be devised in the following manner: if the price of the underlying asset falls or if it stays flat (makes no move) the short position wins: even if it trades higher than the strike price but not through the break-even point you are protected. The position will start to erode only if the price passes beyond the BEP ($73.80). So it is a three-against-one scenario that the short option will be a winning venture.

And then there is the time value effect, which works in favour of the option writer. If at expiration the call option remains out-of-the-money, the entire premium will remain safely in the option writer's trading account.

SELLING PUTS—NAKED PUT WRITING

Key Terms

short put
an option contract that conveys an obligation to its writer to buy specific asset at a set price called the exercise price on or before the fixed date in the future-the expiration date

naked put
an instance when a put option writer does not have a shortposition in the underlying instrument on which the put is written. Also 'uncovered put'

Put writing bears no less risk than call writing—only that the direction of an anticipated price change is inverted. The put writer expects that the price of the underlying will stay where it is or move higher (above the strike price), thus rendering the put worthless. Therefore put writing, the **short put,** is a neutral-to-bullish strategy. If the market reacts in line with the put writer predictions, the option will expire worthless—without assignment—and the profit will be restricted to the amount of the premium received.

For the short put option example we shall take the following data:
Short put exercise price: $72.50
Premium: $3.45

SCENARIO I: PRICE FALL; IN-THE-MONEY

Assignment If the value of the underlying stock declines below the strike price, the put option is said to be in-the-money and is likely to be exercised. If assigned, the put writer will have to buy the shares at a strike price that is substantially higher than its current market value. The loss will reflect the difference between the strike price and the current market price and is restricted only in the sense that price decline cannot go beyond zero.

Net Loss if Assigned: –(Exercise Price – Current UI) + Premium Received

Example: Short Put Assignment

The option writer receives a premium of $345 for writing a put option at $72.50. The price of 3M Co. shares falls to $60, the put options gets "in-the-money" and the writer is assigned an exercise. Writing a naked put means that the investor's portfolio consists only of the short put option. To satisfy the obligation on the put the investor will have to purchase 100 shares of stock at the strike price of $72.50 and simultaneously sell it back to the market at $60.
His net position is –$9.05 per share resulting from –($72.50 – $60.00) + $3.45 = –$12.50 + $3.45 = –$9.05 x 100 = –$905.

SCENARIO II: PRICE RISE; OUT-OF-THE-MONEY

Abandonment The **naked put** is a limited profit strategy. Maximum gain is achieved when the price of the underlying asset at expiration date is above the strike price of the put option sold. The strategy will prove beneficial if the price of underlying shares stays out-of-the-money (remains unchanged or rises moderately), which in terms of market price expectations designates the strategy as bullish. Providing that the underlying stock price is trading at or above the put strike price, the short put option will expire worthless—without assignment—and the option writer will be entitled to retain the premium.

Maximum Profit: Limited to Premium Received

Here is the graph illustrating put writing performance:

Figure 10.4 Short Put Profit & Loss Diagram

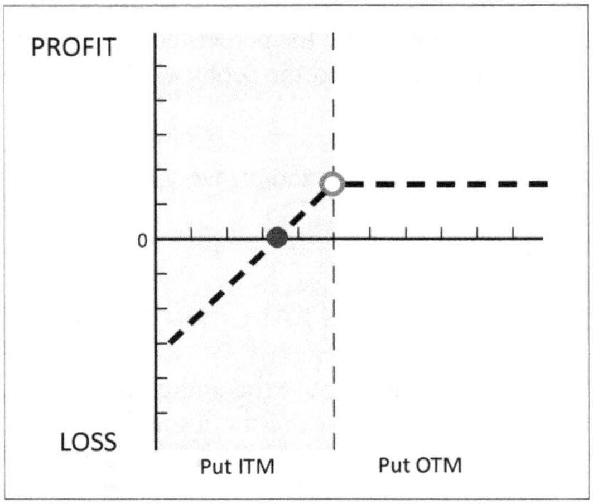

Notations:
- ● BEP
- ○ Exercise Price

BEP and the loss potential are on the downside.

Maximum Loss = Unlimited

The break-even point for the short put option is:

BEP = Exercise Price – Premium Received

As the short put BEP is on the downside, any decrease in the underlying stock price below the strike price produces a negative effect on the option's premium—it will start to erode until it reaches the BEP. At that point the strategy net payoff is equal to zero. If the price of the underlying stock continues to fall below the BEP, the put option writer starts losing dollars one-for-one with the decline of the stock price. What is beneficial for the put option holder is detrimental for the put option writer—and vice versa.

Table 10.4 Short Put Profit & Loss Metrics

Short Put Exercise Price \$72.50 BEP = \$72.50 – \$3.45 = \$69.05			
Stock Price \$	Intrinsic Value	Premium Received	Net P&L
60.00	12.50	3.45	**–9.05**
65.00	7.50	3.45	**–4.05**
67.50	5	3.45	**–1.55**
69.05	3.45	3.45	**0**
72.50	0	3.45	**3.45**
77.50	0	3.45	**3.45**
80.00	0	3.45	**3.45**
82.50	0	3.45	**3.45**

Short Put Exercise Price (X) \$72.50 Resume	
Break-Even Point	Exercise Price – Premium Received
Potential Profit	Limited = Premium when Price of UI is Above BEP
Maximum Loss	Unlimited = UI – BEP if UI is Below BEP
Time Decay	Positive

Aside from selling puts to earn a premium in moderately bullish expectation, there is yet another aspect of analyzing motives for naked put writing.

Writing puts may appear to be a reasonable way of acquiring a stock at a preselected discount price. You sell an out-of-the-money put of your choice and collect the premium. As long as the closing price stays above the strike price the premium remains safe on your account. If the short put expires without assignment you earn the entire premium. If, on the other hand, it fails to perform as expected, and the stock falls below the strike price, you purchase the stock you considered worth owning in your portfolio, at a contentedly discounted price.

N.B. All option transactions, whether on open or close, must go through a brokerage firm so they are subject to transaction fees and commissions.

OPTIONS ONE-PAGE LESSON—THE DIAMOND GRAPH

A four strategies compendium reveals options' antagonistic correlations. The unity of four different strategies is a configuration of affinity and enmity. An image of four parts harmoniously opposed.

If we put some virtual mirrors in between, in the way Figure 10.5 suggests, the logic of opposition unfolds; the starting payoff (upper left) is that of a long call and all other figures clockwise are mirror images of the preceding figure.

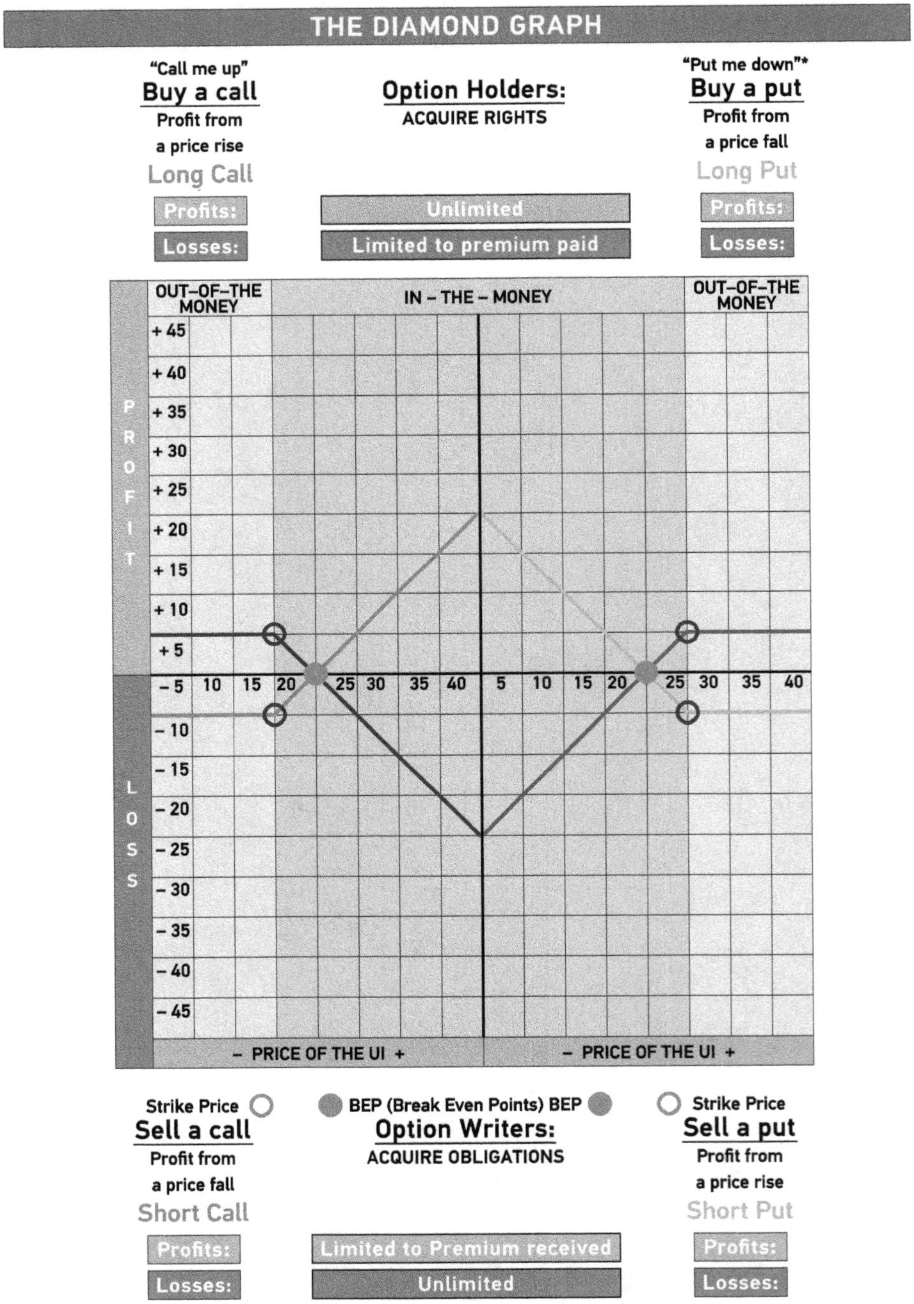

Figure 10.5 Diamond Graph—Mirror Images

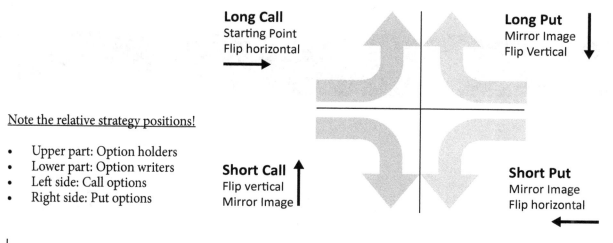

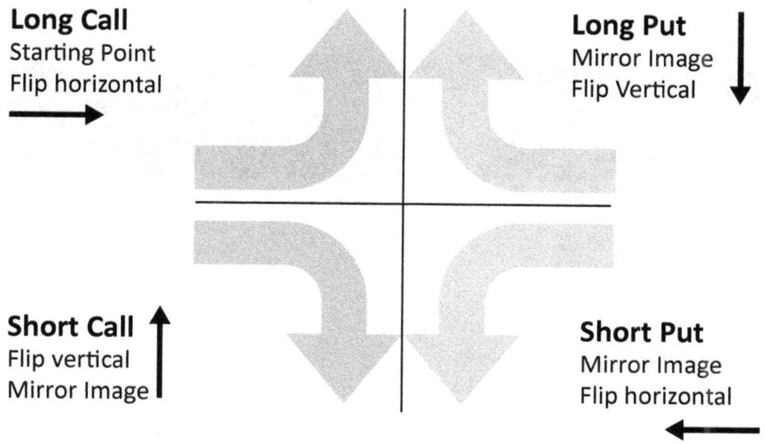

Note the relative strategy positions!

- Upper part: Option holders
- Lower part: Option writers
- Left side: Call options
- Right side: Put options

Figure 10.6: Profit & Loss Antagonistic Correlations

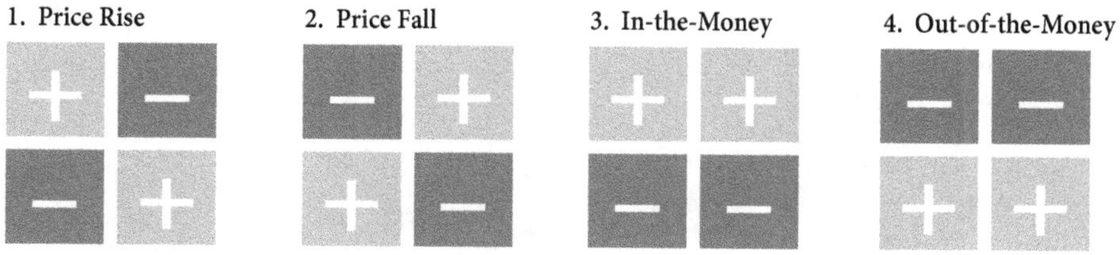

1. Long Call/Short Put: Profit from a **Price Rise.**
2. Long Put/Short Call: Profit from a **Price Fall.**
3. Option Holders: Benefit from **"In-the-Money"** Position.
4. Option Writers: Benefit from **"Out-of-the-Money"** Position.

SUMMARY

In this chapter we have introduced the reader to the basics of options directional trading—outright purchase and sale of four "plain vanilla" option contracts and the repercussions thereof. Each strategy has been illustrated graphically and numerically giving the mechanics of options performance in different market scenarios. Options were treated as an instrument that allowed investors to lever the exposure to the underlying asset price change.

Long options confine risk exposure to their holders to the amount of the premium invested, whereas the profit potential is unlimited.

On the other side, short options limit the profits to the premium received but convey unlimited risk of loss.

Finally we tried to synthesize the basic option characteristics in one figure—the "Options Diamond Graph" aiming to provide a visual representation of major option features.

KEY TERMS

long call	long put	naked put	volume
in-the-money	short call	bid	
out-of-the-money	naked call	ask	
break-even point	short put	open interest	

[redacted]

CHAPTER 11

HEDGE PATTERNS WITH OPTIONS

CHAPTER OBJECTIVES

- To point out and compare differences between futures and futures options
- To illustrate and explain four basic types of options hedging strategies
- To highlight the dissimilarities between the options strategy payoff diagram and the profit-loss diagram
- To emphasize the potential benefits and drawbacks of alternative options strategies
- To learn how to manage market expectation by selecting the strategy best suited to your preferences and risk tolerance

HEDGING POSITIONS CREATED WITH A SINGLE OPTION

Key Terms

option spread
a trading strategy created between options of the same type, only calls or only puts

combination
a trading strategy created with a mixture of calls and puts

synthetic option
an option payoff profile replicated in between a plain vanilla option and an underlying

BASICALLY, WE MAY DIVIDE HEDGING STRATEGIES INTO TWO GROUPS:

1. Hedging position constructed with a single option.
2. Hedging position constructed with an options portfolio; two or more options of the same type—only calls or only puts, or a combination of calls and puts.

In market lingo a strategy initiated with options of the same type is designated an **option spread,** and a mixture of calls and puts is known as a **combination.**

Initiating a hedging position with an option will create the risk-reward profile of another option, a so-called **synthetic option.** This option payout profile is replicated by a combination of a plain vanilla option and the asset underlying the options contract. (The intricacies of causality relation existing between options and their underlying instruments will be treated separately in chapter 17 "Parity Relations.")

In the following figure we depict the diagrams extracted from "Parity Relations" that illustrate the four basic hedging strategies, starting with a plain vanilla option against its underlier:

Figure 11.1 Four Hedging Strategies Created with a Single Option

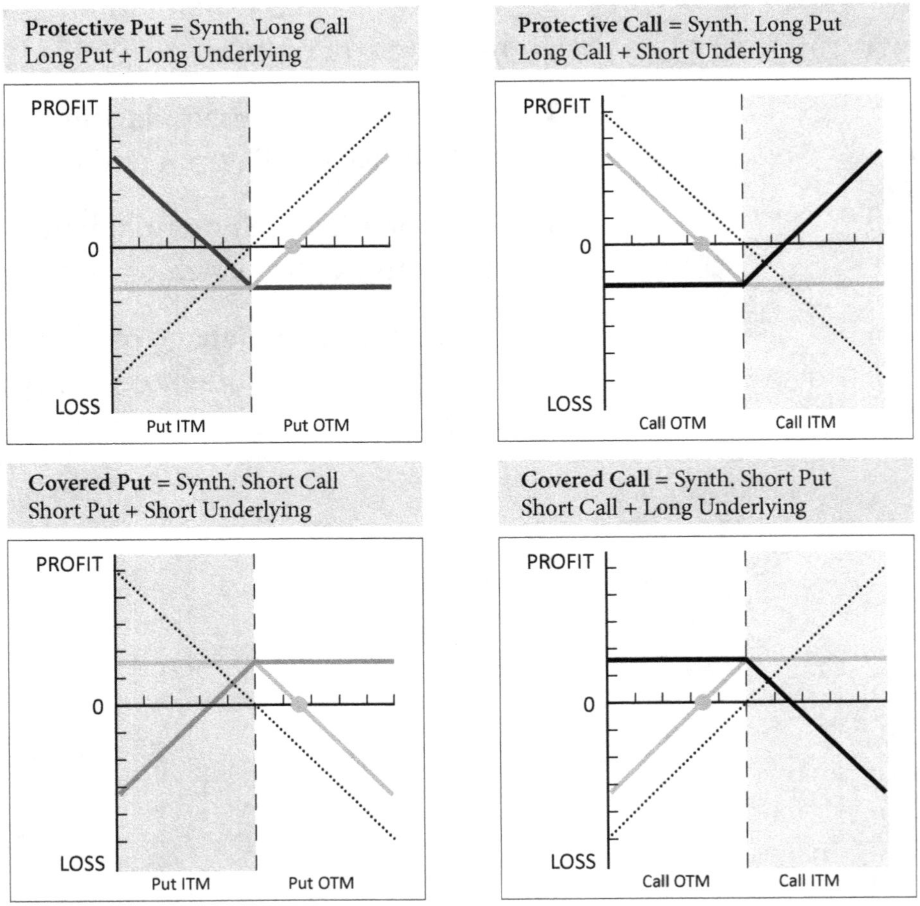

In all the trading strategies depicted in Figure 11.1, options are employed as a hedging instrument to protect an underlying asset position, either from a price rise or a price fall. As these cases represent most common hedging strategies, in the next chapters we shall elaborate each in more detail.

From Figure 11.1 you will observe that plain vanilla options—used as a hedge instrument against the asset at risk—are differentiated with different shades (and line styles), while the resulting strategy is always represented by a grey diagram. The shaded circles denote the break-even point of the strategy and are always located on the opposite side to the plain vanilla option.

These four basic hedging strategies, using options, are analysed and expounded as alternatives to a futures hedge (whose payoff is identical to the X-axis). Why? We thought it was important to relate futures hedge performance to that of an options hedge, in order to explain the basic motive that validates the decision of a potential hedger—to put in place an alternative.

From previous elaborations, we have learned that with futures hedges there is no potential for windfall profit. Gains and losses offset each other and the final outcome usually equals zero. So, you may be tempted to use options instead and to evade the zero effect. An option's hedge protects your existing assets and may leave open the opportunity for additional returns.

In Figure 11.1 we propose an image of four basic options hedging alternatives with distinctive visual generation of the resulting strategy exposures directly confronted with each other—a concise concept of weighing risk against reward.

From the nature of the strategy profile and the risk it implies, options hedge strategies can be divided into two types:

- Strategies that aim to put a limit on a potential loss (in case the price of the underlying you are trying to protect moves adversely), and yet leave the door open for a windfall profit. These goals are afforded by long calls and/or puts, and the respective strategies are designated protective calls and puts.

- Strategies aiming to get additional insurance against an adverse price move at the cost of limiting the profit potential. These goals are afforded by short calls and/or puts and the respective strategies are designated as covered calls and puts.

The prudent hedger's first priority, however, is to become familiar with the hedge strategy risk profile and understand how the hedge outcomes vary with the change in price movement. Additionally, he has to assume the risk-reward ratio and cost considerations associated with the specific strategy chosen, and lastly to decide upon the trade-off between constraints and advantages of each strategy employed.

Key Terms

protective calls & puts
option hedge strategies instituted with a long call or long put option against a short/long underlying

covered calls & puts
options hedge strategies instituted with a short call or short put option against a long/short underlying

FUTURES VS. FUTURES OPTIONS

There is often confusion when it comes to the differences between futures and futures options. Both are agreements between a buyer and seller. At the outset, the costs of entering a futures position are equivalent to a margin specified in the terms of agreement. The risk is unlimited and since its payoff is symmetrical, gains and losses are equal and opposite.

The cost of acquiring a long position in an options contract is equivalent to the premium paid. The premium is paid in advance of acquiring a long call/put option, and is not to be confused with the strike price. The risk is limited to the cost of the premium.

Let us remember briefly that the buyer of an option has purchased the right, but not the obligation, to buy the underlying futures contract—in the case of a call—or to sell the underlying futures—in the case of a put—at a pre-defined strike price. Option buyers are said to be holding the "long" side, and may exercise their right at any time before the option expiration date.

Conversely, option writers inherit no rights and, if assigned an exercise, they are obliged to assume the position that is directly opposite to long option holders.

PAYOFFS AND PROFITS AT EXPIRATION:

Notations:
X – Exercise price
FT – Futures price at expiration

- Call holders acquire the right to go long a futures contract at the exercise price (X). Call writers are obliged to assume a short futures position.

Payoff to Call Holder		Payoff to Call Writer	
(FT – X)	if FT > X	– (FT – X)	if FT > X
0	if FT < X	0	if FT < X

Profit to Call Holder	Profit to Call Writer
Payoff – Premium	Payoff + Premium

- Put holders acquire the right to go short a futures contract at the exercise price (X). Put writers are obliged to go long the futures contract.

Payoff to Put Holder		Payoff to Put Writer	
0	if FT > X	0	if FT > X
(X – FT)	if FT < X	–(X – FT)	if FT < X

Profit to Put Holder	Profit to Put Writer
Payoff – Premium	Payoff + Premium

Figure 11.2 is designed to illustrate graphically the distinction between options payoff and options profit and loss diagrams. The black lines represent option payoff diagrams while the shaded lines represent option profit diagrams.

Figure 11.2 Payoff vs. Profit & Loss Diagrams

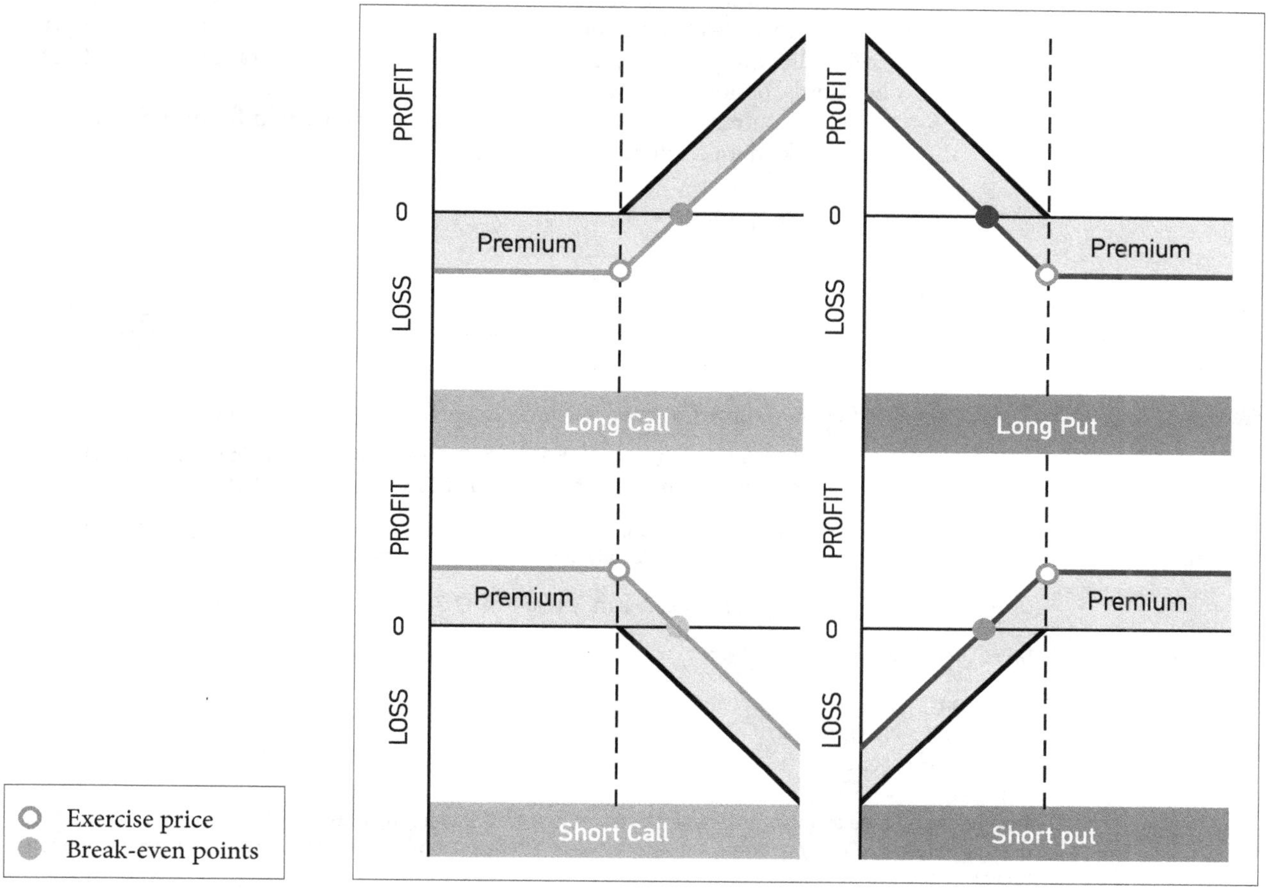

The very first property that you can observe from options diagrams geometry, as ilustrated in Figure 11.2, is that long option diagrams are inversely correlated to those of short options.

Long option payoff is always non-negative (either positive or zero) as the holder's right to exercise will be executed only if options at expiration contain an intrinsic value (in-the-money options).

Conversely, short options expiring in-the-money will produce a negative payoff. Hence, short option payoff diagrams are mirror images of long option payoff diagrams and are either negative or zero.

Profits to option holders are directly commensurate to the losses incurred by option writers.

Options with no intrinsic value at expiration (out-of-the-money options) expire with zero value; hence, exercising is pointless and does not occur.

One of the key dissimilarities between futures and futures options is in how they specify a price.

Futures contracts lock-in the desired target price for a future delivery date based on the current shape of the futures price curve—i.e., based on today's price.

Futures options are different. They are simply options to buy or sell futures contracts at the discretion of the options holder.

Investors entering the options market can avail themselves of an opportunity to decide between a wide range of different expiration months and different strike prices, allowing them to pick an option that suits best their risk tolerance and objectives. In other words, options offer more flexibility.

Option contract buyers therefore may choose the desired future price level they want to lock-in for a future delivery date.

Gold futures options specification:

Underlying Futures	Gold Futures	
Product Symbol	OG	
Venue	CME Globex, CME ClearPort, Open Outcry (New York)	
Hours (All Times are New York Time/ET)	CME Globex:	Sunday - Friday 6:00 p.m. - 5:15 p.m. (5:00 p.m. - 4:15 p.m. Chicago Time/CT) with a 45-minute break each day beginning at 5:15 p.m. (4:15 p.m. CT)
	CME ClearPort:	Sunday - Friday 6:00 p.m. - 5:15 p.m. (5:00 p.m. - 4:15 p.m. Chicago Time/CT) with a 45-minute break each day beginning at 5:15 p.m. (4:15 p.m. CT)
	Open Outcry:	Monday - Friday 8:20 a.m. - 1:30 p.m. (7:20 a.m. - 12:30 p.m. CT)
Contract Size	One COMEX Gold futures contract	
Option Style	American	
Minimum Fluctuation	$0.10 per troy ounce	
Expiration of Trading	Trading terminates on the fourth business day prior to the underlying futures delivery month. If the expiration day falls on a Friday or immediately prior to an Exchange holiday, expiration will occur on the previous business day.	
Listed Contracts	Trading is conducted in the nearest six of the following contract months: February, April, June, August, October and December. Additional contract months - January, March, May, July, September and November - will be listed for trading for a period of two months. A 60-month options contract is added from the current calendar month on a June-December cycle.	
Strike Prices	$10.00 per ounce apart from strike prices below $500, $20.00 per ounce apart from strike prices between $500 and $1,000, $50.00 per ounce apart from strike prices above $1,000. For the nearest six contract months, strike prices will be $5.00, $10.00, and $25.00 apart, respectively.	
Settlement Type	Exercise into futures	
Delivery Period	Delivery may take place on any business day beginning on the first business day of the delivery month or any subsequent business day of the delivery month, but not later than the last business day of the current delivery month.	
Grade and Quality Specifications	Gold delivered under this contract shall assay to a minimum of 999 fineness.	
Position Limits	NYMEX Position Limits	
Rulebook Chapter	115	
Exchange Rule	These contracts are listed with, and subject to, the rules and regulations of NYMEX.	

Once you decide to exercise a futures option, you will be granted an underlying futures contract, virtually inheriting a new commitment attached to the underlying futures. In order to finally close the trade you have to close the futures position. It stands to reason that the right to exercise will be carried out only if acquiring a futures contract is beneficial to the option holder. However, you have to be aware that changes in price direction in subsequent periods may appear to be advantageous, as well as disadvantageous, and consequently have an effect on the ultimate financial result.

In this chapter we will examine in detail the hedging strategies involving futures options—i.e., the CME (COMEX) Gold Futures option contract. COMEX was the very first exchange to offer gold futures options back in 1982.

Gold futures are now traded at three primary global exchanges: Commodity Exchange, Inc (COMEX) in New York, now CME, Tokyo Commodity Exchange (TOCOM) in Tokyo, and MCX India, the world's top gold consumer.

Remember This! Exercising Options on Futures

A call option holder acquires the right to take a long position in the underlying futures contract if he decides to exercise, and the assigned call option writer is obliged to take the corresponding short position in the futures.

Upon exercise, both futures positions—the long futures position in the case of the option holder, and the short futures position in the case of the assigned writer—will be established by the clearing house, at a futures price equal to the strike price and will be marked-to-market.

When the positions are marked-to-market, the margin account (on a long futures position) will be credited with the amount equal to the difference between the current (higher) futures price of the specified asset, and the strike price (FT - X).

At the same time, the other party—the assigned call option writer—will have to deposit corresponding funds to satisfy the variation margin on a short futures position.

A put option holder acquires the right to take a short position in the underlying futures if he decides to exercise and an assigned put option writer is obliged to take the long position.

Upon exercise both futures positions—the short futures position in the case of the option holder and the long futures position in the case of the assigned writer—will be established by the clearinghouse, at a futures price equal to the strike price, and will be marked-to-market.

When the positions are marked-to-market, the margin account (on a short futures position) will be credited with an amount equal to the difference between the strike price and the current (lower) futures settlement price (X - FT).

At the same time, the other party—the assigned put option writer—will have to deposit corresponding funds to satisfy the variation margin on a long futures position.

HEDGE PATTERNS WITH OPTIONS

It will be helpful to keep in mind what we said earlier—a long physical position will generate a loss if the metals price falls. Establishing a short futures position may effectively offset the risk associated with the price fall, but the hedge—depending on the nature of the risk to be eliminated—can also be instituted with options contracts—purchasing a put option and/or writing a call—since they both profit from a price fall.

A short physical position is the opposite—it will generate a loss if the price rises. Establishing a long futures position may effectively offset the risk associated with the price rise, but again, the hedge against a price rise may also be instituted with option contracts—buying a call or writing a put, which both profit from a price rise.

Now, we shall turn our attention to what happens in hedging with options. To some investors using options as a hedging tool is more convenient than hedging with futures. Why is that? Because options hedging offers you an additional 'option'—a possibility, or privilege, that futures hedging is deprived of: the chance of acquiring a windfall profit even if prices are turning against you. If you are hedged against a price rise by going long a futures contract, you will lock-in the purchase price irrespective of how high the spot price might rise. However, you will reap no benefit if the price falls; the commodity being hedged cannot be purchased any cheaper. But, with a long call option contract you can participate in the price fall.

Conversely, if you are using a short futures contract to hedge against the commodity price fall, you will lock-in the sale price irrespective of the spot price decline. But again, you will reap no benefit if the market price turns upwards. The commodity being hedged cannot be sold at a higher price. But with a long put option contract you can participate in the price rise.

In the following section we shall explicate hedging procedures and outcomes of four different hedging strategies ensuing from four different types of options.

These hedging strategies will be presented in the following order:

- **Synthetic Long Put Option Strategy**
  (Hedging against a price rise by purchasing a call)
- **Synthetic Short Put Option Strategy**
  (Hedging against a price fall by writing a call)
- **Synthetic Long Call Option Strategy**
  (Hedging against a price fall by purchasing a put)
- **Synthetic Short Call Option Strategy**
  (Hedging against a price rise by writing a put)

For the purpose of illustrating different hedging scenarios we shall use the prices from the gold futures options chart as published on the "Wall Street Journal" website as of 9 May 2008.

In all four basic hedging scenarios, the hedge strategy performance will be explicated by means of graphic depiction and in tabular form with numeric data. This dual approach makes evaluation of risk against reward easily comparable.

The gold options price chain is presented in the following gold options (COMEX) quotations:

COMEX Gold Close USD/Troy oz 885.80						
Date May, 09.2008				100 troy oz., dollars per troy oz.		
Strike Price	Calls			Puts		
	Jun	July	Aug	Jun	July	Aug
830	57.20	67.00	72.30	1.50	7.20	12.50
835	52.60	–	68.70	1.90	–	14.00
840	48.10	59.30	65.30	2.40	9.40	15.50
845	43.80	–	62.00	3.00	–	17.20
850	39.40	52.00	58.80	3.60	12.10	19.00
855	35.50	–	55.70	4.70	–	20.80
860	31.70	45.20	52.70	5.90	15.30	22.80
865	28.00	–	49.80	7.20	–	24.90
870	24.60	39.10	47.00	8.80	19.20	27.10
875	21.40	36.30	44.40	10.60	21.30	29.50
880	18.40	33.60	41.80	12.60	23.60	31.90
885	15.70	–	39.40	14.90	–	34.40
885.80	GOLD SPOT					
890	13.50	28.60	37.10	17.70	28.60	37.10
895	11.60	–	34.90	20.80	–	39.90
900	9.90	24.40	32.90	24.10	34.30	42.90
910	7.20	20.70	29.10	31.30	40.60	49.00
915	6.10	–		-35.20	–	–
920	5.10	17.40	25.70	39.30		55.60
925	4.00	–	24.20	43.20	–	59.00
930	3.60	14.70	22.70	47.80	54.50	62.50

N.B the above chart is an extract from gold (COMEX) futures options chain as of 9 May, 2008 with a price range selected to be appropriate for the purpose of explaining the hedge strategies involving gold option contracts. Normally the full range of strike prices goes from $500 to $5000.

SYNTHETIC LONG PUT OPTION STRATEGY

Key Terms

synthetic long put
an option strategy acquired by hedging a short underlying position with a long call. Also protective call

HEDGING AGAINST PRICE RISE BY PURCHASING CALL

Motives At the beginning of May a gold artisan accepts an order to deliver jewellery products in two months' time based on the current gold price of $885.80/tr.oz. The gold artisan is therefore said to be short of physical gold and wants to hedge his position against a possible price rise. The physical gold (100 tr. oz.) is required in the month of June. The final selling price is calculated to be profitable providing that the price of physical gold does not rise above $900.00. Since the gold artisan is holding an open cash market position, any increase in the price of gold by June would have a detrimental effect on the artisan's overall profits.

The first alternative is to hedge forward gold purchase by taking a position in the futures market. Suppose that June gold futures are available at $893.00. If he hedges his forward gold purchase by initiating a futures position, he will lock-in the purchase price of $893.00 but he will gain nothing if the gold price falls below that level.

Considering the significant gold market volatility and eventual risk-reward scenarios, the gold artisan decides to replace the futures hedge by purchasing one "at-the-money" June $885.00 gold call option for which he pays a premium of $1570 ($15.70 x 100 tr. oz.). The long call option holder is entitled (if he chooses to exercise his rights) to buy the underlying gold futures contract at the predetermined exercise price ($885.00).

By doing so the gold artisan is setting a limit on the gold purchase price that equals the strike price plus the premium paid for the long call ($885.00 + $15.70 = $900.70). This would be the maximum purchase price guaranteed by the synthetic long put strategy. On the other hand, the portfolio retains an unlimited downside profit potential if the underlying asset price (gold) should decline below the exercise price.

From this point on, the hedger will be monitoring closely the relationship between the option's strike price and the underlying gold futures price, as this correlation is the most distinct determinant influencing the option premium value, and consequently the overall strategy performance.

Here is a brief resume:

Gold entry price (GEP): $885.80
Long call exercise price (X): $885
Premium paid (P_p): $15.70/oz.
Contract size: 100 oz.
Total premium paid: $1570 ($15.70 x 100 tr.oz)
Market expectations: Bearish on the underlying gold
Variable gold futures prices will be designated as (F_t)

How to construct the diagram?

To construct the diagram we need to have only three figures:

1. the exercise price,
2. the premium, and
3. current price of the underlying commodity.

In all figures relating to the basics of hedging strategies with options, we have provided a graphical guidance to these intricate interrelations. The graph notations are as follows:

Notations:
Asset at Risk Payout: ....
Options Payout: ■
Strategy Payout: ■

Each payout is given a different shade for easier visual perception. It was necessary to incorporate different shades in order to differentiate between the strategy payoffs and to understand in which way they are related to each other.

Asset at risk (no-hedge position)—in this particular strategy the short gold P&L diagram is represented as diagonal dotted line that crosses the X-axis at the $885.80 point—the current gold futures price.

We add a long call payout ("black" diagram) respecting the values of a strike price $885 and a premium (Pp) of $15.70;

Determine the long call BEP according to formula:

Long call BEP = Exercise price (X) + premium paid (Pp) which gives the value of:

Long call BEP = ($885 + $15.70) = $900.70

Now you can construct the strategy diagram (net payout; grey diagram) configured as the long call hedging with the help of two additional rules ensuing from Figure 11.3:

Maximum loss = Gold entry price (GEP) – long call BEP
= $885.80 – $900.70 = –$14.90
(the value represented with the flat section of the grey diagram).

Strategy BEP = Gold entry price – premium paid
= ($885.80 – $15.70) = $870.10

The clear graphical and conceptual distinction between short gold (no-hedge) payout and long call option hedge is directly observable from the illustrated compilation of diagrams:

- The short gold payout is presented with a long dotted diagonal from left to right showing that losses are unlimited and associated with the price increase while profits are generated in price decline;
- The synthetic long put (represented by a grey diagram), offers an alternative scenario:

In rising markets—from the exercise price upwards—it locks-in the potential loss—the flat segment of the strategy payout diagram beginning at the strike price, parallel to and below the X-axis.

In falling markets—from the strike price downwards—the long call option expires unexercised and the hedger now avails himself of the privilege to simply abandon the option and fully participate in the underlying gold value gains due to a favourable price decline. The all-in purchase price will be the ultimate gold futures price minus the cost of the premium. The benefit is commensurate with the price decline—the lower the gold futures price the higher the benefit.

Figure 11.3 Synthetic Long Put—Hedging Short Physical with Long Call

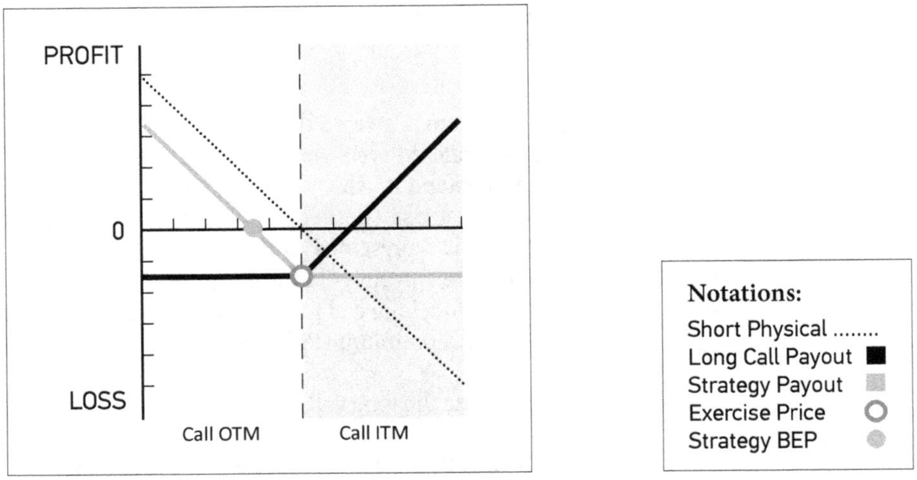

The synthetic long put strategy BEP is on the downside:

Strategy BEP = Gold Entry Price – Pp = \$885.80 – \$15.70 = \$870.10

The long call BEP is on the upside, therefore

Long Call BEP = (\$885 + \$15.70) = \$900.70

The net payout of the strategy, presented with the grey diagram, is, as you can see, identical to the long put payout. For this reason this strategy is designated a synthetic long put. The same strategy is aptly called a "protective call," a term quite consistent with its purpose—to provide 'protection' against losses in a rising market by purchasing a 'call' option.

The primary objective of the protective call strategy is therefore to protect a portfolio (short asset) against losses in rising markets, without losing out on possible price gains in declining markets. Now, let us turn our attention to the synthetic long put performance in two different market scenarios: rising markets and falling markets.

SCENARIO I: FUTURES PRICE RISES TO \$915; ITM

Exercise The synthetic long put is securing an upside protection. Gains on a long call position offset the losses incurred on a short gold position. Therefore, in rising markets, when the current futures price (Ft) exceeds the exercise price (X), losses are limited and the calculation procedure consists of the following steps:

Suppose that the futures price rises to \$915.00, then:

Loss on the short gold position = \$885.80 – \$915.00 =	–\$29.20
Long call intrinsic value =	+\$30
Premium paid =	–\$15.70
Limited loss =	–\$14.90

The above calculation, then, is equivalent to the following equation:

Loss = LIMITED = Gold Entry Price – Long Call BEP

Loss = LIMITED = $885.80 – $900.70 = –$14.90

The formula above is a shortcut for calculating losses in an upward market, so we do not need to go through the step-by-step procedure as the final result would remain invariant to changes in the ultimate futures price (see Table 11.1).

Accordingly, the ultimate purchase price is also limited.

Ultimate Purchase Price = LIMITED = –(X + Pp) = –$900.70

In rising markets, where the underlying futures price exceeds the strike price, the option is in-the-money and the option holder is entitled to exercise his right—to buy the underlying futures.

When a call option is exercised, the hedge unfolds as follows:

By exercising his rights, the call option holder receives the positive difference between the current futures price (Ft) and the exercise price (X), and acquires the gold at a price equal to the exercise price (X), minus the cost of the premium.

Ultimate Purchase Price = (Ft – X) – Ft – Pp

(Ft – X) = (915 – 885) x 100 0z. = +$3000
Acquires long futures: –100 0z. of gold x $915
–Ft = –$91,500
$3000 – $91,500 = –$88,500
–Pp = $1570
–$88,500 – $1570 = –$90,070 : 100 = –$900.70

Risk/ Reward A synthetic long put hedge limits the upside risk—it confines the maximum purchase price to the amount of the strike price plus the premium paid. That is the highest purchase price secured by a long call option hedge. Regardless of the eventual magnitude of the price rise, the synthetic long put option hedge will guarantee that the purchase price never exceeds $900.70. In our example that is $14.30 better than the maturity futures price of $915, or if no hedge had been instituted.

SCENARIO II: FUTURES PRICE FALLS TO $855; OTM

Abandonment With the price fall, the long call option goes out-of-the-money, the option expires worthless, and the premium paid is lost. But now the hedger derives benefit from the falling markets and may participate in price gains as short gold starts to produce a positive return.

In falling markets, when the current futures price (Ft) falls behind the exercise price (X), profits will vary with the price fall. The profit equation is simple and can be expressed as follows:

Profit = VARIABLE = Strategy BEP – Ft

Suppose that the futures price falls to $855.00, then:

Profit = $870.10 – $855.00
= $15.10

Profits are commensurate with the price decline: if the price falls to $835.00, then the profit will rise to $35.10 (the difference between the strategy constituents is clearly evident from Table 11.1).

The profit potential is unlimited, although reduced by the amount of the call premium (it will always be $15.70 less than if the long call hedge has not been initiated).

Accordingly, the ultimate purchase price will also vary with the price of the underlying futures.

Suppose the gold futures price falls to $855:

Gold purchase price = –$855
+ Cost of option premium
–($855 + $15.70) = –$870.70

The above calculation is equivalent to the following equation:

Ultimate Purchase Price = VARIABLE = –(Ft + Premium Paid)

This ultimate purchase price ($870.70) is higher than the current futures price ($855.00), but at the same time it is also $15.10 better relative to the initial short gold price ($885.80).

Benefit Purchasing a call as a substitute for a long futures leaves the hedger an opportunity to participate in the price fall. In our example, if a bear market deepens and prices fall to $855.00, the ultimate purchase price is $870.70, which is $15.10 lower than the short gold spot price of $885.80, so the hedger is left with a windfall profit—the ultimate purchase price acquired is considerably lower. The benefit is commensurate with the price decline. The lower the current futures price the higher the benefit. If the gold futures price declines to $835.00, the profit will increase to $35.10. Note, however, that the synthetic long put will produce a positive return only if the gold futures price declines beyond the strategy BEP (gold entry price – premium paid). Compared to an open cash market position—the physical short gold—the profit potential resulting from a synthetic long put strategy is theoretically unlimited, although reduced (it falls behind the short physical gold position) by the amount of the call premium paid.

In this respect, the net effect of the hedging strategy will be greatly influenced by the option's strike price and the premium the hedger chooses to pay. Performance characteristics of three different scenarios are displayed in Figure 11.4.

The scorecard of individual instruments and the resulting payout of the synthetic long put strategy is summarized in Table 11.1.

Table 11.1 Synthetic Long Put Metrics

Underlying Gold Futures	Long Call 885@15.70 Intrinsic Value	Long Call Premium	Long Call P&L	Short Gold P&L 885.80	Synthetic Long Put P&L
A	B	C	D	E	D + E
835	0	−15.70	−15.70	50.80	35.10
855	0	−15.70	−15.70	30.80	15.10
860	0	−15.70	−15.70	25.80	10.10
870.10	0	−15.70	−15.70	15.70	**0**
880	0	−15.70	−15.70	5.80	−9.90
885	0	−15.70	−15.70	0.80	−14.90
885.80	0.80	−15.70	−14.90	**0**	−14.90
890	5	−15.70	−10.70	−4.20	−14.90
895	10	−15.70	−5.70	−9.20	−14.90
900.70	15.70	−15.70	**0**	−14.90	−14.90
910	25	−15.70	9.30	−24.20	−14.90
915	30	−15.70	14.30	−29.20	−14.90
935	50	−15.70	34.30	−49.20	−14.90

Utterly aware of running the risk of being reiterative we shall bring to your attention the following remark:

In the context of options hedging strategies, the term exercise implies that the market price of the UI (the gold futures price in our example) has moved adversely or unfavourably. Consequently, the option holder exits the hedge in order to limit the damage. The act of exercising substantiates the conclusion that an option's hedge can prevent the detrimental effects of an adverse price move. The act of exercising a long call is an effective protection against an unforeseen price increase. In the case of a protective call hedge it denotes limiting the upside—the maximum purchase price.

Conversely, the term abandonment assumes that the market price of the UI has moved favourably and the option is left to expire worthless. Abandonment inevitably entails a benefit for hedgers employing a long option. Now, the hedgers can exploit the opportunity of a favourable price move to their advantage. In the case of a protective call hedge, abandonment would mean that the option has expired worthless and the underlying gold can now be acquired at a lower market price.

Protective Call Disadvantages:

- Cost of the call option reduces overall profits.
- Time decay: Negative. As time nears expiration, call value portion erodes. The risk of losing the premium invested even if the stock price remains stable.
- Compared to a short cash market position—in declining markets profits fall behind by the amount of the premium paid.
- Compared to a futures hedge— in rising markets the position generates limited losses. On the upside, if the price of the underlying finishes above the strategy BEP, then hedging with futures would be a more beneficial strategy.

Protective Call Advantages:

- The cost to buy the insurance on a short asset (gold) by purchasing a call option is generally cheaper than initiating a futures hedge.
- The protective call allows you to hold on to your short position and participate in the downside potential while at the same time it provides insurance against losses on the upside.
- Compared to an open cash market position: the loss is limited and known in advance; profits are variable and commensurate with the price decrease, although reduced by the cost of the premium.
- Compared to a futures hedge: on the downside, below the strategy BEP, protective call payout is more advantageous than the futures payout.

Advantages ensuing from options flexibility:

Rolling-down long call options A protective call is a bearish strategy as the profit potential is on the downside. If the price of gold drops, there is more than one choice to close the trade. Firstly, you can take a gain by covering the short position and exit the trade. Secondly, you may opt for another alternative. Instead of exiting the trade at a profit you might consider to roll-down the call. Rolling-down would assume selling back the call you own and buying another one closer to the current gold price and with a later expiration date.

By rolling-down the long call, you maintain insurance against upside risk, while at the same time, as you continue being short, the position stays open to reaping benefits from the further price decline.

However, there are several factors to consider (besides the premium) when you are rolling the call: the expiration date, the strike price and the current price of the underlying. Since all the relevant parameters are instantly observable, the decision of whether or not to roll-up is based on a simple upfront calculation.

The mechanics of rolling the call are illustrated in the following example.

Example: Rolling Down Long Call Options

We assume that annualized gold implied volatility is 15%. Since we are dealing with a 30-calendar day option contract we calculate IV for the actual time frame: $885.80 x 0.15 x √30/256 = $132.87 x 0.34 ≈ ±$45. The result of ±$45 would imply that gold prices over a given time frame (from now until options expiration) are expected to range between $840 and $930. Let us suppose that after 10 days, Gold futures first falls to $870.00 and then, at expiration, rallies to $900.00; well beyond a One Standard Deviation Move.
The consequential call price simulation is derived from the BS model.
Gold futures falls from $885.80 to $870.00

Call option goes "out-of-the-money": Premium falls to $6.37
Roll-down → Sell back long put option for $6.37 (the currently held call has not expired yet and therefore will retain some value, which will help reduce the cost of the new call).
(Loss incurred = –$9.33; (+$6.37 – $15.70)
Buy new call (same expiration) at lower strike $870 for $12.42
Total Premium Costs = –$21.75 (–$12.42 – $9.33)
At expiration Gold futures rallies to $900

Call Exercised → Long call converted to long futures; $870.00
Maximum Purchase Price = **–$891.75** = –($870 + $21.75);
Original Maximum Purchase Price = **$900.70**
Overall profit from rolling-up: **$8.95** ($900.70 – $891.75).

To conclude the synthetic long put option strategy, in Table 11.4, we have included a comparison of three different call options quotes from the COMEX Gold Option chart as of 9 May, 2008.

| **Figure 11.4** | Synthetic Long Put—Three Strategies Compared |

GOLD ENTRY PRICE $885,80		
100 troy oz., dollars per troy oz. (COMX)		
Long Call ITM	Long Call ATM	Long Call OTM
Exercise Price (X) $860 Premium Paid ($P_p$) $31.70	Exercise Price (X) $885 Premium Paid ($P_p$) $15.70	Exercise Price (X) $910 Premium Paid ($P_p$) $7.20
Futures Price Rise to $915 EXERCISE	Futures Price Rise to $915 EXERCISE	Futures Price Rise to $915 EXERCISE
Limited Losses **= GEP – Long Call BEP** **1.** –$5.90	Limited Losses **= GEP – Long Call BEP** **2.** –$14.90	Limited Losses **= GEP – Long Call BEP** **3.** –$31.40
Futures Price Fall to $855 ABANDON	Futures Price Fall to $855 ABANDON	Futures Price Fall to $855 ABANDON
Variable Profits **= Strategy BEP – Ft** **3.** –$0.90	Variable Profits **= Strategy BEP – Ft** **2.** $15.10	Variable Profits **= Strategy BEP – Ft** **1.** $23.60
BEP = GEP – P_p = $854.10	**BEP = GEP – P_p = $870.10**	**BEP = GEP – P_p = $878.60**

Notations:

Short Physical
Long Call Payout ■
Strategy Payout ▨
Exercise Price ○
Strategy Payoff ●

Call OTM Call ITM Call OTM Call ITM Call OTM Call ITM

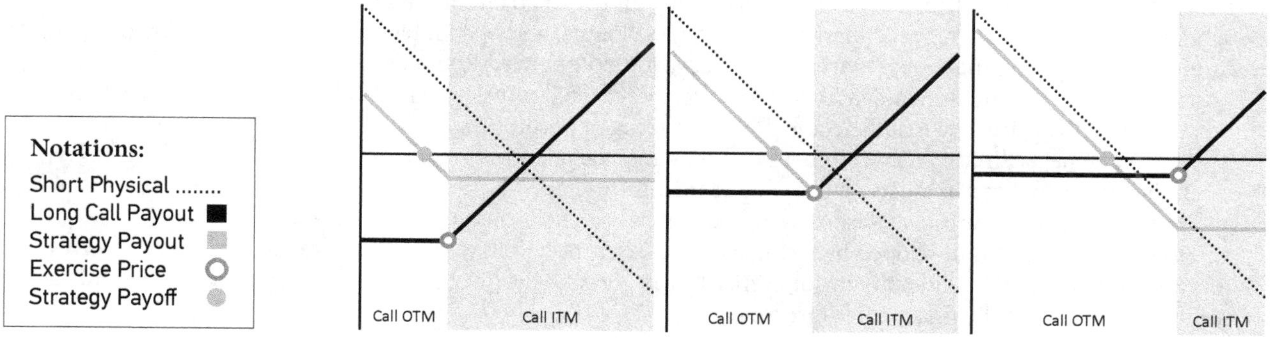

Synthetic Long Put Hedge —Three Strategies Final Comments

Graphic depiction of "Three Strategies Comparison" is meant to provide a clear visual insight and intuitive understanding of options strategy performance and repercussions ensuing from differences in exercise prices employed.

- The synthetic long put is a strategy instituted with the idea of providing protection in rising markets, and at the same time, retains the advantage of participating fully in the eventual price decline.
- If exercised, (in the case of a price increase) the synthetic long put will set a "cap" on portfolio losses. The premium cost in this respect acts as an insurance from a bad event—rising prices. As you can observe from the three strategies comparison, the best protection in rising markets is achieved with an in-the-money call and the poorest with an out-of-the-money call. The higher the premium the higher the protection.

- At the same time, the synthetic long put strategy benefits in declining markets.
- If abandoned, the lowest call premium purchased offers the highest benefit from the price decline.
- Consequently, the maximum benefit is secured with an "out-of the-money" call and the poorest with an "in-the-money" call. The profit potential is inversely related to an option premium: the lower the premium the higher the profit potential.

Remember This! Fundamental Analysis vs. Technical Analysis

The following exposition is merely intended to provide a general overview of two diametrically opposed theories. Both theories declare they accurately developed the method for gauging the forces affecting the market. Both theories claim an exclusive right of possession to the sacrosanct pivotal indicators—signals, the ability to project forward trends, and predict future price performance.

Fundamental Analysis is a doctrine relying upon the significance of economic factors in anticipating forward price trends. Fundamental analysis is unique and inimitable, as it refers to a number of distinctive attributes that allow each commodity to be defined as a specifiable category—one of a kind.

Fundamental Analysis lays emphasis, in the first place, on specific supply/demand factors making each commodity the member of a particular class. It endeavors to evaluate how the macro-economic environment with its array of essential aspects—income, inflation, interest and currency rates, trade balances, political turmoil, social unrest, supply disruptions and strikes, natural catastrophes, seasonal factors etc.—will influence the performance of each particular commodity class.

On a micro-economic level they concentrate on factors such as the quality of a company's management, growth prospects, cash flow, return on equity, the price-to-earnings ratio, etc.

Technical Analysis, in marked contrast, gives priority to non-economic factors, ignoring all the aspects on which fundamenal analysis is based. Technicians rely on the doctrine that market analysis must be based essentially on data derived from the market itself—prices, volume and open interest. This approach contends that, in order to analyze an individual market technically, you do not need to understand its fundamentals. Its basic postulation is that all the fundamental data are already reflected in price charts and that following the patterns created out of the price data is sufficient to identify trading opportunities.

At its extreme, technical analysis implies that fundamental analysis is redundant.

In that respect we may deduce, with apologies to Tolstoy, that:

"Technical Analyses are all alike; every Fundamental Analysis is unique in its own way!"

However, many tools developed by technicians are extensively followed by many traders, hedgers and investors. The ultimate goal is to identify major events, by categorizing the pivotal price influencing factors and indicators, that could shape the future price direction.

Here are some of the most commonly used indicators in technical analysis:

Trend Indicators – trend analysis aims to envisage a direction of price movement over time. A moving average is one of the technical indicators most widely used to discover the overall market trend line and to predict the point of its reversal.

Momentum Indicators – Momentum indicators determine the strength or weakness of a trend as it progresses over time. Usual indicators are RSI, MACD and Stochastics.

Volatility Indicators – measure the magnitude, or size, of daily price fluctuations irrespective of their direction. The most common method is using Bollinger Bands.

SYNTHETIC SHORT PUT OPTION STRATEGY

HEDGING AGAINST PRICE FALL BY WRITING CALL

Motives Consider the gold artisan with 100 tr.oz., of physical metal purchased at the current market price of $885.80. He is planning to release a new line of gold jewellery that will be ready in one month's time (June). He hopes that the new collection will be a market hit but also fears that, in the interim, the gold market may decline considerably, wiping out all of the calculated margin. The gold artisan is said to be "long physical." In order to bridge his open cash market position, his first choice might be to sell the equivalent amount of June futures, thus locking-in the sales price for the gold. Instead, as he is not expecting large moves in prices, he decides to write a call as his hedge. Contrary to the call option holder, he is expecting low volatility and a stable market. If he is right about the gold market trend, and the gold price stays where it is, his strategy will prove profitable. At the same time, as he is virtually taking the other side of the call option holder, the assumptions remain the same:

Long gold entry price (GEP): $885.80
Short call exercise price (X): $885
Premium received (P_r): $15.70/oz.
Contract size: 100 oz.
Total premium received: $1570 ($15.70 x 100 tr.oz)
Market expectations: Neutral to bullish on the underlying gold
Variable gold futures prices will be designated as (F_t)

| **Figure 11.5** | Synthetic Short Put—Hedging Long Physical with Short Call |

Notations:
Long Physical
Short Call Payout ■
Strategy Payout ▨
Exercise Price ○
Strategy BEP ●

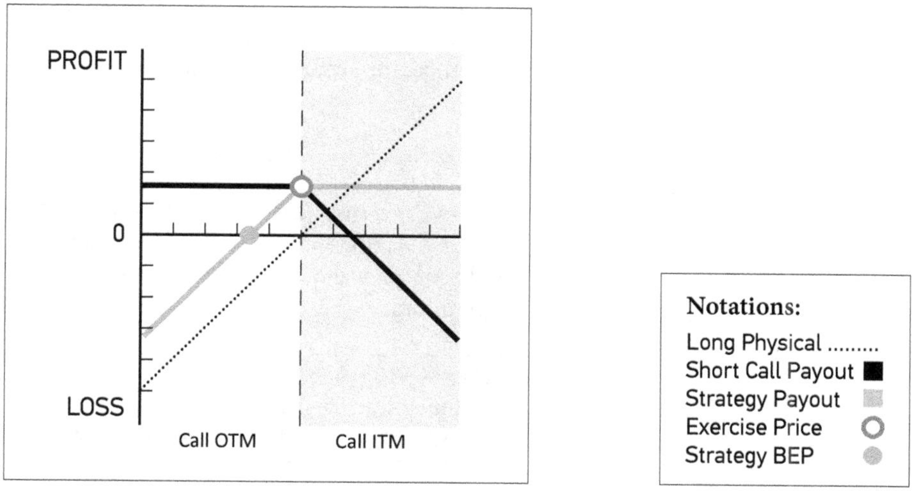

Key Terms

synthetic short put
an option strategy acquired by hedging a long underlying position with a short call, also covered call.

As you can see, the net payout of the strategy, illustrated by the grey diagram, is identical to the short put payout. This is the reason the strategy is designated a **synthetic short put**. The strategies with the same configuration applied typically to equity options are also known as **covered calls**—calls written on stock you own.
Synthetic short put strategy BEP is on the downside, therefore:

Strategy BEP = Gold Entry price – Premium = $885.80 – $15.70 = $870.10

The short call BEP is on the upside, therefore:

Short Call BEP = ($885 + $15.70) = $900.70

SCENARIO I: FUTURES PRICE RISES TO $915; ITM

Assignment With the price rise, the short call option goes in-the-money and the call option writer receives a notice of assignment. He pays the difference between the strike and futures price and acquires a short futures position at the current price of $915. In rising markets, when the current futures price (F_t) exceeds (X), the subsequent profits are limited and the calculation would unfold as follows:

Suppose that futures price rises to $915, then:

Long gold position profit = $915 – $885.80 =	+$29.20
Short call intrinsic value =	–$30
Premium collected =	+$15.70
Ultimate profit =	+$14.90

The above calculation is then equivalent to the following equation:

Profit = LIMITED = Short Call BEP – Gold Entry Price

Profit = Limited = $900.70 – $885.80 = $14.90

A long asset hedged with a short call limits the upside profit potential, hence the ultimate selling price is also limited.

If assigned, the sequence of transactions would unfold as follows:

Ultimate Selling Price = –(Ft – X) + F_t + Premium Received

The futures price rises to $915 and the short call is assigned, therefore the call option writer pays the difference between the current futures price (F_t) and the exercise price (X), and acquires a short futures position at the current futures price (F_t) plus the cost of the premium.

–(F_t – X) = –(915 – 885) x 100 0z. = –$3000
–$3000 (the difference paid)
+F_t = +$91,500 (Sell 100 0z. of gold: +100 x $915)
–$3000 + $91,500 = +$88,500
+ Premium received
$88,500 + $1570 = +$90,070 : 100 = +$900.70

The above calculation is equivalent to the following equation:

Ultimate Selling Price = LIMITED = X + Premium Received

Ultimate selling price = Limited = $885.00 + $15.70 = $900.70

The ultimate gold selling price, irrespective of changes in current futures prices, can never exceed $900.70 (see Table 11.2). This is the highest possible selling price achieved by hedging with a short call. The strategy foregoes the benefit of a price rise. In this case no hedging would prove to be a more beneficial strategy.

Key Terms

buffer effect
in writing a covered call/put strategy, the premiums collected provide an effect of reducing the losses from adverse price movement

Buffer Effect Writing a short call against a long physical position provides insurance against the downside risk. If you look at the grey diagram in Figure 11.5 you will notice that the premium of the short call sold performs as a "buffer" against losses in a downward market.

The so-called "buffer effect" would be proportionate to the amount of the premium sold: the higher the premium the higher the effect.

SCENARIO II: FUTURES PRICE FALLS TO $855; OTM

Abandonment If the underlying futures price falls below the short call strike, the short call option enters the out-of-the-money zone, allowing the short call to expire unexercised. The hedger is left with a long gold position and the losses incurred from the declining prices would be reduced by the amount of the option premium received.

In falling markets, losses vary with the price fall and the equation can be formulated as the following:

$$\text{Loss} = \text{VARIABLE} = F_t - \text{Strategy BEP}$$

In the case where the futures price falls to $855.00, the losses would be simply calculated as follows:

$$\begin{aligned}\text{Loss} &= \$855 - \$870.10\\ &= -\$15.10\end{aligned}$$

If the gold futures price falls to $855.00, then the net strategy loss is $15.10. If the price falls to $835, the loss equals $35.10 (see Table 11.2). Losses are commensurate with the price fall. Comparing to a long gold payout, losses incurred on a synthetic short put strategy always fall behind for exactly $15.70 (the value of the put premium received). The put premium reduces the losses acquired on a long physical position. However, in downward markets a fixed hedge, through selling forward, would prove to be a more advantageous strategy.

Accordingly, the ultimate selling price is also variable and the calculation is equivalent to the following equation:

$$\text{Ultimate Selling Price} = \text{VARIABLE} = F_t + P_r$$

Risk/ Reward The option writer's best result would fall within the range $900.70 on the upside (exercise price + premium received) and $870.10 on the downside (long gold entry price – premium received). The strategy will be greatly influenced by volatility (the lower the better) and the amount of the premium received (the higher the better). If the price rises above $900.70 then no hedge would be more beneficial; if the price falls below $870.10, then hedging with futures is a preferable strategy.

The scorecard of individual constituent gains and losses coalesce to a synthetic short put payoff, as exhibited in the following table:

Table 11.2 Synthetic Short Put Metrics

Underlying Gold Futures	Short Call 885@15.70 Intrinsic Value	Short Call Premium	Short Call P&L	Long Gold P&L 885.80	Synthetic Short Put P&L
A	B	C	D	E	D + E
835	0	15.70	15.70	−50.80	−35.10
855	0	15.70	15.70	−30.80	−15.10
860	0	15.70	15.70	−25.80	−10.10
870.10	0	15.70	15.70	−15.70	**0**
880	0	15.70	15.70	−5.80	9.90
885	0	15.70	15.70	−0.80	14.90
885.80	−0.80	15.70	14.90	**0**	14.90
890	−5	15.70	10.70	4.20	14.90
895	−10	15.70	5.70	9.20	14.90
900.70	−15.70	15.70	**0**	14.90	14.90
910	−25	15.70	−9.30	24.20	14.90
915	−30	15.70	−14.30	29.20	14.90
935	−50	15.70	−34.30	49.20	14.90

Remember This! The History of Gold Fixing

The beginning of gold trading on an organized exchange dates back to 12 Sept 1919 when the first gold price was fixed at GBP 4.9375 per troy ounce among the five principal gold bullion traders and refiners of that time: N M Rothschild & Sons, Mocatta & Goldsmid, Pixley & Abell, Samuel Montagu & Co. and Sharps & Wilkins. Until 2004, the ritual of the Gold Price Fix continued at the premises of N M Rothschild & Sons in St Swithin's Lane, setting twice daily the London "fixing" price, which then becomes a benchmark for gold around the world.

In April 2004 Rothschild withdrew from gold trading and from the London Gold Fixing. So, from 7 June 2004, the fixing procedure moved to Barclays Bank. The actual gold fixing, besides Barclays Bank, is now being done by four other banks: Deutsche Bank, HSBC Bank, Société Générale and Scotia Mocatta (Bank of Nova Scotia). The chairmanship of the meeting rotates annually.

On 19 September 2011 the COMEX Gold price settled at $1923.70 a "new all time high" in nominal terms. However, the gold price fix of $850—reached on 21 January 1980—is still considered to be the record gold price in real terms as this price, indexed for inflation, would equate to $2,479.30 per ounce.

I. SYNTHETIC LONG CALL OPTION STRATEGY

HEDGING AGAINST PRICE FALL BY PURCHASING A PUT

Motives Consider the same gold artisan with 100 tr.oz., of long physical metal acquired at a current market price of $885.80. He is planning to release a new line of gold jewellery that will be ready in one month's time (June). But his view of the short-term market outlook is somewhat different. His expectations are that in the near term gold demand, which traditionally increases in summer months, may drive prices up and he would not like to miss this opportunity. At the same time he is unwilling to bear the losses of an adverse price movement. In order to hedge his long physical position, his first choice might be to sell the equivalent amount of June futures, thus locking-in the gold sales price. Suppose that June gold futures are quoted at $887.00. If he decides to enter into a futures hedge he will lock-in the June futures price of $887.00 but he will forego the opportunity to participate in the eventual price increase. Therefore, instead of fixing a forward sale, he decides to use a put option as a hedge. Hedge strategies which use put options against a long physical position offer an important advantage over the futures hedge: in declining markets, they provide protection against downside risk, while at the same time, in rising markets, retaining unlimited profit potential.

The overall performance of the **synthetic long call** strategy will be critically dependent upon the development between the gold put option's exercise price, at which the hedge is instituted, and the subsequent gold futures price.

Key Terms

synthetic long call
an option strategy acquired by hedging a long underlying with a long put, also known as a protective put

Assumptions are as follows:

Long gold entry price (GEP): $885.80
Long put exercise price (X): $885
Premium paid (P_p): $14.90/oz.
Contract size: 100 oz.
Total premium paid: $1490 ($14.90 x 100 tr.oz)
Market expectations: Bullish on the underlying gold
Variable gold futures prices will be designated as (F_t)

Figure 11.6 illustrates the performance of a synthetic long call strategy.

Figure 11.6 Synthetic Long Call—Hedging Long Physical with Long Put

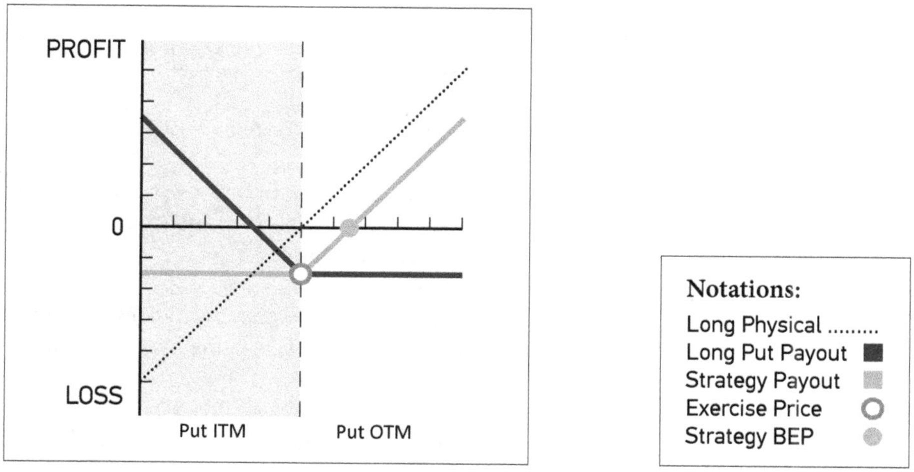

The synthetic long call strategy BEP is on the upside, therefore:

Strategy BEP = Gold Entry Price + Pp = \$885.80 + \$14.90 = \$900.70

The long put BEP is on the downside, therefore:

Long Put BEP = X – Pp = \$885 – \$14.90 = \$870.10

The net payout of the strategy, presented with the grey diagram, as you can see, is identical to the long call payout. For this reason this strategy is designated a **synthetic long call.** The same strategy is also referred to as a protective put, a term quite consistent with its intention—to provide protection against losses in declining markets by purchasing a put option.

The primary objective of the synthetic long call strategy is to protect a portfolio (long asset) against losses in falling markets, without losing out on possible price gains in rising markets.

We can now analyze synthetic long call performance in two different market scenarios: a falling market and a rising market.

SCENARIO I: FUTURES PRICE FALLS TO \$855; ITM

Exercise A synthetic long call is securing downside protection. Gains on a long put position offset the losses incurred on a long gold position; therefore, in declining markets losses are limited.

Suppose the gold futures price declined to \$855.00, the subsequent losses would be calculated as:

Long gold P&L = \$855.00 – \$885.80 =	–\$30.80
Long put intrinsic value =	+\$30.00
Premium paid =	–\$14.90
Ultimate loss =	–\$15.70

The above calculation is then equivalent to the following equation:

Loss = LIMITED = Long Put BEP – Gold Entry Price

Loss = Limited = \$870.10 – \$885.80 = \$15.70

As was the case with a synthetic long put, you do not have to calculate the performance of the strategy's individual constituents as the final result remains invariant to changes in the current futures price.

The ultimate loss, irrespective of changes in current futures prices, can never exceed \$15.70 (see Table 11.3). This is the maximum loss guaranteed by a synthetic long call option hedge.

Accordingly, the ultimate selling price is also limited.

In falling markets, the underlying futures price falls below the strike price, the long put option gets in-the-money and the holder is entitled to exercise his right—to acquire a short futures position at the strike price.

When a put option is exercised, the hedge unfolds as follows:

By exercising his rights the put option holder receives the positive difference between the strike price (X) and the current futures price (Ft), which equals \$3000, and acquires a short futures position at the current futures price (Ft) = \$85,500, minus the cost of the premium = \$1490.
The algebric equation for calculating the hedging outcome in falling markets is:

$$\text{Ultimate Selling Price} = (X - F_t) + F_t - P_p$$

Therefore, in the case of an adverse price movement, the calculating procedure consists of the following steps:

(X – Ft) = (\$885 – \$855) x 100 tr.oz. = +\$3000 (the difference received)
Acquires short futures: +100 x \$855
+Ft = +\$85,500
\$85,500 + \$3000 = +\$88,500
– Pp= –\$1490
\$88,500 – \$1490 = +\$87,010 : 100 = +\$870.10

The above calculation is then equivalent to the following equation:

$$\text{Ultimate Selling Price} = \text{LIMITED} = X - P_p$$

Ultimate selling price = Limited = \$885.00 – \$14.90 = \$870.10

Risk/ Reward A synthetic long call option strategy limits the downside risk; it confines the downfall to the amount of the strike price minus the premium paid. The synthetic long call option hedge will guarantee that the ultimate selling price never falls below \$870.10— the lowest selling price secured by the put option hedge, regardless of the eventual magnitude of the price fall. Compared to an open cash market position, the maximum loss is also limited to the difference between the long put BEP and the gold entry price: –\$15.70.

SCENARIO II: FUTURES PRICE RISES TO \$915; OTM

Abandonment If the stock price rises, the option gets out-of-the-money, the long put option expires unexercised and all of the premium is lost. But remember, rising markets are beneficial to the synthetic long call hedger—now the hedger can participate in the price gains as long gold starts to produce a positive return.

The long put option is therefore abandoned and the gold is sold at the current futures price of \$915.

In rising markets, profits will fluctuate relative to the gold futures price, falling behind exactly by the amount of the premium paid.

The corresponding profit calculation formula is as follows:

Profit = VARIABLE = Ft – Strategy BEP

Therefore, in the case where the futures price rises to \$915.00 the consequent profits would be calculated as follows:

Profit = Ft – Strategy BEP
= \$915.00 – \$900.70
= \$14.30

The profits are commensurate with the price increase (see Table 11.3). If the price rises to \$935.00 the profit would increase to \$34.30, but it will always fall behind for \$14.90 (the cost of the premium paid) compared to long gold P&L.

Accordingly, the ultimate selling price will also vary with the price of the underlying futures.

Ultimate Selling Price = VARIABLE = Ft – Premium Paid

Benefit If the market price rises above the strategy BEP (\$900.70), the synthetic long call position begins to prove beneficial. The put option is allowed to expire unexercised while the long gold position now may be closed at a higher market price. The benefit is commensurate with the price increase. The higher the ultimate futures price the higher the profit. Compared to an open cash market position—the physical long gold—the profit potential resulting from a synthetic long call strategy is also theoretically unlimited, although reduced—it falls behind by the amount of the put premium paid. The scorecard of individual payouts is summarized in Table 11.3:

Table 11.3 Synthetic Long Call Metrics

Underlying Gold Futures	Long Put 885@14.90 Intrinsic Value	Long Put Premium	Long Put P&L	Long Gold P&L 885.80	Synthetic Long Call P&L
A	B	C	D	E	D + E
835	50	–14.90	35.10	–50.80	–15.70
855	30	–14.90	15.10	–30.80	–15.70
860	25	–14.90	10.10	–25.80	–15.70
870.10	14.90	–14.90	0	–15.70	–15.70
880	5	–14.90	–9.90	–5.80	–15.70
885	0	–14.90	–14.90	–0.80	–15.70
885.80	0	–14.90	–14.90	0	–14.90
890	0	–14.90	–14.90	4.20	–10.90
895	0	–14.90	–14.90	9.20	–5.90
900.70	0	–14.90	–14.90	14.90	0
910	0	–14.90	–14.90	24.20	9.30
915	0	–14.90	–14.90	29.20	14.30
935	0	–14.90	–14.90	49.20	34.30

Protective Put Disadvantages:

- Cost of the put option reduces overall profit.
- Time decay: negative. As time nears expiration the call value portion erodes (i.e., decays). There is a risk of losing all of the premium invested even if the price of the stock remains stable.
- Compared to a long cash market position: on the upside, profits fall behind by the amount of the premium paid.
- Compared to a futures hedge: limited losses are generated in falling markets. On the downside, if the price of the underlying declines below the strategy BEP, hedging with futures would be more beneficial.

Protective Put Advantages:

- The cost to buy the insurance on a long asset by purchasing a put option is generally cheaper relative to initiating a futures hedge.
- A protective put allows you to hold on to your long asset and participate in the upside potential while at the same time providing insurance against losses on the downside.
- Compared to a long cash market position: loss is limited and known in advance. Profits are variable and commensurate with the price increase, although reduced by the cost of the premium.
- Compared to a futures hedge: on the upside, above the strategy BEP, the protective put payout is more advantageous than the futures payout.

Advantages ensuing from options flexibility:

Rolling-up Long Put Options Instead of exiting the trade at a profit you might roll-up the put by selling the contract you own and buying another one at a higher strike price. By rolling-up the long put you retain the insurance against downside risk, while at the same time you can participate in upside profit potential.

The mechanics of rolling the call are illustrated in the following example.

Example: Rolling Up Long Put Options

EXAMPLE: We keep the same assumptions as in the protective call example.
Annualized gold implied volatility is 15%, so the gold prices are expected to finish between \$840 and \$930 within a 30 calendar day time frame. Let us suppose that after 10 days, gold futures first rise to \$900.00 and then, at expiration, retreat to \$870.00 .
The consequential call price simulation is derived from the BS model.

Gold futures rally from \$885.80 to \$900

Put option goes "out-of-the-money"; Premium falls to \$6.25 (the put has not expired yet and therefore will retain some value, which will help reduce the cost of the new put).
Roll-up → Sell back long put option for \$6.25
(loss incurred = +\$6.25 – \$14.90 = –\$8.65)
Buy new put (same expiration) at higher strike \$900 for \$12.35.
Total premium cost = –\$21.00 (–\$12.35 – \$8.65)

At expiration gold futures retreats to \$870.00

Put Exercised → Long put converted to short futures: +\$900
Minimum selling price: \$879.00 (\$900.00 – \$21.00);
Original minimum selling price: \$870.10
The overall profit from rolling-up: \$8.90 (\$879.00 – \$870.10)

To conclude the synthetic long call hedging strategy, in Table 11.7, we include the comparison of the three different put options quotes from the COMEX Gold Option chart as of 9 May 2008. The net effects are greatly influenced by the option strike price and the premium the hedger chooses to buy.

Figure 11.7 Synthetic Long Call—Three Strategies Compared

GOLD ENTRY PRICE $885,80
100 troy oz., dollars per troy oz. (COMX)

Long Put OTM	Long Put ATM	Long Put ITM
Exercise Price (X) $860 Premium Paid ($P_P$) $5.90	Exercise Price (X) $885 Premium Paid ($P_P$) $14.90	Exercise Price (X) $910 Premium Paid ($P_P$) $31.30
Futures Price Rise to $915 ABANDON	Futures Price Rise to $915 ABANDON	Futures Price Rise to $915 ABANDON
Variable Profits Formula = Ft – Strategy BEP **1.** $23.30	Variable Profits Formula = Ft – Strategy BEP **2.** $14.30	Variable Profits Formula = Ft – Strategy BEP **3.** –$2.10
Futures Price Fall to $855 EXERCISE	Futures Price Fall to $855 EXERCISE	Futures Price Fall to $855 EXERCISE
Limited Losses = Long Put BEP – GEP **3.** –$25.80	Limited Losses = Long Put BEP – GEP **2.** –$15.70	Limited Losses = Long Put BEP – GEP **1.** –$7.10
BEP = GEP + P_P = $891.70	**BEP** = GEP + P_P = $900.70	**BEP** = GEP + P_P = $917.10

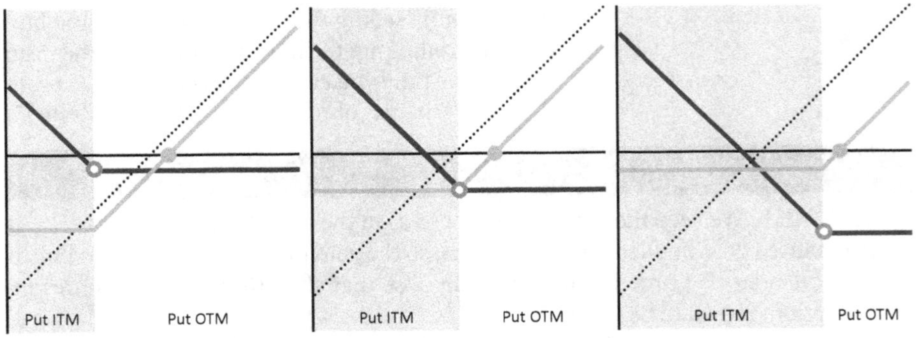

Notations:
Long Physical ....
Long Put Payout ■
Strategy Payout ■
Exercise Price ○
Strategy BEP ●

Synthetic Long Call Hedge —Three Strategies Final Comments

- A synthetic long call hedge (protective put) is a strategy instituted to provide insurance in the case of a price decline while at the same time retaining the advantage of being able to participate fully in a favourable price increase.
- If exercised, in the case of a price decline, a protective put provides a "floor" selling price that can efficiently limit the loss. Hence, the best result is achieved with an in-the-money put and the poorest with an out-of-the-money put. The higher the insurance the higher the cost.
- If abandoned, the lowest put premium purchased offers the highest benefit from the price increase. Therefore the maximum benefit is secured with an out-of the-money put and the poorest with an in-the-money put.

SYNTHETIC SHORT CALL OPTION STRATEGY

HEDGING AGAINST PRICE RISE BY WRITING A PUT

Motives We are following the case of another gold artisan, short of physical gold and with a different view in regard to near-term gold market development. We are at the beginning of May and the physical gold (100 tr. oz.) is required in the month of June. The sale price of gold jewellery is concluded based on the current gold price of $885.80/tr.oz. Now the gold artisan needs to hedge his position against a possible price rise. Before making a final decision he considers several alternatives; one of the choices is to buy the equivalent amount of June futures, thus locking-in the gold purchase price. Instead, as he is not expecting large moves in the price, he decides to write a put as his hedge. He is contrary to the put option holder, expecting low volatility and a stable market. But nevertheless, he wants to get some insurance against an eventual price increase. If he is right about the market trend and the price stays where it is, his strategy will prove profitable. At the same time, he is virtually taking the other side of the put option holder therefore the assumptions remain the same.

Strategy assumptions are as follows:

Gold entry price (**GEP**): $885.80
Short put exercise price (**X**): $885
Premium received (**P**$_r$): $14.90/oz.
Contract size: 100 oz.
Total premium paid: $1570 ($15.70 x 100 tr.oz)
Market expectations: Neutral to bearish on the underlying gold
Variable gold futures prices will be designated as (F$_t$)

| **Figure 11.8** | Synthetic Short Call Hedge-Hedging Short Physical with Short Put |

Notations:
Short Physical
Short Put Payout ■
Strategy Payout ▨
Exercise Price ○
Strategy BEP ●

Key Terms

synthetic short call

an option strategy acquired by hedging a short underlying with a short put, also covered put

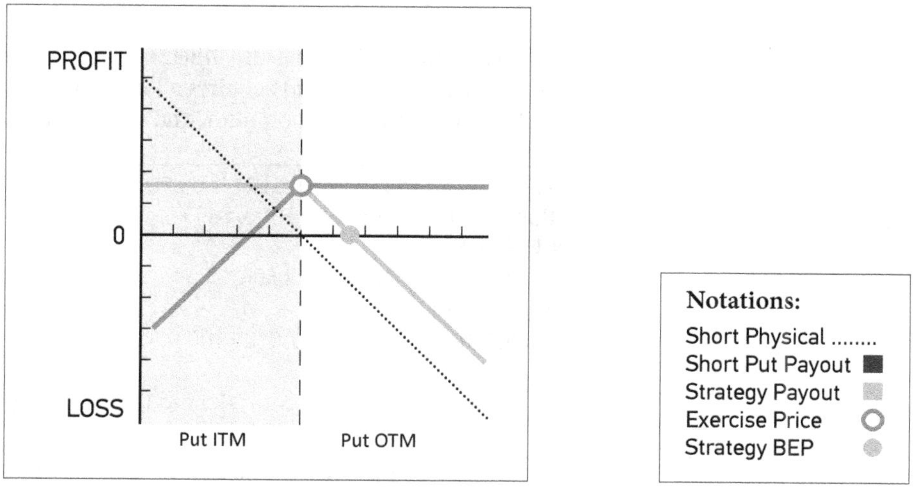

The net payout of the strategy, presented with a grey diagram, as you can see, is identical to a short call payout. This is the reason the strategy is designated a **synthetic short call**. The same strategy is also known as a covered put.

Synthetic short call strategy BEP is on the upside:

Strategy BEP = Gold Entry Price + Premium = \$885.80 + \$14.90 = \$900.70

The short put BEP is on the downside, therefore:

Short Put BEP = (\$885 – \$14.90) = \$870.10

SCENARIO I: FUTURES PRICE FALLS TO \$855; ITM

Assignment The short put option is now in-the-money and the writer receives a notice of assignment, pays the difference between the strike and current futures price and acquires a short futures position at the current price of \$855.

In a falling market synthetic short call strategy profits are limited and may be calculated according to the following formula:

Profit = LIMITED = Gold Entry Price – Short Put BEP

Profit = Limited
Profit = Gold entry price – short put BEP
= \$885.80 – \$870.10
= \$15.70

Writing a short put option against a short asset limits the downside profit potential. Accordingly, the ultimate purchase price is also limited.

If assigned, the sequence of transactions would unfold as follows:

Ultimate Purchase Price = –(X – Ft) – Ft + Premium Received

The put option writer pays the difference between the exercise price (X) and the current futures price (Ft) and acquires a long futures position at the current futures price (Ft) plus the cost of the premium. The step-by-step calculation is as follows:

–(X –Ft) = –(885 – 855) x 100 tr.oz. = –\$3000 (the difference paid)
Buys 100 tr.oz. of gold: –100 x \$855
–Ft = –\$85.500
– \$3000 – \$85.500 = –\$88.500
+ Pr = \$1490
–\$88.500 + \$1490 = –\$87.010 : 100 = –\$870.10

The above calculation is equivalent to the following equation:

Ultimate Purchase Price = LIMITED = $-X + P_r$ = –\$ 870.10

The ultimate purchase price of \$870.10 is also the maximum purchase price locked-in by put writing. That is for \$15.10 higher than the ultimate market price of \$855, but better than \$885.80—the price he would have received if he had entered the hedge with futures. The strategy foregoes the benefit of price decline. In this case no hedging would prove to be the more beneficial strategy.

SCENARIO II: FUTURES PRICE RISES TO $915; OTM

Abandonment If the underlying futures price rises to $915.00, the short put option enters the "out-of-the-money" zone allowing the short put to expire unexercised. The hedger is then left with a short gold position and the losses incurred due to the rising prices would be diminished by the amount of the put option premium received.

In rising markets, a synthetic short call instituted as a hedge against a short physical position generates losses. The losses will fluctuate relative to the gold futures price and the formula for calculating the returns is the following:

Loss = VARIABLE = –(Ft – Strategy BEP)

Following the assumption given in Scenario II, the calculation of the subsequent losses would unwind as follows:

Loss = –(Ft – Strategy BEP)
= –($915 – $900.70)
= –$14.30

If the gold futures price rises to $935.00, then the net strategy loss is $34.30. The losses are commensurate with the price rise (see Table 11.4).

Comparing to short gold payout, losses incurred on the synthetic short call strategy always fall behind for exactly $14.90 (the value of the put premium received). However, in upward markets the fixed hedge through selling forward would prove to be a more advantageous strategy.

Accordingly, the ultimate purchase price is also variable.

Ultimate Purchase Price = VARIABLE = –(Ft – Pr)

Ultimate purchase price = Variable = –($915 – $14.90) = –$900.10

Should the futures price rise to $935, then the ultimate purchase price would be $920.10.

Buffer Effect Writing a short put against a short physical position provides insurance against the upside risk. If you look at the grey diagram in Figure 11.8 you will notice that the premium of the short call sold performs as a "buffer" against losses in an upward market.

The so-called "buffer effect" would be proportionate to the amount of the premium sold: the higher the premium, the higher the protection effect.

Risk/Reward The synthetic short call strategy best results fall within the range $870.10 on the downside (exercise price – premium received) and $900.70 on the upside (June futures + premium received). The strategy will be greatly influenced by volatility (the lower the better) and the amount of the premium received (the higher the better). If prices increase above $900.70 hedging with futures would be the preferable strategy, if prices decline below $870.10 then no hedging would prove to be a more beneficial choice.

The scorecard of individual constituent gains and losses coalesce to a synthetic short call payoff as exhibited in Table 11.4:

Table 11.4 Synthetic Short Call Metrics

Underlying Gold Futures	Short Put 885@14.90 Intrinsic Value	Short Put Premium	Short Put P&L	Short Gold P&L 885.80	Synthetic Short Call P&L
A	B	C	D	E	D + E
835	–50	14.90	–35.10	50.80	15.70
855	–30	14.90	–15.10	30.80	15.70
860	–25	14.90	–10.10	25.80	15.70
870.10	–14.90	14.90	**0**	15.70	15.70
880	–5	14.90	9.90	5.80	15.70
885	0	14.90	14.90	0.80	15.70
885.80	0	14.90	14.90	**0**	14.90
890	0	14.90	14.90	–4.20	10.70
895	0	14.90	14.90	–9.20	5.70
900.70	0	14.90	14.90	–14.90	**0**
910	0	14.90	14.90	–24.20	–9.30
915	0	14.90	14.90	–29.20	–14.30
935	0	14.90	14.90	–49.20	–34.30

We believe that successful investing and management is about diversification of risk and in that respect the full knowledge and understanding of possible alternatives and case scenarios cannot be overstated.

Accordingly, and consistent with our previous research, in Table 11.5 we have included a compendium of risk characteristics associated with the expected risk-reward profile encountered in the four basic hedging strategies using plain vanilla options.

Remember This! LME Traded Options Specifics

In case you intend to use the London Metal Exchange as a medium for price discovery and hedging purposes you have to be aware of the specifics of this particular exchange. On LME, the most recognized non-ferrous metals trading environment, options contracts are backed with a corresponding futures contract.
The "value date" of the underlying futures contract is predetermined at the time of initiating the options contract and remains fixed. Monthly value dates are always set to be the third Wednesday of the "prompt month."
The prompt month is the month during which the contract expires! The holder of the option is entitled to "declare" or "exercise"" the option at any time during the validity of the option until the "declaration date" which designates LME Traded Options as "American-Style Options!" Upon declaration, the option will be converted in the corresponding futures contract. The declaration date (the last date at which you are entitled to exercise the option) at LME is always set to be the first Wednesday of the prompt month. It should also be emphasized that there is hardly ever a practical inducement for declaring an LME option early. On the contrary, you would be much better off to resist declaration, if at all, until the declaration date since holding an option contract provides a protection from an adverse price move while with an open futures contract risk exposure is open on both sides.

Table 11.5 Basic Option Hedging Strategies Resume

Protective Call Hedge Protection From A Price Rise	Covered Call Hedge Protection From A Price Fall
Asset at Risk: Short Gold@$885.80	Asset at Risk: Long Gold@$885.80
Hedge Instrument: Long Call Option	Hedge Instrument: Short Call Option
Strategy Protects from the Price Rise	Strategy Benefits from the Price Rise
Price Rise → Exercise Long Call Option (ITM)	Price Rise → Short Call Assigned (ITM)
Potential Loss Limited = GEP – Long Call BEP	Potential Profit Limited = Short Call BEP – GEP
Strategy Benefits from the Price Fall	Reduced Exposure in case of Price Fall
Price Fall → Abandon Long Call (OTM)	Price Fall → Abandon Short Call (OTM)
Ultimate Profit Variable = Strategy BEP – Ft	Ultimate Loss Variable = –(BEP – Ft)
Protective Call BEP on the Downside = Underlying Gold Entry Price – Premium	Covered Call BEP on the Downside = Underlying Gold Entry Price – Premium

Protective Put Hedge Protection From A Price Fall	Covered Put Hedge Protection From A Price Rise
Asset at Risk: Long Gold@$885.80	Asset at Risk: Short Gold@$885.80
Hedge Instrument: Long Put Option	Hedge Instrument: Short Put Option
Strategy Protects from the Price Fall	Strategy Benefits from the Price Fall
Price Fall → Exercise Long Put Option (ITM)	Price Fall → Short Put Assigned (ITM)
Potential Loss Limited = Long Put BEP – GEP	Potential Profit Limited = GEP – Short Put BEP
Strategy Benefits from the Price Rise	Reduced Exposure in case of Price Rise
Price Rise → Abandon Long Put (OTM)	Price Rise → Abandon Short Put (OTM)
Ultimate Profit Variable = Ft – Strategy BEP	Ultimate Loss Variable = –(Ft – Strategy BEP)
Protective Put BEP on the Upside = Underlying Gold Entry Price + Premium	Covered Put BEP on the Upside = Underlying Gold Entry Price + Premium

3 BASIC ORDER TYPES ON OPTIONS CONTRACTS

The order types on option contracts follow the same logic as order types on futures only that you have to remember that call options gain in value with the underlying price increase while put options gain in value with a price decline.

1. MARKET ORDER

If the market is trading currently at $4.52 your order will be filled immediately at the best available price close to the market price.
Example: Buy 5 Dec. Crude Oil 9300 calls AT THE MARKET TO OPEN (no price specified).

2. LIMIT ORDER

With a limit order you are specifying a price level at which an order must be executed – at limit price or better!

If the market is currently trading at $4.52 and you place an order to buy 5 December call contracts at 4.15, it's a buy limit.
Example: Buy 5 Dec. Crude Oil 9300 calls AT $4.15 LIMIT TO OPEN
If the market is currently trading at 4.52 and you place an order to sell 5 December call contracts at $4.95, it's a sell limit.
Example: Sell 5 Dec. Crude Oil 9300 calls AT $4.95 LIMIT TO OPEN

3. STOP ORDER

By entering the stop order you are setting a certain price level of your choice, needed to be triggered to convert the stop order to market order.
If the market is trading at $4.57 and your order is to buy at $4.90 it's a buy limit instructing your broker to execute only if and when the market breaks the buy stop level.
Example: Buy 5 Dec. Crude Oil 9300 calls AT $4.90 STOP TO OPEN
If the market is trading at $4.57 and your order is to sell at $4.20 it's a sell limit instructing your broker to execute only if and when the market falls through the sell stop level.
Example: Buy 5 Dec. Crude Oil 9300 calls AT $4.20 STOP TO OPEN
This table illustrates the data required for options order placement:
Provisional Options Order Ticket: NYMEX Light Sweet Crude Oil, December 2008 call option 9300 exercise price, "Premium Value" $4.52:

1.	2.	3.	4.	5.	6.	7.	8.	9.	10.	11.
Peter Jones Account 000123	Option Order	Buy or Sell	10	Dec 2008	Strike 93.00	NYMEX Crude oil	Calls	Open	Limit Order 4.45	GTC
NAME & Acc No.	Option Order	Market Action	QTY	Delivery Month	Exercise Price	Exchange Contract	CALL or PUT	Open or Close	Order Type	Order Action

1. State your name and account number.
2. State that you are entering an option order.
3. State market action: whether this order is a buy or sell.
4. State the number of contracts.
5. State the delivery month and year.
6. State the exercise price you choose to trade.

7. State the exchange and contract to be traded.
8. Never fail to state whether this is call or put option.
9. Every step is equally important as it will designate your risk profile, so remember to state whether you are buying or selling to open a new position or to close an existing position
10. Order type. Limit Order (or any of the specific order types available).
11. GTC (Good Till Cancelled).

SUMMARY

Chapter 11 elaborates the four basic hedging strategies using options. Two of them are labelled "protective strategies," implying that an option contract initiated as a hedge against an underlying asset serves as insurance or protection in case the price of the underlying moves contrary to our expectations.

We began our analysis and illustration with the protective call (synthetic long put strategy)—constructed by purchasing a long call against a short gold position. This strategy limits the loss in upward markets but retains potential profits in declining markets. We then explained how to calculate the ultimate purchase prices and relative profits and losses. The net performance of this strategy is presented graphically and numerically. We also tied together a comparison of the three different concepts and repercussions on net strategy payouts, ensuing from different call options' exercise prices. These results are presented in Table 11.4.

Another protective strategy was the protective put strategy (synthetic long call strategy)—constructed by purchasing a long put against a long gold position. This strategy limits the losses in downward markets but retains the potential for profits in rising markets. The same comparative analysis of three concepts ensuing from three different put option exercise prices is included in Table 11.7.

Then, we covered the synthetic short call strategy—constructed with a short put written against a short underlying.

This strategy payout offers limited downside profit potential while reducing upside risk. In that respect, the premium received for put writing serves as a buffer against possible losses in rising markets.

Finally, we discussed the synthetic short put strategy—constructed with a short call written against the long gold position. This strategy payout offers limited upside profit potential while reducing downside risk. In that respect, the premium received for call writing serves as a buffer against possible losses in falling markets.

KEY TERMS

option spread
combination
synthetic option
protective calls & puts
covered calls & puts
synthetic long put
synthetic short put
buffer effect
opportunity cost
synthetic long call
synthetic short call

CHAPTER 12

TYPICAL EQUITY HEDGING STRATEGIES

CHAPTER OBJECTIVES

- To introduce and explain the most popular equity strategies; covered call and covered put.
- To illustrate the "Three Strategies Comparison" and show how the strategy payoff profiles are affected relative to changes in option prices.

COVERED CALL WRITING

Key Terms

covered call

an option strategy acquired by writing a call on a stock you purchase, also synthetic short put

buy write

see covered call

overwrite

a variation of a covered call, it implies writing a call on a stock you already own

ONE OF THE MOST COMMON AND WIDELY USED STRATEGIES RELATED TO STOCK options is definitely **covered call** writing. The concept implies writing a call option and at the same time purchasing an equivalent amount of shares of the underlying stock. With that being the case, the naked call has been collateralized in full (covered), hence—covered call. The same strategy is also known as "**buy write**" and, its modification, distinguished as "**overwrite**", implies writing a call on a stock you already own.

The potential net gain is to be expected on the upside price move and its utmost value attainable is limited to the premium received plus the difference between the strike price and the stock purchase price. This will be realized if the stock price exceeds the call option strike price at the expiration—in which case you should be prepared to execute your obligation to deliver the underlying shares of stock at the option strike price. But the risky assignment is now "covered" by the stock held in the portfolio.

A covered call writer is willingly committed to sacrifice the full profit potential on the long stock in exchange for the premium collected and moderate downside protection.

The eventual profit will, therefore, be greatly influenced by the strike price of the call you choose to sell and the amount of the premium you receive for it. In what follows, we shall exhibit how these different choices affect the resulting exposure.

The protection from a downside price movement is covered only partially by the amount of the premium collected; below the BEP the strategy incurs a one-to-one loss with the long stock. The loss on the long stock position can be substantial, so it is worth noting that writing a covered call is not a very safe way of covering the risk associated with the stock ownership. Nonetheless, it is true that covered writing is less risky than buying the stock outright.

In Figure 12.1 we review the basic concept of a covered call write, employing an at-the-money call—the option strike price equals the stock price purchased. In the next stage we shall expand the analysis by correlating it with other two scenarios: in-the-money and out-of-the-money calls.

Figure 12.1 Covered Call Writing Profit & Loss

Notations:
Long Stock
Short Call Payout ■
Strategy Payout
Exercise Price ○
Strategy BEP ●

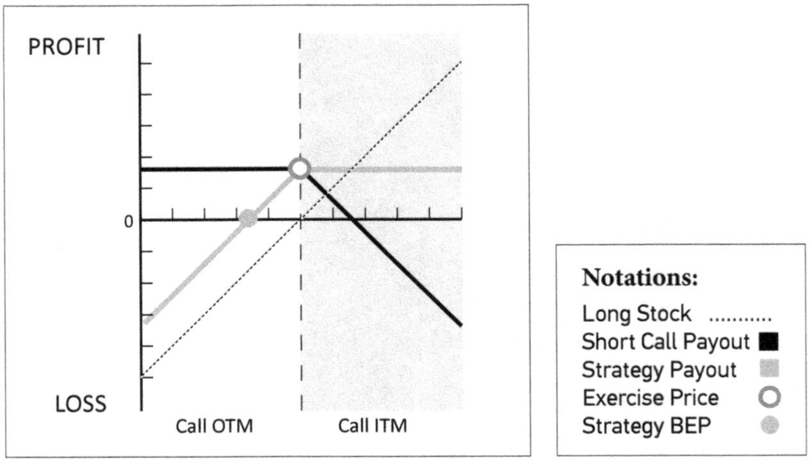

Strategy BEP = Long Stock Price – Premium Received

From the pattern depicted in Figure 12.1, it is easy to see that the covered call payoff corresponds with the payoff of a synthetic short put.
In position equation form: –P = –C + U

To illustrate the performance of the covered call strategy we shall use the same 3M (MMM) option's price chain as from the beginning of Chapter 10:

Stock price: $70.01
Write an ATM short call @70
Premium received: $3.91
Market expectations: Neutral to bullish on the underlying stock
Profit potential: Limited
Loss potential: Substantial

Motives The investor's principal aim is to retain the premium from writing a call, and at the same time, to benefit from stock ownership: dividends and voting rights. The premium received serves as a buffer to potential losses on a long stock position in case the price of the stock declines. If, on the other hand, the price of the underlying stock increases above the option strike price and the stock is called away from you, your overall strategy payoff will yield a limited profit.

SCENARIO I: UNDERLYING STOCK PRICE RISES TO $80; ITM

Call Assigned The stock moves in-the-money and the option writer receives a notice of assignment. You are obliged to deliver the shares at the exercise price. Your maximum profit is limited and can be calculated as per the following formula: exercise price + premium – cost of stock bought which comes to:

$70 + $3.91 – $70.01 = $3.90

Maximum Profit if Exercised = (Exercise Price + Premium) – Stock Cost

SCENARIO II: UNDERLYING STOCK PRICE FALLS TO $60; OTM

Abandonment If the stock price declines to $60 the stock option expires worthless. You retain the stock ownership and you keep the premium received. The premium is your profit but you have an unrealised loss on your long stock position (-$10.01 x 100). This loss is partially offset by the amount of the premium received, i.e., $391 ($3.91 x 100), so that your overall loss is mitigated with the premium ($391) and is only $610.

The strategy BEP is on the downside—the long stock price minus premium received—meaning that a covered call offers only limited protection from the price decline. If the price declines beyond the BEP the hedger will incur a point-to-point loss with the stock price fall.

Maximum Loss = BEP - Current Stock Price

The covered call resulting exposure is illustrated in Figure 12.1.

As should be self-evident from the diagram, in declining markets unrealized losses on the long stock position can be substantial, only mitigated by the premium the hedger receives from the initial call option sale.

A covered call's resulting exposure will be greatly influenced by the choice of the exercise price and corresponding premium. Anticipating the price increase, the investor has every reason to sell a call whose strike is deeper out-of-the-money. Conversely, if price decline seems to be more likely, then selling deeper in-the-money would be a better choice.

Strategy selection is in fact determined by order of preference. Depending on the order of priority, the investor will make a trade-off between the two competing alternatives—risk protection against profit potential. The two alternatives are mutually incompatible—the highest risk protection offers the least profit potential, and vice versa.

To illustrate how the different strike prices affect the overall strategy, we shall tabulate the three strategies, so that the implications of different strike prices and the respective premiums become more obvious.

Figure 12.2 Covered Call Writing–Three Strategies Compared

3M (MMM) Spot Price $70.01
November 2011 Options Chain as of 4 October 2011

Short Call ITM	Short Call ATM	Short Call OTM
Exercise Price (X)$65 Premium Received ($P_R$) $8.12	Exercise Price (X) $70 Premium Received ($P_R$) $3.91	Exercise Price (X) $77.50 Premium Received ($P_R$) $0.78
Spot Price (SP) Rise to $80 CALL ASSIGNED	Spot Price (SP) Rise to $80 CALL ASSIGNED	Spot Price (SP) Rise to $80 CALL ASSIGNED
Limited Selling Price Formula = X + P_R = **$73.12** Overall Profit (73.12 –70.01) 3. $3.11	Limited Selling Price Formula = X + P_R = **$73.91** Overall Profit (73.91 – 70.01) 2. $3.90	Limited Selling Price Formula = X + P_R = **$78.28** Overall Profit (78.28 – 70.01) 1. $8.27
Spot Price (SP) Fall to $60 CALL ABANDONED	Spot Price (SP) Fall to $60 CALL ABANDONED	Spot Price (SP) Fall to $60 CALL ABANDONED
Retain Stock: Unrealized Loss ($1001) Keep Premium $812 1. Overall P&L ($189)	Retain Stock: Unrealized Loss ($1001) Keep Premium $391 2. Overall P&L ($610)	Retain Stock: Unrealized Loss ($1001) Keep Premium $78 3. Overall P&L ($923)
BEP = SP – P_R = $61.89	**BEP = SP – P_R = $66.10**	**BEP = SP – P_R= $69.23**

Notations:
Long Stock
Short Call Payout ■
Strategy Payout ▨
Exercise Price ○
Strategy Pay-off ◉

Call OTM Call ITM Call OTM Call ITM Call OTM Call ITM

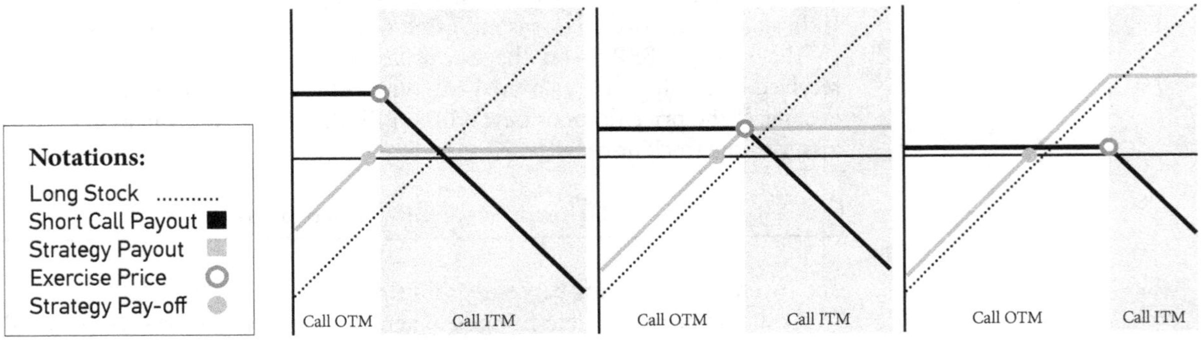

The three strategies comparison graph provides conclusive evidence of the following correlations: if the stock price drops below the strike price the strategy enters the negative zone; the short call expires without assignment, but the long stock position is exposed to unrealised losses—deeper in-the-money calls offer highest protection, whilst out-of-the-money calls offer poorer protection.

Conversely, if the stock prices go up, the short call will be assigned and the investor will be obliged to sell the underlying shares of stock at the strike price—deeper in-the-money calls offer the lowest profit potential, whereas out-of-the-money calls offer the highest.

But there is always a third alternative; the investor can choose to close out the written call with a closing purchase transaction—buy back the call written at the exchange before being assigned—thus cancelling the obligation to sell the underlying shares at the strike price. This would imply that benefits from the stock ownership continue to accrue, but covering the short call position will be realized at a loss, as the cost of call covering—closing purchase—is executed at a premium that is now higher than the premium initially received for the call option sold.

Buffer Effect Writing a short call against a long physical position provides insurance from the downside risk. If you look at the grey diagram in Figure 12.2 you will notice that the premium of the short call sold would perform as a "buffer" against losses in a downward market.

The so-called "buffer effect" would be proportionate with the amount of the premium sold: the higher the premium the higher the effect.

COVERED PUT WRITING

Key Terms

covered put
an option strategy acquired by holding a short stock position and at the same time writing a put on that stock, also synthetic short call

Holding a short stock position is inherently hazardous. To eliminate the imminent danger of price increase, many investors choose to "cover" the stock that is held short by writing a put, thus configuring a covered put strategy. The strategy payoff is identical to the naked call, and with respect to geometry is a mirror image of covered call writing. An inverse payoff geometry has a distinctive character frequently encountered in related option portfolios. Consequently, the idea behind covered put writing is the opposite of covered call writing: it is intended to increase the return on an existing short position commensurate with the premium received, and at the same time maintain a relative protection on the upside.
Observing the diagram depicted in Figure 12.3 it is easy to notice that "covered put strategy" is another term for synthetic short call.

In equation form: $-C = -P - U$

The performance of the covered put writing is demonstrated below.

Assumptions:

Stock price: $70.01
Write an ATM short put @70
Premium received: $2.23
Market expectations: Neutral to bearish on the underlying stock
Profit potential: Limited
Loss potential: Substantial

Figure 12.3 Covered Put Writing Profit and Loss

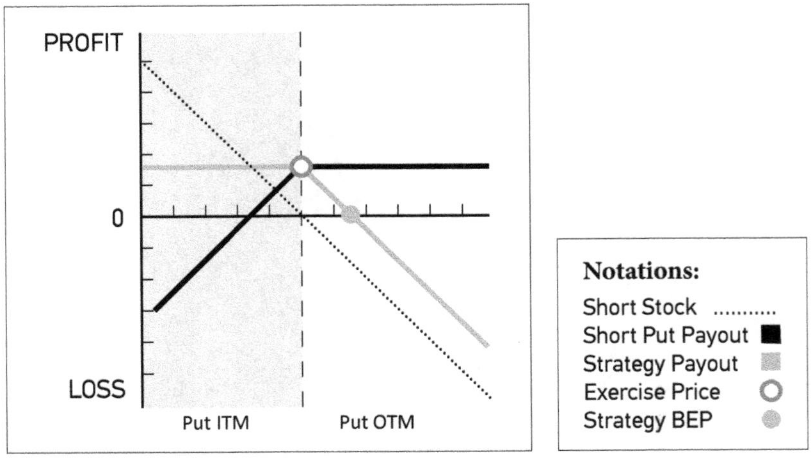

Strategy BEP = Short Stock Price + Premium Received

Motives As in the case of all short writing, the main motive behind option writing comes from the desire of an option writer to retain a premium on the option sold. In the particular case of a covered put the investor's second motive is to partially offset the actual risky position—the short stock—against the price rise. In this respect the amount of option premium sold will serve as a buffer against the undesirable price rise. At the same time, the covered put limits the profit potential of the short stock if the price moves downwards.

SCENARIO I: UNDERLYING STOCK PRICE FALLS TO $60; ITM

Put Assigned The stock moves into the in-the-money zone and the put option writer receives a notice of assignment. He is obliged to take delivery of the shares at the exercise price of $70. He closes the short stock position by delivering the shares at $70.01 for a $0.01 profit plus initial premium of $2.23. The overall strategy profit equals the initial premium plus the difference between the short stock and the put option exercise price of $2.23 + $0.01 = $2. 24

Maximum Profit if Exercised = Premium + (Stock Cost – Exercise Price)

The profit potential of the covered put writing is on the downside, therefore the underlying stock price has to fall below the break-even point in order to be profitable. Maximum profit is achieved when the underlying stock price is at, or falls beyond, the short put strike price.

SCENARIO II: UNDERLYING STOCK PRICE RISES TO $80; OTM

Abandonment If the underlying stock price increases above the exercise price then the put option enters the out-of-the-money zone and the option holder will have no interest in exercising. The option writer is left with the entire premium. But the short stock position initiated begins to lose value and is exposed to substantial losses.

The loss potential is on the upside and it is often quoted that covered put risk of loss is theoretically unlimited as there is no ceiling for the price increase.

The absolute loss is, however, mitigated by the value of the initial premium received from writing a put. In this scenario—a rising stock market—the put premium received serves to partially offset the loss on the short shares.

The price increase, however, has to pass beyond the BEP in order for the position to suffer any losses.

Maximum Loss = BEP – Current Stock Price

Maximum loss = ($70.01 + $2.23) – $80 = –$7.76 x 100 = –$776

To illustrate how the choice of different exercise prices could affect the overall strategy returns, we shall once again make use of the three strategies comparison so that the implications become more obvious.

In Figure 12.4 for illustration purposes we have selected three provisional price levels corresponding to three different option states, namely out-of-the-money, at-the-money and in-the-money.

Characteristics and performance metrics of covered put writing at each state—OTM, ATM and ITM—are disclosed in columns underneath each state, ending up with payoff diagrams of instruments configuring the covered put strategy. The three strategies comparison provides a comprehensive visualisation of the sensitivity and responsiveness of strategies' P&L profiles to a change in the exercise price.

Figure 12.4 Covered Put Writing–Three Strategies Compared

3M (MMM) Spot Price $70.01
November 2011 Options Chain as of 4 October 2011

Short Put OTM	Short Put ATM	Short Put ITM
Exercise Price (X) $65.00 Premium Received (P_R) $1.12	Exercise Price (X) $70.00 Premium Received (P_R) $2.23	Exercise Price (X) $75.00 Premium Received (P_R) $5.11
Spot Price (SP) Falls to $60 PUT ASSIGNED	Spot Price (SP) Falls to $60 PUT ASSIGNED	Spot Price (SP) Falls to $60 PUT ASSIGNED
Limited Purchase Price **Formula = –X + P_R = –$63.88** Overall Profit (70.01 – 63.88) **1.** $6.13	Limited Purchase Price **Formula = –X + P_R = –$67.77** Overall Profit (70.01 – 67.77) **2.** $2.24	Limited Purchase Price **Formula = –X + P_R = –$69.89** Overall Profit (70.01 – 69.89) **3.** $0.12
Spot Price (SP) Rise to $80 PUT ABANDONED	Spot Price (SP) Rise to $80 PUT ABANDONED	Spot Price (SP) Rise to $80 PUT ABANDONED
Close Short Stock ($999) Keep Premium $112 **3.** Overall P&L ($887)	Close Short Stock ($999) Keep Premium $223 **2.** Overall P&L ($776)	Close Short Stock ($999) Keep Premium $511 **1.** Overall P&L ($488)
BEP = SP + P_R = $71.13	**BEP** = SP + P_R = $72.24	**BEP** = SP + P_R = $75.12

Notations:

Short Stock
Short Put Payout ■
Strategy Payout ▨
Exercise Price ○
Strategy Pay-off ◉

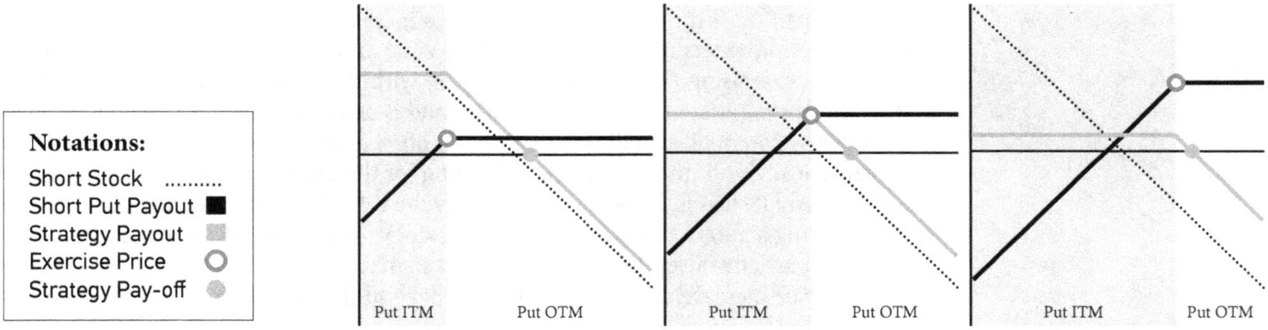

Conclusions ensuing from 12.4, in brief, are as follows: if prices finish beyond the break-even point the strategy stops earning money: deeper in-the-money puts offer the highest protection and less of a return, while out-of-the-money puts offer higher returns and less protection.

Put writing can also be liquidated prematurely. You can exit your short put position before exercise with a closing purchase. This implies that offsetting a short put will generate a loss as the cost of the short put covering—closing purchase—is executed at a premium that is now higher than the premium initially received for the put option sold.

If that is the case, then the investor is left with a short stock position that now generates a profit due to a price decline.

Buffer Effect Writing a short put against a short physical position provides insurance from the downside risk. If you look at the grey diagram in Figure 12.4 you will notice that the premium of the short call sold would perform as a "buffer" against losses in an upward market.

The so-called "buffer effect" would be proportionate to the amount of the premium sold: the higher the premium the higher the effect.

Remember This! Options Account Trading Levels

The stock options market in the USA is regulated by the Securities and Exchange Commission ("SEC") and governed by the rules of the Options Clearing Corporation ("OCC"). Within this framework, brokerage firms have broad discretion under their rules to impose a variety of terms and special requirements with respect to approval of customer accounts and impose restrictions on particular option transactions. As a novice trader, you may be surprised to learn that in advance of opening an options account you will be required to fill a fastidious "risk compliance form." The risk encountered in option trading is categorized in "levels" (the number and order of trading levels may differ subject to particular brokerage house preferences and discretionary rights). Every option trader should inquire scrupulously with his broker and learn about the risk compliance requirements and procedures applicable to the approval and opening of customers' accounts. The main purpose of options account trading levels is (or at least is declared to be) to ensure clients understand the challenges associated with options trading. Before they are allowed to initiate a trade in options issued by the OCC, all brokerage firms are entitled to make an assessment of a client's experience in options trading in order to determine the amount of risk suitable for novice traders and prevent inexperienced customers from applying for high risk and complex strategies.

Here is one example of possible Options Account Trading Levels:

Level 1 in the first place requires you to own stock in order to enter a trade—either a covered call or a protective put, then Level 2 allows you to purchase either a call or a put (debit trades), then, at Level 3, you are allowed to enter a covered put strategy as well as all kinds of debit spreads, at Level 4 you are allowed to use credit spreads, and lastly at Level 5 you are allowed to trade naked short calls and puts (credit trades) and their combinations: straddles and strangles. In seeking observable facts that would justify such a classification we shall find without difficulty that the classification itself is a bit flimsy and may easily be challenged. For example, at Level 3 you are allowed to enter a covered put strategy as well as all kinds of debit spreads, while at Level 4 you are allowed credit spreads, suggesting that "debit strategies" turn out to be less risky and "credit strategies" turn out to be more risky. This division is unsustainable—there is no sound justification for why a debit spread should be less risky than a credit spread; in particular why would a bull call spread and a bear put spread be less risky than a bear call and a bull put spread, while all of them have the same range-bound risk profile? It is also disputable to claim that the long straddle/strangle is less risky than the short straddle/strangle.
So, it seems that the real division lies with the trades paying premium and the trades collecting premium, where the trades paying premium is regarded to be less risky, and the risk of losing the premium is treated as being nonexistent and a rather sustainable write-off. It could be argued then that the purpose of risk assessment is not to provide safety of investment and protect your account from unnecessary losses but simply to gain liquidity by collecting premiums.

STRATEGY	OPTIONS TRADING LEVELS				
	Level 1	Level 2	Level 3	Level 4	Level 5
Covered Call/Protective Puts	x	x	x	x	x
Buying Stock or Index Puts & Calls		x	x	x	x
Covered Put/Debit Spreads			x	x	x
Credit Spreads				x	x
Uncovered Put & Call Writing					x

SUMMARY

Covered call hedge Looking at the three strategies you will observe that the order of strategy payoff resembles a staircase sloping upwards from left to right. This order suggests that profit potential ascends from left to right in sympathy with the increase of the strike price written.

If exercised, in the case of price increase, the covered call limits the profit and the best result is achieved with an out-of-the-money call and the poorest with an in-the-money call.

If abandoned, the highest call premium sold offers the highest protection from the downfall.

Therefore the maximum risk protection is secured with an in-the-money call and the poorest with an out-of the-money call.

The mathematical expression of this relation can be formulated as follows:

Risk protection = Premium/Long stock
1. ITM $8.12 : $70.01 = 11.60%
2. ATM $3.91 : $70.01 = 5.58%
3. OTM $0.78 : $70.01 = 1.11%

Covered put hedge The order of strategy payoffs bears a resemblance to the staircase sloping downwards. The order suggests that the profit potential descends from left to right in opposition to the increase of the strike price written.

If exercised in the case of a price decline a covered put limits the profit and the best result is achieved with an out-of-the-money put and the poorest with an in-the-money put.

If abandoned, the highest put premium sold offers the highest protection from the price increase.

Therefore the maximum risk protection is secured with an in-the-money put and the poorest with an out-of the-money put.

Risk protection = Premium/Short stock
1. ITM $5.11 : $70.01 = 7.30%
2. ATM $2.23 : $70.01 = 3.18%
3. OTM $1.12 : $70.01 = 1.60%

Interpretation of risk protection parameters:

ITM = 7.30%
The stock price has to rise 7.30% before the position begins to lose money $70.01 x 1.073 = $75.12 = BEP

KEY TERMS

covered call
buy write
overwrite
covered put

PART 3

OPTIONS PRICING MODELS

[redacted]

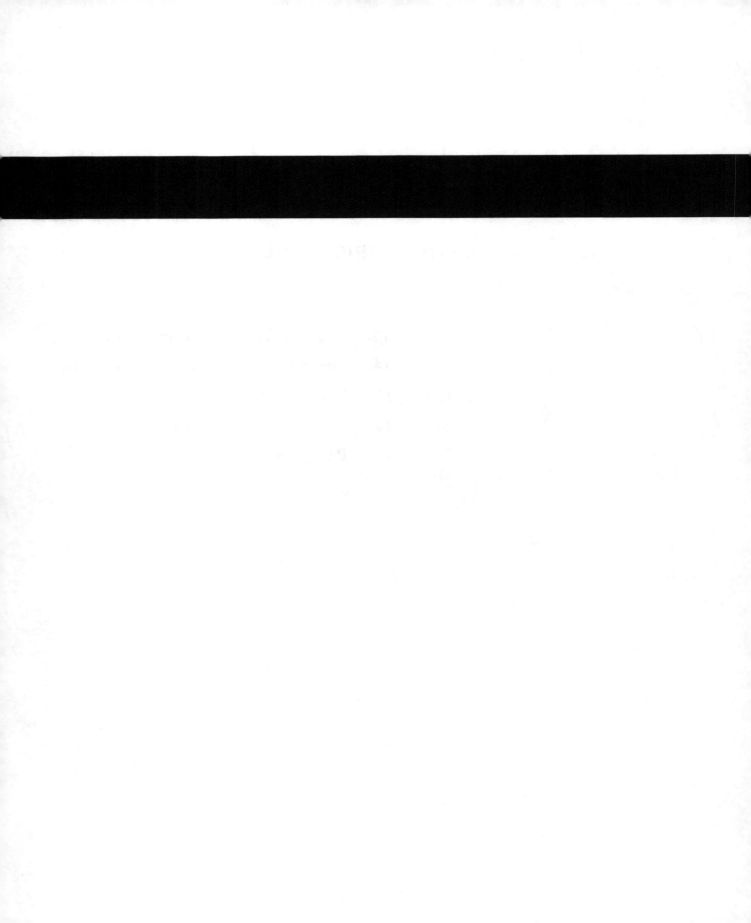

CHAPTER 13

DETERMINANTS OF OPTIONS VALUE

CHAPTER OBJECTIVES

- To identify the four major factors influencing an option's premium: exercise price, underlying instrument price, time decay, and volatility
- To discuss and disclose the main characteristics of each of the four parameters and illustrate how the changes in these factors correlate with the premium
- To focus and examine in particular the volatility issue and highlight the distinction between historical and implied volatility

I MAIN FACTORS INFLUENCING OPTION PREMIUM

THE NEXT STEP IN MASTERING OPTION BASICS WOULD BE THE ACQUAINTANCE with the factors that determine option value. Again we will use the data for 3M Co (MMM) stock options chain taken on 22 December 2011.

3M Co.(MMM) **$80.97**
January 2012 Options Chain as of December 22/2011.

CALLS							Expire at close Friday* January 18, 2012
Strike	Symbol	Last	Chg	Bid	Ask	Vol	Int
70.00	MMM120121C00070000	10.35	+0.95	10.45	11.45	8	935
72.50	MMM120121C00072500	8.82	+1.14	8.40	8.90	2	620
75.00	MMM120121C00075000	6.42	+1.10	6.45	6.55	34	2,049
77.50	MMM120121C00077500	4.30	+0.70	4.30	4.40	100	2,584
80.00	MMM120121C00078000	2.54	+0.49	2.50	2.56	177	8,746
80.97	STOCK PRICE LAST AS OF 12/22/11 - 4:01 PM ET						
82.50	MMM120121C00082500	1.18	+0.26	1.15	1.19	515	6,705
85.00	MMM120121C00085000	0.37	+0.10	0.37	0.41	296	9,849
87.50	MMM120121C00087500	0.10	+0.03	0.08	0.11	45	7,556
90.00	MMM120121C00090000	0.06	+0.01	0.02	0.09	31	5,687
92.50	MMM120121C00092500	0.08	+0.07	0.01	0.08	1	2,304
95.00	MMM120121C00095000	0.07	+0.05	0.01	0.01	3	3,978

PUTS							Expire at close Friday* January 18, 2012
Strike	Symbol	Last	Chg	Bid	Ask	Vol	Int
70.00	MMM120121P00070000	0.27	−0.14	0.27	0.29	63	3,426
72.50	MMM120121P00072500	0.48	−0.21	0.45	0.49	121	6,526
75.00	MMM120121P00075000	0.84	-0.44	0.82	0.85	87	3,580
77.50	MMM120121P00077500	1.53	−0.50	1.48	1.52	167	10,963
80.00	MMM120121P00080000	2.63	−0.78	2.61	2.67	25	2,196
80.97	STOCK PRICE LAST AS OF 12/22/11 - 4:01 PM ET						
82.50	MMM120121P00082500	4.35	−1.15	4.30	4.40	100	5,482
85.00	MMM120121P00085000	6.77	−0.58	6.50	6.65	15	1,673
87.50	MMM120121P00087500	9.00	−1.50	8.90	9.10	5	3,365
90.00	MMM120121P00090000	12.85	+0.45	11.25	11.70	75	1,042
92.50	MMM120121P00092500	16.39	+1.99	13.50	15.50	1	770
95.00	MMM120121P00095000	24.10	+2.60	16.00	18.00	7	442

The main factors influencing the option premium are:

1. Exercise price
2. Underlying instrument price
3. Time decay
4. Implied volatility

EXERCISE PRICE VS. OPTION PREMIUM

Now let us return to the assortment of strike prices and corresponding premiums as can be seen from the 3M Co. NYSE (MMM) Options Chain.

To a careful observer the figures in the two columns: "Strike" and "Last" will reveal some conspicuous and very significant relations.

The lower the exercise price—the higher the premium of the call and conversely, the lower the premium of the put.

The higher the exercise price—the lower the premium of the call and conversely, the higher the premium of the put.

The relationship between strike prices and premiums seems to be logically coherent. Every investor would be willing to pay more premium if the call option strike is below the current price of the underlying. If the call strike is higher than the current underlying you would be willing to pay less premium, as you could buy the underlying spot at a cheaper price. An inverse relationship applies to put options.

Unlike the other pricing factors, the option strike price cannot change during options contract validity. The option exercise price is one of the standardized terms of every option contract: it is fixed and will remain unchanged throughout the life of the option contract. The choice of option strike prices and corresponding premiums, however, is left at the discretion of each individual investor; his estimate of future market performance and the risk appetite the investor is willing to put at stake. On the other hand, the price of the underlying is a free float and is subject to random and continuous change in both directions, up and down.

In options trading, the relationship between the exercise price of an option and the current trading price of its underlying asset is described as the option's **moneyness.** The dynamics of this relationship at any specific point of time is of crucial importance as it determines whether or not option contract contains intrinsic value or time value only.

Consequence options are divided into three categories:

1. In-the-money (ITM)
2. At-the-money or Near-the-money (ATM)
3. Out-of-the-money (OTM)

Table 13.1 Option's Moneyness

Exercise	Put Option		Call Option	
Price (X)	Moneyness	Premium	Premium	Moneyness
87.50	ITM	9.00	0.10	OTM
85.00	ITM	6.77	0.37	OTM
82.50	ITM	4.35	1.18	OTM
80.00	ATM	2.63	2.54	ATM
77.50	OTM	1.53	4.30	ITM
75.00	OTM	0.84	6.42	ITM
72.50	OTM	0.48	8.82	ITM

Key Terms

moneyness
the relationship between the exercise price of an option and the current trading price of its underlying asset

From Table 13.1 we can draw the following conclusions:

- The aggregate of call exercise price and option premium will always exceed the current price of the underlying instrument, for example:

- Option exercise price $75.00 + call premium $6.42 = $81.42 > $80.97 (UI)

> Exercise Price + Call Premium ≥ Current UI Price
> Difference = Extrinsic Value (Time Value + Volatility)

And conversely, the exercise price minus the put option premium will always be less than the current price of the underlying instrument, for example:

- Option exercise price $85.00 – put premium $6.77 = $78.23 < $80.97 (UI)

> Exercise Price – Put Premium ≤ Current UI Price
> Difference = Extrinsic Value (Time Value + Volatility)

Figure 13.1 illustrates the relationship between option's exercise price and premium in a way that will be easy to memorize.

Figure 13.1 Exercise Price vs. Option Premium

Exercise Price (X)	Put Premium	Call Premium
↑	↑	↓

Exercise Price (X)	Put Premium	Call Premium
↓	↓	↑

Put premiums rise and fall in accord with the exercise price, while call premiums are inversely correlated—they rise and fall in the opposite direction.

IN-THE-MONEY OPTIONS

The term refers to those options that would have made a profit if exercised, excluding the amount of initial premium. A call option is said to be in-the-money if the exercise price is lower than the current UI price. You will recall that as a call option holder you have the right to buy the UI at the exercise price. The lower the exercise price, the more profitable the option. If the MMM stock is trading at $80.97, all call options below that level are in-the-money; such as $80 call; $77.50 call, etc. That is the reason why call option buyers will be willing to pay higher premiums.

> Call Option: ITM   if X < UI Price = High Premiums

The converse applies to put option. The in-the-money put option implies that the exercise price is higher than the current UI price. The put option gives you the right to sell, therefore it derives its value from the underlying price fall. If you are holding a put option with an exercise price at $82.50, $85, or $87.50 and above, with the MMM stock trading at $80.97, all the put options are in-the-money. Hence, the option buyers are willing to pay higher premiums.

> Put Options: ITM   if X > UI Price = High Premiums

AT-THE-MONEY OPTIONS

The term refers to those options with exercise prices nearest to the price of UI as the perfect match would rarely be experienced. These options have no intrinsic value and if exercised would leave the trader's initial position unaffected.

Figure 13.2 Graphic Illustration of ITM; ATM & OTM Calls and Puts

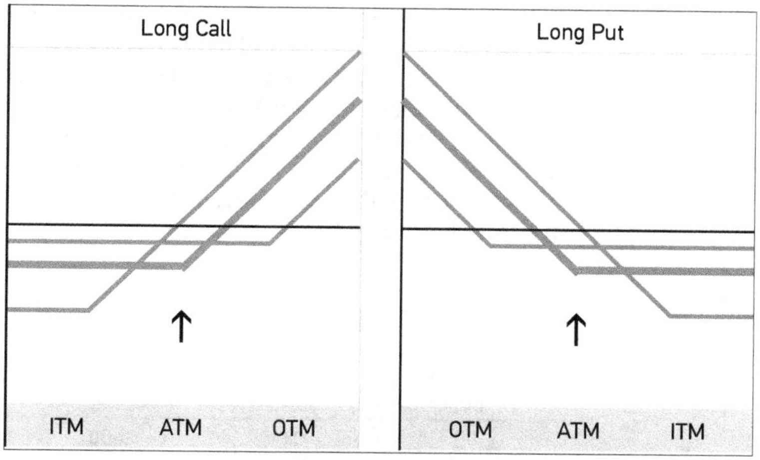

OUT-OF-THE-MONEY OPTIONS

The term refers to those that would generate a loss if exercised. Therefore, these options are left to expire worthless as they contain no intrinsic value. Quite obviously these OTM options cost less than the ITM. A call option is said to be out-of-the-money if the option exercise price is higher than the UI price.

Call Options: OTM	if X > UI Price = Low Premiums

For a put option it implies that the exercise price is lower than the UI price.

Put Options: OTM	if X < UI Price = Low Premiums

UNDERLYING INSTRUMENT VS. OPTION PREMIUM

In the same context, we can display the influence of the underlying instrument price on options premium. Stock prices (as well as any other exchange market security) are subject to constant fluctuations and take a "bumpy ride" each trading day. Changes in underlying stock prices will have diverse effects on the established option position.

Table 13.2 is a simulation of changes in option premiums against a range of different closing stock market prices over time. The model assumes that the stock option position is established at an $80.00 exercise price—with the corresponding premiums $2.54 put and $2.63 call—and varies the theoretical call and put values against fluctuations in the underlying stock price. You can observe the changes in premium for each price level of the underlying stock.

Table 13.2 UI Price vs. Option Premium

Price of Underlying	Put Option		Call Option	
	Moneyness	Premium	Premium	Moneyness
95	OTM	0.002	15.015	ITM
90	OTM	0.013	10.127	ITM
85	OTM	0.655	5.565	ITM
80	ATM	2.54	2.63	ATM
70	ITM	10.065	0.065	OTM
65	ITM	15.003	0.03	OTM
60	ITM	20	0	OTM

In the case of a call option, its premium rises commensurately with the referent stock price rise, and fall with the price decline. The rationale behind this is easy to understand. The spot price of MMM stock is $80.97 and you purchased an MMM $80 call at $2.54; after a rally the share price in the stock market goes to $90. Since you are holding the right to purchase the 3M shares for only $80, it is quite natural that the call premium will increase—its value is not $2.54 any more but say $10.127.

Compared to a put option, the relationship is inverted. The premium of a put will increase if the price of the UI goes down and decrease if it goes up. If you are holding the right to sell the underlying and the share price declines to $60, the put option will gain in value and its premium will rise accordingly to, say, $20—you can exercise the right to sell the asset at $80 while its market price is now worth only $60.

In Figure 13.3 we have illustrated how the change in price of the underlying affects call and put option premiums.

Figure 13.3 Underlying Instrument Price vs. Option Premium

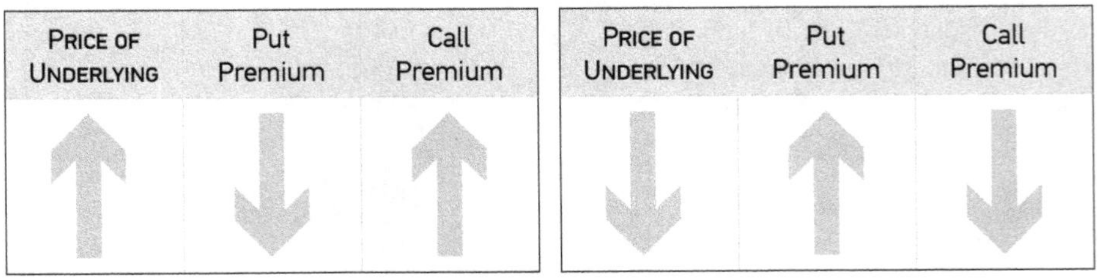

Key Terms

intrinsic value
the positive net value (calculated by taking the the difference between strike price and current market price of the UI) the option would acquire if it were to expire today. It is always either positive or zero

We wish to point out that an ITM option is always the most expensive option, and an OTM is always the least expensive, for obvious reasons. The more the option is ITM the more intrinsic value it has, and the more the option is OTM, the less are the chances that it will gain any value at expiration. Also, if you take a closer look at any option's chain chart you will notice another important relation: namely, you will notice that options with longer time to expiry (July) are a bit more expensive than options with a shorter time to expiry (March). This is because options with a longer time to expiration have increased the probability of larger price fluctuations, thus increasing the likelihood for the option to finish in-the-money—to gain intrinsic value before expiration.

The premium of an option is therefore composed of two components: intrinsic and extrinsic value.

Option Premium = Intrinsic value + Extrinsic Value

The **intrinsic value** is the actual net value the option would acquire if it were to expire today. It reflects the amount the option is in-the-money. Consequently, only in-the-money options contain intrinsic value. It is important to keep in mind that an option's intrinsic value is either positive or zero—in-the-money or not.

The intrinsic value of a call option represents the **positive difference** between the UI price and the exercise price:

Call Intrinsic Value = Current UI Price – Exercise Price

Table 13.3 Call Intrinsic Value

Price of Underlying	Call Option Moneyness	Call Option Premium	Intrinsic Value	Time Value
95	ITM	15.015	15	0.015
90	ITM	10.127	10	0.127
85	ITM	5.565	5	0.565
80	ATM	2.63	0	2.63
70	OTM	0.065	0	0.065
65	OTM	0.03	0	0.03
60	OTM	0	0	0

Table 13.3 shows the relationship between the price of the underlying security and the call option premium. The call premium value is split into its constituent units in separate columns—intrinsic value and time value. ATM option premium consists solely of time value.

Likewise, the intrinsic value of the put option is the **positive difference** between the exercise price and the current UI price:

Put Intrinsic Value = Exercise Price – Current UI Price

Tabular data exhibiting the relationship between the underlying price, put option premium intrinsic value, and time value is presented in Table 13.4.

Table 13.4 Put Intrinsic Value

Price of Underlying	Put Option Moneyness	Put Option Premium	Intrinsic Value	Time Value
95	OTM	0.002	0	0.002
90	OTM	0.013	0	0.013
85	OTM	0.655	0	0.655
80	ATM	2.54	0	2.54
70	ITM	10.065	10	0.65
65	ITM	15.003	15	0.003
60	ITM	20	20	0

A graphical exposition of the call and put intrinsic values (shaded areas) is presented in Figure 13.4:

Figure 13.4 Options Intrinsic Value Chart - Call and Put

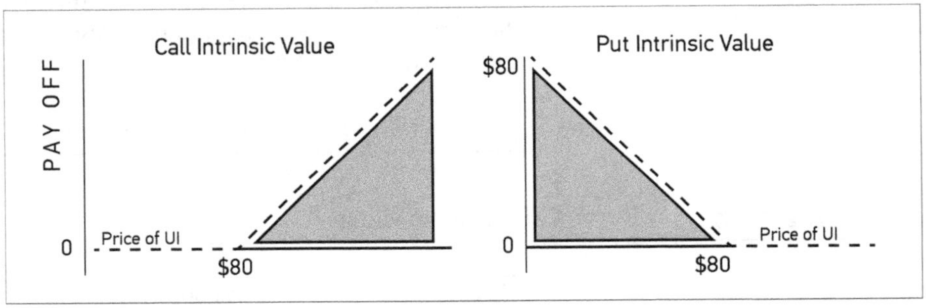

From the Figure 13.4 we can draw the following conclusion:

If the price of underlying stock rises above the call exercise price, the call option earns a positive payout. If the price of underlying stock goes below the exercise price, the call option payout is zero.

If the price of the underlying stock falls below the put exercise price, then the put option earns a positive payout. If the price of the underlying stock rises above the exercise price, the put option payout is zero.

The option's payout is always a non-negative value (either positive or zero).

Yet, a positive payout at expiration does not necessarily mean that your option will be profitable. If you hold a call option—to earn a profit—the price of underlying stock at expiration has to rise above the call option break-even point (exercise price + premium).

Accordingly, if you hold a put option—to earn a profit—the price of underlying stock at expiration has to fall below the put option break-even point (exercise price – premium).

A graphic scheme with combined payoff diagrams—the payoff diagrams (dashed black line) and P&L diagram (solid black line)—is exhibited in Figure 13.5. The empty space that separates the payoff from the P&L diagram denotes the premium value. Shaded triangles enclose the "in-the-money" zone, (beyond the relative break-even points) which is also the zone in which options begin to generate positive returns.

Figure 13.5 Options Profit and Loss Chart – Call and Put

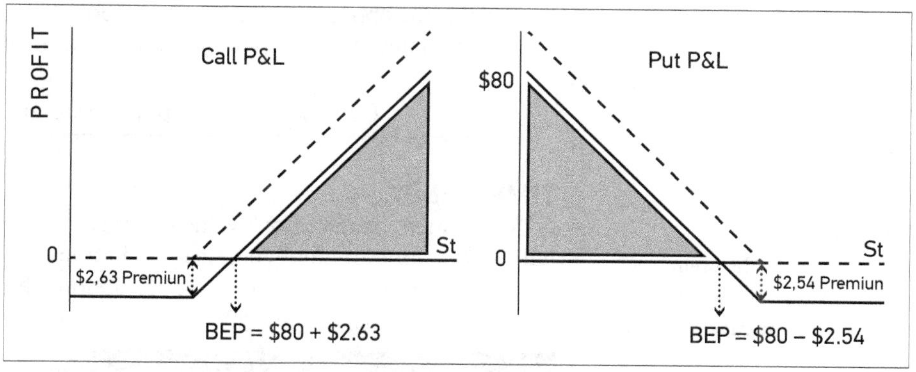

Our emphasis now shifts to the remaining two elements:

- Time decay, and
- Implied volatility.

TIME DECAY VS. OPTION PREMIUM

Key Terms

extrinsic value
the value option is deemed to be worth above its intrinsic value and is attributed to time value and volatility

time value
the fragment in the premium price in excess of any intrinsic value the option may or may not have

The complementary part of an option's premium is its **extrinsic value.** It can be defined as the value the option is deemed to have above its intrinsic value. This is often the case as extrinsic value is made up of time value and volatility.

Extrinsic Value = Option Premium – Intrinsic Value

TIME VALUE

Is the fragment of an option's value in excess of its intrinsic value? At-the-money and out-of-the-money options contain only time value—their intrinsic value is zero. Let us take a quick look at the figures from our options chart, remembering that the intrinsic values of both calls and put can either be positive or zero.

Example: Call Intrinsic Value 3M Stock Option

Current Stock price \$80.97; Exercise Price \$77.50; Premium \$4.30

UI > X (ITM)
\$80.97 (UI) –\$77.50 (X) = \$3.47 (Intrinsic Value)
Extrinsic Value = \$4.30 (Premium) –\$3.47 (Intrinsic Value) = **\$0.83**

Current Stock price \$80.97; Exercise Price \$82.50; Premium \$1.18

UI < X (OTM)
\$80.97 (UI) – \$82.50 (X) = 0 (Intrinsic value)
Extrinsic Value = \$1.18 (Premium) – 0 (Intrinsic Value) = **\$1.18**

The first example displays the case of call premium constiting of two parts: intrinsic value (\$3.47), and extrinsic, or time value in excess of its intrinsic value (\$0.83).

The second example shows the case of an option with zero intrinsic value; the premium is constituted of time value only (\$1.18).

If you were a novice investor you might ask yourself a sound question: Why does this \$82.50 call, with no intrinsic value, cost anything at all? If expired today those options would be worthless. Correct? Yes! But as long as there is any time left to expiration, these options retain the likelihood that the underlying spot price may move favourably in the future, thus making the option contract worth exercising. The only "value" those options contain is the potential of acquiring a positive value. When the time left to expiration is longer, the greater is the probability the price of UI will make a big move and that option will end up in-the-money. Buying time value is actually buying hope. Therefore an option with nine months expiry is worth more than one expiring in three months or one.

The examples that follow exhibit a call and a put option's hypothetical profit and loss diagrams over the course of 90-day expiration and across the range of different underlying asset prices.

Assumptions:
Expiration: 90 days
Long call strike: \$70
Premium: \$800 (\$8.00 x 100)

Table 13.5 exhibits the change in call premium relative to time left to expiration.

Table 13.5 P&L Metrics of 90-day Long Call on Various Dates/Spot Prices

Spot Price	$60	$65	$70	$75	$80	$85
Premium Cost	–$800	–$800	–$800	–$800	–$800	–$800
85-Day Call Value (C1)	$300	$500	$800	$1100	$1500	$1800
P&L (C1–$800)	–$500	–$300	$0	$300	$700	$1000
30-Day Call Value (C2)	$100	$200	$500	$800	$1100	$1600
P&L (C2–$800)	–$700	–$600	–$300	0	$300	$800
Call Value at Expiration (C3)	0	0	0	$500	$1000	$1500
P&L at Expiration (C3–$800)	–$800	–$800	–$800	–$300	$200	$700

Figure 13.6 P&L Diagram of 90-Day Long Call on Various Dates/Spot Prices

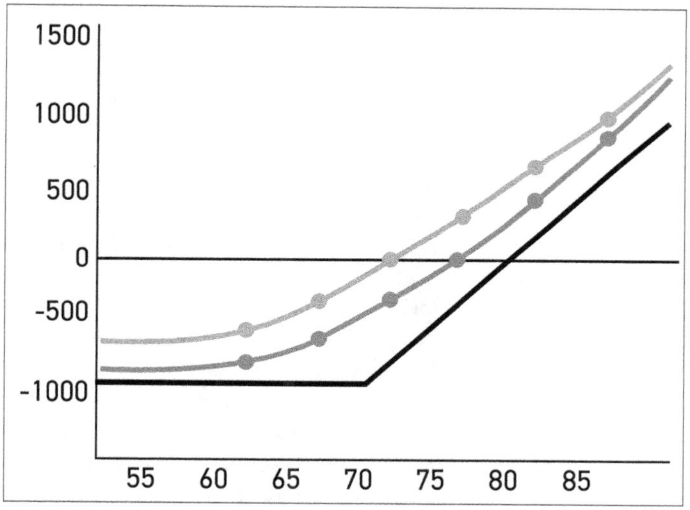

Table 13.6 exhibits the change in put premium relative to time left to expiration.

Assumptions:
Expiration: 90 days
Long put strike: $70
Premium: $700 ($7.00 x 100)

Table 13.6 P/L Metrics of 90-Day Long Put on Various Dates/Spot Prices

Spot Price	$60	$65	$70	$75	$80	$85
Premium Cost	–$700	–$700	–$700	–$700	–$700	–$700
85-Day Put Value (C1)	$1300	$1000	$700	$500	$400	$300
P&L (C1–$700)	$600	$300	$0	–$200	–$300	–$400
30-Day Put Value (C2)	$1100	$700	$400	$200	$100	$100
P&L (C2–$700)	$400	0	–$300	–$500	–$600	–$600
Put Value at Expiration (C3)	$1000	$500	0	0	0	0
P&L at Expiration (C3–$700)	$300	–$200	–$700	–$700	–$700	–$700

Figure 13.7 P/L Diagram of 90-Day Long Put on Various Dates/Spot Prices

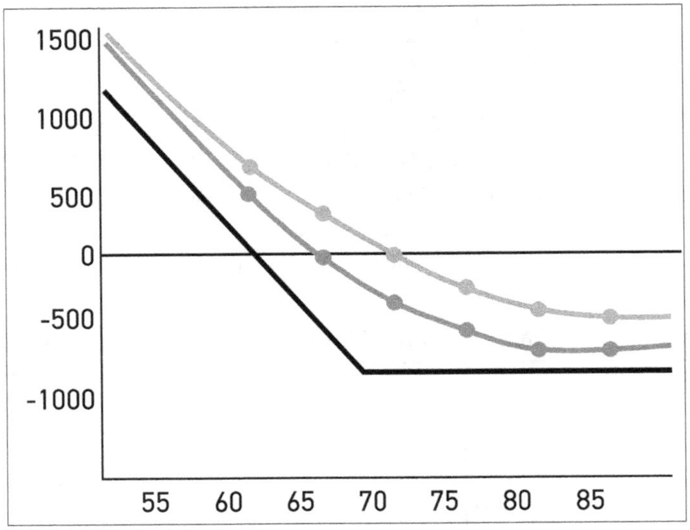

Key Terms

wasting asset
options property implying that after a certain point of time in the future-the expiration date, option contract will have no time value at all

time decay
the progressive decline of options value as the option approaches its expiration date

The above diagrams convincingly show that options with longer time to expiration will be worth more than their intrinsic values, so that you can earn more by offsetting than by exercising. For example—if the price of the underlying asset is at $80, call option at expiration would be worth its intrinsic value = $200; a call with 30-days left to expiration will be priced at $300; and a call with 85-days left to expiration will be worth $700.

This is the appropriate time to remind ourselves what we have discussed at an earlier stage—the life of an option is not indefinite and as the time to expiration nears the time value erodes, causing the value of the option to decline. This brings us to the concept of a **wasting asset:** the option's property denoting that at a certain point of time in the future—the expiration date—the option contract will have no time value at all.

Time value of an option erodes gradually as it approaches expiration date. This phenomenon—"wasting away of time value"—is commonly referred to as **time decay** of an option and can be exhibited graphically as in Figure 13.8:

Figure 13.8 Options Time Decay

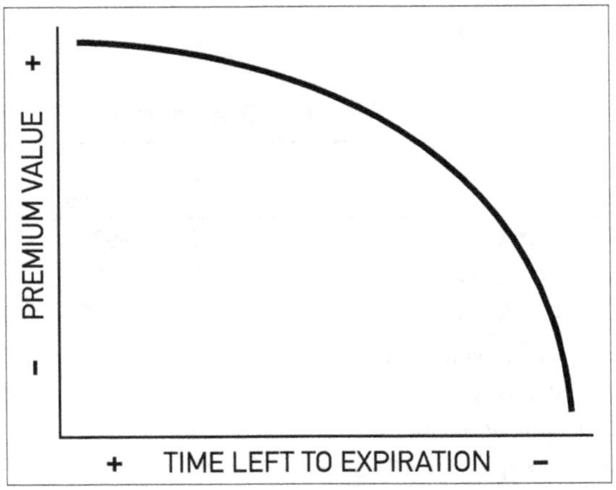

The point to notice from the graph, is that the decay curve falls moderately until it nears the expiration date when—in the very last days—the fall starts to accelaerate dramatically.

The ultimate effect of time decay to option pricing is always negative, for both calls and puts, since the passage of time is an irreversible process causing the time value to move only in one direction—towards expiration. Therefore, as time nears expiration options lose their value.

Figure 13.9 illustrates the effect of time left to expiration on options premium.

Figure 13.9 Time Left to Expiration vs. Option Premium

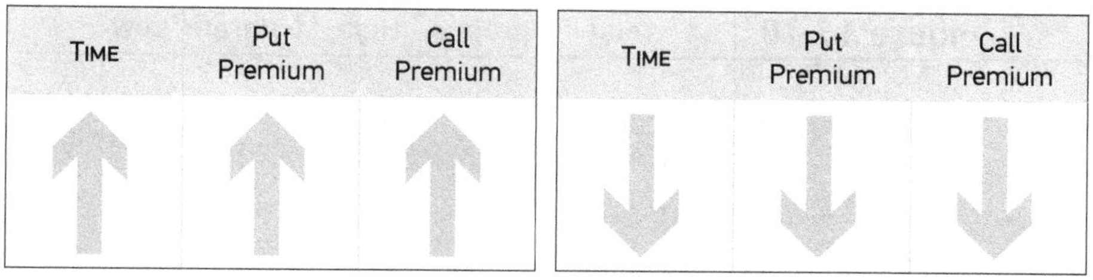

The longer the time to expiration, the higher the premiums of both calls and puts. The nearer the time to expiration, the lower the premiums of both calls and puts.

The conclusion is based on the consensual presumption that the longer the time to expiration the greater are the chances for the price of the underlying to move favourably in the future. Conversely, the lesser the time period to expiration the lesser is the probability.

However, it is worth emphasizing that the above correlation refers only to long options—calls as well as puts. Hence, the effect of time decay on option holders is negative. Developing further consequences of the apparent propensity of time value—to erode as the expiration date nears, would lead us to another logical conclusion: the position of an option writer—with respect to time decay—is opposite to that of the option holder—option writers benefit from time decay. What is detrimental to an option holder is beneficial to the option writer, and vice versa.

Thus, the nearer the time to expiration, the better for option writer. With the time value eroding as the expiration date comes nearer, the chances that the option will move in-the-money are eroding too.

VOLATILITY VS. OPTION PREMIUM

Although the role of volatility has been often and undeservedly underestimated it is by all means the second decisive determinant to option prices—the first being the change in the underlying security price.

Key Terms

volatility
measure of daily prices fluctuation within a given period

Volatility, in its most simplified meaning, is the measure of price fluctuation, or the actual price change in between two points in time, usually a one-year period but it can be measured for shorter periods too—like a month or a week—or any other particular period.

The volatility graphic depiction resembles the shape of a church bell and is commonly referred to as a "bell curve." In Figure 13.10 you may see why:

Figure 13.10 Volatility graphs - High, Moderate, Low

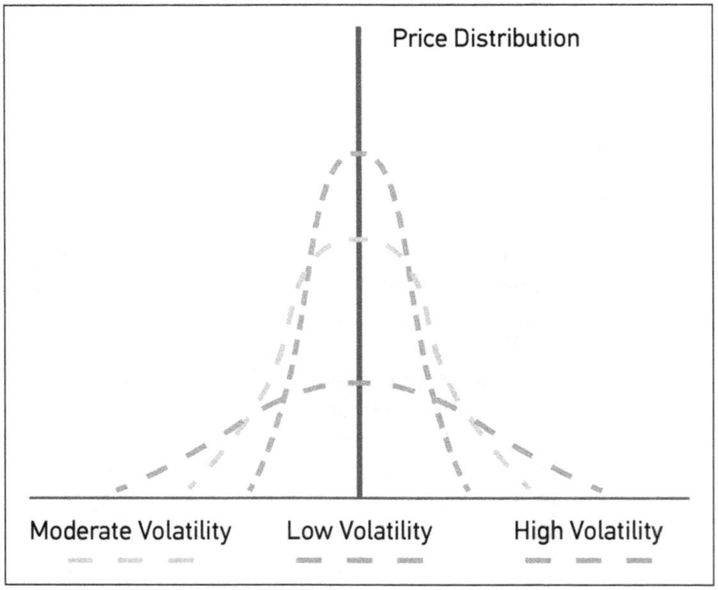

A volatility curve reflects how much the price of an asset fluctuates over time in either direction. In other words, these graphs are telling us that prices ending up below the mean are just as likely as prices ending up above the mean.

High volatility, whether actual or probable, denotes wide price fluctuations, and the possibility that prices will close far away from the mean in any direction are also high.

Low volatility, on the other hand, implies that a narrow range of price fluctuations is more probable.

Moderate volatility conclusively lies in between the two.

Statistical description of the variability of prices around the mean is called **standard deviation** and it measures the degree to which an individual observed price is likely to vary from that mean.

standard deviation
a measurement of volatility associated with price fluctuations. The degree to which an individually observed price is likely to vary from that mean

Volatilities in general are quoted on an annualized basis. To calculate standard deviation for specific time periods less than one year, we use the following formula:

One Standard Deviation Move = UI Price x IV x √ Calendar days/365

Remember This! Standard Deviation

Volatility values are always expressed in percentages and its interpretation will be best to illustrate through a simple example with the following assumptions:

- the price of XYZ stock observed through a one year period, most repeatedly closed at $50.
- the volatility percentage for the same period has been calculated to be 20%.

Having established the mean and the volatility percentage, what standard deviation is telling us is that at the end of the observed period XYZ stock closing price has fallen within:

+/– 1 standard deviation of 20% about 2/3 of the time or about 66%. Explicitly, XYZ stock closed within the range of $40 (–20%) and $ 60 (+20%) about 2/3 of the time. In other words +/– 1 standard deviation contains 66% of all prices within the observed sample. (In terms of implied volatility we could say that the probability of prices falling within the range between $40 and $60 is 66%.)

Inversely, only 1/3 or about 33% of the time it has been outside this range or to put it in another way, only 33% of all prices did fall outside this range.

In extension, the same statistical method has ascertained the second level of price range predictability containing 95% of all possible prices, namely +/– 2 standard deviations. Applied to the same example this would mean that the XYZ stock closing price has fallen within:

+/– 2 standard deviations of 40% 19/20 of the time or about 95%. Explicitly, XYZ stock closed within the range of $30 (–40%) and $70 (+40%) about 19/20 of the time.

Inversely, only 1/20 or about 5% of the time it has been outside this range or to put it in another way, only 5% of all prices did fall outside this range.

There are two main types of volatility. They refer to two different time frames:

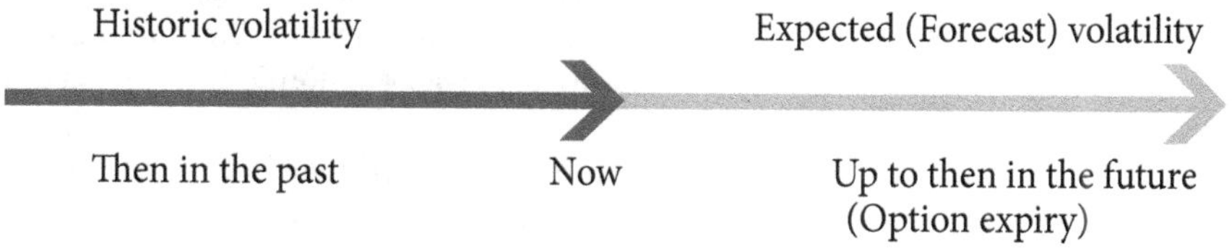

HISTORIC VOLATILITY

Measures the actual price changes between two points of time in the past, most commonly expressed as an annualised number. Its calculation is based typically on a daily record of an asset closing prices over a certain historical time period. A historic volatility calculation model delivers a reliable, indisputable figure related to price fluctuations over a one year time horizon in the past.

EXPECTED VOLATILITY

Every financial forecast is based upon a probability distribution. The single most pronounced parameter that determines an option's payout at expiration is the expected future spot price. Therefore, to value an option contract is to evaluate the probability distribution of its underlying asset. The parameters that define the future probability distribution of an underlying are the time remaining to expiration and the expected volatility.

Key Terms

historic volatility
measures the actual price changes between two points of time in the past

expected volatility
subjective assumption about price fluctuations within a specific time frame (options expiration) in the future

The amount of time remaining to expiration is an observable market input with inevitable and predictable consequences; the greater the time left to expiration the greater the chances that the expected future spot price will be more spread out.

Expected volatility, however, is objectively unobservable. Therefore it is anyone's guess, or subjective assumption, of price fluctuations within some specific time frame (options expiration) in the future.

Key Terms

implied volatility
implied volatility is the forecast volatility implied in the dollar price of an option and as such it shows what volatility level is actually being traded in the market

IMPLIED VOLATILITY

When an expected volatility, assumed by market-makers (professional traders in the market place), is used as an input in an option pricing model it becomes implied volatility. Implied volatility is the forecast volatility implied in the dollar price of an option —it tells you what volatility level is actually being traded in the market. To calculate implied volatility, stock options market predominantly use "Black-Scholes Option's Pricing Model." All that is required is to input the following parameters:

- exercise price of the option,
- price of the underlying asset,
- current option's price,
- option's expiration date, and
- prevailing interest rate.

Factors Influencing Implied Volatility

Except for directly observable parameters, such as the above, implied volatility will also be affected by the following factors:

- Historical volatility; price fluctuations normally evolve gradually and the recent asset performance is a good proxy of potential moves in the near future.
- Demand/supply factors.
- Short-term geopolitical crises.
- Natural catastrophes (floods, hurricanes etc.).
- Political events, economic and financial reports and releases.

Changes in implied volatility correlate directly with option prices. When volatility is high, price fluctuations are also expected to be high, so the model responds with high premiums and vice versa.

It is important to understand that the volatility factor is independent from the market price trend, i.e., it can vary in all market circumstances; bullish, bearish or stagnant.

Figure 13.11 Implied Volatility vs. Option Premium

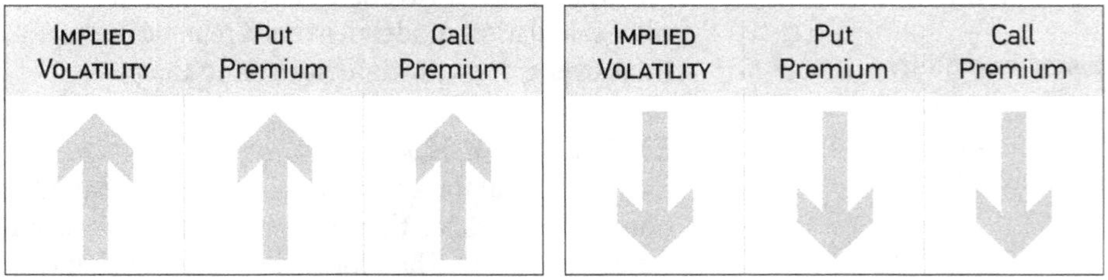

This is easy to understand as it follows the principles of common logic. With volatility declining, the potential range of price changes is narrowing. So is the potential gain. Consequently, investors are willing to pay less in terms of option premium.

Inversely, the more active the market, and with volatility increasing in anticipation of large price fluctuations, the likelihood of a sharp daily price movement is reaffirmed, and so are the chances for the potential gains, with no extra risk, as the eventual loss is contained to the price paid for the option. As a result, investors will be willing to pay more in terms of option premium.

Example

We can explain this relationship using the factual price of Microsoft Corp. at NASDAQ on 10 September 2012. The stock price is at \$29.70

Implied volatility: 26.35%

\$30 ATM Call	\$0.953	\$30 ATM Put	\$1.122

Here are the effects of implied volatility 5% increase/decrease:

Implied volatility: 31.35%

Call value	\$1.149	Put value	\$1.317

Implied volatility: 21.35%

Call value	\$0.757	Put value	\$0.926

and the corresponding Vega = $\delta V/\delta\sigma = 1.149 - 0.953/31.35 - 26.35 = 0.039$

Implied volatility delivered by the Black-Scholes model, deals with predictions—it reflects market consensus in regard to the expected range of price fluctuations in the future; an indication of how volatile the market might be in the future.

In that respect, implied volatility is an important number for analysing and comparing with volatility levels that existed in the past—historical or statistical volatilities—to pre-determine the most probable price the market is supposed to hit on a certain date in the future.

This comparison brings to our attention the concept of an option's **theoretical fair value** or its "fair price."

How do we calculate the "theoretical fair value" of an asset?

First, we need all the inputs required by the Black-Scholes options calculator; we choose option's exercise price and expiration, enter the price of underlying and risk-free interest rate, dividends if any; and then simply enter historical volatility (HV) number for the observed underlying stock. The model will deliver the theoretical fair value for that stock option.

Key Terms

theoretical fair value
a term used to denote the value of an option ensuing from a mathematical model (Black-Scholes); it indicates the price that an option should have if calculation is based on historic volatility

Historical volatility → BS Options Calculator → Theoretical Fair Value

If we calculate backwards, leave out the volatility number, and enter Actual Market Price (everything else being equal), the model will deliver volatility number implied by the option price—Implied Volatility (IV) for the same option.

Actual Market Price → BS Options Calculator → Implied Volatility → the level of future volatility formally acknowledged by the market.

NB: All volatilities are normally quoted on annualized basis.

The level of volatility that is actually implied in an option price, is often biased in one direction or another. Consequently, it may happen that an option pricing model delivers option prices that may be over- or under-valued compared to the theoretical fair value. If this happens to be the case, options are considered to be mispriced.

Actual market price (IV) < Theoretical fair value (HV); Options are undervalued.

Actual market price (IV) > Theoretical fair value (HV); Options are overvalued.

In real time, in terms of volatility, it is not easy to judge which options are bargains and which are overpriced in terms of volatility. It is a fairly arbitrary, subjective approach, which is sometimes based more on a deductive analytical method, emphasizing the historical statistical data of a stock price fluctuation, and sometimes it is based more on speculative expectations of future volatility.

For this reason, skilled options traders will always confront implied volatility with historic volatility, to estimate the risks involved and decide whether or not options actual market price is underpriced or overpriced compared to the theoretical fair value.

Based on these observations, a sound rule of thumb would suggest that there are two basic strategies an investor may undertake in order to exploit mispriced options:

1. If the actual market price (IV) is below theoretical fair value (HV)— it's a good buying opportunity; initiate a strategy involving net long option premium (long call/straddle), and
2. If the actual market price (IV) is above theoretical fair value (HV)—it's a good selling opportunity; initiate a strategy involving net short option premium (short call/straddle),

Implied volatility is lowest when options are at-the-money. Depending on the nature of the underlying asset, the implied volatility curvature may take the shape of a **volatility smile;** when ITM and OTM volatility is higher than for ATM—usually encountered in stock markets—or **volatility skew;** the phenomenon of IV asymmetry is usually depicted as a right skew (if IV is higher for ITM options) or a left skew (if IV is higher for OTM options)—valid predominantly in commodity markets.

Key Terms

volatility smile
graphic characteristic of implied volatility plotted against different strikes showing the shape of a smile. IV is lower for ATM options than ITM and OTM options

volatility skew
asymmetry in volatility curve; right skew if IV is higher for ITM options or left skew if IV is higher for OTM options

Figure 13.12 Volatility Smile & Skew Diagrams

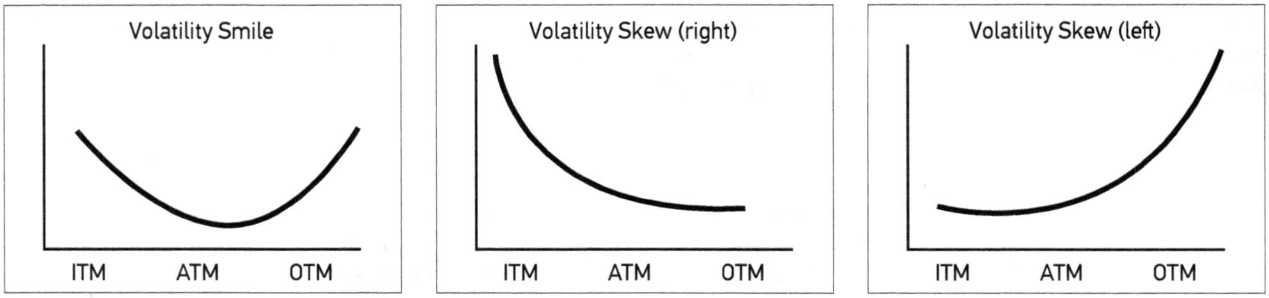

SUMMARY

This chapter has focused on four major parameters that affect an option's value. We began our explanation with the influence of the exercise price. We then exhibited the divergent impact of exercise price level of call and put premiums concluding that the rise and fall of the option exercise price is directly correlated to the rise and fall of the put premium, while the call premium expresses an inverse relationship). An options moneyness is the term that originates from the relationship between option's exercise price and the current price of the underlying instrument. Based on this relationship all options are categorized into three groups: in-the-money (ITM); at-the-money (ATM), and out-of-the-money (OTM) options. Consequently, we explained that ITM options are always more expensive than OTM options.

A second major determinant is the price of the underlying instrument. We have observed that the variation in the price of the UI is directly correlated to a call premium and inversely to a put premium.

It was shown that an option's value is made up of two components: intrinsic value and extrinsic value. Intrinsic value is the in-the-money portion of option's premium. Consequently, only ITM options have intrinsic value and it is always either positive or zero. The intrinsic value of a call option is described as the positive difference between the current UI price and the exercise price, while the intrinsic value of a put option is described as the positive difference between the exercise price the current UI price. We then covered how to calculate options intrinsic and extrinsic values. Further, we have explained the difference between the options payoff diagram and options profit and loss diagram and we briefly analyzed the relative implications.

Time decay was the third element. We began the explanation with an illustration of the option's time eroding progression across different expiration periods showing that as time passes the option loses a portion of its time value. This property designates options as "wasting assets," implying that at expiration the option will lose 100 per cent of their time value.

Volatility is the last parameter analyzed. At the beginning we displayed the volatility graph to introduce the concept visually. We examined the effects of changes in volatility level to call and put premiums affirming positive correlation; call and put premiums rise and fall with the volatility rise and fall. We then delved deeper into the difference between volatility concepts—historic volatility vs. implied volatility—focusing on particular distinctions and applications in regard to option's pricing. We emphasized the concept of overpriced and underpriced options relative to implied volatility level that was actually priced into the options, and eventual trading advantages originating thereof.

As a final summation we are offering the following table:

PARAMETER	RISE	PUT VALUE	CALL VALUE	FALL	PUT VALUE	CALL VALUE
Exercise price	+	+	–	–	–	+
UI price	+	–	+	–	+	–
Time to expiration	+	+	+	–	–	–
Volatility	+	+	+	–	–	–

- Call options are more valuable when the exercise price is lower, when the UI price is higher, when the time to maturity is greater, when the UI volatility is greater, and
- Put options are more valuable when the exercise price is higher, when the UI price is lower, when the time to maturity is greater, when the UI volatility is greater.

KEY TERMS

moneyness
intrinsic value
extrinsic value
time value
wasting asset
time decay
volatility
standard deviation
historic volatility
expected volatility
implied volatility
volatility smile
volatility skew

[redacted]

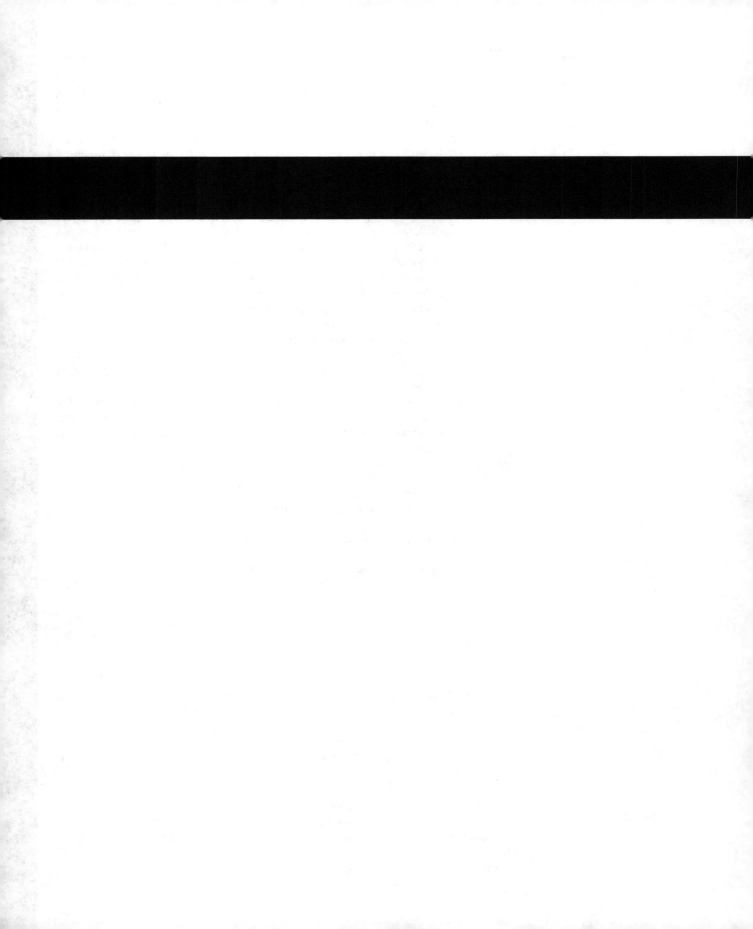

CHAPTER 14

EUROPEAN CALL AND PUT PRICING BOUNDS

CHAPTER OBJECTIVES

- To introduce and explain the concept of call options pricing bounds
- To introduce and explain the concept of put options pricing bounds
- To verify the principles through algebraic examples

EUROPEAN CALL AND PUT PRICING BOUNDS

When it comes to option pricing it is very important to remember that there are certain price bounds that both calls and puts must fit in. Expressed succinctly these bounds state that European put and call options of the same class (i.e., same underlying, exercise price and expiration date) must abide to the following rules:

	European Call Bounds	European Put Bounds
	if **St** = 0, then **Ct** = 0	if **X** = 0, then **Pt** = 0
Upper bound	if **X** = 0, then **Ct** = **St**, $C \leq S$	if **St** = 0, then **Pt** = **X**, $P \leq PV(X)$
Lower bound	$C \leq Max\ [0, S - PV(X)]$	$P > Max\ [0, PV(X) - S]$

EUROPEAN CALL PRICING BOUNDS

The statement that verifies the relationship if St = 0, then Ct = 0, is easiest to understand as it seems to be forcibly logical; it can be translated as follows: If the underlying asset price is zero then the call value is also zero, as nobody would be willing to pay anything for the right to own a worthless asset.

Key Terms

call upper bound states that the call value can never exceed the price of the underlying asset

call lower bound states that the call value must always exceed the difference between the price of the underlying asset and the exercise price

Call Upper Bound Now, let us consider the case of the call upper bound. The holder of a call option is entitled to buy the underlying asset at its exercise price. The lower the exercise price, the more his call is worth. If the exercise price happens to fall to zero, then ask yourself, how much would you be willing to pay for the call? Obviously not more than the price of the underlying asset, because nobody would be prepared to pay for the right to own an asset at a price higher than the asset is readily available for in the market. Therefore, we can intuitively deduce that $C \leq S$: that is to say, the call value can never exceed the price of the underlying asset. In options terminology this imperative is termed as the call options upper bound.

Call Lower Bound This states that the call value must always exceed the difference between the price of the underlying asset and the exercise price, or that $C > Max\ [0, S - PV(X)]$. We can use the simple graphical expositions to illustrate the validity of the arguments.

Figure 14.1 Call Option Pricing Bounds

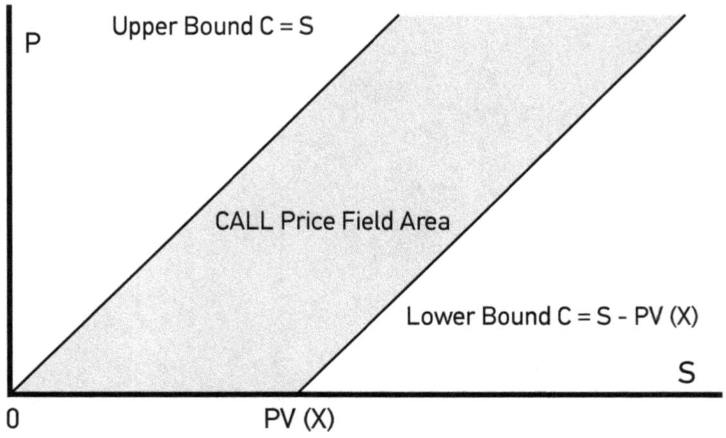

Algebraical verification of this rule can be expressed as follows:

Proof:	Call value ≥ S – PV (X) must hold at all times!
if	C < S – PV (X)
then:	C – S + PV (X) < 0
and	–C + S – PV (X) > 0

An arbitrage is available, no cash is needed to construct a portfolio and there is at least one positive return at expiration.

Algebraic proof:

Time	Present date (t)	Expiration date (T)	
Strategy	State	$S_T > X$	$S_T < X$
Buy Call	– C	(ST – X)	0
Sell Stock	+ S	–ST	–ST
Lend	– PV (X)	+X	+X
Portfolio:	> 0	0	– ST + X > 0

if	C < S – PV (X)
C = $5.00, S = $45, K = $40, r = 6%, T = 3 mos., PV (K) = 39.41	
then:	5.00 – 45 + 39.41 < 0
and	–5.00 + 45.00 – 39.41 > 0

Numeric proof:

Time	Present date (t)	Expiration date (T)	
Strategy	State	$S_T = 46$	$S_T = 38$
Buy Call	–$5.00	+$6.00	0
Sell Stock	+$45.00	–$46.00	–$38.00
Lend	–$39.41	+$40.00	+$40.00
Portfolio:	+$0.59	0	+$2.00

EUROPEAN PUT PRICING BOUNDS

Again, the relationship which states that if X = 0, then $P_t = 0$, is self-explanatory. Why would anyone be willing to pay anything for the right to sell the asset with no value at all (zero value)?

Key Terms

put upper bound
states that put value can never exceed the exercise price

put lower bound
states that put value must always exceed the difference between exercise price and the price of the underlying asset

Put Upper Bound The same logic we used in case of call option bounds may be applied to put option bounds. The upper bound for a put option makes certain that P ≤ X. Why? Because the maximum the holder of the European put option can expect to get upon expiration is the exercise price of the put option or to be more precise, its present value—PV (X). Even if the price of the underlying falls to zero, the return for the put holder will remain PV(X), although it can never exceed the value of the exercise price. Therefore, it stands to reason that P ≤ X must hold at all states.

Put Lower Bound This states that put value must always exceed the difference between the exercise price and the price of the underlying, or that put value must always satisfy the relation P > Max [0, PV (X) – S]

Figure 14.2 Put Option Pricing Bounds

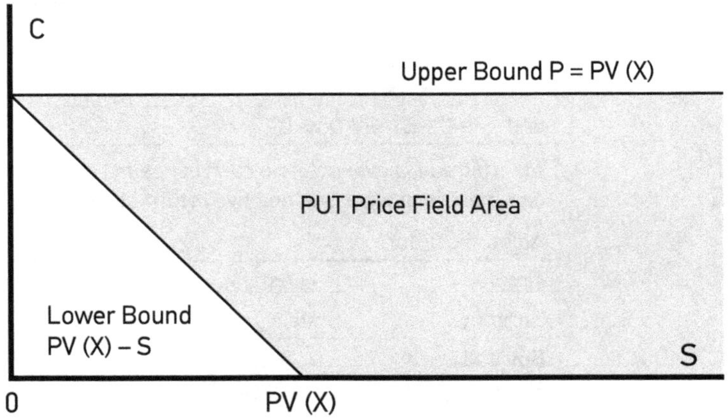

Similarly to call lower bound we can use the same methodology to prove the validity of the dependency relationship, namely that P > Max [0, PV (X) – S].

Proof:	Put value ≥ PV (X) – S must hold at all times!
if	P < PV (X) – S
then:	P – PV (X) + S < 0
and	–P + PV (X) – S > 0

An arbitrage is available, no cash is needed to construct a portfolio and there is at least one positive return at expiration.

Algebraic proof:

Time	Present date (t)	Expiration date (T)	
Strategy	State	$S_T > X$	$S_T < X$
Buy Put	–C	0	(X – ST)
Buy Stock	–S	+ST	+ST
Borrow	+PV (X)	–X	–X
Portfolio:	> 0	ST – X> 0	0

if	C < S – PV (X)
P = $3.00, S = $36, K = $40, r = 6%, T = 3 mos., PV(K) = 39.41	
then:	3.00 – 39.41 + 36 < 0
and	–3.00 + 39.41 – 36 > 0

Numeric proof:

Time	Present date (t)	Expiration date (T)	
Strategy	State	$S_T = 46$	$S_T = 38$
Buy Put	–$3.00	0	+ $6.00
Buy Stock	–$36.00	+$44.00	+$34.00
Borrow	+$39.41	–$40.00	–$40.00
Portfolio:	+$0.41	+$4.00	0

SUMMARY

This chapter has introduced the reader to the concept of options pricing bounds. We thought it was important to treat this matter separately as its fundamentals are important for understanding the theory of options pricing.

A call option is the right to buy an asset at an agreed-upon exercise price. A put option is the right to sell an asset at a given exercise price.

These rights impose certain principles to options pricing. These principles are intuitively logical:

- In case of a call option we asserted that if St = 0, than Ct = 0. This conclusion may be supported with a rhetorical question: "Why would anybody be willing to exercise his right to buy an asset with zero value?"
- In case of a put option we asserted that if X = 0, than Pt = 0, which is inherently logical: "Why would anyone be willing to pay anything for the right to sell the asset with no value at all (zero value)?"

Whatever the pricing model, the pricing bounds rules must be endorsed and validated at all times. If these rules are violated in any possible way, then it would be possible to constitute an arbitrage trade—a portfolio consisting of riskless assets that produce at least one positive return at expiration.

KEY TERMS

call upper bound
call lower bound
put upper bound
put lower bound

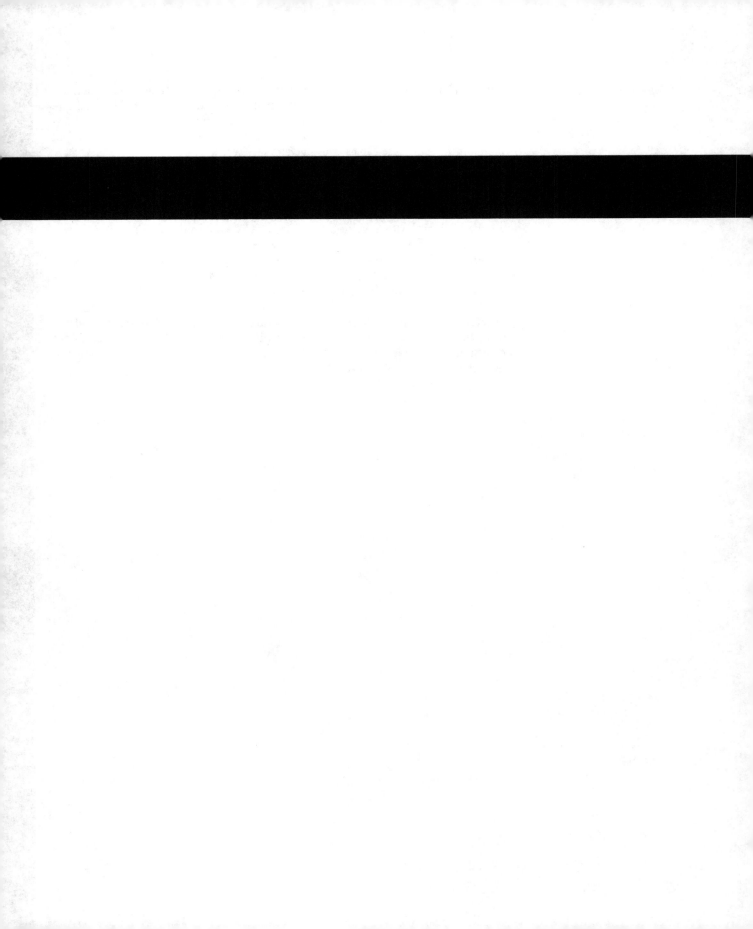

CHAPTER 15

BLACK-SCHOLES PRICING MODEL

CHAPTER OBJECTIVES

- To discuss the fundamentals of the Black-Scholes Pricing Model
- To disclose the intuition behind the famous formula
- To illustrate and explain the calculation process using the model premises
- To outline and explain options Greeks

BLACK-SCHOLES PRICING MODEL

OPTION PRICING MODELS ARE DESIGNED TO OFFER AN ADVANTAGEOUS MATHEMATICAL tool, which enable market participants to judge an option's fair value or theoretical value, and also to use it to simulate and analyse the effects on option prices originating from the complex interrelations among major price determinants.

The most widely-used model for option pricing is Black-Scholes. This formula can be used to calculate a theoretical value for an option taking into account five different factors:

- current stock price,
- option's exercise price,
- implied stock volatility,
- time to expiration, and
- interest rate.

While the presumptions delivered by Black-Scholes do not correspond exactly with real-world market performance, the model is still widely used in options valuation and trading. For three basic reasons:

1. It exploits the valuable and advisable concept of theoretical value.
2. It makes it possible to judge whether the option is under- or over-valued.
3. It allows easy access to "what if?" scenarios in order to assess future strategy performance with different variables.

In this respect it is now possible, with the help of a mathematical formula, to apply reasonably reliable guidance in order to evaluate and compare different option strategies before actually entering the position.

This is made possible in the first place, because the Black-Scholes model is an arbitrage model and undoubtedly one of the imperishable contributions to option pricing analyses.

The arbitrage model is a pricing model in which all the major inputs are related to each other in such a way that it makes it possible to solve the unknown input providing that all the other inputs are recorded. The model manifests the relationship between option premium and major variables, and how the change in any one of them affects the overall position.

The Black-Scholes model is a very sophisticated pricing formula, yet it should not be considered a flawless predictor of future outcome, but rather a fair approximation of reality. All inputs used in the formula are exact and factually evident—the stock price, the exercise price, the interest rate and the time to expiration—and all easily accessible from various daily market data: all except one—the volatility. The Black-Scholes model does not include past volatility performance but rather the volatility expected over the lifetime of the option's contract. This variable is not directly observable as it reflects the anticipation of all market participants. That anticipation of volatility in the future, used as an input in the option pricing model is termed "implied volatility." The implied volatility is therefore the level of expected volatility the market is pricing into the particular class of options.

For example, if a stock option should be trading at $5.75, based on your personal evaluation of time and intrinsic value but is actually trading at $5.95 points, the additional 20 points in the premium can be attributed only to implied volatility. In this instance, the option is overvalued by at least 20 points and may be considered an attractive opportunity for writing. Conversely, if an option is trading at $5.50 but should be trading at around $5.65, then implied volatility is low on that option. It suggests the option is undervalued and may be a good buy.

This brings us to another directly related concept—the "theoretical edge!" The theoretical edge is, as we could learn from the above example, the discrepancy an individual investor recognizes to be the theoretical fair value of an option and the actual price of that same option.

BLACK-SCHOLES MODEL: AN ILLUSTRATION

For those who have not fallen in love with math at first sight, and therefore lack the affinity for differential equations, this formula might look scary.

To make it more friendly we will explain the common logic used by its authors that led to this famous derivation.

Black and Scholes' formula observes the pricing of the European call option that pays no dividend, from the position of an investor that sold short call option (in other words an investor who entered the risky naked short position).

The payoff to call writer is two fold: C max. –(0, ST – X):

1) 0 if ST < X, if the stock price stays where it is or drops in value the option expires worthless and the call writer will keep the premium.
2) –(ST – X) if ST > X, if the stock rallies, short call will lose money.

So, the investor is facing a dilemma—to stay naked or to hedge: that is, to provide some protection on the upside. If he stays naked short, he will benefit from the price decline but the position will suffer a loss if the price goes up.

The other alternative is to hedge. Hedging a short call can be achieved by buying the long stock outright—thus, covering the naked call. If the stock goes up, the gains on the long stock will offset the loss on the short call; but if the stock price declines the position will generate a loss.

We see that both choices have their advantages and disadvantages. It turns out that for the investor it would be best to get a "cover" if the stock price rallies, and remain naked if it falls. So, the payoff that would reconcile both choices is in fact that of the long call.

Is it possible to create a portfolio of stocks and bonds so as to replicate the payoff of a long call option? The Black-Scholes formula gives the answer.

The payoff of the long underlying stock matches the "variable" part of the call option option's payoff.

The risk-free bond payoff matches the "flat" part of the call option's payoff.

It follows that a call option payoff can be replicated by using an appropriate combination of the long underlying stock and borrowing—short selling the zero coupon bonds. That is, we can trade the position of a stock in such a way that its performance operates just like the payoff of a long call option.

If the stock price increases, increase the number of shares purchased; if the price goes further up, buy more shares. If the share price declines, sell back the corresponding number of shares; if it goes down further, sell more.

In this way, by continuously adjusting the "long stock-short bond" ratio, we ensure that the value of the portfolio, at any point in time, mimics the exposure of the long call option.

The Black-Scholes formula*:

$C0 = S0N(d^1) - Xe^{-rT} N(d2)$

Where:

$d_1 = [\ln(S0 / X) + (r + \sigma^2/2) T] / \sigma \sqrt{T}$

And:

$d2 = d1 - \sigma \sqrt{T}$

* Originally developed by Fisher Black & Myron Scholes in 1973 for European securities options and later amended by Black for futures options

Notations:

C0 = current option value

S0 = current stock price

N (d1) and N (d2) are probabilities, estimated by using a cumulative standardized normal distribution and the values of d_1 and d_2 obtained for an option.

X = exercise price

e = 2.71828, is the discount (present valuing) factor

r = risk-free interest rate (annualized continuously compounded rate on a zero coupon bond with the same maturity as the expiration of the option;

T = time to options maturity, in years

ln = natural logarithm function

σ = volatility, standard deviation of the annualized continuously compounded rate of return on the stock

Example:

Assumptions:

Exercise price is at $95

Current price of the XYZ shares is $100

Option expires in three months (one-quarter year).

Volatility of the stock is 30% on a yearly basis.

Risk-free rate is 6% per year

Dividend yield = 0

First we calculate d_1:

$d_1 = [\ln(S0 / X) + (r + \sigma^2 / 2) T] / \sigma \sqrt{T}$

$d_1 = [\ln(\$100 / \$95) + (0.06 + 0.3^2 / 2) 0.25] / 0.3\sqrt{0.25}$

$d_1 = [\ln(1.0526) + (0.06 + 0.045) 0.25] / 0.15$

$d_1 = [0.05129 + (0.105 \times 0.25)] / 0.15$

$d_1 = [0.05129 + 0.02625)] / 0.15$

$d_1 = 0.07754 / 0.15$

$d_1 = 0.5169$

Then we calculate d_2:

$d_2 = d_1 - \sigma \sqrt{T}$

$d_2 = 0.5169 - 0.3\sqrt{.25} = 0.3669$

From the Normdist we find that:

$N(d_1) = N(0.5169) = 0.6974 = \delta$ (delta of an option)

$N(d_2) = N(0.3669) = 0.6431$

Thus, when we substitute the values for Nd_1 and Nd_2 the value of the call option is:

$C0 = S0N(d_1) - Xe^{-rT} N(d_2)$
C0 = \$100 x 0.6974 – \$95e –0.06 x 0.25 x 0.6431
Co = \$69.74 – \$60.18
C0 = \$9.56

What the formula is telling us is that the option's fair value will rise or fall in tandem with the rise or fall in the share price S, the volatility of the share price (sigma σ, measured by its standard deviation), the risk-free interest rate r, the time to maturity t, and the probability that the option will be exercised—and would perform in reverse relative to the exercise price X: the higher the exercise price, the lower the call value and vice versa.

Consequently the value of the put can be derived from the put-call parity equation formula:

P = C0 + PV (X) – S0
P = C0 + Xe –rT – S0
P = \$9.56 + 95e–0.06 x 0.25 – \$100
P = \$3.14

Key Terms

options greeks
measures derived from the Black-Scholes formula denoting the sensitivity of option prices to various inputs

delta
measures the change in an option value given a \$1 unit change in the underlying asset price

OPTIONS GREEKS

The so-called Greeks are measures derived from the Black-Scholes formula denoting the sensitivity of option prices to various inputs. They are also called risk parameters and there are five of them:

δ, γ, τ, v and ρ.

Delta **(δ)**: Of all option pricing parameters, Delta seems to be the most conspicuous. It is an indication of how much the theoretical option value (option premium) changes, given a \$1 unit change in the underlying asset price. Delta is often interpreted as the probability that option will be in-the-money by expiration. The higher the Delta, the higher the probability.

Long Call Options have positive Delta range from 0 and 1 (zero and 100%).
Long Put Options have negative Delta range from –1 and 0 (–100% and zero).

Delta is normally expressed as a percentage change ranging from 0 to 100 per cent (for example, 50%), or it may be expressed as a ratio (0.50), or simply in points (50 points): the figure 50 in this case, tells us that given a \$1 rise (or fall) in the price of the stock the option price will increase (decrease) by approximately 0.50 cents.

Formula: Delta (Δ) = (DP0 – DP1) / (UP0 – UP1)

DP0 = Derivative price now
DP1 = Derivative price previous
UP0 = Underlying price now
UP1 = Underlying price previous

Figure 15.1 Option's Delta

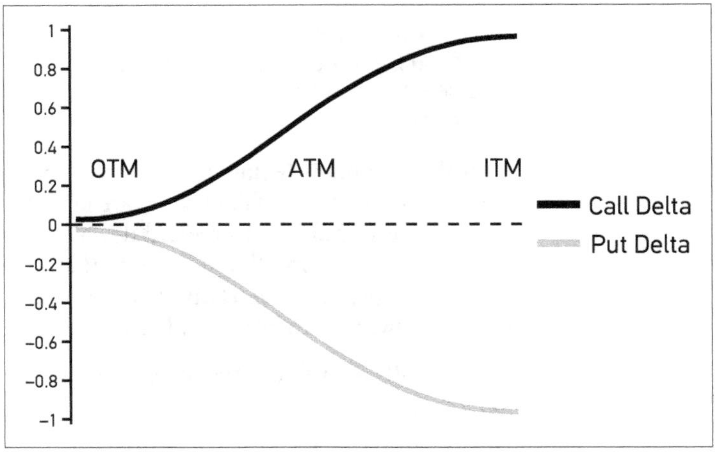

ITM Delta ranges from 0.50 to 1 for call options, and −0.50% and −1 for puts.
ATM Delta is around 0.50% for call options and around −0.50% for puts.
OTM Delta ranges from 0.50% and zero for calls and −0.50% and 0 for puts.

Positive Delta Values Indicate that long call options and short put options will theoretically rise in value with a rise in underlying stock price, and will fall in value with a fall in underlying stock price, thereby constituting a positive association. The Delta of the long underlying itself is always positive (+1).

Negative Delta Values Indicate that long put options and short call options will theoretically rise in value as the underlying stock price declines, and decline in value as the underlying stock price rises, thereby constituting a negative association. The Delta of the short underlying itself is always negative (−1).

Table 15.1 Options Delta

XYZ STOCK Last Trade: $100	10.12.2008
XYZ stock price $100; Expiration in 90 days	
$95 Call is priced at $9.55	$95 Put is priced at $3.13
Call Delta is 0.6974	Put Delta is −0.303
if stock price rise to $101	
$95 Call is priced at $10.258	$95 Put is priced at $2.831
if stock price fall to $99	
$95 Call is priced at $8.863	$95 Put is priced at $3.449

An interesting feature of Delta that should be carefully observed is its sensitivity to the decrease in option's time to expiration. As an option's expiration nears the value of Delta it accelerates either to 1 or 0—ITM option's delta gets nearer to 1, and OTM options delta gets nearer to zero.

A decrease in an option's time to expiration will also have another side effect that can be clearly monitored from the BS formula itself. Namely, when the time to expiration gets shorter the options volatility will fall in a ratio determined by the formula's $\sigma \sqrt{T}$, which translates into one of the very important BS formula's rules:

"The standard deviation of volatility varies with the square root of time."

This simply means the shorter the time to expiration, the lower the volatility.

The decrease in volatility, for its part, will push the Deltas of ITM calls closer to 1 (−1 for puts), and the OTM options Delta closer to zero. The logic behind this is straightforward—lower volatility assumes that the future stock price fluctuation is expected to fade away, hence the lower the volatility, the higher the probability of the ITM options to remain in-the-money at expiration. And vice versa, the lower the volatility, the higher the probability of the OTM options to remain out-of-the-money at expiration.

Comparison of increase/decrease in an option value relative to increase/decrease in the value of the underlying asset may also be viewed in terms of percentage change. In that respect we arrive at the concept of **option elasticity**—the percentage change in an option's value resulting from a one per cent change in the value of the underlying asset.

Key Terms

options elasticity
the percentage change in an option's value resulting from a 1 per cent change in the value of the underlying asset

Example: Options Elasticity

Stock price \$71; Call Strike \$70@3.91; Delta 0.60
Stock price → \$72; Strike → \$4.51
0.60/4.51 = 13.30%; 1/71 = 1.4%
13.30/1.4 = 9.52%
For every 1% increase in the underlying price the call option price increases 9.52%. The ratio that compares the percentage increase in an option's value versus a 1 percentage point change in the value of underlying asset is called option elasticity. Although the nominal dollar movement in the option price (\$0.60) is lower compared to a one dollar increase in the asset price, the percentage rate of return in the option's price (0.60/4.5 = 13.30%) is far greater than that in the asset price (1/71 = 1.4%).

There are two more concepts directly associated with options Delta:

1. Hedge Ratio (or Delta Hedge), and
2. Delta Neutral Concept.

1. Hedge Ratio Delta of an option is an indication of how much the theoretical option value will change relative to a small change in the price of the underlying stock. Options with a high Delta will have high responsiveness to the change in the price of underlying instrument. Options with low Delta will have low responsiveness to the underlying asset price.

The situation is represented graphically in Figure 15.4. We have drawn a price curve representing a call option with a line at point "A" marking the at-the-money position. We have also drawn a tangent at this point. The slope of the tangent corresponds to the Delta of an at-the-money call option. A long call Delta is always positive (between 0 and +1). The tangent on the left corresponds to a low Delta (approaching zero as the underlying price falls) and low option price sensitivity. The tangent on the right corresponds to a high Delta (approaching +1) and high option price sensitivity relative to changes in the underlying asset price.

Figure 15.2 Option's Delta – Tangent to a Slope

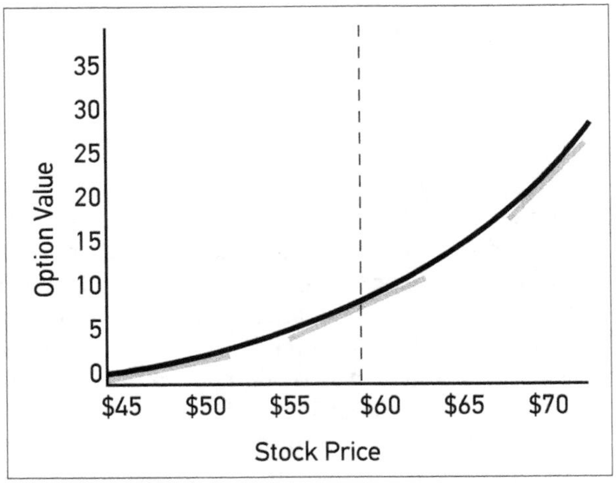

For hedgers, Delta is an important indicator as it determines how many contracts are needed to hedge the particular underlying instrument. **Hedge ratio** is a calculation pointing to the number of option contracts needed to hedge the value of an asset at risk.

A stock call option with, for example, 50 Delta (at-the-money call), indicates that the option price will move 50 cents for every $1 move in the underlying stock. Hence, in order to hedge 100 shares of stock, you would need to buy twice as many option contracts (2 x 100 shares) in order to fully hedge your position. This computation is simple and looks like this:

> **Key Terms**
>
> **hedge ratio**
> a calculation that points to the number of option contracts needed to hedge the value of an asset at risk, also Delta Hedge

The value of 100 shares of stock increases by $1 x 100 = $100
The value of two option contracts (2 x 100 shares) increases by $0.50 x 200 = $100

For a long call and a short put option, the Delta value is positive, hence

Number of contracts = Total Stock Value/Delta Per Contract

For a long put and a short call option, the Delta value is negative, hence

Number of contracts = Total Stock Value x –1/Delta Per Contract

2. Delta Neutral Concept Further derivation ensuing from a hedge ratio model is frequently designated as a **delta neutral concept**. The concept is related to and used in association with complex options strategies. With no intentions to delve into the versatility and complexity of implementing Delta neutral strategies, suffice it to say the following:

A Delta neutral strategy is any option strategy which aimes to eliminate the exposure of a position relative to price change in the underlying instrument. It is constructed in a such a way that the sum of the deltas is set initially to zero. In this way, any gain/loss in the value of the shares held due to a rise or a fall in the share price, would be exactly offset by a loss/gain on the value of the options purchased or sold. Change in the shares price leaves the position value unaffected.

> **Key Terms**
>
> **delta neutral concept**
> any options strategy aimed to eliminate exposure of the position relative to change in the price of the underlying instrument

The Delta of a long stock position is (100). To establish a Delta neutral strategy, we need to hedge a long stock position with a negative Delta equivalent—for example, two short call options with a Delta of –50 each—will have a combined total Delta of –100.

Delta Neutral Formula: $H = -1$

However, in order to remain Delta neutral, as markets are changing continually, we need to make adjustments in the Delta position throughout the validity of the contract.

Key Terms

options gamma
a measure of the sensitivity of delta to unit change in the underlying asset price

Gamma (γ): A measure of the sensitivity of Delta to unit change in the underlying asset price. Gamma is a number that indicates a theoretical change in Delta with a 1 per cent change in the underlying price. Long calls and puts are always Gamma positive, while short calls and puts are always Gamma negative. Options with long term are less sensitive than short term options.

The option's Gamma is highest for at-the-money options and lowest for deep in-the-money and out-of-the-money options.

Formula: Gamma $(\Gamma) = (\Delta_0 - \Delta_1)/(UP_0 - UP_1)$

Δ_0 = Delta now
Δ_1 = Delta previous
UP_0 = Underlying price now
UP_1 = Underlying price previous

In our example with Microsoft Corp. we can find the following data:

Table 15.2 Option's Gamma

XYZ STOCK
Last Trade: $100 10.12.2008

XYZ stock price $100; Expiration in 90 days	
$95 Call Delta is 0.6974	$95 Put Delta is –0.3026
$95 Call Gamma is 0.023	$95 Put Gamma is 0.023
if stock price rise to $101	
$95 Call Delta is 0.7204	$95 Put Delta is –0.2796
if stock price fall to $99	
$95 Call Delta is 0.6744	$95 Put Delta is –0.3256

From the figures displayed we can draw two conclusions:

Calls and puts Delta move inversely relative to the up and down move in the underlying price:

- As the underlying price increases the long call nears the maximum Delta value of (+1), while the long put will be near the lowest Delta value—zero.

- In case the underlying price decreases the long call is nearing zero Delta and the long put will be near its maximum value (–1). The reverse holds for short call and put positions.

Key Terms

options vega
a measure of an option's price sensitivity as implied volatility varies

Vega (**v**): A measure of an option's price sensitivity as implied volatility varies. Vega is an indication of how much the option value will change when the volatility factor moves up or down by 1 per cent.

The higher the Vega the higher the change in option's price as implied volatility changes. Vega value is highest for ATM options and then progressively declines as options go ITM and OTM. Therefore the curvature for options Vega is the same as for options Gamma. The long calls and puts have positive Vega's while short calls and puts have negative Vega's.

Let us take a look at our Microsoft example:

Table 15.3 Options Vega

XYZ STOCK
Last Trade: $100 10.12.2008

XYZ stock price $100; Expiration in 90 days	
$95 Call is priced at $9.55	$95 Put is priced at $3.13
$95 Call Vega is 0.175	$95 Put Vega is 0.175
Implied Volatility is 30%	
if Implied Volatility rises to 31%	
$95 Call is priced at $9.725	$95 Put is priced at $3.305
if Implied Volatility falls to 29%	
$95 Call is priced at $9.375	$95 Put is priced at $2.955

Formula: Vega (V) = $(DP_0 - DP_1)/(V_0 - V_1)$

DP_0 = Derivative price now
DP_1 = Derivative price previous
V_0 = Underlying volatility now
V_1 = Underlying volatility previous

Option buyers benefit from an increase in volatility while option writers benefit from the fall in volatility. The Vega of long-term options, as a general rule, is higher than the Vega for short-term options.

Key Terms

options theta
a measure of an option's price sensitivity with respect to the passage of time

Theta (**τ**): A measure of an option's price sensitivity with respect to the passage of time. In mathematical terms, Theta is the derivative of the option price equation with respect to the remaining time to expiration. Theta, or time decay, is usually expressed as cents of the dollar value of a one-day passage of time, and is always negative since time only moves in one direction. Theta impact is most pronounced near the expiration and is higher for ATM options than ITM and OTM.

In our example the values of call and put Theta's are –$14.083 and –$8.468 respectively. What it means is that the value today of a $9.55 call expiring in 90 days, will tomorrow theoretically be worth $9.41 ($14.083 less due to the time decay), and the value of the $3.13 put tomorrow will be worth $3.045 ($8.468 less).

The rate of time decay is a nonlinear process and it increases as expiration nears. Let us take a look at our Microsoft option, all other parameters being unchanged:

Formula: Theta = $(DP_0 - DP_1)/(T_0 - T_1)$

DP_0 = Derivative price now
DP_1 = Derivative price previous
T_0 = Time now
T_1 = Time previous

NB: Literally, **Vega** is not a letter belonging to the Greek alphabet, in many instances λ, κ or ω are used instead.

Theta values will be as follows:

Table 15.4 Options Theta

XYZ Stock Last Trade $100	10.12.2008
Expiry at 90 days	Expiry at 180 days
Theta value	Theta value
Call: −14.083	Call: −10.878
Put: −8.468	Put: −5.346

Key Terms

options rho
a measure of the sensitivity of option's value as interest rate changes by 1 per cent

Rho (ρ): Rho is one of the least significant Greeks as its impact on the theoretical option value is the most inconsiderable. It measures the sensitivity of option's value as interest rate changes by 1 per cent. An increase in interest rates increases the value of calls and decreases the value of puts. A decrease in interest rates decreases the value of calls and increases the value of puts.

Remember This! Black's 76 Model

Option contracts traded on LME are available monthly to 120 months.
Options Declaration (Expiration) Date: 1st Wednesday of the relevant month
Prompt Date: 3rd Wednesday of the relevant month
So that declared option becomes futures positions for the 3rd Wednesday.

In view of these specifics, LME Traded Options are calculated according to Black's '76 option pricing model which is very similar to the Black-Scholes formula for valuing stock options, except for the following three points:

- The spot price of the underlying is replaced by futures price F.
- Discounted factor is modified to $e^{-r_{continuous}(T+2/52)}$ to correspond to 2 weeks time span between declaration date and prompt date.
- Conversion of annually compounded interest rate to continuously compounded is according to the formula $r_{continuous} = \ln(1 + r_{annualized})$.

According to Black's '76 model, the call option pricing formula is
$c = e^{-r(T+2/52)}[FN(d_1) - XN(d_2)]$
and the corresponding put formula is

$p = e^{-r(T+2/52)}[XN(-d_2) - FN(-d_1)]$
where d_1 and d_2 are calculated in the same way as in the original Black-Scholes Model.

SUMMARY

The most widely used model for option pricing is the Black-Scholes. This famous model relates to a paper "Pricing of Options and Corporate Liabilities" co-authored by Myron Scholes and Fischer Black and later improved by Robert Merton, a finance professor at Harvard. In 1997 Robert Merton and Myron Scholes received the Nobel Prize in Economics; Fisher Black died in 1995.

This elegant formula, sublime in its simplicity, correlates the price of the option to five other determinants: options strike price; price of the underlying stock; volatility of the underlying stock; time left to options expiration; interest rates (the cost of money).

Using the Black-Scholes model, investors are able to calculate the theoretical call price expressed as the rate of change of the call option price subject to the rates at which the other four variables are changing.

Although the formula provides the most essential logic for evaluating options prices, it should be noted that the model has its limitations. Critics of the model usually emphasise the following shortcomings: continuous rebalancing, infinitely divisible quantities, no arbitrage, no transaction costs, no limits on short-selling, unrestricted access to lending and borrowing at a risk-free interest rate: and on top of that probably the most pronounced weaknesses—the drift and volatility are constant and variables change smoothly.

Due to inflexible assumptions and simplifications, the model occasionally drifts away from market reality, as on the oft quoted Black Monday (19 October 1987), when the world's stock markets plummeted 20% within a few hours. In terms of the Black-Scholes model's assumptions, characterized by geometric Brownian motion, this event was utterly impossible to predict.

Acknowledging the verity that theory does not always match reality, many experienced investors use the model with caution, and accordingly, compare the option's price delivered by the model to that based on historic volatility in order to gain an idea of the real value and decide whether the option is under- or over-valued.

The numbers, collectively known as the "Greeks", estimate the risk exposure of an option: Delta measures the change in the option price relative to a change in the stock price; Gamma measures the change in the option delta relative to a change in the stock price; Theta measures the change in the option price with respect to a one-day decrease in time to expiration; Vega measures the change in the option price due to one percentage point change in volatility; and Rho measures the change in the option price relative to one percentage point change in the risk-free interest rates.

KEY TERMS

options elasticity	Greeks	Vega
hedge ratio	delta	Theta
delta neutral	gamma	Rho

CHAPTER 16

BINOMIAL OPTIONS PRICING MODEL

CHAPTER OBJECTIVES

- To explain the binomial option pricing model
- To define basic terms used in binomial valuation
- To introduce two basic concepts for valuing options: the Riskless and Risk-neutral models
- To demonstrate how to construct a multi-binomial tree and explain step-by-step how to calculate option prices
- To explicate Pascal's Triangle's exponential pattern and demonstrate how it can aid in computing option prices

BINOMIAL OPTIONS PRICING MODEL

Key Terms

BOPM
methodology used to estimate the theoretical fair value of an option that rests upon the assumption of the no arbitrage principle and given the inputs that determine the stock price expansion process in a binomial tree

binomial tree
graphic exposition of multiple stock price movements across a predetermined number of steps

THE BINOMIAL OPTION PRICING MODEL (BOPM), AS PROPOSED BY RUBINSTEIN, Cox and Ross in 1979, is a popular discrete time numerical model that is used in the pricing of financial derivatives—options.

The BOPM maps out the expansion of the asset underlying the derivative under the assumption that at each time interval (step of the tree) the asset price increases by some predetermined fixed proportion or decreases by another fixed proportion. Mathematically the BOPM is a methodology used to estimate the theoretical fair value of an option that rests upon the assumption of no arbitrage and given the inputs that determine the stock price expansion process in a binomial tree.

Some notations and definitions:

Binomial: Polynomial with two terms (x + y) n.
Binomial Expansion Theorem: Explains what happens when you multiply a binomial by itself.
Binomial Tree: In its graphical exposition the model assumes the form of a so-called "binomial tree" or "lattice". A tree of asset prices is initially produced working forward from the present to expiration. The BOPM may be calibrated in such a way as to break down the time to expiration into a potentially very large number of sub-intervals.

Formula for calibrating the volatility of a binomial step:

$$\sigma_{step} = \sigma\sqrt{t}$$

Su – increase, stock price going up, or
Sd – decrease, stock price going down, where:

up factor u > 1
down factor d = 1/u < 1

(Up and down movements are calculated based on volatility and the desired number of binomial steps—subintervals in one year)

In our pragmatic case, we are following the development of the tree and the relevant asset values in three time intervals, or steps, taking the values for up and down factors to be as follows:

up factor > 1	u = 1.25
down factor d = 1/u < 1	d = 0.80

Example Figure 16.1 illustrates the expansion of the underlying asset in a "Three step binomial tree." The initial asset price is taken arbitrarily to be $100 and the time period t, is taken to be one year, so that each time interval step corresponds to a one-year period, ending with Step 3 which equates to the third-year period. This one year time period, is selected only for the purpose of emphasizing the progress of expansion, which would be less conspicuous in the case of smaller time periods.

| Figure 16.1 | Three Step Binomial Tree |

	Step I	Step II	Step III
			S = $195.31
		S = $156.25	
	S = $125		S = $125
S = $100.00		S = $100.00	
	S = $80		S = $80
		S = 64	
			S = $51.20
Period 0	*Period 1*	*Period 2*	*Period 3*

NB: A tree of asset prices is produced working forward step by step from initial state towards expiration.

The tree depicts the scheme of all the possible paths that the asset price could take during the designated time period. Each node in the binomial tree—or lattice— represents the price of the underlying asset at that particular point in time.

PROPERTIES OF THE TREE

This tree is labelled as **multiplicative,** referring to the pattern of the tree that interprets the evolution of the "multiplicative geometric binomial process". This means that the asset price's up and down movements are proportional to the asset value at the node from which a binomial step originates. At each node you can calculate upward as well as downward values using either an up factor (u = 1.25) or a down factor (d = 0.80) as shown in the graph above.

This tree is also designated a **recombining tree;** signifying that at each node you can calculate upward and/or backward values using either an up factor or a down factor so that an up or down movement will bring you back to the node value where it started.

Take for example the stock value at node S = $156.25:

Example: Recombining Property

Upward move:
$156.25 x 1.25 = $195.31 and $195.31/1.25 = $156.25

Downward move:
$156.25/1.25 = $125 and $125 x 1.25 = $156.25

This property is embedded into the tree structure; it also implies that at each step (n), the tree will have (n + 1) nodes end-values.

n = no. of steps, time intervals
nodes of the tree: at each step (n), the tree will have (n + 1) nodes

If we conceive a tree with a great many time intervals or steps—rather than only three, as depicted in our example—we would witness that the distribution of asset prices resembles a "log-normal distribution", i.e., a symmetric bell-shaped curve on a log-normal scale.

Key Terms

multiplicative binomial tree
the model of computation implicitly incorporated in the BOPM in which up and down movements are defined as a predetermined proportion to the asset value from the initial node of the related binomial expansion tree

recombining tree
a computational property of the tree securing that an up/down movement will bring us back to the value at the node where it started

BINOMIAL VALUATION

Think for a moment about alternatives to hedging a short call. The naked short call position is a very risky investment. If the price goes up and your short call ends up in-the-money you will be called away—that is you will have to deliver 100 shares of stock—and you will have to do it at a loss equal to the difference between the market price and exercise price, less the premium received. On the other hand, if the price of the underlying goes down, the call will end up out-of-the-money. The option will expire without assignment—worthless—and you won't be obliged to deliver anything, therefore you will not need to have any shares at all.

Obviously you can hedge a short call with a long call. You will be perfectly hedged except for the commissions and fees. But by hedging a short call with a long call—if a call happens to be mispriced—then you cannot take advantage of constructing an arbitrage portfolio.

Hence you would actually need to create a synthetic instrument that replicates a payoff of the long call option. To hedge a short call you would need to create a portfolio that would accomplish what seems to be an irreconcilable solution—to provide a hedge on the upside, and at the same time to be off-hedged on the downside.

Is this kind of portfolio possible? Is it possible to mimic a payoff of a derivative — the long call—with a portfolio consisting only of an underlying asset (a stock) plus the appropriate sum in cash (a bond)? How many shares of stock do you need at the outset to be fully hedged at maturity? The binomial pricing model is the answer.

I. RISKLESS HEDGE MODEL

Step 1.	Find a replicating portfolio
Step 2.	Exhibit the performance of a risk-free hedge
Step 3.	Verification of no-arbitrage principle; Deviations from fair value
Step 4.	Construct multi-binomial tree

II. RISK NEUTRAL HEDGE MODEL

Step 1.	Explain "Pascal's Triangle"
Step 2.	Computing risk neutral probabilities
Step 3.	Construct multi-binomial tree
Step 4.	Dynamic hedge primer; A random walk through a binomial tree

I. RISKLESS HEDGE MODEL

Model assumptions: "One Step Binomial Model."

> S = \$100
> X = \$100
> r = 0.0833 (annual risk free 8% rate continuously compounded!)
> up factor > 1 u = 1.25
> down factor d = 1/u <1 d = 0.80

The binomial model implies that an instrument (a financial asset) may take on only two possible outcomes at the end of the relevant period—the expiration date.

One Step Binomial Model

Stock Payoff:

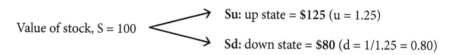

Value of stock, S = 100 → **Su:** up state = **\$125** (u = 1.25)
→ **Sd:** down state = **\$80** (d = 1/1.25 = 0.80)

Under the circumstances the call option payoff will also take only two possible values:

Call Payoff:

Value of call, C = ? →
Su: = \$125
Cu = \$25 max (uS – X, 0)
→
Sd: = \$80
Cd = 0 max (dS – X, 0)

FIND A REPLICATING PORTFOLIO

We are looking for a portfolio whose payoff is the same as the call option that we want to price. Put-call parity implies that, if two portfolios have the same payoffs at expiration then the initial cost of the two portfolios needs to be the same.

> Payoff of Replicating Portfolio = Payoff of Call Option

Hence, if we can price the replicating portfolio we can price the call option too.

Let us remember for a moment a call payoff's characteristics.

The value of the call increases with the increase in the price of the underlying asset—the variable segment of a call option payoff; if the underlying price decreases the value of the call remains constant—the flat segment of a call option payoff.

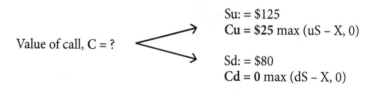

Figure 16.2 Long Call Option – Asymmetric Payoff

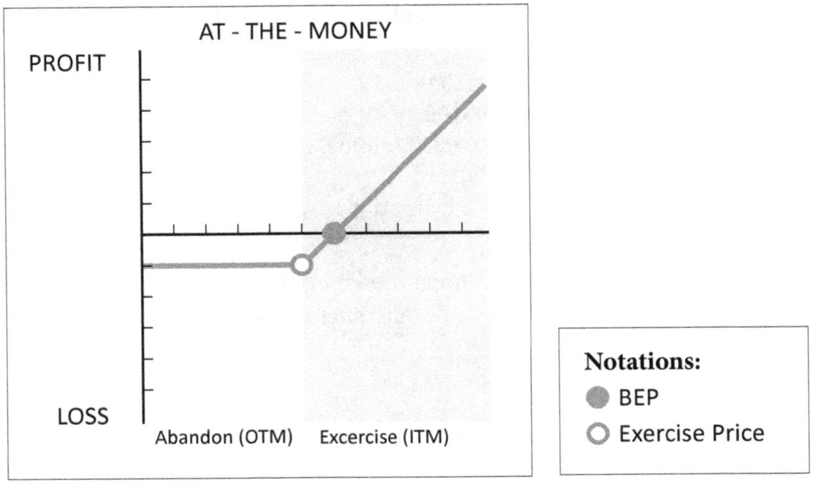

So the question is: Can we replicate a call payoff with a portfolio consisting of an underlying asset (a stock) and a riskless asset (a bond)? The binomial model proves that we can. Why these two instruments? Because buying a call is like buying stock at the discretion of the call holder—if the call option is exercised it ends up in underlying stock ownership. Stock purchase is normally financed with borrowed money—with a bond. Thus we have a combination of two different assets with two different payoffs that we can use to replicate the "asymmetric payoff" of the call. Underlying assets (shares of stock) would mimic the variable part of the call option payoff, and a riskless asset (a bond) would mimic the flat segment of the option payoff.

In the next step we shall demonstrate how to construct a replicating portfolio.

The key to the solution is in finding the right proportion—the number of units of S (the appropriate delta ratio for a stock), and the corresponding amount of borrowed money (a bond) that would satisfy the following equations:

Value of Investment

Initial Investment	At Expiration
No. of units x S_t (100) – B_t	up state: no. of units x S_T (\$125) – B_t(1+r) = \$25
	down state: no. of units x S_T (\$80) – B_t(1+r) = 0

Mathematically, the no. of units of stock are defined as the "delta ratio" for a stock. Formula for delta:

$$\Delta = \frac{Cu - Cd}{(u - d)\, S_t}$$

Solving for delta (Δ) we get:

$$\Delta = \frac{25 - 0}{125 - 80} = 0.5556, \quad \mathbf{\Delta = 0.5556}$$

Solving for B_t at maturity we get:

$1.0833B_T = \$69.45 - \$25 = \$44.45 = FV(B)$

$1.0833B_T = \$44.45 - 0 \quad = \$44.45 = FV(B)$

Now we shall verify if we have replicated the call payoff.

Replicating Portfolio Performance, Stock + Bond Payoff

	down state $80	up state $125
Stock	0.5556 x $80 = +$44.45	0.5556 x $125 = +$69.45
Bond	–$44.45	–$44.45
Payoff	**0**	**+$25.00**

Replicating Portfolio Payoff

0.5556St – PV(B) → up state: $69.45 – $44.45 = $25

0.5556St – PV(B) → down state: $44.45 – $44.45 = 0

The graphical interpretation of the construction of the replicating portfolio is presented in two phases in two figures—Figure 16.3 and Figure 16.4. These schemes reveal, by means of geometric depiction, how the major constituents of the portfolio are interrelated to each other:

Phase I (Figure 16.3) shows four separate payoffs: the payoff of a regular long stock position (solid black diagonal diagram); the payoff of long delta shares (dashed line diagram); short bond (flat diagram); and the payoff of a long call option (thick grey diagram).

As can be clearly seen from the graph, the slope of the stock payoff is determined by the number of shares purchased—its delta value—which is 0.5556. Following the one-step BOPM assumptions, the delta value of the shares in down-state ($80) translates to $44.45 and in up-state ($125) to 69.45.

The bond payoff is negative as it represents a liability: by selling a bond today (i.e., borrowing) we enter into an obligation to repay the par value of the bond—$44.45 at the bond's maturity. The repayment of the bond value has no relevance to the prevailing stock price at maturity—the fixed payoff equals $44.45 no matter if the stock price is at $80 or $125.

The call option diagram is depicted as the payoff of the long call, with the strike price (X) at $100. In a declining market the long call payoff is zero (as $ST \leq X$, flat part of the diagram from $100 downwards), while in rising markets ($ST \geq X$, from $100 upwards) the call value will rise in a direct one-to-one proportion with the rise in the underlying stock market price.

Figure 16.3 Replicating Portfolio – Phase I

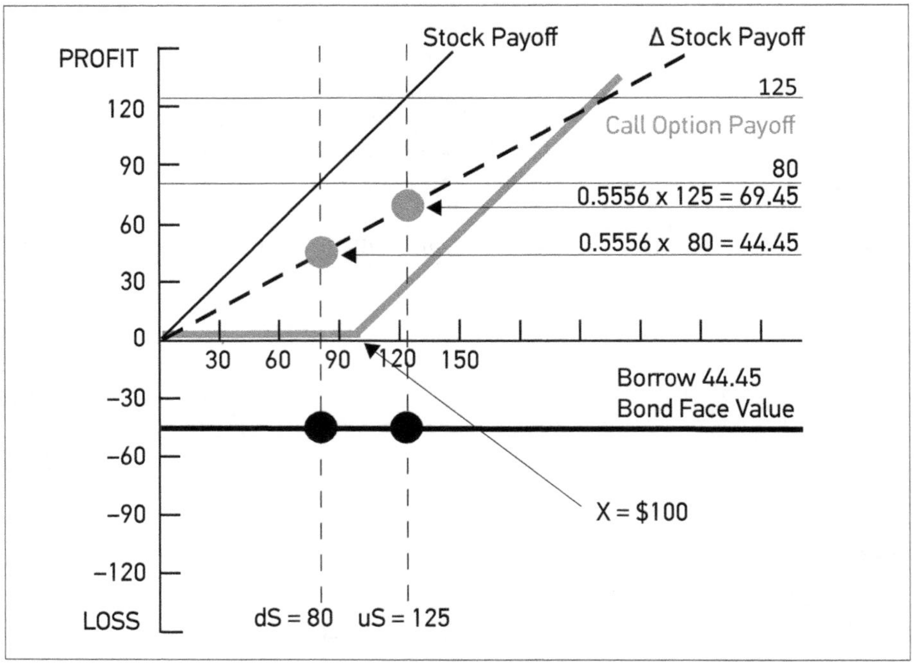

In phase II we are showing the combined Δstock + bond payoff being the only line that replicates the payoff of the call option.

Figure 16.4 Replicating Portfolio – Phase II (ΔStock + Bond Payoff)

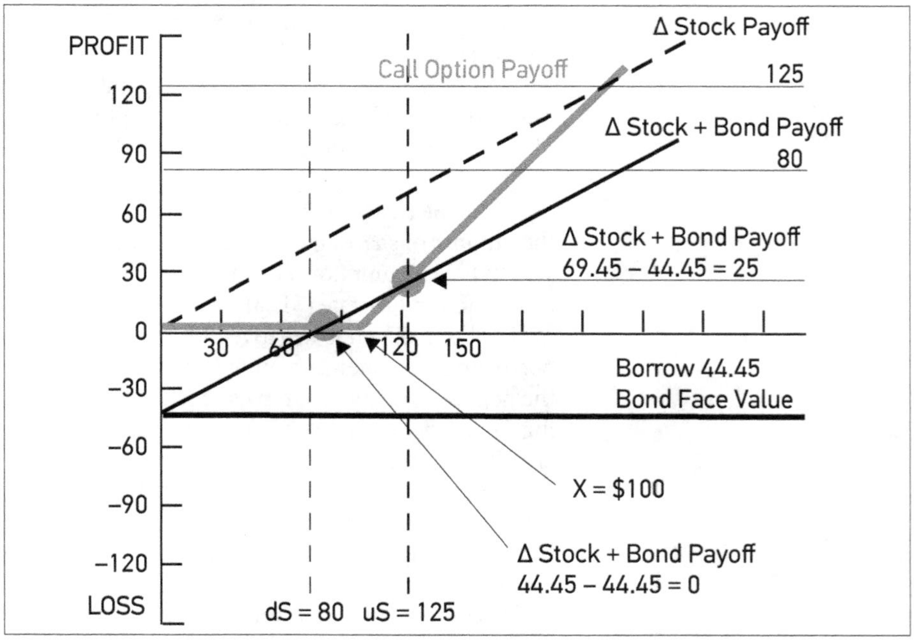

Remember This! Zero-Coupon Bonds

In most part of this work we are referring to "bonds" implying the particular type of bond known as a zero-coupon bond. The principal distinction between a zero-coupon bond and regular bonds (Treasury Notes and Treasury Bonds) is that zero-coupon bonds (often referred to as "discount bonds" or "deep discount bonds") do not make interest payments each month like regular bonds. Instead, zero-coupon bonds are sold out at a discount to their par or face value, whereas the issuer promises to pay you back on a particular day—the "maturity date"—all of the compounded interest, plus the principal.

The generalized formula for yield on a discount basis for Treasury bills is the following:
Discount Yield(%) = (Face Value – Purchase Price/Face Value) x 360/Days Till Maturity x 100%
The most recognized example of a zero-coupon bond is a US Treasury Bill that matures in one year or less (Bills with 91-day and 182-day maturities), which are commonly considered to be "riskless" because they are backed by "the full faith and credit" of the US government.

Bonds are also known "fixed-income" investments. Unlike stocks—which make no promises in regard to forward returns—if you buy a bond and hold it, you know exactly how much you're going to earn at maturity.
Treasury bills are sold by single price auctions, held weekly. After T-Bills have been issued in the primary market, you can buy and sell bonds in the secondary market. Individuals are now able to trade T-Bills online and have the funds debited from and credited directly to their personal bank accounts.

The portfolio (the grey diagram) constructed with Δ stock position and borrowing (short bond B) intercepts the payoff of the call precisely at two critical points, the only two values that a stock might take after one binomial step, which are: dS = 80 and uS = 125. Hence we have managed to create a synthetic instrument (combination of a long stock, short bond) that exactly mimics the payoff of a call.

Δ STOCK + BOND Payoff = CALL Payoff

And since the face value of the bond (FV(B) = Bt x 1.0833) will be paid out only on the expiration date, then the amount we borrow today must equal PV(B)—the present value of the bond (the bond discounted to its present value at the risk-free rate).

Bt = $44.45/1.0833
Bt = $41.03 = PV(B) present value of bond

Generalized formula for PV(B):

$$PV(B) = \frac{uCd - dCu}{(u - d)(1 + r)} = \frac{1.25\,(0) - 0.80\,(25)}{(1.25 - 0.80)\,1.0833} = \frac{20}{0.4874} = \$41.03$$

Because the replicating portfolio and the call option have identical payoffs after one binomial period—according to the no arbitrage principle—they must have the same cost today. The cost of acquiring the delta amount of shares of stock at current price St, and borrowing a certain amount of a bond discounted at the risk-free rate, must equal the fair value of the call option.

$$\Delta St + PV(B) = C$$

NB: (B) is a liability and as such always negative, always between 0 and the present value of borrowing.

Consequently, the left-hand side—the initial cost of the replicating portfolio, $\Delta St + PV(B) = (0.5556 \times \$100) - (\$44.45/1.0833) = \$14.53$, must be equal to the right hand side—the cost of the call option, C = $14.53.

Call Fair Value = $14.53

The portfolio constructed by buying delta shares of stock and selling the risk-free bond (borrowing) is the one that mimics exactly the payoff of the call. Therefore it is rightfully referred to as a **replicating portfolio.**

Key Terms

replicating portfolio
a portfolio consisting of an underlying asset and the riskless asset that yields exactly the same cash flows as a call or put option

Two distinctive features designate the replicating portfolio:

1. Number of shares: Δ (delta), and
2. Face value of bond: **FVB**

ΔStock Payoff + Bond Payoff → Replicating Portfolio → Call Payoff

Replication of risk is possible.
Leveraged equity position (S x no. shares of stock + bond) → fair value of a European call option = $\Delta S - PV(B)$

CREATING THE PERFORMANCE OF RISK-FREE HEDGING

Now we can use this replicating portfolio to convert a risky short call position into a risk-free strategy that returns FV(B) = $44.45 regardless of the underlying stock price at the expiration.

Let's check it out! We sell a call and receive a premium—$14.53. We need to borrow additional funds to be able to invest in S x no. of shares of stock that will perfectly hedge the risky position in both states; up as well as down.

Composition of the risk-free hedge portfolio:

Initial Investment	At Expiration
ΔS – Call Option →	Δ shares of stock – uC (call option at up state) Δ x $125 – Max [125 – 100.00]
ΔS – Call Option →	Δ shares of stock – dC (call option at down state) Δ x $80 – Max [80 – 100.00]

In the up state, St > X, the short call payoff will generate a loss equal to –(ST – X) so that the value of the hedged portfolio would be; Δ x $125 – $25.
In the down state, St ≤ X, the short call payoff will generate a zero return, so that the value of the hedged portfolio would be; Δ x $80 – 0.

Value of the Hedged Portfolio

Initial Investment		At Expiration
$55.56 – $14.53 = PV (B)	→	Δ shares of stock – uC 69.45 – 25 = $44.45 FV (B)
	→	Δ shares of stock – dC 44.45 – 0 = $44.45 FV (B)

Key Terms

hedged portfolio
a proportion of a portfolio consisting of an underlying asset and the riskless asset that returns exactly the risk-free rate

In this way we have created a **hedged portfolio**—one that earns a risk-free return—regardless of the price of the stock going up or down!

Since the value B will be paid out only at expiration date, the value of investment (delta no. of shares less the call value) must equal the present value of the Bond = PV(B)—the bond discounted to its present value at the risk-free rate.

PV(B) = $44.45/1.0833 = $41.03

In order to have a zero initial investment we need to borrow an amount PV(B) that equals the value of delta shares of stock minus the price that we get for the call.

PVB = ΔS – C
$41.03 = 0.5556 x $100 – $14.53

> With investing PV(B) = $4103
> You earned FV(B) = $4445
> A 8.33% difference, which is exactly the Risk-Free Return Rate.

It means that all derivatives can be valued by assuming that the return from their underlying assets is the risk-free rate.

The key postulation is that we find and form a risk-free hedge that can be priced directly and thereafter price the option off that risk-free hedge. The riskless hedge will be priced in such a way that at maturity it earns exactly the risk-free rate of return, which is where arbitrageurs come into play.

Call option value:

C = ΔS + PVB
C = 0.5556 x $100 – $44.45/1.0833
= $14.53

Call value = $14.53

In the next stage, we shall illustrate: firstly, how to configure a relevant portfolio to validate the no arbitrage principle, assuming that the call option price delivered by BOPM corresponds to the theoretical fair value; and secondly, the hypothetical cases in which the call option price deviates from the theoretical fair value, thus allowing the construction of an arbitrage portfolio.

VERIFICATION OF NO-ARBITRAGE PRINCIPLE

SCENARIO I: In case of share price increase to $125

Portfolio	Time (t)	Time (T) = $125
Short Call (14.53 x 100)	+$1453	
Borrow (Sell Bond)	+$4103	
Buy 55.56 Shares x 100	–$5556	
Buy more 44.44 Shares at $125		–$5555
Deliver 100 Shares@$100		+$10,000
Return Bond		–$4445
Portfolio Value:	0	0

At Time (t) you would not need to have the full funds to pay for the shares of stock but only a portion of this amount—delta Δ = 55.56 x 100.

Alternatively at Time (T) you may buy all 100 shares@125 = –$12.500 + deliver 100 shares for $10.000—incurring a loss of $2500).

Your total borrowing now is $2500 + $4445 = $6945.

You bought 55.56 shares at the outset. Sell the 55.56 shares @125 (current market price) = $69.45, and repay the indebtedness (the total borrowing of $6945). The result is the same = 0.

SCENARIO II: In case of share price decrease to $80

Portfolio	Time (t)	Time (T) = $80
Short Call (14.53 x 100)	+$1453	
Borrow (Sell Bond)	+$4103	
Buy 55.56 Shares x 100	–$5556	
Short Call Payoff		0
Sell 55.56 Shares at $80		+$4445
Return Bond		–$4445
Portfolio Value:	0	0

Irrespective of the underlying asset price direction (whether the stock price rises or falls) after writing a call—the hedged portfolio at expiration will always produce the same result.

Deviations from Fair Value Deviations from fair value of a European call option lead to arbitrage-free profit.

If the contract premium is anything other than $14.53 (the value derived by the model), then you have a chance of locking in a pure arbitrage profit—aka "free money." By adhering strictly to the rules ensuing from a put-call parity equation, you have a chance to earn money without risking any of your own.

For example, let us suppose that the call premium is $15.50. To take advantage of a mispriced call option you should deploy the strategy as follows:

Assumption:
Call overpriced = $15.50

SCENARIO I: If share price increases to $125

Portfolio	Time (t)	Time (T) = $125
Short Call (15.50 x 100)	+$1550	
Borrow (Sell Bond)	+$4006	
Buy 55.56 Shares x 100	–$5556	
Buy more 44.44 Shares at $125		–$5555
Deliver 100 Shares@$100		+$10,000
Return Bond ($4006 x 1.08333)		–$4340
Portfolio Value:	0	+$105

SCENARIO II: If share price decreases to $80

Portfolio	Time (t)	Time (T) = $80
Short Call (15.50 x 100)	+$1550	
Borrow (Sell Bond)	+$4006	
Buy 55.56 Shares x 100	–$5556	
Short Call Payoff		0
Sell 55.56 Shares at $80		+$4445
Return Bond ($4006 x 1.08333)		–$4340
Portfolio Value:	0	+$105

If the call turns to be overpriced, with zero initial investment you end up with a riskless profit of $105.

You are getting 97 cents per stock ($15.50 – $14.53) x $100 x 1.0833 = $105

If the option premium is $14.00 then you deploy the opposite strategy: short 50 XYZ; buy one contract (call); and invest the money in the money market.

Assumption:
Call underpriced = $14.00

SCENARIO I: If share price increases to $125:

Portfolio	Time (t)	Time (T) = $125
Sell Short 55.56 Shares x 100	+$5556	
Buy Call ($14 x 100)	–$1400	
Lend (Buy Bond)	–$4156	
Buy back 55.56 Shares at $125		–$6945
Sell Back Call ($125 – $100)		+$2500
Collect Bond ($4156 x 1.08333)		+$4502
Portfolio Value:	0	+$57

SCENARIO II: If share price decreases to $80

Portfolio	Time (t)	Time (T) = $80
Sell Short 55.56 Shares x 100	+$5556	
Buy Call ($14 x 100)	–$1400	
Lend (Buy Bond)	–$4156	
Buy back 55.56 Shares at $80		–$4445
Long Call Payoff		0
Collect Bond ($4156 x 1.08333)		+$4502
Portfolio Value:	0	+$57

In case the call happens to be underpriced with zero initial investment you end up with a riskless profit of $57.

You are getting 53 cents per stock ($14.53 – $14.00) x $100 x 1.0833 = $57

MULTIPLE BINOMIAL TREE

We assume that an option contract expires at time t3. Firstly, we calculate the asset prices working forward from the present time—period 0—all the way through to period 3, based on notations as shown below.

Figure 16.5 Multi-Binomial Tree Notations

	Step I	Step II	Step III
			Cuuu
		Cuu	
	Cu		Cuud
C		Cud	
	Cd		Cudd
		Cdd	
			Cddd
Period 0	*Period 1*	*Period 2*	*Period 3*

Computation of option prices at each node goes in the opposite direction from that used to compute the prices of the underlying instrument. We apply an iterative technique called **backward induction,** which starts from the last step of the binomial tree and goes backward to the present.

At the end of the tree (time t3, final step), all option payouts are the payouts at expiration, hence all option prices at each final node are known as they simply equal their terminal intrinsic values. This is consistently logical as the payout of the option is a function only of the underlying value at expiration.

Now we can enter call prices at expiration that equal their terminal intrinsic values. No calculation is required.

Note that in this example we have chosen the option exercise price to be **X = $95,** therefore the corresponding option values (C) would be as follows:

Key Terms

backward induction
iterative process of calculating option prices starting from the option payouts at expiration of the given binomial tree and then working back to the present value

Figure 16.6 3 Step Binomial Tree

	Step I	Step II	Step III
			112.74
			C=17.74
		108.32	
	104.08		104.08
			C=9.08
100		100	
	96.08		96.08
			C=1.08
		92.31	
			88.69
			C=0
Period 0	*Period 1*	*Period 2*	*Period 3*

Assumptions for calculating the hedge ratio and call option prices:

S = \$100
X = \$95
r = 0.0005
u = 1.0408
d = 0.9608

Inputs for calculating **u** and **d**:

$\sigma = 40\%$
t = 1/100 = 0.01
σ step = $0.4\sqrt{0.01}$
σ step = 0.4 x 0.1
σ step = 0.04
u = exp (0.04) ≈ 1.0408
d = exp (−0.04) ≈ 0.9608

Backward Induction Calculus As all remaining nodes of the tree are not payouts at expiration, the option values must be calculated. Therefore, we move one step back and calculate option values for each of the three nodes at time t_2 (step II) using terminal intrinsic values from time t_3 (step III).

We start with the top of Step II where we find the stock value to be, S = \$108.32. For easier understanding we may attach the following notations to each node, starting with the first column:

t_0 – S = \$100 **(A)**,
t_1 – S = \$96.08 **(B)**, S = \$104.08 **(C)**,
t_2 – S = \$92.31 **(D)**, S = \$100.00 **(E)**, S = \$108.32 **(F)**,
t_3 – S = \$88.69 **(G)**, S = \$96.08 **(H)**, S = \$104.08 **(I)** S = \$112.74 **(J)**

We extract the first triangle (F), (J), (I), and apply the same mathematical reasoning as in the case of the one-step binomial tree.

Price@time t_2	Terminal Values	Intrinsic Values
	\$112.74 (J)	\$17.74
\$108.32 (F)		
	\$104.08 (I)	\$9.08

First, we calculate the hedge ratio, Δ (delta):

Δ = \$17.74 – \$9.08/\$112.74 – \$104.08 = **1**

We then calculate the value for B by creating a "hedged portfolio"—the one with the risk-free payoff:

B = 1 x \$112.74 – \$17.74
= 1 x \$104.08 – \$9.08
= **\$95**

Validate that the "replicating portfolio" is correct (the one that replicates the call option payoff at terminal states; J & I).

Portfolio (J) = ΔS (J) – B
Portfolio (J) = 1 x \$112.74 – \$95 = **17.74**

Portfolio (I) = ΔS (I) – B
Portfolio (I) = 1 x \$104.08 – \$95 = **\$9.08**

Finally, we calculate the value of the call at (F) by discounting the value of the bond at the risk-free rate according to the formula:

$$C = \Delta S + B / (1 + r)$$

C = 1 x \$108.32 – \$95/1.0005 = **\$13.3675**

We move down to the next sub-period—node **(E)**, S = \$100 and extract the triangle defined by (E), (I), (H):

Price@time II	Terminal Values	Intrinsic Values
	\$104.08 (I)	\$9.08
\$100.00 (E)		
	\$96.08 (H)	\$1.08

We calculate the new hedge ratio: Δ(delta) for node (E):
Δ = \$9.08 – \$1.08/\$104.08 – \$96.08 = **1**

We formulate the replicating portfolio:
1 x \$104.08 – \$9.08 = \$96.08 – \$1.08 = **\$95**

And again, we calculate the value of the call at (E):
C = 1 x $100.00 – $95/1.0005
= **$5.0475**

We complete Step II with the final sub-period which happens to be the node (D), S = $92.31. The corresponding triangle is defined as (D), (H), (G).

Repeating the same calculus, we find that the value of the call at the node (D) is:
C = **$0.535**
Applying the analogous "one period" methodology for each node, we finally arrive to the following option values:

Figure 16.7 3 Step Binomial Tree: Final Values

	Step I	Step II	Step III
			(J) C = $17.74
		(F) C = $13.3675	
	(C) C = $9.175		(I) C = $9.08
(A) C = $5.95		(E) C = $5.0475	
	(B) C = $2.774		(H) C = $1.08
		(D) C = $0.535	
			(G) C = 0
Period 0	*Period 1*	*Period 2*	*Period 3*

II. RISK-NEUTRAL HEDGE MODEL

The risk-neutral hedge approach is an alternative technique for an option's valuation that lead to the same result. This method is faster than risk-free hedging as it exploits risk-neutral valuation based on probabilities of underlying prices and corresponds directly to the properties of the binomial tree.

For this reason we shall delve deeper into the features embedded in the binomial tree and binomial expansion theorem.

PASCAL'S TRIANGLE

Pascal's triangle is a remarkable visual aid aimed to facilitate understanding of two key features of the binomial expansion theorem with compelling and unambiguous logic.

We begin with an elaboration of the logic behind Pascal's Triangle coefficients hierarchy:

- Triangle begins with 1 because (x + y) 0 = 1;
- Row no.1, is all 1, because when the exponent is 1 you get the original polynomial unchanged; (x + y) 1 = x + y;
- All edge figures below begin and end with term 1;
- In between, each subsequent term is the addition of a pair of terms right above it;
- For example, row no. 3: 3 is obtained from 1 and 2 above;
- Row no. 5: 5 is obtained from 1 and 4 right above; 10 is obtained from 6 and 4 right above, and so on and so forth;
- Coefficients are symmetric.

Figure 16.8 Pascal's Triangle – Coefficient Pattern

1

1 1

1 2 1

1 3 3 1

1 4 6 4 1

1 5 10 10 5 1

Raising binomial to a power:

(x + y) 0 = 1
(x + y) 1 = 1 x + 1y
(x + y) 2 = 1 x^2 + 2 xy + 1y^2
(x + y) 3 = 1x3 + 3x2y + 3xy2 + 1y3

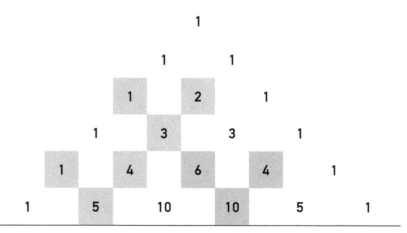

$(x + y)\ 4 = 1x^4 + 4x^3y + 6x^2y^2 + 4xy^3 + 1y^4$
$(x + y)\ 5 = 1x^5 + 5x^4y + 10x^3y^2 + 10x^2y^3 + 5xy^4 + 1y^5$

Exponents pattern:

Take a careful look, for example, at step no. 4, (x + y) 4: exponents of "x" start with 4 and go down to zero; $x^4, x^3, x^2, x^1 = x, x^0 = 1$, whereas exponents of "y" start with 0 and go upwards to 5 as illustrated in step no. 5, $(x + y)^5$: $y^0 = 1, y^1 = y, y^2, y^3, y^4, y^5$.

Figure 16.9 Pascal's Triangle – Exponents Pattern Example

$(x + y)\ 0 = 1$

$(x + y)\ 1 = x + y$

$(x + y)\ 2 = x^2 + 2xy + y^2$

$(x + y)\ 3 = x^3 + 3x^2y + 3xy^2 + y^3$

$(x + y)\ 4 = x^4 + 4x^3y + 6x^2y^2 + 4x^1y^3 + x^0y^4$

$(x + y)\ 5 = x^5\ y^0 + 5x^4\ y^1 + 10x^3\ y^2 + 10x^2\ y^3 + 5x\ y^4 + y^5$

Based on these premises a formula has been developed that allows "easy" calculation of a binomial raised to a power of "n", which is as follows:

Synthesized expression of the binomial theorem no. 1

$$(x + y)^n = \sum_{k=0}^{n} \binom{n}{k} x^k\, y^{n-k}$$

The upper index **n** is the exponent of the expansion; the lower index **k** refers to which term.

Example:

when n = 5, each term in the expansion of $(a + b)^5$ will look like this:

$(5/0)\ a^{5-k}b^k$

k will successively take on the values 0 through 5.

$(a + b)^5 = (5/0)\ a^5 + (5/1)\ a^4b + (5/2)\ a^3b^2 + (5/3)\ a^2b^3 + (5/4)\ ab^4 + (5/5)\ b^5 = 1a^5 + 5\ a^4b + 10\ a^3b^2 + 10\ a^2b^3 + 5\ ab^4 + 1\ b^5$!

You will also notice that the coefficient of the first term is always 1, and the coefficient of the second term is always the same as the exponent of (a + b), which is 5 in this example.

The term (5/3), for example, is calculated as follows: 5 x 4 x 3/1 x 2 x 3 = 60/6 = 10

Another generalized formula expressing the same relationship introduces the "sigma" notation with the factorials:

Synthesized expression of the binomial theorem no. 2

$$(a+b)^n = \sum_{k=0}^{n} \frac{n!}{(n-k)!\,k!} a^{n-k} b^k$$

The factorial notation "*n!*" means; the product of all the whole numbers between 1 and n, so, for instance, $6! = 1 \times 2 \times 3 \times 4 \times 5 \times 6$.

COMPUTING RISK-NEUTRAL PROBABILITIES

We begin with a "One-Step Binomial Model" using the same model assumptions as in the riskless valuation model, therefore:

Notations:
S = \$100
X = \$100
r = 0.0833 (annual risk free 8% rate continuously compounded)
up factor >1 u = 1.25
down factor d = 1/u <1 d = 0.80

Call payoff:

Value of stock, S_0 = 100

→ uS = \$125
Cu = \$25 max (uS – X, 0)

→ dS = \$80
Cd = 0 max (dS – X, 0)

A risk-neutral valuation is a complementary model to that which we have encountered in the "replication of risk" model and as such it hinges upon a premise of a "risk-neutral economy"—in which all investors are indifferent to risk, and where the expected rate of return on the stock equals the risk-free rate:

We assign the probabilities "**p**" for the stock price going up, and (1 – **p**) for the stock price going down, so that "**p**" values satisfy the following equilibrium condition:

$$puS + (1 - p)\,dS = (1 + r)\,S0$$

We derive the "p" value:

p = (1 + r) – d/u – d
= 1.08333 – 0.80/1.25 – 0.80
= **0.6296,** and
(1 – p) = **0.3704**

Substituting the "p" values in the above equation we can verify that the expected rate of return on the stock equals the risk-free rate.

(**0.6296** x \$125) + (**0.3704** x \$80) = \$78.7 + \$29.632 = **\$108.333**

Alternatively, we could have computed the probability values (**p; 1 – p**) with a slightly different method, the one which postulates that the stock price equals the expected value of the terminal payoff, discounted by the risk-free rate.

$$S0 = [125p + (1 - p)\ 80] \times 1 / (1 + r)$$

p = S0/0.923079 – dS/uS – dS
= \$100/0.923079 – \$80/\$125 – \$80
= 28.333/45
= **0.6296**, and
(1 – p) = **0.3704**

By substituting the probabilities we can validate that the stock price equals the expected value of the terminal payment, discounted at the risk-free rate:

\$100 = [\$125 x 0.6296 + 0.3704 x \$80] x 0.923079
= \$108.333 x 0.923079
= \$100

Consequently, if all investors were risk neutral, then it must follow that the option price would be equal to the probability-weighted potential payouts, or the cash flows discounted at risk-free rate.

$$C = pCu + (1 - p)\ Cd / (1 + r)$$

C = [(0.6296 x \$25) + (0.3704 x 0)]/1.08333
= (\$15.74 + 0)/1.08333
= \$14.53

Thus we may assume that the formula derived from risk-neutral assumptions is just a mathematical validation expressing the obvious particulars:

The option value is the sum of the probability-weighted intrinsic values discounted at the risk-free rate.

CONSTRUCTING THE MULTI-BINOMIAL TREE

If we recall the call payoffs at expiration, we shall observe that only the higher price paths create option intrinsic values at expiration [(St – X) if St > X]. All the low price paths—stock prices that are lower than the exercise price at expiration—do not add to option value and their payoff simply equals zero; (0 if St < X).

For the sake of comparison, we keep the same data as in the Risk Neutral Model.

S = 100
X = 95
(1 + r) = R = 1.0005
(1 + r) 3 = 1.0015
u = exp (.04) ≈ 1.0408
d = exp (−.04) ≈ 0.9608

and we work out underlying instrument values:

Figure 16.10 Multi-Binomial Tree

Underlying Instrument Values			
			(J) S = 112.74
		(F) S = 108.32	
	(C) S = 104.08		(I) S = 104.08
(A) S = 100		(E) S = 100	
	(B) S = 96.08		(H) S = 96.08
		(D) S = 92.31	
			(G) S = 88.69
Call Values			
			(J) C = 17.74
		(F) C = 13.37	
	(C) C = 9.175		**(I) C = 9.08**
(A) C = 5.95		(E) C = 5.05	
	(B) C = 2.774		**(H) C = 1.08**
		(D) C = 0.535	
			(G) C = 0
Period 0	*Period 1*	*Period 2*	*Period 3*

Accordingly, we may enter call prices at expiration at the end of the tree (Period 3) as they equal their payouts at expiration. All remaining nodes of the tree have to be calculated.

In the next step, we calculate the respective probabilities, according to the formula:

$$p = R - d/u - d$$

p = 1.0005 − 0.9608/1.0408 − 0.9608
= 0.49625, and
(1 − p) = 0.50375
Next, we apply the formula from the "Binomial Expansion Theorem," Pascal's triangle for the row no. 3 (Period 3):

$$(x + y)^3 = 1x^3 + 3x^2y + 3xy^2 + 1y^3$$

$C = \{1 \text{ x } (0.49625)^3 \text{ x } \$17.74 + [3(0.49625)^2 (0.50375)] \text{ x } \$9.08 + [3 (0.49625)(0.50375)^2] \text{ x } \$1.08 + [1 \text{ x } (0.50375)^3 \text{ x } 0]\}/(1+0.0005)^3$

$C = [(0.1222 \text{ x } \$17.74) + (0.3722 \text{ x } \$9.08) + (0.3778 \text{ x } \$1.08) + (0.1278 \text{ x } 0)]/0.0015$

The sum of probabilities must equal 1: 0.1222 + 0.3722 + 0.3778 + 0.1278 = 1

$C = (2.1678 + 3.3796 + 0.4080 + 0)/1.0015$
$= 5.9465 \approx \$5.95$

Voila! Using the risk neutral approach, we have arrived at exactly the same call price as in the riskless hedge model. The advantage of the "Binomial expansion theorem" becomes obvious.

Verification of the model:

$$pSu + (1 - p)\ Sd = (1 + r)\ S0$$

$(0.49625 \text{ x } \$104.08) + (1 - 0.49625) \text{ x } \$96.08 = 1.0005 \text{ x } \$100 = \$100.05$

$$pu + (1 - p)\ d = (1 + r) \text{ or } R$$

$(0.49625 \text{ x } 1.0408) + (1 - 0.49625) \text{ x } 0.9608 = 1.0005$

Check C value; for example, at F node:

$CF = [(0.49625 \text{ x } \$17.74) + (0.50375 \text{ x } \$9.08)]/1.0005$
$= \$8.803475 + \$4.57405$
$= \$13.377525/1.0005$
$= \$13.37$

DYNAMIC HEDGE PRIMER; A RANDOM WALK THROUGH THE BINOMIAL TREE

The following is an attempt designed to illustrate how we could use the model to our advantage in the case where real-world option prices deviate from those suggested by the model.

In a risk-neutral world, the risk associated with asset prices moving up or down loses its significance. The asset itself—due to the possibility of re-balancing the portfolio dynamically and perfectly—behaves like a bond.

We shall try to verify this statement in the illustration that follows below with one remark related to dynamic hedging.

Dynamic hedging in its very essence is a process of continuous re-balancing. It is worth mentioning that the term "continuous" in this construction refers more to a theoretical connotation rather than empirical reality as in practice we are only able to re-balance the portfolio at discrete time intervals.

In order to fully understand the logic behind the continuous re-balancing process that we are intending to illustrate, we need to remind ourselves of how the change of the stock price affects delta.

Near expiration the value of delta accelerates towards 1 (one)—if the option is in-the-money—or towards 0 (zero)—if the option is out-of-the-money. Therefore, at expiration delta may only take two values—either 1 (one) or 0 (zero).

If the option finishes out-of-the-money, the delta value finishes at 0 (zero): the number of shares purchased declines to 0 (zero); and the amount of bond declines to 0 (zero) too. Why? Because at different points of time as the stock was declining we were selling the stock back to pay down the bond. So, at expiration the portfolio should contain 0 (zero) shares and 0 (zero) bond.

If the stock finishes in-the-money, delta value is 1 (one): the call option writer is assigned and he will have to deliver the shares. Then the number of shares in the portfolio must be exactly equal to the number of shares required by the owner of the option. How do we achieve that? At different points in time as the stock increases we increase the purchase of delta shares of the stock, financed by increased borrowing. The funds received against the delivered shares of stock will have to be exactly enough to offset the outstanding bond liability. The initial portfolio constructed with the delta amount of shares of stock at current price and shorting a certain amount of bond is referred to as a **self-financing/replicating** portfolio—after initiating the strategy we do not need to invest more funds as all eventual requirements for additional payments are financed through borrowing.

In order to exemplify the characteristics of the dynamic hedging process with continuous re-balancing we shall use rather exaggerated values respectively:

S = \$90
X = \$100
u = 1.25
d = 0.80
R = 1.10

Figure 16.11 Random Walk through 3 Step Binomial Tree

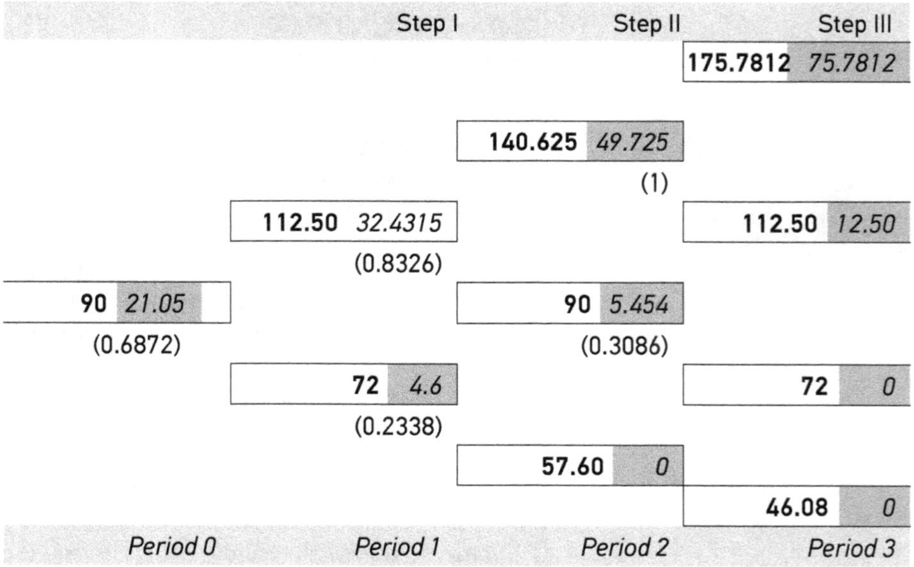

Notations:
bold numbers denote stock prices
numbers in brackets denote delta values
shaded numbers denote call values

Now we can start our "random walk."

The model, as we can see, defines the fair value of the call to be \$21.05. Suppose that the current market price of the call on the same share of stock and with the same strike (\$90) is selling at \$23.00. This would imply that the call is overpriced and that we may initiate an arbitrage portfolio to our advantage:

Time t_0. Initiate the hedge. We sell the overpriced call at \$23, and construct a riskless hedge portfolio by purchasing delta shares of stock less the value of the call = (0.6872 x \$90.00) – \$21.05 = \$40.798. We short sell the bond = \$40.798 to finance the purchase of a partial amount of stock. The difference between \$23 and \$21.05 = \$1.95 rests safely deposited in the bank.

Time t_1. Now, we may choose arbitrarily our next step. We may follow the stock path going up or down. Let us assume that the stock price in the next time period went down to \$72.00. The stock price decline is reflected in the change of delta so that new delta is now 0.2338. We have to adjust our "long stock-short bond" portfolio to reflect that change. To do that, we sell a partial amount of shares (0.6872 – 0.2338 = 0.4534) at \$72.00 per share for a total value of 0.4534 x \$72 = \$32.6448. We use these funds to pay back the liability from the previous step—time t0—which is now equal to \$40.798 x 1.1 = \$44.8778. The repayment reduces our total liability to \$44.8778 – \$32.6448 = \$12.233.

Time t_2. Again we may choose the next step according to our preferences. Suppose we decide to follow the up path and the stock price at the next time interval—time t_2— is at 90.00. The corresponding delta value is 0.3086. We buy a partial amount of shares (0.3086 – 0.2338 = 0.0748) at \$90.00 per share for a total value of \$6.732. We borrow \$6.732 to finance the purchase. Our total indebtedness is 12.233 x 1.1 = \$13.4563 + \$6.732 = \$20.1883.

Time t_3. At this point we may choose two alternatives—the stock shall either expire in-the-money (\$112.50), or it will finish out-of-the-money (\$72). Let us check out both scenarios:

- If the stock finishes in-the-money (\$112.50). The delta at expiration equals 1. The call you sold has been assigned and you are obliged to deliver. You buy 1 share of stock at 1 x \$112.50 = \$112.50 incurring a loss of \$12.50 (\$112.50 – \$100 = \$12.50). You borrow additional funds = \$12.50 to cover the loss. Your total liability is \$20.1883 x 1.1 = \$22.20713 + 12.50 = \$34.71. You are also left with 0.3086 shares. Sell this at \$112.50 per share for a total value of \$34.71 and use the proceeds to repay the liability.

- If the stock finishes out-of-the-money (\$72) the stock expires worthless. You are left with 0.3086 shares worth \$72.00 per share. Sell this for a total amount of \$22.21 and cover the borrowing of \$20.1883 x 1.1 = \$22.21.

In both cases you break even. You go to the bank and recover your deposit which has grown safely to $1.95 \times (1.1)^3 = \$2.60$.

SUMMARY

This chapter explaines the concept of the Binomial Options Pricing Model or BOPM. We use this model to determine the theoretical fair value of an option under the assumption that the stock price expansion process assumes the form of a binomial tree or lattice. The process of "binomial valuation" is split into two models: "Riskless hedge model" and "Risk neutral model."

Explanation of the riskless hedge model began with constructing a one-step binomial tree which assumes that an asset (stock) may take on only two possible values at expiration. We then proceeded by finding a replicating portfolio whose payoff is the same as the call payoff that we want to price. We discovered that the call payoff may be replicated combining a stock and a bond. In an attempt to find an observable model to prove this proposition we developed graphic schemes (Figure 16.3 and 16.4) to help elucidate this seemingly elusive and delicate relationship. Next, we offered the proofs for the no arbitrage principle and illustrated how the eventual deviations from the fair value may be exploited to your advantage. Finally, we described the step by step method for constructing the multi-binomial tree.

The next model, the risk-neutral model, is entered with the explication of Pascal's Triangle—a model that explains the logic of raising a binomial to a power leading to a generalized binomial theorem formula used to calculate an asset value at any binomial tree node.

We also covered characteristics of computing risk-neutral probabilities and the process of constructing a multi-binomial tree based on the premises of Pascal's Triangle.

The last entry, the dynamic hedge primer, completed our overview of the binomial option pricing model. This example was meant to illustrate the process of continuous rebalancing, and how the deviations of real-world option prices from the fair value suggested by the model might be employed in constituting an arbitrage portfolio.

KEY TERMS

BOPM
binomial tree
multiplicative tree
recombining tree
replicating portfolio
hedged portfolio
backward induction

CHAPTER 17

PARITY RELATIONS

CHAPTER OBJECTIVES

- To introduce the concept of derivatives parity relations
- To discuss the fundamental relationship between options and underlying instruments
- To introduce basic equations resulting from payoff geometry diagrams
- To highlight the differences between put and call option payoffs
- To define and illustrate put-call parity geometry and the equations ensuing thereof
- To display arbitrage opportunities arising from mispriced options
- To illustrate the case of conversion strategy
- To illustrate the case of reverse conversion or reversal strategy

PARITY RELATIONS BETWEEN OPTIONS AND UNDERLYING ASSETS

THIS CHAPTER INTRODUCES THE CONCEPT OF PARITY RELATIONS. These can be summed up as a correlation existing between a put and a call option of the same class (the same exercise price and expiration date), and an underlying asset configured in such a manner as to preclude arbitrage opportunities—the existence of riskless profit. If you manage to grasp this concept in its entirety, further understanding of basic hedging strategies discussed in the next chapter will be much facilitated. The best way to delve into the intricacies of the phenomena we are exploring and to unveil the complexity of positions that can be created between elements constituting the parity relations is through a graphical depiction.

Now, imagine the payoff diagrams of long and short underlying assets together with all four types of options with no premium—where premiums are equal to zero—on the same underlying asset, with the same expiration date and the same exercise price presented together in a single graph.

The figure would look something like this:

Figure 17.1 Parity Relations Between Options And Underlying Assets

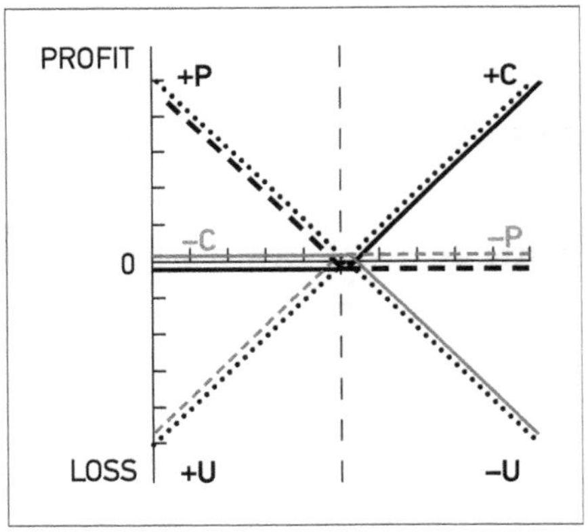

The graphical exposition above encapsulates the plurality of the relationship existing between singular payoffs and their entwined causality. Although it may resemble a railroad crossing sign, the constellation of different payoffs as presented in the figure is a fine example of geometry and algebra in harmonious agreement.

Abstraction of the put-call parity relations now becomes perceptible and may be monitored at a glance. The visual display is designed to achieve three objectives:

1. To show the complexity of locked-in relations,
2. To offer the key to unravel the hidden patterns existing between puts and calls on the one side and underlying securities on the other, and
3. To demonstrate how this underlying geometric conjunction ultimately converges on their algebraic equations.

We begin to decipher the graph by outlining the graphic representation of options payoff diagrams:

+C = solid black	+P = dashed black	-C = solid grey	-P = dashed grey

The remaining two—the underlying instrument payoffs (long and short)—will be represented with the dotted black diagonals.
Letter symbols remain unchanged:

Long Call + C	**Long Put + P**	**Short Call - C**	**Short Put - P**

Long Underlying: + U	**Short Underlaying: -U**

Thanks to the graphic and symbolic identity assigned to each payoff profile, we may now differentiate between them.

So, then, let's get back to Figure 17.1 and see what would happen if we take the long underlying out of the scene. What is left in its place is the same payoff replicated by two options payoffs—long call and short put—thus creating a **synthetic long** position.

+C -P = +U long call and short put equal the long underlying.

Applying the same procedure to the short underlying we shall discover the following causation:

-C +P = -U short call and long put equal the short underlying,

this leads us to the conclusion that the above equations, manipulated in symbolic form, correspond to the rules of geometry as exhibited in Figure 17.2.

Figure 17.2 Put-Call Parity P/L Illustrations-Synthetic Underlying

Long Underlying: + U = +C – P **Short Underlying: -U = +P – C**

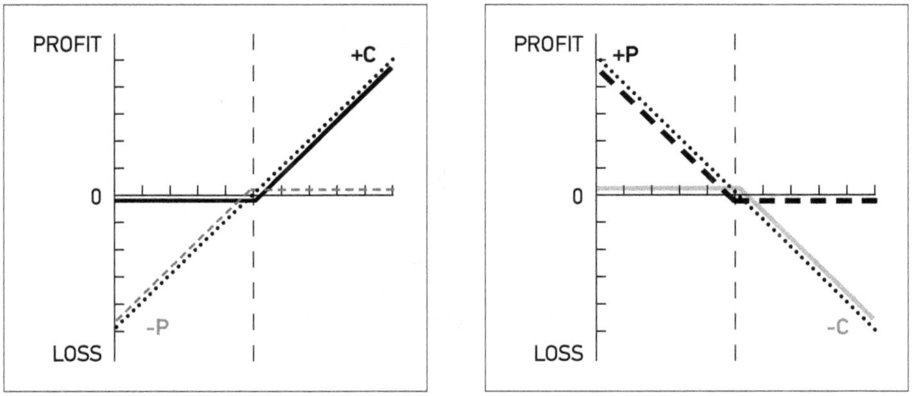

We may carry this farther, and affirm that each of the displayed options constituents can be replicated by a combination of the other two related elements. The following equations are simple derivatives ensuing from the parity relations geometry manipulated according to the rules of arithmetic:

+C = +P + U; -C = -P – U
+P = +C – U; -P = -C + U

Now, let's prove that the above algebraic equations are also manipulated according to the rules of geometry.

In Figure 17.3 we shall extract each of the option payoffs in order to unveil the arcane constellation between an option payoff and an underlying payoff that allows the creation of **synthetic options.**

Figure 17.3 Put-Call Parity P/L Illustrations-Synthetic Options

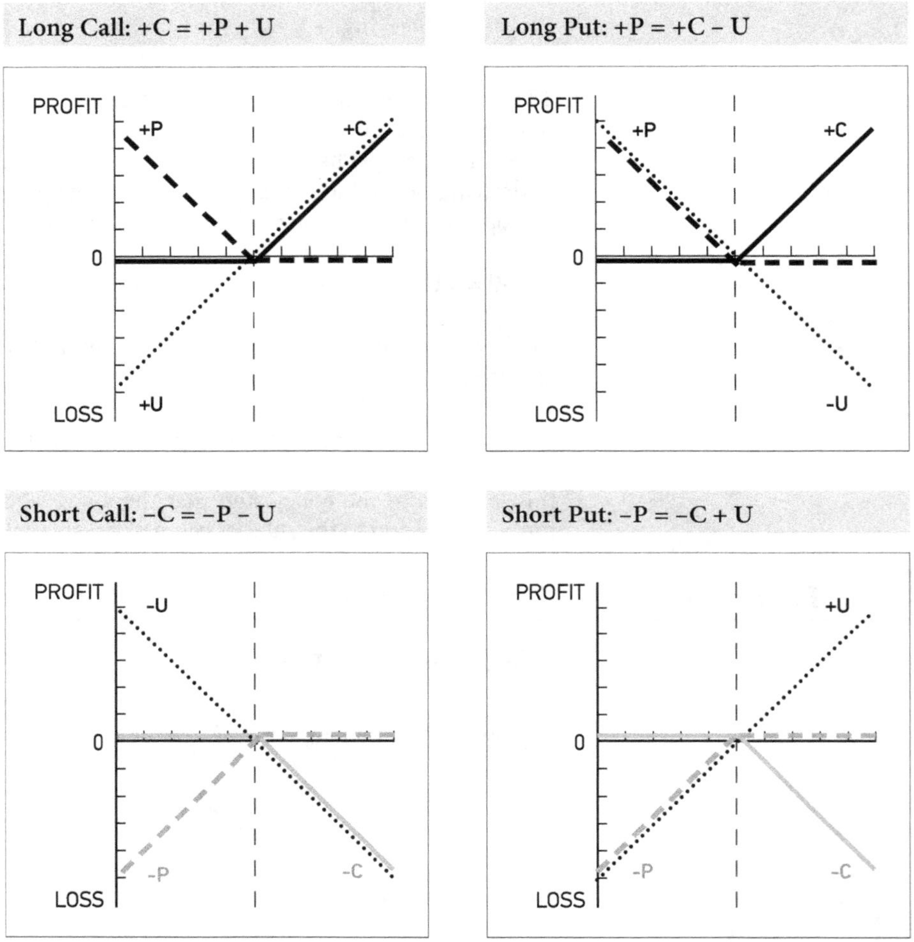

From the graphical presentation we can unreservedly assert that each option payoff may be replicated synthetically in between two correlated instruments:

- Long call = Long put + long underlying
- Short call = Short put + short underlying
- Long put = Long call + short underlying
- Short put = Short call + long underlying

So far we have discovered six synthetic positions in aggregate:

- two positions that combine a put and a call option and coalesce into a single synthetically created underlying instrument payoff, and

Key Terms

synthetic option
an option payoff profile replicated in between a plain vanilla option and an underlying

- four positions that combine put and call options with an underlying and coalesce into a synthetic option payoff

We are missing two more configurations:

- long put and short call against long underlying coalesce to zero; +P –C +U = 0
- long call and short put against short underlying coalesce to zero; +C –P –U = 0

The put-call parity graphic geometries provide the most beneficial tool intended to help you, firstly, to understand these complex interrelations, and secondly, to grasp the variety of all possible alternatives. It is our firm belief that if you manage to memorize the position diagram compendium exhibited in Figure 17.1 and the geometric inference offered, you will be able to compose and recreate mentally any of the synthetic equations. The only thing needed is to choose one of the synthetically created position diagrams—by virtue of your personal affinity—the one you consider to be the basic or fundamental—and then based on that single configuration you should be able to build infallibly all others.

Recapitulation ensuing from the payoff geometry We arrive at the concept of a put-call parity which explicates, in geometrical terms, the causality between the different constituent payoffs (options and underlying instruments), stating that every single constituent payoff may be replicated by combining the other two.

Algebraic recapitulation of the entire put-call parity complex:

Table 17.1 Put-Call Parity P/L Equations

–U = +P –C	**+U** = +C –P
+P = +C –U	**+C** = +P +U
–P = –C +U	**–C** = – P –U
+P –C +U = 0	+C –P –U = 0

PUT-CALL PARITY

Up to this point we have concentrated on developing a visual elucidation of the complex relationship that exists between options and their underlying instruments. For this purpose we have articulated the importance of the P/L diagrams compendium (Figure 17.1) to outline the diversity and complexity of parity relations.

A foundational constituent of the put-call parity model is the no arbitrage principle—the hallmark of efficient markets—that prevents the incidence of a riskless investment: a portfolio that could earn the riskless rate of interest.

Extracting shared characteristics from the put-call parity examples, the model conclusively substantiates the hypothesis that equivalent assets—actuals and their synthetically created equivalents—with identical payoff diagrams at every state and point in time, must sell for the same price. If not, there is an arbitrage opportunity—existence of riskless profit.

If we want to go one step further and translate this relationship into its quantitative terms we need to assign a price to each component. By introducing the "fourth element" in our parity equations we arrive at the so-called "put-call parity equations."

Therefore in addition to put and call options and underlying instruments we have to include also the payoff of the asset that is considered to be "risk-free"—a bond. The involvement of the bond instrument is crucial for understanding the put-call parity and will be discussed shortly.

Different position diagrams may be easily compared and analysed by determining the portfolio payoff at expiration as a function of the price of the underlying instrument.

The option's value at expiration is determined by the ultimate spot price of the underlying instrument. As a consequence of option moneyness, at expiration date the only value that matters for valuing a European option is its intrinsic value. Note, however, that options with no intrinsic value at expiration are considered worthless—their value is considered to be zero.

Table 17.2 is an exposition of the payoff multiple causal relations: stocks, bonds and option resulting exposures relative to the ultimate price variations—an alternative to geometric methods of payoff generation exhibited in Figure 17.4.

Key Terms

put call parity
states that equivalent assets (actuals and their synthetically created equivalents) with identical payoff diagrams at every state and point in time, must sell for the same price

Table 17.2 Payoff Metrics of Stocks, Bonds & Options

Stock Price	+S	−S	+X	−X	+C	−C	+P	−P
0	0	0	25	−25	0	0	25	−25
5	5	−5	25	−25	0	0	20	−20
10	10	−10	25	−25	0	0	15	−15
15	15	−15	25	−25	0	0	10	−10
20	20	−20	25	−25	0	0	5	−5
25	25	−25	25	−25	0	0	0	0
30	30	−30	25	−25	5	−5	0	0
35	35	−35	25	−25	10	−10	0	0
40	40	−40	25	−25	15	−15	0	0
45	45	−45	25	−25	20	−20	0	0
50	50	−50	25	−25	25	−25	0	0

This synthetized guide is a numerical verification of the position diagrams as illustrated in Table 17.4 and of the put-call parity equations ensuing thereof.

Its main goal is to provide a simple and convincing proof that assets—actual and their synthetically created equivalent constituting the put-call parity equation—are in the state of equilibrium and therefore, deliver the same payoff diagram.

Values given in Table 17.2 suggest that the cost of the option—its premium—is not germane to the payoff metrics and could be ignored. So, in the case of call options we have that if S < X—the call option is OTM, and therefore will not be exercised (the value of the call is considered to be worthless) hence, its value is 0 (zero). Accordingly, in the case of put options, if S >X—the put option is OTM, and will not be exercised (the value of the put is considered to be worthless), hence its value is 0 (zero). In summary:

- If the stock price at expiration is above the call exercise price, you get a payoff.
- If the stock price at expiration is below the call strike, the value of the call is 0 (zero).
- If the stock price at expiration is below the put exercise price, you get a payoff.
- If the stock price at expiration is above the put exercise price, the value of the put is 0 (zero).
- Long stock payoff is +X; the payoff increases linearly one-for-one as the stock price increases.
- Short stock payoff is –X; the payoff decreases linearly one-for-one as the stock price increases.
- Risk-free asset, Long bond payoff is +X—positive in the case of lending; risk-free asset, Short bond payoff is –X—negative in the case of borrowing (both payoffs are constant; invariant to change in stock prices).

Algebraic interpretation of the call and put option payoffs is as follows:

Payoffs at Expiration: Calls	Payoffs at Expiration: Puts
Payoff to Call Holder max (0,ST – X) (ST – X) if ST > X, 0 if ST < X	Payoff to Put Holder max (0,X – ST) 0 if ST > X, (X – ST) if ST < X
Profit to Call Holder at Expiration Payoff – Premium	Profit to Put Holder at Expiration Payoff – Premium
Payoff to Call Holder max (0,ST – X) –(ST – X) if ST > X, 0 if ST < X	Payoff to Put Holder max (0,X – ST) 0 if ST > X, –(X – ST) if ST < X
Profit to Call Writer at Expiration Payoff + Premium	Profit to Put Writer at Expiration Payoff + Premium

POSITION DIAGRAMS

The geometric exhibition of the portfolio payoff versus the price at expiration is called a position diagram.

Figure 17.4 Position diagrams

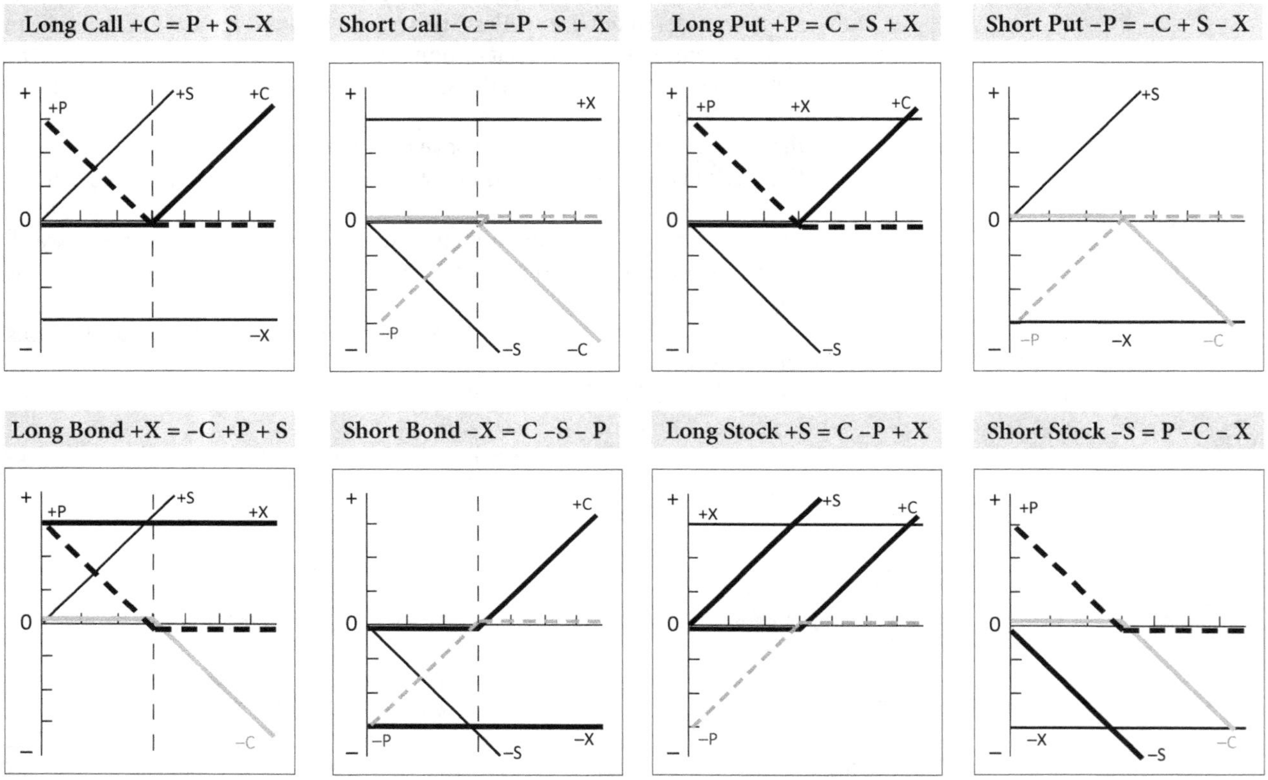

Figure 17.4 is a compilation of the position diagrams—single instrument payoffs created synthetically. These graphs demonstrate the plurality of parity relationships and their entwined causality.

The significance of these info-graphics is that relatively simple means of linear correlations could exhibit the manifold causal paths that exsist between spot prices, options, actuals, and bonds.

We believe that by focusing on these distinctive geometry features one can benefit significantly and develop sharpened understanding of these complex parity relations. This geometric approach also compares favorably with the put-call parity equations ensuing thereof.

Now let's explore how the two position diagrams—put-call parity P/L diagram (P – C + U = 0), and a payoff diagram with the same constituents (P – C + U = X)—relate to each other, and then, we shall generalize the arguments.

So, let's go back to the following equation:

$$P - C + U = 0$$

Key Terms

position diagrams
geometric expression of the portfolio payoff versus the price at expiration

This equation states that profit/loss from the left-hand side portfolio (LHS)—consisting of a long underlying (stock) plus a long put and a call written on the stock (put and call sharing the same exercise price X, and expiration date T)—produces a zero result. The graphic interpretation of this relationship is presented in Figure 17.5.

Figure 17.5 Position Profit/Loss Diagram +P −C +U = 0

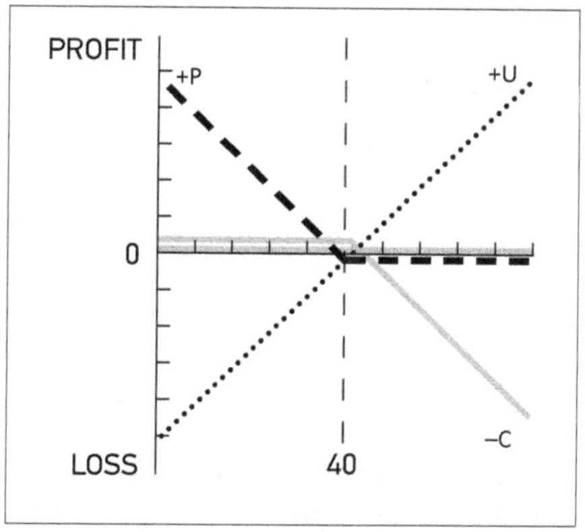

From Figure 17.4 we can extract the position diagram with the same constituents: P − C + S as exhibited in Figure 17.6

Figure 17.6 Position Payoff Diagram +P −C +U = X

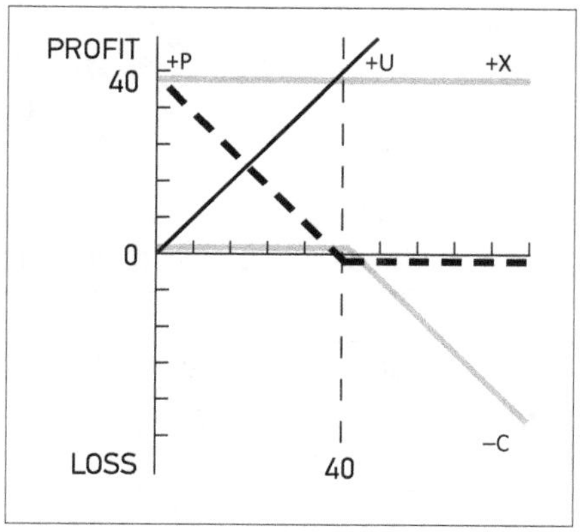

The ensuing equation is:

$$P - C + S = X$$

The equation above states that the left-hand side portfolio (LHS)—consisting of a long stock plus a long put and a call written on the stock (put and call sharing the same exercise price X, and expiration date T)—is equivalent to the right-hand side (RHS) portfolio consisting of a zero-coupon bond that pays X at date T.

The comparison of the two portfolio diagrams: buy one share of stock, buy one put option on the stock and sell one call option on the stock (same exercise price and expiration date) is given in Figure 17.7:

Figure 17.7 Payoff Diagram and Profit/Loss Diagram

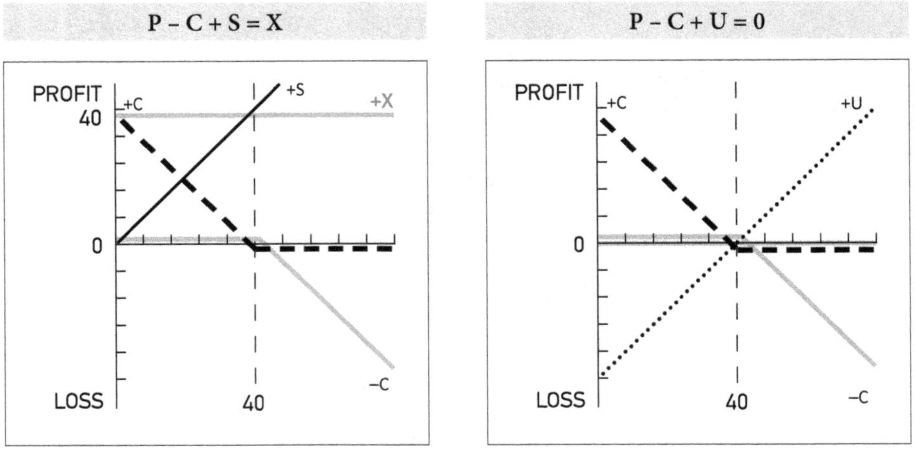

From the figure above we can conclude that, although the payoff diagram and the profit/loss diagram are configured differently, the return of both portfolios, at every possible state and time, is unchanged—both portfolios produce a constant payoff.

Put-Call Parity payoff: $S + P - C = X$ Algebraic expression

Time	Expiration date (T)	
Position	$S_T < X$	$S_T > X$
Buy Stock	ST	ST
Buy Put	X − ST	0
Sell Call	0	−(ST − X)
Portfolio:	X	X

Put-Call Parity payoff: $S + P - C = X$ Numerical expression

Position	0	10	20	35	40	45	50
Buy 1 share of stock at $40	0	10	20	35	40	45	50
Buy 1 Jan 40 Put	40	30	20	5	0	0	0
Sell 1 Jan 40 Call	0	0	0	0	0	−5	-10
Portfolio	40	40	40	40	40	40	40

Now it becomes clear that at every possible state and time, the return of the portfolio is unaffected. Irrelevant to a spot price change, you end up with a constant payoff—the exercise price X.

Pursuing the mathematical line of reasoning we can arrive at the conclusion that a call and a put with the same exercise prices, expiration date and underlying stock, must respond to a consistent logical relationship in terms of their value.

In other words the theorem says that if two portfolios have the same payoffs in every possible state and time, and consequently the same expiration value, then their present values also must be the same.

In a put-call parity theorem, no arbitrage assumption implies that:

- If put-call parity holds at expiration, it also must hold before expiration.
- If any of the elements is mispriced then a risk-free arbitrage would be available.

The exercise price is identified as the "face value" of the risk-free bond, therefore the present value of the bond PV(X) equals (exercise price – interest). Algebraic notation for PV(X) is most commonly taken to be either X/(1 + r)T or X e^{-rT} (where e^{-rT} is the discount—present valuing factor continuously compounded with e = 2.7182818). Substituting X in the formula in accordance with this principle we arrive at one of the most relevant put-call parity equations:

$$S + P - C = PV\ (X)$$

Or

$$S + P - C = X\, e^{-rT}$$

Interlocked in the relationship of rigorous causality, put-call parity equations imply that any of the four elements (stock, risk-free bond, put, and call), can be created synthetically, combining the appropriate quantity and state (long/short) of the remaining three constituents.

Subsequently we can derive all of the eight possible put-call parity equations:

Synthetic Long Positions	
PV (X) = S + P – C	Synthetic Long Bond
S = C – P + PV (X)	Synthetic Long Stock
P = C – S + PV (X)	Synthetic Long Put
C = S + P – PV (X)	Synthetic Long Call

And their reversals:

Synthetic Short Positions	
–PV (X) = –S – P + C	Synthetic Short Bond
–S = –C + P – PV (X)	Synthetic Short Stock
–P = –C + S – PV (X)	Synthetic Short Put
–C = –S – P + PV (X)	Synthetic Short Call

Expressed succinctly, there is a synthetic equivalent for every basic instrument payoff.

A synthetic position is simply the combination of instruments that replicates the resulting exposure of another single instrument.

At this point, it might be worth emphasizing that by financial market convention there are 3 different meanings associated with the +/– notations.

- The plus sign (+) indicates a long position in the case of the underlying asset, call or put and lending in case of the bond, whereas the minus sign (–), indicates a short position of the above instruments and borrowing in the case of the bond,
- These signs may as well denote the final outcome of the strategy payoff: profit (+); and loss (–) and finally,
- They also may indicate the immediate cash flow—the cash flow at time t = 0. In this respect, the plus sign (+) indicates the positive cash flow (cash inflow) or the selling position of the call/put, the underlying asset, and a sale of a zero

coupon bond (borrowing), whereas, the minus sign (–) indicates the negative cash flow (cash outflow) or buying position of the call/put, the underlying asset, and a purchase of the zero coupon bond (lending).

This distinction becomes essential when constructing the arbitrage portfolio as will be soon explicated. In particular, it is very important to differentiate between borrowing and lending, so here is an additional note of clarification.

By buying a bond today (lending) we are contracting an acceptance of a fixed payoff at time (T), equal to bond value plus interest; initial outflow, sign (–X); payoff profile positive (+).

Payoff Diagram – Lending

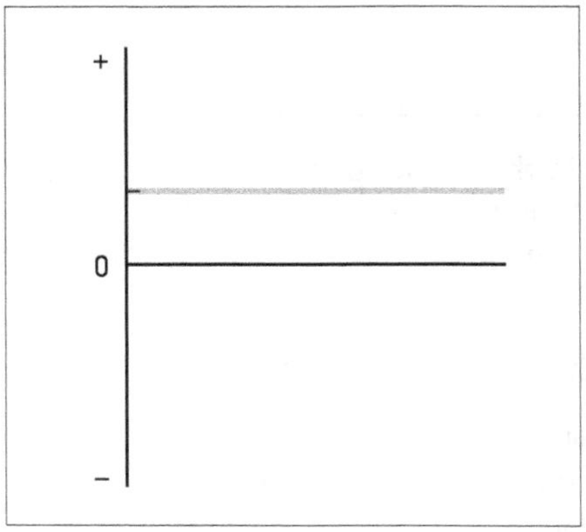

By selling a bond today (borrowing) we are contracting a repayment of a fixed payoff at time (T), equal to bond value plus interest; initial inflow, sign (+X); payoff profile negative (–).

Payoff Diagram – Borrowing

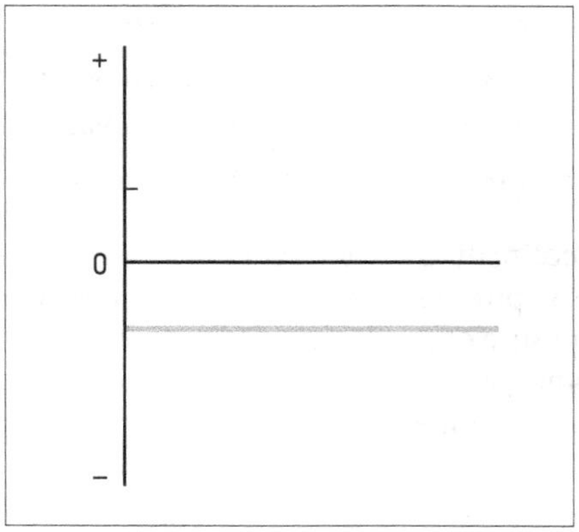

After getting an insight to all these "parities" you may be wondering why all this stuff? Why synthesize? What do we achieve by using the synthetic instruments? What is the point? Why do we care about synthetics at all?

The point is that if this principal rule is violated and if any of the elements of the equation is mispriced relative to "other constituents," then it would be possible to make a riskless profit by acquiring the low-cost alternative and selling the high-cost alternative.

I PUT-CALL PARITY THEOREM PROOFS

There are multiple ways to demonstrate the put-call parity theorem. One of the possible propositions states the following:

I. FIDUCIARY CALL = PROTECTIVE PUT

Fiduciary call (C + X)—a portfolio consisting of a riskless zero-coupon bond (that pays X at date T) and the right to buy one share (long call) of the underlying stock for exercise price X at time T, is equivalent to
Protective put (S + P)—a portfolio of one share of the underlying stock and the right to sell that share (long put) for exercise price X and time T

Table 17.3 Put Call Parity C + X = S + P

+C	+X	= LHS	+S	+P	= RHS
0	25	25	0	25	25
0	25	25	5	20	25
0	25	25	10	15	25
0	25	25	15	10	25
0	25	25	20	5	25
0	25	25	25	0	25
5	25	30	30	0	30
10	25	35	35	0	35
15	25	40	40	0	40
20	25	45	45	0	45
25	25	50	50	0	50

Hence, as the payoffs at maturity from the two portfolios are equal, the present value of the two portfolios at any date prior to maturity must be equal too.

Figure 17.8 is a geometry structure reflecting the relationship between the two portfolios—fiduciary call and protective put:

Figure 17.8 Position Diagram C + X = S + P

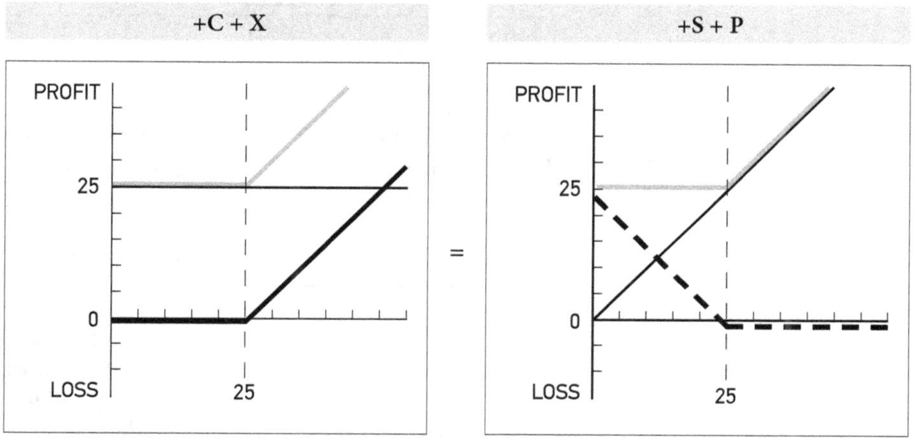

Key Terms

fiduciary call
a portfolio consisting of a long call and an equivalent PV of the strike price invested in a bond

protective put
a portfolio consisting of one share of stock and one long put option—this strategy payoff profile is identical to a long call

If the PV (X) denotes the present value of a bond (exercise price – interest) that will pay X at date T, then the appropriate formula claiming that the present value of the two portfolios is equal at any date prior to maturity is:

Long Call + Exercise Price – Interest = Long Stock + Long Put

Whereas the algebraic equivalent of the same portfolio can be expressed as follows:

$$C + Xe^{-rT} = S_0 + P$$

If two portfolios have the same payoffs at every possible state and time in the future, their prices must be equal.

Assume that we have the following inputs:

C = \$3.25, P = \$0.65, S0 = \$42, X = \$40, r = 6%
T = 3 months (0.25);
PV(X) = \$39.40

then

\$3.25 + \$39.40 = \$42 + \$0.65
\$42.65 = \$42.65

In order to prove that the LHS = RHS you should do the following:
move everything to the LHS so that C + X – S – P = 0
\$3.25 + \$39.40 – \$42 – \$0.65 = 0

Algebraic interpretation:

Time	t_0	Expiration date (T)	
Position	state	$S_T < X = 37$	$S_T > X = 44$
Sell Call	\$3.25	0	–\$4
Sell Bond (Borrow)	\$39.40	–\$40	–\$40
Buy Stock	–\$42.00	\$37	\$44
Buy Put	–\$0.65	\$3	0
Portfolio:	0	0	0

II. SYNTHETIC LONG UNDERLYING = LEVERAGED EQUITY

This relationship is another way of proving the put-call parity theorem—its algebraic expression is as follows:

$$C - P = S0 - X$$

LHS: Long call and short put = RHS: buy one share with borrowed money
We can replicate the payoff of a long call and a short put by:

- Going long one share of stock today and holding it to expiration (T);
- Borrowing the amount of Xe^{-rT} that pays X at expiration (T);

Table 17.4 Put Call Parity C – P = S – X

+C	–P	= LHS	+S	–X	= RHS
0	–25	–25	0	–25	–25
0	–20	–20	5	–25	–20
0	–15	–15	10	–25	–15
0	–10	–10	15	–25	–10
0	–5	–5	20	–25	–5
0	0	0	25	–25	0
5	0	5	30	–25	5
10	0	10	35	–25	10
15	0	15	40	–25	15
20	0	20	45	–25	20
25	0	25	50	–25	25

The payoff of the LHS (long call + short put) equals the long forward position.
The payoff of the RHS (long stock – short bond) also equals the long forward position.

Figure 17.9 Position Diagram C – P = S – X

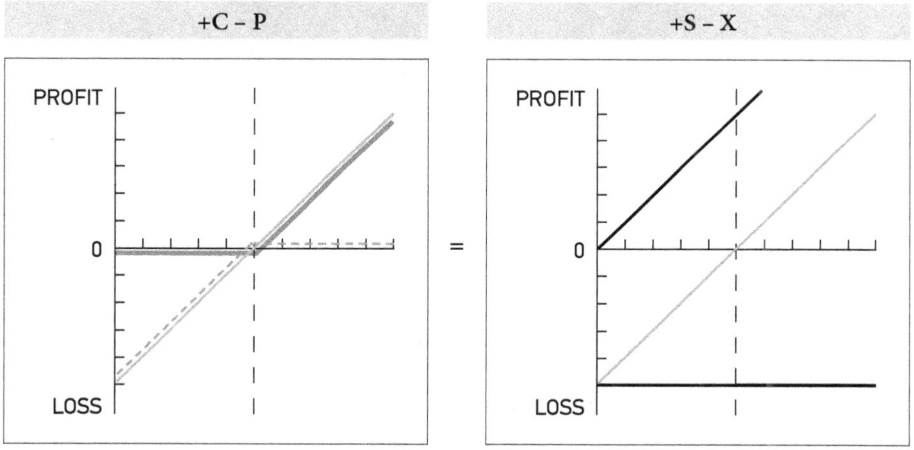

Key Terms

leveraged equity
portfolio constructed with a long stock and a short bond (borrowing)

The portfolio constructed as above (S – X) is referred to as **leveraged equity.**

Since the payoff of a long call and a short put are equivalent to leveraged equity at every state and point of time, their present values must be equal:

$$C - P = S0 - Xe^{-rT}$$

If at the expiration date S > X, the call is exercised—you get one share and pay X.

If at the expiration date, S < X, the put is assigned, you pay X, and get one share.

Note that the synthetic long forward contract results in owning the asset, irrelevant of the underlying price position at the expiration, just as the actual long.

Proof of the basic put-call parity proposition:

if $C - P = S - Xe^{-rT}$
then $C - P - S + Xe^{-rT} = 0$

Algebraic interpretation:

Time	t_0	Expiration date (T)	
Position	state	$S_T < X$	$S_T > X$
Sell Call	+C	0	–(ST – X)
Buy Put	–P	(X – ST)	0
Buy Stock	–S	+ST	+ST
Sell Bond (Borrow)	$+Xe^{-rt}$	–X	–X
Portfolio:	0	0	0

If a portfolio, on either side of these equations, can be sold for a higher price than the other is bought, then prospective investors may avail themselves of the opportunity to construct a portfolio that will lock-in a riskless profit.

The following two examples illustrate the provisional risk-free trades—arbitrage.

I. ARBITRAGE OPPORTUNITIES

Arbitrage, in general, refers to an investment concept that can describe several different strategies. So, not surprisingly, the use of the term varies: some authors relate arbitrage to trading opportunities originating from competitive advantages in fundamental factors—capital and labour—in cross-border markets producing outsized profits. In financial markets, the term relates to any set of simultaneous trades that manage to produce a less risky or riskless profits by exploiting the unjustifiable price discrepancies existing in identical or similar securities traded in two separate exchange markets.

In a narrower sense, in the context of a "Put-call Parity Theorem" specifically, arbitrage may be defined as a portfolio that aims at exploiting the phenomenon of price differentials—a mispriced instrument (either a call or a put) configuring the put-call parity equation.

Key Terms

arbitrage
a portfolio that aims at exploiting the phenomenon of a mispriced instrument (either a call or a put) configuring the put-call parity equation

Remember This! Arbitrage

There are at least 3 conditions that determine an arbitrage portfolio:

1. no initial investment (cash out-flow)
2. no risk of loss
3. at least at one state there is a positive return.

FIDUCIARY CALL ≠ PROTECTIVE PUT

The following two examples illustrate the provisional profitable trades:

$$C + Xe^{-rT} \# S0 + P$$

Conversion Consider now that LHS of the equation is overpriced relative to the RHS. A mispriced instrument—call option (C = \$3.85), so that:

$$C + Xe^{-rT} > S0 + P$$

\$3.85 + \$39.40 > \$42 + \$0.65
\$43.25 > \$42.65

Overpriced call option.

To construct the arbitrage portfolio shift the RHS to the LHS so that,
$\mathbf{C + Xe^{-rT} - S0 - P > 0}$
\$3.85 + \$39.40 – \$42 – \$0.65 > 0
\$0.60 > 0

To construct the arbitrage portfolio we should:

1. Sell call option
2. Sell zero coupon bond (borrow)
3. Buy one share of stock
4. Buy put option

Performance metrics of the portfolio constructed as above are demonstrated below.

Algebraic interpretation:

Time	t_0	Expiration date (T)	
Position	state	$S_T < X = 37$	$S_T > X = 44$
Sell Call	\$3.85	0	−\$4
Sell Bond (Borrow)	\$39.40	−\$40	−\$40
Buy Stock	−\$42.00	+\$37	+\$44
Buy Put	−\$0.65	+\$3	0
Portfolio:	\$0.60	0	0

Key Terms

conversion
a specific arbitrage portfolio created with a long underlying and an opposite synthetic short position (long put + short call)

In the market lingo an arbitrage portfolio constructed with the long underlying stock (asset) is referred to as a "**conversion.**" The conversion is a specific arbitrage portfolio consisting of a long underlying instrument confronted with its synthetically created counterpart (long put/short call), aiming to take the advantage of the mispriced constituent—the call option.

Reverse Conversion Consider now an example in which the LHS of the equation is underpriced relative to the RHS ensuing from a mispriced instrument—put option (P = \$1.50), so that:

$$C + Xe^{-rT} < S0 + P$$

\$3.25 + \$39.40 < \$42 +\$1.50
\$3.25 + \$39.40 < \$42 +\$1.50
\$42.65 < \$43.50

Overpriced put option.

In this case you should shift the **LHS** to the **RHS** and construct the following portfolio:

S0 + P – C – Xe-rT > 0
\$42 + \$1.50 – \$3.25 – \$39.40 > 0
\$0.85 > 0

To construct the arbitrage portfolio we should

1. Sell one share of stock
2. Sell put option
3. Buy call option
4. Buy zero coupon bond (Lend)

Algebraic interpretation:

Time	t_0	Expiration date (T)	
Position	state	$S_T < X = 37$	$S_T > X = 44$
Buy Call	−\$3.25	0	\$4
Buy Bond (Lend)	−\$39.40	\$40	\$40
Sell Stock	\$42.00	−\$37	−\$44
Sell Put	\$1.50	−\$3	0
Portfolio:	+\$0.85	0	0

Key Terms

reverse conversion
a specific arbitrage portfolio consisting of a short underlying and its synthetically created counterpart with a purpose to take advantage of the mispriced instrument configuring a put-call parity equation

In the market lingo the arbitrage portfolio constructed by shorting the underlying stock (asset) is referred to as a "**reversal**" or "**reverse conversion.**" Hence, the reverse conversion is the opposite strategy referring to a specific arbitrage portfolio consisting of a short underlying instrument and its synthetically created counterpart (short put, long call) aiming to take advantage of the mispriced constituent configuring a put-call parity equation—the put option.

SYNTHETIC LONG UNDERLYING ≠ LEVERAGED EQUITY

The following two examples illustrate the provisional arbitrage trades:

$$C - P \# S0 - Xe^{-rT}$$

Conversion Consider now that the LHS of the equation is overpriced relative to the RHS:

$$C - P > S0 - Xe^{-rT}$$

then $C - P - S + Xe^{-rT} > 0$

Assumption: $C = \$4.50$, $P = \$0.65$, $S = \$42$, $X = \$40$
$r = 6\%$, $T = 3$ mos.,
$Xe^{-rT} = \$39.40$.
$C - P > S - Xe^{-rT}$

$\$4.5 - \$0.65 > \$42 - \$39.40 = \$3.85 > \$2.60$
$\$4.5 - \$0.65 - \$42 + \$39.40 > 0$
$\$1.25 > 0$

To construct the arbitrage portfolio we should:

1. Sell call option
2. Buy put option
3. Buy one share of stock
4. Sell zero coupon bond (Borrow)

Algebraic interpretation:

Time	t_0	Expiration date (T)	
Position	state	$S_T < X = 33$	$S_T > X = 46$
Sell Call	\$4.50	0	–\$6
Buy Put	–\$0.65	\$7	0
Buy Stock	–\$42.00	\$33	\$46
Sell Bond (Borrow)	\$39.40	–\$40	–\$40
Portfolio:	+\$1.25	0	0

As you can read from the table, a conversion portfolio simply involves buying an underlying stock (asset), and then utilizing the remaining three constituents to replicate synthetically an equal and opposite short position (sell call, buy put, borrow).

Therefore, if $C - P > S - Xe^{-rT}$, an arbitrage portfolio can be created. The investor earns a price differential today—a cash inflow ($1.25), but the cash outflow at the expiration—in both states—is zero.

Reverse Conversion Consider now that the LHS of the equation is underpriced relative to the RHS:

$$C - P < S0 - Xe^{-rT}$$

then $\mathbf{S - Xe^{-rT} - C + P > 0}$

Assumption:
$C = \$3.25$, $P = \$2.50$, $S = \$42$, $X = \$40$,
$r = 6\%$, $T = 3$ mos.,
$Xe^{-rT} = \$39.40$
$C - P < S - Xe^{-rT} = 3.25 - 2.5 < 42 - 39.40 = 0.75 < 2.60$

then
$\$42 - \$39.40 - \$3.25 + \$2.5 > 0$
$\$1.85 > 0$

To construct the arbitrage portfolio we should:

1. Buy call option
2. Buy zero coupon bond (Lend)
3. Sell one share of stock
4. Sell put option

Algebraic interpretation:

Time	t_0	Expiration date (T)	
Position	state	$S_T < X = 33$	$S_T > X = 46$
Buy Call	–$3.25	0	$6
Buy Bond (Lend)	–$39.40	$40	$40
Sell Stock	$42.00	–$33	–$46
Sell Put	$2.50	–$7	0
Portfolio:	+$1.85	0	0

A reverse conversion portfolio, logically, is doing the opposite—it involves shorting the underlying stock (asset) and then utilizing the remaining three constituents to replicate synthetically an equal and opposite long position (buy call, sell put, lend).

The investor earns a price differential today—a cash inflow ($1.85), but the cash outflow at the expiration—in both states—is zero.

You may very well have noticed by now that an incidence of a mispriced instrument may appear in any market, in any of the synthetically created positions. Consequently, you may easily check if there is a price disparity—the existence of the mispriced instrument in put-call parity equations—by constituting a provisional portfolio.

Every time the disequilibrium is triggered there would be an arbitrage opportunity. The proof of any violation of the put-call parity must converge to either one of the two possible portfolios—a conversion or a reverse conversion.

Conversion: $C - P - S + X > 0$

Reverse Conversion: $S - X - C + P > 0$

An infallible guide to a quick check of a properly constructed portfolio are the following relations:

C and X signs are always identical
P and S signs are always identical

or

C and P signs are always opposite to each other
S and X signs are always opposite to each other

SUMMARY

Chapter 17 attempted to elucidate the concept of parity relations. We defined parity relations as a correlation existing between a put and a call option of the same class (the same exercise price and expiration date) and the underlying asset in such a manner as to preclude arbitrage opportunity—the existence of riskless profit.

At the very beginning we introduced a graphic "Parity Relations Between Options and Underlying Assets" aiming to visualize the complexity of put-call parity relations. Next, we analyzed the constellations ensuing from the graphic exposition, using two different approaches—geometric and algebraic. We ascertained that every singular payoff (of an option or underlying instrument) may be replicated synthetically combining the payoffs of another two instruments.

The put-call parity is defined as a dependant relationship that is locking-in the prices of an underlying contract and a call and a put with the same exercise price and expiration date. The parity equation infers that equivalent assets ("actuals" and the synthetically created equivalent) having identical payoff diagrams, must sell for the same price, if not, there is an arbitrage opportunity—the existence of a riskless profit. The proofs verifying the put-call parity theorem are derived from the causality existing between the two paradigmatic equations:

1. Fiduciary call and protective put, on one side, and
2. Synthetic long underlying and leveraged equity, on the other.

We then focused on how to detect and uncover arbitrage opportunities and specifics of enacting an arbitrage portfolio—either a Conversion or a Reverse conversion.

KEY TERMS

synthetic underlying
synthetic options
put call parity
position diagrams
fiduciary call
protective put
leveraged equity
arbitrage
conversion
reverse conversion

Most Prominent Stock and Futures Exchanges

Ten Biggest Stock Exchanges:

1. New York Stock Exchange (NYSE): $9.57 trillion in market value
2. Tokyo Stock Exchange (TSE): $3.10 trillion in market value
3. National Association of Securities Dealers Automated Quotations (NASDAQ) Stock Exchange: $2.77 trillion in market value
4. NYSE Euronext: $2.26 trillion in market value
5. London Stock Exchange (LSE): $2.20 trillion in market value
6. Shanghai Stock Exchange: $2.07 trillion in market value
7. Hong Kong Stock Exchange: $1.77 trillion in market value
8. Toronto Stock Exchange: $1.35 trillion in market value
9. Frankfurt Stock Exchange (Deutsche Börse): $1.13 trillion in market value
10. Madrid Stock Exchange: $1.08 trillion in market value

Futures Exchanges:

USA

* Chicago Board Options Exchange (CBOE)
* Chicago Mercantile Exchange (CME)
* Chicago Board of Trade (CBOT) [Merged 2007, now CME Group]
* Chicago Climate Exchange
* ELX Electronic Liquidity Exchange
* International Securities Exchange (Eurex ISE)
* ICE Futures U.S. (Formerly New York Board of Trade or NYBOT)
* Kansas City Board of Trade (KCBT)
* Minneapolis Grain Exchange (MGEX)
* Nadex (formerly Hedge Street)
* NASDAQ OMX Futures Exchange (formerly Philadelphia Board of Trade)
* NASDAQ OMX PHLX (formerly Philadelphia Stock Exchange)
* New York Mercantile Exchange (NYMEX) [Acquired, August 2008, now CME Group]
* NYSE Liffe US
* One Chicago (Single-stock futures (SSF's) and Futures on ETFs)

PAN-EUROPEAN

* Eurex
* Euronext.liffe
* European Climate Exchange
* OMX
* BELFOX (Belgian Futures and Options Exchange)
* NYSE Euronext – Euronext Brussels Derivatives Exchange

UNITED KINGDOM

* ICE Futures Europe
* London International Financial Futures and Options Exchange (LIFFE), precursor to Euronext.liffe
* London Metal Exchange (LME)
* NYMEX Europe

CHINA

* Dalian Commodity Exchange (DCE)
* Shanghai Futures Exchange (SHFE)
* Zhengzhou Commodity Exchange (ZCE)
* China Financial Futures Exchange (CFFEX)
* Hong Kong Exchanges and Clearing (HKEx)
* Hong Kong Futures Exchange (HKFE)

PART 4

ADVANCED HEDGING STRATEGIES

CHAPTER 18

HEDGING LONG UNDERLYING WITH A BEAR CALL SPREAD

CHAPTER OBJECTIVES

- To introduce the concept of hedging a long position in the physical market with a bear call spread
- To describe the performance of the strategy relative to changes in market prices
- To define key features of the strategy
- To exhibit the payoff profile of the strategy and highlight its profit and loss characteristics

I INTRODUCTION

YOU CAN USE OPTIONS OR OPTIONS COMBINATIONS TO HEDGE A CASH COMMODITY position in many interesting ways. In this chapter we have prepared a choice of hedge strategies divided into two groups: one involving a long underlying asset and the second involving a short underlying asset. This classification looks as follows:

I. HEDGE STRATEGIES INVOLVING LONG UNDERLYING

HEDGING INSTRUMENT	STRATEGY DESIGNATION	PAYOFF
	SIMPLE HEDGING STRATEGIES	
Long Put	Protective Put (Synthetic Long Call)	Long Call
Short Call	Covered Call (Synthetic Short Put)	Short Put
	ADVANCED HEDGING STRATEGIES	
Bear Call Spread	None	Long Split Combo
Short Split Combo	Collar	Bull Spread
Short Combo	Conversion	Long Bond

Protective puts and covered calls have already been elaborated in Chapter 11 while the remaining strategies designated as "advanced" will be elaborated in the following chapters.

II. HEDGE STRATEGIES INVOLVING SHORT UNDERLYING

HEDGING INSTRUMENT	STRATEGY DESIGNATION	PAYOFF
	SIMPLE HEDGING STRATEGIES	
Long Call	Protective Call (Synthetic Long Put)	Long Put
Short Put	Covered Put (Synthetic Short Call)	Short Call
	ADVANCED HEDGING STRATEGIES	
Bull Call Spread	None	Short Split Combo
Long Split Combo	Fence	Bear Spread
Long Combo	Reversal	Long Bond

The protective call and covered put have also been elaborated in Chapter 11 while the remaining "advanced" strategies as illustrated above will be exhibited in separate chapters that follow hereafter.

The choice of the strategies elaborated here, will allow you to evaluate hedge structure alternatives and select a risk management approach that delivers the most appropriate risk-adjusted returns.

All strategies will be illustrated using real data for the COMEX Options Copper Contract as announced on 12 February 2010.

HI GRADE COPPER (COMEX) (USd/lb.) 310.200 25,000 lbs., cents per lb. 12. February 2010						
Strike	Calls			Puts		
	Jun	July	Aug	Jun	July	Aug
305	7.75	15.95	21.30	4.50	11.70	16.10
306	7.20	15.40	20.80	4.95	12.15	16.60
307	6.65	14.90	20.30	5.40	12.65	17.10
308	6.15	14.40	19.80	5.90	13.15	17.60
309	5.65	13.90	19.35	6.40	13.65	18.15
310	5.20	13.45	18.85	6.95	14.20	18.65
310.200	COPPER SPOT					
311	4.75	13.00	18.40	7.50	14.75	19.20
312	4.35	12.55	17.95	8.10	15.30	19.75
313	4.00	12.10	17.50	8.75	15.85	20.30
314	3.65	11.65	17.05	9.40	16.40	20.85
315	3.30	11.25	16.60	10.05	17.00	21.40

HEDGING LONG UNDERLYING WITH A BEAR CALL SPREAD

Key Terms

open-ended risk profile
refers to a payoff profile implying that the strategy, at its extremes, will be open to unlimited profits, or unlimited losses

long split strikes combo
a payoff configured with a higher strike long call and a lower strike short put

You may decide to use a bear call spread in order to hedge an existing long position in a commodity—copper for example. This type of protection will produce an **open-ended risk profile** implying that the strategy, at its extremes, will be open to unlimited profits—in upward markets, or unlimited losses—in downward markets.

The performance of the strategy is very sensitive to exercise prices chosen and effects on profits and losses will vary considerably.

We shall use two arbitrary examples to illustrate how the choice of exercise prices influences the final strategy result.

As you will notice, a bear call spread against a long underlying will produce a risk-reward profile which is identical to a **long split strikes combo**—a payoff configured with a higher strike long call and a lower strike short put.

STRATEGY CONFIGURATION; CASE I

The strategy is constructed as follows:
Long underlying $310.200
Long call $311@4.75
Short call $309@5.65
Net credit: $0.90

The performance of a hedging strategy, configured with the above data, is summarized in Table 18.1.

Table 18.1 Hedging Long Underlying with a Bear Call Spread (Case I)

UI Value $/lb 310.200	Long UI Payoff	Short Call 309@5.65 –(St – X)	Long Call 311@4.75 (St – X)	Premium Net Credit	Bear Call Total Return	Position Total Return $
A	B	C	D	E	F	B + F
315	4.80	–6	4	0.90	–1.10	3.70
314	3.80	–5	3	0.90	–1.10	2.70
313	2.80	–4	2	0.90	–1.10	1.70
311.30	1.10	–2.30	0.30	0.90	–1.10	0
311	0.80	–2	0	0.90	–1.10	–0.30
310.200	0	–1.20	0	0.90	–0.30	–0.30
309.90	–0.30	–0.90	0	0.90	**0**	–0.30
309	–1.20	0	0	0.90	0.90	–0.30
308	–2.20	0	0	0.90	0.90	–1.30
307	–3.20	0	0	0.90	0.90	–2.30
306	–4.20	0	0	0.90	0.90	–3.30
305	–5.20	0	0	0.90	0.90	–4.30

Hedging a long underlying with a bear call spread delivers an "open-ended" payoff profile, as depicted in Figure 18.1, signifying unlimited loss/unlimited profit potential with a characteristic flat part (in between the two strikes) which we arbitrarily identified as a "plateau."

Figure 18.1 Hedging Long Underlying with a Bear Call Spread (Case I)

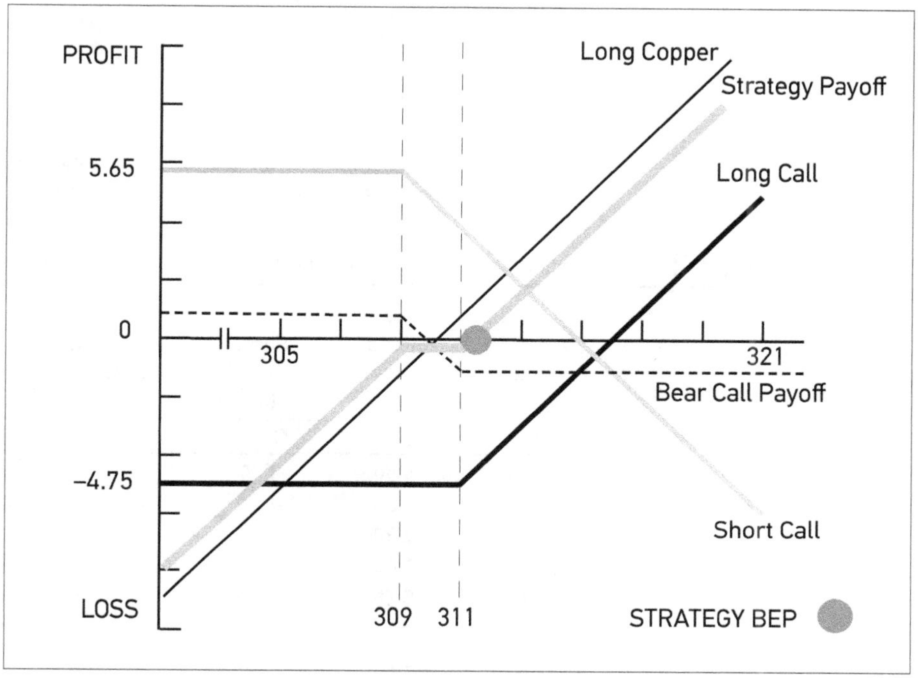

Strategy Key Features

Plateau In between lower exercise price $309 and higher exercise price $311
= Bear call BEP ($309.90) – UI ($310.200)
= –$0.30

BEP One on the upside
= HS price + (Difference between UI and the bear call BEP)
= $311 + ($310.20 –$309.90)
= $311.30

Profit and Loss Characteristics

On the downside:

Loss Buffer From the lower exercise price downward
= Net credit
= $0.90

On the upside:

Profit Lag Strategy profit falls behind the UI payoff from BEP upwards
= Difference between strikes – net credit
= $2 – $0.90
= $1.10

The configuration of the same strategy may have been enacted using different strikes. In the next example, Case II, we shall illustrate how the change in strike prices alters the basic payoff diagram.

STRATEGY CONFIGURATION; CASE II

The strategy is constructed as follows:
Long underlying $310.200
Long call $312@4.35
Short call $310@5.20
Net credit: $0.85

In Table 18.2 we have demonstrated the results of a hedging strategy, configured with alternative data—different strikes, as shown under Case II.

Table 18.2 Hedging Long Underlying with a Bear Call Spread (Case II)

UI Value $/lb 310.200	Long UI Payoff	Short Call 310@5.20 −(St − X)	Long Call 312@4.35 (St − X)	Premium Net Credit	Bear Call Total Return	Position Total Return $
A	B	C	D	E	F	B + F
315	4.80	−5	3	0.85	−1.15	3.65
314	3.80	−4	2	0.85	−1.15	2.65
313	2.80	−3	1	0.85	−1.15	1.65
312	1.80	−2	0	0.85	−1.15	0.65
310.85	0.65	−0.85	0	0.85	**0**	0.65
310.200	**0**	−0.20	0	0.85	0. 65	0.65
310	−0.20	0	0	0.85	0.85	0.65
309.35	−0.85	0	0	0.85	0.85	0
308	−2.20	0	0	0.85	0.85	−1.35
307	−3.20	0	0	0.85	0.85	−2.35
306	−4.20	0	0	0.85	0.85	−3.35
305	−5.20	0	0	0.85	0.85	−4.35

In Figure 18.2, you may notice the alteration in the payoff diagram relative to different strike prices ($310 and $312), configuring the bear call spread.

The Case II scenario modifies the strategy payoff to the hedger's advantage. The complete strategy payoff diagram seems to have been lifted so that the plateau now sits above the x-axis, shifting the break-even point down from $311.30 to $309.35. This is a considerable improvement, as now the risk of loss will not be triggered unless the price of the underlying asset passes beyond $309.35.

On the other side, from the break-even point upwards, the portfolio begins to generate positive returns which rise commensurately with the rise in the underlying asset price.

However, from the higher call strike price purchased, the return on the portfolio will consistently fall behind the unhedged copper position. The gap is reflected in column F (−$1.15), which represents the bear call position returns.

The graphic convincingly points to the conclusion that the hedger would be much better off choosing the strikes given in Case II, relative to Case I, endorsing the importance of analyzing the risk to expected reward profile in advance of the hedging transaction.

Using graphic depiction to simulate different market scenarios is a smart way to protect your risky asset and generate increased returns.

Figure 18.2 Hedging Long Underlying with a Bear Call Spread (Case II)

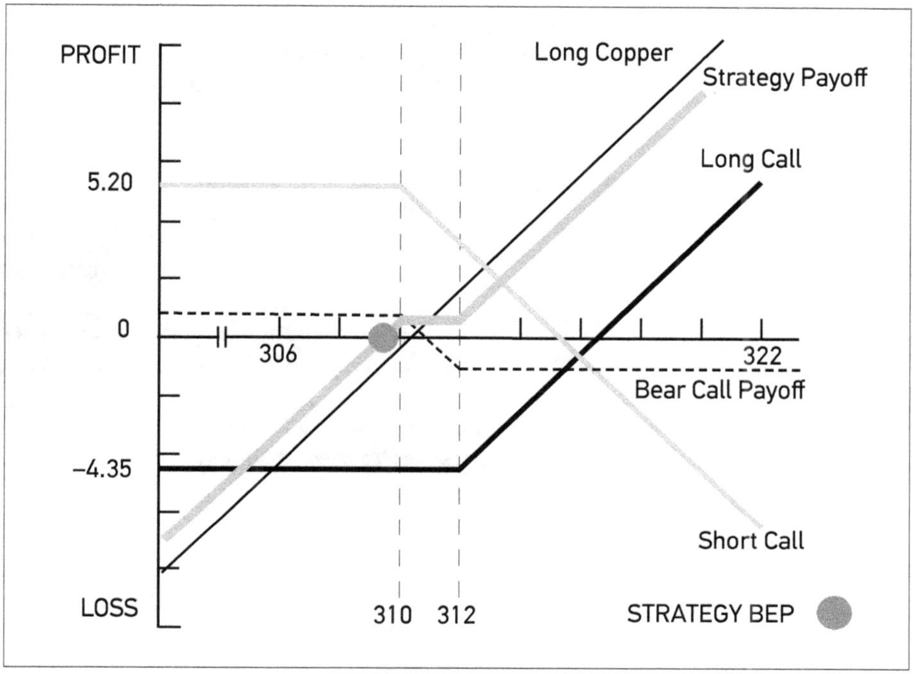

Strategy Key Features

Plateau In between lower exercise $310 and higher exercise $312
= Bear call BEP ($310.85) – UI ($310.200)
= +$0.65

BEP One on the downside
= LS price – (bear call BEP – UI)
= 310 – ($310.85 – $310.200)
= $309.35

Profit and Loss Characteristics

On the downside:

Loss Buffer From BEP downwards
= Net credit
= $0.85

On the upside:

Profit Lag The strategy profit falls behind the UI from the higher strike upwards
= Difference between strikes – net credit
= $2 – $0.85
= $1.15

SUMMARY

Chapter 18 introduced the characteristics of hedging a long physical copper position using a bear call spread. We exhibited the risk to reward profile of the strategy that delivers unlimited profits on the upside as well as unlimited losses on the downside. This strategy diagram, which is identical to "long split strike combo," for obvious reasons is termed as "open-ended risk profile."

We have shown the basic features of the strategy, introducing the three characteristic expressions:

- Plateau—the flat part of the strategy diagram in between the strikes of the bear call spread,
- Profit lag—the profits of the strategy fall behind the long physical position payoff; the value of the "lag" is expressed as the difference between the strikes less the net credit; and
- Loss buffer—the amount of the net credit serves as a buffer in downward markets, reducing the losses relative to an unhedged long copper position.

We have also pointed to the sensitivity of strategy end-results relative to the choice of the strike prices used to configure the hedging instrument—the bear call spread.

KEY TERMS

open-ended risk profile

long split strikes combo

CHAPTER 19

HEDGING SHORT UNDERLYING WITH A BULL CALL SPREAD

CHAPTER OBJECTIVES

- To introduce the concept of hedging a short position in the physical market with a bull call spread.
- To describe the performance of the strategy relative to changes in market prices.
- To define the key features of the strategy.
- To exhibit the payoff profile of the strategy and highlight its profit and loss characteristics.

HEDGING SHORT UNDERLYING WITH A BULL CALL SPREAD

Key Terms

short split strikes combo
a payoff configured with a lower strike long put and a higher strike short call

HEDGING A SHORT UNDERLYING WITH A BULL CALL SPREAD WILL PRODUCE INVERTED results to that in the previous example. The resulting exposure of this strategy is also an "open-ended" risk profile, only this time it is a **short split strikes combo**—a strategy whose payoff profile is characterized by unlimited gains in downward markets and unlimited losses in upward markets.

STRATEGY CONFIGURATION; CASE I

The strategy is constructed as follows:
Long underlying $310.200
Long call $310@5.20
Short call $312@4.35
Net debit: -$0.85

In Table 19.1 we have exhibited the performance metrics of the portfolio constituents contracted at the same option price levels as in the previous example. If you compare the metrics with those exhibited in Table 18.2 you will notice that they are reciprocally interrelated. The break-even point is at the same level ($309.35), only the direction of profit and losses is inverted. The maximum profits of a strategy—hedging the long underlying with a bear call spread, compare to the maximum losses of the strategy—hedging a short underlying with a bull call spread, and vice versa.

Table 19.1 Hedging Short Underlying with a Bull Call Spread (Case I)

UI Value $/lb (310.200)	Short UI Payoff	Long Call 310@5.20 (St – X)	Short Call 312@4.35 –(St – X)	Premium Net (Debit)	Bull Call Total Return	Position Total Return $
A	B	C	D	E	F	B + F
305	5.20	0	0	–0.85	–0.85	4.35
306	4.20	0	0	–0.85	–0.85	3.35
307	3.20	0	0	–0.85	–0.85	2.35
308	2.20	0	0	–0.85	–0.85	1.35
309.35	0.85	0	0	–0.85	–0.85	0
310	0.20	0	0	–0.85	–0.85	–0.65
310.200	**0**	0.20	0	–0.85	–0.65	–0.65
310.85	–0.65	0.85	0	–0.85	**0**	–0.65
312	–1.80	2	0	–0.85	1.15	–0.65
313	–2.80	3	–1	–0.85	1.15	–1.65
314	–3.80	4	–2	–0.85	1.15	–2.65
315	–4.80	5	–3	–0.85	1.15	–3.65

Accordingly, the resulting payoff diagram is the mirror image of the payoff diagram depicted in Figure 18.2. This is because the constituent call options are contracted at the same strikes ($310 and $312), only this time they are configured as a bull call spread instead of a bear call spread.

In Figure 19.1 we have illustrated the characteristic "open-ended" risk to reward payout diagram created with a bull call spread.

Figure 19.1 Hedging Short Underlying with a Bull Call Spread (Case I)

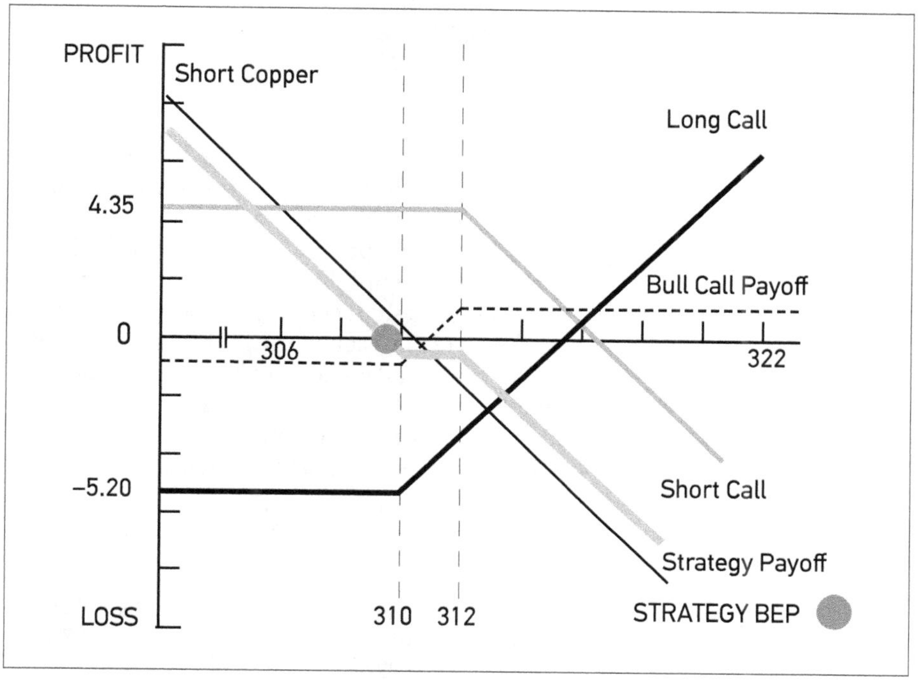

Strategy Key Features

Plateau Located in between lower exercise $310 and higher exercise $312
= UI ($310.200) – bull call BEP ($310.85)
= –$0.65

BEP One on the downside
= LS price – (Difference between bull call BEP and UI)
= $310 – ($310.85 – $310.20)
= $309.35

Profit and Loss Characteristics

On the downside:

Profit Lag Falls behind the UI from BEP downwards
= Net debit
= $0.85

On the upside:

Loss Buffer From higher exercise price upwards
= Difference between strikes – net debit
= $2 – $0.85
= $1.15

We continue to explore how the alternative choice of strike prices constituting the short split combo affects the performance metrics of the portfolio.

STRATEGY CONFIGURATION; CASE II

The strategy is constructed as follows:
Short underlying \$310.200
Long call \$309@5.65
Short call \$311@4.75
Net debit: –\$0.90

The choice of the strikes in Case II is arbitrary but it proves the point. The typical profit-loss results ensuing from an alternative choice of strike prices configuring a bull call spread are presented in Table 19.2.

Likewise, the performance metrics exhibited in this table are reciprocally interrelated to those in Table 18.1. Again the reciprocity is due to the fact that the portfolio consisting of a short copper position against a bull call spread is contracted at the same strikes as options configuring the bear call spread against a long copper position. The break-even point remains in the same position (\$311.30), while the direction of profits and losses is inverted. Hedging a long underlying with a bear call spread maximises profits, compared to the maximum losses produced by hedging a short underlying with a bull call spread, and vice versa.

Table 19.2 Hedging Short Underlying with a Bull Call Spread (Case II)

UI Value \$/lb (310.200)	Short UI Payoff	Long Call 309@5.65 (St – X)	Short Call 311@4.75 –(St – X)	Premium Net (Debit)	Bull Call Total Return	Position Total Return \$
A	B	C	D	E	F	B + F
305	5.20	0	0	–0.90	–0.90	4.30
306	4.20	0	0	–0.90	–0.90	3.30
307	3.20	0	0	–0.90	–0.90	2.30
308	2.20	0	0	–0.90	–0.90	1.30
309	1.20	0	0	–0.90	–0.90	0.30
309.90	0.30	0.90	0	–0.90	0	0.30
310.200	0	1.20	0	–0.90	0.30	0.30
311	–0.80	2	0	–0.90	1.10	0.30
311.30	–1.10	2.30	–1	–0.90	1.10	0
313	–2.80	4	–2	–0.90	1.10	–1.70x
314	–3.80	5	–3	–0.90	1.10	–2.70
315	–4.80	6	–4	–0.90	1.10	–3.70

Accordingly, the resulting payoff diagram is the mirror image of the payoff diagram depicted in Figure 18.1. This is because the constitutuent call options are contracted at the same strikes (\$309 and \$311), only this time they are configured as a bull call spread instead of a bear call spread.

In comparison to the Case I scenario, employing a bull call spread with different strikes (\$309 and \$311) offers a clear advantage. The "plateau" sits above the x-axis, the break-even point is shifted to the right so that the strategy will start losing only if the price of the underlying goes above \$311.30.

In Figure 19.2 you can follow and compare how the selected strike prices alternate the risk to reward profile of the strategy.

Figure 19.2 Hedging Short Underlying with a Bull Call Spread (Case II)

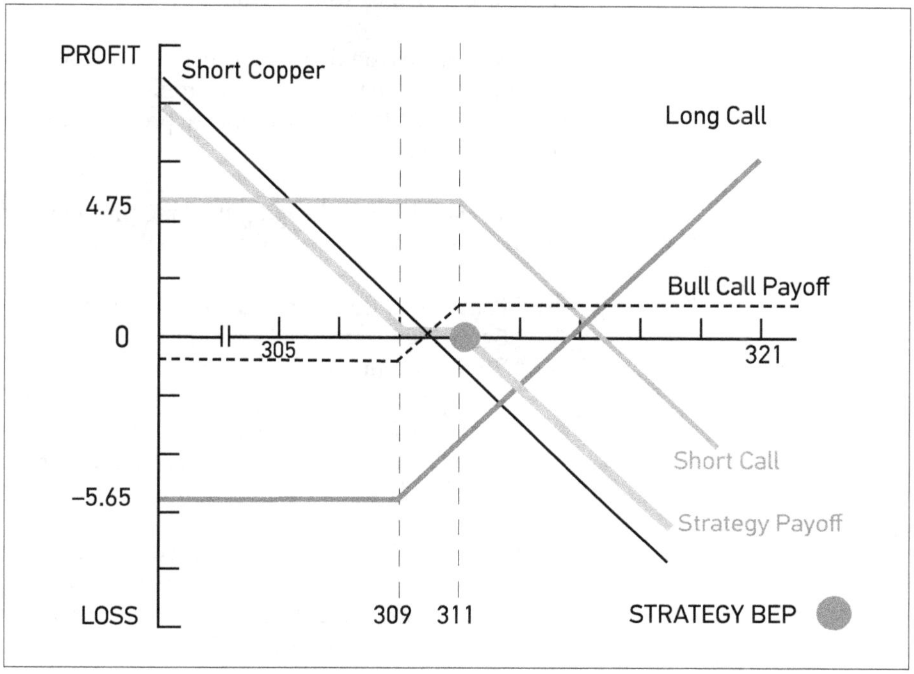

SUMMARY

To manage the market risk exposure companies can call on various hedging concepts. In this chapter we have covered the characteristics of hedging the short position in the physical market by using a bull call spread.

This strategy payoff diagram, which is an explicit "short split strike combo," is also an example of an "open-ended" risk profile. The risk to reward profile, as you may observe from Figure 19.1, delivers unlimited profits on the downside as well as unlimited losses on the up-side.

As was the case with hedging the long position using a bear call spread, the strategy characteristics are explicated through the three essential strategy features:

- Plateau—in this particular configuration, the plateau sits below the x-axis, in between the two strikes.
- Profit lag—the profits of the strategy are on the down-side and fall behind the short physical position payoff; the value of the "lag" is equal to net debit ($0.85).
- Loss buffer—is expressed as the difference between the strikes less the net debit and reduces the losses in upward markets relative to an unhedged short copper position.

As the choice of the strike prices used to configure the hedging instrument—the bull call spread—will affect the outcome of the strategy's profits and losses for better or worse, companies should tailor their risk-management subject to various scenario analyses.

KEY TERMS

short split strikes combo

CHAPTER 20

COLLARS AND FENCES

CHAPTER OBJECTIVES

- To explain and illustrate a collar strategy
- To exhibit the payoff profile of a collar strategy and highlight its profit and loss characteristics
- To explain and illustrate a fence strategy
- To exhibit the payoff profile of the fence strategy and highlight its profit and loss characteristics
- To emphasize the differences between performance metrics of collars and fences

I INTRODUCTION

To avoid confusion related to the terminology used to define collar and fence strategies it would be sensible to issue a word of warning in advance.

To be exact, the collar strategy (the long underlying hedged with a short split combo) is associated with more than one term—a "cylinder" or "window" to begin with. In exchange markets jargon this is a common occurrence: different authors label the same strategy configuration—with the same constituents and referring to exactly the same phenomenon—with different names that replace each other as being synonymous.

And in many other instances we have the opposite situation: instead of having one name/title as a unique identifier of an object, phenomenon or a strategy composition, we often find that a wide swathe of strategies—with different constitutive elements—are given the same term. This only proliferates perplexity. For example, the term "fence" (short underlying hedged with a long split combo) is particularly conspicuous as in some instances, the same term is used also to define quite the opposite strategy:

- Long underlying + short split combo (short OTM call + long OTM put)

which "de facto" is a collar! So we have the situation where the term fence refers to strategy "A" but may also be applied to strategy "B." And since a collar, a "cylinder," a "window" and a "fence" are used also as synonyms it turns out that all of these terms may be used to denote strategy A as well as strategy B.

The confusion peaks when you stumble upon the term "long collar" referring to a "long split combo" and "short collar" referring to "short split combo." In yet another instance—the "long split combo" and the "short split combo" are also designated respectively as a "bull fence" and a "bear fence."

To illustrate these examples in a real-world context we shall revert again to the options price chart used in our previous cases.

HI GRADE COPPER (COMEX) (USd/lb.) 310.200

25,000 lbs., cents per lb. 12. February 2010

Strike	Calls			Puts		
	Jun	July	Aug	Jun	July	Aug
305	7.75	15.95	21.30	4.50	11.70	16.10
306	7.20	15.40	20.80	4.95	12.15	16.60
307	6.65	14.90	20.30	5.40	12.65	17.10
308	6.15	14.40	19.80	5.90	13.15	17.60
309	5.65	13.90	19.35	6.40	13.65	18.15
310	5.20	13.45	18.85	6.95	14.20	18.65
310.200	COPPER SPOT					
311	4.75	13.00	18.40	7.50	14.75	19.20
312	4.35	12.55	17.95	8.10	15.30	19.75
313	4.00	12.10	17.50	8.75	15.85	20.30
314	3.65	11.65	17.05	9.40	16.40	20.85
315	3.30	11.25	16.60	10.05	17.00	21.40

I COLLAR STRATEGY

Key Terms

collar
refers to a hedging strategy instituted to hedge a long underlying position with a short split combo – a combination of a long put option plus a short call option drawn on the same underlying and same expiry but with different strike prices

The lexical ambiguity forms an intricate knot that calls for an "Alexandrian solution."

Therefore within the scope of this topic, the term **collar** shall refer to a strategy instituted to hedge a long underlying position with a short split combo (a combination of a long put option plus a short call option with the same expiry but different strikes, both out-of-the money), drawn on the same underlying.

The resulting P&L profile of the strategy described above is that of the bull put spread.

There are two different paths of configuration for a collar strategy delivering the identical resulting exposure.

1. Hedging long underlying with short split combo (short semi-futures)
A collar is a strategy aimed to protect an actual long physical position using a short split combo (long put + short call, different strikes) as a hedging instrument. The collar strategy is a limited loss/limited profit undertaking and the resulting P&L diagram is identical to a bull put spread P&L profile.

2. Covered call + Long put
This strategy can also be viewed from another perspective. If you pay attention to the elements that constitute the collar, you will notice the following three instruments: the long underlying, the long put and the short call. As you will recall, writing a call on a long underlying designates a covered call strategy with a P&L diagram of a short put. Adding a long put (entered at a lower exercise price) to the existing portfolio will deliver a payoff of a bull put spread.

The advantage of the collar strategy is derived from the cost reduction in the strategy initiation—the cost of the put option is reduced by the proceeds received from selling the call option so that the premiums preferably tend to net out. Sometimes it would even be possible to achieve what is designated as "costless collar" or a "zero cost collar" strategy in which the income from selling a call evens out the costs of purchasing a put.

What segregates these two pathways is the choice of steps and their timing, but at the end both will produce an identical strategy profile—a bull put spread.

COLLAR STRATEGY CONFIGURATION

Long underlying $310.200
Short call $314@3.65
Long put $310@6.95
Net debit: $3.30

Table 20.1 shows collar profit-loss results, which are, as you may notice, restricted in both directions. This property of a resulting payoff diagram designates the collar as a "range-bound" strategy, delivering a limited risk-reward ratio.

The range-bound profile of the collar strategy locks-in the profit and loss potential of the strategy (between an upper limit of $0.50 and a lower limit of –$3.50). The range–bound profile delivered by a collar strategy is irrelevant to the prevailing market price of the underlying instrument. But again, the hedger should be aware of the fact that the choice of strikes will modify the strategy total return for better or worse.

Table 20.1 Collar Strategy Metrics

UI Value $/lb 310.200	Long UI Payoff	Long Put 310@6.95 (X – St)	Short Call 314@3.65 –(St – X)	Premium Net (Debit)	Short Combo Return	Position Total Return $
A	B	C	D	E	F	B + F
317.65	7.45	0	–3.65	–3.30	–6.95	0.50
314	3.80	0	0	–3.30	–3.30	0.50
313.50	3.30	0	0	–3.30	–3.30	0
313	2.80	0	0	–3.30	–3.30	–0.50
312	1.80	0	0	–3.30	–3.30	–1.50
311	0.80	0	0	–3.30	–3.30	–2.50
310.200	**0**	0	0	–3.30	–3.30	–3.30
310	–0.20	0	0	–3.30	–3.30	–3.50
309	–1.20	1	0	–3.30	–2.30	–3.50
308	–2.20	2	0	–3.30	–1.30	–3.50
307	–3.20	3	0	–3.30	–0.30	–3.50
306.70	–3.50	3.30	0	–3.30	0	–3.50
303.05	–7.15	6.95	0	–3.30	3.65	–3.50
300	–10.20	10	0	–3.30	6.70	–3.50

The collar strategy payoff profile is depicted in Figure 20.1.

Figure 20.1 Collar Strategy Payoff

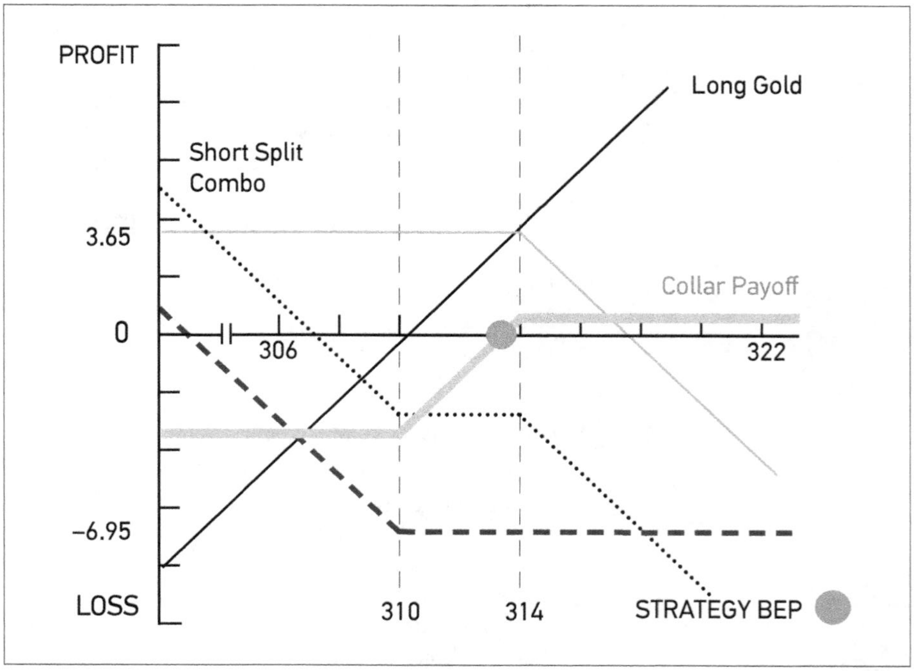

Key Terms

range-bound risk profile
an option strategy profile implying that the potential of possible gains and losses is confined within the predefined limits of the exercise prices selected

As we can see from Figure 20.1, the collar strategy P&L diagram is identical to a bull spread. They both secure a **range-bound risk profile** implying that the potential of possible gains and losses is confined within the predefined limits of the exercise prices selected. This is achieved by purchasing a put option—to set a price "floor"— and at the same time writing a call option—to set a "ceiling" or a "cap" price (both strikes being out-of-the-money).

The range of selected exercise prices will of course affect the performance of the strategy. The example offered here can be summarized as follows:

Risk/ Reward Collar strategy returns will be determined decisively by the choice of the exercise prices and the respective premiums. Whatever the choice, the strategy will always produce a bull spread payoff.

Covered call writing sets a "cap" on a selling price:

Guaranteed cap price = $310.70
Call exercise price minus net debit = $314 – $3.30 = $310.70 or $310.20 + $0.50 = $310.70

You will earn only $0.50 in the case where the price breaks above the higher price limit of $314. If unhedged your gain would be $3.80. Your opportunity loss at that price level equals a net debit of $3.30 and goes higher as the price increases. The potential profits on the upside are forfeited on behalf of the protection from the price decline.

Protective put sets a "floor" on a selling price:

Guaranteed floor price = $306.70
Put exercise price minus net debit = $310 – $3.30 = $306.70 or $310.200 – $3.50 = $306.70

At this point, the loss on the stock position equals the loss of the collar portfolio (–$3.50). The protection offered with a collar will start to pay off only if price breaks beyond $306.70 level.

The range-bound profile of the collar strategy is locked-in (between the lower selling price of $306.70 and the upper selling price of $310.70), irrespective of the actual market price level.

Profit and Loss Characteristics of Short Split Combo

The difference between the long put return and short combo return on the downside = $3.65 = Short call premium.

Example:

UI Value $307
Long put profit/loss = Payoff – premium = $3 – $6.95 = –$3.95
Short split combo profit/loss = –$0.30
Difference: -$3.95 – (–$0.30) = –$3.65

The difference between the short call return and short combo return on the upside =

Example:

UI value $316
Short call profit and loss = Payoff + premium = –$2 + $3.65 = $1.65
Short split combo profit & loss = –$5.30
Difference: $1.65 – (–$5.30) = $6.95

6.95 = Long put premium

Portfolio Key Features

Nominal sum of profits and losses ($3.50 + $0.50) equals the options spread (difference between the strikes): $314 – $310 = $4
Maximum profit (on the up-side) = (Short call exercise price – UI price) – net debit = ($314 – $310.20) – $3.30 = $0.50
Maximum loss (on the down-side) = (Long put exercise price – UI price) – net debit = ($310 – $310.20) –$3.30 = –$3.50
BEP = Purchase price of underlying + net debit

PUT SPREAD COLLAR

A collar risk/reward profile as demonstrated herewith is obviously deficient in desirable profit expectations, but its meagre performance presents a good opportunity to emphasize one of the major options advantages—its flexibility. You can tailor your investment strategy precisely to your requirements and adapt it to take advantage of prevailing market circumstances.

Now, let us illustrate this point following the collar strategy example:

Collar portfolio
Long underlying $310.200
Short call $314@3.65
Long put $310@6.95
Net debit = $3.30

Assume we add a short put option on an existing collar:
+ Short March put $307@5.40

Overall net credit = $2.10

In Figure 20.2 we have offered the comparison between the two payout diagrams—the collar payout (black dashed line) and the resulting diagram of the put spread collar (solid grey line). Adding a short put option on an existing collar spread will morph the payout profile to the advantage of the hedger. A graphical scheme as depicted in Figure 20.2 offers instant visual recognition of payout profile transformation.

First you should take notice of the radical shift in BEP position: the old break-even point was at $313.50 and the new break-even point is at $304.90:

Put Spread Collar BEP = Put Exercise Price – Net credit = $307 – $2.10 = $304.90

This has caused the risk/reward aspect of the new portfolio to change dramatically.

Now you can easily evaluate and compare the performance metrics of the two strategies.

Figure 20.2 Put Spread Collar Payoff

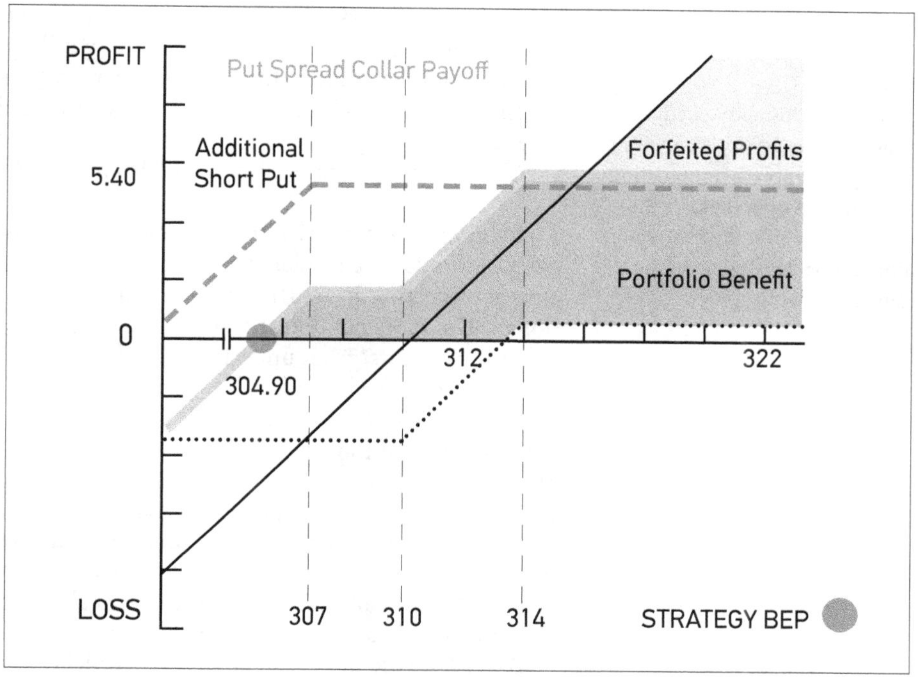

Key Terms

put spread collar
a strategy configured by adding a put option on an existing collar

The profit potential of the new portfolio—**put spread collar,** will grow up to a limit of $5.90, compared to collar strategy limit of only $0.50, meaning that upward price movement will be now "capped" at $316.10 ($310.20 + $0.50 + $5.40 = $316.10). Above that level the put spread collar portfolio will stop earning money, i.e., it will underperform compared to an unhedged copper owner (forfeited profit zone above $316.10 point = opportunity loss).

On the downside the portfolio will start losing money only below the level of the new BEP at $304.90. If the price declines all the way to $301.40 ($304.90 – $3.50), the put spread collar portfolio losses will equal that of the original collar strategy losses of $3.50. Below that point (301.40) the put spread collar payoff will cross beyond the range-bound shelter and its losses will exceed those of the collar strategy.

FENCE STRATEGY

Key Terms

fence
a strategy instituted to hedge a short underlying position with a long split combo; a combination of a long call option plus a short put option with same expiry but different strikes drawn on the same underlying

The term **fence** refers to a strategy instituted to hedge a short underlying position with a long split combo—a combination of a long call option plus a short put option with the same expiry but different strikes—drawn on the same underlying.

The resulting P&L profile of the strategy described above is that of a bear call spread.

A fence strategy can be also viewed from two different perspectives:

1. Hedging short underlying with long split combo (long semi-futures)
A fence should be considered as the complementing opposition of a collar strategy. It aims at protecting an actual short physical or futures position using a long split combo (long call + short put different strikes) as a hedging instrument. The fence strategy is also a limited loss/profit undertaking and the resulting P&L diagram is identical to a bear spread.

2. Covered put + long call
This strategy can also be viewed from another perspective. If you pay attention to the elements that constitute the collar, you will notice the following three instruments: short underlying/futures, long call and short put. As you will recall, short put against short futures and/or underlying will produce a covered put strategy with a P&L diagram of a short call. Adding a higher long call exercise price to the existing portfolio will produce a bear call spread P&L profile.

As in the case of the collar strategy, whichever way you choose to construct the fence, both will produce an identical strategy profile—a bear call spread.

Collars and fences clearly differ in constitutive elements and their performance is reciprocally interrelated—they fit together as two parts of the whole, mutually supplying what the other lacks.

FENCE STRATEGY CONFIGURATION

Short underlying $310.200
Long call $314@3.65
Short put $310@6.95
Net credit = $3.30
The profit-loss metrics of the fence strategy are presented in Table 20.2.

Risk/Reward The two strategies—collars and fences, being a complementary pairing, will consequently produce results that are inversely correlated to each other; the collar strategy maximum profit compares to the maximum loss of the fence strategy ($0.50), whereas the maximum loss of the collar strategy compares to the maximum profit of the fence strategy ($3.50).

The break-even point of the fence strategy is positioned at the same spot ($313.50) as in the collar strategy payoff diagram, only that profit and loss range-bound limits are in an inverse order.

You will lose only $0.50 if the price breaks above the higher price limit $314. If unhedged your loss would be $3.80.

The gains will be limited to only $3.50 if the price breaks below the lower price limit $310. Beyond that point downwards, the hedger will be faced with "opportunity loss" as the profits of an unhedged position would exceed those of a hedged strategy.

Table 20.2 Fence Strategy Metrics

UI Value $/lb 310.200	Short UI Payoff	Short Put 310@6.95 –(X – St)	Long Call 314@3.65 (St – X)	Premium Net Credit	Long Combo Return	Position Total Return $
A	B	C	D	E	F	B + F
305	5.20	–5	0	3.30	–1.70	3.50
306.70	3.50	–3.30	0	3.30	0	3.50
307	3.20	–3	0	3.30	0.30	3.50
308	2.20	–2	0	3.30	1.30	3.50
309	1.20	–1	0	3.30	2.30	3.50
310	0.20	0	0	3.30	3.30	3.50
310.200	**0**	0	0	3.30	3.30	3.30
311	–0.80	0	0	3.30	3.30	2.50
312	–1.80	0	0	3.30	3.30	1.50
313	–2.80	0	0	3.30	3.30	0.50
313.50	–3.30	0	0	3.30	3.30	0
314	–3.80	0	0	3.30	3.30	–0.50
315	–4.80	0	1	3.30	4.30	–0.50
320	–9.80	0	6	3.30	9.30	–0.50

Figure 20.3 illustrates the payout profile of the fence strategy which is identical to a bear spread.

Figure 20.3 Fence Strategy Payoff

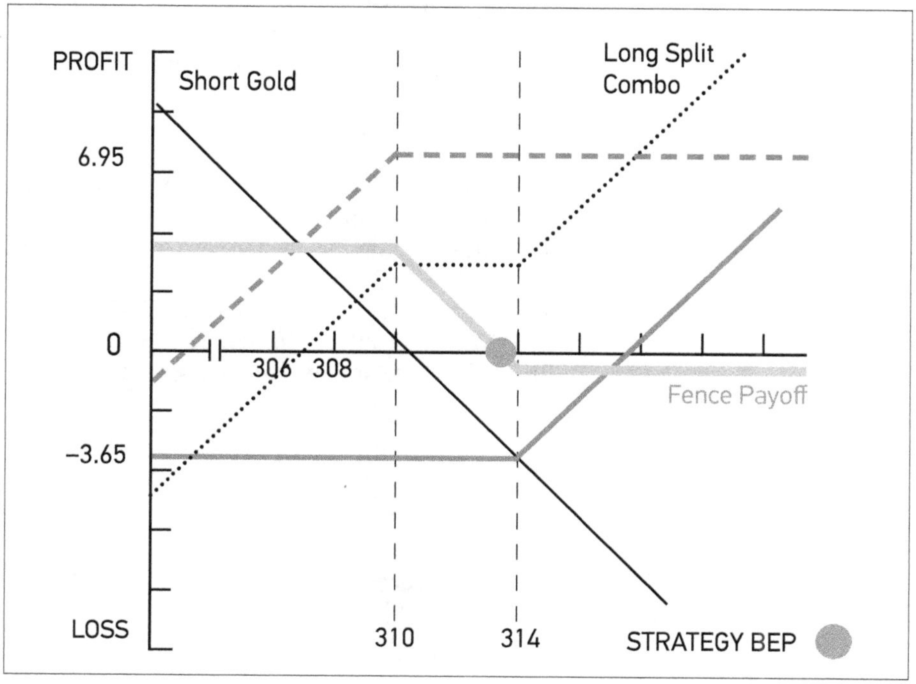

In the example offered here with the strategy, payout looks as follows:

SCENARIO I: In the case of price decline

Lowest purchase price = –$306.70
Put exercise price plus net credit = –$310 + $3.30 = –$306.70 or – $310.20 + $3.50 = –$306.70

At the $310 price level you will pay $3.50 less for copper because of a fence! Below $306.70 the strategy witnesses an opportunity loss (compared to an unhedged position!). If the price breaks the lower limit set up with a short put, the strategy will forfeit the benefit from a further price fall as the potential returns would be offset by a short put.

SCENARIO II: In the case of price increase

Highest purchase price = –$310.70
Call exercise price plus net credit = –$314 + $3.30 = –$310.70 or – $310.200 – $0.50 = –$310.70

On the other side, as compensation for opportunity loss suffered in an eventual price decline beyond $306.70, a fence strategy effectively limits the potential losses if prices were supposed to rally above the higher limit imposed by the long call option.

A fence strategy ensures that you will pay only $0.50 more for copper if the price increases to the $314 limit or beyond. At $314 the benefit from the fence equals net credit = $3.30.

The range-bound profile—between the lowest purchase price of $306.70 and the highest purchase price of $310.70—is locked-in, no matter what happens with the actual market price.

Profit and Loss Characteristics of Long Split Combo

The difference between the long call return and long combo return on the upside = $6.95 = Short put premium.
The difference between the short put return and long combo return on the downside = $3.65 = Long call premium.

Portfolio Key Features

Nominal sum of profits and losses ($3.50 + $0.50) equals the options spread (difference between the strikes): $314 – $310 = $4
Maximum loss (on the up-side) = (UI price + net credit) – long call exercise price = ($310.20 + $3.30) – $314 = –$0.50
Maximum profit (on the down-side) = (UI price + net credit) – short put exercise price = ($310.20 + $3.30) – $310 = $3.50
BEP = Purchase price of underlying + net credit

SUMMARY

This chapter has focussed on two distinctive strategies—collars and fences. In the very beginning of the chapter we pointed out the miscellany of terms associated with the strategies that we finally differentiated as "collars" and "fences." Both strategies use split strike combos as hedging instruments but they are inversely related to each other in every respect. How to differentiate? The simplest way is to associate "a collar" with a long physical position and "a fence" with a short physical position. A collar strategy implies adding a hedging instrument—a short split strike combo—to a long physical position. Therefore the collar payoff profile is identical to a bull spread—a spread strategy profiting in rising markets.

The inverse applies to "a fence" strategy—a short physical position is protected with a long split strike combo.

Consequently, the fence strategy will produce a payoff profile identical to a bear spread—a strategy profiting in declining markets.

Both strategies deliver a "range-bound" risk to reward profile, implying that profit and loss potential is limited in both directions. We then discussed strategy key features illustrating how the profit and loss characteristics vary when the price changes. We then covered a special case portfolio—put spread collar—which delivers added diversification: an example of multiple opportunities available to option hedgers.

KEY TERMS

Collar

Range-bound risk profile

Put Spread Collar

Fence

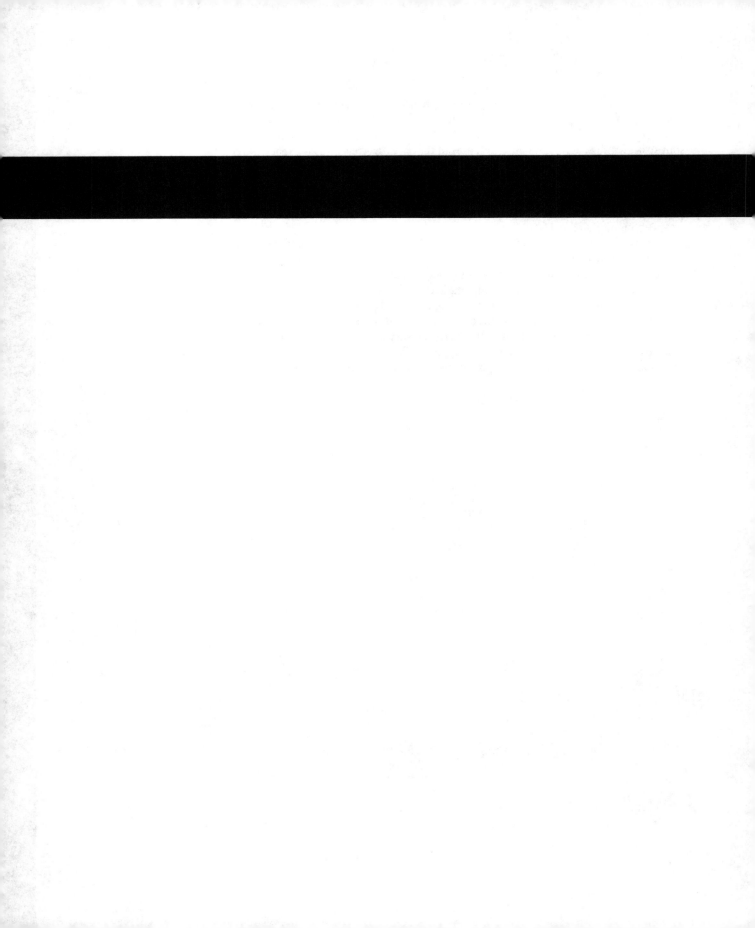

CHAPTER 21

CONVERSIONS AND REVERSALS

CHAPTER OBJECTIVES

- To explain and illustrate the conversion strategy
- To explain and illustrate the reversal strategy
- To explain the causality existing between conversions and reversals and interpret the illustrated relationship

I INTRODUCTION

Conversions and reversals (aka "reverse conversions"), are arbitrage strategies configured with the purpose of taking advantage of a price differential in options trading resulting in a limited risk-free profit. The theory of efficient markets postulates that the put/call parity is in force perfectly, and no arbitrage trade between actual instruments and synthetically created equivalents would be possible. The total amount of extrinsic value in the actual instrument and the amount of extrinsic value in the synthetic position should be exactly the same. For example, a synthetically created long call/put option should have the same amount of extrinsic value as the actual call/put option itself.

However, there are occasions when this equilibrium is disrupted so that actuals and their equivalent synthetics do not hold to the put call parity theorem and the existence of a price differential in extrinsic values could be exploited to lock-in the riskless profit —to strike an arbitrage trade. Each of the four basic designs exhibited may be closed out with a single opposite option, performing the role of a closing instrument. In the following Figure 21.1, we build-up the transformation of an existing synthetically created option into the consequential conversions and reversals.

Figure 21.1 Synthetically Created Options + Plain Vanilla Options

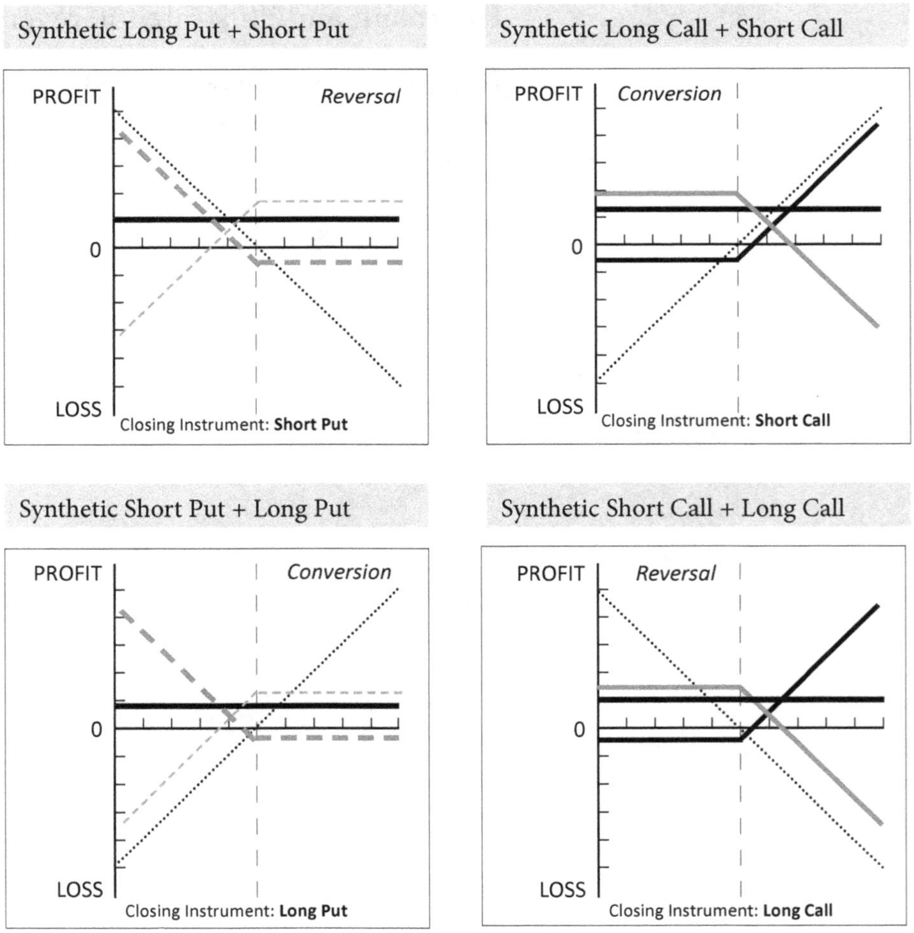

I. CONVERSIONS AND REVERSALS – MULTIPLE CASE EXAMPLES

Initial Position	Components	Closing Instrument	Classification
1. Synthetic long put	Short UI + long call	Short put	Reversal
2. Synthetic long call	Long UI + long put	Short call	Conversion
3. Synthetic short put	Long UI + short call	Long put	Conversion
4. Synthetic short call	Short UI + short put	Long call	Reversal

Characteristics of conversion and reversal arbitrage: as you can observe from the position diagrams, the closing instrument in each individual case has to be entered at the same exercise price and expiration as the existing synthetically created option.

To contract an arbitrage however, there is one precondition to be fulfilled: a positive price differential between the extrinsic values in the synthetically created option and its offsetting plain vanilla option. When such a position is closed at a net credit the strategy will produce a limited profit invariant to the price direction of the underlying asset.

Synthetic long calls and puts use short calls and puts as closing instruments. Conversions and reversals would be feasible if the extrinsic value of the short plain vanilla calls and puts exceed the extrinsic value of the synthetic equivalent (offsetting short options are overvalued relative to the synthetic equivalent).

In the case of synthetic short calls and puts the situation is reversed. The extrinsic value of long plain vanilla options used as offsetting instruments have to be lower than their synthetic equivalent (offsetting long options are undervalued relative to the synthetic equivalent).

These opportunities are difficult to spot and are not always available but the search is much facilitated when you know exactly what you are looking for and when you are able to develop a corresponding routine in exploiting favourable circumstances.

If we take the empirical data from the table below, then the following configurations will be available:

Position no 1. Synthetic Long Put + Short Put
Extrinsic value of the synthetic long put = \$0.20 – \$5.20 = –\$5.00
Extrinsic value of the short put = \$6.95
Reversal arbitrage is possible. The risk-free profit is locked-in at \$1.95

Position no 2. Synthetic Long Call + Short Call
Extrinsic value of the synthetic long call = -\$0.20 – \$6.95 = –\$7.15
Extrinsic value of the short call = \$5.20
Conversion is not possible. Loss locked-in at \$1.95

Position no 3. Synthetic Short Put + Long Put
Extrinsic value of the synthetic short put = -\$0.20 + \$5.20 = \$5.00
Extrinsic value of the long put =-6.95
Conversion is not possible. Loss locked-in at \$1.95

Position no 4. Synthetic Short Call+ Long Call
Extrinsic value of the synthetic short call = \$0.20 + \$6.95 = \$7.15
Extrinsic value of the short call = –\$5.20
Reversal arbitrage is possible. The risk-free profit is locked-in at \$1.95

Reversal maximum profit is constant = to the positive price differential between a synthetically created option and its offsetting counterpart.

HI GRADE COPPER (COMEX) (USd/lb.) 310.200

25,000 lbs., cents per lb. 12. February 2010

Strike	Calls			Puts		
	Jun	July	Aug	Jun	July	Aug
305	7.75	15.95	21.30	4.50	11.70	16.10
306	7.20	15.40	20.80	4.95	12.15	16.60
307	6.65	14.90	20.30	5.40	12.65	17.10
308	6.15	14.40	19.80	5.90	13.15	17.60
309	5.65	13.90	19.35	6.40	13.65	18.15
310	5.20	13.45	18.85	6.95	14.20	18.65
310.200	COPPER SPOT					
311	4.75	13.00	18.40	7.50	14.75	19.20
312	4.35	12.55	17.95	8.10	15.30	19.75
313	4.00	12.10	17.50	8.75	15.85	20.30
314	3.65	11.65	17.05	9.40	16.40	20.85
315	3.30	11.25	16.60	10.05	17.00	21.40

COPPER FUTURE (US$/lb.) 310.200
25,000 lbs., cents per lb. 12 February 2010
To round up the various methods of employing conversions or reversals we shall consider two more concepts which could be summarized as follows:

Initial Position	Closing Instrument	Classification	Payoff
5. Long underlying	Short combo	Conversion	Long bond
6. Short underlying	Long combo	Reversal	Long bond

CONVERSION STRATEGY

Key Terms

conversion
a specific arbitrage portfolio created with a long underlying and an opposite synthetic short position (long put + short call)

Commodity markets are not perfect. In every market where trades are available for cash and the derivative alternative, instances of pricing discrepancies and anomalies occur over the short run. Spotting and tracking these anomalies in real time data is a painstaking assignment. However, they do occur and may exist temporarily. Pricing discrepancies lead to profit opportunities and the prospect of implementing arbitrage. One such arbitrage is called a **conversion**—a strategy constructed with the idea of taking advantage of mispriced constituents in which profits are locked-in immediately.

To create a conversion, the investor should buy the underlying asset (copper) and at the same time initiate an offsetting synthetic short position—short combo (long put + short call)—with same exercise prices and expiry. Taking into account the data from the Hi Grade Copper Options Price Chart above, let's look at whether the real-time price constellation would allow for the conversion strategy.

CONVERSION STRATEGY CONFIGURATION

Long underlying $310.200
Short call $310@5.20
Long put $310@6.95
Net debit: $1.75

Using the data from our real-world example, the position would produce the results which are summarized in Table 21.1.

Table 21.1 Conversion Strategy Metrics

UI Value $/lb 310.200	Long UI Payoff	Short Call 310@5.20 −(St − X)	Long Put 301@6.95 (X − St)	Premium Net (Debit)	Short Combo Return	Position Total Return $
A	B	C	D	E	F	B + F
315	4.80	−5	0	−1.75	−6.75	−1.95
314	3.80	−4	0	−1.75	−5.75	−1.95
313	2.80	−3	0	−1.75	−4.75	−1.95
312	1.80	−2	0	−1.75	−3.75	−1.95
311	0.80	−1	0	−1.75	−2.75	−1.95
310.200	**0**	−0.2	0	−1.75	−1.95	−1.95
310	−0.20	0	0	−1.75	−1.75	−1.95
309	−1.20	0	1	−1.75	−0.75	−1.95
308.25	−1.95	0	2	−1.75	0	−1.95
307	−3.20	0	3	−1.75	1.25	−1.95
306	−4.20	0	4	−1.75	2.25	−1.95
305	−5.20	0	5	−1.75	3.25	−1.95
300	−10.20	0	10	−1.75	8.25	−1.95

The payout profile of a conversion strategy is exhibited in Figure 21.2.

Figure 21.2 Conversion Strategy Payoff: Long Underlying + Short Combo

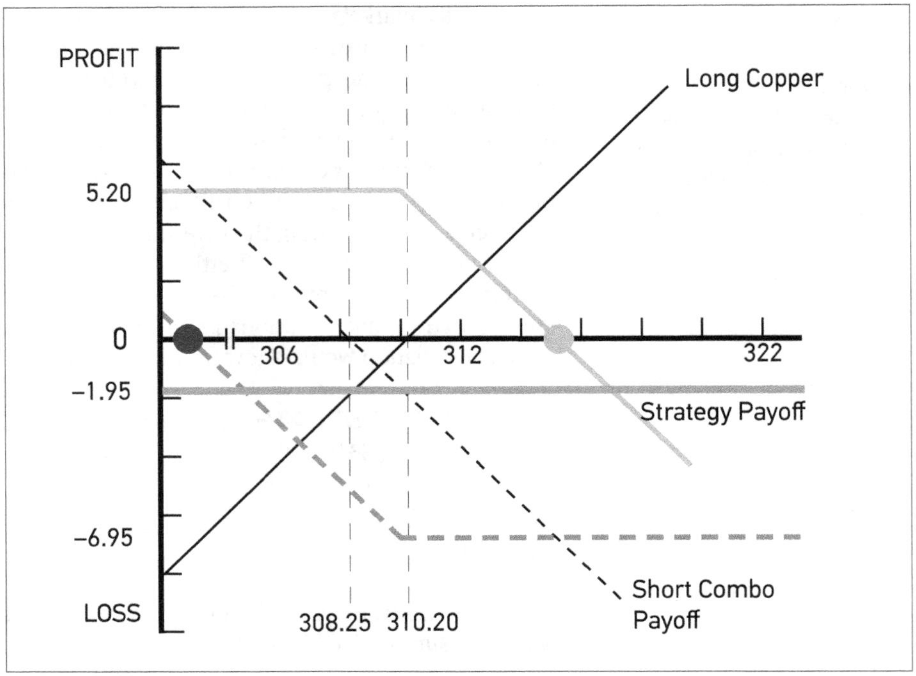

Key Terms

selling a bond (borrowing)
by selling a bond today we are committed to repaying a fixed payoff at maturity (principal + compounded interest)

The above graph supports the conclusion that, although the strategy is properly configured from a technical point of view—the synthetic short position (short combo) offsets the long underlying position (long copper)—in prevailing market circumstances, the conversion strategy is not possible—the strategy generates a negative return (-$1.95).

Profit/ Loss Characteristics:

Maximum loss = Locked in (-$1.95)
This is equal to the price differential between the exercise price of a long underlying (310.200) and the synthetic short combo break-even point ($308.25)
Short combo BEP = Short combo exercise price - net credit
= $310.00 - $1.75
= $308.25
Profit = Not possible

A strategy constructed as above—initiated at net debit—generates a continuous loss instead of profit. The resulting exposure of the strategy is in the negative zone, identical to the payoff profile when **selling a bond** (borrowing).

So, if the actual market prices do not allow configuration of a conversion strategy, then there might be a "reverse conversion" opportunity.

I REVERSAL STRATEGY

Key Terms

reversal or reverse conversion
a strategy created with a short underlying and an opposite synthetic long position (long call + short put)

To create a reverse conversion—a short underlying plus long combo, with the same exercise prices and expiry—you should do exactly the opposite: sell the underlying asset and initiate an offsetting synthetic long position—the long combo (long call + short put).

REVERSAL STRATEGY CONFIGURATION

Long underlying $310.200
Long call $310@5.20
Short put $310@6.95

Net credit: $1.75

The scorecard of the performance metrics for reverse conversion constituents looks like this:

Table 21.2 Revers Conversion Strategy Metrics

UI Value $/lb (310.200)	Short UI Payoff	Long Call 310@5.20 (St – X)	Short Put 310@6.95 –(X – St)	Premium Net Credit	Long Combo Return	Position Total Return $
A	B	C	D	E	F	B + F
315	–4.80	5	0	1.75	6.75	1.95
314	–3.80	4	0	1.75	5.75	1.95
313	–2.80	3	0	1.75	4.75	1.95
312	–1.80	2	0	1.75	3.75	1.95
311	–0.80	1	0	1.75	2.75	1.95
310.200	**0**	0.20	0	1.75	1.95	1.95
310	0.20	0	0	1.75	1.75	1.95
309	1.20	0	–1	1.75	0.75	1.95
308.25	1.95	0	–1.75	1.75	**0**	1.95
307	3.20	0	–3	1.75	–1.25	1.95
306	4.20	0	–4	1.75	–2.25	1.95
305	5.20	0	–5	1.75	–3.25	1.95
300	10.20	0	–10	1.75	–8.25	1.95

From the table metrics we can see that in actual market circumstances, using the real-time prices, we managed to configure an arbitrage—profit is locked-in immediately—implying that the reverse conversion portfolio delivers positive returns invariant to price direction. Given that the short physical risk exposure is protected with an offsetting counterpart (the long combo), its returns are not exposed to market risk.

The related application presented hereafter points to an obvious conclusion: pricing discrepancies reflect a market anomaly that is short-lived. Therefore, you cannot transact an arbitrage in any trading day. Conversions and reversals are two sides of the same coin, aiming to exploit an instance of a mispriced option. The more the markets are in favour of one strategy the less they are in favour of its complementary counterpart.

Figure 21.3 illustrates a reversal strategy configuration.

Figure 21.3 Reversal Payoff: Short Underlying + Long Combo

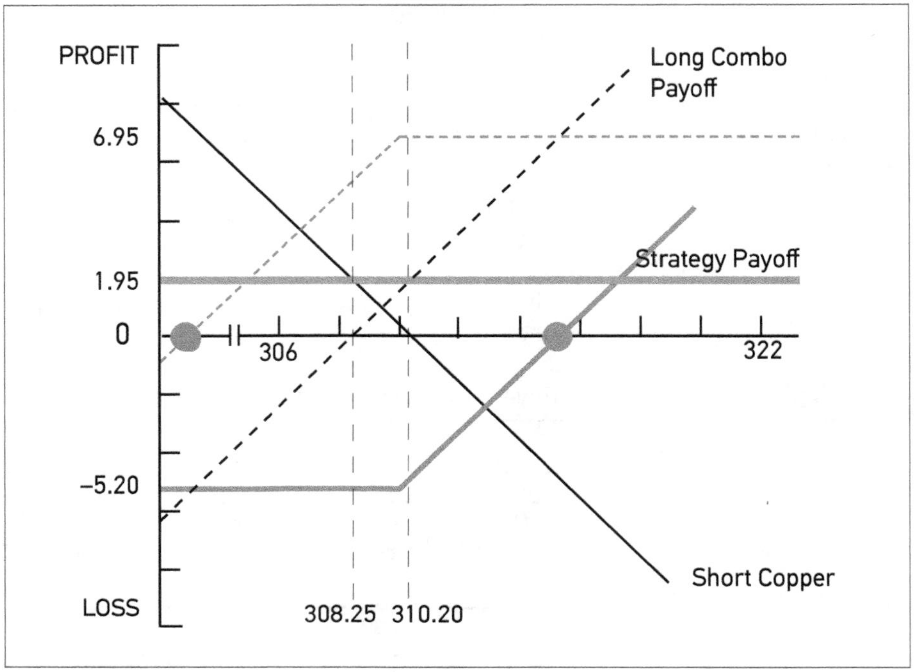

As you can see in the above figure, the reversal strategy delivers a payoff diagram that is identical to **buying a bond** (lending).

Key Terms

buying a bond (lending)
by buying a bond today we are committed to receiving a fixed payoff at maturity (principal + compounded interest)

Profit/ Loss Characteristics:

Maximum profit = Locked in (+$1.95)
This is equal to the price differential between the exercise price of a short underlying (310.200) and the synthetic long combo break-even point ($308.25).
Long combo BEP = Short combo exercise price – net credit
= $310.00 – $1.75
= $308.25
Loss = Not possible

"Seesaw" effect
Conversions and reversals are reciprocally interrelated, mutually exclusive and exhaustive events. The accessibility of one strategy precludes the incidence of the other.

SUMMARY

A conversion is a specific arbitrage portfolio constructed with a long underlying **instrument** and its synthetically created counterpart—the short combo—with the intention of taking advantage of the mispriced instrument configuring a put call parity equation and locking-in profits immediately. Given that the long underlying instrument is protected with an offsetting counterpart (short combo), portfolio returns are not exposed to market risk.

A reverse conversion or reversal is a specific arbitrage portfolio constructed with a **short underlying instrument** and its synthetically created counterpart—the long combo—with the intention of taking advantage of the mispriced instrument configuring a put call parity equation and locking-in profits immediately. Given that the short underlying instrument is protected with an offsetting counterpart (long combo), portfolio returns are not exposed to market risk.

Both strategies deliver a payoff profile—a positive flat diagram—identical to buying a bond (lending).

KEY TERMS

conversion
reversal or reverse conversion
selling a bond (borrowing)
buying a bond (lending)

[redacted]

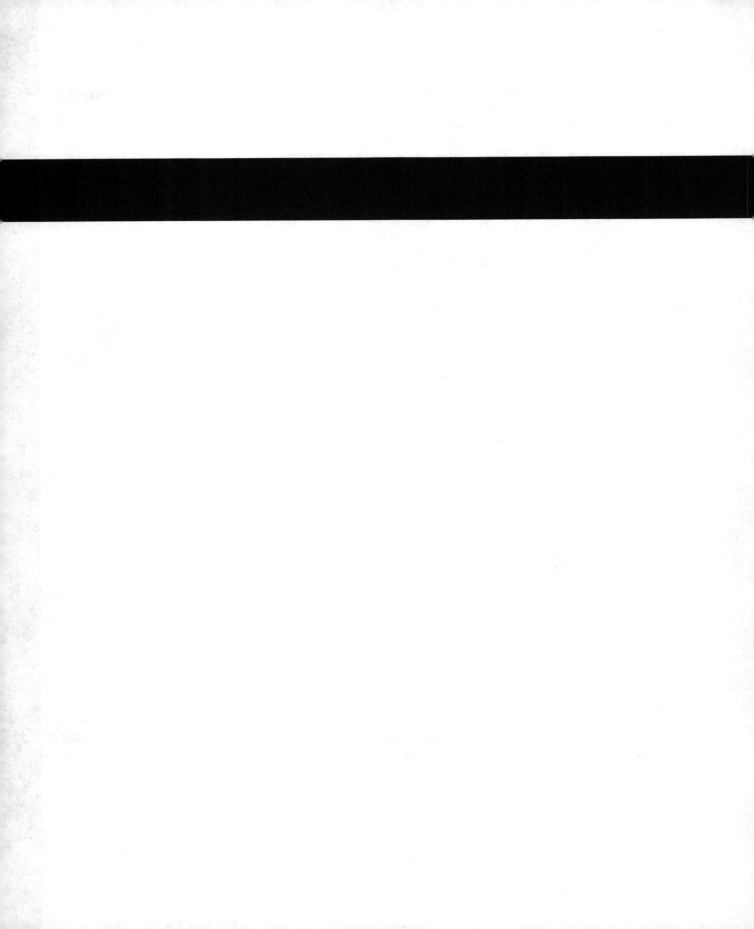

CHAPTER 22

COVERED SHORT STRADDLES AND STRANGLES

CHAPTER OBJECTIVES

- To explain the concept of a covered short straddle
- To illustrate how to configure a covered short straddle
- To explain the concept of a covered short strangle
- To illustrate how to configure a covered short strangle

COVERED SHORT STRADDLE

Key Terms

covered short straddle
selling the same strike call and a put option against a long underlying asset

THE "STRADDLE" IS AN OPTION STRATEGY THAT IS CONSTRUCTED WITH A CALL AND a put on the same strike. The straddle strategy and its variations will be covered in detail in Chapter 26.

The **covered short straddle** is a modification of the simple straddle as it uses the same constituents (the short call and a short put option entered on the same strike and expiration) except that the investor at the same time holds a long position on the commodity underlying the option contract.

This strategy is classified by many commentators as very risky and as such unsuitable for most traders. It requires a very good understanding of the relative market and an excellent knowledge of all the critical parameters affecting the change in price direction of the specific commodity. For this reason mainly, we decided to place it in the category of advanced strategies.

In configuring a covered short straddle, the investor sells both a call and a put on the same underlying, strike and expiration, but at the same time, he also owns the equivalent quantity of the asset underlying the options contract, in our example 25,000 lbs. of copper.

Covered short straddle assumptions:

Buy 25,000 lbs. of copper at $310.200.
Sell the June 2010 312 call strike for $4.35.
Sell the June 2010 312 put strike call for $8.10.

As usual, to understand the logic of the strategy and demonstrate its performance, we begin with the hypothetical case scenarios.

SCENARIO I: In case of price decline

If the price of the copper is below the option's strike price at expiration, then the call option sold expires "out-of-the-money" allowing the investor to retain the call premium collected, but the put option sold expires "in-the-money" and will be exercised. The put writer is assigned a long futures position and obliged to take delivery of copper at the strike price. This would be a very unfavourable scenario as the portfolio generates losses not only on the long copper position but also on the uncovered put written. The losses accelerate progressively with the price decline.

SCENARIO II: In case of price increase

However, if the copper price advances and is above the call option strike price at expiration, then the investor's position is inverted: the sold put expires out-of-the-money and becomes worthless, but the short call is now in-the-money and therefore destined to be exercised. The call writer is assigned an exercise and acquires a short futures contract obliging him to deliver 25,000 lbs. of copper at $312c/lb. Since the short call is covered, the hedger simply delivers the copper he already owns.

The repercussions of both scenarios are demonstrated in Table 22.1.

Now, let's take a look at the portfolio performance metrics. As you can see the strategy delivers a limited profit potential on the upside, while at the same time it suffers serious losses in a declining market.

Table 22.1 Covered Short Straddle Performance Metrics

UI Value $/lb 310.200	Long UI Payoff	Short Call 312@4.35 −(St − X)	Short Put 312@8.10 −(X − St)	Premium Net Credit	Covered Call Return	Position Total Return $
A	B	C	D	E	F	B+C+D+E
320	9.80	−8	0	12.45	6.15	14.25
316.35	6.15	−4.35	0	12.45	6.15	14.25
314	3.80	−2	0	12.45	6.15	14.25
313	2.80	−1	0	12.45	6.15	14.25
312	1.80	0	0	12.45	6.15	14.25
310.200	**0**	0	−1.80	12.45	4.35	10.65
309	−1.20	0	−3	12.45	3.15	8.25
308	−2.20	0	−4	12.45	2.15	6.25
307	−3.20	0	−5	12.45	1.15	4.25
305.85	−4.35	0	−6.15	12.45	**0**	2.25
304.875	−5.325	0	−7.125	12.45	−0.975	0
300	−10.20	0	−12	12.45	−5.85	−9.75
290	−20.20	0	−22	12.45	−15.85	−29.75
250	−60.20	0	−62	12.45	−55.85	−109.75

In view of the configuring process we can split the strategy into two phases:

- phase I sees the construction of a covered call strategy—writing a call ($312) on a long copper position ($310.200).
- phase II simply implies an additional short put at the same strike ($312).

Figure 22.1 shows the configuration of a covered call.

Figure 22.1 Covered Short Straddle; Phase I (Covered Call)

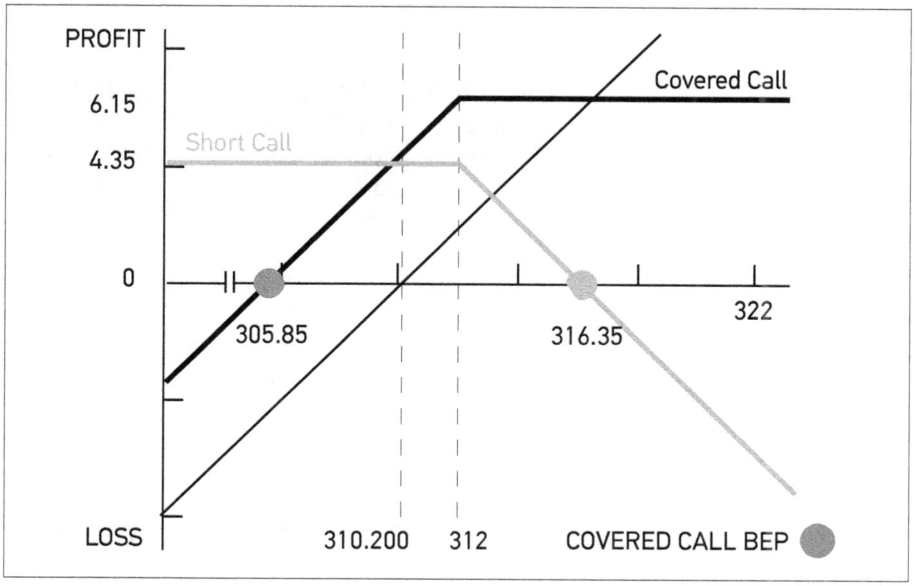

Figure 22.2 Covered Short Straddle; Phase II (Covered Call + Short Put)

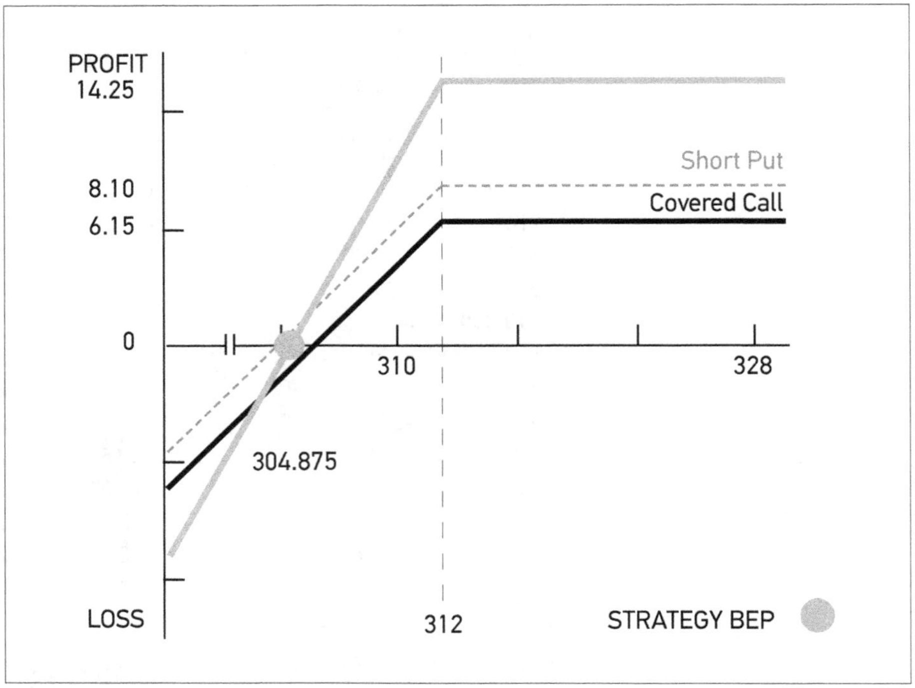

The payoff obtained by adding an additional short put on existing covered call is depicted in Figure 22.2.
The risk profile of the covered short straddle is very similar in appearance to that of the covered call, except that adding an extra put to a covered call modifies the steepness of the payoff diagram, so that the decline of the portfolios resulting exposure accelerates at approximately double the speed compared to a simple covered call.

The performance metrics exhibited in Table 22.1 evidently support the graphic interpretation.

COVERED SHORT STRADDLE PORTFOLIO KEY FEATURES

On the upside: limited profit potential.
The nominal amount of position's total return exceeds that of a covered call.
The spread is equal to a put option premium:
$14.25 – $6.15 = $8.10

On the downside: unlimited loss potential.
Maximum loss exceeds that of a covered call.
Portfolio losses accelerate at almost double the speed compared to a covered call.
BEP = (Purchase price of underlying + short put strike price – net premium received)/2
= ($310.200 + $312 – $12.45)/2
= $304.875

Profit & Loss Characteristics

Maximum profit is achieved when the price of the underlying at expiration date exceeds the strike price sold:

Maximum profit = Strike price – long copper purchase price + net premium collected
= \$312 – \$310.200 + \$12.45
= \$14.25

Maximum loss is achieved when the price of underlying at expiration date is below the strike price sold:

If the actual gold price = \$250
Maximum loss = Copper purchase price + strike price – (2 x actual copper purchase price) – net premium collected:
= \$310.200 + \$312 – (2 x \$250) – \$12.45
= 109.75

COVERED SHORT STRANGLE

Key Terms

covered short strangle
selling a call and put option at different strikes against the long underlying asset

The covered short strangle may be considered a special case of the covered short straddle: both strategies are bullish in regard to market expectations, maintaining limited profit potential in rising markets and unlimited risk potential in declining markets. The resulting payoff profile is therefore very similar to a covered short straddle.

The major difference between the two is that an additional short put is entered at a different strike price.

Performance metrics of a covered short strangle are demonstrated in Table 22.2.

Table 22.2 Covered Short Strangle Performance Metrics

UI Value $/lb 310.200	Long UI Payoff	Short Call 312@4.35 −(St − X)	Short Put 308@5.90 −(X − St)	Premium Net Credit	Covered Call Return	Position Total Return $
A	B	C	D	E	F	B+C+D+E
320	9.80	−8	0	10.25	6.15	12.05
316.35	6.15	−4.35	0	10.25	6.15	12.05
314	3.80	−2	0	10.25	6.15	12.05
313	2.80	−1	0	10.25	6.15	12.05
312	1.80	0	0	10.25	6.15	12.05
310.200	**0**	0	0	10.25	4.35	10.25
309	−1.20	0	0	10.25	3.15	9.05
308	−2.20	0	0	10.25	2.15	8.05
307	−3.20	0	−1	10.25	1.15	6.05
305.85	−4.35	0	−2.15	10.25	0	3.75
303.975	−6.225	0	−4.025	10.25	−1.875	0
300	−10.20	0	−8	10.25	−5.85	−7.95
290	−20.20	0	−18	10.25	−15.85	−17.95
250	−60.20	0	−58	10.25	−55.85	−57.95

The dissimilarity of the risk to reward profiles between the two strategies is clear from the graphic depiction. Hence, in Figure 22.3 and 22.4 we repeat the set of transactions relevant for configuring the covered short strangle.

The risk profile of the covered short strangle deviates from the covered short straddle in that it involves a different strike, namely the additional short put is entered at the lower strike of $0.308. The second strike modifies the risk payoff in that in between the strikes, the downfall in portfolio returns is commensurate with the fall in the price of the underlying. Below the lower strike price, the portfolio downfall accelerates at approximately double the speed of the covered call.

The performance metrics exhibited in Table 22.1 endorse the graphic interpretation.

The following figures depict the configuration of a covered short strangle split in two phases:

- phase I illustrates the constitution of a covered call (short call against long underlying), and
- phase II which simply adds a short put to the existing covered call portfolio.

Figure 22.3 Covered Short Strangle; Phase I (Covered Call)

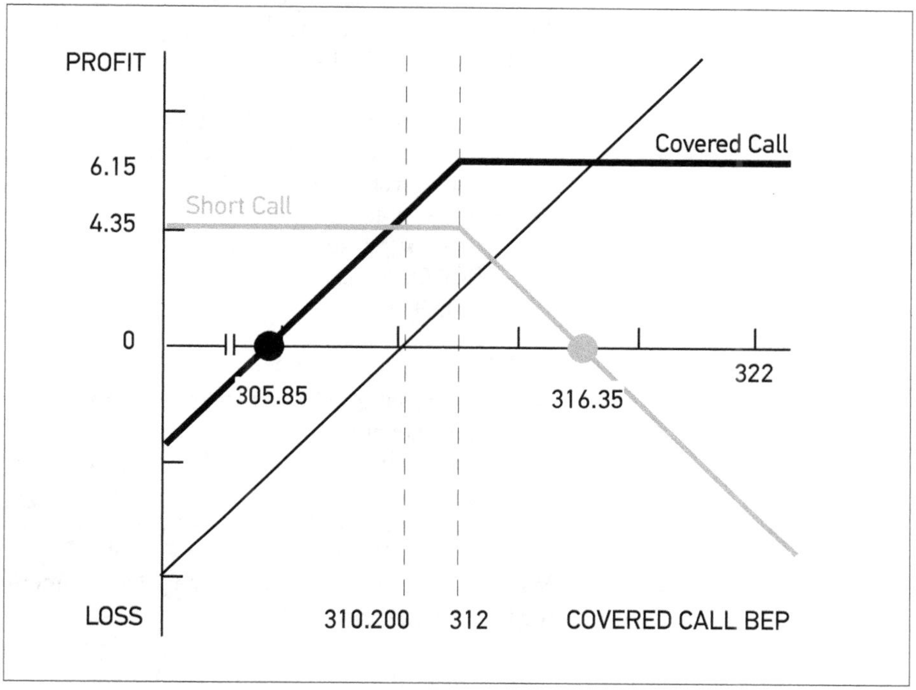

Figure 22.4 Covered Short Strangle; Phase I (Covered Call + Short Put)

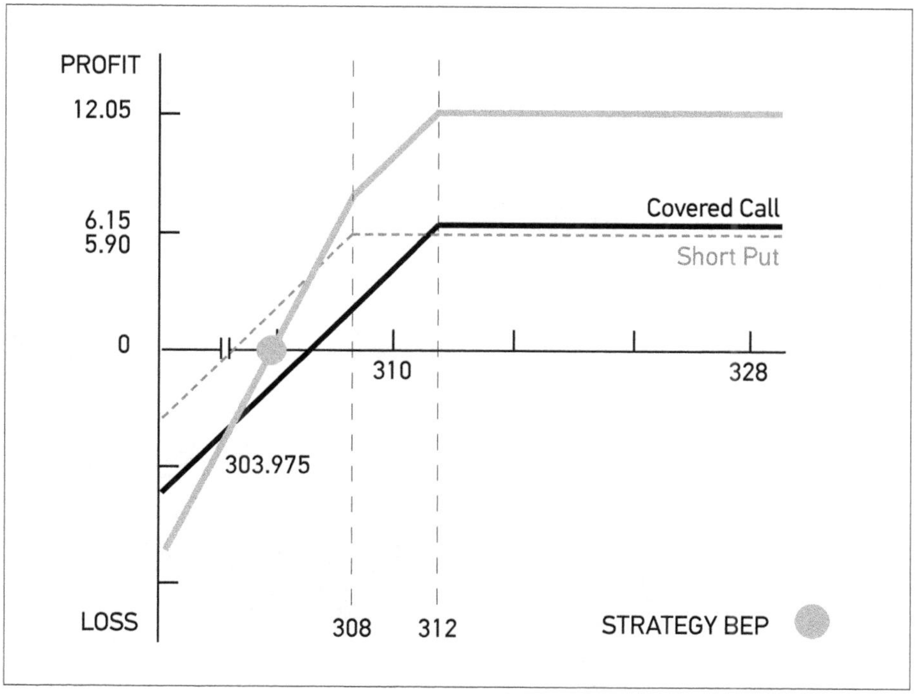

COVERED SHORT STRANGLE PORTFOLIO KEY FEATURES

On the upside: limited profit potential.
Nominal amount of the position's total return exceeds that of a covered call.
The spread is equal to the short put option premium:
$12.05 – $6.15 = $5.90

On the downside: unlimited loss potential.
Maximum loss exceeds that of a covered call.
Bellow the short put strike, portfolio losses accelerate at almost double the speed compared to a covered call.
BEP = [{(Short put strike) – (stock price – net credit)}]/2 – (stock price – net credit)
= [{($308) – ($310.200 – $10.25)/2 – ($310.200 – $10.25)
= $303.975

Profit & Loss Characteristics

Maximum profit is achieved when the price of the underlying at expiration date exceeds the strike price sold:
Maximum profit = Short call strike price – long copper purchase price + net premium collected
= $312 – $310.200 + $10.25
= $12.05
Maximum loss is achieved when the price of underlying at the expiration date is below the lower strike price sold:

If the actual copper price = $250
Maximum loss = Copper purchase price + put strike price – (2 x actual copper purchase price) – net premium collected
= $310.200 + $308 – (2 x $250) – $10.25
= 107.95

SUMMARY

This chapter focused on two similar strategies: covered short straddle and covered short strangle. A closer look at these strategies discovered their similarities and dissimilarities. Both strategies are designated as being neutral to bullish, and very risky if the market breaks-out in the opposite direction. The risk profiles illustrated endorse this conclusion.

We hope that this elaboration helps investors envisage the multiple ways of covering the risks associated with holding a long position.

Comparing different hypothetical strategy scenarios along with back-testing the performance metrics allows investors to develop a reliable method of measuring risk against expected return and to finally refine the portfolio parameters, relative to prevailing market conditions, in an attempt to achieve superior results.

KEY TERMS

covered short straddle

covered short strangle

[redacted]

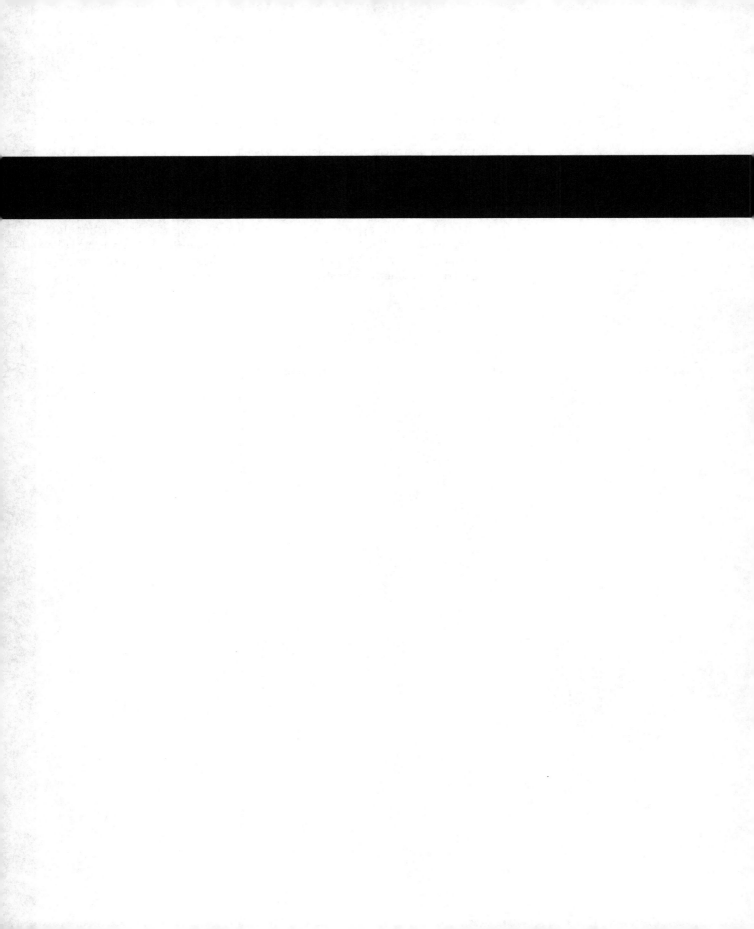

CHAPTER 23

ACCRUED PROFITS PROTECTION

CHAPTER OBJECTIVES

- To examine how different instruments may be used to provide protection on accrued profits
- To show the characteristics of each protection portfolio
- To tie together different concepts and risk to expected reward profiles in a comparative analysis resume

I ACCRUED PROFITS PROTECTION

SAFEGUARDING PROFITS ACCRUED IN COMMODITY MARKETS, WITH THEIR ERRATIC and capricious price movements, is an absolute, indispensable priority of the prudent investor. This chapter introduces the reader to different alternatives that can be used to protect the accrued profit so that the returns of the combined portfolio will not be exposed to market risk.

We assume that you have invested in copper by purchasing May COMEX futures at an effective price of 310.200. Today, on March 22, 2010, the copper price has increased to 336.10. You want to protect your accrued profits ($25.90) at this actual price level and you are considering five possible alternative strategies:

I. Hedge with a short futures
II. Protective put hedge
III. Covered call hedge
IV. Short combo hedge
V. Short split combo hedge (short semi-futures)

I. HEDGE WITH A SHORT FUTURES

We initiate the protection by shorting a copper futures: the market is in contango and three months (May) futures are available at $337.20.

Example: Sell May futures @337.20

Table 23.1 Protection with a Short Futures

Copper at Expiration $/lb	300	**310.20**	320	336.10	**337.20**	350	360
Long Copper Payoff	(10.20)	0	9.80	25.90	27	39.80	49.80
Short Futures Payoff	37.20	27	17.20	1.10	0	(12.80)	(22.80)
Portfolio P&L	27	27	27	27	27	27	27

Long asset payoff = ST – X
Short futures payoff = F – ST
Portfolio payoff = F – ST + ST – X = F > X = Positive constant (if F < X = Negative constant)
Portfolio payoff = $337.20 – ST + ST – $310.20 = +$27

Portfolio P&L diagram = Positive constant (Bond)

The remaining four strategies involve options. We select "near-the-money"option contracts with May expiry to match the maturity of the futures contract.

The actual options quotations for Monday, March 22, 2010, are given in the following chart.

HI GRADE COPPER (COMEX) (USd/lb.) 336.100
25,000 lbs., cents per lb. 22 March 2010

Exercise Price	CALLS			PUTS		
	Apr	May	June	Apr	May	June
300	37.45	39.95	44.00	0.05	1.95	5.00
331	8.30	17.00	22.85	1.85	9.95	14.85
332	7.60	16.45	22.30	2.15	10.40	15.35
333	6.90	15.90	21.80	2.45	10.85	15.80
334	6.30	15.35	21.30	2.85	11.30	16.30
335	5.70	14.80	20.75	3.25	11.75	16.75
336	5.10	14.30	20.25	3.65	12.25	17.25
3336.100	HI GRADE COPPER (COMEX) SPOT					
337	4.60	13.80	19.75	4.15	12.75	17.75
338	4.10	13.35	19.30	4.65	13.30	18.30
339	3.65	12.85	18.80	5.20	13.80	18.80
340	3.25	12.40	18.35	5.80	14.35	19.35
341	2.85	11.95	17.90	6.40	14.90	19.90
342	2.50	11.50	17.45	7.05	15.45	20.45
343	2.15	11.05	17.00	7.70	16.00	21.00
344	1.90	10.65	16.55	8.45	16.60	21.55
345	1.65	10.25	16.15	9.20	17.20	22.15

In the relevant tables accompanying each strategy described we have shown the potential profits and losses at various copper price levels with the following observations:

- The table gives an insight into the payoffs of the constitutent elements at arbitrary copper price levels.
- The row marked "portfolio" gives the actual value of the portfolio at various price levels obtained as the sum of the corresponding payoffs, and the related premium (either credit or debit).
- In the row marked "portfolio P&L" we have exhibited the profit and/or loss potential of the portfolio in comparison to the initial copper price level of $310.200.

With this preamble in mind, we can now elaborate briefly the characteristics of each particular strategy.

II. PROTECTIVE PUT HEDGE

There are many creative alternatives that might be employed to protect accrued profits. In general, exploiting options' flexibility to this effect proliferates opportunities for market participants.

One of the choices to discuss in this respect is to ensure accrued profits by employing a long put option as a protective instrument.

Portfolio P&L diagram = Synthetic long call
Limited profit on the downside; variable profit on the upside
(it depends upon the choice of the put exercise price)
Example: May $336 Long Put @12.25

Table 23.2 Protective Put Protection

Copper at Expiration	300	**310.20**	320	336	336.10	350	360
Long Copper Payoff	(10.20)	0	9.80	25.80	25.90	39.80	49.80
Long Put Payoff	36	25.80	16	0	0	0	0
Premium	(12.25)	(12.25)	(12.25)	(12.25)	(12.25)	(12.25)	(12.25)
Portfolio	323.75	323.75	323.75	323.75	323.85	337.75	347.75
Portfolio P&L	13.55	13.55	13.55	13.55	13.65	27.55	37.55

The purchase of a put option establishes a floor price in a downward market—the protection is triggered at the point of the put exercise price purchased—$336. In this particular example it means that a protective put, within its validity, secures the floor selling price of $323.75 regardless of the actual price decline.

If the copper price moves in another direction—from the exercise price level upwards—this strategy retains the benefit of a favourable price increase. Although increasing with the price rise the portfolio profit, as you may have noticed, will consistently fall $12.25 behind the copper spot price, which is exactly the value of the put premium paid.

III. COVERED CALL HEDGE

Next, we consider using a short call as a protective instrument.

Portfolio P&L diagram = Synthetic short put
Variable profit & loss on the downside! Limited profit on the upside;
(it depends on the choice of the call exercise price)

Table 23.3 Covered Call Protection

Copper at Expiration	250	295.90	**310.20**	336	336.10	350	360
Long Copper Payoff	(60.20)	(14.30)	0	25.80	25.90	39.80	49.80
Short Call Payoff	0	0	0	0	(0.10)	(14)	(24)
Premium	14.30	14.30	14.30	14.30	14.30	14.30	14.30
Portfolio	264.30	310.20	324.50	350.30	350.30	350.30	350.30
Portfolio P&L	(45.90)	0	14.30	40.10	40.10	40.10	40.10

The writing of the call option locks-in the price ceiling— $350.30. That is the maximum net selling price you receive in case of being exercised (if market finishes above the short call exercise price). Consequently, writing a covered call forfeits the full benefit of the favourable price increase. As the copper selling price is limited so are the potential profits. If you opt for this solution, the implication is that you will face an "opportunity loss" in the rising market—equal to the difference between the actual spot price and the short call BEP point ($350.30).

However, if the copper market turns in another direction and starts to plummet, the net premium received for writing the call will serve as a "buffer" in the declining market—the loss in the portfolio value originating from the price decline will be reduced by $14.30, which is exactly the value of the premium received.

IV. SHORT COMBO HEDGE

We may establish a protection using a short combo instrument.

Portfolio P&L diagram = Positive constant (Bond)
Locked-in profit of $.05 = Net credit

Example: May $338 long put @13.30; May $338 short call @13.35
Net credit: $.05

Table 23.4 Short Combo Protection

Copper at Expiration	300	**310.20**	320	336.10	338 / 338	340	350
Long Copper Payoff	(10.20)	0	9.80	25.90	27.80	29.80	39.80
Long Put Payoff	38	27.80	18	1.90	0	0	0
Short Call Payoff	0	0	0	0	0	(2)	(12)
Net Credit	0.05	0.05	0.05	0.05.	0.05	0.05	0.05
Portfolio	338.05	338.05	338.05	338.05	338.05	338.05	338.05
Portfolio P&L	27.85	27.85	27.85	27.85	27.85	27.85	27.85

Table 23.4 illustrates the performance of a short combo hedge. This strategy provides an effective portfolio value of $338.05 fixed at all price levels. Compared to the copper price of $336.10, the portfolio will produce a constant return of $1.95—the difference between the exercise price plus the net credit, and the copper price ($338 + $.05 – $336.10 = $1.95)—invariant to a change in copper prices. Compared to the initial (entry) price of $310.20, this strategy affords the efficient profit confined to $27.85 ($338.05 – $310.20).

V. SHORT SPLIT COMBO HEDGE (SHORT SEMI-FUTURES)

Lastly, we analyse the result of a portfolio implemented with a short split combo.

Portfolio P&L diagram = Bull put spread
Range-bound risk to reward profile. Profits locked-in in both directions.

Example: May $336 long put @12.25; May $342 short call @14.30
Net credit: $2.05

Table 23.5 Short Split Combo Protection

Copper at Expiration	300	**310.20**	320	336	336.10	342	350
Long Copper Payoff	(10.20)	0	9.80	25.80	25.90	31.80	39.80
Long Put Payoff	36	25.80	16	0	0	0	0
Short Call Payoff	0	0	0	0	0	0	(8)
Net Credit	2.05	2.05	2.05	2.05	2.05	2.05	2.05
Portfolio	338.05	338.05	338.05	338.05	338.15	344.05	344.05
Portfolio P&L	27.85	27.85	27.85	27.85	27.95	33.85	33.85

The portfolio will also produce a constant range-bound return without regard to the change in the underlying asset price, only this time divided into two segments: below the long put exercise price of $336—the protection with a short split combo locks in the price of $338.05 ($1.95 better than $336.10); and above the short call exercise price of $342—the price is locked-in at the $344.05 level ($7.95 above $336.10).

As you may notice that if the market rallies above the $342.20 level, this strategy would forfeit the full benefit of a favourable price increase.

SUMMARY

In this chapter we have introduced different concepts that might be implemented in various market circumstances, to protect a position that acquired a positive return. We identified 5 different portfolios, each providing a distinctive protection delivering specific risk-reward ratios.

Finally, we tied together the end results of different portfolios and analyzed correlated inputs under the premise of a copper price falling or rising within a range of $0 to $450.

Portfolio 1: Hedge with a short futures
Portfolio 2: Hedge with a protective put
Portfolio 3: Hedge with a covered call writing
Portfolio 4: Hedge with a short combo
Portfolio 5: Hedge with a short split combo

Within these hypothetical limits, different strategies would deliver different results. A tabular scorecard that comprehensively captures the correlated inputs is shown below:

	Potential Losses	Losses Avoided	Accrued Profits	Extra Profits	Foregone Profits
Portfolio 1		310.20	25.90	1.10	112.80
Portfolio 2		310.20	13.55	114	12.25
Portfolio 3	295.90	14.30	25.90	14.20	99.70
Portfolio 4		310.20	25.90	1.95	111.95
Portfolio 5		310.20	27.85	6.00	105.95

PART 5

OPTION SPREADS AND COMBINATIONS

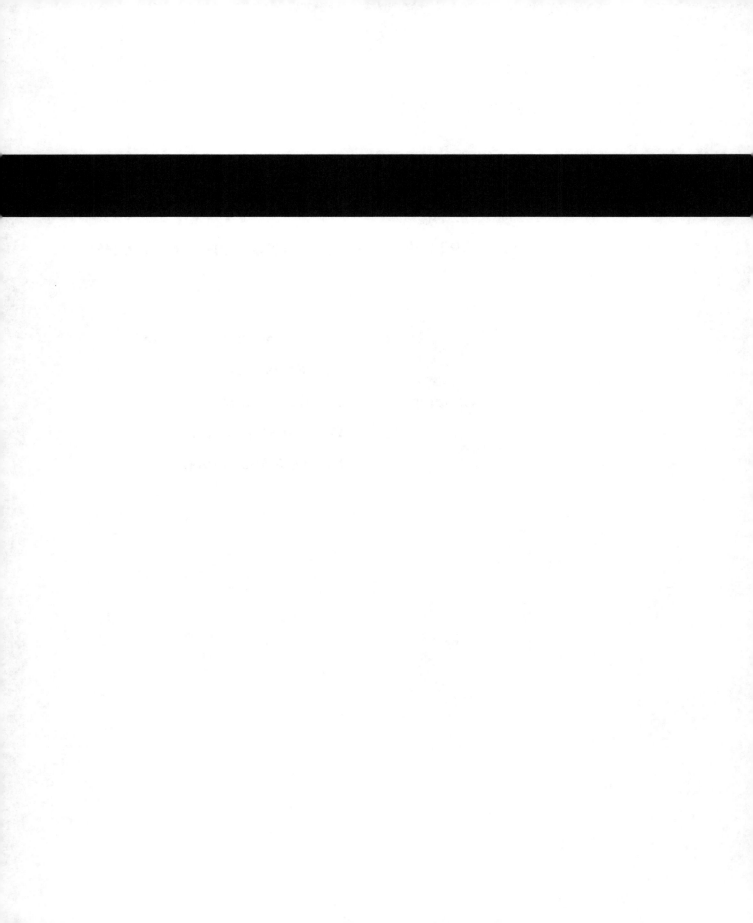

CHAPTER 24

OPTIONS SPREAD STRATEGIES

CHAPTER OBJECTIVES

- To introduce the family of Spread Strategies
- To identify and explain the differences between various spread types
- To illustrate and define the basic characteristics of the most common strategies:
    - Bull Call Spread
    - Bull Put Spread
    - Bear Call Spread
    - Bear Put Spread
    - Butterfly Spreads
    - Condor Spreads

I INTRODUCTION

In most general terms a spread is a trade combination which refers to simultaneous purchase and sale of related derivative instruments and/or cash positions. There are two principal reasons for entering a spread position:

- To confine risk: two parts of the trade offset each other, and/or
- To profit from the change in the price relationship

At the beginning we will provide an initial guide to the distinctive terms most commonly encountered in option markets:

Call and Put Spreads Differentiation of option spreads consisting of only calls or only puts.

Bull and Bear Spreads Option spreads designated as bull spreads aim to profit from an increase in the underlying price. If an option spread is intended to profit in the falling market, it is designated a bear spread.

Credit and Debit Spreads Option spreads may also be differentiated as a credit and debit subject to the net premium outlay resulting from options sold and purchased. If the premium of the sold options is higher than the premium of the options purchased, then it is a credit spread. If the premium sold is less then the premium purchased then it is a debit spread.

Ratio Spreads and Backspreads These refer to option spreads constructed with an unequal number of options purchased and sold. Ratio spreads imply that a strategy is constructed with more options sold then purchased. An inversed ratio—more options purchased than sold—is designated ratio backspread.

Horizontal or Calendar Spread Refers to a strategy constructed with options of the same type—either calls or puts—the same underlying and strike price, but with a different expiry.

Vertical Spread A type of option spread in which a pair of calls (or puts) on the same underlying and with the same expiry but different strike is simultaneously bought and sold.

Diagonal Spread A type of option spread with the simultaneous purchase and sale of a pair of calls (or puts) on the same underlying but with different strikes and different expiry dates.

Options Combinations In many cases a trader will try to exploit favourable market opportunities and take advantage of the option's inherent property— its flexibility. This is made possible by constructing a combination of call and put options, as will be discussed under a separate entry.

If we take a look at the HI Grade Copper (COMEX) futures options price chart the differences between the last three option spread types will become obvious.

Key Terms

bull spread
a type of option spread where the lower strike option is purchased and the higher strike option is sold. The strategy is beneficial in case of price increase

bear spread
a type of option spread where the higher strike option is purchased and the lower strike option is sold. The strategy is beneficial in case of price decline

horizontal or calendar spread
transaction where an option, either call or put, is purchased and another call or put on the same underlying and the same strike, but a different expiry is sold

vertical spread
a type of option spread in which a pair of calls (or puts) on the same underlying and with the same expiry but different strike is simultaneously bought and sold

diagonal spread
a type of option spread referring to a simultaneous purchase and sale of a pair of calls (or puts) on the same underlying but with different strikes and different expiry dates

options combinations
a strategy configured with a combination of calls and puts

Hi Grade Copper (COMEX)
25,000 lbs., cents per lb. Options Chain as of February 12, 2010

	CALLS			PUTS		
Strike	Mar	Apr	May	Mar	Apr	May
301	10.25	18.15	23.45	3.00	9.95	14.25
302	9.60	17.55	22.90	3.35	10.30	14.70
303	8.95	17.00	22.35	3.70	10.75	15.15
304	8.35	16.45	21.85	4.10	11.20	15.65
305	7.75	15.95	21.30	4.50	11.70	16.10
306	7.20	15.40	20.80	4.95	12.15	16.60
307	6.65	14.90	20.30	5.40	12.65	17.10
308	6.15	14.40	19.80	5.90	13.15	17.60
309	5.65	13.90	19.35	6.40	13.65	18.15
310	5.20	13.45	18.85	6.95	14.20	18.65
310.200 HI GRADE COPPER (COMEX) (cents/lb.) 310.20						
311	4.75	13.00	18.40	7.50	14.75	19.20
312	4.35	12.55	17.95	8.10	15.30	19.75
313	4.00	12.10	17.50	8.75	15.85	20.30
314	3.65	11.65	17.05	9.40	16.40	20.85
315	3.30	11.25	16.60	10.05	17.00	21.40

1. Horizontal (Time) Call Spread   2. Diagonal Put Spread   3. Vertical Put Spread

1. Same strikes ($311), different expiration (Apr $13.00; May $18.40)
2. Different expiration (Mar $6.40; Apr $12.65), different strikes ($309; $307)
3. Same expiration May, different strikes ($309; $305)

In the following section we shall acquaint you with the four most common and most popular vertical spread strategies:

I. Vertical spreads basic patterns:		
1.	Bull call spread	Figure 24.1
2.	Bull put spread	Figure 24.2
3.	Bear call spread	Figure 24.3
4.	Bear put spread	Figure 24.4

BULL CALL SPREAD

Key Terms

bull call spread
a type of option spread where the lower call strike option is purchased and the higher call strike option is sold

An example of a vertical spread where a lower strike call is purchased and a higher strike call is sold, both initiated on the same underlying and having the same delivery (expiry) months. The strategy is configured by purchasing a lower strike, or nearer out-of-the-money call (A), and simultaneously selling a higher strike, or farther out-of-the-money call (B). It is usually enacted when the trader is moderately bullish on the market price direction since the strategy limits the profit potential. Should the market turn to be very bullish, this strategy will limit your upside potential and you will not be in a position to fully participate in a favourable price increase.

The popularity of the strategy comes from the low investment requirements and the fact that the risk exposure is generally lower than buying a naked call and definitely lower than selling a call.

STRATEGY KEY FEATURES

Break-even point for a call option is on the upside, therefore:
Break-even point = A (lower strike) + net debit.
Maximum loss: Limited to the net debit paid
Maximum profit: Difference between strike prices – net debit.

From the graph below it is easy to observe the range-bound profile; the maximum loss is reached below the point (A), and the maximum profit is reached above the point (B).

Figure 24.1 Bull Call Spread–Long Lower Strike, Short Higher Strike

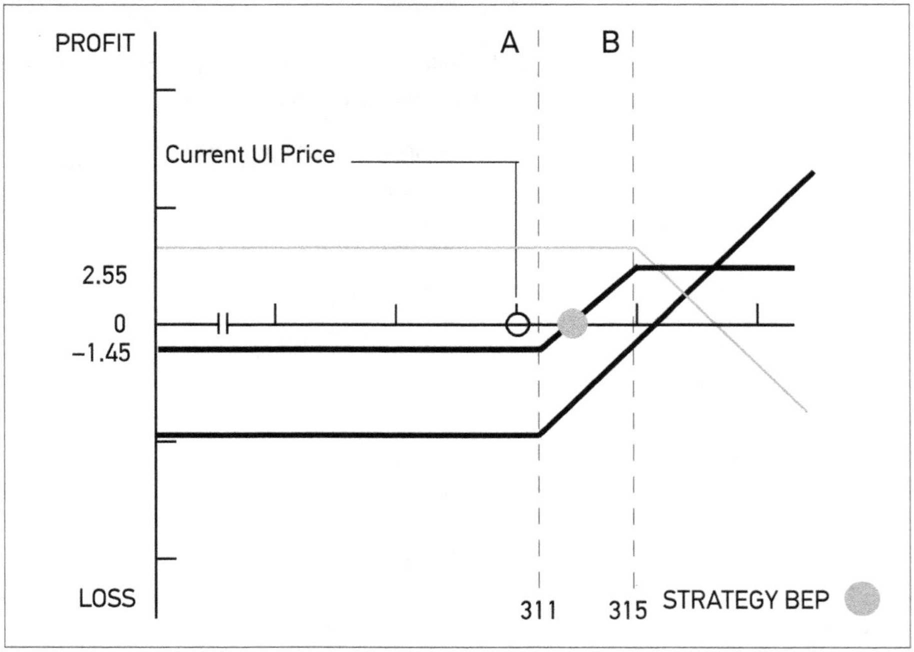

Bull call spread is also distinguished as a debit strategy since higher strike calls must always be cheaper than the lower strike calls. The logic is straightforward: the strike price of a call is inversely correlated with its premium (is correlated with its premium in a manner of inverse order)—the higher the call strike the lower the call premium.

For the sake of illustrating the risk to reward payoff profile of spread strategies we shall use HI Grade Copper (COMEX) options chain as of 12 February 2010:

Bull call strategy is configured as follows:

HI GRADE COPPER (COMEX) (cents/lb.) $310.20
A point—buy lower strike March $311 call at $4.75
B point—write higher strike March $315 call at $3.30
Net debit: $1.45
Here is the resume of bull call strategy performance:

SCENARIO I Copper Futures Price Stays Below A point	
Both Call Options are OTM Both Call Options Abandoned	
Premium Paid	$4.75
Premium Collected	$3.30
Net Return: Debit (cents/lb)	($1.45)

SCENARIO II Copper Futures Price Stays Above B point	
A – Long Call Exercised B – Short Call Assigned	
A – Purchase Copper B – Deliver Copper	–$311 +$315
Proceeds Less Debit	+$4 –$1.45
Net Return: Credit (cents/lb)	+$2.55

Remember This! Origins of the name "Copper"

1. **Chalkos** - Greek historians argue that copper was found at Cachous on the island of Euboea, near the town of Chalkos, and that the name "chalkos" is given by the ancient historian Homer. Hence, the transitional period between Stone Age and the Bronze Age was called the "calcolitic period" (from the Greek Chalkos). The island of Cyprus (Kythira)—halfway between Greece and Egypt—was consecrated to the ancient goddess of love and beauty Aphrodite.

2. **Cuprum** - Romans knew copper by the name of "cyprum", which was later changed to "cuprum", both names being derived from the Latin form of the name of the island of Cyprus (in Greek Κυπρος [Kypros]), where copper was mined. The English word copper, the French *cuivre*, the Spanish *cobre* and the German *kapfer* were introduced into those languages about the tenth century and are modifications of the old Latin *cuprum.*

The astronomical symbol for Venus is the same as that used in biology for the female sex: a circle with a small cross beneath. The Venus symbol, the coalescence of the mythology and alchemy, derivation of the **Egyptian Ankh symbol** (the symbol of Isis, the goddess of motherhood, healing and immortality) was subsequently adopted by Carl Linne to represent femininity, and in western alchemy stood for the metal copper. Polished copper has been used for mirrors from antiquity, and the symbol for Venus has sometimes been understood to stand for the mirror of the goddess.

In astrology alchemy the seven heavenly bodies known to the ancients were associated with seven metals also known in antiquity:

Sun (Sol)	Gold (Aurum)
Mercury (Mercurius)	Mercury (Hydrargyrum)
Venus	Copper (Cuprum)
Moon (Luna)	Silver (Argentum)
Mars	Iron (Ferrum)
Jupiter	Tin (Stannum)
Saturn	Lead (Plumbum)

BULL PUT SPREAD

Key Terms

bull put spread
a type of option spread where the lower put strike option is purchased and the higher put strike option is sold

An example of a vertical spread where a lower strike put is purchased and a higher strike put is sold, both being on the same underlying and having the same delivery (expiry) month. The strategy can be implemented by purchasing a lower strike or farther out-of-the-money put (A), and simultaneously selling a higher strike or nearer out-of-the-money put (B). It is usually initiated when the trader is only moderately bullish on the market price direction since the maximum profit potential is limited to the credit received upon initiating the trade. Should the market turn to be very bullish, this strategy will impose a limit on the upside potential and you will not be in a position to fully participate in a favourable price increase.

Unlike the bull call spread, a bull put spread is distinguished as a credit strategy since the higher strike puts are always more expensive than the lower strike puts: the strike price of a put is directly correlated with its premium—the higher the put strike the higher the put premium. (For correlations between strike prices versus call and put premium see Table 5.1).

STRATEGY KEY FEATURES

Break-even point for a put option is on the downside, therefore:

Break-even point = B (higher strike) – net credit
Maximum loss: difference between strike prices – net credit.
Maximum profit: limited to net credit received.

Figure 24.2 displays the payoff profile of bull put spread.

Figure 24.2 Bull Put Spread–Long Lower Strike, Short Higher Strike

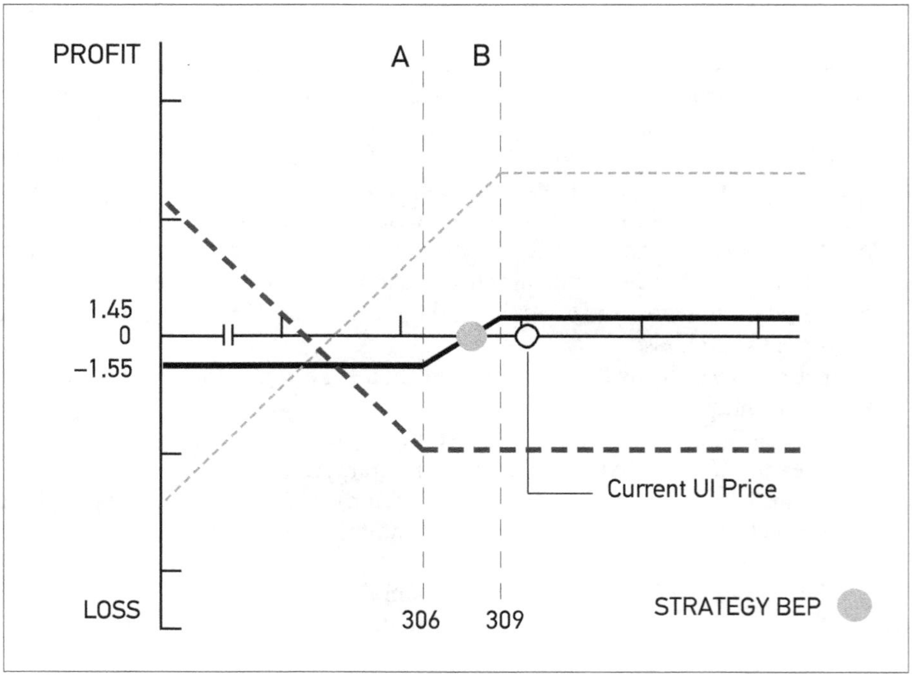

Bull put strategy is configured as follows:

HI GRADE COPPER (COMEX) (cents/lb.) 310.20
A point—buy lower strike March $306 put at $4.95
B point—write higher strike March $309 put at $6.40
Net credit: $1.45

SCENARIO I Copper Futures Price Stays Above B point	
Both Put Options are OTM Both Put Options Abandoned	
Premium Paid	$4.95
Premium Collected	$6.40
Net Return: Credit (cents/lb)	$1.45

SCENARIO II Copper Futures Price Stays Below A point	
A – Long Put Exercised B – Short Put Assigned	
A – Deliver Copper B – Purchase Copper	+$306 –$309
Proceeds Less Credit	–$3 $1.45
Net Return: Debit (cents/lb)	($1.55)

Remember This! Codelco History

Chile is one of Latin America's most important mining countries and maintains its role as the world's largest copper producer. As a result, apart from Codelco and the private Chilean mining company Antofagasta Minerals, all the major international mining houses are active in Chile (BHP Billiton, Anglo American, Rio Tinto, Placer Dome, Phelps Dodge, Falconbridge, Freeport-McMoRan, Barrick Gold, Newmont, Mitsui, etc.)

Company History:

The state-owned Corporacion Nacional del Cobre de Chile (Codelco) is the world's largest producer of copper, accounting for more than 18 percent of Chile's exports. Codelco controls one-fifth of the world's known reserves of copper and was producing over 1.6 million metric tons of copper a year at the end of the 20th century. Its largest two mines, Chuquicamata and El Teniente, are the world's largest open-pit and underground copper mines, respectively. Codelco is also the world's second largest producer of molybdenum, a byproduct of copper mining.

Key Dates:

1810: The year of independence, Chile produced 19,000 tons of copper.

1909: U.S. mining engineer William Braden sells controlling share of his Braden Copper Co. to the Guggenheim Exploration Co. (Guggenex); the site of the operation is El Teniente in the Andes Mountains.

1910: In that year, Guggenheim Bros. acquired control over the Chuquicamata fields for $25 millions and created the Chile Exploration Company.

1915: The Chuquicamata and El Teniente mines, owned by the Kennecott Utah Copper Corporation, are in operation.

1966: Guggenheim-controlled Kennecott sells 51 percent of its mining operations in Chile to the Chilean government.

1971: Four mines, including the aforementioned two, have been fully nationalized under the rule of Salvador Allende.

1976: Corporacion Nacional del Cobre de Chile (Codelco) is established to operate the four mines for the Chilean government.

1983: Codelco's production for the first time broke 1 million tons and reached 1.1 million metric tons.

1996: El Abra mine opens about 30 miles north of Chuquicamata, 49 percent owned by Codelco, 51 percent of the El Abra property was sold to Cyprus Amax Minerals Co.

1998: Codelco opens its newest copper mine, Radomiro Tomic.

2008: During this year a new project called Gaby, Gabriela Mistral, is in the process of finishing construction and is starting production.

BEAR CALL SPREAD

Key Terms

bear call spread
a type of option spread where the lower call strike option is sold and the higher call strike option is purchased

Bear spreads in general demonstrate an inverse relation. This type of spread is an example of a vertical spread where a higher strike call is purchased and a lower strike call is sold, both being on the same underlying and having the same delivery (expiry) months. The strategy is employed by purchasing a farther out-of-the-money call (B) and simultaneously selling a closer out-of-the-money call (A). Typically, option traders enter this range-bound strategy when expecting that the underlying asset price will fall only moderately in the near future since the strategy is limiting the profit potential. If the market turns to be very bearish this strategy will limit your downside potential and the full profit potential will be forfeited.

STRATEGY KEY FEATURES

Break-even point for a call option is on the upside, therefore:

Break-even point = A (lower strike) + net credit
Maximum loss: difference between strike prices – net credit.
Maximum profit: limited to net credit received.

From Figure 24.3 it is easy to observe that the maximum loss is reached at point B—the higher strike—and the maximum profit is reached at point A—the lower strike.

The bear call spread is a credit strategy since higher strike calls must always be cheaper than the lower strike calls. The logic is straightforward as the strike price of a call is inversely correlated with its premium—the higher the call strike the lower the call premium.

The bear call spread risk-to-reward profile is depicted in Figure 24.3.

Figure 24.3 Bear Call Spread–Long Higher Strike, Short Lower Strike

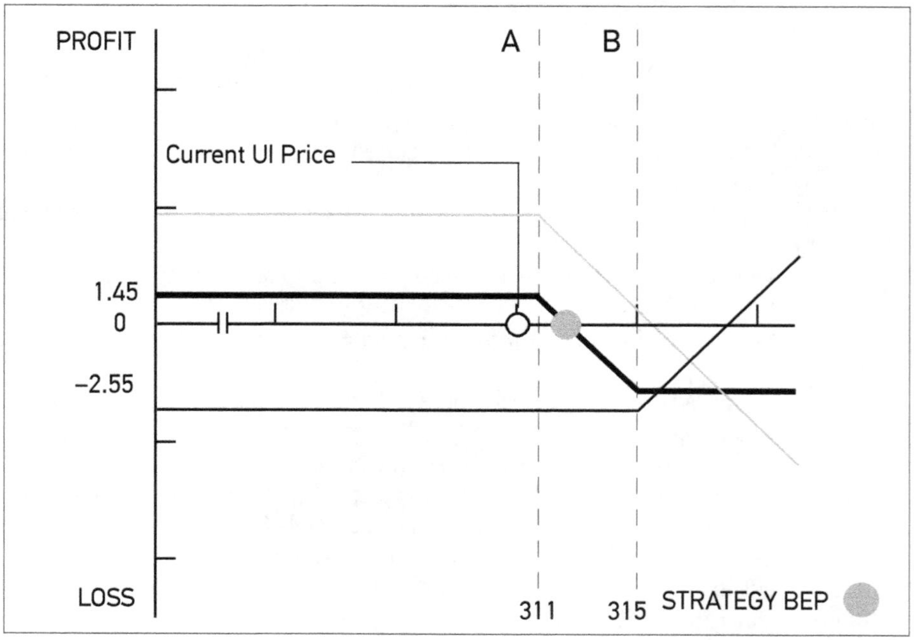

Bear call strategy is configured as follows:

HI GRADE COPPER (COMEX) (cents/lb.) 310.20
A point—sell the lower strike March $311 call at $4.75
B point—buy the higher strike March $315 call at $3.30
Net credit: $1.45

SCENARIO I Copper Futures Price Stays Below A point	
Both Call Options are OTM Both Call Options Abandoned	
Premium Collected	$4.75
Premium Paid	$3.30
Net Return: Credit (cents/lb)	$1.45

SCENARIO II Copper Future Price Stays Above B point	
A – Short Call Assigned B – Long Call Exercised	
A – Deliver Copper B – Purchase Copper	+$311 –$315
Proceeds Less Credit	–$4 +$1.45
Net Return: Debit (cents/lb)	($2.55)

Remember This! Chilenization of Copper

The nationalization of the Chilean copper industry was the progressive process in which the Chilean government acquired total control of the copper industry from the hands of a few multinational corporations, especially those from the United States. The process started under the government of President Carlos Ibanez del Campo, and culminated during the government of President Salvador Allende, who completed the nationalization.

There were two distinctive phases through which the Chilean government managed to acquire the control of its mineral resources. The first phase was known as "negotiated nationalization" and it started during the administration of President Eduardo Frei Montalva. On January 25, 1966, Congress sanctioned law 16.425 and transformed the "Copper Office" into the "Copper Corporation of Chile" (Codelco - Corporacion Nacional del Cobre de Chile).

On June 26, 1969, President Eduardo Frei Montalva signed an agreement with the Anaconda Copper Company. In this agreement, the government acquired 51% of the remaining two major mines (Chuquicamata and El Salvador) and also the right for Codelco to consolidate the international sales of Chilean copper.

In the agreement, it was established that the Chilean government could buy within the next 13 years (starting from 1970) the remaining 49% from the multinational corporations.

The second phase, "the outright nationalization" without compensation (also known as "**Chilenization of copper**", is linked with newly elected president Salvador Allende. In 1970 he had great support from the leftist political parties as well as the Christian Democratic Party.

At the beginning of 1971, he sent Congress a proposal for a constitutional amendment that would allow him to nationalize all mines outright, and to transfer all present and future copper fields to the state. Congress passed this amendment on July 11, 1971, by a unanimous vote and on July 16, 1971, the law 17.450 was promulgated, and became effective immediately.

Codelco operates one of the largest open pit mines in the world, Chuquicamata, in northern Chile's Atacama Desert and also the largest underground mine, El Teniente, a dormant volcano on the western slope of the Andes Mountains about 50 miles north of Santiago, the capital of Chile.

Principal Divisions: Codelco Norte (Chuquicamata & RadomiroTomic); Andina; El Teniente; Salvador; El Abra; Gaby

YEAR 2006		
World Total	Chile 35%	Codelco 35%
15,3 Mil.Tons	5,4 Mil.Tons	1,8 Mil.Tons

BEAR PUT SPREAD

Key Terms

bear put spread
a type of option spread where the lower put strike option is sold and the higher put strike option is purchased

A bear put spread is an example of a vertical spread where an equal number of put options, on the same underlying and having the same delivery (expiry) month, are simultaneously bought and sold. The strategy is entered at a net debit and the maximum gain is expected on the downside. To set up this strategy we need to write a lower strike put at (A) and simultaneously buy a higher strike put or closer at-the-money put at (B).

STRATEGY KEY FEATURES

Break-even point for a put option is on the downside, therefore:

Break-even point = B (higher strike) – net debit
Maximum loss: Limited to net debit paid.
Maximum profit: Difference between strike prices – net debit.

Unlike the bear call spread, the bear put spread is distinguished as a debit strategy since the higher strike puts are always more expensive than the lower strike puts: the strike price of a put is directly correlated with its premium—the higher the put strike the higher the put premium.

The bear put spread risk profile is depicted in Figure 24.4.

Figure 24.4: Bear Put Spread–Long Higher Strike, Short Lower Strike

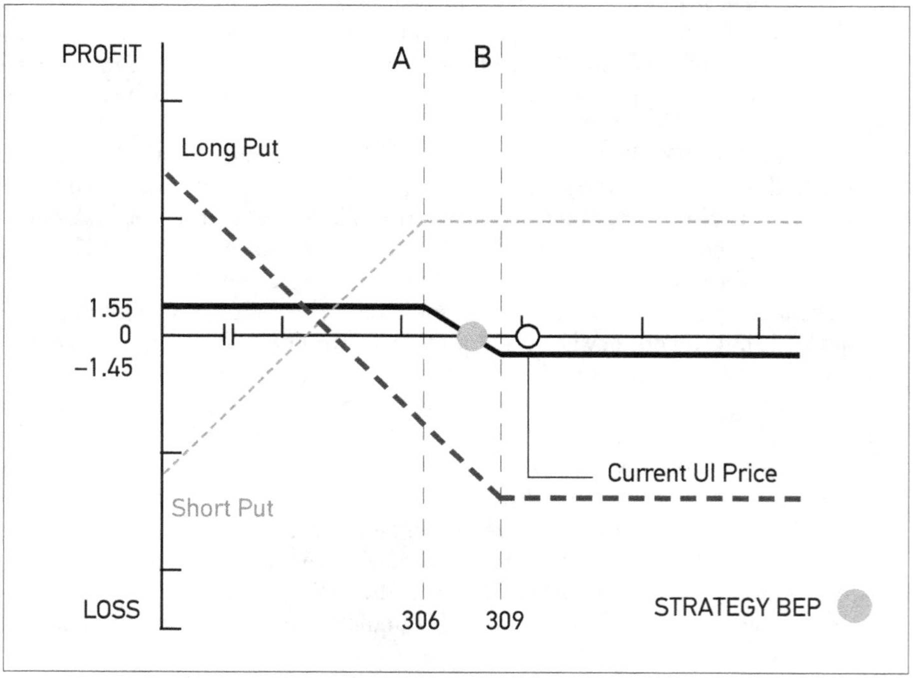

The bear put spread delivers a "range-bound" profile. Profit potential is on the downside with the maximum $1.55 reached below the lower strike. The potential loss above the higher strike purchased is also limited to –$1.45.

The bear put strategy is configured as follows:

HI GRADE COPPER (COMEX) (cents/lb.) $310.20
A point—sell lower strike March $306 Put at $4.95
B point—buy higher strike March $309 Put at $6.40
Net debit: $1.45

SCENARIO I Copper Futures Price Stays Above B point		SCENARIO II Copper Futures Price Stays Below A point	
Both Put Options are OTM Both Put Options Abandoned		A – Short Put Assigned B – Long Put Exercised	
Premium Paid	$6.40	A – Purchase Copper B – Deliver Copper	–$306 +$309
Premium Collected	$4.95	Proceeds Less Debit	+$3 $1.45
Net Return: Debit (cents/lb)	($1.45)	Net Return: Credit (cents/lb)	$1.55

The comparative analysis of vertical spread strategies is presented in Table 24.1.

Table 24.1 Vertical Spreads Resume

COMPONENTS				BEP	MAX LOSS	MAX PROFIT
Bull Call	Long Lower Strike Call	Short Higher Strike Call	Debit	Lower Strike + Net Debit	Net Debit	(HS – LS) – Net Debit
Bull Put	Long Lower Strike Put	Short Higher Strike Put	Credit	Higher Strike – Net Credit	(HS – LS) – Net Credit	Net Credit
Bear Call	Short Lower Strike Call	Long Higher Strike Call	Credit	Lower Strike + Net Credit	(HS – LS) – Net Credit	Net Credit
Bear Put	Short Lower Strike Put	Long Higher Strike Put	Debit	Higher Strike – Net Debit	Net Debit	(HS – LS) – Net Debit

In Figure 24.5 we illustrate the payoff profiles of bull spreads and bear spread relative to strike prices used to construct the position.

Figure 24.5 Profit Potential of Vertical Spreads

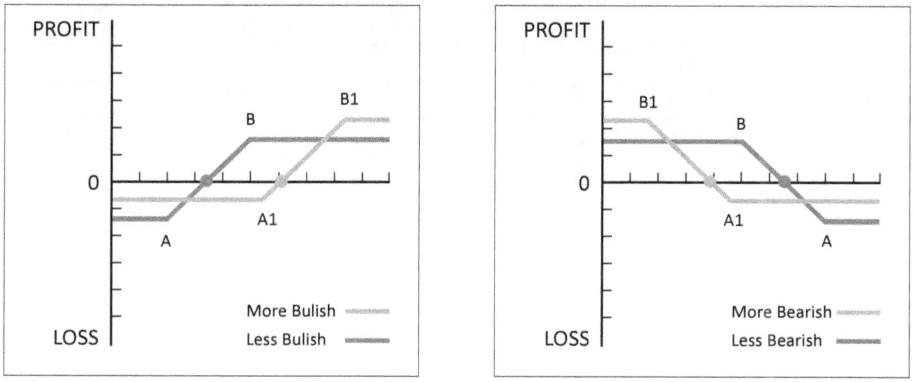

PAY-OFF DIAGRAMS

The staircase ascending from left to right	The staircase ascending from right to left
Higher profit – higher break-even point	Higher profit – lower break-even point
Max. profit at or above higher strike price	Max. profit at or below lower strike price
Max. loss at or below lower strike price	Max. loss at or below higher strike price

DISAMBIGUATION

Buying Call Spread	= Long Call Vertical	= Bull Call Spread	Debit
Selling Call Spread	= Short Call Vertical	= Bear Call Spread	Credit
Selling Put Spread	= Short Put Vertical	= Bull Put Spread	Credit
Buying Put Spread	= Long Put Vertical	= Bear Put Spread	Debit

Remember This: World's Largest Copper Producers (2011)

Copper has played a large role in the Chilean economy since at least 1825, when the British and Americans were already competing with other foreign investors to control Chile's copper and silver market. By the end of World War I, one generation of Guggenheims (the family business run by Meyer Guggenheim, just thirty-seven years old, and his seven sons) controlled more than 75% of the world's supply of silver, copper, and lead and was worth an estimated $300 million. In 1910 they acquired one of the largest, and richest, copper deposits ever discovered in Chuquicamata Chile, for US$25 million, along with the Kennecott Creek, Alaska, to form the Kennecott Copper Corporation—a world famous partnership with JPMorgan. These two copper mines, it turned out, would bring the Guggenheim's some of their highest profits. The brothers eventually sold the Chile Copper Corporation to Anaconda Copper for $70 million cash, the largest private sale of a mining property in history, cashing in on a profit, in modern dollars, of more than $800 million.

By the late 1950s, the three principal copper mines in Chile were: Chuquicamata, El Salvador and El Teniente. Chuquicamata and El Salvador were owned by the Anaconda Copper Company and El Teniente was owned by the Kennecott Utah Copper Corporation. The La Exotica mine was added to these big mines in 1966.

1.	CODELCO Chile	1,74 million tons
2.	Freeport-McMoRan	1,68
3.	BHP Billiton	1,64
4.	Xstrata	0.889
5.	Anglo American	0.645
6.	Glencore	0.628
7.	Grupo Mexico	0.598
8.	Rio Tinto	0.591
9.	Southern Copper	0.587
10.	KGHM poland	0.543

LONG CALL BUTTERFLY

Key Terms

long call butterfly
a type of option spread constructed by buying 1 in-the-money call; selling 2 at-the-money calls and buying 1 further out-of-the money call

The strategy is characterized with a modest net premium outlay and low volatility expectations as it profits only if the prices move within a very narrow range.
To illustrate the performance of a butterfly spread we shall use the ABN Amro Stock Price Chart as of July 9, 2007.

Example: ABN Amro Stock Price $34.68 9 July 2007

Call Close	Series	Put Close
$2.85	July 07 $32	$0.05
$1.10	July 07 $34	$0.35
$0.55	July 07 $35	$0.80
$0.25	July 07 $36	$1.50
$0.05	July 07 $38	$3.25

The long Call Butterfly position is constructed as follows:

1 x Long call	ITM	$34	A	at $1.10	–$1.10
2 x Short calls	ATM	$35	B	at $0.55	+$1.10
1 x Long call	OTM	$36	C	at $0.25	–$0.25

Net debit: $0.25

The loss is limited to the net premium outlay. The maximum profit being at the point (B), or the strike of 2 x at-the-money calls sold. The two break-even points are also equidistant from the middle strike price—the one on the downside would be the lower call or in-the-money call strike at (A) plus the debit (or the cost of the spread)—and the upside break-even would be the higher call or out-of-the-money call strike at (C), less the cost of the spread.

The payoff profile of the long call butterfly is illustrated in Figure 24.6.

Figure 24.6 Long Call Butterfly

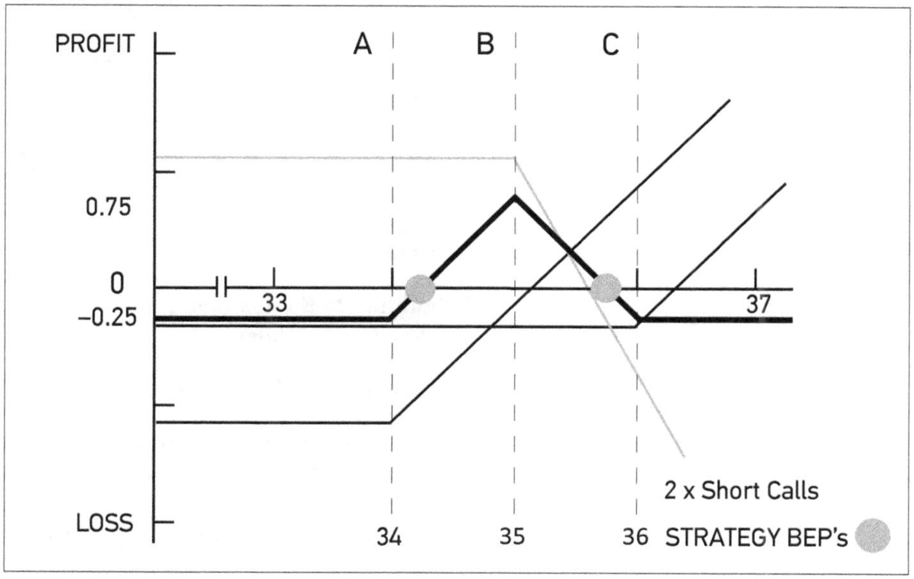

STRATEGY KEY FEATURES

Break-even points = Two
On the upside = Higher call at C – Net debit = \$36 – \$0.25 =\$ 35.75
On the downside = Lower call at A + Net debit = \$34 + \$0.25 = \$34.25
Maximum loss: limited to the net premium outlay
Maximum profit: limited to the difference in strikes
I. High strike – middle strike – net debit = \$36 – \$35 – \$0.25 = \$0.75
II. Middle strike – low strike – net debit = \$35 – \$34 – \$0.25 = \$0.75
Volatility outlook: bearish
Market outlook: neutral
Time decay: benefits position

In Table 24.2 we exhibit the performance metrics of the long call butterfly.

Table 24.2 Long Call Butterfly Performance Metrics

Price of Underlying	1 x Long Call at A \$34@1.10	2 x Short Calls at B \$35@0.55	1 x Long Call at C \$36@0.25	Long Butterfly Payoff \$
A	B	C	D	B+C+D
32	−1.10	1.10	−0.25	−0.25
33	−1.10	1.10	−0.25	−0.25
34	−1.10	1.10	−0.25	−0.25
34.25	−0.85	1.10	−0.25	0
34.45	−0.65	1.10	−0.25	0.20
34.90	−0.20	1.10	−0.25	0.65
35	−0.10	1.10	−0.25	**0.75**
35.10	0	0.90	−0.25	0.65
35.55	0.45	0	−0.25	0.20
35.75	0.65	−0.40	−0.25	0
36	0.90	−0.90	−0.25	−0.25
36.25	1.15	−1.40	0	−0.25
37	1.90	−2.90	0.75	−0.25

Maximum profit = Difference in strikes:
I. High strike – middle strike – net debit = \$36 – \$35 – \$0.25 = \$0.75
II. Middle strike – low strike – net debit = \$35 – \$34 – \$0.25 = \$0.75
Maximum loss = Net debit = \$0.25

There are several ways to configure the long butterfly strategy:

1. In addition to the example exhibited here, it may be constructed just as well using only put options:

   Long 1 put at A; Short 2 puts at B; Long 1 put at C.

2. But it also may be constructed using a mixture of calls and puts:
   Long 1 put at A; Short 1 put and 1 call at B; Long 1 call at C

When we use a combination of calls and puts we speak about iron butterflies.

Key Terms

iron butterfly
a type of option spread constructed by purchasing one out-of-the-money put; selling an at-the-money put and call and buying one further out-of-the-money call

wingspreads
a family of spread strategies with a payoff resembling a flying creature

IRON BUTTERFLY

An iron butterfly is a distinguished variation of a butterfly spread that belongs literally to a category of "options combinations" (strategies combining calls and puts), but since its payoff profile is identical to a common butterfly strategy we thought it would be more convenient to exemplify the distinction within this chapter. One additional reason to place the iron butterfly together with ordinary butterflies is that they both belong to so-called **wingspreads**—a family of spread strategies with a payoff resembling a flying creature. Condors and iron condors are also of the same family.

The iron butterfly is a strategy consisting of four legs spread over three different strikes—A (lower strike), B (mid strike) and C (higher strike).

IRON BUTTERFLY = Long 1 Put at A; Short 1 Put and 1 Call at B; Long 1 Call at C

The major attraction and popularity of the iron butterfly among experienced investors, comes from the fact that the position is entered with an initial credit. In this respect, the iron butterfly may be viewed from a different perspective—as a combination of two credit spreads—bull put and a bear call, having the same mid strike. To illustrate the performance of an iron butterfly we shall use data from the ABN Amro price chart:

1 x Long put	ITM	$34	A	at $0.35	–$0.35
Short call/put	ATM	$35	B	at $0.55 + $0.80	+$1.35
1 x Long call	OTM	$36	C	at $0.25	–$0.25
Net credit: $0.75					

The risk profile of the iron butterfly suggests it would be most beneficial in low volatility or so-called "flat markets." The portfolio delivers the same profile—limited profit versus limited risk—so the key strategy features remain the same as those explicated under the long butterfly strategy. In order to make the strategy profitable, the particular underlying will have to remain neutral, or trade in a narrow range—in between the two BEPs ($34.25 and $35.75).

Table 24.3 Iron Butterfly Performance Metrics

Price of Underlying	1 x Long Put at A $34@0.35	1 x Short Put at B $35@0.80	1 x Short Call at B $35@0.55	1 x Long Call at C $36@0.25	Long Condor Payoff $
A	B	C	D	E	B+C+D+E
30	3.65	–4.20	0.55	–0.25	–0.25
31	2.65	–3.20	0.55	–0.25	–0.25
32	1.65	–2.20	0.55	–0.25	–0.25
33.65	0	–0.55	0.55	–0.25	–0.25
34.20	–0.35	0	0.55	–0.25	–0.05
34.25	–0.35	0.05	0.55	–0.25	0
34.45	–0.35	0.25	0.55	–0.25	0.20
35	–0.35	0.80	0.55	–0.25	0.75
35.55	–0.35	0.80	0	–0.25	0.20
35.75	–0.35	0.80	–0.20	–0.25	0
36.25	–0.35	0.80	–0.70	0	–0.25
38	–0.35	0.80	–2.45	1.75	–0.25
40	–0.35	0.80	–4.45	3.75	–0.25

SHORT CALL BUTTERFLY

Key Terms

short call butterfly
a type of option spread constructed by selling 1 in-the-money call; buying 2 at-the-money calls and selling 1 further out-of-the-money call

This is the reverse of the long butterfly, so it is bullish on volatility and initiated at a net credit.

The strategy is constructed as follows:

Sell 1 x in-the-money call at A
Buy 2 x at-the-money calls at B
Sell 1 x out-of-the-money call at C
A and C calls are equidistant.

The maximum loss occurs if at expiry the market is pinned to the original at-the-money calls purchased, which will be equal to: B minus A minus the original credit received for entering the trade. The maximum profit is limited to the net premium received. This would be obtained if the market at expiration passed below (A) or above (C). The break-even is at point (A) plus the net premium income, and at point (C) less the net premium income.

Figure 24.7 illustrates the payoff profile of the short call butterfly.

Figure 24.7 Short Call Butterfly

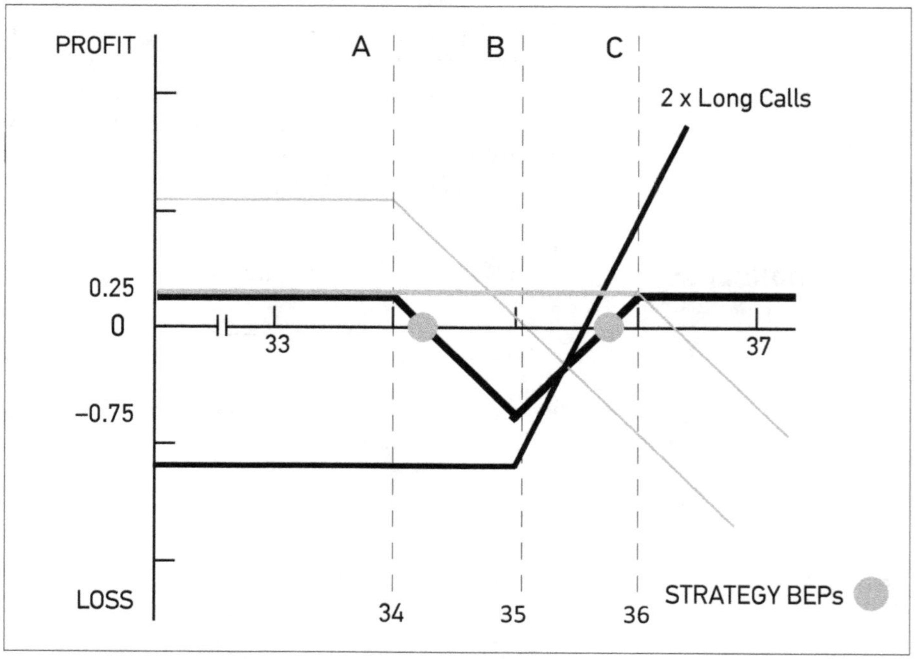

STRATEGY KEY FEATURES

Break-even points = Two
On the upside = Highest strike short call – net premium received
On the downside = Lowest strike short call + net premium received
Maximum loss: strike price of the long call – lower strike short call – net premium received

Maximum profit: net premium received
Volatility outlook: bullish
Market outlook: neutral
Time decay: hurts position

This strategy also can be constructed with different components:
Short 1 put at A; Long 2 puts at B; Short 1 put at C.
Short 1 call at A; Long 1 call and 1 put at B; Short 1 put at C.
Short 1 put at A; Long 1 put and 1 call at B; Short 1 call at C.

If we use the same data from the ABN Amro stock chart we can illustrate the performance of the short call butterfly strategy.

ABN Amro Stock					
1 x Short call	ITM	$34	A	at $1.10	+$1.10
2 x Long calls	ATM	$35	B	at $0.55	–$1.10
1 x Short call	OTM	$36	C	at $0.25	+$0.25
Net credit: $0.25					

The data is summarized in Table 24.4.

Table 24.4 Short Call Butterfly Performance Metrics

Price of Underlying	1 x Short Call at A $34@1.10	2 x Long Calls at B $35@0.55	1 x Short Call at C $36@0.25	Short Butterfly Payoff $
A	B	C	D	B+C+D
32	1.10	–1.10	0.25	0.25
33	1.10	–1.10	0.25	0.25
34	1.10	–1.10	0.25	0.25
34.25	0.85	–1.10	0.25	0
34.45	0.65	–1.10	0.25	–0.20
34.90	0.20	–1.10	0.25	–0.65
35	0.10	–1.10	0.25	**–0.75**
35.10	0	–0.90	0.25	–0.65
35.55	–0.45	0	0.25	–0.20
35.75	–0.65	0.40	0.25	0
36	–0.90	0.90	0.25	0.25
36.25	–1.15	1.40	0	0.25
37	–1.90	2.90	–0.75	0.25

LONG CALL CONDOR

Key Terms

long call condor
a type of option spread constructed as follows: Buy 1 ITM Call (Lower Strike), Sell 1 ITM Call; Sell 1 OTM Call; Buy 1 OTM Call (Higher Strike). This is a combination of a Bull Call plus Bear Call spread

The payoff profile of a long call condor strategy is very similar to the Butterfly payoff and is used in similar conditions, but yields a wider and relatively more attractive range of profitability. It can be made up of either calls or puts. Being an overall long position the loss is limited to the net premium cost which occurs at expiration—if the market is below (A) or above (D).

This strategy is constructed out of four legs spread over four different strikes as follows:

Buy 1 x in-the-money call at A
Sell 1 x slightly in-the-money call at B
Sell 1 x slightly out-of-the-money call at C
Buy 1 x out-of-the-money call at D

All strikes are equidistant from each other.

The break-even on the downside is at (A) plus the net debit or on the upside at (D) less the net debit. The maximum profit is between (B) and (C)—this being equal to the difference in strikes [(B minus A) – net debit]. The Maximum risk is limited to the net debit paid for initiating the strategy.

The payoff profile of the long call condor is displayed in Figure 24.8.

Figure 24.8 Long Call Condor

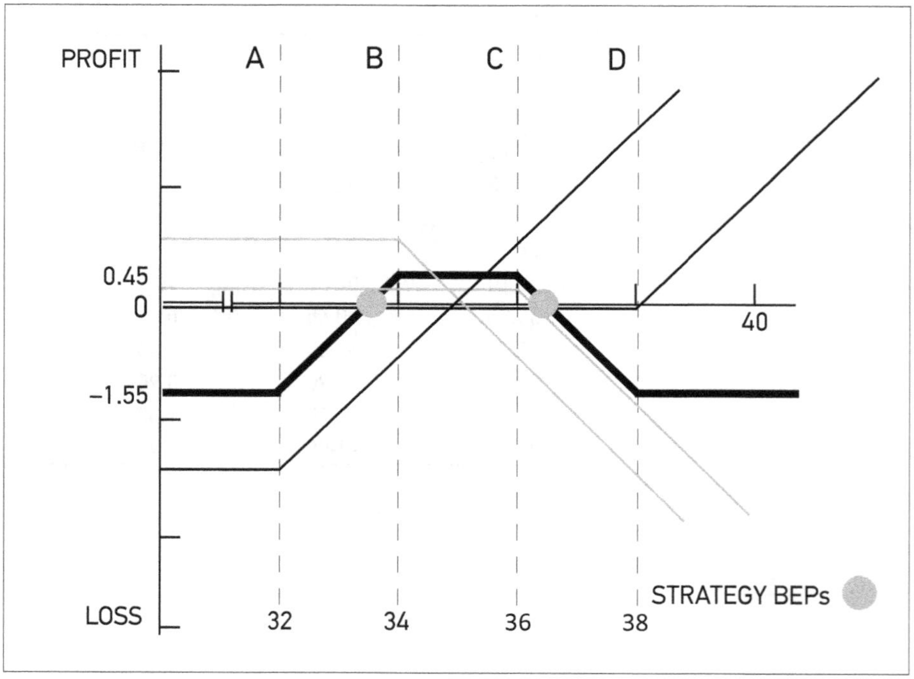

STRATEGY KEY FEATURES

Break-even points = Two
On the upside = Highest strike long call – net premium paid
On the downside = Lowest strike long call + net premium paid
Maximum Loss: net premium paid
Maximum Profit: lower strike short call – lower strike long call – net premium paid
Volatility outlook: bearish
Market outlook: neutral
Time decay: benefits position

This strategy can be constructed with the different components:
Long 1 put at A; Short 1 put at B and 1 put at C; Long 1 put at D
Long 1 call at A; Short 1 call at B and 1 put at C; Long 1 put at D
Long 1 put at A; Short 1 put at B and 1 call at C; Long 1 call at D

To illustrate the performance of a long condor strategy we shall use the data from the ABN Amro stock chart.

ABN Amro Stock Price

1 x Long call $32	at	$2.85	A	–$2.85
1 x Short call $34	at	$1.10	B	+$1.10
1 x Short call $36	at	$0.25	C	+$0.25
1 x Long call $38	at	$0.05	D	–$0.05
Net debit: $1.55				

The performance of a long call condor, configured with the above data, is summarized in Table 24.5.

Table 24.5 Long Call Condor Performance Metrics

Price of Underlying	1 x Long Call at A $32@2.85	1 x Short Call at B $34@1.10	1 x Short Call at C $36@0.25	1 x Long Call at D $38@.05	Long Condor Payoff $
A	B	C	D	E	B+C+D+E
30	–2.85	1.10	0.25	–0.05	–1.55
31.95	–2.85	1.10	0.25	–0.05	–1.55
33.55	–1.30	1.10	0.25	–0.05	0
33.75	–1.10	1.10	0.25	–0.05	0.20
34	–0.85	1.10	0.25	–0.05	0.45
34.85	0	0.25	0.25	–0.05	0.45
35	0.15	0.10	0.25	–0.05	0.45
35.10	0.25	0	0.25	–0.05	0.45
36	1.15	–0.90	0.25	–0.05	0.45
36.25	1.40	–1.15	0	–0.05	0.20
36.45	1.60	–1.35	–0.20	–0.05	0
38.05	3.20	–2.95	–1.80	0	–1.55
40	5.15	–4.90	–3.75	1.95	–1.55

Key Terms

iron condor
an option strategy composed of two vertical credit spreads, namely a Bull Put and a Bear Call, with different mid strikes, as opposed to an Iron Butterfly, a strategy that shares the same mid strike price

IRON CONDOR

An iron condor is equivalent to an iron butterfly with all the basic characteristics attributable to a common long condor.

An iron condor consists of four legs spread over four different strikes: A (lower strike), B (mid strike), C (higher mid strike) and D (the highest strike). Usually the strikes spread between long and short puts and long and short calls are equidistant.

IRON CONDOR = Long 1 Put at A; Short 1 Put at B; Short 1 Call at C; Long 1 Call at D

If you split the above selection of puts and calls into two parts—left and right—you will notice that a left pair of puts configures a bull put spread while the right pair of calls configures a bear call spread. Together in one portfolio they deliver an iron condor spread.

This is a neutral strategy configuring a risk-to-reward profile characterized by a profit potential spread out between the two mid strike prices and with limited losses. Its major advantage compared to the common condor is just the same as for the iron butterfly—the iron condor position consists of two credit spreads collecting an initial net premium.

The portfolio delivers the same payoff profile of a long condor, therefore retaining the same characteristics and key strategy features. The maximum profits are limited to net premium collected ($0.50), which is attained between the two mid-strikes—short put ($34) and short call ($35)—since all options within this range, constituting the iron condor, expire worthless. To illustrate the performance of an iron condor we shall use the same data from the ABN Amro price chart:

1 x Long put	OTM	$32	A	at $0.05	-$0.05
1 x Short put	OTM	$34	B	at $0.35	+$0.35
1 x Short call	OTM	$36	C	at $0.25	+$0.25
1 x Long call	OTM	$38	D	at $0.05	-$0.05

Net credit: $0.50

Table 24.6 Iron Condor Performance Metrics

Price of Underlying	1 x Long Put at A $32@.05	1 x Short Put at B $34@0.35	1 x Short Call at C $36@0.25	1 x Long Call at D $38@.05	Long Condor Payoff $
A	B	C	D	E	B+C+D+E
30	1.95	−3.65	0.25	−0.05	−1.50
31.95	0	−1.70	0.25	−0.05	−1.50
33.50	−0.05	−0.15	0.25	−0.05	0
33.65	−0.05	0	0.25	−0.05	0.15
34	−0.05	0.35	0.25	−0.05	0.50
34.85	−0.05	0.35	0.25	−0.05	0.50
35	−0.05	0.35	0.25	−0.05	0.50
35.10	−0.05	0.35	0.25	−0.05	0.50
36	−0.05	0.35	0.25	−0.05	0.50
36.25	−0.05	0.35	0	−0.05	0.25
36.50	−0.05	0.35	−0.20	−0.05	0
38.05	−0.05	0.35	−1.80	0	−1.50
40	−0.05	0.35	−3.75	1.95	−1.50

SHORT CALL CONDOR

Key Terms

short call condor
a type of option spread constructed as follows: Sell 1 ITM Call (Lower Strike), Buy 1 ITM Call; Buy 1 OTM Call, Sell 1 OTM Call (Higher Strike). This is a combination of a Bear Call plus Bull Call spread

A short call condor is the opposite of the long condor and is usually initiated in anticipation of a sharp move in either direction—below (B) or above (C). The maximum loss at expiry occurs between (B) and (C) which is equivalent to B less A less the premium credit received. The maximum profit occurs if the market at expiration moves either below (A) or above (D), and will be limited to the net premium received.

The short call condor strategy is constructed as follows:

Selling 1 x in-the-money call at A
Buying 1 x slightly in-the-money call at B
Buying 1 x slightly out-of-the-money call at C
Selling 1 x out-of-the-money call at D

Figure 24.9 illustrates the payoff profile of a short call condor.

Figure 24.9 Short Call Condor

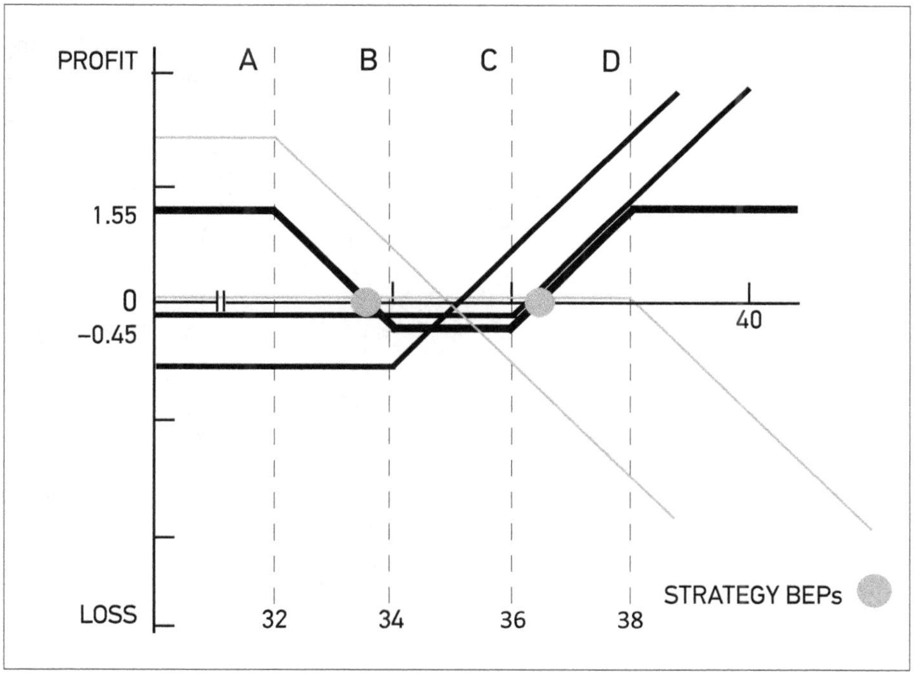

STRATEGY KEY FEATURES

Break-even points = Two
On the upside = Highest strike short call – net premium paid
On the downside = Lowest strike short call + net premium paid
Maximum loss: lower strike long call – lower strike short call – net premium received
Maximum profit: net premium received
Volatility outlook: bullish

Market outlook: neutral
Time Decay: hurts position

This strategy can also be constructed with the different components:
Short 1 put at A; Long 1 put at B and 1 put at C; Short 1 put at D
Short 1 call at A; Long 1 call at B and 1 put at C; Short 1 put at D
Short 1 put at A; Long 1 put at B and 1 call at C; Short 1 call at D

Useing the same data from the ABN Amro stock chart we can illustrate the performance of the short call condor strategy. The data is summarized in Table 24.7.

ABN Amro Stock Price				
1 x Short call	$32	at $2.85	A	+$2.85
1 x Long call	$34	at $1.10	B	−$1.10
1 x Long call	$36	at $0.25	C	−$0.25
1 x Short call	$38	at $0.05	D	+$0.05
Net credit: $1.55				

Table 24.7 Short Call Condor Metrics

Price of Underlying	1 x Short Call at A $32@2.85	1 x Long Call at B $34@1.10	1 x Long Call at C $36@0.25	1 x Short Call at D $38@.05	Short Condor Payoff $
A	B	C	D	E	B+C+D+E
30	2.85	−1.10	−0.25	0.05	1.55
31.95	2.85	−1.10	−0.25	0.05	1.55
33.55	1.30	−1.10	−0.25	0.05	0
33.75	1.10	−1.10	−0.25	0.05	−0.20
34	0.85	−1.10	−0.25	0.05	−0.45
34.85	0	−0.25	−0.25	0.05	−0.45
35	−0.15	−0.10	−0.25	0.05	−0.45
35.10	−0.25	0	−0.25	0.05	−0.45
36	−1.15	0.90	−0.25	0.05	−0.45
36.25	−1.40	1.15	0	0.05	−0.20
36.45	−1.60	1.35	−0.20	0.05	0
38.05	−3.20	2.95	1.80	0	1.55
40	−5.15	4.90	3.75	−1.95	1.55

SUMMARY

In deciding what type of price protection to implement in a risky environment, companies should consider various hedging ideas depending on the proximity of risk impact and its potential magnitude. The choices are many and they should be carefully observed. In this Chapter we have presented a variety of strategies and their risk profiles for you to reflect on before making your final decision. Here are the most important strategies covered:

Bull call spread—refers to a strategy configured in between call options; the lower strike call is purchased and the higher strike call is sold; the resulting payoff is designated as a "range-bound" profile.
Bull put spread—refers to a strategy configured in between put options; the lower strike put is purchased and the higher strike put is sold; the resulting payoff is also a range-bound profile.
Bear call spread—refers to a strategy configured in between call options; the lower strike call is sold and the higher strike call is purchased; the resulting payoff is an inverted bull call spread.
Bear put spread—refers to a strategy configured in between put options; the lower strike put is sold and the higher strike put is purchased; the resulting payoff is an inverted bull put spread.
Long call butterfly spread—refers to a strategy configured in between call options; buy 1 ITM call, sell 2 ATM calls and buy 1 OTM call; the strategy limits profits as well as losses and the strategy payoff is a variant of a range-bound profile; option strike prices used to configure this strategy are equidistant; this strategy may also be regarded as a combination of a bull call and a bear call spread sharing the same mid strike price.
Iron butterfly—a variation of a butterfly spread configured between calls and puts resulting in a net credit; the strategy profile is the same as the butterfly spread.
Short call butterfly spread—is an inverse of the long call butterfly spread; sell 1 ITM call, buy 2 ATM calls and sell 1 OTM call; options strike prices used to configure this strategy are also equidistant, and the strategy payoff is a mirror image to that of a long butterfly; this strategy may also be regarded as a fusion of a bear call and a bull call spread, sharing the same mid strike price.
Long call condor spread—refers to a strategy configured in between four call options with equidistant strikes; buy 1 ITM call, sell 1 higher ITM call, sell 1 OTM call, buy another higher OTM call; the strategy delivers an exceptional variant of a range-bound profile with limited profits and limited losses; this strategy may also be regarded as a combination of a bull call and a bear call spread.
Iron condor— a variation of a condor spread configured between calls and puts resulting in a net credit; the strategy profile is the same as the condor spread.
Short call condor spread—is an inverse of the long call condor spread; the strategy is configured in between four call options with equidistant strike prices; sell 1 ITM call, buy 1 higher ITM call, buy 1 OTM call, sell 1 higher OTM call; the strategy delivers a variant of a range-bound profile with limited profits and limited losses; this strategy may also be regarded as a combination of a bear call and a bull call spread. Due to their resemblance to a flying creature, the payoff profiles produced by the family of butterflies and condors are designated as "wingspreads."

KEY TERMS

bull spread
bear spread
horizontal or calendar spread
vertical spread
diagonal spread
options combinations
options combinations
bull call spread
bull put spread
bear call spread
bear put spread
long call butterfly
iron butterfly
wingspreads
short call butterfly
long call condor
iron condor
short call condor

CHAPTER 25

CALL RATIO SPREADS

CHAPTER OBJECTIVES

- To identify and explain the concept of call ratio spreads
- To examine and illustrate how to configure a call ratio spread
- To define and illustrate the characteristics of three basic types in regard to initial outlay
- To demonstrate how to configure a call ratio backspread and explain its basic characteristics

I CALL (BULL) RATIO SPREADS

Key Terms

bull call ratio spread
refers to a strategy constructed with long lower strike calls and more short higher strike calls

A BULL CALL RATIO SPREAD IS A STRATEGY EMPLOYED TO TAKE ADVANTAGE OF AN expected price increase. The strategy—designed to suit investors' specific preferences and perceptions—is built upon a simple bull call spread adjusted for an additional short call to create one of those distinguished risk-averse payoffs. Anticipation of a rising market gives justification for the bullish profile of the strategy.

This strategy is constructed exclusively with call options: buying lower strike calls—usually ITM or ATM—and simultaneously selling more higher strike OTM calls.

<u>Buy ITM calls, sell more OTM calls:</u>
Long lower strike calls
Short **more** higher strike calls

The configuration of 1:2 bull call ratio spread is demonstrated below.

We begin by creating a simple bull call spread—buying the lower strike price and selling the higher strike price as shown below:

Long 1 call $309@5.65
Short 1 call $311@4.75
Net debit: $0.90

This strategy is designated a "debit spread" since the price of the lower strike call purchased must always be more expensive than the higher strike call sold.

In the next stage we add an extra short call with the same strike and expiry (311@4.75).

The final result of a portfolio which consists of a bull call spread plus an extra short call is that of a bull call ratio spread.

The graphical exposition in Figure 25.1 is straightforward: on the left is the P&L graph of the bull call spread; then we add an extra short call with the same strike and expiration and compile the results in the final P&L diagram—a bull call ratio spread.

Figure 25.1 Call Bull Ratio Spread Configuration

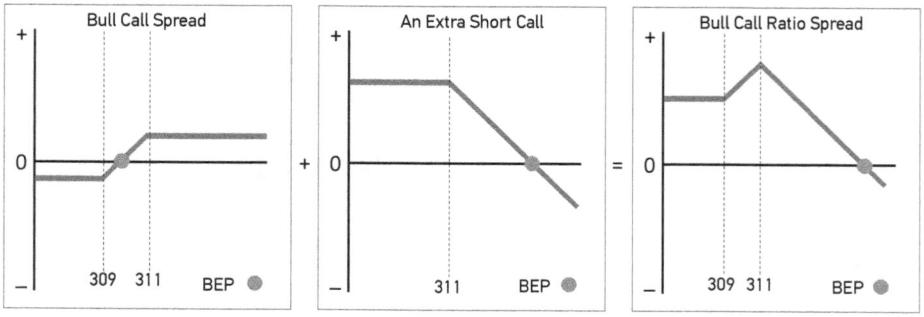

Maximum loss=0.90	Maximum gain=4.75	Limited gain=4.75-0.90=3.75
Maximum gain=1.10	BEP=311+4.75=315.75	Max. gain=4.75+1.10=5.85
BEP=309+0.90=309.90	Max. loss=above BEP	BEP=311+5.85=316.85
		Unlimited loss=above BEP

The ratio between long and short calls need not be 1:2—it can take literally any combination of which the more usual are 1:3; 2:3; 2:4; 4:7; 4:10, and so on. Regardless of the ratio, as long as you use more short calls than long calls, the strategy profile in its critical construct will remain the same.

From the standpoint of financial outlay ensuing from the different ratios of long/short calls which is used to configure the strategy, we can distinguish three different types of bull call ratio spreads:

- Credit – cash inflow (the value of short calls exceeds the value of long calls)
- Debit – cash outflow (the value of long calls exceeds the value of short calls)
- Even Money – premiums of long and short call exactly offset each other

I. CALL (BULL) RATIO SPREADS

1. Call (Bull) ratio spreads (Credit) Figure 25.2. / 25.3
2. Call (Bull) ratio spread (Even Money) Figure 25.4
3. Call (Bull) ratio spread (Debit) Figure 25.5
4. Call (Bull) ratio backspreads Figure 25.6 / 25.7

For the sake of illustration, in the following examples we took the (COMEX) copper price chart as of February 12, 2010. The copper futures price on that particular day for March expiry was $310.200 cents/lb.

HI GRADE COPPER (COMEX) (cents/lb.) $310.200
25,000 lbs., cents per lb. 12. February 2010

	CALLS			PUTS		
Strike	Mar	Apr	May	Mar	Apr	May
305	7.75	15.95	21.30	4.50	11.70	16.10
306	7.20	15.40	20.80	4.95	12.15	16.60
307	6.65	14.90	20.30	5.40	12.65	17.10
308	6.15	14.40	19.80	5.90	13.15	17.60
309	5.65	13.90	19.35	6.40	13.65	18.15
310	5.20	13.45	18.85	6.95	14.20	18.65
310.200	HI GRADE COPPER (COMEX) (USd/lb.) 310.20					
311	4.75	13.00	18.40	7.50	14.75	19.20
312	4.35	12.55	17.95	8.10	15.30	19.75
313	4.00	12.10	17.50	8.75	15.85	20.30
314	3.65	11.65	17.05	9.40	16.40	20.85
315	3.30	11.25	16.60	10.05	17.00	21.40

Different shades used in the options chain are intended to distinguish the price pairs used in three different types of bull call ratio spreads:

1. Credit Spread	2. Even Money Spread	3. Debit Spread

1. Value of short calls (2 x \$4.75) exceeds the value of long call (1 x \$5.65).
2. Long call (\$7.20) and short call premiums (2 x \$3.65) nearly offset each other.
3. Value of long call (\$7.75) exceeds the value of short calls (2 x \$3.30).

1. BULL CALL RATIO SPREAD (CREDIT)

Firstly, we shall focus on a bull ratio spread constructed at a net credit implying that the value of the short calls (the sum of its premiums) exceeds the value of the long call premium.

Key Terms

credit ratio spread
the premiums sold exceed the premiums purchased

The strategy is constructed as follows:

Long 1 call \$309@5.65
Short 2 calls \$311@4.75 x 2 = \$9.50
Net credit: \$3.85

The performance of a bull call ratio spread (credit) is exhibited in Table 25.1.

Table 25.1 Call Bull Ratio Spread (Credit)–Expiration Results

Underlying Price \$310.200	Long LS Call \$309 (St – X) x 1	Short HS Call \$311 –(St – X) x 2	Premium Net Credit	Position Total Payoff cents/lb
A	B	C	D	B+C+D
305	0	0	3.85	3.85
306	0	0	3.85	3.85
307	0	0	3.85	3.85
308	0	0	3.85	3.85
309	0	0	3.85	3.85
310	1	0	3.85	4.85
311	2	0	3.85	**5.85**
312	3	–2	3.85	4.85
313	4	–4	3.85	3.85
314	5	–6	3.85	2.85
315	6	–8	3.85	1.85
316.85	7.85	–11.70	3.85	0
320	11	–18	3.85	–3.15
330	21	–38	3.85	–13.15

A bull call ratio spread delivers a distinguished asymmetric risk-to-reward profile which is depicted in Figure 25.2.

The maximum profit potential (\$5.85) sits at the higher strike—above the price of the underlying \$310.200—designating the "bull" part of the strategy title. Beyond the lower strike price the strategy gains control of a further price decline, confining the profits to a \$3.85 price level. On the upside—beyond the \$311 price level—the strategy profit declines proportionally with the fall of the underlying asset price. From the break-even point (\$316.85) onward, the strategy enters into the negative zone, producing losses commensurate with the price decline.

Figure 25.2 Call Bull Ratio Spread (Credit)

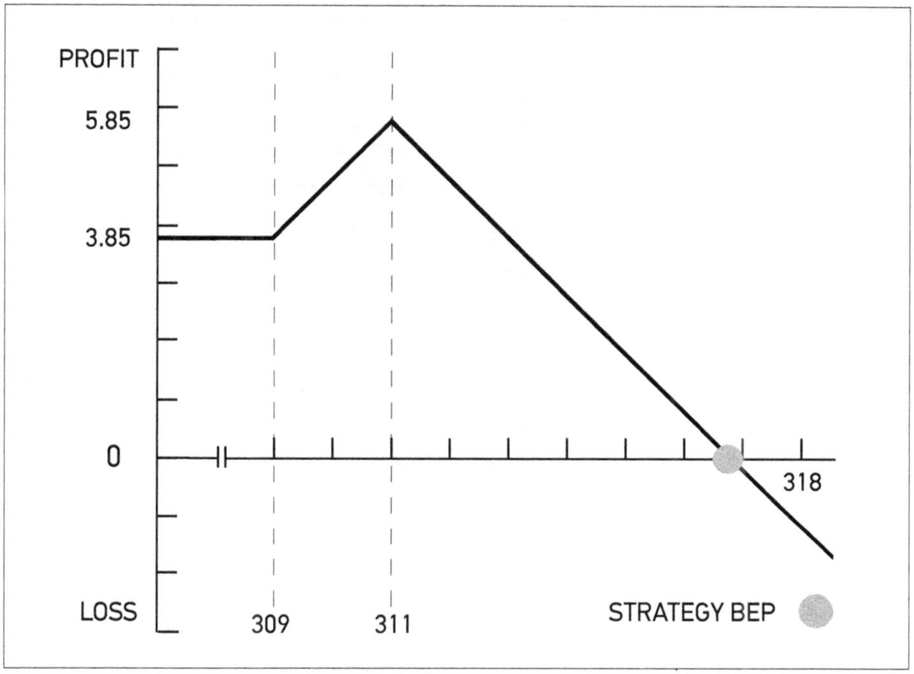

Strategy Key Features

Limited return (below the lower strike) = Net credit

Maximum return = (total short call premium received + [(difference in strikes – price of long call) x number of long call contracts])

Maximum loss = Unlimited above BEP

BEP = Short call strike price + [maximum profit /(number of short call contracts – number of long call contracts)]

Algebraic verification:

Limited return = \$9.50 – \$5.65 = \$3.85

Maximum return = \$9.50 + (\$311 – \$309 – \$ 5.65) x 1 = \$5.85

BEP = \$311 + [\$5.85/(2 – 1)] = \$316.85

Call Bull Ratio Spread (Credit) – Increased Number of Calls

The following example shows a variation of a bull call ratio spread with an increased number of short calls creating a strategy of 1:3 ratio spread. The increased number of short calls in this particular case—three instead of two—affects the steepness of the payoff diagram as illustrated in Figure 25.3.

The strategy is constructed as follows:

Long 1 call \$309@5.65
Short 3 calls \$311@4.75 x 3 = \$14.25
Net credit: \$8.60
The repercussions of this strategy are presented in Table 25.2.

The specific 1:3 payoff profile of a credit call ratio spread is exhibited in Figure 25.3.

Table 25.2 Call Bull Ratio Spread(Credit) Increased no. of Calls 1:3

Underlying Price $310.200	Long LS Call $309 (St – X) x 1	Short HS Call $311 –(St – X) x 3	Premium Net Credit	Position Total Payoff cents/lb
A	B	C	D	B+C+D
305	0	0	8.60	8.60
306	0	0	8.60	8.60
307	0	0	8.60	8.60
308	0	0	8.60	8.60
309	0	0	8.60	8.60
310	1	0	8.60	9.60
311	2	0	8.60	**10.60**
312	3	–3	8.60	8.60
313	4	–6	8.60	6.60
314	5	–9	8.60	4.60
315	6	–12	8.60	2.60
316.30	7.30	–15.90	8.60	0
320	11	–27	8.60	–7.40
330	21	–57	8.60	–27.40

Figure 25.3 Call Bull Ratio Spread (Credit) Increased no. of Calls 1:3

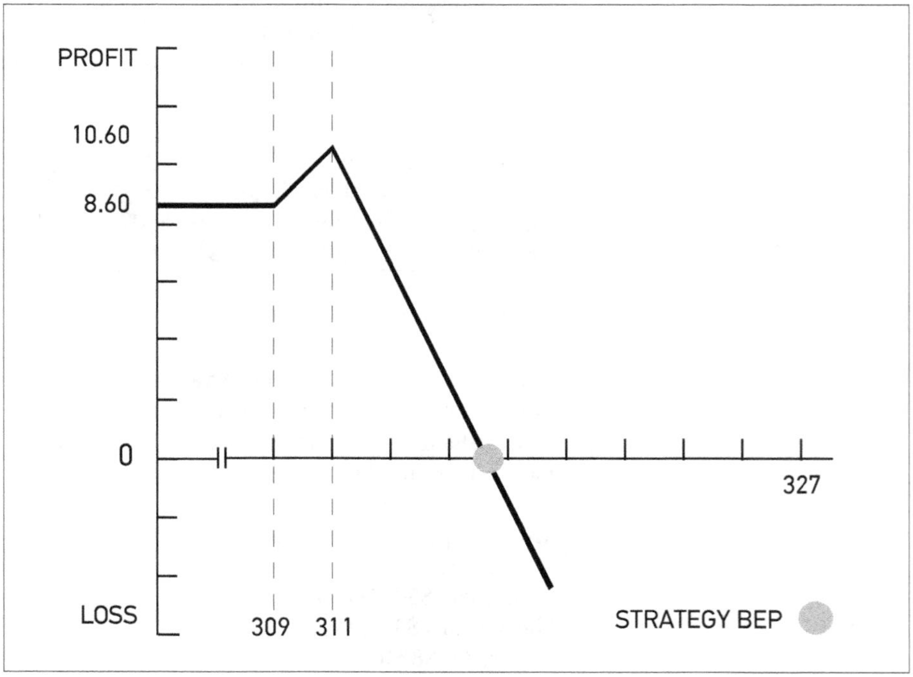

Strategy Key Features
Limited return (below the lower strike) = Net credit
Maximum return = (Total credit from short call options + [(difference in strikes – price of long call) x number of long call contracts])
BEP: Strike price of short call options + [maximum profit / (number of short call options – number of long call options)]

Algebraic verification:
Limited return = $14.25 – $5.65 = $8.60
Maximum return = $14.25 + ($311 – $309) – $5.65 x 1 = $10.60
BEP = $311 + $10.60/(3 – 1) = $316.30

Resume: the maximum profit sits higher, the BEP goes a bit lower, the loss accelerates!

2. BULL CALL RATIO SPREAD (EVEN MONEY)

Key Terms

even-money ratio spread
the premiums sold and the premiums purchased even out

In the next example we examine the case of a bull ratio spread constructed at even money implying that the value of the short call premiums and the value of the long call premium almost exactly offset each other. In an ideal match the limited loss—from the lower strike downwards—would be exactly 0 (zero), while in our example this part of the graph sits a bit above the zero level—at $0.10.

The strategy is constructed as follows:

Long 1 call $306@7.20
Short 2 calls $314@3.65 x 2 = $7.30
Net credit: $0.10

The performance of a bull call ratio spread configured at even money is displayed in Table 25.3.

Table 25.3 Call Bull Ratio Spread (Even Money) - Expiration Results

Underlying Price $310.200	Long LS Call $306 (St – X) x 1	Short HS Call $314 –(St – X) x 2	Premium Net Even	Position Total Payoff cents/lb
A	B	C	D	B+C+D
305	0	0	0.10	0.10
306	0	0	0.10	0.10
308	0	0	0.10	2.10
309	0	0	0.10	3.10
310	0	0	0.10	4.10
311	1	0	0.10	5.10
314	2	0	0.10	**8.10**
317	3	0	0.10	5.10
318	4	–6	0.10	4.10
319	5	–8	0.10	3.10
320	6	–8	0.10	2.10
322.10	7.85	–11.70	0.10	0
330	11	–18	0.10	–7.90
340	21	–38	0.10	–17.90

And the payoff profile will take the following shape:

Figure 25.4 Call Bull Ratio Spread (Even Money)

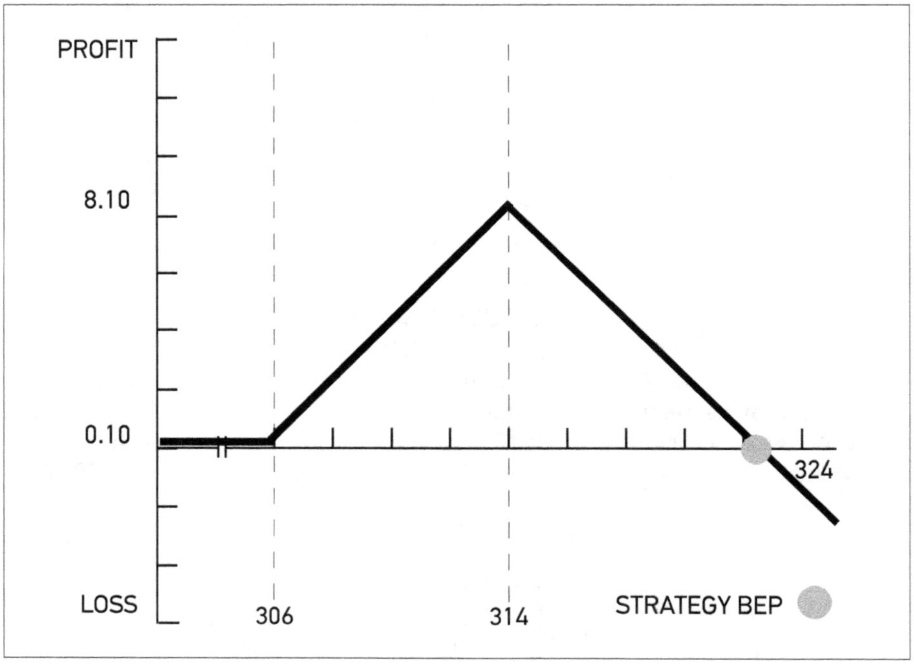

Strategy Key Features
Limited return (below the lower strike) = Net credit
Maximum return = (Total short call premium received + [(difference in strikes – price of long call) x number of long call contracts])
Unlimited loss = Above BEP
BEP = Short call strike price + [maximum profit/(number of short call contracts – number of long call contracts)]

Algebraic verification:
Limited return = $7.30 – $7.20 = $0.10
Maximum return = $7.30 + ($314 – $306 – $7.20) x 1 = $8.10
BEP = $314 + ($8.10/(2 – 1)) = $322.10

3. BULL CALL RATIO SPREAD (DEBIT)

Key Terms

debit ratio spread
the premiums purchased exceed the premiums sold

The third and final case of a bull call ratio spread is the one constructed at a debit, denoting that the value of the long call ($7.75) exceeds the value of the short calls ($6.60).

The strategy is constructed as follows:

Long 1 call $305@7.75
Short 2 calls $315@3.30 x 2 = $6.60
Net debit: $1.15

The performance of a call bull ratio spread configured at a debit is displayed in Table 25.4.

Table 25.4 Call Bull Ratio Spread (Debit) -Expiration Results

Underlying Price $310.200	Long LS Call $305 (St – X) x 1	Short HS Call $315 –(St – X) x 2	Premium Net Debit	Position Total Payoff cents/lb
A	B	C	D	B+C+D
305	0	0	–1.15	–1.15
306.15	1.15	0	–1.15	0
310	5	0	–1.15	3.85
312	7	0	–1.15	5.85
313	8	0	–1.15	6.85
314	9	0	–1.15	7.85
315	10	0	–1.15	**8.85**
316	11	–2	–1.15	7.85
317	12	–4	–1.15	6.85
318	13	–6	–1.15	5.85
320	15	–10	–1.15	3.85
323.85	18.85	–17.70	–1.15	0
330	25	–30	–1.15	–6.65
340	35	–50	–1.15	–16.65

The payoff profile of a bull call ratio spread configured at a "debit" is illustrated in Figure 25.5.

Figure 25.5 Call Bull Ratio Spread (Debit)

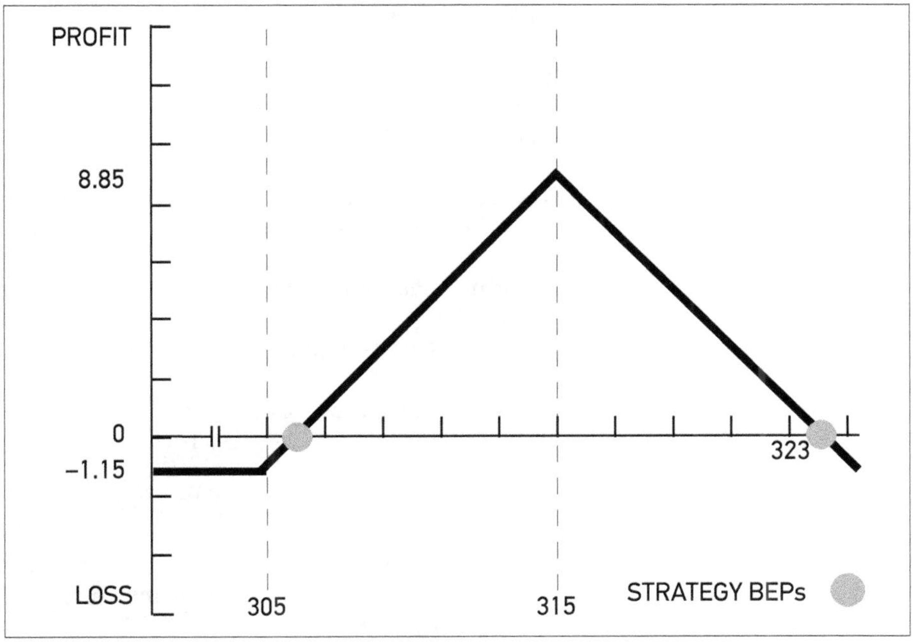

Strategy Key Features
Limited loss (below the lower strike) = Net debit
Unlimited loss = Above upper BEP
Maximum return = (Total short call premium received + [(difference in strikes – price of long call) x number of long call contracts])
Two BEPs:
Lower BEP = Lower strike + net debit
Higher BEP = Short call strike price + [maximum profit /(number of short call contracts – number of long call contracts)]

Algebraic verification:
Limited loss (below the lower strike) = \$7.75 – \$6.6 = –\$1.15
Maximum return = \$6.60 + (\$315 – \$305 – \$7.75) x 1 = \$8.85
Lower BEP = \$305 + \$1.15 = \$306.15
Higher BEP = \$315 + [\$8.85/(2 – 1)] = \$323.85

Key Terms

call ratio backspread
refers to a strategy constructed with short lower strike calls and more long higher strike calls

4. CALL RATIO BACKSPREAD

There is of course also the case of the bull call spread, which can be attuned in a similar fashion, to create what is commonly designated a **call ratio backspread** or a bull ratio backspread. The strategy structure is built upon a simple bear call spread attuned to a specific ratio to reflect investors' specific preferences. In this particular case, short options are used to finance the purchase of multiple long options!

This strategy is constructed by selling ITM or ATM call options and at the same time purchasing more long OTM options thus creating in effect an "upside-down" call ratio spread:

Short lower strike calls
Long **more** higher strike calls

As in the previous example we begin by creating a bear call spread—selling the lower strike price and buying the higher strike price as shown below:

Short 1 call \$305@7.75
Long 1 call \$315@3.30
Net credit: \$4.45

The bear call spread is designated a credit spread since the price of the lower strike sold must always be more expensive than the higher strike call purchased.

In the next stage we add an extra long call with the same strike and expiry. This addition of a long call transforms the strategy from bear to bull creating a type of a vertical ratio spread with unlimited upside potential.

The resulting exposure of the portfolio consisting of a bear call spread and an extra long call is that of a bull call ratio backspread.

In the graphical explication below, Figure 25.6, we follow the same configuration process. The sequence of graphs begins with the P&L diagram of the bear call spread (short one lower strike call, long one higher strike call), then we add an extra long call with the same strike and expiration and compile results in a final P&L diagram of a bull call ratio backspread.

Figure 25.6 Call Ratio Backspread Configuration

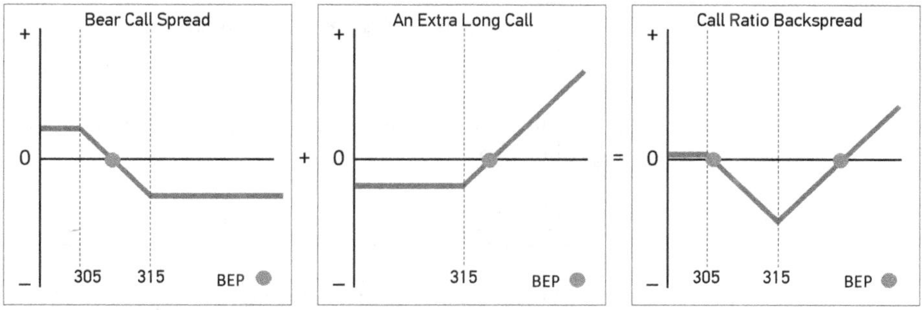

Maximum Loss=5.55
Maximum Gain=4.45
BEP=305+4.45

Maximum Loss=3.30
BEP=315+3.30=318.30
Max. Gain=above BEP

Limited Gain=4.45–3.30=1.15
Max. Loss=5.55+3.30=8.85
Lower BEP=305+1.15=306.15
Upper BEP=315+8.85=323.85
Unlimited Gain=above BEP

From the graph you can easily deduce that in the case of bull ratio backspread there is not much sense in creating a debit spread since the strategy will effectively lock-in the losses—generating a negative return at all points below the upper BEP—while profits will be recorded only if prices surge above the higher BEP. So, you would be much better off if you simply bought a call instead. Consequently, the bull call ratio backspreads should always be established as credit spreads.

The performance and characteristics of a call ratio backspread configured at a "credit" are discussed below.

4.1 CALL RATIO BACKSPREAD (CREDIT)—SELL 1 ITM CALL, BUY 2 OTM CALLS

To analyse the performance of the call ratio backspread we will use the same data:

HI GRADE COPPER (COMEX) (cents/lb.) $310.200
25,000 lbs., cents per lb. 12 February 2010

	CALLS			PUTS		
Strike	Mar	Apr	May	Mar	Apr	May
305	7.75	15.95	21.30	4.50	11.70	16.10
306	7.20	15.40	20.80	4.95	12.15	16.60
307	6.65	14.90	20.30	5.40	12.65	17.10
308	6.15	14.40	19.80	5.90	13.15	17.60
309	5.65	13.90	19.35	6.40	13.65	18.15
310	5.20	13.45	18.85	6.95	14.20	18.65
310.200 HI GRADE COPPER (COMEX) (USd/lb.) 310.20						
311	4.75	13.00	18.40	7.50	14.75	19.20
312	4.35	12.55	17.95	8.10	15.30	19.75
313	4.00	12.10	17.50	8.75	15.85	20.30
314	3.65	11.65	17.05	9.40	16.40	20.85
315	3.30	11.25	16.60	10.05	17.00	21.40

The strategy is constructed as follows:

Short 1 call $305@7.75
Long 2 calls $315@3.30 x 2 = $6.60
Net credit: $1.15

The performance of the strategy configured with the above data is summarized in Table 25.5.

Table 25.5 Call Ratio Backspread - Expiration Results

Underlying Price $310.200	Long HS Call $315 (St – X) x 2	Short LS Call $305 –(St – X) x 1	Premium Net Credit	Position Total Payoff cents/lb
A	B	C	D	B + C + D
305	0	0	1.15	1.15
306.15	0	–1.15	1.15	0
310	0	–5	1.15	–3.85
312	0	–7	1.15	–5.85
313	0	–8	1.15	–6.85
314	0	–9	1.15	–7.85
315	0	–10	1.15	**–8.85**
316	2	–11	1.15	–7.85
317	4	–12	1.15	–6.85
318	6	–13	1.15	–5.85
320	10	–15	1.15	–3.85
323.85	17.70	–18.85	1.15	0
330	30	–25	1.15	6.15
340	50	–35	1.15	16.15

The risk-reward profile of the call ratio backspread, as you can see from Figure 25.7, is an inverted diagram relative to a bull call ratio spread—flipped vertically—hence the term "backspread."

The call ratio backspread delivers an interesting combination of asymmetric "range-bound" profiles—from zero price level until the higher BEP $323.85— and an "open-ended" risk profile beyond that point.

On the downside—beyond the lower BEP ($306.15)—the strategy profits are secured but limited ($1.15). In between the BEPs, strategy losses are confined (0 to -$8.85)—pinned at the higher call strike purchased ($315).

If the price of the underlying asset breaks sharply through beyond the BEP ($323.85), the strategy enters the positive zone and begins to generate profits commensurate with the price increase. However, if you analyze the P&L profile of this strategy you will see that its profit potential is very inferior compared to that of a call option for example.

In this particular configuration, the call ratio backspread P&L clearly indicates that this would be a very risky venture: it requires an extremely volatile market—it offers very limited benefit on the downside, while on the upside it calls for erratic price movement far beyond the actual market price ($310.200).

Figure 25.7 Call Ratio Backspread

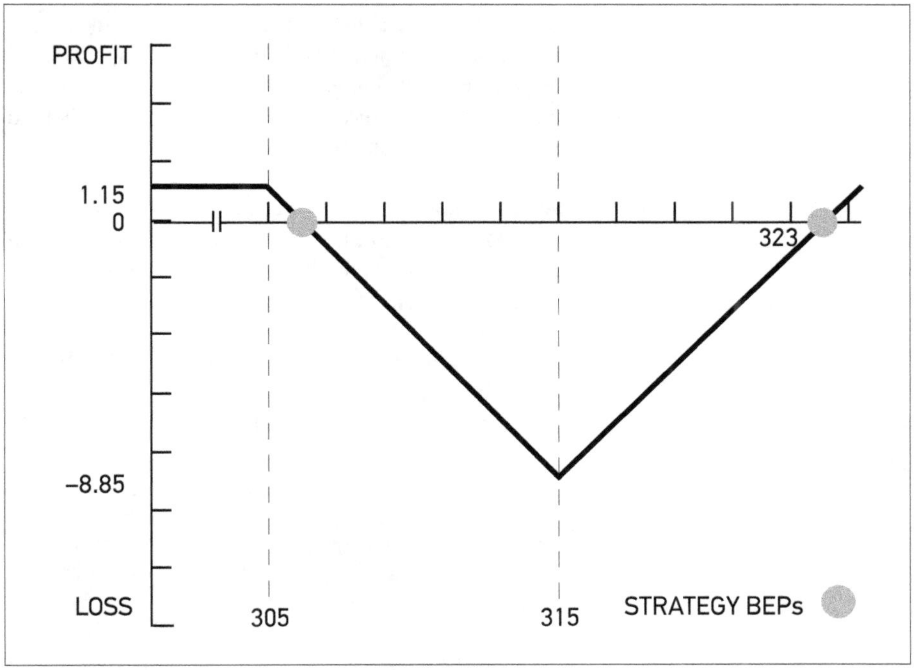

Strategy Key Features

Maximum loss = Difference in strikes – net credit received
Limited return = Net credit
Unlimited return = Above upper BEP
Two BEPs:
Lower BEP = Lower strike call + net credit/number of contracts sold
Upper BEP = Long call strike + (number of contracts sold x difference in strikes) – net credit

Algebraic verification:
Maximum loss = (\$315 – \$305) – \$1.15= –\$8.85
Lower BEP = \$305 + \$1.15 = \$306.15
Upper BEP = \$315 + (1 x \$10) – \$1.15 = \$323.85

SUMMARY

Chapter 25 has explored strategies which are configured exclusively in between call options that deliver an amalgam of "open-ended" and "range-bound" risk profiles. The call ratio spread configuration may vary in the number of long and short calls. The governing rule states that lower strike calls are purchased (normally ITM or ATM) and the higher strike calls (OTM) are sold. The strategy configuration may be interpreted as a two-phase process: first, initiate a simple bull call spread (long 1 lower strike call and short 1 higher strike call) and then add an extra short call entered at the same short call strike.

We then identified the three basic variants: credit, even money, and debit spread. Each strategy was elaborated by means of graphical and numerical terms. It was shown that the shape of the payoff diagram and ensuing expiration results are markedly influenced by the choice of strike prices configuring the particular strategy.

The call ratio spread is also designated as the "bull" strategy, signifying that the highest profit potential and the break-even point of the strategy is on the upside. Hence, the strategy should be employed in an anticipation of rising markets.

In the last section we discussed the characteristics and main features of call ratio backspread. The strategy is configured in a directly opposite manner to that of a call ratio spread; the lower strike calls are sold and the higher strike calls are purchased. Accordingly the shape of the call ratio backspread risk profile is an inverse image of a call ratio spread.

In terms of the market price direction, the call ratio backspread is also characterized as the bull strategy indicating that the unlimited profit potential lays on the upside—beyond the higher break-even point.

KEY TERMS

- bull (call) ratio spread
- credit ratio spread
- call ratio backspread
- even-money ratio spread
- debit ratio spread

CHAPTER 26

PUT RATIO SPREADS

CHAPTER OBJECTIVES

- To identify and explain the concept of put ratio spreads
- To explain and illustrate how to configure a put ratio spread
- To define and illustrate the characteristics of three basic types in regard to initial outlay
- To demonstrate how to configure a put ratio backspread and explain its basic characteristics

| PUT (BEAR) RATIO SPREADS

Key Terms

put (bear) ratio spread
refers to a strategy configured with long higher strike puts and more short lower strike puts

THE PUT RATIO SPREAD IS A STRATEGY EMPLOYED TO TAKE ADVANTAGE OF AN expected price decline. Anticipation of a declining market justifies the bearish character of the strategy. Contrary to a bull call ratio spread, this strategy is built upon a bear put spread adjusted for a specific ratio of put options. The payoff delivered is an inverted image of the bull call ratio spread. The strategy is constructed by buying higher strike puts—usually ITM or ATM—and simultaneously selling more lower strike OTM puts.

Buy ITM Puts, Sell more OTM Puts:
Long higher strike puts
Short **more** lower strike puts

For the sake of clarification let us consider the construction of a 1:2 bear put ratio spread.

We begin by creating a simple bear put spread, that is by buying the lower strike price and selling the higher strike price as shown below:

Long 1 put $311@7.50
Short 1 put $303@3.70
Net debit: $3.80

This strategy is always designated a "debit spread" as the lower put strike price purchased must always be less expensive than the higher strike put sold.

Next, we implement an additional short put with the same strike and expiration (303@3.70).

The graphical exposition in Figure 26.1 illustrates the put bear ratio spread in three steps: the P&L diagram on the left is the bear put spread; than we add an extra short put with a same strike and expiration (the diagam in the middle); and compile the results in the final P&L diagram—the bear put ratio spread on the right.

Figure 26.1 Put Bear Ratio Spread Configuration

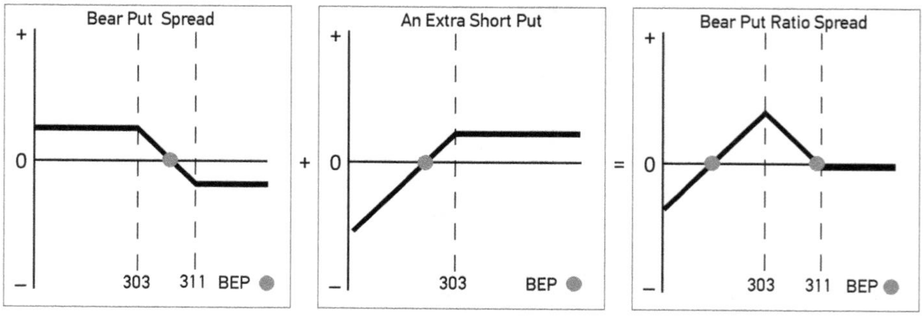

Maximum Loss=3.80	Maximum Gain=3.70	Limited Loss=3.70-3.80=-0.10
Maximum Gain=4.20	BEP=303-3.70=299.30	Max. Gain=4.20+3.70=7.90
BEP=311-3.70=307.20	Max. Loss=below BEP	Lower BEP=303-7.90=295.10
		Upper BEP=311-0.10=310.90

The ratio between long and short puts depends on the investor's preference and the particular investment goal. Therefore, as in the case of bull ratio spreads, it can take literally any combination, other than 1:2. As long as you use more short puts than long puts—regardless of the ratio applied—the strategy profile, in its critical construct, will remain the same. The flat part of the diagram may be positioned as debit (below the x-axis), even money (x-axis) or credit (above x-axis). The maximum profit will always be reached at the lower strike put, with break-even points taking varying positions subject to the strike prices selected.

From the standpoint of the strategy's financial outlay ensuing from a different ratio of long/short calls used, we can distinguish between three different types of bear put ratio spreads:

- Credit—cash inflow (the value of short puts exceeds the value of long puts).
- Debit—cash outflow (the value of long puts exceeds the value of short calls).
- Even Money—premiums of long and short puts exactly offset each other.

I. PUT BEAR RATIO SPREAD (CREDIT)

1. Put (Bear) ratio spread (Credit)	Figure 26.2
2. Put (Bear) ratio spread (Even Money)	Figure 26.3
3. Put (Bear) ratio spread (Debit)	Figure 26.4
4. Put (Bear) ratio backspread	Figure 26.5 / 26.5

The performance and characteristics of each type are displayed below in more detail.

PUT BEAR RATIO SPREAD (CREDIT)

Buy ITM put, sell more OTM puts

HI GRADE COPPER (COMEX)
COPPER FUTURES OPTIONS (cents/lb.) $310.200
25,000 lbs., cents per lb. 12 February 2010

	CALLS			PUTS		
Strike	Mar	Apr	May	Mar	Apr	May
301	10.25	18.15	23.45	3.00	9.95	14.25
302	9.60	17.55	22.90	3.35	10.30	14.70
303	8.95	17.00	22.35	3.70	10.75	15.15
304	8.35	16.45	21.85	4.10	11.20	15.65
305	7.75	15.95	21.30	4.50	11.70	16.10
306	7.20	15.40	20.80	4.95	12.15	16.60
307	6.65	14.90	20.30	5.40	12.65	17.10
308	6.15	14.40	19.80	5.90	13.15	17.60
309	5.65	13.90	19.35	6.40	13.65	18.15
310	5.20	13.45	18.85	6.95	14.20	18.65
310.200 HI GRADE COPPER (COMEX) (cents/lb.) 310.20						
311	4.75	13.00	18.40	7.50	14.75	19.20
312	4.35	12.55	17.95	8.10	15.30	19.75
313	4.00	12.10	17.50	8.75	15.85	20.30
314	3.65	11.65	17.05	9.40	16.40	20.85
315	3.30	11.25	16.60	10.05	17.00	21.40

As in previous call ratio spread examples, the variation of shades used in the price chart fields is intended to distinguish the price pairs used in constructing the three different types of bear put ratio spreads:

1. Credit Spread	2. Even Money Spread	3. Debit Spread

1. Value of short puts (3 x $3.70) exceeds the value of long puts ($7.50).
2. Long puts (2 x $8.10) and short put premiums (3 x $5.40) exactly offset each other.
3. Value of long puts (2 x $10.05) exceeds the value of short puts (4 x $4.50).

The strategy is constructed as follows:

Long 1 put $311@7.50
Short 3 puts $303@3.70 x 3 = $11.10
Net credit: $3.60

In Table 26.1 we have summarized the results of a bear put ratio spread configured at a credit.

Table 26.1 Put Bear Ratio Spread (Credit)–Expiration Results

Underlying Price $310.200	Long HS Put $311 (X– St) x 2	Short LS Put $303 –(X–St) x 3	Premium Net Credit	Position Total Payoff cents/lb
A	B	C	D	B+C+D
312	0	0	3.60	3.60
311	0	0	3.60	3.60
310	1	0	3.60	4.60
306	5	0	3.60	8.60
305	6	0	3.60	9.60
304	7	0	3.60	10.60
303	8	0	3.60	**11.60**
302	9	–3	3.60	10.60
301	10	–6	3.60	9.60
300	11	–9	3.60	8.60
297.20	13.80	–17.40	3.60	0
290	21	–39	3.60	–14.40
285	26	–54	3.60	–24.40
270	41	–99	3.60	–54.40

The payoff profile of a bear put ratio spread is illustrated in Figure 26.2. Since the maximum profit potential is reached on the downside—pinned at the lower strike price—the nature of the strategy profile is designated "bearish." Hence, the "bear" part of the title.

The strategy is protected from the downfall up to the break-even point ($297.20), which is well beyond the actual market price $310.200. However, the strategy risk is also on the downside (note well the steepness of the payoff diagram from the lower strike price down). The profits accelerate downwards twice as much as the market price decline.

Figure 26.2 Put Bear Ratio Spread (Credit)

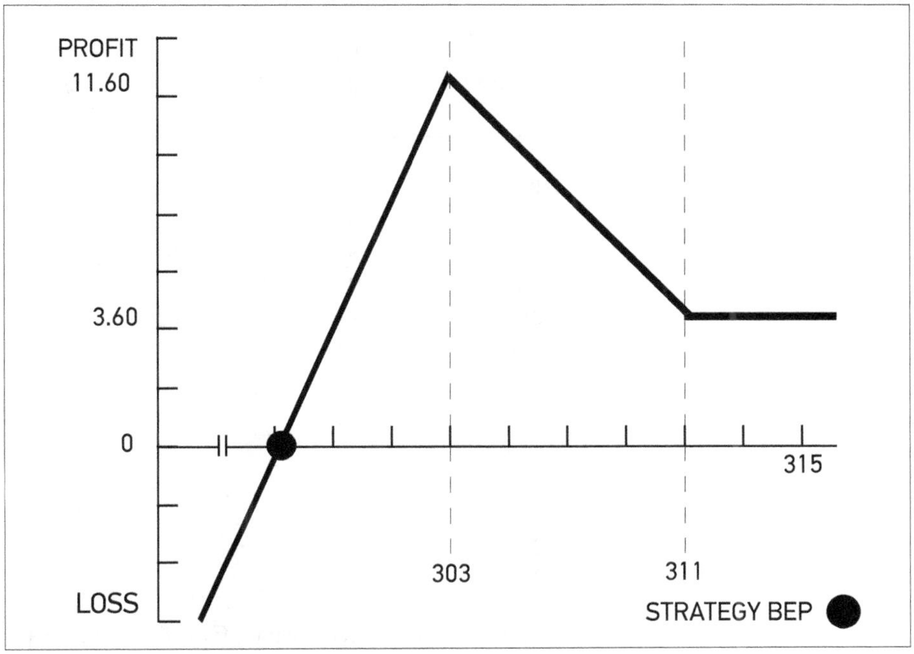

Strategy Key Features
Limited return = Net credit
Maximum return = (Total credit from short put options + [(difference in strikes - price of long put) x number of long put contracts])
BEP: Strike price of short put options – [maximum profit/(number of short put options - number of long put options)]

Algebraic verification:
Limited return = \$11.10 – \$7.50 = \$3.60
Maximum return = \$11.10 + (\$311 – \$303 – \$7.50) x 1 =\$ 11.60
BEP = \$303 – \$11.60/3 – 1 = \$297.20

2. PUT BEAR RATIO SPREAD (EVEN MONEY)

In our HI GRADE COPPER (COMEX) Options Chain chart we were able to find the perfect match in put premium values allowing the "even money" put bear ratio spread.

The strategy is constructed using the following data:

Long 2 puts \$312@8.10 x 2 = \$16.20
Short 3 puts \$307@5.40 x 3 =\$16.20
Net even money: 0

In Table 26.2 we have summarized the performance of a bear put ratio spread configured at even money.

Table 26.2 Put Bear Ratio Spread (Even Money)–Expiration Results

Underlying Price $310.200	Long HS Put $312 (X – St) x 2	Short LS Put $307 –(X – St) x 3	Premium Net Even	Position Total Payoff cents/lb
A	B	C	D	B+C+D
312	0	0	0	0
311	2	0	0	2
310	4	0	0	4
309	6	0	0	6
308	8	0	0	8
307	10	0	0	**10**
306	12	–3	0	9
305	14	–6	0	8
304	16	–9	0	7
300	24	–21	0	3
297	30	–30	0	0
290	44	–51	0	–7
285	54	–66	0	–12
270	84	–111	0	–27

Figure 26.3 illustrates the payoff profile of a bear put ratio spread constructed at even money.

Figure 26.3 Put Bear Ratio Spread (Even Money)

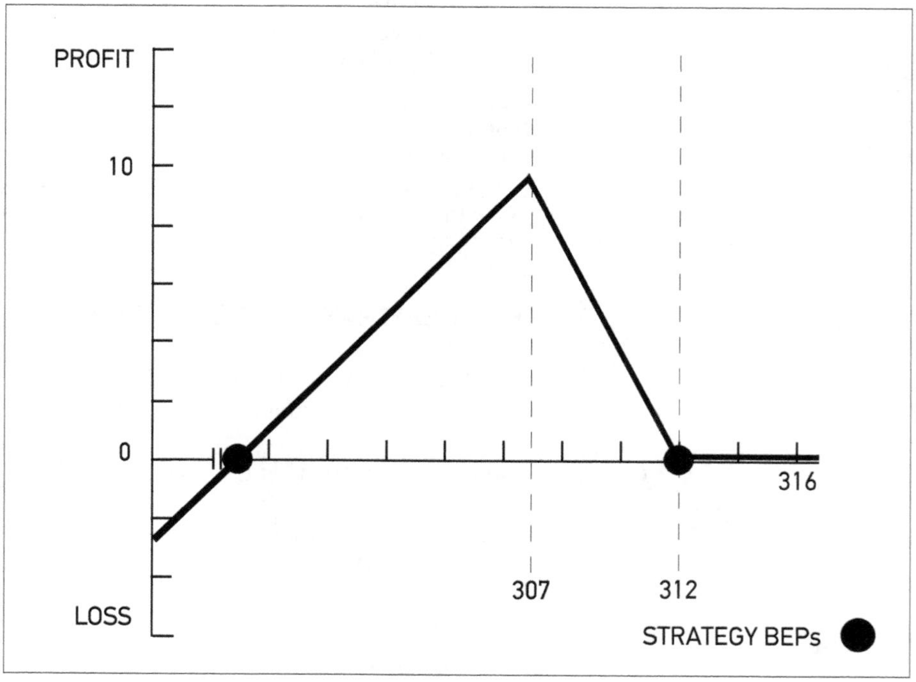

Strategy Key Features

Limited return = Net even money

Maximum return = (Total credit from short put options + [(difference in strikes - price of long put) x number of long put contracts])

BEP: Strike price of short put options – [maximum profit/(number of short put options – number of long put options)]

Algebraic verification:

Limited return = \$16.20 – \$16.20 = 0

Maximum return = \$16.20 + (\$312 – \$307 – \$8.10) x 2 = \$10

BEP = \$307 – 10/3 – 2 = \$297

3. PUT BEAR RATIO SPREAD (DEBIT)

To construct the "debit" spread we used the following data:

Long 2 puts \$315@10.05 x 2 = \$20.10
Short 4 puts \$305@4.50 x 4 = \$18.00
Net debit: \$2.10

In Table 26.3 you can monitor the performance of a bear put ratio spread configured as debit. Now, the strategy delivers a negative payout beyond the break-even points—in any direction—and limited profits in between the two BEPs with the highest point pinned at the lower strike put option.

Table 26.3 Put Bear Ratio Spread (Debit) - Expiration Results

Underlying Price \$310.200	Long HS Put \$315 (X – St) x 2	Short LS Put \$305 –(X – St) x 4	Premium Net Debit	Position Total Payoff cents/lb
A	B	C	D	B+C+D
320	0	0	–2.10	–2.10
315	0	0	–2.10	–2.10
313.95	2.10	0	–2.10	0
310	10	0	–2.10	7.90
308	14	0	–2.10	11.90
306	18	0	–2.10	15.90
305	20	0	–2.10	**17.90**
304	22	–4	–2.10	15.90
302	26	–12	–2.10	11.90
300	30	–20	–2.10	7.90
296.05	37.90	–35.80	–2.10	0
295	40	–40	–2.10	–2.10
285	60	–80	–2.10	–22.10
270	90	–140	–2.10	–52.10

Figure 26.4 illustrates the payoff profile of a bear put ratio spread constructed at a "debit."

Figure 26.4 Put Bear Ratio Spread (Debit)

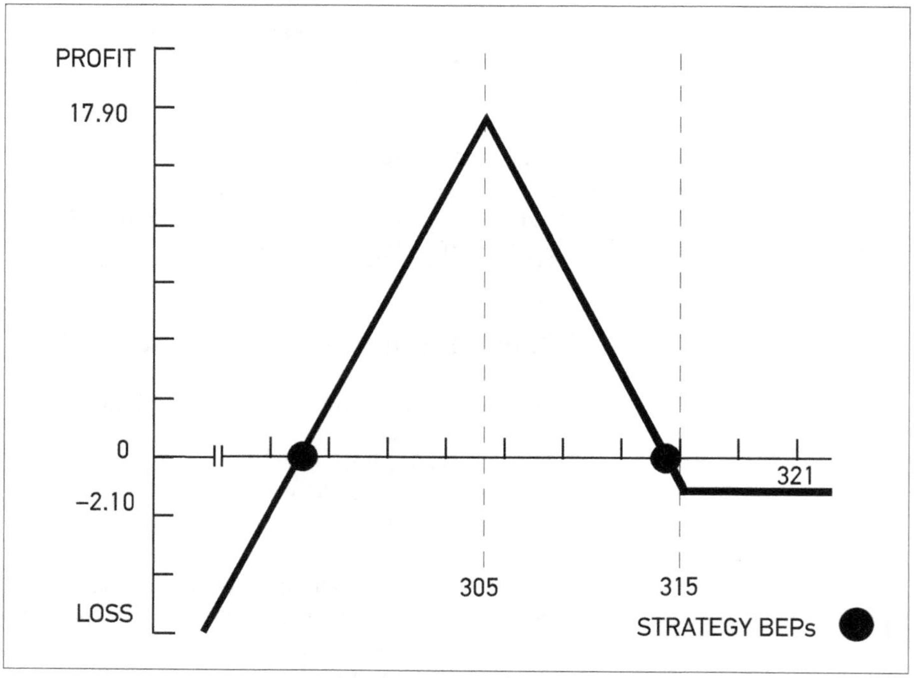

Strategy Key Features
Limited loss = Net debit
Maximum return = (Total credit from short put options + [(difference in strikes - price of long put) x number of long put contracts])

Two BEPs:
Lower BEP = Strike price of short put options – [maximum profit /(number of short put options – number of long put options)]
Upper BEP = Higher strike – net debit/number of long put options

Algebraic verification:
Limited loss = \$20.10 – \$18.00 = \$2.10
Maximum return = \$18 + (\$315 – \$305 – \$10.05) x 2 = \$17.90
Lower BEP = \$305 – [\$17.90/(4 – 2)] = \$296.05
Upper BEP = \$315 – \$2.10/2 = \$313.95

Key Terms

put ratio backspread
refers to a strategy configured with short higher strike puts and more long lower strike puts

4. PUT RATIO BACKSPREADS

The inverted strategy of a bear put ratio spread is of course the bear put ratio backspread which can be attuned in a similar fashion to create a payoff profile which in many respects is an alternative of the plain vanilla long put.

The structure of the strategy is built upon a simple bull put spread adjusted in a specific ratio that transforms the character of the strategy from bull to bear. In this particular case, short options are used to finance the purchase of multiple long options. This strategy is constructed by selling ITM or ATM put options and at the same time purchasing more long OTM options, thus creating in effect an "upside-down" payoff profile compared to the bear put ratio spread:

Short higher strike puts
Long more lower strike puts

As in the previous example we begin by creating a bull put spread by selling the higher strike put and buying the lower strike put as shown below:

Short 1 ITM put \$312@8.10
Long 1 OTM put \$303@3.70
Net credit: \$4.40

The bull put spread is always designated a "credit spread" as the higher put strike sold must always be more expensive than the lower strike put purchased.

We follow the same graphic method—we begin with the P&L graph of the bull put spread, then we add an extra long put with a same strike and expiration and resume the final results in a P&L diagram of a put ratio backspread:

Figure 26.5 Put Ratio Backspread Configuration

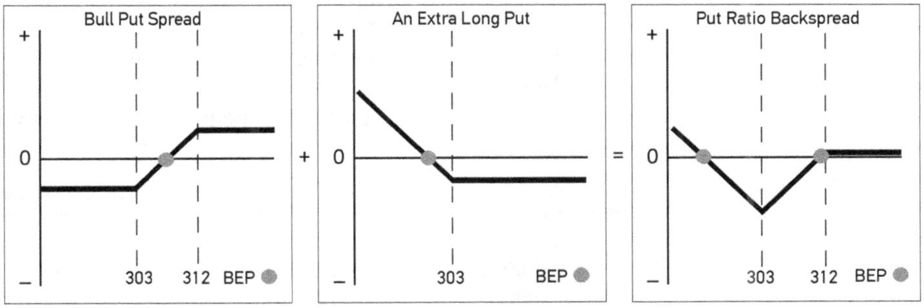

Bull Put Spread	An Extra Long Put	Put Ratio Backspread
Maximum Gain=4.40	Maximum Loss=3.70	Limited Gain=4.40-3.70=0.70
Maximum Loss=4.60	BEP=303-3.70=299.30	Max. Loss=4.60+3.70=-8.30
BEP=312-4.40=307.60	Max. Gain=below BEP	Lower BEP=303-8.30=294.70
		Upper BEP=312-0.70=311.30

From the graph you can easily deduce there is not much sense in creating a debit spread since the strategy will effectively lock-in the losses and generate a negative return at all points below the lower BEP, while the profits will be recorded only if prices surge above, so you would be much better off simply buying a put instead.

Consequently, put ratio backspreads, by definition, are always established as credit spreads.

4.1 PUT RATIO BACKSPREAD (CREDIT)—SELL 1 ITM PUT, BUY 2 OTM PUTS

HI GRADE COPPER (COMEX)
COPPER FUTURES (cents/lb.) \$310.200
25,000 lbs., cents per lb. 12 February 2010

	CALLS			PUTS		
Strike	Mar	Apr	May	Mar	Apr	May
301	10.25	18.15	23.45	3.00	9.95	14.25
302	9.60	17.55	22.90	3.35	10.30	14.70
303	8.95	17.00	22.35	3.70	10.75	15.15
304	8.35	16.45	21.85	4.10	11.20	15.65
305	7.75	15.95	21.30	4.50	11.70	16.10
306	7.20	15.40	20.80	4.95	12.15	16.60
307	6.65	14.90	20.30	5.40	12.65	17.10
308	6.15	14.40	19.80	5.90	13.15	17.60
309	5.65	13.90	19.35	6.40	13.65	18.15
310	5.20	13.45	18.85	6.95	14.20	18.65
310.200 HI GRADE COPPER (COMEX) (cents/lb.) 310.20						
311	4.75	13.00	18.40	7.50	14.75	19.20
312	4.35	12.55	17.95	8.10	15.30	19.75
313	4.00	12.10	17.50	8.75	15.85	20.30
314	3.65	11.65	17.05	9.40	16.40	20.85
315	3.30	11.25	16.60	10.05	17.00	21.40

Using the data from the above chart we constructed the put ratio backspread at a "credit."

Short 1 ITM put $312@8.10
Long 2 OTM puts $303@3.70 x 2 = $7.40
Net credit: $0.70
The performance metrics of the put ratio backspread are demonstrated in Table 26.4.

Table 26.4 Put Ratio Backspread (Credit)–Expiration Results

Underlying Price $310.200	Short HS Put $312 −(X – St) x 1	Long LS Put $303 (X – St) x 2	Premium Net Credit	Position Total Payoff cents/lb
A	B	C	D	B+C+D
320	0	0	0.70	0.70
315	0	0	0.70	0.70
312	0	0	0.70	0.70
311.30	−0.70	0	0.70	0
311	−1	0	0.70	−0.30
308	−4	0	0.70	−3.30
306	−6	0	0.70	−5.30
303	−9	0	0.70	**−8.30**
300	−12	6	0.70	−5.30
298	−14	10	0.70	−3.30
295	−17	16	0.70	−0.30
294.70	−17.30	16.60	0.70	0
285	−27	36	0.70	9.70
270	−42	66	0.70	24.70

In Figure 26.6 we have depicted the payoff profile of a put ratio backspread constructed at a credit.

Figure 26.6 Put Ratio Backspread (Credit)

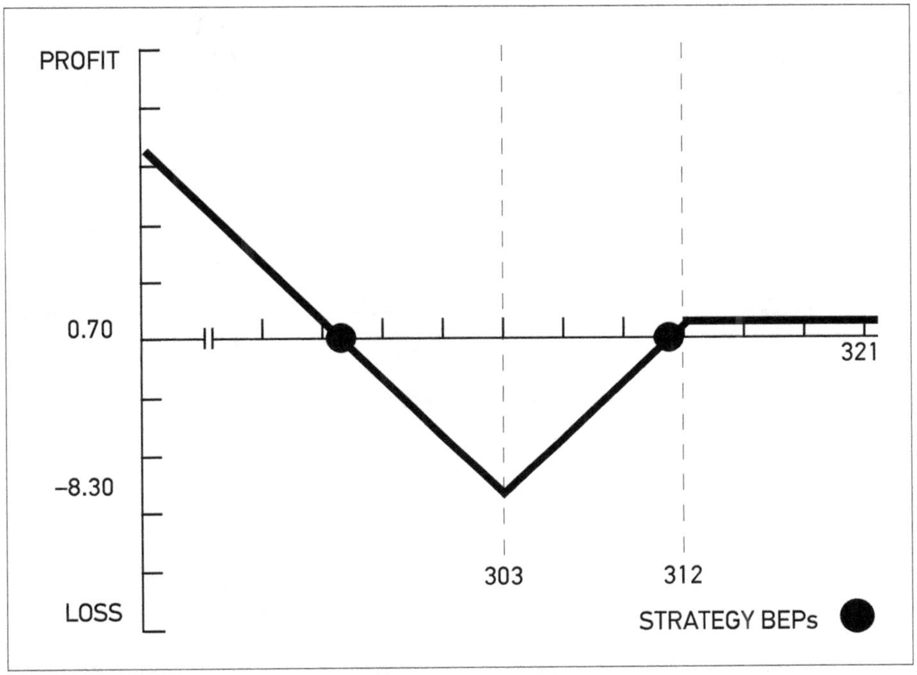

The put ratio backspread strategy constructed in 1:2 ratio delivers the P&L profile that is in effect an "upside-down" put ratio spread.

Figure 26.6 provides some insight into the strategy nature and expectations: the diagram highlights the fact that an investor enacting this type of strategy must feel very bearish on the underlying copper price—expect the price to pass beyond $294.70 (the lower BEP)—and if not, be prepared to take a loss up to $8.30.

However, if the copper price moves in oppsite direction—above $311.30 (the higher BEP)—the strategy will earn a modest return ($0.70).

Strategy Key Features

Maximum loss = Difference in strikes – net credit received
Maximum return = Unlimited (below lower BEP)

Two BEPs:
Lower BEP = Long put strike – (number of contracts sold x difference in strikes) + net credit
Upper BEP = Short put strike – net credit/number of put contracts sold

Algebraic verification:
Maximum loss = $312 – $303 – $0.70 = –$8.30
Lower BEP = $303 – ($312 – $303) x 1 + $0.70 = $294.70
Upper BEP = $312 – $0.70/1 = $311.30

RATIO SPREADS RESUME AND DISAMBIGUATION

1. Call ratio spread 1:2 ratio (involves more short options!)
Bull call spread + 1 short call option

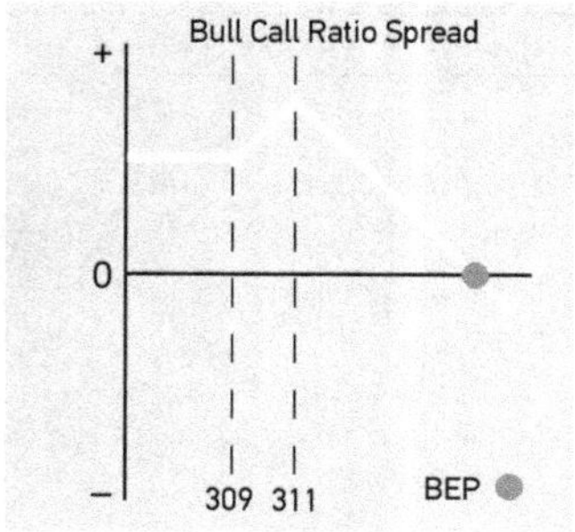

Three alternative P/L Diagrams:

1. Bull (Call) ratio spread (Credit)
2. Bull (Call) ratio spread (Even money)
3. Bull (Call) ratio spread (Debit)

Plethora of alternative titles:

Call ratio spread
Call ratio vertical spread
Bull call ratio spread
Call front spread
Positive ratio spread
Long call ratio spread
Christmas tree

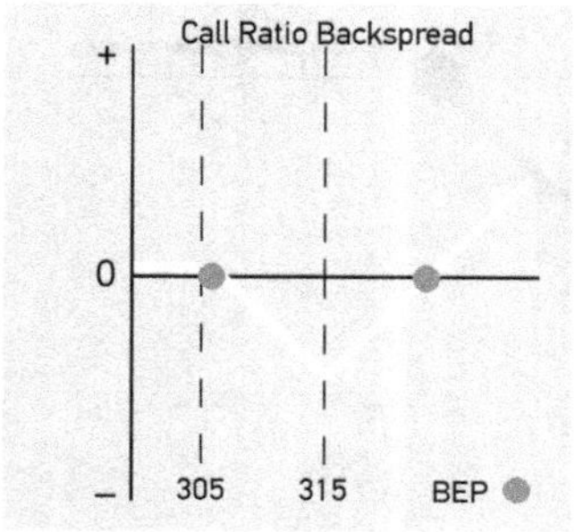

1.1 Call Ratio Backspread 1:2 Ratio (Involves more Long Options!)
Bear call spread + 1 long call option

An "upside-down" call ratio spread

Plethora of alternative titles:

Call ratio backspread
Short bull ratio spread
Call back spread
Positive backspread
Short call ratio spread

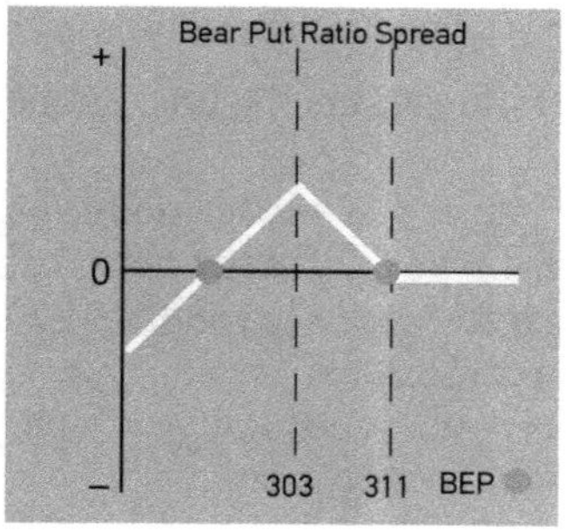

2. Put Ratio Spread 1:2 Ratio (Involves more Short Options!)
Bear put spread + 1 short put

Three Alternative P/L Diagrams:

1. Put (Bear) ratio spread (Credit)
2. Put (Bear) ratio spread (Even Money)
3. Put (Bear) ratio spread (Debit)

Plethora of alternative titles:

Put ratio spread
Put ratio vertical spread
Bear put ratio spread
Put front spread
Negative ratio spread

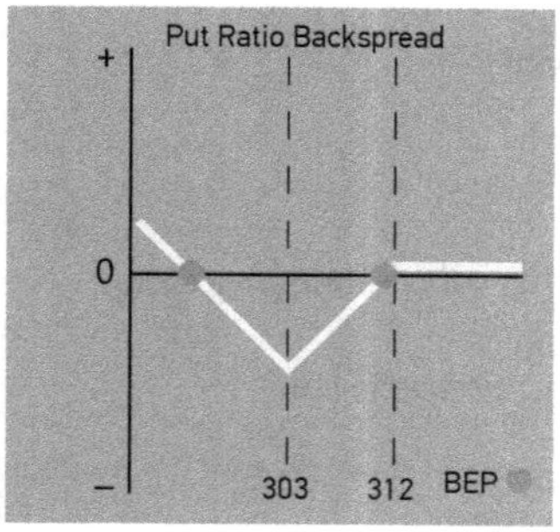

2.2 Put ratio backspread 1:2 ratio (involves more long options!)
Bull put spread + 1 long put

An "upside-down" put ratio spread

Plethora of alternative titles:

Put ratio backspread
Short bear ratio spread
Put back spread
Negative backspread
Short put ratio spread

SUMMARY

This chapter has covered the concept and characteristics of a complementary strategy—the put (bear) ratio spread. The strategy consists entirely of put options and its configuration may also vary in the number of long and short puts employed. The governing rule states that higher strike puts are purchased (normally ITM or ATM) and the lower strike puts (OTM) are sold.

A put ratio spread is initiated around a simple bear put spread (long 1 higher strike put and short 1 lower strike put) with the addition of an extra short put entered at the same short put strike.

The three basic strategies—credit, even-money and debit spreads—were exhibited with complete characterization interpreted graphically and numerically.

As in call ratio spreads, you can manipulate the number of puts and their strike prices in view of risk preferences and market expectations to accomplish the most suitable risk-to-reward strategy profile.

This strategy is also known as a bear ratio spread, signifying that the profit potential of the strategy is on the downside. Hence, this type of strategy will produce the best results in declining markets.

The put ratio backspread is the opposite of the put ratio spread strategy, producing an inverted payoff profile that will work only in extremely bearish markets.

KEY TERMS

put (bear) ratio spread

put ratio backspread

[redacted]

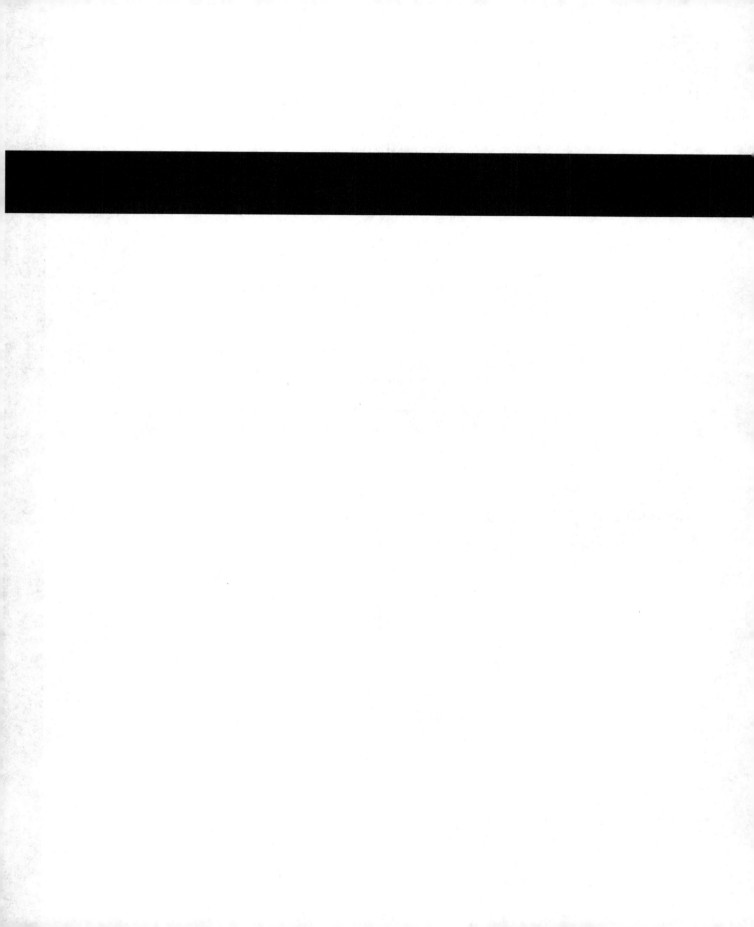

CHAPTER 27

OPTIONS COMBINATIONS

CHAPTER OBJECTIVES

- To introduce and discuss the family of option spread combinations
- To illustrate and define basic characteristics of the most common strategies:
  - Straddles
  - Strangles
- To explain different ways of configuring a straddle synthetically
- To introduce and explain characteristics of strips and straps
- To exhibit and highlight the comparison between straddles' and strangles' performance metrics

LONG STRADDLE

WITH OPTIONS, IT IS POSSIBLE TO CONSTRUCT STRATEGIES IN VERY MANY different ways. Versatility of options combinations is one of the most attractive features in options trading. Options combinations allow you to configure P&L profiles that are not imaginable in futures trading.

In this chapter we shall introduce some concepts of weighing risk against rewards that are most commonly encountered in options exchange markets.

The term straddle refers to simultaneous purchase, or sale, of a call and a put at the same strike price, same expiration date and same underlying asset.

Long Straddle strategies are normally constituted with at-the-money options—one long call and one long put.

Paying two at-the-money option premiums consisting of only time values makes the straddle quite an expensive strategy.

Straddles, along with strangles, are generally designated "volatility play", implying that investors who initiate these types of strategies are indifferent to the price direction—hoping only for a significant move. They take a view of future volatility, confronting their own intuitive assessment of options' theoretical fair value with that indicated by the market. Options traders entering long straddles or strangles are expecting a substantial price change or an increase in volatility, whereas those who are selling straddles and/or strangles are expecting quiet market conditions or a decrease in volatility. This ever-present dichotomy of choices has keept the market alive, increasing its liquidity.

For example if an option's exercise price is currently trading at $5.50 but you feel the actual market price—compared to its historic volatility—should not be above $5.30 then this means that the current option price is implying an additional 0.20 points. This can be attributed solely to volatility factors. So, that option is 0.20 points overvalued and is hence suitable for writing.

If your calculations should lead to the conclusion that the option is undervalued —should be trading at $5.80—then it is actually trading at 0.30 points less, implying that the overall market volatility perception of that stock is currently low and therefore it is a good purchase opportunity.

Assuming a high probability of a major market move, irrespective of its direction, an investor could construct a long straddle—buy simultaneously an at-the-money call and put. The initial outlay is equal to the cost of the two premiums paid. The graphical expression of a long straddle, also referred to as a "bottom straddle", resembles a spike or a pen point, as depicted in Figure 26.1.

Key Terms

long straddle
a type of option spread constructed by simultaneous purchase of a call and a put at the same strike

LONG STRADDLE CONFIGURATION

Buy 1 x at-the-money put at A
Buy 1 x at-the-money call at A
Net debit

The loss of this strategy is limited to the total premium paid peaking up at point A, the price level at which the strategy is initiated (or if no price change occurs). If the share price closes anywhere between break-even points (a and b) the strategy loses money.

Although the profit potential is unlimited, the price of underlying needs a substantial breakout, beyond the upper or lower break-even point, before it starts generating profits. The long straddle—mainly because of the net debit outlay—is a rather risky strategy that should be entered only if excessive price moves are expected or in market conditions where apparent volatility prevails. Time decay, obviously, is your enemy, as the at-the-money option premium consists solely of time value. Should the underlying asset price remain unchanged the time decay will wipe out all of the premium paid.

In Figure 27.1 we have depicted the P&L profile of a long straddle.

Figure 27.1 Long Straddle

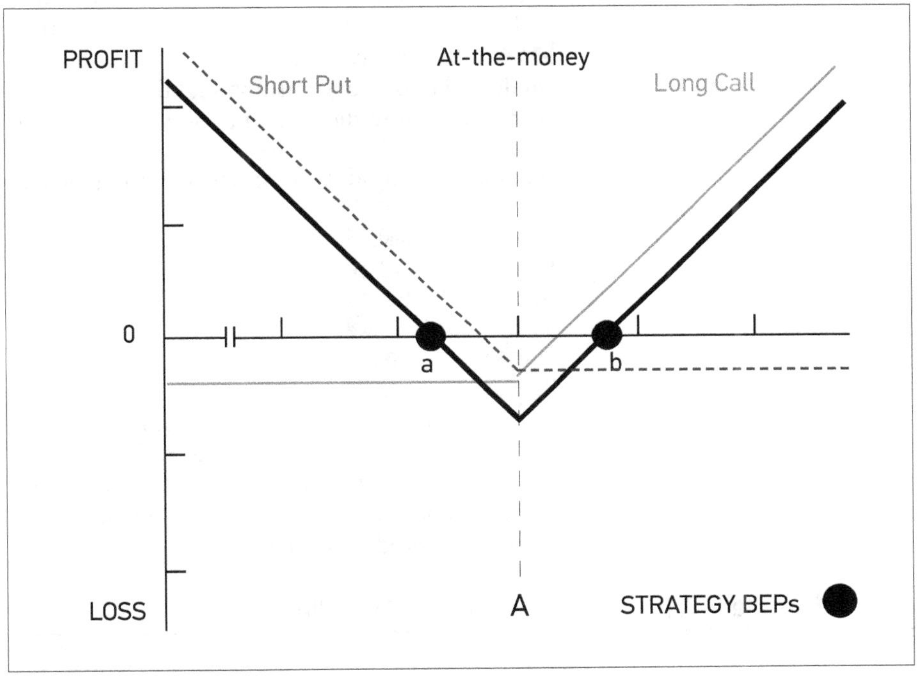

Strategy Key Features
Break-even points = Two

a. On the downside = Strike price – net debit
b. On the upside = Strike price + net debit

Maximum loss: Confined to premium debit
Maximum profit: Unlimited in both directions
Volatility outlook: High on the price of the underlying
Time decay: Erodes position

Key Terms

bullish long straddle
a type of straddle constructed by simultaneous purchase of an in-the-money call and a put at the same strike

BULLISH LONG STRADDLE

It is worth emphasizing that in real market situations you would rarely be in a position to buy or sell exactly an at-the-money call or put. It is more likely that you will be faced with the situation that the range of possible strike prices does not match precisely the current market price. The real time options chain of ABN Amro Stock Price taken on 9 July 2007 illustrates this point:

Example: ABN Amro Stock Price $34.68, 9 July 2007

Call Close	Series	Put Close
$2.85	July 07 $32.00	$0.05
$1.10	July 07 $34.00	$0.35
$0.55	July 07 $35.00	$0.80
$0.25	July 07 $36.00	$1.50
$0.05	July 07 $38.00	$3.25

Consequently you will have to make a choice between being more bullish or more bearish in regard to the expected market direction.

If you select a strike at $34.00, below the current price of ABN AMRO Stock (A = $34.68), then the call is in-the-money and the put option is out-of-the-money which would make your long position slightly more bullish—the upside break-even point (b) becomes closer to the current underlying price (A)—as shown in Figure 27.2.

A bullish long straddle is constructed using the following data:

Long put $34@0.35
Long call $34@1.10
Net debit: $1.45

Strategy Key Features
Break-even points:
a. On the downside = $34 – $1.45 = $32.55
b. On the upside = $34 + $1.45 = $35.45
Maximum loss: confined to premium debit = $1.45
Maximum profit: unlimited in both directions
Time decay: erodes position

Figure 27.2 Bullish Long Straddle

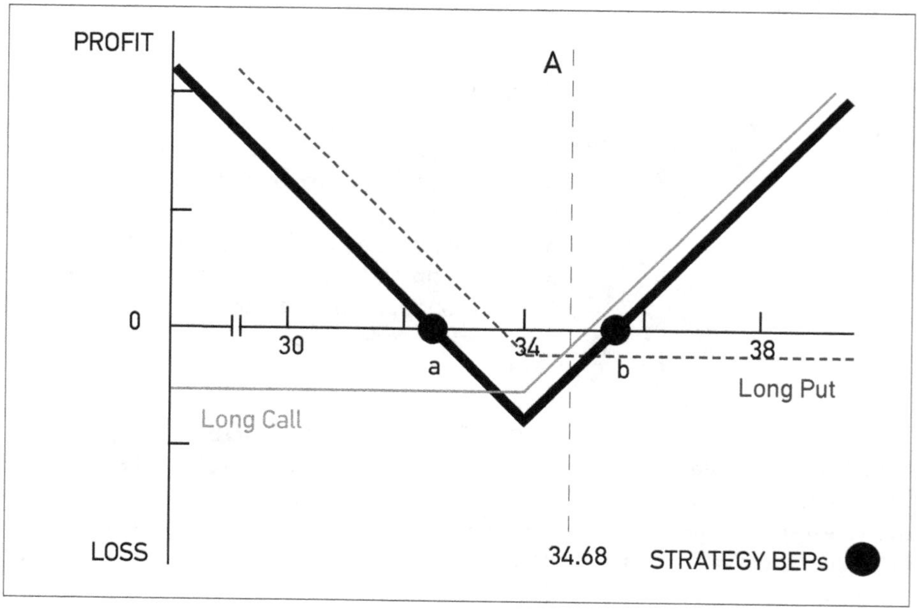

Profit and Loss Characteristics

On the downside:

In order to generate profits, the price of the ABN AMRO stock would have to fall significantly further down the x-axis—beyond the lower BEP.

On the upside:

The higher BEP sits closer to the ABN AMRO stock current price, so that a lower increase in price is needed for the strategy to generate profits.

Key Terms

bearish long straddle
a type of straddle constructed by simultaneous purchase of an out-of-the-money call and a put at the same strike

BEARISH LONG STRADDLE

If, on the other hand, your choice is the strike at $36.00, then your call option is out-of-the money and your put is in-the-money, which makes your long position more bearish—the break-even point on the down-side (a) becomes closer to the current market price (A)—and since less price fall is required to make your strategy profitable the strategy is designated more "bearish," as illustrated in Figure 27.3.

The bearish long straddle is constructed using the following data:
Long put $36@1.50
Long call $36@0.25
Net debit: $1.75

Strategy Key Features
Break-even points:
a. On the downside = $36 – $1.75 = $34.25
b. On the upside = $36 + $1.75 = $37.75
Maximum loss: confined to premium debit = $1.75
Maximum profit: unlimited in both directions
Time decay: erodes position

Figure 27.3 Bearish Long Straddle

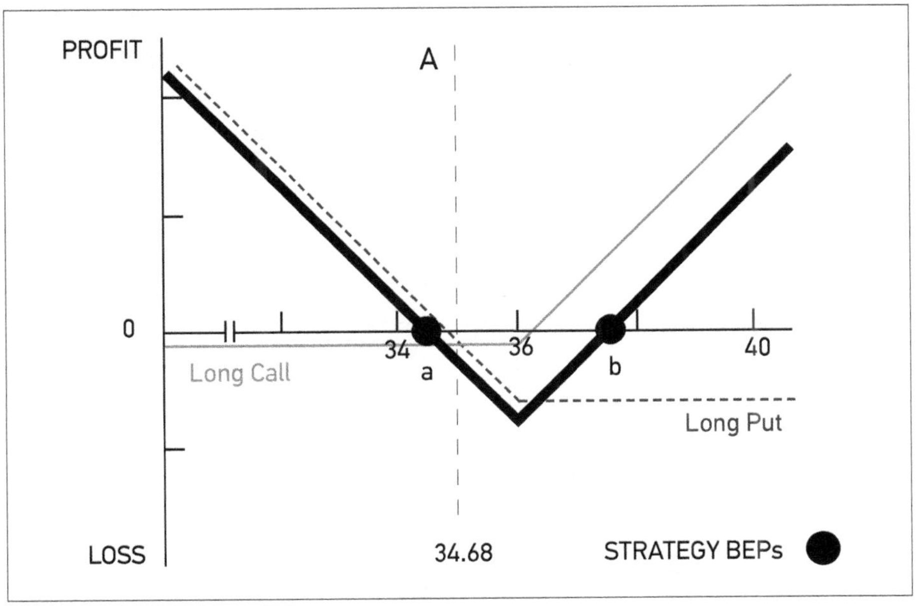

Profit and Loss Characteristics

On the downside:

In order to generate profits, the price of the ABN AMRO stock would have to rise significantly further up the x-axis—beyond the higher BEP.

On the upside:

The lower BEP sits closer to the ABN AMRO stock current price, so that a smaller fall in the price is needed for the strategy to generate profits.

SHORT STRADDLE

Key Terms

short straddle
a type of option spread constructed by simultaneous sale of a call and a put on the same underlying instrument at the same strike

The payoff of a short straddle is an inverse image of the long straddle, so market expectations are also inverted compared to long straddles. At a time when the market is starting to slow up after a period of activity, a trader anticipating a volatility slowdown may look for an opportunity to sell a straddle and receive a combined premium. Any drop in volatility is in the investor's favour and the longer the option runs locked within the two BEPs, the better for this short strategy, as time decay is its ally. While the maximum profit is confined to the aggregate premiums received, in this trade there is no limit for the potential loss in either direction.

SHORT STRADDLE CONFIGURATION

Selling 1 x at-the-money put at A
Selling 1 x at-the-money call at A

The payoff profile of a long straddle is depicted in Figure 27.4.

Figure 27.4 Short Straddle

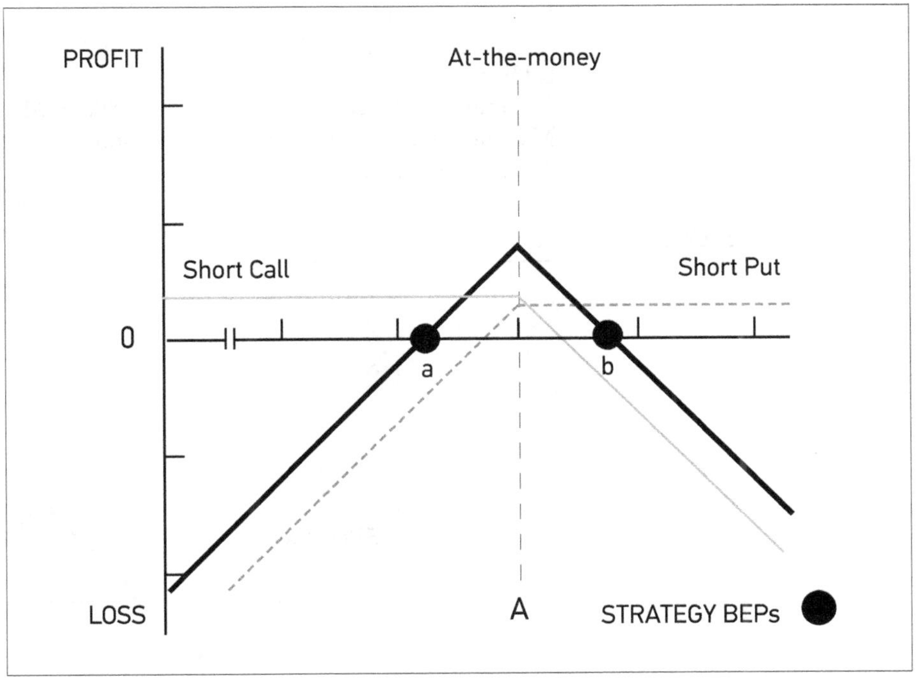

Strategy Key Features
Break-even points:
a. On the downside = Strike price – net credit
b. On the upside = Strike price + net credit
Maximum loss: unlimited in both directions
Maximum profit: confined to premium credit

Volatility outlook: low on the underlying stock
Time decay: benefits position

BULLISH SHORT STRADDLE

Key Terms

bullish short straddle
a type of straddle constructed by simultaneous selling of an in-the- money put and a call at the same strike

As is the case with long straddles, short straddles—relative to the current market price of the underlying asset—may also be differentiated as bullish and bearish. In our case, with ABN AMRO Stock, the bullish short straddle would be constructed by choosing the strike price above the current stock price ($34.68)—for example, $36.00. In this scenario, the short call is out-of-the-money and the short put is in-the-money, so that the lower break-even point (a) comes closer to the current stock price (A). Consequently, the ABN AMRO stock price would have to rise above the current price level (A) in order to maximize profits. Since the maximum profit potential is on the upside the strategy is designated "bullish." Figure 27.5 illustrates the P&L profile of a bullish short straddle. The bullish short straddle is constructed using the following data:

Bullish short straddle is constructed using the following data:
Short put $36@1.50
Short call $36@0.25
Net credit: $1.75

Strategy Key Features
Break-even points:
a. On the downside = $36 – $1.75 = $34.25
b. On the upside = $36 + $1.75 = $37.75
Maximum profit: confined to premium credit = $1.75
Maximum loss: unlimited in both directions
Time decay: benefits position

Figure 27.5 Bullish Short Straddle

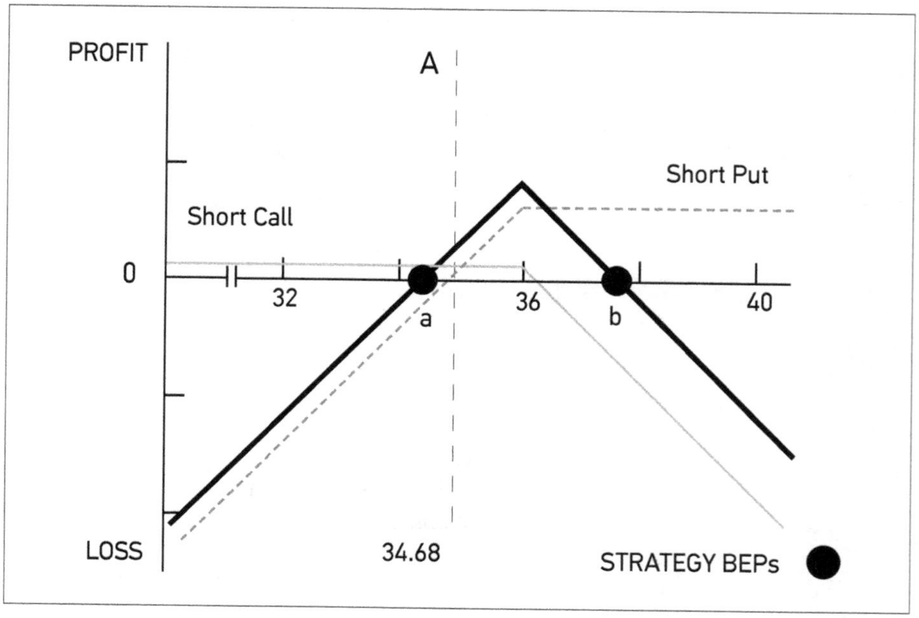

On the downside:

Losses are more probable on the downside as the lower BEP is closer to ABN stock price.

On the upside:

Losses on the upside are less probable as the higher BEP sits further from the ABN AMRO stock price, so that a major breakout is needed before the strategy begins to lose money.

Key Terms

bearish short straddle
a type of straddle constructed by simultaneous sale of in-the-money call and put at the same strike

BEARISH SHORT STRADDLE

Conversely the bearish short straddle would be constructed by choosing the strike price below the current ABN AMRO price ($34.68)—for example, $34.00. In this scenario the short call is slightly in-the-money and the short put is slightly out-of-the-money. The higher break-even point (b) comes closer to (A), so that prices would have to fall below the current underlying in order to maximize profits. Since the maximum profit potential is on the down-side the strategy is designated "bearish".

Figure 27.6 illustrates the P&L profile of a bearish short straddle.

A bearish short straddle is constructed using the following data:
Short put $34@0.35
Short call $34@1.10
Net credit: $1.45

Strategy Key Features

Break-even points:
a. On the downside = $34 – $1.45 = $32.55
b. On the upside = $34 + $1.45 = $35.45
Maximum loss: confined to premium debit = $1.45
Maximum profit: unlimited in both directions

Figure 27.6 Bearish Short Straddle

Time decay: Erodes position

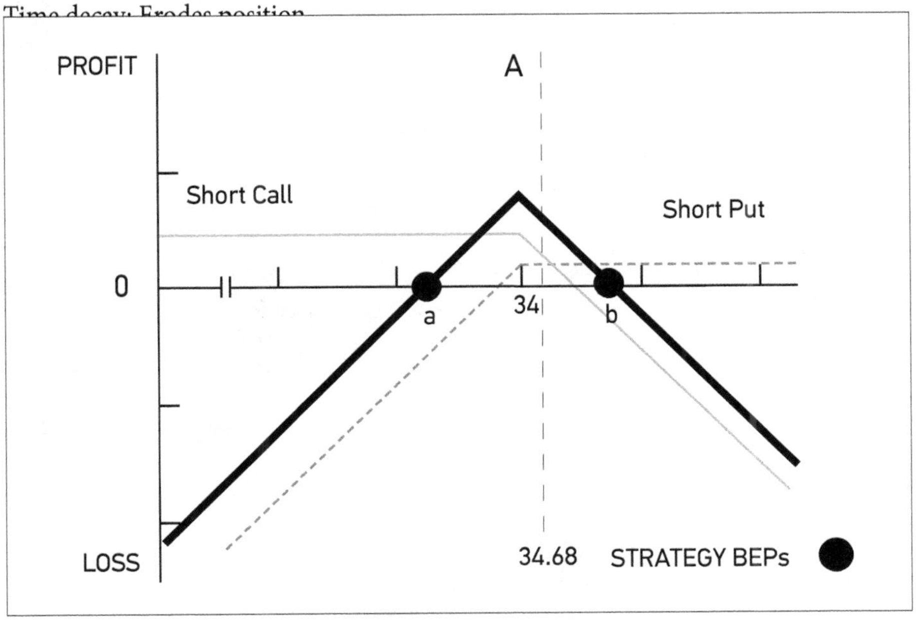

Profit and Loss Characteristics

On the downside:

The lower BEP is further from the current ABN AMRO stock price so that a significant breakout on the downside is needed before the strategy begins to lose money.

On the upside:

The higher BEP sits closer to the ABN AMRO stock current price so that losses are more probable on the upside.

LONG AND SHORT SYNTHETIC STRADDLES

OPTIONS FLEXIBILITY

When using options instruments, the enacted risk profile may easily be converted into another risk profile: one of the option's great advantages—its flexibility. For example, each of the synthetically constructed options illustrated in this chapter may be transformed into another strategy with a different risk profile. In this section we shall acquaint you with the transformation of four basic synthetically produced options into synthetic straddles.

Variations of configuring synthetic long and short straddles are presented in Figures 27.7 and 27.8.

Figure 27.7 Synthetic Long Straddles (Case I)

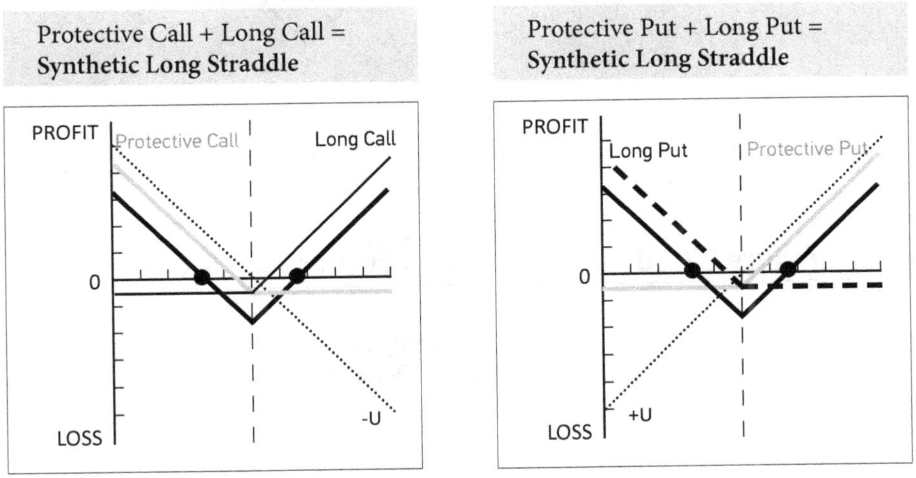

Figure 27.8 Synthetic Short Straddles (Case I)

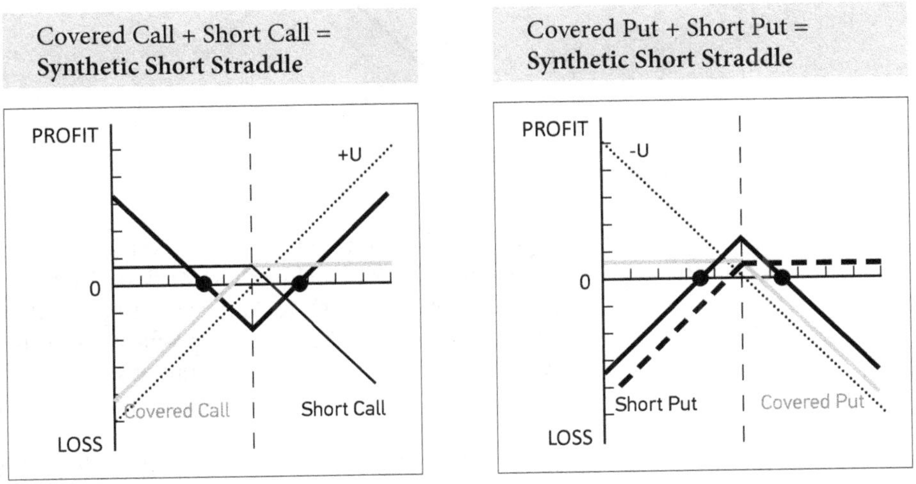

Configuring a synthetic straddle may also be regarded as a combination of two options with the same strikes and expiry instituted simultaneously against short and long instruments respectively, as depicted below. The risk profile delivered is that of a straddle.

Figure 27.9 Synthetic Long Straddles (Case II)

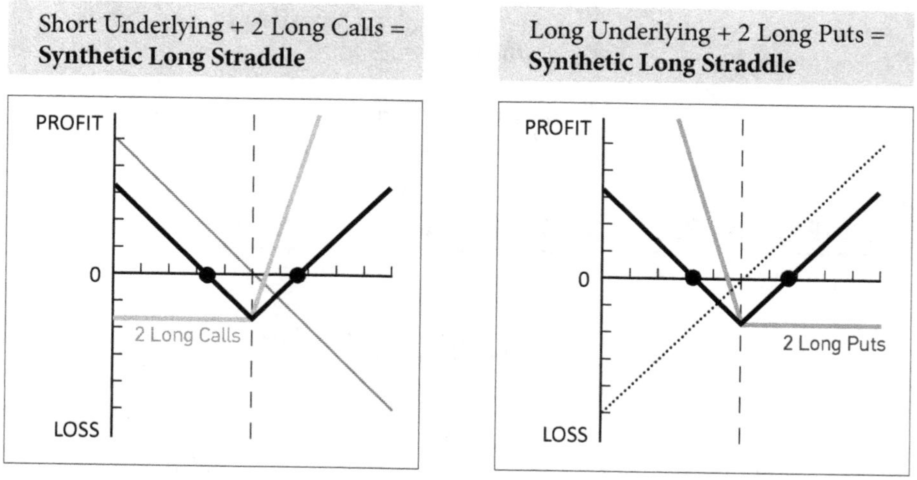

Figure 27.10 Synthetic Short Straddles (Case II)

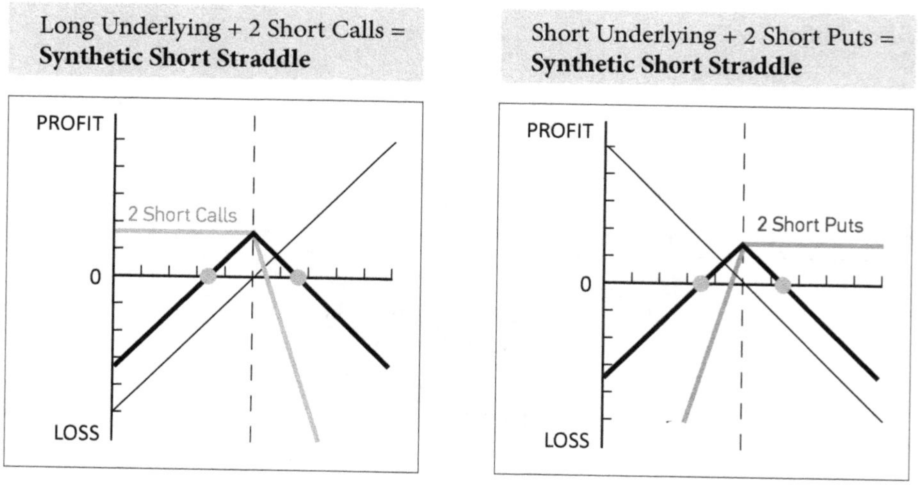

Figure 27.9 illustrates the configuration of a synthetic long straddle: on the left diagram, an investor holding a short stock position enters the market by purchasing two long calls on that short stock, thus creating a P&L profile of a straddle. The graph on the right shows that the same risk profile can be generated by different constituents—a long underlying and two long put options.

Figure 27.10 proves that the same rationale can be applied in constituting a synthetic short straddle.

The profit and loss metrics of a synthetic long straddle are presented in Table 27.1.

Table 27.1 Synthetic Long Straddle Profit/Loss Metrics

Short Stock@25 + 2 x Long Calls 25@5

Stock Price	-S	+C	+C	Premium 2 x $5	P&L
0	25	0	0	−10	15
5	20	0	0	−10	10
10	15	0	0	−10	5
15	10	0	0	−10	0
20	5	0	0	−10	−5
25	0	0	0	−10	−10
30	−5	5	5	−10	−5
35	−10	10	10	−10	0
40	−15	15	15	−10	5
45	−20	20	20	−10	10
50	−25	25	25	−10	15

Long Stock@25 + 2 x Long Puts 25@5

Stock Price	+S	+P	+P	Premium 2 x $5	P&L
0	−25	25	25	−10	15
5	−20	20	20	−10	10
10	−15	15	15	−10	5
15	−10	10	10	−10	0
20	−5	5	5	−10	−5
25	0	0	0	−10	−10
30	5	0	0	−10	−5
35	10	0	0	−10	0
40	15	0	0	−10	5
45	20	0	0	−10	10
50	25	0	0	−10	15

The P&L metrics of a synthetic short straddle are presented in Table 27.2.

Table 27.2 Synthetic Short Straddle Profit/Loss Metrics

Long Stock@25 + 2 x Short Calls 25@5

Stock Price	+S	-C	-C	Premium 2 x $5	P&L
0	−25	0	0	10	−15
5	−20	0	0	10	−10
10	−15	0	0	10	−5
15	−10	0	0	10	0
20	−5	0	0	10	5
25	0	0	0	10	10
30	5	−5	−5	10	5
35	10	−10	−10	10	0
40	15	−15	−15	10	−5
45	20	−20	−20	10	−10
50	25	−25	−25	10	−15

Short Stock@25 + 2 x Short Puts 25@5

Stock Price	-S	-P	-P	Premium 2 x $5	P&L
0	25	−25	−25	10	−15
5	20	−20	−20	10	−10
10	15	−15	−15	10	−5
15	10	−10	−10	10	0
20	5	−5	−5	10	5
25	0	0	0	10	10
30	−5	0	0	10	5
35	−10	0	0	10	0
40	−15	0	0	10	−5
45	−20	0	0	10	−10
50	−25	0	0	10	−15

STRIP AND STRAP STRATEGIES

Key Terms

strip strategy
a type of straddle constructed by adding another put to a straddle; one long call + two long puts at the same strikes

strap strategy
a type of straddle constructed by adding another call to a straddle; one long put + two long calls at the same strikes

Further variations of a common straddle—in regard to an investor's bias towards price direction—are available in the form of "strips" and "straps." In case our investor shares the sentiment that one direction seems to be more probable than the other he would add another (third) long option to a straddle. Consequently, these strategies are referred to as "triple options." Since they involve an additional option, strips and straps cost more than common straddles.

Once the decision on price direction is confirmed, an investor would choose either a strip—if he is more bearish, or a strap—if he feels more bullish.

LONG STRIP STRATEGY

A strip is a strategy created by adding another long put to a straddle. So, the investor explicitly buys one call and two puts all with the same strike price, maturity and underlying asset.

Buy 1 ATM call
Buy 2 ATM puts

The additional put affects the steepness on the bearish side of the strategy profile and it amplifies the gains if the price of the stock falls sharply below the lower BEP. The two put options will double the profit due to the decrease in the stock's market price.

LONG STRAP STRATEGY

A strap is basically the opposite of the strip: it is created by adding another long call to a straddle. So, the investor explicitly buys one call and two puts all with the exact same strike price, maturity and underlying asset.

Buy 1 ATM put
Buy 2 ATM calls

The additional call affects the steepness on the bullish side of the strategy profile and it amplifies the gains if the price of the stock rises sharply above the higher strike BEP. Two call options will double the profits from any increase in the stock's market price.

Comparing the profit and loss metrics of strips and straps with a common straddle:

Assuming the investor paid $8.00 for the common straddle positions, the profit and loss aftermath will look like this:

Strike Price = $50
Lower BEP = $42 (Strike price – $8);
Higher BEP = $58 (Strike price + $8)
Maximum loss = Net outlay = $8
Maximum profit below lower BEP = $42
Maximum profit above higher BEP = Stock price – BEP

Strip and strap P&L profiles are exhibited in Figure 27.11.

Figure 27.11 Strips and Straps

Long Strip

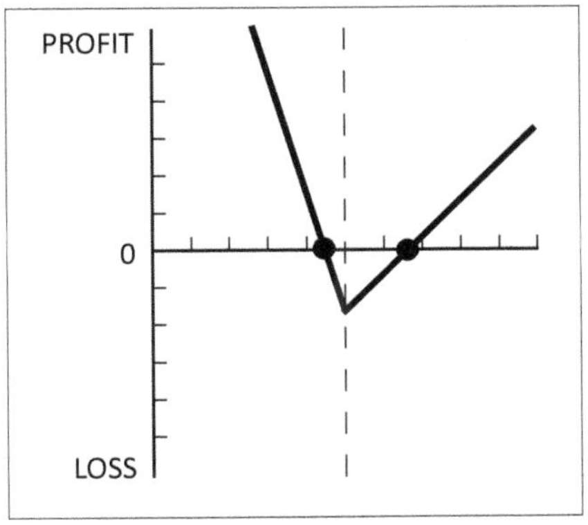

Lower BEP = Strike Price – Net Outlay
Higher BEP = Strike Price + Net Outlay/2

Strips

If you think that the price of the underlying is going to decrease, you can buy two puts and, for protection, buy one call. This takes the view that the stock price will go down, but protects you if the stock price goes up.

Long Strap

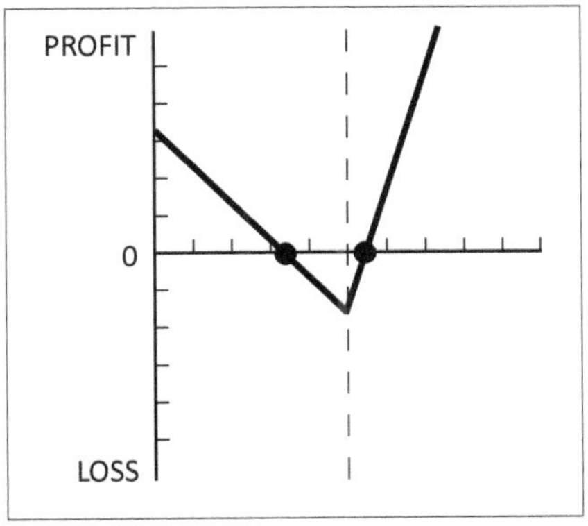

Lower BEP = Strike Price – Net Outlay/2
Higher BEP = Strike Price + Net Outlay

Straps

If you think that the price of the underlying is going to increase, you can buy two calls and, for protection, buy one put. This takes the view that the stock price will go up, but protects you if the stock price goes down.

For the strip, because it has two puts instead of one, the strategy payout will look like this:

The net outlay is now $12 therefore:

Lower BEP = $44 (Strike price – net outlay/2)
Higher BEP = $62 (Strike price + net outlay)
Maximum loss = Net outlay = $12
Maximum profit below lower BEP: limited = (BEP – stock price) x 2 = $44 x 2 = $88
Maximum profit above higher BEP: unlimited = Stock price – BEP

For the strap, because it has two calls instead of one, the strategy payout will look like this:

The net outlay is also $12 therefore:

Lower BEP = $38 (Strike price – net outlay)
Higher BEP = $56 (Strike price + net outlay/2)
Maximum loss = Net outlay = $12
Maximum profit below lower BEP: limited = (BEP – stock price) = $38
Maximum profit above higher BEP: unlimited = (Stock price – BEP) x 2

Payoff to a Strip	ST < X	ST > X
2 Puts	2 (X – ST)	0
1 Call	0	ST – X

Payoff to a Strap	ST < X	ST > X
1 Put	X – ST	0
2 Calls	0	2 (ST – X)

LONG STRANGLE

Key Terms

long strangle
a type of option spread constructed by purchasing a call and a put on the same UI and same expiry but at different strike prices

If you cut off the nib of the straddle you will get the payoff diagram as shown below—a strangle. This strategy is constructed when a call and a put option—on the same underlying asset with the same expiry date, but different strike prices—are either purchased—long strangle, or sold—short strangle.

Both options—a call with a higher strike and a put with a lower strike—are out-of-the-money. The strategy seems as if it is embracing the range between a higher call and a lower put, thus making a "strangle." In a long strangle, breaking up from the strangled range—in either direction—would lead to unlimited profits as the diagram directly suggests, but the prices would have to move either through the lower strike A minus the total premium outlay, or the higher strike B plus the total premium paid.

The loss outlay is "strangled"—confined to the aggregate cost of the premiums paid.

LONG STRANGLE CONFIGURATION

Buying 1 x out-of-the-money put at A (lower strike)
Buying 1 x out-of-the-money call at B (higher strike)
A and B points are equidistant.
Strategy profile: Net debit

Strangle strategies are generally less expensive than straddles, as the strikes chosen—both being out-of-the-money—are cheaper than at-the-money strikes typical for straddles. Also time decay in strangle strategies is of less influence than in straddles.

Figure 27.12 Long Strangle

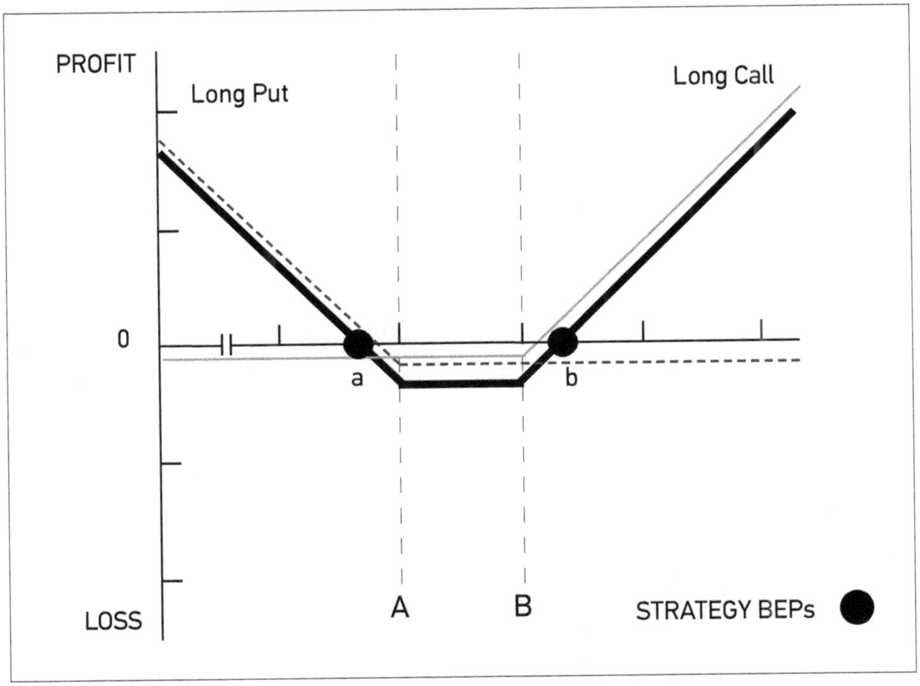

Key Terms

synthetic long strangle
a strategy created with a short underlying plus a long ITM call, and a long OTM call

Strategy Key Features
Break-even points = Two
I. On the upside = Higher strike price (B) + net debit
II. On the downside = Lower strike price (A) – net debit
Maximum loss: limited to premium debit
Maximum profit: unlimited
Volatility outlook: high on the underlying asset
Time decay: erodes position

You can transform the short physical position into a synthetic long strangle:

Synthetic long strangle: –UI + C (ITM) +C (OTM)

SHORT STRANGLE

Key Terms

short strangle
a type of option spread constructed by selling a call and a put on the same underlying instrument and at the same expiry but at different strike prices

support
price level used in technical analysis to indicate a floor price that is unlikely to be penetrated

resistance
price level used in technical analysis to indicate a ceiling price that is unlikely to be penetrated

The short strangle is of course the inverse image of the long strangle except that in this strategy both options are sold. When a market is static or locked in a trading range—unlikely to break in either direction—then it may seem opportune to implement a short strangle rather than long.

SHORT STRANGLE CONFIGURATION

Selling 1 x out-of-the-money put at A (Lower Strike)
Selling 1 x out-of-the-money call at B (higher strike)
A and B points are equidistant.
Strategy profile: net credit

The most you can make with this trade, is to "strangle" the range between the two strikes. The price of the underlying asset would require a large move—whether up or down—to negate the net premium received. However, if the market penetrates the range in any direction, it may lead to a considerable loss. This strategy should be exploited in a sideways moving market in which prices remain in a narrow range for a considerable time span. This is a market environment with a predictably close distance between **support** and **resistance** price levels.

Figure 27.13 Short Strangle

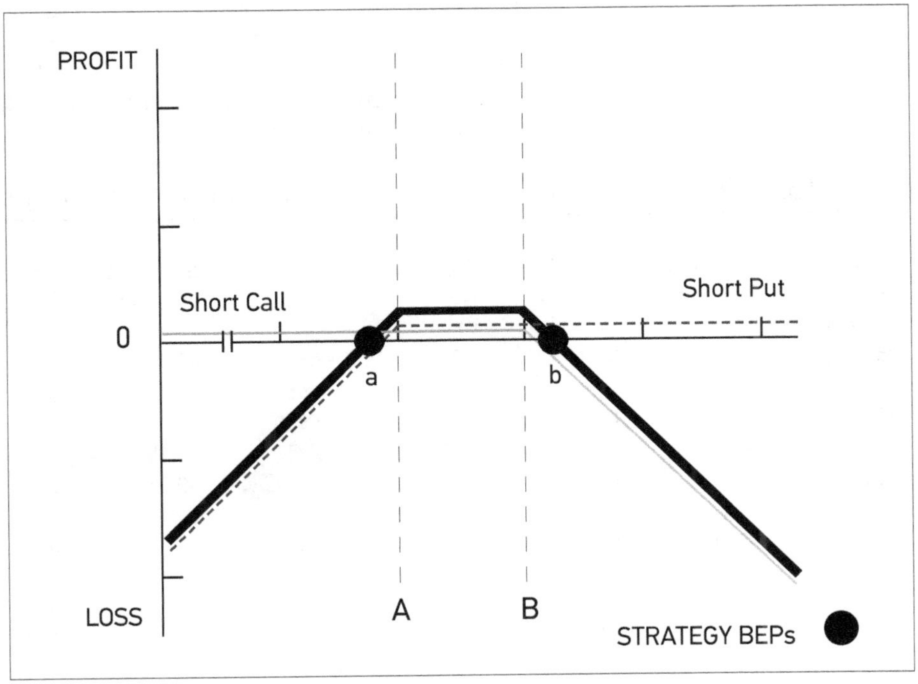

Strategy Key Features
Break-even points = Two
I. On the upside = Higher strike price (B) + net credit

Key Terms

synthetic short strangle
a strategy created with a short underlying against a short ITM put, and a short OTM put

II. On the downside = Lower strike price (A) – net credit
Maximum loss: unlimited
Maximum profit: limited to premium credit
Volatility outlook: low on the underlying asset
Time decay: benefits position

You can transform the short physical position into a **synthetic short strangle.**
Synthetic short strangle: –UI –P (ITM) –P (OTM)

Table 27.3 offers a comparison between the "straddles" and the "strangles" essential characteristics of the straddle and the strangle.

Table 27.3 Straddles and Strangles Resume

COMPONENTS			BEP	MAX LOSS	MAX PROFIT
Short Straddle	Sell Short Call and Short Put Same Strikes	Credit	SP + Credit SP – Credit	Unlimited	Net Credit
Long Straddle	Sell Long Call and Long Put Same Strikes	Debit	SP + Debit SP – Debit	Net Debit	Unlimited
Short Strangle	Sell Lower Strike Put Sell Higher Strike Call	Credit	LS – Credit HS + Credit	Unlimited	Net Credit
Long Strangle	Buy Lower Strike Put Buy Higher Strike Call	Debit	LS – Debit HS + Debit	Net Debit	Unlimited

To compare investment strategies we have developed tabular data with butterfly and condor performance metrics. Table 27.4 is a numerical exposition of the performance metrics of long straddles and strangles relative to change in price of the underlying instrument. It aims to capture instant visual recognition of differences between the two strategies' expiration results.

Table 27.4 Long and Short Straddle/Strangle Performance Metrics

Price of Underlying	Short Put 35@0.55 (X – St)	Short Call 35@0.80 (St – X)	Premium Net Debit	Short Straddle Return $	Short Put 34@0.35 (X – St)	Short Call 36@0.25 (St – X)	Premium Net Debit	Short Strangle Return $
25	–10	0	1.35	–8.65	–9	0	0.60	–8.40
32	–3	0	1.35	–1.65	–2	0	0.60	–1.40
33	–2	0	1.35	–0.65	–1	0	0.60	–0.40
33.40	–1.60	0	1.35	–0.25	–0.60	0	0.60	0
33.65	–1.35	0	1.35	0	–0.35	0	0.60	0.25
34	–1	0	1.35	0.35	0	0	0.60	0.60
34.40	–0.60	0	1.35	0.75	0	0	0.60	0.60
35	0	0	1.35	**1.35**	0	0	0.60	0.60
35.60	0	–0.60	1.35	0.75	0	0	0.60	0.60
36	0	–1	1.35	0.35	0	0	0.60	0.60
36.35	0	–1.35	1.35	0	0	–0.35	0.60	0.25
36.60	0	–1.60	1.35	–0.25	0	–0.60	0.60	0
37	0	–2	1.35	–0.65	0	–1	0.60	–0.40
38	0	–3	1.35	–1.65	0	–2	0.60	–1.40
45	0	–10	1.35	–8.65	0	–9	0.60	–8.40

The inverse relationship in performance metrics between long and short strategies follows the logic depicted in payoff diagrams.

The comparison criteria between straddles and strangles may be divided into two categories—long straddles/strangles and short straddles/strangles—and their corresponding similarities and dissimilarities:

1. Long straddles and strangles

Similarities—both long strategies are entered at net debit and both are positioned as highly volatile strategies with limited losses attained within the range of the premiums sold, and an unlimited risk beyond the two break-even points. The risk-reward profile of both strategies is designated as "open-ended."

Dissimilarities—the long straddle loss occurs between a limited price range ($33.65 and $36.35), while the maximum loss (if the UI finishes at the exact strike price of $35 at expiration) sits at a lower price level (–$1.35) compared to the strangle loss maximum (–$0.60).

If the underlying price breaks out beyond the break-even points, in either direction, straddle profits would be a bit steeper than those of a strangle.

2. Short straddles and strangles

Similarities—if the opposite set of transactions is put in place, than both strategies are entered at net credit and both are positioned as neutral strategies with limited profits (attained within the range of the premiums sold) and unlimited risk (beyond break-even points in either direction). The risk/reward profiles of short straddles/strangles also belong to a category marked as "open-ended."

Dissimilarities—however, short straddles deliver profits over a slightly contracted price range ($33.65 and $36.35) while the maximum profit (if the UI finishes at the exact price of $35 at expiration) sits at a higher price level ($1.35) compared to the strangle maximum ($0.60).

If the price of underlying breaks out beyond break-even points in either direction, straddle losses would be a bit steeper than those of a strangle.

In conclusion, we have prepared a compendium with the list of the most frequently used options strategies.

The order of the strategies in this compendium is just one of various choices, compiled relative to subjective preferences assumed to be inherently logical. Although it could be arranged in an alternative sequence, its aim would be the same—to call attention to the wider implications of strategy selection based on the risk profiles they deliver, and to help manage market challenges.

In Table 27.5 we have proposed a comprehensive array of tools and strategies designed to contain, reduce or completely eliminate the implicit risks in commodity trading.

Table 27.5 Options Spreads and Combinations Compendium

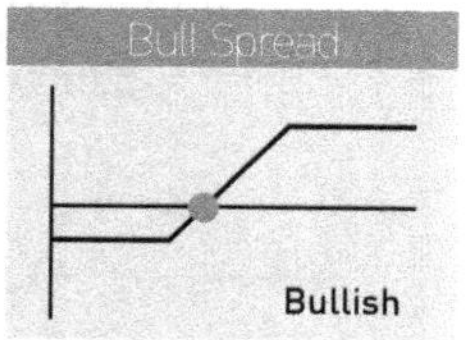

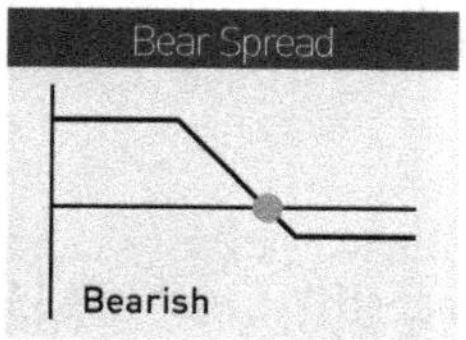

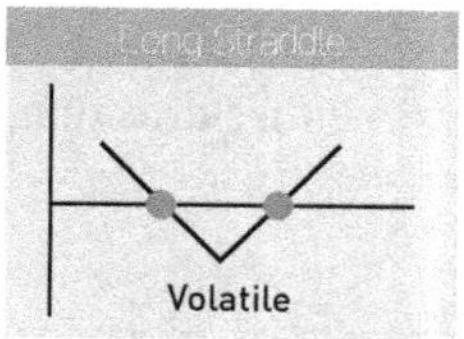

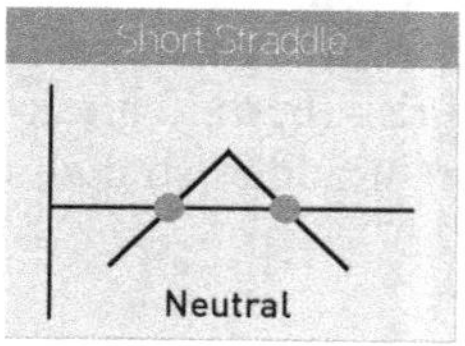

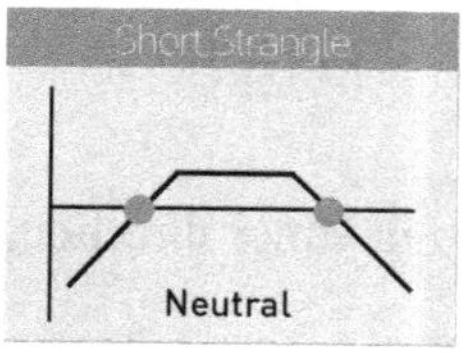

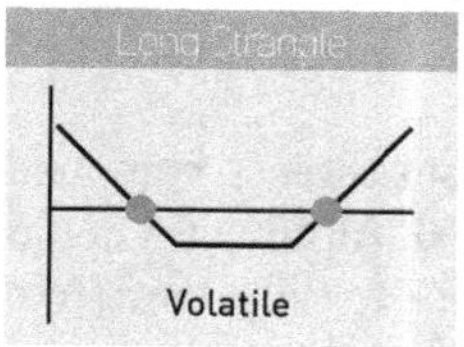

Call Options		ITM	ITM	ATM	OTM	OTM
Premiums		6.15	5.65	5.20	4.75	4.35
Strike Prices		308	309	310	311	312
Put Options		OTM	OTM	ATM	ITM	ITM
Premiums		5.90	6.40	6.95	7.50	8.10
Strategy Title	D/C	Strategy Components				
Bull Call Spread	D				+C	−C
Bull Put Spread	C	+P	−P			
Bear Call Spread	C				−C	+C
Bear Put Spread	D	−P	+P			
Long Straddle	D			+C+P		
Short Straddle	C			−C−P		
Long Strangle	D		+P		+C	
Short Strangle	C		−P		−C	
Call Ratio Spread	C		+C		−C−C	
Call Ratio Backspread	D		−C		+C+C	
Put Ratio Spread	C		−P−P		+P	
Put Ratio Backspread	D		+P+P		−P	
Long Call Butterfly	D	+C		−C−C		+C
Long Put Butterfly	D	+P		−P−P		+P
Short Call Butterfly	C	−C		+C+C		−C
Short Put Butterfly	C	−P		+P+P		−P
Iron Butterfly	C	+P		−P−C		+C
Reverse Iron Butterfly	D	−P		+P+C		−C
Long Call Condor	D	+C	−C		−C	+C
Long Put Condor	D	+P	−P		−P	+P
Short Call Condor	C	−C	+C		+C	−C
Short Put Condor	C	−P	+P		+P	−P
Iron Condor	C	+P	−P		−C	+C
Reverse Iron Condor	D	−P	+P		+C	−C

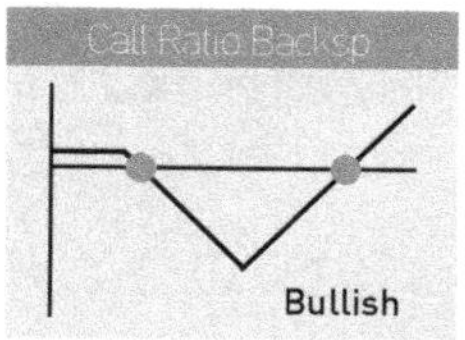

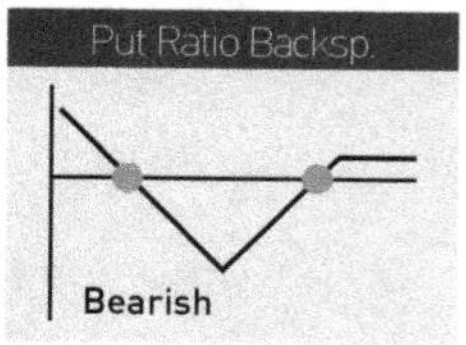

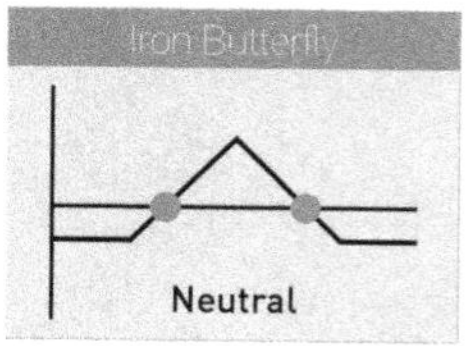

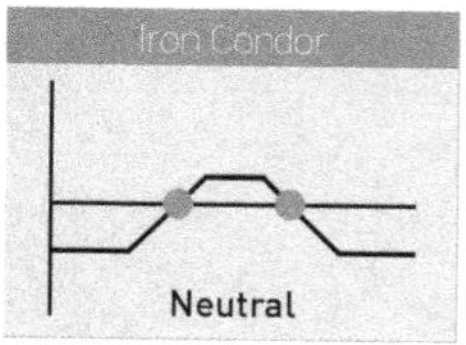

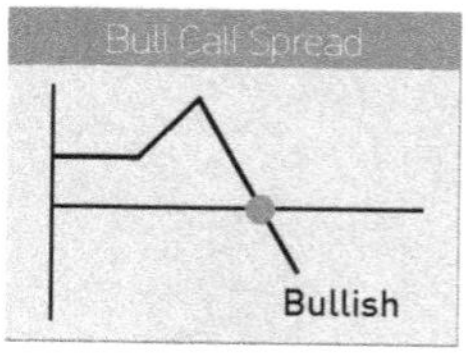

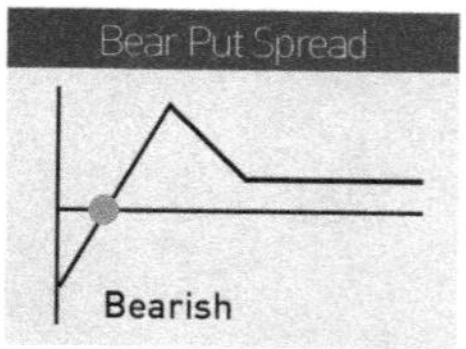

SUMMARY

The main goal of this chapter has been to explain some of the most popular spread strategies which are most frequently used. The choice of such strategies is subjective, as it only could be, bearing in mind the fact that there are more then 70 of them. Each strategy outlined is a small world of its own and would definitely deserve more extensive elaboration. But we had to draw a line somewhere and have sufficed with accentuating only the basic characteristics.

We began the chapter illustrating the long straddle strategy. The profile of the strategy is designated as "open-ended", pointing to its potential to earn profits in either direction. This strategy requires an increase in volatility, otherwise, if the market remains dull this will affect the position adversely and lock-in the loss equivalent to the combined option premiums paid. The short straddle is a mirror image with performance characteristics directly opposed to those of the long straddle—the maximum profit is confined to the combined premiums received while there is no limit for the potential losses.

We then covered variations of straddles in regard to market outlook, making the strategy diagram either more bullish or more bearish.

Further variations of straddle strategies are covered under the topic Strips and Straps.

Next, we discussed the strangle strategy, pointing to the similarities and dissimilarities to the straddle. A long strangle is comparable to a long straddle (limited losses anywhere between the aggregate strike prices bought and unlimited profits beyond break-even points on either side) while a short strangle retains most of the characteristics of a short straddle (maximum profit occurs anywhere between the aggregate strike prices sold and unlimited losses beyond break-even points in either direction).

Enclosing the exposition of these intricate topics, we thought it might be advantageous to prepare a compendium of all strategies discussed in this article primarily for two reasons:

- Firstly, the table compendium is designed in a way to provide the reader with quick reference to numerous strategies, their constituting elements and the resulting exposure they deliver, and
- Secondly, it aspires to emphasize the interlocked inverse relationship existing between relevant strategy pairs that become more apparent if exposed in a comparable manner.

KEY TERMS

long straddle
bullish long straddle
bearish long straddle
short straddle
bullish short straddle
bearish short straddle
straps
strips
long strangle
synthetic short strangle
short strangle
support
resistance
synthetic short strangle

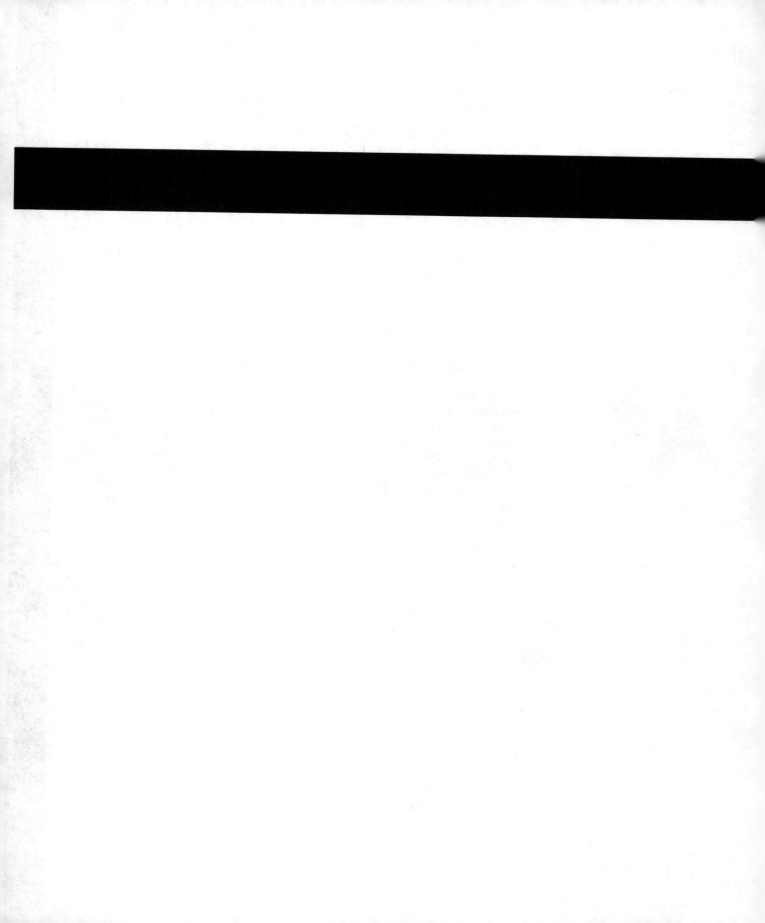

CHAPTER 28

SYNTHETIC INSTRUMENTS

CHAPTER OBJECTIVES

- To explain the logic of creating a synthetic instrument
- To explicate combinations between options and an underlying instrument
- To explicate synthetically created long and short combos with same strikes
- To explicate synthetically created long and short combos with split strikes
- To explicate synthetics excluding options

SYNTHETICS CREATED BETWEEN OPTIONS AND UNDERLYING INSTRUMENTS

Key Terms

synthetics
a financial instrument whose payoff is replicated artificially, combining features of a mixture of single assets

In financial jargon the term "synthetics" refers to a financial instrument whose payoff is replicated artificially, combining features of a mixture of single assets. The risk-reward profile of every single financial instrument, be it stock, bond, futures, call or put option, can be imitated (or exactly replicated) by blending the payoffs of two different instruments. Accordingly, there are manifold ways to create synthetic positions.

It was due to the versatility of synthetic combinations that we thought this topic deserved to be treated as an exclusive single reference and in one place. From the viewpoint of constituting elements we may classify all synthetics into three large groups:

1. Synthetics created between options and an underlying instrument,
2. Synthetics created between options only, and
3. Synthetics excluding options

The first compilation exhibited in Figure 28.1 must look familiar. These cases have been elaborated extensively in Chapter 13 so on this visit we shall outline only the most characteristic features.

Figure 28.1 Synthetically Created Options

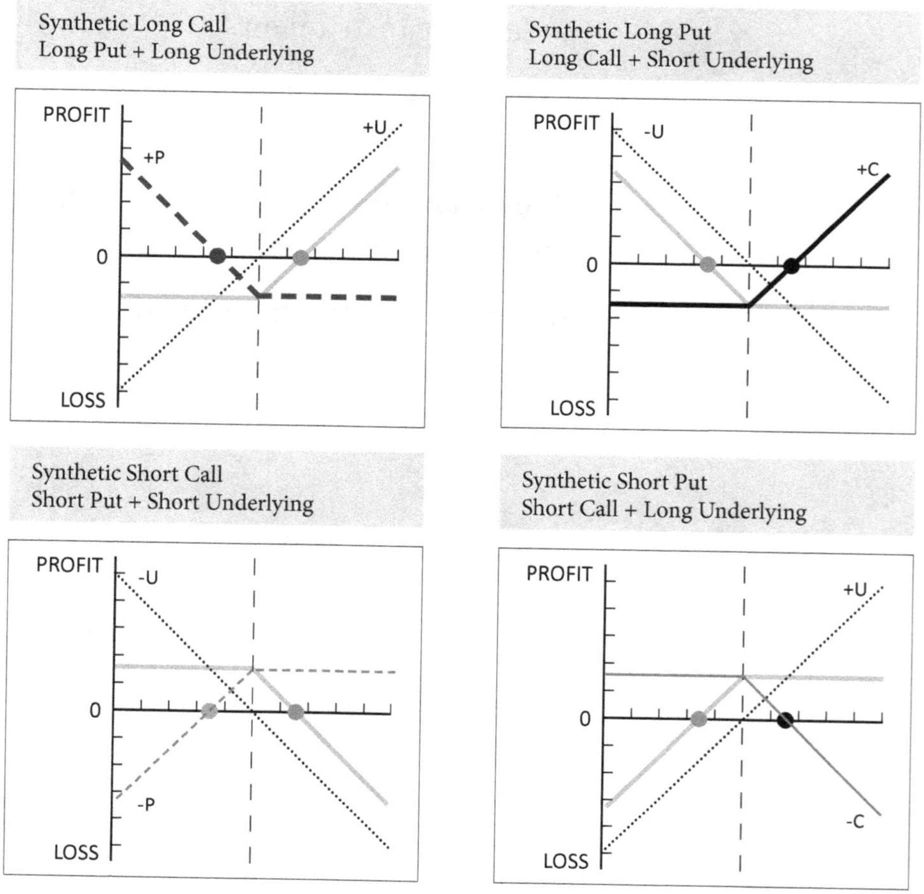

I SYNTHETICS CREATED BETWEEN ONLY OPTIONS

Key Terms

long combo
synthetic instrument created with a long call and put, with the same strikes and expiration

LONG/SHORT COMBOS: SAME STRIKES

Long and short combos are combinations of call and put options on the same underlying and with the same time to expiration, and with the same strike prices. Options' strikes are always ATM. The diagram created with synthetic combos replicates either a long or short asset position.

The risk-reward profile of every single instrument and the risk-reward profile of its synthetically created equivalent are virtually identical, though they are not to be considered as being absolutely equal.

The graphs below aim to enhance our ability to understand delicate differences between various risk exposures, to identify their distinctive features, and compare their performance.

In the case of synthetic combos, quick perception of the differences is readily noticeable if you compare their BEPs. So, let's take a look at their BEPs.

Memorizing these BEP equations that determine the strategy P&L profile could be a tricky business because the outcomes rely on fine differences.

Figure 28.2 Long Combos – Same Strikes

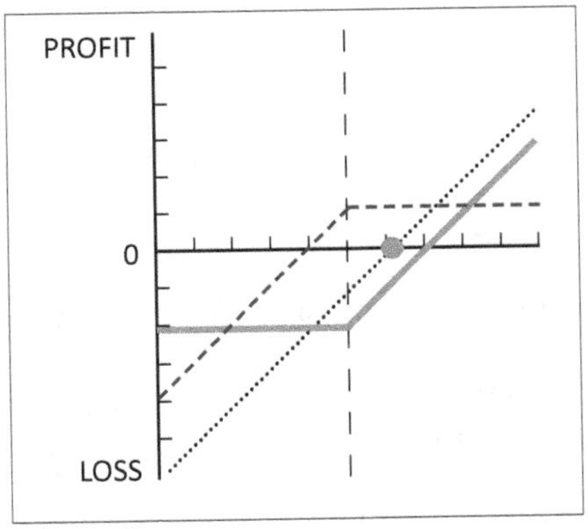

Buy call/sell put: same strikes

BEP = Strike + net debit

Synthetic position profits are consistently behind the stock purchase.
Synthetic position losses are consistently ahead of the stock purchase.

Long combo: **Debit**

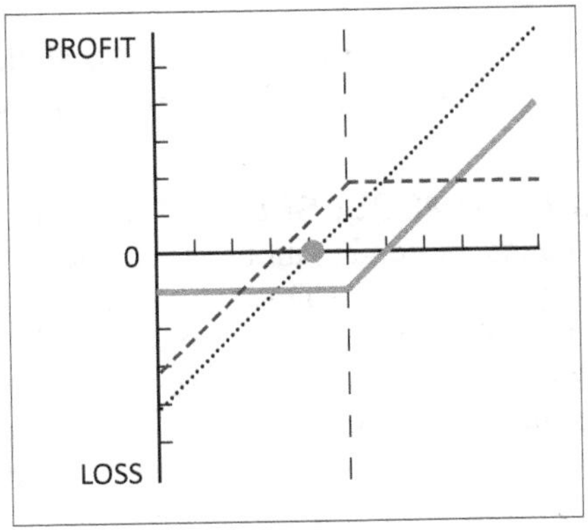

Buy call/sell put: same strikes

BEP = Strike – net credit

Synthetic position profits are consistently ahead of the stock purchase.
Synthetic position losses are consistently behind the stock purchase.

Long combo: **Credit**

In the next example, Figure 28.3, we demonstrate the configuration and characteristics of a short combo. The payoff of the short combo is the exact opposite of the long combo that virtually replicates an "open-ended" short asset or short futures position.

Figure 28.3 Short Combos - Same Strikes

Key Terms

short combo
a synthetic instrument created with a short call and put, with the same strikes and expiration

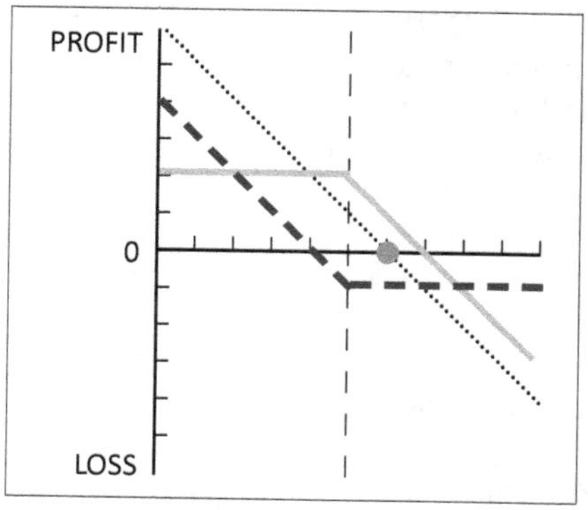

Sell call/buy put: same strikes

BEP = Strike + net credit

Synthetic position profits are consistently ahead of the stock sale.
Synthetic position losses are consistently behind the stock sale.

Short combo: **Credit**

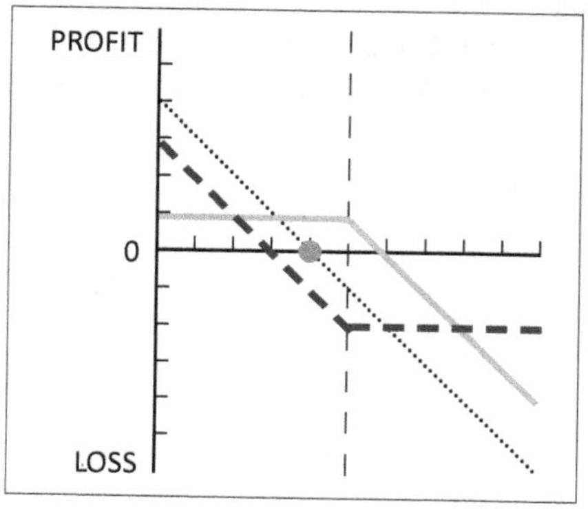

Sell call/buy put: same strikes
BEP = Strike – net debit

Synthetic position profits are consistently behind the stock sale.
Synthetic position losses are consistently ahead of the stock sale.

Short combo: **Debit**

Graphic expositions, in many cases, demonstrate the superiority of descriptive explanations.

The ultimate significance of these diagrams is that they are credible tools: a visual guidance that points towards an infallible yet very obvious conclusion.

The resultant combo diagram is always shifted towards the higher premium diagonal.

Comparing the BEP of a synthetic equivalent with the BEP of the actual instrument is a simple way to evaluate the payoff discrepancies and their effects.

LONG/SHORT COMBOS: SPLIT STRIKES

plateau
the flat part of an option's diagram in between option strike prices

Split strike combos are combinations of call and put options on the same underlying and with the same time to expiration, but with different strike prices. The diagram created with the split strike combos replicates either a long or a short asset position with one striking difference—due to the difference in strike prices, split strike combos' profit and loss diagrams form a "plateau"—the flat area in between option strike prices.

Depending on the net outlay of the position, the plateau sits either below the X-axis (in the case of a debit spread), or above the X-axis (in the case of a credit spread). The position of the plateau is determined by the strikes involved: combos created at a net credit will have a plateau positioned above the X-axis; combos created at a net debit will have the plateau positioned below the X-axis.

The profit/loss diagram is "open-ended" both ways, implying that the strategy is open to unlimited profits as well as losses.

Figure 28.4 illustrates the configuration process and the main characteristics.

Figure 28.4 Long Combos - Split Strikes

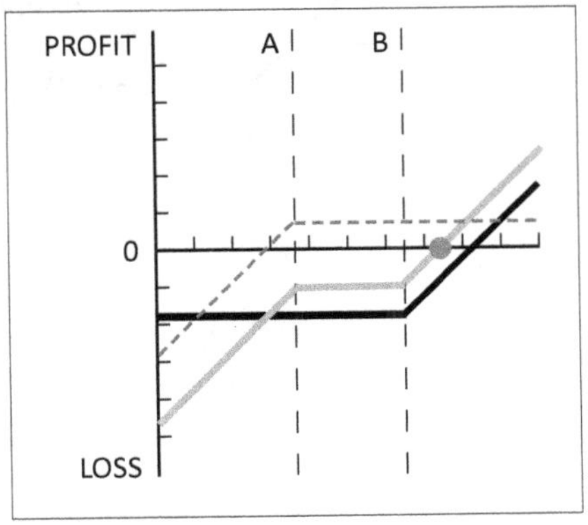

Buy OTM call (B); Sell OTM put (A)
BEP = Call strike B + net debit

Profits: S > BEP
Low plateau; sits below X-axis

aka "Bull Fence"

Long split combo: **Debit**

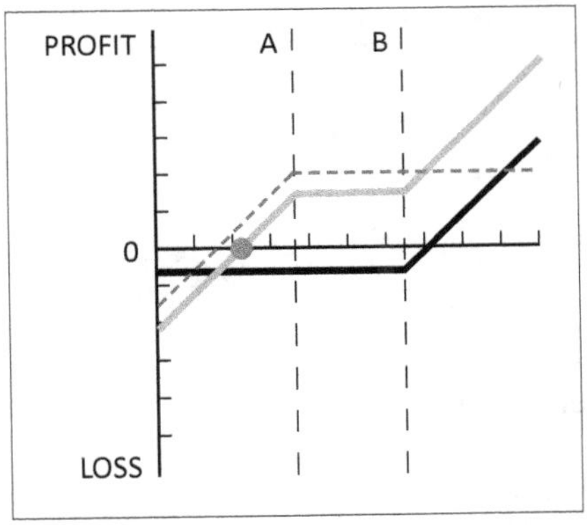

Buy OTM call (B); Sell OTM put (A)
BEP = Put strike A – net credit

Profits: S > BEP
High plateau; sits above X-axis

aka "Bull Fence"

Long split combo: **Credit**

Key Terms

long split combo
a synthetic instrument created with a long call and put, with the same expiration and different strikes; also known as a bull split-strike combo

What are the risks associated with this strategy? Since your expectations are generally bullish, let's first consider the outcome if the market rallies: the put option is out-of-the-money and the call option is in-the-money; you abandon the put and you exercise the call option; your ultimate profits equal the difference between the stock market price and the synthetic break-even point.

If the stock market declines: the call option is out-of-the money and the put option is in-the-money; you abandon the call option but your put option is assigned, obliging you to purchase the stock at the put strike; your ultimate loss equals the difference between the stock market price and the synthetic break-even point.

Either way, you end up owning a stock. The advantage of this strategy is that you invoke a position that replicates a stock ownership without having to pay the full cost of the stocks, and yet you participate in unlimited profits if there is a price increase.

On the other side, if the market drifts in the other direction, the strategy's justification is substantiated by the fact that you are obliged to purchase those particular underlying shares of stock at the put strike that is lower (since you sold an OTM put) than the stock market price when the long split strikes combo was initiated.

Figure 28.5 Short Combos - Split Strikes

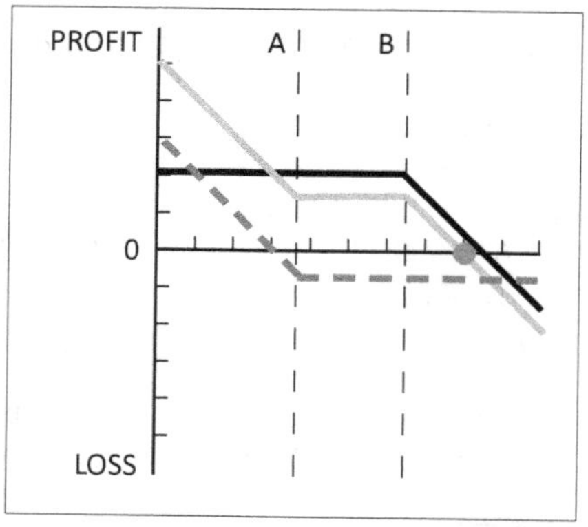

Sell OTM call (B); Buy OTM put (A)
BEP = Call strike B + Net credit

Profit = S < BEP
High plateau; sits above X-axis

aka "Bear Fence"

Short split combo: **Credit**

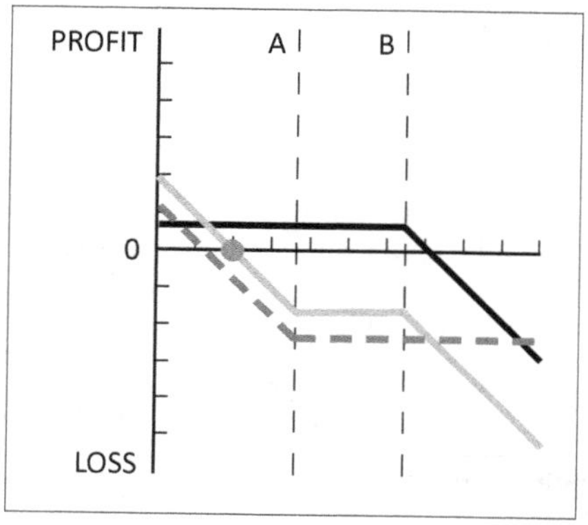

Sell OTM call (B); Buy OTM put (A)
BEP = Put strike A – net debit

Profit = S < BEP
Low plateau; sits below X-axis

aka "Bear Fence"

Short split combo: **Debit**

Key Terms

short split combo
a synthetic instrument created with a short call and put with the same expiration amd different strikes; also known as a bear split-strike combo

If your market expectations are bearish, you may choose a short split-strike combo.

As was the case with Figure 28.4, the diagrams exhibited in Figure 28.5—critically examining the P&L profile sensitivity and responsiveness to strike prices constellation—transcend their dramatically different implications by means of causal relations based on the principles of geometry.

The choice of the strikes entered to initiate a position will affect the strategy's P&L profile in a way that is clearly perceptible:

- If entered at a credit, the strategy retains unlimited profit potential in falling markets—below the strategy BEP, and substantial losses in rising markets—above the strategy BEP

- If entered at a debit—although retaining the same directional exposure—the strategy's risk-to-reward profile is considerably inferior to that of a credit combo.

SYNTHETICS EXCLUDING OPTIONS

Lastly, we shall exhibit synthetic instruments created by combining the payoff diagrams between actuals (long/short physical positions), futures and bonds.

The graphical explications are separated into two groups:

- Synthetically-created long instruments – Figure 28.6
- Synthetically-created short instruments – Figure 28.7

Figure 28.6 Outright Long Positions and Synthetic Equivalents

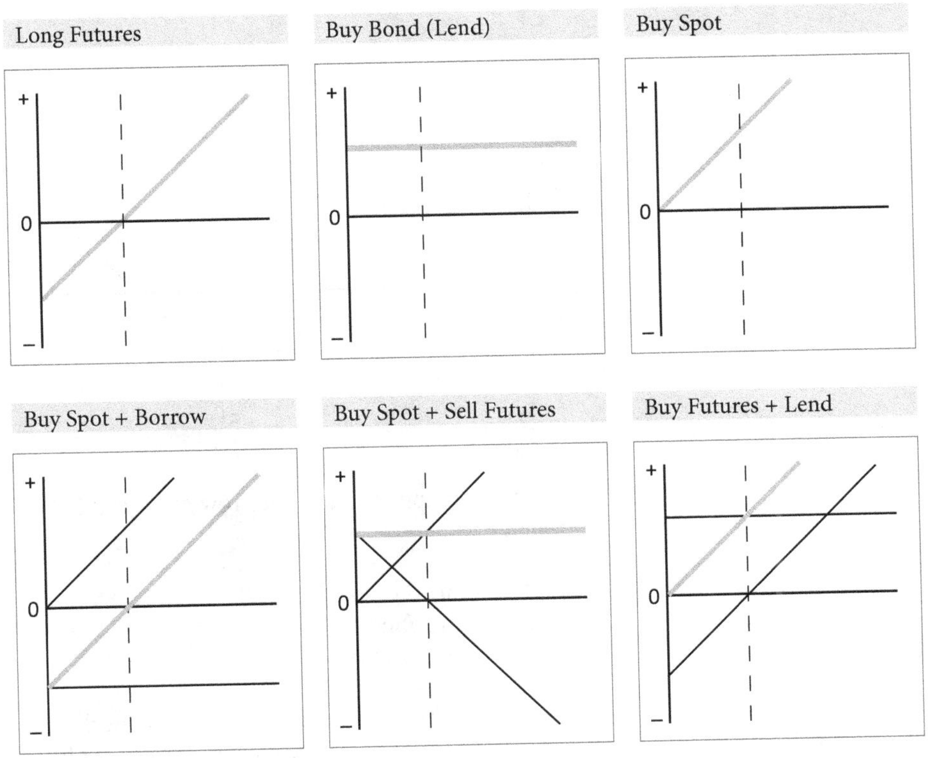

The graphs in the upper row show the three outright long positions:

1. Long futures,
2. Long bond, and
3. Long asset (stock).

The graphs beneath are synthetically created payoff profiles which mimic exactly the cash flow of the conventional long financial instruments.

We should emphasise here that the word "mimic" is used in its literal sense, signifying that aside from virtually identical P&L profiles, the financial instruments' outright positions and synthetic equivalents differ substantially.

Figure 28.7 Outright Short Positions and Synthetic Equivalents

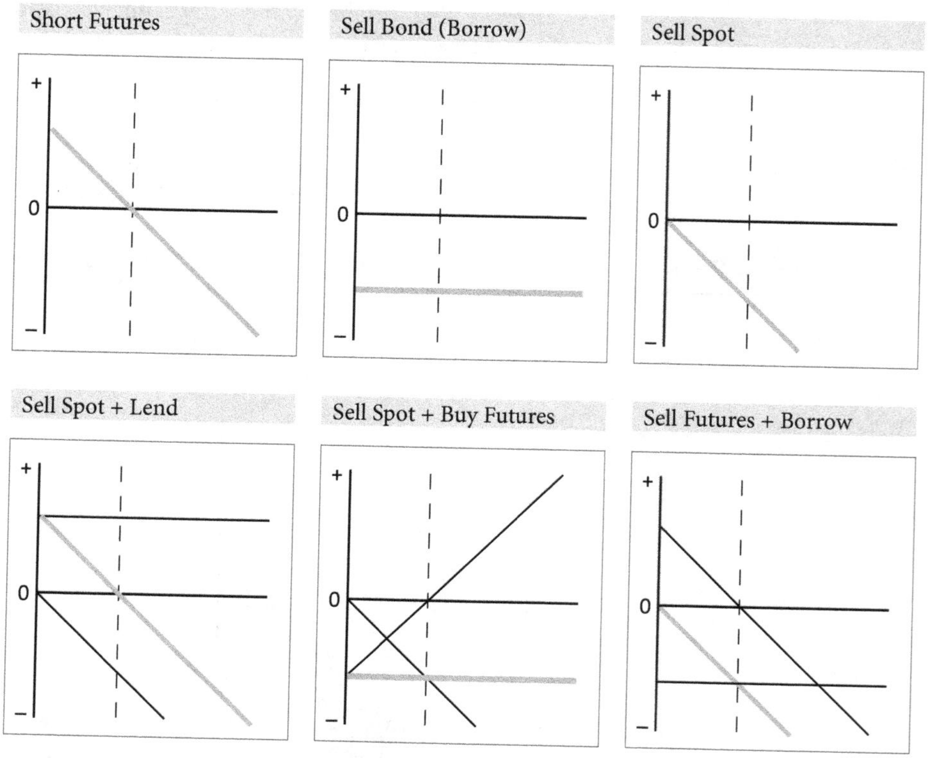

Likewise, graphs in the upper row of Figure 28.7 show the three outright short positions :

1. Short futures,
2. Short bond, and
3. Short asset (stock).

The graphs beneath depict the synthetically created payoff profiles which mimic exactly the cash flow of the conventional short financial instruments.

Synthetics are just another way of imitating (or exactly replicating) the cash flow of an existing financial instrument—amalgams of two different payoffs preserving the same directional exposure.

SUMMARY

In the last chapter we covered the class of so-called "synthetic instruments." The term synthetics refers to creation of a financial position, generated artificially, by combining the payoff features of different single instruments. The payoff diagram of a synthetic instrument is an amalgam of risk profiles that replicates exactly the price exposure of another conventional instrument.

From the viewpoint of constituting elements we have classified all synthetics into three large groups:

- Synthetics created between options and an underlying instrument; the combination in between these instruments produces a payoff of an option,
- Synthetics created between options only; the combination in between these instruments produces a payoff of a long/short instrument (long/short combos, same strikes), or a payoff designated as long/short combos, split strikes,
- Synthetics excluding options refers to combinations created in between a long/short physical position (or a futures) and a bond. The result of these combinations are the payoff diagrams of a single instrument: an actual, a futures, or a bond.

By examining the multiple range of outcomes that may arise from blending the payoffs of different instruments, we wanted to point to a variety of approachable strategies that should be considered in managing market risk exposure. In exceedingly uncertain and unpredictable occurrences and events related to commodity markets, it becomes crucially important to tailor the risk-management processes with a full knowledge and awareness of diverse hedging alternatives.

KEY TERMS

synthetics
long combo
short combo
long split combo
short split combo

INDEX

D

E

F

G

H

I